America
Religions and Religion

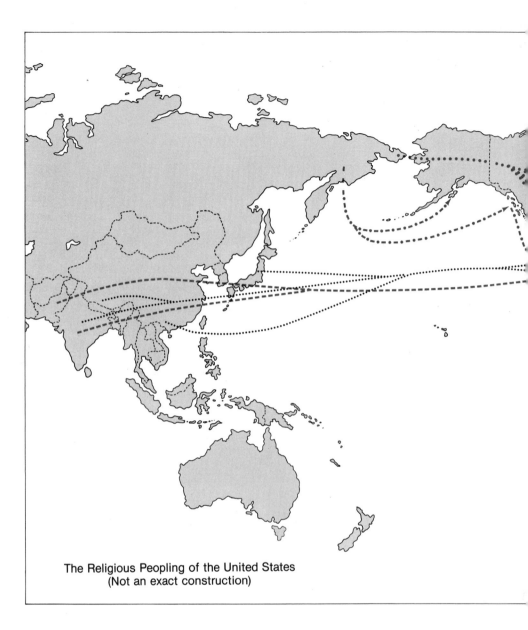

The Religious Peopling of the United States
(Not an exact construction)

American Indians
Jews
Roman Catholics
Protestants

African-Americans

Nearer Easterners (Eastern Orthodox)

Middle Easterners (Muslim)

Farther Easterners (Buddhist and Hindu)

WADSWORTH RELIGIOUS STUDIES
TITLES OF RELATED INTEREST

Denise and John Carmody, *Ways to the Center: An Introduction to World Religions*, 3rd edition

David Chidester, *Patterns of Action: Religion and Ethics in Comparative Perspective*

Nancy Falk and Rita Gross, *Unspoken Worlds: Women's Religious Lives*

Meredith McGuire, *Religion: The Social Context*, 2nd edition

Roger Schmidt, *Exploring Religion*, 2nd edition

AMERICA
RELIGIONS AND RELIGION

Second Edition

Catherine L. Albanese
University of California, Santa Barbara

Wadsworth Publishing Company
Belmont, California
A Division of Wadsworth, Inc.

Religion Editor: *Peggy Adams*
Editorial Assistant: *Amy Havel*
Production Editor: *Jerilyn Emori*
Interior and Cover Designer: *Cynthia Schultz*
Print Buyer: *Randy Hurst*
Permissions Editor: *Robert Kauser*
Compositor: *TypeLink, Inc.*
Printer: *Fairfield Graphics*
Cover: *Algonkian Copper Gorget, New Hampshire. This throat covering, the work of an unknown American Indian artist, suggests the later symbol of the American eagle but gives the representation an almost numinous quality. Photograph by Hillel Burger (Peabody Museum, Harvard University)*

Illustration Credits: **Page 8:** Museum of the City of New York, The Harry T. Peters Collection. **Page 20:** California Museum of Photography, Keystone-Mast Collection, University of California, Riverside. **Page 40:** Museum of Northern Arizona. **Page 52:** © John Hopf. **Page 88:** © 1983 Arnold Zann/Black Star. **Page 114:** © Steve Rosenthal. **Page 162:** Courtesy of the Library of Congress. **Page 204:** Bequest of Maxim Karolik, courtesy Museum of Fine Arts, Boston. **Page 227:** First published in William E. Smythe, *The Conquest of Arid America, 1900.* **Page 243:** The Western Reserve Historical Society, Cleveland, Ohio. **Page 263:** Wellcome Institute Library, London. **Page 287:** California Museum of Photography, Keystone-Mast Collection, University of California, Riverside. **Page 309:** Raymond B. Williams. **Pages 330 and 331:** Catherine L. Albanese. **Page 360:** Sun Bear, California Medicine Wheel Gathering. Photograph by Marti Kranzberg, 1982, courtesy Bear Tribe Medicine Society. **Page 380:** *Fundamentalist Journal,* September 1983. **Pages 394 and 400:** Courtesy of the Library of Congress. **Page 412:** Courtesy of Billy Graham Center Museum. **Page 444:** The Metropolitan Museum of Art, New York, gift of William H. Huntington. **Page 490:** American Antiquarian Society, Worcester, MA. **Page 507:** Courtesy of the Library of Congress.

This book is printed on acid-free paper that meets Environmental Protection Agency standards for recycled paper.

Printed in the United States of America

5 6 7 8 9 10

Library of Congress Cataloging-in-Publication Data
Albanese, Catherine L.
    America, religions and religion / Catherine L. Albanese. — 2nd ed.
        p.   cm.
    Includes bibliographical references and index.
    ISBN 0-534-16488-9
    1. United States — Religion.   I. Title.
BL2530.U6A43   1992
291′.0973 — dc20   91-21694

To the memory of my grandfather,
Frank S. Spiziri (1878–1958), one among the many

CONTENTS

FOREWORD

This book is unique: within one volume the author has brought together informed and informative treatments of the most significant of the multiple and diverse religious groups and traditions in America and insightful discussions of those religious elements that bind together diverse people of this nation. The result is twofold: (1) an accurate (and very readable) single volume overview of a lively and significant subject and (2) a landmark among such surveys. The strengths of the first edition are enhanced in this new edition by the inclusion of additional material that is timely and by its simpler style.

Those who set out to deal authoritatively and coherently with the subject of religion (and religions) in America must, if they are to succeed, master both detail and synthesis. In the course of such efforts over more than a century, treatment of detail has both widened and deepened while the synthetic framework has changed markedly. Most early treatments deal primarily with the major Christian denominations, groups that had evolved almost entirely out of the context of Christendom in Europe. Subsequently, some attention was also given to Judaism, then to such indigenous groups as Mormonism and Christian Science, then to groups and emphases with Oriental or Asian roots, and, more recently, to African-American religion. Dr. Albanese goes a few steps further by including systematic treatment of Native American traditions, the distinctive religion of one region of the United States, New Age religion, and fundamentalist-evangelical Protestantism.

Organizing assumptions in the treatment of religion (and religions) in America have ranged from stress on the providential coincidence of the Protestant Reformation with the discovery and early settlement of America to stress on the uniqueness of the American religious scene due to the separation of church and state and the resultant importance of "voluntaryism" in the American religious experience. Some have fixed upon a sociological approach that tends to see religion in America as shaped primarily by economic and other environmental factors. Dr. Albanese's approach is informed by a view that understands that religion encompasses all of life—both the ordinary and the extraordinary, and both the detail of a particular religious denomination and the generality of unifying and cohesive assumptions and beliefs in our pluralistic society. This approach draws from the methods and resources of the history, sociology, and anthropology of religion and ably applies these specifically to the American scene.

Robert S. Michaelsen
University of California, Santa Barbara

PREFACE

Americans during their formative years were a people in movement through space. . . . This is the mighty saga of the outward acts, told and retold until it has overshadowed and suppressed the equally vital, but more somber, story of the inner experience. Americans have so presented to view and celebrated the external and material side of their pilgrims' progress that they have tended to conceal even from themselves the inner, spiritual pilgrimage, with its more subtle dimensions and profound depths.

Sidney E. Mead, The Lively Experiment, pp. 7–8

So wrote Sidney Mead in his classic work as he explored the space, time, and religion of the American people. There was a "one story" to be celebrated, an epic tale of triumph written, as Mead said, "with cosmic quill." Yet in the midst of the heroic narrative, inner experience remained unexplored, even by the doers of the mighty deeds.

Mead knew then, and we know now, that not all of these Americans were alike. Over and over again, we have grown familiar with clichés about the fact and experience of pluralism in the United States. To be plural means to be more than one, to be many. To be a pluralistic land means to be one country made up of many peoples and many religious faiths. Yet when we look at America's history books — and more to the point here, America's religious history books — we find that they generally tell one major story, incorporating the separate stories of many peoples into a single story line arranged chronologically. The one story is the "mighty saga of the outward acts," as Mead so clearly saw. For if you tell the one story of America, perforce, it will center on the history-makers, the Anglo-Saxon and Protestant majority — and perhaps those most like them — who dominated the continent and its culture into the later twentieth century. To keep the story line going, you will focus on exemplary deeds and overall achievements while looking only briefly, if at all, at the deeper, more hidden dimension of spirituality.

There is surely a point to such single-line storytelling, for it conveys the idea of a common culture shared by all Americans. At its best, it binds many diverse peoples into one political community, one nation. It does so by picking up the threads of their separate stories and showing how the many encounter and assimilate with the dominant group, always to form part of the one continuous narrative. However, to face up to the implications of pluralism means to recognize that it is problematic to recite, even if artfully and inclusively, one story *before* exploring the realities of the many stories. Like it or not, to do so suppresses the distinctive identities of the many peoples who count themselves part of the American venture. True, some accounting of their presence can be and, in contemporary versions, usually is expressed through the single story plot. Still, the inner and spiritual stories of these diverse peoples are swept away into the march of mainstream American history. Telling merely one story, without first telling many stories, is possible only at a considerable cost — that of losing touch with the richness and texture of American pluralism.

This book arises from a conviction that the cost is too high. Standing within the pluralistic experiment, the book tells, first, not one but many stories. Only thereafter does it search for the tentative oneness amidst the manyness of the United States. Moreover, it seeks to tell a different kind of story by viewing religious history as a complex recital that leads to the inner world of the human spirit and imagination. In other words, the text deals with two kinds of events.

First are the simple, clear-cut, and short-term events with which most history usually deals. Where useful and available, dates will be noted and leaders named; new organizations and popular configurations will be recorded and outer achievements marked. Second, and just as important for the history of religions, are inner events of consciousness that find outer expression in religious settings. Unlike the names and dates of a more politically oriented history, these sets of events are not neat, tidy, and easily comprehended in conventional historical summaries. Most of the time, they unfold gradually, over centuries. To borrow — and modify — an idea from the French historian Fernand Braudel, they are events of "long duration." Such long-term events do not have sharp and precise edges, like a frame around a battle painting of the Civil War. Rather, these events are grasped as emerging out of the experience of a people, vocalized and expressed through sacred story and ritual, everyday behavior, and sometimes institutions. Hence, this book tries to follow the pathways from outer expression to inner experience. It assumes that the inner stories are immensely significant in American religious history.

In keeping with the goal of relating the religious stories of the many and the one, the text is concerned with popular religion, the religion of the people. It aims to explore each religious world from the point of view of its entire community. For that reason, issues of more concern to leaders than to other participants — governance and politics, for example — are downplayed, although they are not wholly ignored. For the same reason, considering the many stories before the single story has added significance. Although ordinary people are aware of pluralism, they usually do not choose to confront it head on. Rather, they live in their own separate centers of religious meaning constructed from an inherited past and a necessary present.

However, the book also recognizes that people *do* live out their particular religious histories within the larger society — in an ultimately public space that involves other groups of people. Therefore, a general sociological framework forms a kind of horizon for the text. Although problems exist with any typology of religious groups, the framework of this book is based on conventional understandings of churches, denominations, sects, and cult movements (defined in the Introduction and thereafter). More important, the book implicitly works from ideas derived from the sociology of knowledge. When, for example, Americans are called strangers in the land, the background of the social setting for their experience is never far away in the text. The social reasons why Americans know what they know are seen as important to the religious question. Finally, in the formulation of its basic theme the book has profited from anthropological insights concerning the importance of boundaries. As social spaces where two peoples or two realities meet, boundaries assume monumental importance in America. They are discussed further in the Introduction, and, in this context, so is the understanding of religion that governs the text.

As background for this discussion, it is assumed that definitions of religion can be divided into three types: substantive, functional, and formal. *Substantive* definitions of religion focus on the inner core, essence, or nature of religion and define it by this thing-in-itself. They tend to emphasize a relationship with a higher being or beings (God or the Gods) and to be favored by theologians and philosophers. *Functional* definitions of religion emphasize the effects of religion in actual life. They stress the systems of meaning-making that religion provides and how it helps people deal with the ills, insecurities, and catastrophes of living. Functional definitions are favored by scholars in the social sciences. Lastly, *formal* definitions of religion look for typically religious forms gleaned from the comparative study of religions and find the presence of religion where such forms can be identified. Religious forms include sacred stories, rituals, moral codes, and communities; and formal definitions of religion tend to be favored by historians of religions. Since this book is not a theoretical work, in the strict sense it does not define religion. But it does *describe* religion working from the discipline of the history of religions, and so its understanding of religion is formal. Because the book is as much about "plain" religious history and is likewise open to sociological and anthropological categories, its understanding is also functional.

The order of chapters in Part I is mostly historical, as the introduction explains. The first six chapters introduce the early cast of characters — Native Americans, Jews (who arrived with Christopher Columbus), Catholics, Protestants (in two chapters), and African-Americans — more or less in the order of their appearance. The following chapters trace new religious developments in the chronological order in which they became significant. The chapter on regional religion focuses on a religious culture of long duration — that of Southern Appalachia. A major function of the chapter is to introduce the concept of regional religion as a fruitful way to study a religious people, but the chapter also views an emphasis on regionalism in religion as part of a distinctly modern "moment" in American religious history. Seeing the inward-turning growth of religious regionalism juxtaposed to the cultural stretch toward religions of the East tells us more than seeing either of these two phenomena alone. Similarly, a final chapter in this section views two contemporary religious movements together. Looking at conservative Protestantism and New Age religion in concert throws important light on American religion in the present as a cultural system.

Like that of Southern Appalachia, other case studies are included in many of the chapters. The criterion for their selection has tended to be intrinsic religious interest more than the numerical size of the group. Indeed, if the text were to operate on the numerical principle in Part I, most of the material would be about Protestants, with a section on Catholics and a brief mention of African-Americans, Jews, and other groups close in size. From the viewpoint of an interest in religious forms and meanings, however, counting people is not the best approach to the study of religion in America. More than that, such an approach may be exceedingly deceptive since, of necessity, it favors those religions whose members build strong, enduring organizations that keep conventional written records. Many religions in nineteenth- and twentieth-century America were structurally too diffuse for such endeavors and, besides, were ideologically alienated from these kinds of concerns regarding number. Yet their presence in our culture may be far greater than we would at first suspect. For example, we will see that this is true for metaphysical traditions like New Thought and for Asian disciplines like yoga.

In contrast to Part I, Part II examines the "one story" of religion in America and therefore uses a more topical approach. The one story here has three aspects, and a pedagogic logic suggests that the sequence move from the most clearly recognizable and familiar face of religion to its less noticed manifestations. Within the chapters, the narrative runs from past to present when that is possible. However, dominating movement in short-term events is the continuing presence of the long-term event that is the one religion of America. From the seventeenth century, the basic structure of that religion was, in rough form, present. So the text aims to trace the elements of structure, form, and content according to methods that, it is hoped, will disclose something of the religious nature of America. A concluding chapter, which deals with the one religion and the many religions of America, works historically within a thematic framework. It surveys the history of the relationships among the many and the one as, again, a long-term event.

Notes are avoided throughout the book in order not to burden the beginning student. At the end of each chapter, however, is a short and selective bibliography that serves two purposes. First, it suggests sources to the student for further and more extensive discussion of material in the preceding chapter. Second, it indicates, in a general but not exhaustive way, sources that the text itself reflects. As a rule, new terms are explained when used initially, avoiding the necessity for a glossary. Biblical quotations are from the King James Version for historical reasons. Any reference to God or the Gods in the text is capitalized because the book acknowledges the truth of all of the Gods in the power that they hold in people's lives. The past tense is generally employed throughout the text as well. This does not in itself imply that religious beliefs and practices discussed have fallen into disuse but rather that they are events of long duration begun, in most cases, before our time. The present tense is used only sparingly for contemporary religious phenomena.

In its goal of bringing to readers a faithful report of the many religious people in America, the book has profited from the insights of many individuals. If writing this work has taught me anything, it has brought home how much scholarship is a community affair. Charles H. Long introduced me to the distinction between ordinary and extraordinary religion on which subsequent chapters rest. Martin E. Marty influenced me with his own wide interest in questions of pluralism. Numerous friends and colleagues knowledgeable in specific traditions read and criticized, with painstaking care, earlier drafts of sections of the text. For their advice and encouragement in doing so for the first edition, I thank Jonathan M. Butler, Theodore Chamberlain, Jay P. Dolan, Robert S. Ellwood, Jr., Eric L. Friedland, Sam D. Gill, Philip Gleason, Stephen Gottschalk, Richard A. Humphrey, Charles H. Long, Alfonso Ortiz, Sharon Welch Patton, Albert J. Raboteau, Frank E. Reynolds, Ernest R. Sandeen (unhappily now deceased), Jan Shipps, Jane S. Weeks, Rose Wendel, and Ronald M. White. In addition, I owe other debts to the scholars who read the entire first-edition text and made helpful suggestions for its improvement. For these good offices, I thank Sandra Sizer Frankiel, Martin E. Marty, Robert S. Michaelsen, Frank E. Reynolds, the late Ernest R. Sandeen, J. Benton White, and Peter W. Williams. I thank, too, Sidney E. Mead, who granted me permission to quote from *The Lively Experiment* and ably criticized this preface. For this second edition, I thank for their reading and comments Kay Alexander, Katharine L. Dvoràk, Stephen Gottschalk, Richard L. Hoch, Laurie Maffly-Kipp, Robert S. Michaelsen, Timothy Miller, Carlton T. Mitchell, Grant Wacker, and J. Benton White. All of these people have enlightened and assisted me in many ways, but I hasten to add that I alone am responsible for any remaining errors and omissions. I am also responsible for the interpretive stance the text reflects.

Now over a decade ago, the Liberal Arts College of Wright State University was tremendously supportive of the first edition, allowing me to rearrange and lighten my teaching schedule in order to have the spring quarter of 1979 free for research and writing, and extending a research grant to me to aid in manuscript preparation. That assistance brought me Virginia Blakelock, whose helpfulness extended far beyond the excellence of her typing. Patricia A. Schwab and

Veda D. Horton in the Religion Department also assisted generously with the typing. David L. Barr, my colleague at the time in the department, was an invaluable consultant on points concerning biblical matters, and all of my colleagues cheered and supported me. Dean Eugene B. Cantelupe and his office assumed the financial burden for my seemingly endless photocopying requests; Margaret Roach of the university library prepared the original index; and Stephen Haas and others also at the library rendered many services.

For the second edition, Gregor Goethals offered helpful suggestions for illustrations, for which I remain grateful. I am grateful, too, to Lynne Williamson, who, several years ago and in another context, introduced me to the Algonkian copper gorget whose representation appears on the cover and elsewhere in this book. For use of the photograph itself, I thank the Peabody Museum of Harvard University, and—as important—I thank the anonymous Algonkian artist of long ago whose elegant and eloquent artifact I have borrowed in its representation. Meanwhile, I owe a continuing debt to Sheryl Fullerton, former Religion Editor at Wadsworth, for the help, support, and encouragement that have made both first and second editions possible. And I thank my new friends at Wadsworth, Jerilyn Emori and Cynthia Schultz, who have patiently worked with a seemingly eternally tardy author in the production of the second-edition text.

My present colleagues at the University of California, Santa Barbara, have also supported and encouraged me as I worked to produce this new edition, and I remain grateful for the intellectual climate they have created in my world. I also owe a debt of a different order to the multitalented photocopying machine in Santa Barbara's Department of Religious Studies. And I acknowledge the many students there and elsewhere over the years who have responded to material in the first edition and so helped to shape the changes resulting here.

Finally, to my parents, Louis and Theresa Albanese, who were my earliest teachers, I owe debts still larger. It was they who gave me my first understanding of the vitality of a community of one people against the backdrop of pluralism. And that is also why I have chosen to dedicate this book to an ancestor whom I remember dearly and whose memory I cherish.

The Elephant in the Dark

There is a story that both Buddhists and some Muslims claim as their own and like to use as a teaching device. It is about an elephant and a group of blind men who had never before encountered one. Each of the men felt the elephant, took note of his sensations, and later described the experience. Some, who had felt the head of the animal, claimed that an elephant was like a pot. Others, who had felt an ear, claimed that an elephant was like a harvest basket used to separate grain. Still others had touched a tusk, and they announced that an elephant was part of a plow, while, finally, another group that had patted the trunk thought an elephant was a plow, whole and complete. The moral of the story, of course, goes beyond elephants, to the secrets of the universe and of life. Each individual tries to fathom these secrets from a place of personal darkness. Each describes the portion experienced, and none can speak about the whole. The lesson is to accept the fact of human limitation with humility and the fact of cosmic complexity with awe. Nobody will ever know the whole story, because the vastness that surrounds us far exceeds our senses or our ability to understand.

What does all of this have to do with American religious history? Quite a bit. In our study, we will in some sense be like blind people trying to feel an elephant. First, there will be so much elephant to feel: there will be so many American religions to explore. Each Native American nation in the land before the Europeans came had its own form of religion. In turn, each later immigrant group brought to the new country religious commitments from the Old World. Europeans brought Judaism, Roman Catholicism, and many forms of Protestantism. Africans brought Islam and the remembered beliefs and practices of many smaller ethnic religions. Orientals, by the late nineteenth and early twentieth centuries, contributed forms of Buddhism, Hinduism, and other Eastern religions.

1

Meanwhile, conditions in America favored the growth of new religions, native to this continent, thus adding to the picture of religious diversity.

Second, we will be feeling our religious elephant in the dark. We will be in the dark because even as we try to study American religious history, there is an ongoing debate among scholars about what we mean by religion in the first place. While this uncertainty about the meaning of religion may seem surprising and even shocking, it is a more ordinary experience in scholarship than we might suspect. In fact, in our own everyday lives we have probably known similar uncertainty, although not perhaps about religion. We have all at one time or another stared into a landscape or into the distance of a city street. As we stood or sat, thinking of nothing in particular, just looking at the scene, we may have noticed after a while that the finely chiseled outlines of separate objects seemed to disappear. We may have experienced an optical effect in which the borders that separated one thing from another were not so solid anymore. The world, which five minutes ago was fixed and stable, had dissolved its firm boundaries, and one reality mixed itself with the next, to our confusion.

In the same way, staring long and hard at what we call religion tends to dissolve its firm boundaries. Scholars have become less certain about what should be counted as religion, and so our study of American religious history must reflect that ambiguity. In other words, our task will in some ways be like trying to see an elephant in the dark. Initially, we will need to understand what we mean by religion. If we are to make progress in our study, that understanding will have to help us see American religious history. After we settle—for our purposes—the question of religion, for most of the book we will need to look at the United States of America, studying the main examples of religion that we find there.

Both of these tasks—trying to understand what religion means and trying to understand specific religious systems—are the work of a field of study called the history of religions. The further task of trying to understand religious continuity and change in the course of time is the work of "plain" religious history. This text is a study of religion in America from the perspectives of the history of religions and of general religious history. We will be asking three questions in the following pages. First, we will want to know what is *religious* about American religious history. Second, we will seek to discover what is *American* about American religious history. Third, we will ask about continuities and sketch the direction of changes in the course of American religious history. We begin with the task of trying to understand, in a general sense, what we mean by religion.

Defining Religion

From the viewpoint of common sense, every one of us knows what religion is. Surely, it is one of those obvious realities that we have either grown up practicing or observing others practice. It is just there—a fact as unavoidable in the social landscape as a mountain or a tree would be in a natural setting. Everyone knows what religion is—that is, until someone tries to define it. It is in the act of defining that religion seems to slip away.

We might want to limit religion to a relationship that humans consider themselves to have had with God or the Gods, but someone could point out that the oldest Buddhists did not believe in any God, while another person might ask if atheists were religious. We might want to call religion a way of living, an ethical system such as Confucius taught, but somebody could counter that all people had some way of living or other and that many of these ways were not, in any recognizable sense, religions. We might say that religion had to do with a quality of experience, a powerful feeling that people have had when they have confronted something totally "other." Yet a few in our group would be sure to suggest that the most powerful experience they could remember at a religious service on many a Saturday or Sunday morning was being lost in a daydream. We might become very brave and venture that religion was the thing in life a person was most ultimately concerned about, but one sarcastic member of our group would be sure to ask if that meant racehorses or the lottery as well as less material realities.

Why is it that so common a feature of human life proves so baffling? What is it about religion that eludes our grasp? Is the inability to define, like the optical illusion, simply caused by staring too long into the religious landscape? Or are there other problems as well, intrinsic to the nature of religion? A definition, says *Webster's Third New International Dictionary,* is an "act of determining or settling." It is "the action or the power of making definite and clear or of bringing into sharp relief." Definition, in fact, comes from the Latin word *finis,* which means an end or limit—a boundary. A definition tells us where some reality ends; it separates the world into what is and what is not that reality. So a definition certainly works to end optical illusions, firming up the object in its landscape rather than dissolving it.

But there is a special reason why religion eludes definition, and this reason moves beyond the general problem of staring at it too long. Religion cannot be defined very easily because it thrives both within and outside of boundaries. It crosses and crisscrosses the boundaries that definitions want to set because, paradoxically, it, too, concerns boundaries. The boundaries of religion, however, are different from the logical boundaries of good definitions. In the end, religion is a feature that encompasses *all* of human life, and therefore it is difficult if not impossible to define it.

Rather than continuing to try to square the religious circle, it may be more fruitful to think not of defining religion but, instead, of trying to describe it. To describe something is to say what it generally looks like and how it usually works. It is not to say what its innermost realities are, and it is not to say definitely what separates these realities from every other object in the world. Still, describing a thing can tell us much about what it is. Looking at the past and present appearances of religion can tell us what functions and forms go along with it. Learning to recognize these functions and forms helps us know when we are looking at religion. Hence, in what follows, we will not so much try to define religion as to describe it.

Religion and Boundaries

What we know about various religions suggests that they arose in the context of dealing with boundaries. For many peoples, physical boundaries that marked the limits of the territory of another group were highly charged with emotional significance. They divided land that was safe, the source of nurture and sustenance, from land that was alien and unfriendly, the home of hostile spirits and strange or warring peoples. So it was that any exchanges conducted across these boundaries were stressful occasions and that people strengthened themselves for these exchanges through the use of ritual. In the formula of word and act, people at a dangerous place in the physical landscape could call on special help; they could ease their encounter with whatever was alien to themselves.

This assistance seemed to come from the unknown, from forces that transcended, or went beyond, ordinary life. In other words, alien land and people were countered by a second form of "otherness," more powerful than the first. By enlisting the help of this second otherness, the first was overcome, and life could go on as intended. These "other" forces that saved a difficult situation by their power were called religious. And the rituals through which they were contacted were religious rituals.

But territorial boundaries were only one kind of border with which people dealt. There were also the limits of their own bodies, the boundaries of skin and tissue that separated each person in a group from every other person. Crossing the boundary of one's body could not be avoided: it happened every day in the simple acts of eating and drinking, of defecating, or of having sexual intercourse. It occurred even when words passed from one person out to the next, and rituals like prayer before a solemn speech or meeting grew up around these exchanges of language. In many cultures, prayer also accompanied the taking of food and drink. Similarly, the products of human bodies at their boundaries — hair, spittle, nail parings, feces — were invested with a power that made them dangerous or helpful, depending on the circumstances and the talents of the user. Thus, in a number of cultures, people feared that an enemy who found strands of their hair or their nail parings could bring evil upon their persons. Hair and nail parings, along with other "boundary" products of the body, possessed a mysterious energy that made them focuses for ritual. Religious specialists learned to use them in magical ceremonies, and people stood in awe of these products of their bodies.

Finally, there were the temporal boundaries in the life cycle that any person passed through. In the events of birth, puberty, marriage, and death, a person crossed the border between one form of life, which was known and secure, and a new kind of life, which was perhaps somewhat fearful. These were crisis events, and so there were rites that would ease the passage across the boundaries from one stage in the life cycle to another. In our own society, we are familiar with ceremonies of baptism for infants and with Bar or Bat Mitzvahs and confirmation rites at adolescence. Marriage brings its solemnity as, even in the simplest of ceremonies, two people exchange their commitment to each other. At death, both wakes and funerals form the usual rites of passing.

This concern for boundaries has been apparent throughout the history of human societies. Borders continued to be places invested with religious significance—for example, by the imposing, birdlike *garudas* at the entrances of Hindu temples or the equally arresting gargoyles at the outside corners of medieval Christian cathedrals. These signs and boundary markers warned all comers that they were crossing a frontier into a sacred precinct. They effectively divided one world from another. In a striking example from the United States, many Roman Catholics in the Upper Midwest placed on their lawns statues of the Virgin Mary, which performed a similar function. Anyone who has seen the vast sameness of the prairie and has imagined its unending wildness for Europeans before the creation of their towns can understand why a Virgin would be wanted on the lawn—defining the sacred space of the family and separating it from the far reaches of unnamed territory.

Even in the realm of language, religious or theological discourse has tried to speak about the unspeakable. It has been "limit" language, language that pushes to the edge of human knowledge and tries to talk about what goes beyond. Death, judgment, heaven, hell—these were critical events for Christian theology. They were also words to cross the boundary of the world we know, attempts to make sense of mysterious realities from a different world. When religious people used such language, they were trying to describe a landscape they had only seen, as the biblical Paul said, "through a glass, darkly" (I Cor. 13:12). They were trying to name, through linguistic signs and symbols, features of a country they had not seen with bodily eyes.

It should be clear by now that we are part of a long tradition of mixing boundary questions with religious questions. Thus, our religion concerns the way we locate ourselves in space through the arrangement of sacred rites and holy places as boundary markers. It concerns, too, the way we locate ourselves in time through origin stories or theological traditions that also express boundaries. But location is always social. It concerns our place among other human beings, and it means staking out a claim on the landscape of identity.

The internal landscape of identity provides a new territory in which boundaries become important. So an important modern version of the religion–boundary theme is the quest for identity. As social beings who turn within, people act out the same concerns about boundaries that they do in external space. By searching for identity and finding it, individuals metaphorically establish inner boundaries, discover through testing who they are not, and begin to affirm who they are. In the process, each individual finds that these personal boundaries overlap with those of others, so that there can be a free process of exchange. In other words, a person locates those who occupy the same inner territory and, because of the shared internal space, feels at one with them and their concerns. This is the meaning of identification with others.

Religion through the ages has tried to answer the continuing human question "Who am I?" More particularly, religious writers of our century have made much of the issue of identity, since the intense pluralism of the modern world has given people many choices about the boundaries of the inner space they will occupy. In more traditional societies, most people grew up in a culture that took outer and inner worlds for granted, with ancient and prescribed rules for living. But in a mobile society, as in our postindustrial era, this picture of fixed space disappears. The presence of many possibilities for finding an inner world of one's own means that many decisions have to be made. Many interior regions must be denied, and others must be affirmed. Hence, in our era, identity has become a problem in a way that it was not during much of the past.

Two Kinds of Religion

The preoccupation with boundaries that comes with the search for identity points to an important fact: people are concerned not just about how to cross boundaries but also about how to live well within them. Finding one's identity means finding the inner space and social space within which it is possible to thrive and grow. And so, if religion is about boundaries, it is not just about crossing them but, as in the question of identity, about respecting them, too. Therefore, learning to live well within boundaries and learning how to cross them safely gives rise to two kinds of religion. The first kind is *ordinary religion* — the religion that is more or less synonymous with culture. Ordinary religion shows people how to live well within boundaries. The second is *extraordinary religion* — the religion that helps people to transcend, or move beyond, their everyday culture and concerns. Extraordinary religion grows at the frontiers of life as we know it and seeks to cross over into another country and another form of life. In the West, extraordinary religion helps us to contact God. Let us look briefly at each of these two kinds of religion.

Ordinary religion, we might say with the scholar Joachim Wach, is the trunk of the tree of culture. In the most general sense, ordinary religion is the source of distinguishable cultural forms and the background out of which the norms arise that guide us in our everyday lives. Yet ordinary religion resists precise definition. The reason is that it is the taken-for-granted reality that we all assume, the statements and actions that make up our picture of the way the world is and is not, the things we do not have to think about or would not dream of arguing over because they are so obvious. Ordinary religion puts its premium on the things that are deeply present and unconsciously revered here within the borders of everyday culture. So this kind of religion can reveal itself in intuitive statements and vague sayings about the meaning of life: "Whatever will be, will be"; "It is better to give than to receive"; "Every cloud has its silver lining"; and the like. This kind of religion is better at being implicit than explicit.

In a more specific sense, ordinary religion can reveal itself in the many customs and folkways that are part of a culture: expected ways of greeting people; wedding etiquette concerning clothes, manners, and obligations; habits of diet; and holiday behavior, to mention a few. Each of these, if examined, can tell worlds about the main values of a society. Each is a concrete expression of the way in which people are accustomed to think and act. As such, each is a boundary marker that helps people to locate themselves and to make sense of the everyday world. For example, a bridal gown suggests the traditional values of the importance of marriage and family. The distinctiveness of wedding attire speaks for how significant such values still are in America, for how strongly the bride — and the culture — uses the institution of marriage to mark social space.

In other words, ordinary religion is at home with the way things are. It functions as the (mostly unexamined) religion of a community as community. Because it is about living well within boundaries, it values the social distinctions that define life in the community and respects the social roles that people play. It honors the ranks that they hold and the general institutions of government, education, family, and recreation to which they assent. In sum, ordinary religion is the religion that reinforces the bonds between members of a society, that provides social "glue" to make people cohere.

On the other hand, extraordinary religion is, as the term literally announces, extra ordinary, *outside* the ordinary *circle of society*. Indeed, extraordinary religion involves an encounter with some form of otherness, whether natural or supernatural. It is specific and particular, easily recognizable as religion, and possible to separate from the rest of culture. Thus, if ordinary religion is diffused throughout culture, extraordinary religion is condensed — present in clear and strongly identified religious forms that stand out from their background. Extraordinary religion encourages a special language that also distinguishes it from the rest of culture, and its sense of going beyond the boundaries often finds expression in universal statements, intended to apply to all peoples. The special language of extraordinary religion maps a landscape that people have not clearly seen. It gives people names for the unknown and then provides access to a world beyond. It assures people that the "other" world does touch this one but is never merely the same as it. In Christianity, for example, language of God, grace, and salvation posits realities beyond the material world. These terms chart the unknown and suggest how it beckons people away from their more ordinary concerns. Moreover, extraordinary religion often encourages religious activity not only on the part of the community as a whole but also on the part of separate individuals who attune themselves with particular intensity to the message delivered to the community. Mystics and prophets, who say they have seen visions and experienced special mental states, are its heroes and heroines.

The Ladder of Fortune. This Currier & Ives lithograph from 1875 provides a useful illustration of ordinary religion. The print lists virtues to aid the ambitious who seek business success. Prints such as this hung on the walls of family dwellings and were also used in Sunday schools.

Yet we call this religion extraordinary not because it is hard to find or to express but because it concerns itself with what is extraordinary in our day-to-day existence. It deals with how to negotiate boundaries and still return to the ordinary world. It may involve ecstasy, but it may also involve a simple and uneventful Sunday morning church service. The point is that people in some symbolic way voice their concern with crossing boundaries to the "other" side. Such concern is what makes the religion extraordinary, and as we will see, such concern is what makes it visible and easy to find.

As we move through the religious landscape of the United States, we will find that here, as elsewhere, ordinary and extraordinary religion are often difficult to separate. In fact, in traditional societies the two were often very closely blended, and people used the same or similar symbols to express both everyday and transcendent concerns. For instance, in Judaism the most repeated ritual of extraordinary religion was the Sabbath meal, a weekly family observance that joined a formal framework of prayer and blessings to ordinary conversation and enjoyment around the dinner table.

One sign of modernity in the West has been the increasing separation of extraordinary from ordinary religion. And as we will notice, Protestantism, more than any other religious movement, tried to make a clear distinction between the two. However, even with this Protestant goal and even with the overall Protestant character of the United States, there were numerous examples of the fusion of ordinary and extraordinary religion. Sometimes, as in the Jewish example of the Sabbath meal, people tried to make the extraordinary world easy and familiar by setting it in the midst of ordinary reality. At other times, people became so involved in the extraordinary claims of an "other" world that they drew everything possible along with them. For example, in the new religious movements of the later twentieth century, many people were making a radical break with their former lives to embrace a total commitment to extraordinary concerns.

Components of a Religious System

Both ordinary and extraordinary religion exist as religious systems; that is, they are composed of parts related to other parts, which together add up to one whole. For convenience, we can think of these parts as the four Cs: creed, code, cultus, and community. These four terms, taken together, express the collection of related symbols that make up a religious system. Each of these, therefore, is present in both ordinary and extraordinary religion.

First, religion is expressed in *creeds*, or explanations about the meaning or meanings of human life. Such creeds may take various forms, from highly developed theologies and sacred stories of origin to informal oral traditions and unconscious affirmations that surface in casual conversation. Second, religion is expressed in *codes*, which are rules that govern everyday behavior. These may take the form of articulated moral and ethical systems, but they may also be the customs that have become acceptable in a society, the ethos by which people live. Third, religion is expressed in *cultuses*, which are rituals to act out the insights and understandings that are expressed in creeds and codes. Not to be confused with small and intense religious groups sometimes called cults, ritual cultuses, with their formal and repeated character, underline and reinforce the meanings evoked by creeds and codes.

Finally, religion is expressed in *communities*, groups of people either formally or informally bound together by the creed, code, and cultus they share. In ordinary religion, such communities tend to be ethnic or cultural (Indians, blacks, Polish people), informally knitting together people who share a common land, history, and language. In extraordinary religion, such communities, especially in the West, have tended to be formal institutions (Catholicism, Methodism, Adventism), designated in terms of their social organization as churches, denominations, sects, or cult movements.

In the chapters that follow, we will learn more about each of these forms of extraordinary religious community. For now, let it be clear that these descriptive terms reflect the level and kind of organization in the different groups. Churches (which in our sense include non-Christian groups) are the most broadly inclusive, and denominations are more or less inclusive. Meanwhile, sects and, finally, cult movements, at the other end of the spectrum, are the most exclusive and so have the fewest members. Similarly, churches are the most accommodating to the rest of culture and the least demanding of their members, while cult movements deliberately try to cut themselves off from the rest of society and make the most radical demands on members. Churches are most at home in settings in which there is a national religion; and therefore, properly speaking, Old World churches have become denominations — voluntary communities of believers — in the United States. Here separation of church and state has meant that there can be no official national religion.

We learn from the components of a religious system that religious beliefs — ideas — are only one part of a religion. Code, cultus, and even community all refer to concrete ways in which religion is acted out. More than a form of belief, religion is a matter of practice, an *action system*. Body and emotions play as large a role in a living religion as philosophical concepts. Perhaps, in fact, they play a larger role. Of course, there are connections between all parts of a religious system. Religious practice in code, cultus, and community organization expresses the ideas of the religious creed. Similarly, the religious creed provides an intellectual rationale for why people act in the religious ways that they do. Mind and body are both necessary to human religious life.

A Short Description of Religion

So far, we have noticed that the history of religions has been a history of how to deal with boundaries. We have seen that in ordinary religion people learned how to live well within the boundaries of their world and that in extraordinary religion they learned to cross them to reach an "other" world. We have found that in both of these kinds of religion, people have followed a systematic path in expressing their religion through creeds, codes, cultuses, and communities.

It is time now to sum up what we have learned in a short descriptive statement (some might call it a "working definition") to guide us as we explore religious history in America. Religion here can be understood as *a system of symbols (creed, code, cultus) by means of which people (a community) orient themselves in the world with reference to both ordinary and extraordinary powers, meanings, and values.* Orientation means taking note of where the boundaries are and placing oneself in relation to them. This may mean carefully within the boundaries, out on the frontier, or some of each. The point is that the process goes on continually wherever people are. From this perspective, while many people live without Gods, nobody lives without religion. Moreover, many people absorb seemingly contradictory elements and live comfortably in more than one religious system.

Describing religion in this way will be helpful to us later, because it gives priority in understanding religion to concrete human experience and expression. It does not tell us what the substance, or core, of religion is, but it tells us how religion functions (to deal with boundaries), and it tells us what forms (creed, code, cultus, community) it takes. Describing religion in this way also avoids making religious ideas the most important part of religion. As we will see in our study of the United States, for many people religion was not so much thought about as acted out. By contrast, the problem with many attempts to define religion has been that, in one way or another, they have fallen into the trap of making the specific content of people's ideas essential to the meaning of religion. That is, definitions of religion have traditionally ended by assuming that religion *had* to be about the Gods, the transcendent world, or a sacred realm. Then people could feel and do as they were inspired with reference to this intellectual object of religion. Body and emotions were always second to the intellectual contents of the mind — contents expressed in a special language that was recognizably religious.

Finding Religion in America

We have been pursuing at some length the meaning of the term *religion*, but thus far we have paid little attention to the theme that will be uppermost as our study progresses. We have not begun to consider the United States. The silence, in fact, has been deliberate because we will be trying to look not simply for the external features of church or sect in the United States but for what is *religious* about American religion. Now it is time to discuss more carefully the scope of the project in seeking to understand religion *in America.*

The phrase "in America" is here used as a shorthand for the political boundaries of the United States and all that happens within them. It is true that the phrase "in America" may have arisen initially to reflect the cultural imperial-ism of the United States—as if our neighbors to the north and south did not exist. In this study, however, the expressions "Americans" and "in America" are used to refer to the people and territory of the United States simply for conve-nience. We should recognize that the story of religion in the United States can-not be told fully until it becomes part of the larger story of religion on the North American continent. At the same time, limitations of space in this text will force us to stick to the borders of the continental United States. We will follow people across boundaries to deal with extraordinary religion, but with some re-gret we will not cross boundaries to deal with Canada or Mexico.

Many Religions and One Religion

American religious history, in this text, is the paradoxical story of the manyness of religions and the oneness of religion in the United States. The *manyness of religions* means religious pluralism. It refers to the distinct religions of the many peoples who have come to call the United States their homeland. Conversely, the *oneness of religion* means the religious unity among Americans. It refers to the dominant public cluster of organizations, ideas, and moral values that have char-acterized this country. We begin, therefore, with a short examination of religious manyness and oneness in America. In so doing, we hope to gain an overall glimpse of the religious elephant with which we began.

Religious manyness, or pluralism, is so much at the center of this story that, if it did not smack of irreverence, we might expand the elephant analogy to call America a religious "zoo," a menagerie of many religious animals of some-times altogether different species. Each of these "species" is a form of extraordi-nary religion. But each has also included generous portions of ordinary religion, coming from the cultural roots of the extraordinary religion, usually in a foreign land. Thus, the many religions have repeatedly introduced novelty into the existing situation, and they have done so both historically and geographically.

Historically, as each new native or immigrant group affirmed its religious independence on American soil, it brought an added element. People had to take account of a new religious group and make room for it. Moreover, other Americans had to find a way to include it in the script and operating procedures that governed religious liberty. Geographically, as different areas of the United States became the home of diverse peoples, a particular group might give the life and style of the area a regional flavor that was, in fact, a religious flavor from the group. Thus, the Amish left an indelible impression on the life of Lancaster County, Pennsylvania, as did the Hopi Indians on northeastern Arizona and Jewish immigrants on parts of Los Angeles.

Further, each people that became part of the United States, whether na-tive or immigrant, changed through time. More important, each people changed by, in, and through its relationships with the public mainstream that gave Amer-ica its religious oneness. So we need to take account of the interaction of the many (other) centers with the one (public) center in which the many were shaped by the one. We will see, too, as our study progresses, that the one was shaped by the many and, also, that the many were shaped by their mutual condition of "otherness" and their exchanges with one another. If every religion was about boundaries, the story of religion in the United States was doubly so. Perhaps this was the reason why European observers in the nineteenth century reported that America seemed more religious than any other nation they had known. Newcomers who might, in the land of their origin, have taken religion for granted and not have been actively involved in its institutional forms, in America might practice their inherited faith with self-conscious deliberateness. Again, the boundary issue might be the reason why many of the groups were so strongly impressed by the geographical reality of the land. Working out a relationship to the land became, in symbolic fashion, a way of working out a relationship with the one public center and with other peoples among the many — a way to discover an American identity.

Meanwhile, the religion of oneness supplied the continuing theme in both time and space, the collapse of boundaries (again) between peoples to transform them all into partisans of the center. Although the Roman Catholic tradition was strong in both the West and Southwest, historically this religion of oneness has been mostly Protestant, Anglo-Saxon, and white. It has, however, picked up many fellow travelers along the way, especially among the Northern European immigrants. New realities and events have made their impressions on it, but it has nonetheless maintained a clear and lasting identity.

This religion of oneness inherits the concerns of extraordinary religion from its Protestant heritage. But it is, above all, the ordinary religion of American culture, which comes to us through the media, the public-school system, government communications, and commercial networks. In both its ordinary and extraordinary forms, it is the religion of a kind of "ruling" elite among Americans — those who through their past history, education, and leadership roles control the main carriers of our culture. This ruling elite, whether it has intended to or not, has shaped the mainstream of American culture.

To cite but one example, for several centuries the influence of the elite dominated the textbooks of our land. Far and away the earliest and most striking attempts at public education were made in seventeenth-century New England. There the plans for each new town were required to include plans for its schoolhouse. As each small schoolhouse in New England came into existence, it needed books, and so texts were supplied, at first from overseas and then from American authors. These texts included affirmations of the theological beliefs of Puritans regarding Adam's sin and the grace of God (extraordinary religion). More significantly in the long run, they also included observations about human behavior and success as, for instance, in classics like Aesop's fables (ordinary religion). It was natural that when other communities sought to establish schools, they looked to New England for books or at least for models of how to write them. Then in the nineteenth century, when the common-school movement spread across America demanding free public schools for all, again there was a search for adequate texts. And again the models came from New England. Thus, it is not surprising that millions of American schoolchildren learned far more about Puritanism in New England than, say, about the Moravian or Cherokee Indian religions in Georgia.

Historically, sheer numbers *were* on the side of the religion of oneness. Many people, especially among the early immigrants to the nation, embodied the values that it taught. Therefore, from another point of view the religion of oneness is not so much the religion of a ruling elite as that of a democratic majority. It contains the assumptions, understandings, and moral judgments that made their greatest mark on the early American community because they were shared by the largest single group of people. It reflects, in short, the public face of America. At the same time, geographically, the religion of oneness means the ways of looking at religion and the styles of religious behavior that are generally present throughout the country. Even in places where the religion of oneness is now relatively unimportant, at least it commands the public media. In other words, even though Catholics and Indians predominate in the Southwest and even though African-Americans make up the majority in some inner cities, that picture is not clearly reflected in the dominant image that religion in America presents.

More about Boundaries

Like the meaning of religion itself, the meaning of religion in America is linked to the question of boundaries. Earlier in our discussion of boundaries, we viewed the issue of identity as a problem of setting up and respecting inner boundaries. This internal process, however, has external and social results; that is, we tend to act out our inner struggles and decisions. We like to give them flesh by creating concrete social expressions of them in the world. The existence of many religions and one religion in America is an example of this process. Hence, whether religion is ordinary or extraordinary, as we have already seen, it is expressed in communities.

From this perspective, the many religions and one religion of America are engaged in a dispute concerning boundaries. The many religions, each of them distinct, want to draw clear boundaries between themselves and others. Indeed, the clearer the boundaries, the tighter and more cohesive the religious group becomes — a fact that we noticed in our brief treatment of the differences among religious groups ranging from churches to cult movements. Meanwhile, the one religion seeks unity by including everyone within its religious landscape and drawing one great boundary around the whole. In its quest for unity, it aims to lessen the diversity that separate boundaries help to guarantee.

The difference between these boundaries, disputed by the many religions and the one religion, and that "other" boundary, which extraordinary religion seeks to cross, is great. The boundaries of the many religions and one religion are *social:* they concern problems about the relationships among people in ordinary life. On the other hand, the boundaries of extraordinary religion go beyond social arrangements: they present people with the goal of crossing into a sacred and otherworldly domain. Thus, the quarrel over boundaries between the many religions and the one religion helps us especially to understand what is *American* about American religion. But the goal of crossing worldly boundaries in extraordinary religion emphasizes what is *religious* about American religion. To put the matter another way, the dispute between the many religions and the one religion concerning boundaries takes place mostly within the boundaries of ordinary religion.

The Manyness of Religions in America

The text that follows is divided into two parts. In Part I, which is the longer section, we look in some detail at the manyness of religions in America. The approach is topical and at the same time historical. Thus, we begin with a series of chapters on what might be called the "original cast"—those groups whose presence together created the initial mix of religious and ethnic traditions that marked America. We start with the religions of Native Americans, the peoples who originally dwelled in the land. As we will see, the manyness of these first religions prefigured the religious and ethnic pluralism that would later characterize the United States. After the account of American Indian religions, we turn to the major European religions that came to the New World. Beginning with the Jews who took ship with Christopher Columbus, we continue with the Spanish and French Roman Catholics who maintained an early presence in the land.

Then, in two chapters, we examine the Protestants, who arrived as English colonists and thereafter dominated the political and religious history of the country. In the Old World, from a social perspective, both Jews and Roman Catholics had been organized in churches, religious communities that included everyone born within a given ethnic group or territory. By contrast, Protestants, although they at first followed the territorial idea of churches, later introduced the beginnings of personal choice in religion. From them arose the denominations, more selective and voluntary than churches but still broad and inclusive in a total cultural setting. From them, too, came major impulses toward *both* liberalism and conservatism in religion that came to characterize other religions as well.

With the religions of Native Americans and Europeans introduced, the text turns next to an account of the third major group among the first to arrive: African-Americans. Present from the early seventeenth century, these people brought with them the heritage of their indigenous African religions and also of Islam. In the New World, much of the heritage was lost, but much still remained, blending with the American experience and Protestant Christianity to form an authentic religion of blackness.

Now the text moves on to consider the effects of the American environment on religious creativity. In two chapters we examine a number of distinctive "newmade" religions that arose, mostly in the nineteenth century. We see, therefore, what happened religiously during a middle period in American history. At this time new religious sects and communes absorbed the tensions of pluralism and transformed them—into original solutions to problems that plagued people in a world that seemed to grow less friendly. In the occult and metaphysical traditions, which are treated next, we see people deal with these issues by turning not to sectarian communities where ethnic bonds could be cultivated but instead to other homesteads in their minds. By turning within, people sought a fixed and sure abode as America continually changed and seemed less understandable.

Then, by the end of the nineteenth century, Eastern peoples began to immigrate in greater numbers, bringing their native religions with them. At the same time, some non-Oriental Americans who had been seeking inner homesteads were attracted to some aspects of these Eastern religions. So a pattern of expansion—of cultural stretching—became more clearly a major theme in American religious history. This discussion of Eastern religions in America brings us to the 1860s and 1870s, when the manyness of new religious movements became a non-Protestant revival for many Americans. Next, we look at the inverse side of religious expansion in the "contraction" of regional religion. Although regionalism was always a feature of American religion, it became still more prominent in an era when more and more religious choices intensified pluralism for many. As one example of religious regionalism, we focus on the religion of the Southern Appalachian Mountains. Here we see an instance of how land and people blended to produce a distinct religious ethos that expressed a separate identity and spirituality. In the final chapter in Part I, we bring our study of expansion and contraction—and of American religious history—to the late twentieth century. We look at New Age religion as a key to the theme of expansiveness and contemporary Protestant conservatism as an important instance of the theme of contraction.

The Oneness of Religion in America

If the picture that emerges from Part I is largely that of many unconnected religious groups, that is part of the thrust of the story. In some sense, American religious history is like the short notes of musical staccato, a series of sounds, touching each other but not necessarily blending—at least not at the beginning. But played against the staccato, there is another theme that has woven itself through American religious history. This is the theme of the religion of oneness, and in Part II we listen to its major expressions.

First, we hear the theme of the Protestant mainstream, that public voice with which religion in America sounded. We learn its characteristics, all of which seem to blend with ease. We learn, for instance, how separation of church and state produced a situation in which every religious society was a voluntary organization, leading, in turn, to a need for religious activism to guarantee membership amid religious competition. We learn, too, about how a concern for moral rules to govern such activity led to increasing moralism in the mainstream religion of the United States, of how intellectual difficulties in religious thought were avoided in order to appeal to the greatest audience of active people, and of how revivalism emerged to capture the religious feeling that was preferred to religious thought.

Second, we hear the theme of civil religion, the religion of the nation–state, in which the idea of America itself became a center for religious worship. We listen to the early Puritans, who gave us the beginnings of civil religion in communities where church and state were fused into one. We hear, too, the new voices of the American Revolution, which joined the old Puritan notion of the New Israel to the God of the Declaration of Independence, ruling by natural law and granting natural rights to all. We follow the message through the years of the nineteenth and twentieth centuries into our own era, listening to presidential speeches and foreign-policy decisions that confirmed the religion of nationalism. We hear it at Fourth of July celebrations and at times of national crisis when patriotic voices grew strong.

Finally, the message of the civil religion persuades us to listen for still a third theme — the larger cultural religion of the United States. Civil religion in one way was a form of this religion, but it had also been deliberately shaped by legislators and government leaders. In the less self-conscious forms of cultural religion, people themselves created an ordinary religion to express the specifically American ways in which they found meaning in life. So we learn how nature and the land have become religiously significant for many Americans, while others have turned to technology and the machine as sources of direction and value. We hear religion in the shouts from baseball and football stadiums, and we find a religious dimension to the evening news. We listen, too, to American heroes from Davy Crockett to Elvis Presley for the clues they give to the ordinary cultural religion of Americans. Then we listen for the rhythms of the annual calendar with its cycle of feasts from Thanksgiving to Halloween, each of them telling us something about the religion of oneness in America.

As we listen, we begin to see. Although there is darkness, we can begin to trace the dimensions of the American religious elephant. The manyness and the oneness are interconnected, each affecting the other and both together writing American religious history. In the concluding chapter, we examine some of the relationships between manyness and oneness — relationships in which the one influenced the many, the many made changes in the one, and the many also transformed their ways of life in the presence of one another.

In Overview

We have been thinking about American religious history partly from the perspective of a discipline called the history of religions. One task in the ongoing work of that discipline is to understand what makes something religious. Although it has proved extremely difficult for scholars to tell us completely, we have seen that the question of boundaries is important to answering the question of religion. The boundaries are both external and internal; they are also both social boundaries between different peoples and spiritual boundaries between this world and one thought to go beyond it. The last two kinds of boundaries (social and spiritual) correspond roughly to two kinds of religion. The first of these, ordinary religion (concerned with social boundaries), is what we normally refer to as culture. The second, extraordinary religion (concerned with spiritual boundaries), tries to reach beyond culture to encounter an "other" dimension to life, such as the God or Gods a people claims. Both ordinary and extraordinary religion express themselves as religious systems. As such, both contain creeds (belief systems), codes (norms for behavior), and cultuses (ritual actions), which combine to give a community a language for naming and expressing various powers, meanings, and values in life.

When we apply this understanding to the United States, we find that it is complicated by the importance of the social boundaries in this country and by the changes that history has brought. Mostly related to ordinary religion, these social boundaries establish a "one" religion that has been historically dominant from the point of view of share of population, power in government and supporting institutions, and social prestige. The social boundaries also indicate the presence of many religions, the expressions of various peoples who live within the United States. In the chapters that follow, we deal with the many religions in Part I and the one religion in Part II. Then, in a conclusion, we explore the complex series of relationships between one and many.

Studying American religions and religion in this way *is* aiming for a good deal. And we have to admit at the outset that we will only partially succeed. Sometimes, factual records will be lacking, and more times the elusive records of people's experiences will defy recovery. Sometimes, the subtleties and intricacies of response and reaction in the pluralistic situation will all but prevent a refined analysis (further elephants? further darkness?). But the "messiness" of the materials is not an excuse for refusing to try to understand them, and it is in this spirit that we need to go forward. We begin at the beginning, therefore, with the religions of Native Americans.

SUGGESTIONS FOR FURTHER READING: DEFINING RELIGION IN AMERICA

Comstock, W. Richard. *The Study of Religions and Primitive Religion.* New York: Harper & Row, 1972.

Eliade, Mircea. *The Sacred and the Profane.* New York: Harcourt, Brace & World, Harvest Books, 1959.

Evans-Pritchard, E. E. *Theories of Primitive Religion.* Oxford: Clarendon Press, 1965.

Marty, Martin E. *A Nation of Behavers.* Chicago: University of Chicago Press, 1976.

Mead, Sidney E. *The Lively Experiment: The Shaping of Christianity in America.* New York: Harper & Row, 1963.

Niebuhr, H. Richard. *The Social Sources of Denominationalism* (1929). New York: New American Library, Meridian Books, 1975.

Streng, Frederick J. *Understanding Religious Life.* 2d ed. Belmont, CA: Dickenson, 1976.

Troeltsch, Ernst. *The Social Teaching of the Christian Churches* (1911). 2 vols. Translated by Olive Wyon. Chicago: University of Chicago Press, 1976.

Van Gennep, Arnold. *The Rites of Passage* (1909). Translated by Monika B. Vizedom and Gabrielle L. Caffee. Chicago: University of Chicago Press, 1960.

Wach, Joachim. *Sociology of Religion* (1944). Chicago: University of Chicago Press, Phoenix Books, 1962.

Ellis Island, 1907. New York's Ellis Island was the main port of entry for
European immigrants at the turn of the century.

Part One

THE MANYNESS OF RELIGIONS IN AMERICA

From the first, a central feature of American history was the manyness of American religions. Religious pluralism was present with the aboriginal inhabitants: Native Americans were organized in separate nations, and each nation possessed its distinctive religion. Jews, Roman Catholics, and Protestants also added to the manyness as they immigrated. They brought not only external differences with one another but also internal divisions within each group because of the different ways they came to interpret the themes of their given religions. Similarly, African-Americans added to the complexity with religious constructions of their own.

Nor did the pluralism end with the original actors in what became American religious history. New forms of old religions flourished, and so did religions that were radically new — with new founders, claims of revelation, and behavioral prescriptions. By the nineteenth century, the presence of new immigrants and their religions contributed another dimension to the manyness. Eastern forms of religion became more available, and religious eclecticism as well as occult-metaphysical themes became more prominent. In the twentieth century, pluralism seemed stronger than ever. There were noticeable patterns of stretching toward religions that seemed "other" from the point of view of a hypothetical mainstream. At the same time, there were identifiable patterns of contraction, of turning within to seek a purity and definition that many otherwise found missing.

THE ORIGINAL CAST

Native Americans—American Indians—were the first human inhabitants of the Americas. For centuries, in separate nations, they nurtured and developed their own cultures without serious interruption by European or other peoples. But by the late fifteenth century that situation began to change, and by the seventeenth century a series of other peoples had arrived in the land to stay. The sixteenth century saw Spanish Catholics and their missionaries in Florida and New Mexico, while the seventeenth century brought French Jesuit missionaries south of the St. Lawrence River. Meanwhile, Jews of mostly Portuguese origin were settled in Brazil until wartime circumstance forced them to flee in 1654—many to the Dutch colony of New Amsterdam that would later become New York. By this time, English Protestants of broadly Puritan leanings had dug in on the Eastern seaboard, and African-Americans were supplying forced labor to New World English masters.

Five religious groups, broadly conceived, were now present in the land that would become the United States. Native Americans had been joined by Jews, Roman Catholics, English Protestants, and African-Americans. Throughout the eighteenth century, this original religious "cast" would occupy the stage of American history largely unchallenged by new religious players. Already, though, the diversity was impressive, with significant differences, especially, among Native Americans, English Protestants, and African-Americans inherited from their respective pasts. And already, changes were afoot, and new religious configurations could be seen.

Chapter 1

Original Manyness:
Native American Traditions

At one time or another, each of us has probably seen a photograph of a tired Indian warrior idling his horse or of an ancient Indian woman, wrinkles lining her face, looking into the sunset. The message was clear enough: Indians had come to the end of their trail. They were a vanishing race, and while remnants of their cultures had survived, it was up to scholars to collect them and up to others to appreciate them with dutiful nostalgia. Yet if we are to take seriously the record of events in the second half of the twentieth century, the message was wrong. Native Americans, along with many other ethnic minorities in America, enjoy a new vigor as they demonstrate that their cultures have endured and grown in the face of the dominant Euro-American mainstream. In fact, in law courts and public demonstrations, Indians have signaled militancy, and they are also reclaiming the relics of their ancestors that whites have displayed on museum shelves.

Central to these manifestations of Indian cultural health have been Native American religions. Articulate representatives of Indian people have seen the ancient beliefs and rituals as a strong foundation for contemporary political endeavors. While we may argue that politicized religions are changed religions, the point is that the religions have shown themselves as the source of Native American identity and vitality. Any study of American Indian experience must begin and end in religion. It must learn to trace the sacred circles the Indians themselves did.

The resiliency of these Native American religious traditions in the midst of the political battles of the twentieth century is already a clue to something we will meet again and again. For Indians, until recent times, ordinary religion — the cultural religion within boundaries — and extraordinary religion — the clear attempt to reach beyond them — were fused. Indian nations such as the Oglala Sioux had no word for *religion* in their native language because they had not separated the ordinary details of living from the mysterious forces that they believed surrounded them. They saw their beliefs and activities as part of the same whole.

Native American Diversity

If the picture of the tired warrior at the end of the trail is wrong, however, it is wrong not just because it speaks of the death of Indian cultures. It is also wrong because it suggests that there is any one Indian to represent all Indians or any one Native American tradition to represent them all. Native American culture, in the singular; Native American religion, in the singular; or discussion of "the American Indian," again in the singular, is mostly a convenient fiction when we need to contrast Native Americans with Euro-Americans. In reality, about 550 different Indian societies and distinct languages have been identified in North America, and even four decades ago, about 150 Native American languages were still being used north of the Rio Grande.

Indian languages have been divided into five major groups, a fact that, in itself, suggests the diversity of Indian cultures. To the east were Algonkian speakers, among them the peoples who first encountered the English on the shores of Massachusetts Bay and Virginia. Still others who spoke Algonkian dwelled in the eastern part of the Midwest and in a far western pocket. Running like a wedge between the eastern and midwestern Algonkian speakers were the Six Nations of the Iroquois, who spoke varieties of Hokan-Sioux, the language group of vast areas in the southeastern United States, the central prairies, and portions of southern California as well. In parts of the Southwest and the West, Uto-Aztecan, which had affinities to cultures farther south, was spoken, while also in the Southwest and parts of the Northwest, Athabascan was the language family for many Indian nations. Meanwhile, Penutian speakers dwelled in the Northwest, and, if we include Alaska, we introduce a sixth language family, that of the Eskimo-Aleut, which flourished in broad coastal belts alongside the Athabascan spoken farther inland.

Just as languages and geographical areas expressed the diversity of the Indians, so did cultural characteristics. Some Native Americans were hunter-gatherers, others were agriculturalists, and still others were various combinations of the two. Some societies were highly organized, while others were loosely knit. Some seemed to absorb elements from the cultures of their neighbors, but others remained more isolated. Some gave prominence to women in kinship organization and in actual responsibility. Others were, as anthropologists say, patrilineal (taking their rights from the man's side of the family) and patrilocal (living after marriage in the man's household, or village/band). Basketry, pottery, and weaving flourished among many groups, but in others, if they existed, they were not too important. Shelters were erected in various styles and sizes and materials. Some groups were warlike, and others fought only with great reluctance, regarding the slaughter of another human being as a form of pollution.

In such a picture of manyness, it seems fair to ask if there were as many Native American religions as there were Native American languages and cultures. The question, however, already betrays a Euro-American way of seeing and organizing things, and its answer is present in the fusion of the ordinary and the extraordinary we have mentioned in Native American cultures. For Native Americans, culture was tradition was religion; so there were as many American Indian religions as there were separate peoples and societies. As a matter of fact, one of the strongest points of cultural collision between Indians and whites was in their understanding of what whites called religion. Indians thought that every *people* had its sacred stories and rituals on which its world was based. Euro-American Christians argued that their religion was the universal truth for all. Even though in mission practice they spread the values of European culture along with Christianity, in theory, at least, they thought Christianity transcended culture. Indians, in other words, would hardly ride a country circuit to win converts whom they could not adopt wholesale into their communities. On the other hand, Euro-Americans saw converting the "heathen" as one of the reasons they should settle the New World.

Common Characteristics in Religion

Although there was an ethnic profusion of American Indian religions, it is possible to talk provisionally about common characteristics that run through most, if not all, of them. Looking at these common characteristics is most helpful when we want to see Native American religions as a related series that can be contrasted with Euro-American religions. Because so much of our later discussion will deal with Euro-American religions, we need to look at these mutual elements in Indian religions. We also need to have some sense of the differences among them and some sense of how later historical developments have changed them, but let us begin by noticing what traditional Native American religions have had in common.

In general, Native American religions possessed a strong sense of continuity with the things that people held sacred. Both in space and in time, Native Americans saw what they conceived as holy and mysterious as very closely related to their daily existence. In space, whereas Euro-Americans conceived of a three-level universe with God, human beings, and nature inhabiting different realms, Native Americans thought of a world to which they were bound by ties of kinship. There were the Grandfathers who were Thunder Beings; there was Grandmother Spider; and there was the Corn Mother. There were animals who took on human form such as Coyote the Trickster or sacred birds or sacred buffalo. There were gifted human beings such as shamans—holy people who, as sacred healers, mystics, and magicians incorporated into one, were said to fly like birds and talk to the animals. Among the Plains Indians, even ordinary people were thought to speak to guardian animal spirits in vision quests. The world, in short, was a huge extended family network, with the Indians existing as younger and humbler brothers and sisters among their more venerable relations.

In time, too, the Indians saw powerful ties of continuity that bound them to sacred events they believed had occurred before the coming of the present world. These events, shrouded for them in mystery, were the acts of creation that had caused the world and Indian peoples to be. For Native Americans, these events were the enduring models on which life was to be based in the years that followed. There was no break between these models and the happenings that made up the ordinary history of a group. History, indeed, was considered sacred; and it was thought to begin in the origin account of the people. When N. Scott Momaday, a twentieth-century Kiowa Indian, tried to explain what his people meant to him, he did so in a narrative (*The Way to Rainy Mountain*) that combined the Kiowa traditional account of origins with historical traditions, recollected stories of his immediate ancestors, and his personal appropriation of all three sets of traditions. When Edmund Nequatewa, a twentieth-century Hopi, attempted to describe Hopi "truth" for outsiders (*Truth of a Hopi*), he began with Birdmen in the original Hopi underworld and included the twentieth-century founding of the village of Hotevilla. Traditional account and recent event were collapsed because, just as Indian space existed as one whole, so, too, did Indian time.

In such a world in which metaphors of kinship abounded and tradition was as real as clashes with the government of the United States, the material world was, above all, holy. While Euro-Americans tended to separate material from spiritual things and in their religions to exalt the spiritual, Native Americans expressed in many ways their sense of the sacredness of matter. The distinction between a natural and a supernatural realm, an easy shorthand for describing Euro-American religions, was forced and strained when applied to the religions of Native Americans. They saw power at work, awesomely and mysteriously, in every portion of nature. It was, for them, personal power, and the forces of the universe could be named as relatives. But it was never or hardly ever abstract power that in its "real" form was separate from nature. The sacred beings were conceived as animal and plant guardians who, in a pact long ago, had pledged the bodies of their species as food for Indian peoples. Thus, Pacific Coast Indians had to be careful in taking flesh from the salmon, for they believed that the skeleton, when placed in the river waters, would receive new flesh as the sacred beings reproduced themselves. Other Native Americans evolved elaborate rules of courtesy for hunting or planting, apologizing to the spirits of the life forms they took, offering first "fruits" to these spirits, and being careful to use every portion of what they killed. Because nature — the material world — was thought sacred, Indians mostly tended to be natural ecologists from an age before the Euro-American concept was born.

If the outer world that surrounded Native American peoples was held to be sacred, so, too, was the inner one. For them, dreams revealed holy, hidden things that often would not be known in other ways. The Iroquois had their dream-guessing rite in which individuals presented themselves to the tribal council so that personal dreams and their meanings could be discerned. On the Plains, leaders of the hunt were men who had prayed for months and had dreams they believed were significant. For the Mohave in the West, the warrior who would take scalps must first have had the "good dream for taking scalps," regarded as the sign of religious power for the undertaking. Sometimes, for native peoples, in dreams the free soul traveled to distant places to learn, and at other times dreams brought visions from guardian spirits.

This inner world that dreams disclosed was intimately related to the one outside. Bridging the space between inner and outer, an Indian person should have a name that indicated his or her kinship with nature and at the same time told something of inner essence. For many Native Americans, names were changed as significant deeds and happenings etched new marks in the story of their character. So there could be Black Hawk, or Afraid of Horses, White Rabbit, or Moves from Your Sight Little Red Star. The colors were significant here, for each of the four directions had its color, which brought with it certain qualities as gifts of the direction. Thus, the red of the north might be the color of wisdom, while the white of the south might be thought to give innocence and trust. The black of the west might be held to bring deep thought and introspection, and the yellow of the east might be the sign for inner light.

Changing a name, however, was only one form of a process that Native Americans saw all around them. Transformation was almost in European terms a law, and Indian lore was filled with accounts of animal–human changes, as we have noted. Trickster figures such as Hare or Raven or Coyote were shapeshifters who could assume any form they chose in the midst of their adventures. They were seen as beings of creative power who had helped to put the present world in order. At the same time, they seemed to embody a principle of disorder that continually disturbed the regular workings of society.

The "hero" of the Winnebago Trickster cycle, for example, violated the first rule of a warrior: that he must keep himself away from women, who possessed an alien power capable of interfering with the warrior's power. Trickster, in other words, could change from world maker to world breaker and back again. He could also shift from the sly, cunning creature who could outwit Bear or Coyote to the fool who fought himself because his right arm and left arm did not know that they belonged to each other and who burned his own anus to punish it for not standing guard while he slept. He was male, yet he became female, married a chief's son, and bore him three little boys. Most of the time, as a male, he carried his penis around in a box with him and did not quite know how to treat it. Yet when Chipmunk managed to gnaw most of it up, Trickster used the pieces to make potatoes, artichokes, ground-beans, and rice for the people.

Trickster, in short, was the epitome of existence without boundaries, thrown open in every direction to become what inspiration and circumstance decreed. He posed the major issue for Native American religions directly. Continuity and discontinuity, identity and transformation were statements about boundaries and frontiers. Indians seemed to be saying that the lines that bound them in the sacred circles of their communities were all-important, and yet, at the same time, they were admitting how fragile and, indeed, fictive these lines were. Belief in transformations implied a world that was one substance, and Trickster figures continually reminded Indian people of this.

Native Americans highlighted the importance of transformation in their ceremonies. Many societies had sacred clowns who were at once funny and terrible beings. They could do foolish things, such as dressing themselves backwards and acting in a backward and upside-down manner. They could embarrass others by sexual joking or mimicking, and they could tease mercilessly. Yet they were very serious figures, such as the Sioux clown, or *heyoka*, who assumed his calling because of his sense of visionary power from a Thunder Being. Sometimes clowns brought retribution to the people, like the Fool Dancers of the Kwakiutl, who threw stones, or the False Faces of the Iroquois, who sprayed hot cinders. Indeed, clowns were to ritual what Tricksters were to cycles of traditional story, and by turning the standing order inside out, they pointed to the permeability of boundaries and the necessity, sometimes felt, of destroying them. Creative disorder, they seemed to be saying, could and would regenerate the order on which religion and society depended.

Often, in ceremonies, masked dancers carried transformation further still as they impersonated different Gods and guardian spirits and sometimes, in the course of the dance, felt they became the figure they impersonated. In the Pueblo villages of the Southwest, according to tradition, the Kachina dancers came from the mountains to perform on ritual occasions during the year. Meanwhile, in hunter societies, shamans were seen to transform illness into material objects that could be sucked or drawn out of their patients. Special dreams were transformed into ceremonies by being acted out, among the Plains people, in ritual dramas. Sacred story became history, and history was changed into sacred story. In sum, it was the deceptiveness of appearances that Native American religions proclaimed. This ordinary world for them touched another; in fact, it *was* another. Sacredness, the transformations told, was never far away.

Living in such a world, Native Americans conceived of their religious task as the process of bringing themselves into harmony with nature, which surrounded them. Harmony with the natural (and sacred) world, they believed, conferred power in the hunt, in the field, in war, or in government. Power was thought to come from the solemn recitation of origin accounts that brought Indian peoples into harmony with their beginnings. Power was found, too, in sacred objects and forces that manifested themselves in ritual — in the sweat lodge, in a sun dance, or in a sacred game of ball — and led to harmony with the universe.

In these ceremonies and even in more mundane tasks such as constructing a dwelling, Indians were preoccupied with the directional points. They lived out their sense of the importance of orientation toward boundaries in graphic ways. Four — for the four directions — was a privileged number that appeared again and again in story and legend as well as in ceremony. The number five was privileged as well, for it added the center to the four corners. So, too, was seven, since to the four directions of the horizontal plane, seven added a vertical dimension: there was the zenith, or highest point, the nadir, or lowest depth, and the center, where the Indian person stood. Understood in this way, religion became a centering process in which Native Americans learned to maintain harmony by living equidistant from all the boundaries. For them life blossomed not just on the edges of society, as transformation had hinted, but also in the middle.

Standing in the middle with the six directions at equal points around him or her, the Native American described a three-dimensional circle. It was like the circles traced by vegetation or like the circles that figured so frequently in ceremonies and also in the construction of dwelling places. Circles were sacred for Indians because they reflected and imitated shapes they saw in nature. To be in harmony, for Indian people, meant to live as part of the circle, or the medicine wheel, of the world. Thus, in their religions, Native American peoples were living out their own versions of the ancient idea of correspondence. Their societies were understood to be small-scale replicas of a larger reality that surrounded them. They believed that it was up to them to be the manifest expression of the powers that were nature's secrets. At the same time, by looking at the picture as painted on the larger canvas, the canvas of nature, they believed they could better comprehend life's meaning and appropriate work. Because they saw themselves as made of the same stuff as the natural and sacred world, the boundaries were always permeable and could easily be crossed. Yet because the natural and sacred world was seen as one of centers and circumferences and directions, Indian peoples could plant themselves securely in the middle place, in the ordinary world where they did not venture toward the frontiers.

Euro-Americans, on the other hand, tended to see the world in more divided ways. The sacred world of divine power was for them separated from the profane one of ordinary existence. God, they believed, had caused the world to be, and his law governed its movements; in that sense, he could be said to dwell within it. Yet for them he also far transcended it, and meanwhile his human creatures had increased the separation between God and the world by the fall in the Garden of Eden. In this understanding, sin had entered the world, and it had affected not just human beings but all of nature. For Euro-Americans, the world had become a three-level affair. God tried to control human beings, and human beings tried to control nature. If there was rebellion in both cases, it only emphasized the fact that the seamless garment of one creation had been, in the Euro-American view, pulled apart. That there were important values attached to the divisions of creation and creator we will see when we begin to consider Euro-American religions in more detail.

Differences in Religion

For now, however, our task is to understand what we can about Native American religious traditions. For the most part, we have been viewing them in terms of what they had in common, and beyond indicating the vast array of Indian societies and languages, we have paid very little attention to their differences. It is, of course, difficult to touch on the differences in a study such as this, but in order to give some sense of the range that has existed in American Indian religions we will briefly take up the religions of two distinct Indian societies, the Oglala Sioux and the Hopi. The first is a hunter-gatherer society of the Plains, and the second is an agricultural Pueblo culture from the Southwest. By looking at what religion means among each of these peoples, we will gain some sense of the differences that have made American Indian religions separate and distinctive traditions.

The Oglala Sioux

The Oglala Sioux, who were victims of the United States military in the Wounded Knee Massacre of 1890, are perhaps the best-known single group of American Indian people. They were one of the thirty-one or so Indian nations who in the nineteenth century roamed the prairies of North America between the Mississippi River and the Rocky Mountains, setting up temporary camps and moving them as the seasons changed and they pursued the buffalo. More specifically, the Oglala Sioux belonged to the Teton division of the Seven Fireplaces of the Sioux family. They dwelled in the western portion of Sioux territory and, along with other nations of the Teton Sioux, spoke Lakota.

Like the other Tetons, too, the Oglala had originated in what is now the state of Minnesota and had come onto the Plains, where in about 1750 they obtained horses, an event that changed their fortunes and led to their wealth and fame as buffalo hunters. With horses they no longer had to travel and hunt on foot, carrying their belongings on their backs or with their dog travoys. Ironically, the horses had come from whites — from the Spanish of the Southwest from whom the animals had strayed or been stolen or traded. Thus, the beginning and end of the flowering of Sioux culture were linked to Euro-Americans. But in this heyday of their fortunes, the religion that the Oglala lived reflected the centrality of the buffalo and taught lessons of a sacred world in terms of the values of Native American hunters. Like American Indian religions in general, it blended ordinary and extraordinary worlds together.

The traditional account of the Oglala's origin, like that of many another Indian people, concerns their emergence from the earth — in this case through the intrigues of a Trickster figure, Inktomi the Spider. Through a wolf, Inktomi wooed the people with food and clothing until Tokahe and three strong companions came to the upper world to investigate its virtues for themselves. Here, Inktomi plied them with more gifts and promised them youth, so that they returned to the people in the world below with glowing tales of what they had experienced. Although the old chief and an old woman warned of cold wind and the need for hunting in the upper realm, Tokahe led out six families. The results were not so fortunate as they had hoped, and the children cried for food while Inktomi laughed. Yet all was not lost, for they met Old Man and Old Woman, who taught them to hunt, clothe themselves, and make tipis. Oglala life had begun: for the tradition, Tokahe and the six families were the first people in the world.

This is but one of a cycle of sacred stories that explained the origins of things in intricate detail. In the beginning, according to account, there had been Skan, who gave movement to all, but it was Inktomi the Trickster who performed the real work of transformation that made the Oglala a people on the earth instead of under it. In other words, there was the vanishing God, Skan, and then a culture hero, Inktomi, who provided the creative impetus for the present world. Such a pattern was frequent among Native American accounts of origin, but what is important here is that this particular sacred story told of *Oglala* beginnings. It was about a specific people, not about the world in general. Like all sacred accounts, the story this one told is true in the sense that it explained the meaning of existence in the world as the Oglala knew it. We are a people of the earth, they were saying, and although creation was a kind of trick that was played on us (we did not really know what it meant to be born; we did not really have any choice), still we have learned to feed and clothe and shelter ourselves. Our life goes on.

The origins of life, however, concerned not only physical existence. There were origins, too, for the rituals that acted out the meaning of being Oglala Sioux. So tradition explained the gift of a sacred pipe to the people when once two of the men were approached by a beautiful woman in white buckskin with a bundle on her back. Later, the sacred story told, she entered the Oglala Sioux camp, came to the lodge, and with ritual attention to the directions, presented the sacred pipe to the chief. "With this sacred pipe," she said, "you will walk upon the Earth; for the Earth is your Grandmother and Mother and She is sacred." Since before the beginning of the nineteenth century, the pipe has figured in the rituals of the Oglala — the sign of their felt bond to one another and to the earth, their common source. In the tradition, the pipe, in fact, accompanied the gift of ritual. For the mysterious woman also offered the people a round stone containing seven inscribed circles, each of the circles representing a rite that they would receive. After she had taught them the first of these rites — a ceremony meant to keep spirits of the dead — she walked away, turned into a red and brown buffalo calf, rolled over and became a white buffalo calf, and then became a black one.

This White Buffalo Calf Woman, it was said, had given the Oglala a ceremonial repertoire, with the sacred pipe at its center, for the expression of all their religious needs. Thus, in the first rite of ghost keeping, the Oglala were able to deal more easily with death. The soul, or spirit, of a deceased person, it was believed, could be kept for a period of time ranging from six months to two or more years. A kept "ghost," instead of starting immediately on the ghost road to its fate, was thought to remain close to relatives. Keeping the ghost in this way was said to enable it, through the proper rites, to be sure of return to its beginnings. At the same time, ghost keeping served as a reminder to others of the fact of death. Elaborate ceremonies surrounded the making and keeping of a ghost bundle, including a lock of hair from the dead person. Members of the family observed ritual taboos, and a special dwelling was built for the bundle. When the day arrived on which the spirit was meant to be released, the ceremonies were equally elaborate.

The other rituals of the Oglala have included the sweat lodge ceremony, the vision quest, the sun dance, the "making of relatives," the girl's puberty ritual, and a sacred ball game. Each of them was characterized by minute prescriptions for word and gesture, hinging always on the use of the directional points. Each ritual, in other words, located the Oglala in a world of meaning by a centering process with regard to space. As religious people, they paid attention to the directions, because in ordering themselves properly in relationship to the cardinal points, they sought to create the harmony that was the essence of their way. In the sweat lodge ritual, for instance, there were rules that governed the construction of the lodge, the use of space within it, and the roles that those who participated played. The leader had to move sunwise as he entered the lodge; the heated stones placed at the bottom of the special hole were four in number for the four directions; the two stones placed on top represented zenith and nadir; and the very top stone of all signified Spotted Eagle. There were thus seven stones (again, a sacred number), and prayers had to be offered over them before more stones could be added to give the necessary heat for the ritual purification. Later, after the door had been sealed, the ritual went forward with attention to the four directions as various gestures and actions were performed.

The vision quest, or *hanbleceya* ("crying for a vision"), gave men — and sometimes women — in the community the opportunity to use the power of ritual in a situation that was tailored to individual character. The ritual in its central part was performed alone on a sacred hill away from the camp, usually for the first time in adolescence. It was meant to enable the person who undertook the quest to gain power through a vision in which guardian spirits would reveal their relationship to the seeker and bestow the knowledge/power he desired. The ritual was conducted under the guidance of a holy man and involved the smoking of a sacred pipe, preliminary purifications in the sweat lodge, fasting, and prayer. Once the seeker reached the sacred hill, there was the same attention to directions we have previously seen: four saplings formed poles at the four directions, and the seeker traced a cross by returning to the center from each of the four.

Because the heart of the ritual occurred with the seeker alone for one to four days and because it was expected to yield knowledge and power for a particular seeker, the vision quest has often been cited as a sign of the individualistic nature of the religion of hunters. Yet to speak of the individualism of Oglala Sioux religion or its vision quest is a bit misleading. The vision quest, despite the loneliness of the seeker's encounter with the sacred, began and ended in community. The holy man who guided the quest embodied the spiritual wisdom of the Oglala as a people. The purification in the sweat lodge was never solitary but always the collective work of those who supported the questing individual — usually his relatives and the holy man. And when at last the seeker believed that the vision had been granted and that he had heard the Thunder Beings, or the animals and birds had spoken, he had to return, relate his experience in the presence of the others, and listen as the guiding holy man interpreted its meaning. In short, the vision became "flesh" when it had been ratified by the community through its authorized representatives. If there was a place for the individual in Oglala religion, it was a place that was very carefully circumscribed. The gift of the seven rites was conceived as a gift to all the people.

The communal character of Oglala religion was especially evident in the sun dance. The only ritual that occurred at a special time of year, the sun dance was held in the early summer after the buffalo "harvest." Often it was an intertribal affair involving a huge encampment in which many people came together. The ritual extended over four days, and each day had its proper ritual tasks, its formal and necessary ceremonies. A lodge was constructed, a cottonwood tree selected and trimmed according to prescription to form the sacred pole at the center, and the pole painted and decorated with symbolic offerings, among them reminders of the buffalo. In a dance that followed, warriors in their finest attire circled the pole, running to each of the directions to flatten the ground and symbolically "killing" the images of a man and a buffalo at the pole. But the culmination was the actual dance around the pole that gave the lengthy rite its name. The dancers were literally bound to the sacred center, attached by thongs to the pole. They performed either gazing at the sun from morning until night or with skewers digging into their flesh. Under their leader they danced themselves into an ecstasy of sacrifice until they fell exhausted or the flesh was pulled from their bodies and they were released. They fasted for the duration of the dance, demonstrating in this hunting version of a first-fruits festival that, in return for the gift of life they acknowledged, they would give themselves in the flesh.

The remaining rituals of the Oglala did not stint in their prescriptions for careful and symbolically elaborate ceremonial behavior. The "making of relatives" was designed to unite two people to each other in a bond considered closer than that between relatives, committing them to dying for each other, if necessary. The puberty ritual for girls, the buffalo ceremony, was performed at first menstruation with the intention of placing young women in the care of the sacred buffalo and of securing for them a relationship with White Buffalo Calf Woman. At their menstrual periods thereafter, women lived temporarily alone, a practice common among Native Americans, who believed that women possessed a power that, if it came into contact with that of the hunter-warriors, could damage it. The religious power seen in women figured in the seventh rite of the Oglala as well. In a ritual that perhaps symbolized the game of life, a young girl threw out a ball to people standing at the four directions. The ball stood for knowledge, and the people trying to catch it were struggling, said the Oglala, to free themselves from ignorance.

The ball used in the seventh rite, like so many of the objects that were part of the rituals, was considered *wakan*, or holy. *Wakan* was a quality thought to be possessed by the elements such as thunder and lightning, by the animals or plants, sometimes by human beings, and sometimes even by objects. For the Oglala, *wakan* was that dimension of reality that caused transformation. It was the mysterious force that surrounded them in the world the sacred buffalo had given, and in its culminating aspect it was *Wakantanka*, sometimes equated with the God of Christianity and Judaism. Yet it is difficult to translate into Euro-American terms the nuances of *wakan* and *Wakantanka*. Both may be said to be more adjectival — more qualifying — than substantive — fixed entities or things. *Wakantanka* perhaps means something like "holy, sacred," and yet *Wakantanka* also meant sixteen different godly beings who collectively were *Wakantanka*. The difficulty in understanding or conceiving of *Wakantanka* rests ultimately with the different models of relationship to what is held sacred that characterize Indians and Euro-Americans. Indians tend to see sacredness as a quality suffusing all things and to personify their Gods ambiguously so that at the same time they both are and are not separate from nature. Euro-Americans tend toward more precision — and separation — in their concept of the supernatural.

It should be evident, however, that if any being was *wakan* among the Oglala, it was the buffalo. Sacred story and ritual together demonstrated how central the buffalo was. Oglala religion, like Oglala life, revolved around the being from which, or whom, they drew all of their sustenance — economic, in the buffalo hunt and the many uses for buffalo meat, hide, and even teeth thereafter, but even more, spiritual. The buffalo gave the Oglala a center and an identity. If they were people of the earth, it was because they were people of the buffalo.

The people of the buffalo traveled a long path from 1700 to the twentieth century. Despite the advances of an alien Euro-American culture that threatened to take away their lands and livelihood, the Oglala proved stubborn in the maintenance of their identity. No longer depending for their survival on the leadership of a hunter-warrior, twentieth-century Oglala survive as a people because of their religion. The pipe is still an Oglala means of prayer, and prayer today, as in the past, is addressed to *Wakantanka*. Sweat lodge, vision quest, and sun dance all continue, and in the contemporary Oglala community there is a strong reawakening of religious traditionalism. Meanwhile, traditional religious practices have been joined by others: for some people, the peyote religion, which, in a communion ritual, sees and uses the plant as a sacred power person (see the section later in this chapter on "Change in Native American Traditions");

for a few, traces of the ghost dance (see the same discussion); and for most, Christianity. Usually, contemporary Oglala belong to one or another Christian denomination, and many traditionalist leaders see no conflict between Christian adherence and the older ways. In sum, with their canon of sacred story, with the presence of the buffalo through the sacred pipe and the seven rites that were seen as its gift, the Oglala have also adapted to change and have come to know themselves as one among the many peoples of the United States.

The Hopi

Although our look at the religion of the Oglala has been all too brief, we move now to a consideration of a much different group of Native Americans. We do this to gain some sense of the diversity that has existed in the religions of Native Americans, similar as they have been in overall ideas and ethics. The Hopi are numbered among the Pueblo, or "village," Indians of the American Southwest, so named because they dwelled together in adobe and stone apartment villages. River, or eastern, Pueblo peoples, the Tanoans and the Keresans, settled along the Rio Grande in what is now the state of New Mexico, but to the west in the desert was the country of the Zuni (New Mexico) and the Hopi (Arizona). Life in the desert proved to favor cultural continuity, for, with greater isolation from Spanish, Mexican, and Anglo-American conquerors than their eastern cousins, the Hopi for most of their history maintained an identity and ritual life largely untouched by Christianity.

Hopi origins are veiled in mystery. Some scholarship has suggested that over 2,000 years ago, their ancestors came into the Southwest. Groups of hunter-gatherers who learned to farm, the Basketmakers, as they have also been called, dug pits in the floors of caves to store their food and eventually began to live in pit houses in the caves or out in the open. Other scholars say that the Hopi came from the California desert to their present-day land from about A.D. 500 to 700. And the Hopi themselves tell of crossing the water to the New World on rafts or, as we will see, of emerging from the earth. What is clear, though, is that from about A.D. 900 to 1300, their culture reached its heights. This was the era of the cliff dwellings, carved into the sides of the mountains at places that were easy to defend, and the apartment terraces, villages that are still characteristic of the Pueblo peoples. Old Oraibi, the ancient ceremonial village of the Hopi, dates back to this time, having been built mostly after 1300, with beginnings, though, as early as 1150.

Most important, the Hopi have had ancient agricultural traditions behind them. While they were also hunters and gatherers in the past, particularly when their crops failed, hunting and gathering gradually declined. The Hopi continued to be farmers, growing crops of corn, beans, and squash as staples. Tilling the soil was a man's job in this society, but social organization revolved around women, since the communities were organized in matrilineal clans. The Hopi villagers spoke Shoshonean, which belonged to the Uto-Aztecan language family, and some of their beliefs and customs reflected the influence of Mezo-American Indian cultures. But they also inherited a variety of hunter-gatherer values, such as awe of the dead, and of practices, such as reliance on healers. Their villages were ceremonial centers in which the terrace apartments were grouped around the plazas, the sites of outdoor dances and formalities, and the kivas, the sacred pit houses where the various clans conducted rituals from which women were excluded.

Yet, although women had been barred from participation in kiva rites, Hopi tradition expressed the prominence of feminine symbolism. The Hopi had emerged from the womb of Mother Earth, their most sacred stories told them, and the kiva itself, essentially a large hole dug in the earth, was a forceful reminder. Each Hopi village had its own slightly different version of the origins of things, but there was general agreement on the major motifs. In one version from Oraibi, two Hard Being women (deities of hard objects such as shells, corals, turquoise, and beads) caused dry land to appear and then created birds, animals, a woman, and a man.

In another sacred story that related subsequent events, the people enjoyed a good life in the world below until evil entered into the hearts of the chiefs and the people, sexuality ran rampant, and hatred and quarreling grew apace. In their plight the chiefs tried to find an escape, and they fashioned a Pawaokaya bird, singing over him to give him life. Meanwhile, the chiefs planted a pine tree and a reed beside it to reach the hole into the upper world. The bird flew in circles around the two "ladders," found the opening but found nothing else, and returned exhausted. So, according to the story, the chiefs made a hummingbird and then a hawk who, in turn, repeated the search and also came back unsuccessful and exhausted. Finally, the chiefs created Motsni, who flew through to the upper world, found the site of present-day Oraibi, and also encountered, sitting there alone, Masauwuu, or Skeleton. When he heard Motsni's tale, Skeleton explained that he was living in poverty but that the people were welcome to join him. So they came, emerging from their plant ladders to the world above. Later, aided by Spider Woman, they fashioned a symbol that turned into the moon and another that became the sun. The people had begun to make their way, and given in the story the gift of corn, small though it was, the Hopi were also given an identity. After a series of migrations, the clans arrived at their villages, and life, as the Hopi knew it, began.

As if to corroborate the tradition, on a rock to the south of Old Oraibi the symbol of the emergence is said to be carved. It is an abstract symbol representing the womb of Mother Earth by means of a maze intersected at its opening with a cross line. The line is seen as the umbilical cord that connects the Hopi to the womb of the Earth Mother, and at the same time it is understood as the way through which they came out into the world. Meanwhile, in each sacred kiva of the Hopi was a *sipapu*, thought to open to the world below. Most times covered by a stone, it was opened at the initiation ceremonies at the end of the year with the belief that the dead could leave the womb of Earth to participate.

Blending folk memory and folk philosophy, the Hopi account fused history with interpretation. Emergence from the earth had been historical truth for the Hopi, if their ancestors had dwelled in the pit houses that were replicated in the kivas. Similarly, matrilineal organization must have existed for a long time, for it was said that in the beginning the Hard Being women (deities) had created a woman first and then a man. And the sequence was a model for customs in Hopi society by which women owned their houses and household goods and, in a sense, their children, who derived their clan kinship from their mothers. Finally, Skeleton and the small gift of corn suggested the precariousness of life in the desert growing subsistence crops. Yet, as with the Oglala, the truth of Hopi tradition did not depend on historical recollection. Once again, it was the statement of identity that made the account true, for in telling who they were, the Hopi were also telling what meaning and significance they attached to their lives. Like the Oglala, although in the particularity of their own sacred story, the Hopi were saying that they were people of the earth.

The Hopi were like the Oglala in being people of the earth, but unlike the Plains people they were farmers. Nowhere was this more clearly demonstrated than in the cycle of rituals that formed a ceremonial year in the Hopi villages. While the Sioux possessed only one calendric ritual in the sun dance, for the Hopi every rite depended on the cycle of the seasons. Desire for harmony with nature, in their case, was expressed in ritual harmony with its changing seasons: transformation, so central for all Native Americans, here meant following the movements of nature through cyclic time. The motivating force behind the calendar of rites was the ever-present need for water to make crops grow in this desert region. Once again, as for the Oglala, religion and everyday economic need were not strangers. Just as the buffalo was central for the Sioux, water was primary for the Hopi. In both cases, ordinary religion and extraordinary religion had been fused. Rituals were the vehicles for maintaining the boundaries so that life could be lived within the safe fences of economic and social organization. Rituals were also the way to cross over the farthest frontiers and experience what they felt as the power of the sacred.

In general, the rites of the Hopi year possessed certain common features. In a pattern that showed the fragmentation of the clan system and yet managed to effect some degree of reconciliation, each of the ceremonies was conducted by one or more hereditary chiefs and clans. At its most basic level, therefore, it might be appropriate to talk about the religions of the Hopi: each clan had its specific area of religious responsibility and, thus, its particular religious truth and action to teach. One might say that all got the chance to "do their thing" during the Hopi ceremonial year. All of the ceremonies aimed at the production of rain, as we noticed, for fertility and growth. All utilized, as well, similar ritual techniques: the offering of prayer sticks called *pahos*, the building of an altar of sacred objects, the sprinkling of corn as medicine to lead to the transformations of nature that the people desired, the recitation of the emergence story, the verbal forms of prayer, attention to the four directions, and the use of song and dance. Finally, the ceremonies usually followed a similar time pattern with eight days of preparation and then eight days of secret rites culminating in a public dance on the ninth day. With a full calendar of annual ceremonies, the Hopi were spending roughly one-third to one-half of the year in ritual concerns. Ritual work was, in short, at the center of their lives.

The major division in the ceremonial year was between the Kachina rituals from December through July and the non-Kachina ones from August through November. In order to understand the significance of the Kachinas during their portion of the ceremonial year, we need to look more closely at Hopi belief. Actually, the word *Kachina* might refer to any one of three different phenomena in Hopi society. Kachinas were, first, thought to be spiritual beings. Inner and invisible forms, they were understood to give a spiritual dimension to outer and physical existence. They were not considered Gods in the Euro-American sense but were honored as spirits — of the dead; of minerals, plants, and animals; even of the planets. They were said to be intermediaries from the sacred world who, during the second half of the year, dwelled in the San Francisco peaks on the outer edge of Hopi country (the border, once more) and visited the Hopi villages during the first half when the Kachina rituals were held. Well over 250 in number (some say as many as 600 have been known), the Kachinas were never worshiped but rather looked upon as friends and endowed with a variety of human qualities. New ones were continually appearing as old ones were forgotten, so that the catalog of Kachina spirits was fluid and variable. So, too, were their personalities, ranging from benevolent, kindly spirits to others who inspired fear by their whippings to punish offenders in Hopi society.

Such reported physical contact with them suggested the second meaning of *Kachinas* for the Hopi. Kachinas were also the male dancers who, during the Kachina ceremonies, impersonated both male and female Kachinas. Wearing masks that represented particular Kachinas and were thought to confer sacred power, often believing they inherited a right to identify with these Kachinas, the performers sought to dance themselves into a state in which they lost all sense of separate self and felt that they *became* the Kachinas they impersonated. Kachina dancers, in other words, desired to achieve the transformation that Native Americans felt was all around them, crossing the frontier that divided ordinary reality from the extraordinary.

In its third and final usage, *Kachinas* referred to the elaborate and exquisitely carved dolls that the Kachina dancers gave to Hopi children during the ceremonies to teach them about the Kachina beings. Made in traditional and highly stylized patterns from cottonwood root, the Kachina dolls were not toys in the modern American sense, but neither were they sacred objects believed to contain power. Rather, they were perhaps "show" objects that would grace the Hopi home, reminding all, and especially the children, of the Kachinas the dolls represented. Beings, dancers, and dolls, all the Kachinas pointed to the

Crow Mother Kachina. Kachina doll representing the Crow Mother, known as the mother of the Hu Kachinas. At the February Powamu, or bean dance, the Crow Mother appeared through the performance of a male Hopi dancer.

extraordinary reality that for the Hopi lay behind the ordinary world. The grotesqueness of carved masks and dolls suggested a world beyond this one, imbued with a power that was other.

We return here to a consideration of the ritual calendar of the Hopi, divided into times for Kachina and non-Kachina ceremonies. By now it should be evident that Kachina ceremonies were those held to be visited by the Kachina beings as impersonated by Hopi dancers. The Hopi thought that the dual calendar was necessary because they believed that, in the world below this one, life corresponded to arrangements in Hopi society. Thus, whatever rituals occurred during the first part of the year above were replicated during the second half in the world below. The Kachinas had to be elsewhere in the summer and fall: this was why they could not dance in the village plazas with the Hopi.

The Kachina rituals included the Soyal, before the winter solstice, when the sun ceased its journey southward; the Powamu, or bean dance, in February; and the Niman, or home dance, in July. First came Soyal. In its culminating rituals, a cornhusk, which symbolized fertility, was brought to every person in the village so that all might breathe on it, sending a message to the spirit beings. After a ceremony in which sexual intercourse was simulated ritually by the male corn collector to encourage a corresponding fertility in nature, seed corn was gathered from the villagers and blessed. Later in a kiva dance, the Kachina Muyingwa, who embodied vegetation, leaped and danced. Prayer sticks were distributed to every house so that their presence throughout the year would provide a continuing plea to the spirit beings for the fertility the Hopi desired.

Then, for the February Powamu, preparations included a secret planting of beans in the kivas, where, kept warm and moist, the plants began to grow. Kachinas thereafter distributed the bean plants through the village as gifts to the people, promises of what was to come. Early in spring came the ceremony to honor the Great Serpent Palulukong, said to confer fertility on crops and also on people. In a dramatic sequence, his voice was simulated in the ritual, and within the kiva, puppets with huge serpent heads made from corn represented him and knocked over rows of corn plants to represent the future harvest. Finally, Niman, at summer solstice, marked the time when the Kachinas were said to leave the villages. By now, the first corn had come, and the Kachinas danced as a group for the Hopi as the people expressed their gratitude.

The disappearance of the Kachinas did not signal the disappearance of ritual. In August, Flute and Snake-Antelope ceremonies were held in alternate years with the hope that they would bring some final rain, supplying suitable soil for the Hopi to plant their corn a second time. Executed like all the Hopi rites by the clan or clans that had given their ceremony to the pueblo, the Flute ceremony featured distinctive music, elaborate symbolic adornment to represent the Hopi universe, and a procession to the sacred Flute Spring to procure water to be offered in prayers for rain. Meanwhile, the Snake and Antelope societies performed a ritual dance with snakes and then released the snakes into the desert to carry the Hopi prayers for rain. The Hopi intended to bring back the Snake people, according to tradition once driven in anger from one of their villages. As in the Flute ceremony, they were seeking a reconciliation with nature so that nature, restored to harmony, would give nourishment and life.

Later, in September and October, three ceremonies were performed by the women's societies. Since women were seen as passive beings who received the male seed and carried it to term, their prominence in ceremonies at this time seemed especially important. In this way of thinking, they should be open and ready to receive the seed so that human society would grow and blossom. So, too, the earth should begin to be ready, for soon it would be planting time again when, as the womb of nature, the earth would nourish the beginnings of life.

Finally, in November, came the Wuwuchim, the last of the non-Kachina ceremonies but actually the first of the three major winter ceremonies. Wuwuchim was the initiation ritual of the Hopi, when the *sipapu* was kept open so that, as the Hopi believed, the spirits of the dead could take part. Its symbolism of death and rebirth was apparent with the presence of a new fire, the closing of roads to the four directions (signifying death that must precede rebirth), a night of ritual washing of hair, and the recitation of the Hopi account of emergence. The candidates for initiation, young Hopi ready to become "men," remained in the kiva enveloped in their blankets, as they heard the sacred account of origins and experienced in themselves, it was hoped, the mysteries of spiritual death and rebirth. For the Hopi, harmony with nature meant that just as the cycle of the seasons brought death and rebirth to the natural world, so, too, the Hopi should conform their lives to the seasonal rhythms by undergoing an inner form of dying and being reborn.

It should be clear that with their attention to the planting cycle, their masked Kachinas, and the content of their religious concerns, the Hopi had a traditional religion that was significantly different from that of the Oglala. This is the case not only for the Hopi but also for the numerous other Indian societies that have flourished in what is now the United States. In many instances, it is true, people who were more closely related in culture have had similar religious systems. The point, however, is still that each was a distinct entity, not the same as the others. Each Indian nation had its traditions of origin, its ceremonial cycle, and its identity as "the people," cherished by the sacred powers and cherishing them. Each people saw itself as the collected children of nature.

In the case of the Hopi, erosions in the ceremonial life of the villages began to occur. At the same time, witchcraft grew with the spread of anxiety. Beliefs in witchcraft and sorcery had, indeed, been of long duration: the traditional account of the emergence, in its complete form, had spoken of the presence of sorcery both in the world below and in the world above. But as time passed, witches and sorcerers seemed to multiply everywhere, and fear and dissension struck at the heart of Hopi society. Old prophecies associated the coming of whites with the end of the Hopi way in the present world and the beginning of a time of purification.

From 1862 on, Mormons, with their accounts of Indian descent from the tribes of Israel (see Chapter 7), became the most successful among missionaries to the Hopi. It was not necessary, though, to abandon Hopi tradition and ceremony to embrace Mormonism or to follow other Christian denominations: a Hopi could participate in traditional religion and new (Christian) religion at the same time. On the other hand, at least one Hopi prophecy taught the coming of a new—and true—religion and counseled rejecting the traditional past to follow it.

More broadly, from 1870 on there was no avoiding the cultural presence of the United States. Religious and cultural compartmentalization became a continuing feature of Hopi life, with "blocks" of thinking and acting that remained traditionally Hopi and other "blocks" that accommodated the alien culture and its Christian religion. While the Hopi have demonstrated into our own time the persistence of their rituals, the strength of their religious bond can dilute, but not destroy, the acids of modernity. Like the religion of the Oglala, the religion of the Hopi has sought to preserve and protect the ordinary even as it conducts believers into the mysteries of the extraordinary world. Still, the decline of the Hopi ceremonial cycle, the increase of witchcraft beliefs and practices, and the expectations of the fulfillment of prophecy suggest the action of history on this Native American religion. With the resurgence of Native American religious traditions, however, decline is not the last word to be spoken. Hopi prophecies of the end are also prophecies of the beginning.

Change in Native American Traditions

Although we can only glance at the subject here, it is important to note the evidence that, for the Hopi and for all Native Americans, religion does not stand still while the world changes around it. Like the Hopi, who struggled to maintain their traditional ways and yet changed, other Native Americans continued, with greater or lesser success, to hold to their traditional religions. When change came, however, general responses to the new cultural forces were threefold. First, Native Americans might keep up the practices of their traditional religions but add to them a syncretistic blend of elements derived from Christianity. Second, Native Americans might express their anguish, and their hope, by taking up a variety of new religions. Third, Native Americans might be converted to various denominational forms of Christianity, either maintaining their traditional religion alongside and separate from the new or renouncing the old completely in favor of the new.

Syncretism (the mixing and harmonizing of elements from different religions) occurred in those regions that had been missionized by Spanish Roman Catholic priests, that is, in the Southwest and California. In the Rio Grande Pueblos of New Mexico, for example, after the initial period of encounter from 1540, there was little or no contact with Catholic priests in the late eighteenth century and through most of the nineteenth. Thus, the Pueblos for a period of about 150 years were free to modify the new rituals that Roman Catholicism had brought so that they might serve Native American ends. The result was ceremonial calendars in the various pueblos that for the most part were based on traditional Native American beliefs and practices. But added to them was an amalgam of Catholic ceremonies that seemed to satisfy Pueblo needs. There was little interest in Jesus or the Virgin, in heaven and hell, or in the Christian understanding of God. Yet a saint's day became an occasion for festivity, and Holy Week and Christmas, while not historical commemorations of events in the life of Jesus, were times for prayer. Similarly, the Roman Catholic All Souls' Day provided an opportunity to honor departed ancestors with gifts.

Perhaps the most prominent example of a new religion was the millennial religion (preaching the imminent end of the present world and the birth of a new one) of the ghost dance, which swept the Plains in the late nineteenth century. When the old religions seemed to fail as the whites pushed the Indians out of their lands, new religious prophets arose to proclaim rites and ceremonies that would bring the power to end white ascendancy and to restore the Indians to harmony with the earth and themselves. Among these new religious prophets was a Paiute Indian from Nevada named Jack Wilson, or Wovoka. He claimed to have died twice and to have seen God. Thereafter, he began to predict that the earth and whites would be destroyed by flood and that the Indians should perform the ceremony of their ancient round dance so that the flood would wash under them and they would survive. Then, predicted Wovoka, the earth would spring to life with the abundance of new creation, and in the fresh, green land that succeeded the arid Nevada terrain the Indians would be reunited with their deceased ancestors and dwell together in plenty.

The ghost dance, as it was called, spread rapidly among other Native American peoples as delegations from various Indian nations came to learn the ceremony. It had its most stark repercussions among the Oglala Sioux, who reshaped the dance to their own ritual sense and life needs. They began to wear ghost shirts as they danced — long white garments that, decorated with red-colored symbols and eagle feathers, they believed were bulletproof. This conviction contributed to their decimation at Wounded Knee as the Oglala, wearing their ghost shirts, thought they could not be harmed by the bullets of the U.S. Seventh Cavalry.

Other new religions among American Indians did not lead to such results. For example, the nineteenth-century Seneca religion led by the prophet Handsome Lake (d. 1815) resulted in the enduring organization of *Gaiwiio*, the Old Way of Handsome Lake. Indeed, even during his lifetime the religion of Handsome Lake spread from the Seneca to all Six Nations of the Iroquois. Based on three visions that he told he had had, Handsome Lake preached, first, an apocalyptic gospel that stressed the imminent destruction of the world, the reality of sin, and the need for salvation. Later he added a second social gospel that emphasized a series of moral reforms, including temperance, peace, model economic enterprise, and domestic rules and requirements. Beginning in the 1840s the Code of Handsome Lake combined a traditional account of the late prophet's visionary experience and teaching with ritual prescriptions for a longhouse (the traditional Iroquois structure) church and with moral guidance that underscored the sacredness of the family. In the latter part of this century, it has been estimated that perhaps one-quarter of all reservation Iroquois are following the Code of Handsome Lake.

In the twentieth century, too, the peyote religion has flourished, in the form of the Native American Church and independently. With a 1990 Supreme Court decision in *Oregon v. Smith*, the "free exercise" of peyote religion has not been supported at a national level. But although serious constitutional questions remain, the peyote religion is legal in some states, and its right to exist has long been tacitly acknowledged in others. More important than legal issues for us, though, is the strong evidence that ceremonial peyote use gives of Native American religious change.

A pan-Indian movement, peyote religion grew beginning in the second half of the nineteenth century and spread northward onto the Plains. By the early years of this century, it had been carried across the Mississippi River eastward by Indian people who lived on Oklahoma reservations. Peyote religion now exists from the Plains cultures of the Sioux to the reservations of the Navajo and Pueblo peoples: it has become the most widespread among contemporary Indian religions. The Peyote Way, as it is often called, centers on a communion ritual involving the ingestion of some form of the peyote cactus (*Lophophora williamsi*) in a ceremony that usually lasts for a night. There is prayer, song, meditation, sacramental consumption of peyote, and — when the communicant is said to be favored by the spirit power of the plant — extraordinary visual and auditory experience. Communicants say that peyote heals and gives knowledge, and they are also aware of the Christian elements in their religion. But they have actively *used* Christianity to express their own religious vision, and so they have strongly bent Christian material to Native American beliefs and values.

The Christian elements in peyote religion point to the fact that the new religions discussed here all contain Christian elements. What makes them new religions, though, and different from the syncretism of the earlier Pueblo example, is the presence of a strikingly new vision, even if shaped from older materials. It is a vision borne by the authority of a new leader or leaders who proclaim the distinct teaching; by the intensity of the new organizational commitment; and, most importantly, by the introduction of a distinctive new ceremony or ceremonies to integrate all of these elements.

Different from the amalgams that produced syncretistic religions and new religions was Native Americans' turn in a more direct way toward Christianity. Denominational Christianity had sprung up in various forms with the first presence of Euro-American Christians. Every European people that settled in the New World had as a conscious objective the conversion of the "heathen" to Christianity. The Spanish and French brought their priests, and the English sent Protestant missionaries. So there were "praying Indians" in colonial New England towns such as Natick, Massachusetts (see Chapter 5), while later (1769), in California, Franciscan missionaries created segregated mission communities of Christian Indians. Throughout the nineteenth century, with the development of the reservation system, knowledge of Christianity was introduced to the Indians. Today it would be difficult to find a reservation without the presence of one or more Christian churches.

Take, for example, the case of the Eastern Cherokee, who live on the Qualla Boundary Reservation in western North Carolina. In the early nineteenth century the Cherokee were spread across a series of southern states, and Christian missionary work began among them in 1801 with a Moravian center and school. By 1804 the Presbyterians came, and later the Cherokee allowed Baptists, Methodists, and Congregationalists (the last, along with the Presbyterians, as representatives of the American Board of Commissioners for Foreign Missions). When the federal government forced the bulk of the Cherokee Nation to resettle west of the Mississippi in 1838, a small remnant escaped the deportation to remain in the East. A decade later, isolated in the mountains of western North Carolina, they were, according to one visitor, mostly Baptists and Methodists. Indeed, even before the Removal, by 1829 the Gospel of Matthew was available in an authoritative Cherokee translation, and so was a hymnal.

Still earlier, in 1820, the Baptists, with their missionary Evon Jones, had been present; and eventually the Baptists won the most adherents among the Eastern Cherokee. Baptist strength continued into the twentieth century, so that by 1960, out of twenty-one Christian congregations on what was now the Qualla Boundary Reservation, fifteen were Baptist. In keeping with the mid-twentieth-century Baptist message throughout the South, it was fundamentalist Christianity that the Eastern Cherokee were taught. Predominating themes were human sinfulness and the need to believe in salvation through Jesus Christ to escape the torments of hell. The Cherokee attended services faithfully and listened to the preaching.

Still, there was more to this Cherokee embrace of Christianity than first meets the eye. The Cherokee could relate to the Christian message of kinship and love because, in their own clans and extended families, they already felt they experienced both. Similarly, they could relate to the message of guilt and the need for atonement because, in their traditional religion, the quest for purity had been an important theme. In fact, the ritual of baptism, so central to the Baptist form of Christianity, echoed, for the Cherokee, their traditional cold baths in streams, the purification they knew as "going to water." Observers of Cherokee worshipers in the later twentieth century reported that they sat impassively through sermons and revivals and that men sometimes dozed as a preacher reached the emotional heights of his sermon.

Moreover, the prevalence of common-law marriage among twentieth-century Cherokee may be linked to the ancient custom of acknowledging a marriage, without clerical help, by the bride and groom's symbolic exchange of gifts and uniting of their blankets. And, in time of death, twentieth-century Cherokee mourners have been reported as keeping to a funeral ceremony outside the church. The body of the dead person has been laid out at home with an all-night vigil including ritual preaching by ministers or lay exhorters and the singing of Christian hymns. But the vigil probably has roots in the traditional Cherokee fear that witches might otherwise violate the corpse. And in an account from the early part of the twentieth century, after a Cherokee funeral, the near relatives would "go to water" as a Cherokee priest-conjurer prayed for their purification. Later, a new fire was ignited at the cabin of the dead person, and pine branches were burned so that the smoke would purify the interior.

Given this and similar evidence, it is clear that Cherokee Christianity has actually been a blending of Christian and traditional themes. In the Cherokee as in other Native American examples, the blending is often perhaps too subtle to be called syncretism, but nonetheless each Indian people that turns to Christianity does so in terms of prior beliefs and commitments that make the new religion plausible. Then, after conversion, the worshipers shape the Christianity in quiet ways to their own requirements.

Moreover, as we have already noted, in recent times the traditional religions have enjoyed a new prestige as vehicles for maintaining Native American identity and encouraging political action. The "Longest Walk" of 1978, for instance, was a political march across the continent to Washington, D.C., to demand Indian rights. Yet leaders of the march spoke of their pilgrimage as a spiritual one that had renewed their religious energies and restored them to contact with their ancient traditions. Significantly, the same year saw the passage of the American Indian Religious Freedom Act, in which Congress resolved that "it shall be the policy of the United States to protect and preserve for American Indians their inherent right of freedom to believe, express, and exercise [their] traditional religions." Since then, a series of court challenges by Indian peoples has invoked the congressional resolution, but to little avail. Still, the court cases have been instructive because what has been at stake is land, which for Indian peoples means sacred sites associated with traditional religious beliefs and ceremonies.

In the case of *Lyng v. Northwest Indian Cemetery Protective Association*, for example, the U.S. Supreme Court in 1988 decided against Native American plaintiffs. The U.S. Forest Service proposed to build a paved road between Gaston and Orleans, California (the "G-O Road"), to be used for logging and other commercial and recreational purposes. This road was to cross land in the Six Rivers National Forest and pass through an area considered highly sacred by Yurok, Karok, and Tolowa Indians. The Indians argued that centrally important ceremonies required that religious leaders have access to the "high country" and that the proposed road would violate the undisturbed sacredness of the space. The Indians won their case in U.S. District Court, but the Supreme Court reversed the decision.

It is important, though, that Native American seriousness about traditional religion has been noticed by official representatives of the U.S. government. And the American Indian Religious Freedom Act is indicative of a climate in which traditional religion has become a vehicle for Indian political voice. For although the courts have not generally been supportive (the peyote case — *Oregon v. Smith* — is a good example), Indian peoples have by no means given up. Their own understanding of sacred space and their political will to express their views and work to achieve their goals are likely to continue for the foreseeable future.

In Overview

The traditions of Native Americans were diverse, as we have seen, but Indians held many things in common. Their sense of continuity with the sacred world was expressed in beliefs regarding kinship with nature and in traditional sacred stories that reflected no break between the events of creation and the ordinary history of the people. For American Indians, the outer, material world was holy in itself, and so, too, was the inner world of dreams. Moving between the different worlds meant existence without firm boundaries. Hence, transformations were important, and holy beings were seen as shapeshifters, able to assume new form or change the world around them. Living in harmony with nature was the great religious requirement, for the human world, it was thought, should correspond with the model nature provided.

Among the Oglala Sioux of the North American Plains and the Hopi of the Southwest, different versions of Native American religion gave ordinary and extraordinary meaning to existence. Thus, like Indian societies in general, both collapsed ordinary and extraordinary religion into one. At the same time, the Oglala, a hunter-gatherer society, and the Hopi, an agricultural people, are case studies in diversity. Their respective traditions show us how American Indian religion really means American Indian religions. Still further, American Indians experienced religious change especially after the coming of Europeans. Sometimes there was a syncretism in which elements from European Christianity were grafted onto the Native American growth. At other times, new religions sprang up, while in still different cases Native Americans became converts to various Christian denominations.

The story of American Indian religions is a microcosm of the religious encounters that would confront each of the immigrant peoples to America. All would come with the ways of their ancestors; all would intend to preserve them. Yet each people was one among many "nations" present in the New World, and the presence of other ways led to changes in traditional religions. Syncretistic religion, new religion, and conversion were not confined to Native Americans, but were widespread.

If other peoples shared the Indian experience, the people of Israel—the Jews—were a special case in point. Like Native Americans, for centuries they had been sojourners more than settlers, and also like Native Americans, they sought to preserve their historic destiny even as they emulated their Protestant neighbors.

SUGGESTIONS FOR FURTHER READING: AMERICAN INDIAN RELIGIONS

Beck, Peggy V., and Walters, A. L. *The Sacred: Ways of Knowledge, Sources of Life.* Tsaile, AZ: Navajo Community College, 1977.

Brown, Joseph Epes. *The Sacred Pipe.* Baltimore: Penguin Books, 1971.

Courlander, Harold. *The Fourth World of the Hopis.* New York: Crown, 1971.

Deloria, Vine, Jr. *God Is Red.* New York: Grosset & Dunlap, 1973.

DeMallie, Raymond J., ed. *The Sixth Grandfather: Black Elk's Teachings Given to John G. Neihardt.* Lincoln: University of Nebraska Press, 1984.

_____, **and Parks, Douglas R., eds.** *Sioux Indian Religion: Tradition and Innovation.* Norman: University of Oklahoma Press, 1987.

Gill, Sam D. *Native American Religions: An Introduction.* The Religious Life of Man Series. Belmont, CA: Wadsworth, 1982.

_____. *Native American Traditions: Sources and Interpretations.* The Religious Life of Man Series. Belmont, CA: Wadsworth, 1983.

Loftin, John D. *Religion and Hopi Life in the Twentieth Century.* Religion in North America. Bloomington: Indiana University Press, 1991.

Momaday, N. Scott. *The Way to Rainy Mountain.* New York: Ballantine Books, 1970.

Neihardt, John G. *Black Elk Speaks.* Lincoln: University of Nebraska Press, 1961.

Nequatewa, Edmund. *Truth of a Hopi.* 1936. Reprint. Flagstaff, AZ: Northland Press, 1967.

Page, Jake. *Hopi.* New York: Harry Abrams, 1982.

Powers, William K. *Oglala Religion.* Lincoln: University of Nebraska Press, 1977.

Silko, Leslie Marmon. *Ceremony.* New York: Viking Press, 1977.

Tedlock, Dennis, and Tedlock, Barbara, eds. *Teachings from the American Earth: Indian Religion and Philosophy.* New York: Liveright, 1975.

Underhill, Ruth M. *Red Man's Religion.* Chicago: University of Chicago Press, 1965.

Vecsey, Christopher. *Imagine Ourselves Richly: Mythic Narratives of North American Indians.* New York: Crossroad, 1988.

Voth, H. R. *The Traditions of the Hopi.* 1905. Reprint. Millwood, NY: Kraus Reprint, 1973.

Israel in a Promised Land:
Jewish Religion and Peoplehood

When Christopher Columbus touched land in the New World in 1492, among his crew were Marranos, Spanish Jews who in fear of the Inquisition had converted to Christianity but secretly continued to practice Judaism. Their presence was one of those accidents of history that, in retrospect, seem especially fitting. Ancient Israel had, in its time, begun a religious revolution that became the source not only of later Judaism but of Christianity as well. So it was appropriate that the descendants of ancient Israel should be among the first Europeans to see the Americas.

The late fifteenth century had given some European Jews pressing reasons to venture across the Atlantic. In 1492, the same year that Columbus sailed, Jews were expelled as a people from Spain, and in 1497 the same fate befell them in Portugal. Thus, Jews sought refuge in whatever lands seemed likely to welcome or, at least, tolerate them. While many fled the Mediterranean basin to Palestine and, notably, to Italy and Turkey, others turned to liberal Holland, where they flourished as the largest Spanish-Portuguese Jewish community in exile. After the Dutch won their political independence in the 1590s, they began to establish a far-flung colonial empire. Jews participated in the new Dutch success, and when in 1630 the Dutch moved into eastern Brazil, the Jews, with some Marranos already there, were partly responsible. So began a prospering Jewish settlement in the New World—only to be cut short suddenly in 1654 when the Portuguese reconquered their territory in Brazil. Once again, the Jews fled, some to Dutch colonies in the Caribbean, some back to Amsterdam in Holland, and some to New Amsterdam, a young Dutch colony in North America.

Peter Stuyvesant, the Dutch governor of this colony on the Hudson River, was not pleased. He was overruled, however, by the Dutch of old Amsterdam. As proprietors of the Dutch West India Company, which had Jewish shareholders, they urged that the Jews be permitted to stay. Thus, within ten years, Jewish people were not only engaging in trade and commerce but also buying property, bearing arms, and joining the militia in defense of the colony. Yet the Dutch future in New Amsterdam was limited, and in 1664 the colony fell to the British. It became New York, and little more than a century later it would be one of the thirteen British colonies that formed the United States. The Jews had become one group among the many who would help to shape American religious history.

Moreover, from the beginning of their history in the New World, the Jews had repeated an age-old pattern of wandering. Moving from place to place through European history, they had no land that, without reservation, they could call home. Indeed, their history of wandering was more ancient still. One of the oldest verses in the Bible reads, in the Revised Standard Version, "A wandering Aramean was my father" (Deut. 26:5); and although the origins of the Hebrew people are shrouded, their earliest representatives were nomads. As we will see, this nomadic sense was not only an external condition but also became internalized to shape Jewish religious experience and expression throughout history. Like Native Americans, the Jews were often forced to wander by the misfortunes of history. Like Native Americans, too, they dwelled in small, homogeneous communities in which religion and peoplehood were inextricably blended. Indeed, some Americans told tales of a kinship between Jews and Indians. As early as the seventeenth century, stories circulated in the United States describing Native Americans as remnants of the lost tribes of Israel. Somewhere, a chord had been struck, and Americans in symbolic ways pointed to a likeness between Indian and Jewish peoples.

Yet, as we will notice, there were many ways in which the Jews were unlike Indians and more like other Europeans who immigrated to the New World. The story of their arrival in America is an epic that bears striking resemblances to the history of other ethnic groups, and we turn now to a brief sketch of the Jewish entry into this new promised land, America.

The Jewish Immigrations

We have already seen that the oldest Jewish immigrants came from Brazil to New Amsterdam, which became New York. These Jews were Sephardim, and their religious culture and ritual practice followed the Babylonian tradition of Jewish law and observance. Evolved in the sixth century A.D. in Persian rabbinic academies, this Babylonian tradition has been consciously so designated to recall the legacy of the Jews from the time of their Babylonian exile from their homeland. Further, as the Sephardic Jews inherited the tradition, it was influenced by the period of Muslim domination of Spain. Distinctive in law and observance, the Sephardim also spoke a distinctive Jewish dialect called Ladino, a blend of

Touro Synagogue of Congregation Jeshuat Israel, Newport. Exterior and interior views of Touro synagogue, dedicated in Rhode Island in 1763 and the nation's oldest synagogue. Note, in the interior lower left, the *bimah*, or sanctuary reading desk, for the Torah.

medieval Spanish with Hebrew, Arabic, and other elements; and their religious music was known for its rich, melodious chants.

The Sephardic Jews of New York were at first a very small community. They were mainly tradespeople, lacked a rabbi and synagogue, and frequently intermarried with the local population. By 1692, however, they had established the first synagogue in North America; and although they were never expressly granted the right to worship publicly, they literally took it, and no one in British New York objected. Meanwhile, other Sephardic Jews had settled in Newport, Rhode Island, where they acquired a burial ground in 1677 and less than a century later (1763) built Touro synagogue. Gradually, the Sephardim, along with a small number of Northern European Jews who had arrived by this time, established small congregations in eastern seacoast cities from Boston to Charleston, South Carolina.

After 1820 a new and much larger wave of Jewish immigration swept into America. The newcomers were Ashkenazim, Jews of German origin who followed a combined Babylonian (from the exile) and Palestinian (from their homeland) tradition in law and ritual practice, using Northern European forms in their religious services. When these German Jews came, there were only about 5,000 Jews in the United States out of a total population of some 13 million. Within the next half century, though, between 200,000 and 400,000 Jews from Central Europe entered the country, and the sheer size of their presence transformed Jewish life in the New World. Sephardic ascendancy faded, although the Sephardim continued as a kind of Jewish aristocracy throughout the nineteenth century. Meanwhile, the Germans brought with them not only Ashkenazic customs and practices but also a movement toward the reform of Judaism.

In order to understand the budding Reform movement the immigrants brought with them from Germany, we need to understand what happened to European Judaism as a result of the eighteenth-century intellectual movement known as the Enlightenment. With its emphasis on human reason and the law of nature, the Enlightenment thrived in the new spirit of liberty, equality, and brotherhood that the revolutions in the United States and France promoted. As a result the Jews found that, as the eighteenth century became the nineteenth, various European countries began to invite them out of their ghettos—the segregated communities in which they had been forced to live. Now, they were told, they could experience the full enjoyment of civil rights. This Emancipation, as it was called, slowly eroded the close-knit Jewish communities of the past, as more and more Jews became middle-class citizens of their respective countries.

In this context, many Jews became concerned about what was called "passing" in Gentile society. They did not wish to attract attention to themselves by strange habits and antiquated customs. Thus, a new emphasis on decorum began to affect the way some Jews conducted their synagogue services. The long, drawn-out chanting, the absence of a sermon, the alien Hebrew language, the prayer shawls that covered members of the congregation—all these seemed outmoded to a number among the self-conscious and recently emancipated Jewry.

This primary emphasis on practice, on what a Jew should *do* to be religious, was in keeping with the oldest traditions of Judaism, as we will see later in more detail. But proper practice was linked to proper thought. The Jewish Reform movement of Germany began to question the authority of the rabbinic tradition as established in the Talmud, the huge compilation that elaborates or amplifies Jewish law. Reform Jews also repudiated the old expectation of a personal Messiah who would lead the Jews back to Palestine, hoping instead for a messianic age, an era of justice, compassion, and peace for the world. Jewish people had no country, they declared, except the land in which they were born, bred, and exercised rights as citizens.

In the United States, the Reform movement grew among the German immigrants, fueled by their desire to "pass" in the adopted land. With the promise of a civic and social status more secure than their position in Germany had ever been, the Jews strived to blend unobtrusively with their Protestant neighbors. In the twin lights of modernity and the American flag, much that had seemed acceptable in the old country came under new scrutiny—and was changed. When Isaac M. Wise (1819–1900) arrived in 1846, he quickly became the leader of the Reform party, and by midcentury, Reform had become the most prominent Jewish movement in the national life.

The majority of the new immigrants were modest peddlers and shopkeepers. The spoke their own dialect, called Judeo-German; and in spite of the presence among them of some rabbis attracted to America from Europe, they produced no learned class. Instead of restricting themselves to the eastern seacoast as the earliest immigrants had done, these Ashkenazim spread out across the country, so that soon cities like Cincinnati and San Francisco could boast flourishing Jewish communities. Despite their liberalism, most Reform rabbis strongly disapproved when immigrants intermarried with other Americans and lost their ties to the Jewish community. In the dominant spirit of the Reform movement, however, most were eager to embrace American culture.

The German immigration was outnumbered, however, by a third wave of Jewish immigration, more than 1.7 million strong. The newcomers arrived, beginning in about 1880 and continuing until 1914, when the outbreak of the First World War and, a decade later, the enactment into law of immigration quotas (the National Origins Act) effectively ended massive Jewish immigration. This third influx of Jewish people was far different in character from the other two. These Jews were Eastern Europeans, from countries like Russia, Rumania, Poland, and Austria. Here they had endured hardship and persecution, living in the *shtetls*, towns and communities within a designated area where Jews were permitted to dwell. No tempting bait of suffrage and civil rights had been held out to these people, and their mental world, formed through years of alienation, did not include the desire of their German and Sephardic cousins to mingle freely with Protestants and other mainstream Americans. They came to the New World in order to be free, and in the beginning they did not think that having freedom meant becoming otherwise like mainstream Americans. They were poor and mostly illiterate in English, and they settled in huge numbers in major cities such as New York and Chicago, becoming part of a vast army of workers in factories or struggling along as artisans and small shopkeepers. It was many of these people who were to form the backbone of the deliberate and self-conscious Orthodox Judaism that in America became the strictest form of Judaism.

Clearly, the new immigrants were an embarrassment to the thriving American Jewish community already in the United States. Beyond that, the transition from the traditional Judaism of the *shtetl* to the suave, Americanized version promoted by Reform-minded rabbis seemed impossible to imagine, let alone perform. Still, despite the poverty and seeming social awkwardness of the immigrants, the bond of Jewishness meant that the older American Jewish community could not look away. There was a warmth and inner meaning to the old ways that the immigrants brought, and the attraction of tradition, the responsibility of relationship, and, among some, a growing disenchantment with Reform encouraged the growth of yet a third form of Judaism. Out of this mix Conservative Judaism was born.

The story after the Eastern European influx is one of growth and material prosperity, of education and involvement in the social and political life of America. It is also a story of a continuing search for the meaning of Jewishness in the American context, and it is one to which we will return later. For now, however, we need to ask the question of what Jewishness and Judaism mean in themselves. Our question is in some sense artificial, for as wanderers, Jews had dwelled in many lands and had absorbed into their traditions many foreign and Gentile customs. Still, we need to take a general look at the outlines of Jewish experience and expression before we relate them further to the sojourn in an American Zion.

Jewishness and Peoplehood

Being Jewish has always meant being a people as well as serving a God. The two notions were really one notion in the minds of the Jews of history, and that understanding was articulated from biblical times in ancient Israel's confidence that its God had bound himself to the nation in a covenant. In this irrevocable agreement, the Jewish people believed, he had promised to be the God of Israel, even as Israel pledged to be his people. Thus, religious blessings and benefits were understood to come to the community as a particular historical group. And thus, the origins of Jewry were tied to an ethnic and a religious identity that were fused. To state the matter in the terms of the text, ordinary and extraordinary coalesced in traditional Jewish experience. It was only post-Enlightenment modernity that tried to bring about a separation, dividing Jewishness, an ethnic and cultural reality, from Judaism, a religion. Let us pursue the distinction briefly.

First, Jews were a people because they viewed themselves as the inheritors of a common history. Their oldest remembrances, recorded in the Hebrew Bible, told of their descent from Abraham, their sojourn in Egypt and exodus under the leadership of Moses and the power of God, their acceptance of the gift of the Law at Sinai, and their eventual entry into Canaan, the land God had promised them. Other recollections dwelled on their exile in Babylon and their return to Jerusalem, where they raised up the Temple that had been destroyed by foreign troops. Still later, the rabbinic tradition would record the destruction of the Temple for a second time in A.D. 70. With the devastation of the homeland, popular memory would continue to recall the stories of the faithful who remained in Palestine and of the remnants who scattered throughout the Roman Empire, making their way to parts of Europe, the Middle East, and Northern Africa.

Second, Jews were a people because their common history had been one of suffering. From earliest times, because their land lay on the connecting routes that joined the Tigris–Euphrates valley of Mesopotamia to the valley of the Nile in Egypt, the ancestors of the Jews had borne years of war and insecurity. Later, when they no longer had a land to call their own, they still perpetuated the memory of Israel. Their strict monotheism and refusal to give up their distinctive customs and practices in the host countries where they settled led to persecution. As Christianity broke away from Judaism, its early scriptures reflected its struggle to be free of the synagogue, and anti-Semitism was spread by accusations that the Jews had killed Jesus. In this climate, the history of medieval Jewry was one of segregation, exclusion, and sporadic attempts at extinction. Pogroms tried to wipe out Jewish communities at intermittent intervals; and ultimately, as we have already seen in Spain and Portugal, a number of governments ordered mass expulsions of the Jews.

Moreover, the Enlightenment was hardly an unalloyed blessing. Jews found their old and segregated communities no longer legally and socially recognized. Instead, they possessed a set of civil rights that in most cases, they discovered, did not confer social equality or even, practically speaking, legal equity. The ultimate horror occurred in "enlightened" Germany under Adolf Hitler (1889–1945): it is the event we call the Holocaust, and it meant the destruction of 6 million Jewish people for no other reason than that they were Jewish.

Finally, Jews were a people because their history and their suffering were indissolubly bound to their sense of having been chosen by God for special tasks. From the beginning, when they had expressed this relationship with God in terms of a covenant, they had seen themselves as different. The covenant, they believed, marked them off from other nations: it drew boundaries that identified them as a people united in their commitment to the Law of God. At the same time, the covenant separated them from the rest of the world. Moreover, for the Jews, Israel's God was not like other Gods. In their teaching, he demanded an exclusive allegiance, and by the time of the classical prophets in the eighth century B.C., he was proclaimed the only God for all the nations. When Christianity and, later, Islam drew their monotheism from Jewish roots, the Jewish sense of chosenness was reinforced. Jews believed that they were the people to whom God had disclosed his true nature: he had told them his name, and they would never be the same because of that. In one sense, they thought, Jewish suffering came because, as the prophets had warned, the Jews had transgressed the Law, failing to fulfill the special tasks God required of them. Yet in a second sense, why Jews should suffer in being the keepers of the Law and revelation of God was, for them, a divine mystery. Their faithfulness, they believed, came in enduring, in respecting the secrets of God and proving themselves loyal.

Hence, Jewishness was born in the dynamic tension among a common history, mutual suffering, and a sense of being chosen. Did the sense of being chosen lead necessarily to the history of suffering? Did the suffering bring about the idea of being chosen as a way to give meaning to the inexplicable? And did the idea of chosenness itself excite the enmity of others so that persecution grew apace? Had the Jews, in choosing to maintain their identity as a separate people, chosen as well their history as an oppressed people? We will never know the answers to these questions because they are circular in nature. But they do point up sharply the relationship between Jewishness and questions of boundary.

As "others" throughout their history, Jews have been people on the boundary, living their lives in two worlds with a foot, so to speak, in each. As a marginal people, the Jews have experienced the strain of separateness, but they have also experienced its stimulation. Through the centuries, they have been remarkable for their creativity, in our own times advancing knowledge in the sciences and sensitivity in the arts. Likewise, through the centuries, they have been in a nearly ideal position to render criticism to a host culture and society. In every land where they settled, Jews knew enough to understand, but they also preserved a set of values that prevented them from being uncritical of cultural routine. They could penetrate cultural assumptions to find new models for understanding or acting, and the results of this blend of creativity and criticism have given the world such intellectual leaders as Sigmund Freud and Albert Einstein.

From a religious studies point of view, Jewish existence on the boundary leads us back to the blend of ordinary and extraordinary that characterizes Judaism. If the two kinds of religious experience were fused for the Jews, it was because their history had taught them the advantages of living at the place where two contexts met and mingled. We turn now to a closer look at what Judaism, the revealed religion, traditionally represented.

Judaism and Revealed Religion

In our discussion of Native American traditions, we saw that Indians in their emphasis on harmony with nature lived according to a religious belief in correspondence. For Indian societies, the human community was a microcosm, a small-scale reflection of the macrocosm of nature that surrounded them. Religion meant adjusting any disruptions of the cosmic rhythms in the human sphere, restoring wholeness through the power of sacred story and ritual. The earliest recollections of the Jewish people, present in the Hebrew Bible, suggest that they viewed the world in similar terms, seeing, for example, a close relationship between the fertility of land and crops and the reproductive fruitfulness of women and men. But something happened to the religious consciousness of Israel, and that something was tied to the cultural revolution that gave us the Judeo-Christian tradition. Gradually, Israel shifted the way it thought about the macrocosm by replacing metaphors of space with metaphors of time. In other words, instead of continuing to speak of the space of nature, people began to dwell on the time of history.

This shift was reflected in the transformation of the religious festivals that the Jews celebrated. Although in their earliest forms the festivals were probably seasonal rites following the agricultural cycle of planting and harvest, they came to have historical meaning. For example, Passover originally seemed to be a ritual event to mark the release of the earth from the grip of winter, the sowing of seed, and the renewal of clan and kinship ties. But as time passed, new interpretations were added, and the Jews came to see Passover as a historical feast to relive the exodus from Egypt and the birth of the Jewish nation: the Jews had passed over from slavery to freedom, even as the Angel of Death had slain the Egyptians but passed over the firstborn among the infant sons of Israel. So this feast — and the other feasts that followed a similar pattern — made a traditionally understood event the plan and model for Jewish existence. The macrocosm lay no longer in space but was instead in time.

Along with this shift from space to time came a sense of a greater separation between the divine and the human than the old model of correspondence had expressed. Briefly, in the new model of causality, Israel held that God had *caused* the world — but not out of his own "body." There was a gap between the sacred and the profane worlds, a gap reflected in the account in Genesis of the fall of Adam and Eve from paradise. In this way of thinking, it therefore became necessary that things be done by God or the Jews to insure that, though separate from God, the world would still experience his power. Nature had been demoted, while the Jews saw themselves as creatures made in the image of God and given by God the right and duty of controlling and subduing nature.

In its full expression, this conception parted radically from the older notion of correspondence, present as well in Native American societies. When Christianity, the child of later Judaism, broke away from its parent stock, it took with it the heritage of causality, and in the differences between correspondence and causality we have in rough outline the patterns that would lead to cultural collision between Indians and Europeans in the New World. Thus, if Jews were in some ways like Indians, they were also in very significant respects different from them.

To return to the Jewish religious understanding, however, we need to see that for the Jews the community of Israel — without God — would be in the same plight as nature. Therefore, it was thought, steps had to be taken either by God or by the people to establish some relationship, to turn the gap between divine and human into a bridge between them. Jews believed that God had done just this in his revelation and had bound Israel to himself with the covenant. Hence, the Jews could respond to God and tighten the bond by their faithful observance of the Law. In this simple and incisive explanation of the nature of things, Judaism, the religion, found its identity.

The sense of a relationship with God expressed in the covenant also started Israel on a path that led to the pure monotheism of the eighth-century prophets. From the time of the Abraham tradition in the third millennium, the ancestors of the Jewish people had begun to express their devotion to a single clan or tribal deity. In the late second millennium, the Moses tradition only underlined how exclusive should be Israel's adherence to one God. But the religion of Moses was henotheism more than monotheism; that is, it emphasized worship of one God but still held that other nations worshiped different deities. It was only when the prophets began to interpret the history of Israel in light of the covenant that they came to see the God of Israel as the universal God of all the nations, an idea that contained the essence of monotheism. Briefly, when the armies of foreign nations marched against Israel, the prophets saw these events as God's punishment for his people's unfaithfulness to the covenant. This meant that nations such as Persia and Assyria were seen as controlled by the divine hand and as belonging, in effect, to the same God as the God of Israel. It was only a short leap to the belief that no other God existed and the God of Israel was the God of all.

Similarly, the sense of a relationship with God expressed in the covenant led Israel to the discovery of history that lay behind the idea of causality. By pledging his commitment to the Jewish people in the Hebrew Bible, God, for the Jews, had entered history, establishing a pattern in which, at each new crisis, he would intervene in human affairs. And if the Almighty was seen to act in human events, then acting and doing became especially important. The God who acted led in a logical trajectory to a people who acted. As the notion of the covenant had already implied, *how* people acted became a significant question.

It was in this context that the Jewish people developed their traditions gathered in the Law. Implicit in the idea of God's covenant with Abraham, the Law became explicit in the first five books of the Hebrew Bible, called the Torah. Here, rules for living, prescriptions for both ceremonial and moral righteousness, were recorded for future generations. To be a Jew, then as now, meant to accept the burden of the Law. Indeed, it was more what people *did* in their observation of the Law that made them Jewish than what they *believed*.

To sum up, Judaism as a religion grew out of a strong Jewish belief in the covenant between God and Israel. For Jews, the covenant healed the widening rift between the divine and the human that had been expressed in the idea of causality. It expressed for Israel the significance of time as a new kind of "space" in which God acted. Because Jews saw God as acting, they came to see action and human history as important. Hence, belief in their covenant with God led the Jews to affirm their further belief in the importance of religious practice, of observance of the Jewish Law.

Jewish Tradition and the Consecration of Time

With this short survey of Jewishness and Judaism as background, we return to the Jewish immigrants who entered the United States. Like other Europeans, they shared basic insights and beliefs that characterized the Judeo-Christian tradition. But Jewish immigrants differed from many of their fellow Europeans or Euro-Americans in the emphasis they placed on the *doing* of the Torah. While Christians in America tended to be activists, as we will see in Part II, their theological tradition still stressed the importance of right, or correct, belief. In Judaism, on the other hand, there was no theological tradition in the Christian sense but, rather, a rabbinic tradition of interpretation of the Torah. Thus, Judaism in America meant a series of concrete acts that led to the Jewish consecration of time.

For the early immigrants who followed the uncontested orthodoxy of the past — and later for observant Reform and Conservative Jews as well — the consecration of time meant two kinds of things. First, it meant ritual action in a regular communal cycle of feasts and historical commemorations and in an individual life cycle marked for each person by significant times of passage from one stage of maturation to the next. Second and equally, the consecration of time meant consistent dedication in moral action. For later immigrants, as we have already seen to some extent, the rise of the different forms of Judaism was linked to arguments in the American Jewish community about *how* time should be consecrated and about what role traditional ritual should play.

The Ceremonial Cycle

Perhaps the most compelling symbol of the Jewish consecration of time among the early immigrants was the Sabbath. The creation narrative of the biblical book of Genesis had led, step by step, to the climactic account of how on the seventh day God rested (Gen. 2:2), thus establishing the seventh-day Sabbath as a holy day. Yet the Sabbath holiness did not require for the Jews a temple or church. Since the sixth century B.C., when they were exiled in Babylon, they had learned to live without the animal sacrifices of the Temple in Jerusalem. Sometime in that era the beginnings of the later synagogue had developed. A special place in which the Torah could be read and studied, the synagogue had its chief presider in a religious teacher and leader called a rabbi. But even though the scrolls of the Torah were kept in an honored place in the synagogue, the heart of Judaism lay in the home. Perhaps it took the earliest Jews nearly forty years to establish their first synagogue in North America because, as long as they had their homes and families, they felt that they had the essentials of Judaism in their midst.

A high point of the traditional Sabbath was — and is — a ritual meal eaten after sundown on Friday evening to inaugurate the feast. Previously, the house was cleaned, a white cloth was laid on the table, and the best dishes and utensils were spread. The choicest foods were prepared, there was wine, and twisted loaves of Sabbath bread (called *hallah*) were placed under an embroidered napkin. The mistress of the house then lit the Sabbath candles (at least two) and spoke the blessing: "Blessed art Thou, O Lord our God, King of the Universe, Who hast hallowed us by Thy commandments and commanded us to kindle the Sabbath lamp." At the beginning of the meal, the head of the household (the father) read or chanted a scriptural text, pronounced the *Kiddush*, or sanctification, and blessing the bread, began to break it and distribute it to members of his family, all of whom had previously ritually washed their hands. The dinner that followed was far from solemn, for the Sabbath was a time of festival.

At sundown on Saturday evening, the Sabbath closed with another home-centered ritual to mark the end of its light. In the *havdalah*, or separating, the head of the household took a special candle made of two or more plaited pieces of wax and, reciting a prayer to thank God for the separation of the sacred from the profane, which the Sabbath symbolized, extinguished it in a full glass of wine. In between, the Sabbath was traditionally observed with a strict separation from work and everyday activity. No travel was allowed, no business transacted, no money exchanged, no writing accomplished, and no other chores performed. At the same time, the Sabbath called for leisure and recreation through visiting family and friends, going on strolls, and the like. But above all, it called for mental and spiritual re-creation through the reading and study of the Torah. This is why on Saturday morning it became customary to hold a synagogue service.

With its symbolism of separation to mark it off from the rest of time, the Sabbath was the time of extraordinary religion. For Jews, its roots lay in the revelation of the transcendent God of Israel, who had created human beings out of nothing. As a memorial to the God who acted in history, the Sabbath aimed to bring transcendence into time, establishing there a religious monument that was to time what a cathedral was to space. And yet, because in the Jewish scheme of things religion and peoplehood were one, the Sabbath was extraordinary time made ordinary. In fact, in the Sabbath meal with its blend of ritual formality and unstudied family conversation, we can see, encapsulated, the Jewish fusion of ordinary and extraordinary religion. Because the Jews saw their religion as what had made them a people, because they saw their God as one who had made a covenant, they believed that transcendent reality had entered their ordinary world.

If the Sabbath made time holy at weekly intervals, it was — and continues to be — joined by a cycle of seasonal feasts that made time holy on an annual basis. Judaism observed these feasts according to a lunar calendar of 353 or 354 days, with an extra month added at set intervals to bring the reckoning into line with the solar calendar that determined planting and harvest seasons. Three major observances, originally attached to the agricultural cycle, provided the foundation for the yearly cycle. These were Passover (*Pesach*), at the beginning of the planting season, which had been historicized to recall the exodus from Egypt; Weeks (also called *Shavuot* or Pentecost), at the end of the barley harvest, which commemorated the giving of the Law (Torah) to Moses on Mount Sinai; and Booths (also called *Sukkot* or Tabernacles), at the end of all agricultural work for the year and just before the beginning of winter rains, which commemorated the wandering of the Jews in the desert before they entered Canaan.

Both agriculture and history shared a chronology in which Passover came first, logically followed by Weeks and then Booths. From the religious point of view, however, it was the autumn season of Booths that marked the beginning of the Jewish year. Booths looked toward the future, for the wilderness wandering of the Jews had been the final preliminary to entry into their promised land. Thus, the feast was prospective: it told of the inauguration of new things, and it was fitting that *Rosh Hashanah*, the Jewish New Year, should occur just before the feast of Booths. Indeed, so named because the Jews had constructed and lived temporarily in huts, or booths, to remind them of their desert sojourn, Booths was the third stage in a long and solemn festival season. The New Year, *Rosh Hashanah*, came first. Ten days later, it was followed by the Day of Atonement, *Yom Kippur*, in which Jews fasted, did penance, and confessed what they considered their sinfulness before God. Finally, four days later came the week-long Booths with its theme of new hope and confidence for the future.

Perhaps the most solemn moments of the Jewish ceremonial year occurred on the Days of Awe, *Rosh Hashanah* and *Yom Kippur*, when the shofar, a special trumpet made of a ram's horn, was blown. Both the New Year and the Day of Atonement were days of religious remembrance in which, Jews believed, both God and humans recollected their past and gathered the fruits of such remembrance to shape the future. In this view, God recalled the deeds of his people, while the people remembered their creation and covenant with God, their chosenness as his Israel, and their successes and failures in faithfulness. The shofar blew to remind Israel of its calling, piercing time to bring year after year into the covenant. Hence, while the Jews did not kneel at any other time of year, on *Rosh Hashanah* and *Yom Kippur* an important part of the synagogue services was the ritual prostration, usually performed by the rabbi and the cantor in the name of the congregation, to acknowledge God's lordship over the earth as creator.

Finally, like all the solemnities of the Jewish year, the New Year and the Day of Atonement were not simply remembrances in the ordinary way in which we use that term. They were recollections that aspired to bring times of origin back again. That is, they aimed to destroy the work of time to bring pious Jews in touch with the religious acts of tradition. They aimed to re-create past time so that its imputed power could be tapped in the present and the future. Again, the blast of the shofar helped to bring these intentions home. Its extraordinary sound, unheard at any other time of year, signaled a desire to break through profane time to bring Jews into the presence of what they held to be sacred and timeless truth.

Similarly, it was significant that at the other "beginning" of Jewish festivals, the springtime Passover, the solemn ritual meal carried the same message.

The meal, called a *seder*, was a remembrance of the meal the ancestors were said to have eaten on the night they fled from Egypt. In this historicized version of the ancient Palestinian harvest festival, the Jews used unleavened bread (*matzah*) because in the biblical exodus story they had no time to wait for bread to rise. They ate bitter herbs to remind them of the story's bitter journey and a mix of chopped nuts, apples, raisins, and cinnamon, like the mortar they had placed between bricks in the account of slavery in Egypt. Parsley dipped in salted water, a roasted egg, the shank bone of a lamb, and four ceremonial cups of wine — all had symbolic meaning, and all were meant to re-create, as vividly as possible, the story of the exodus. At the heart of the ritual was a recitation of the sacred narrative of the flight from Egypt. To introduce the telling, the youngest boy in the family asked a question that, like the horn of the shofar, aimed to cut through time to make the past present again: "Why *is* this night different from all other nights?" The boy's father answered in kind: "This *is* the night we fled the Egyptians" — and went on to tell the story. If the ritual succeeded, time and its work had been undone; the family and its guests felt as if transported to the moment of the exodus; they could experience renewal as they continued their ordinary lives.

Beyond these celebrations, there were a number of other feasts and fasts linking the parts of the year to one another, making the entire year holy, and, as we have seen, rendering the extraordinary an ordinary event. Most important among these minor commemorations were *Purim* and *Hanukkah*. *Purim* was based on an account contained in the biblical Book of Esther. Read formally from a scroll, or *megillah*, on the evening and the morning of this winter feast, the story told how Esther and Mordecai triumphed over Haman of Persia on the very day on which he planned to exterminate the Jews. Once again, Jews brought sacred and extraordinary events into everyday reality by making *Purim* a time of carnival. Among the Ashkenazim in Europe, children had dressed in masquerade costumes, often representing figures from Jewish history, and had gone door to door begging. The custom came to the New World with the immigrants, and *Purim* carnivals continued to be popular, especially among the young.

Hanukkah, called the Feast of Lights or Dedication, was not biblical but still became one of the most popular of Jewish festivals. Occurring at the time of winter solstice, *Hanukkah* recalled not the natural return of the sun in length-ened daylight hours but the rekindling of the candelabrum in the Temple of Jerusalem by Judas Maccabeus and his followers (165 B.C.). The Syrian–Greek monarch, Antiochus IV, who held Jerusalem under his sway, had tried to make the Temple into a shrine to the Greek deity Zeus. Judas with his brothers and other followers stormed the hill of the Temple, drove out the Greek troops, purified the sanctuary, and restored the traditional services. The eight-day festi-val that, according to tradition, the Maccabees then inaugurated was perpetu-ated in Jewish homes by the lighting each evening for eight days of the *menorah*, or candelabrum. On the first evening, only one candle was lit, on the second, two, on the third, three, and so on until the eighth night, when all of the candles had been kindled. It was a festival of remembrance, and it celebrated the Jewish right to be different. The deed of the Maccabees proclaimed that because the Jews lived in the middle of a Greek culture, they did not also have to be Greek.

Just as the Jewish year had its cycle, so, too, did the life of an individual, and the key events in a Jew's lifetime were marked by ritual and solemnity. From the first, a Jew should be a son or daughter of the Law, and so it had been a custom to carry the scroll of the Torah to the very door of the lying-in chamber where mother and infant were resting. If the child was a boy, he was circumcised on the eighth day, so that, now formally admitted to the community of kinship, he would bear in his flesh a sign of the covenant that Jews affirmed between God and Israel. At thirteen, the same boy would become Bar Mitzvah, a "son of the commandment." In effect, he became an adult from the religious point of view and demonstrated his maturity by reading from the scroll of the Torah in the synagogue. In America, among many Conservative and Reform congregations, his sister might become Bat Mitzvah, a "daughter of the commandment," as well.

At marriage, ritual worked to express to bride and groom the importance of the human duty they were to undertake. As they stood together under the bridal canopy of white silk or satin, the marriage contract was read to them, the Seven Blessings were pronounced, the pair drank from the cup of betrothal, and then the glass was smashed to recall the destruction of the ancient Temple. Meanwhile, at death, austere and simple rituals marked the event, and there was burial in the earth. Family and community would not forget, however. After the prescribed mourning period, there would be yearly commemorations of the dead when, on the anniversary of passing, the *kaddish*, or prayer of praise, would be recited by the surviving kin. In addition to these individual services, there would be an annual collective remembrance, the *Yizkor* service. Especially popular in the United States, the "*Yizkor* days" recalled for Eastern European Jews not only their dead but also their traditional ways, often for the most part laid aside in the rush of business and, as we will see, in the process of becoming American.

Thus, ritual interpreted the meaning of natural growth and change at the highpoints in the life cycle of each individual Jew. But ritual also told the devout the meaning of their Jewishness in everyday life. The dietary laws prescribed just what foods should be eaten and how they should be consumed. Animals were divided into the clean and unclean, and only those that had a cloven hoof and chewed the cud could be consumed. Most specifically, in terms of American dietary habits, pork was forbidden. In the case of seafood, any aquatic creatures had to possess fins and scales, hence eliminating shellfish from Jewish cuisine. Finally, meat and milk dishes could not be eaten together, and at least several hours must expire before an observant Jew could consume milk after having eaten meat.

The origins of these practices are lost in history, and speculation on their development has produced a host of intriguing explanations. In the post-Enlightenment American context, however, they quickly became a badge of Jewishness, separating out this one group among the many and affirming its distinctiveness. Inherited from a biblical past in which, Jews believed, God had acted in history in an extraordinary manner, the dietary laws recalled in ordinary time belief in the extraordinary mission of Israel. They were one more example of how, for Jews, just as ethnicity and religion went together, so, too, did life within the boundaries of this world and life that aimed to transcend them.

The Moral Law

We have seen that the consecration of time meant fulfillment of the ceremonial requirements of the Torah. But equally, the consecration of time meant that Jews should live the life of moral righteousness that the Law demanded. According to the biblical account, there were two tablets to the Law that God had given to Moses on Sinai. The second, and longer, promulgated the ethic by which Jews should live in their *human* relationships. If God was the God of justice and mercy, Jews thought, they should emulate him in their regard for one another. The myriad ceremonial prescriptions of the Law were to bring home the meaning of the *shema* (Deut. 6:4–9, Deut. 11:13–21, and Num. 15:37–41), the solemn summary of the covenant — of belief in God's unity and the duty of loving and serving him — recited morning and evening by the pious Jew. Love for the creator was meant to lead to love for the fellow creature, and Judaism as a religion expressed collective concern for the widow, the orphan, and all those in need.

Still more, the commandments of the Law went beyond external behavior to the inner spirit that motivated it. Biblical teaching held that a person could sin, even without acting, if he or she looked with envy on the life of another. In the writings of the prophet Ezekiel, God had promised the Jews to change their hearts of stone for hearts of flesh (Ezek. 11:20), and in the writings of Jeremiah, he had announced that he would write his Law deep within the hearts of his people (Jer. 31:33). Thus, for Jews the covenant began and ended *within*, and right behavior without a right heart was not sufficient. Reversing the equation, for Jews a right heart *always* led out into the world where deeds were done. With their preaching of social justice and compassion toward all, the prophets extended the meaning of the covenant and announced a universal ethical message — one that could apply to every people.

The Moral Law in America

As Jews responded to their new situation in America, it was the ethical prescriptions of the Law that assumed added importance. The mid-nineteenth-century Reformers found the ethical teachings of the prophets more and more central, and they held that "outmoded" ritual practices should fall away to reveal the true essence of Judaism. Thus, Isaac M. Wise maintained that Jewish chosenness meant a divine mission to spread throughout the world the prophetic call for justice and mercy. Indeed, he thought there was a special congruity between Judaism and America, for with its ideal of democracy the United States offered the perfect stage for the ethical action and idealism that the ancient Jewish prophets had demanded.

Later, Kaufmann Kohler (1843–1926), Wise's successor as president of Cincinnati's Hebrew Union College, took his ideas to still more radical conclusions. Divine revelation, Kohler argued, occurred in the natural historical process. Hence, the revelation of Judaism was natural and historical. Its essence lay in its ethics, and its true aim was to bring in the messianic age by the salvation of human beings in history. In 1885 a conference of Reform rabbis called by Kohler met in Pittsburgh to adopt the widely influential Pittsburgh Platform. This statement of Reform principles, while rejecting the vast body of Mosaic and rabbinic law, held to the moral law taught in the Torah and expressed a commitment on that basis to the struggle of the poor for equality with the rich. The mission of Israel, as Kohler and other Reformers saw it, was the moral redemption of society.

In their transformation of Judaism in America, the Reformers received assistance from an unexpected source. This aid was indirect and unintentional, but it added to the Reform emphasis on the true essence of Judaism as the quest for righteousness in social relationships. The assistance came from one segment of the Eastern European immigrants after the 1880s. While many Eastern European Jews retained as nearly as they could their Orthodox customs and practices, others substituted social radicalism for Jewish ceremonialism. This had happened for some in the old countries, when they responded to anti-Semitic harassment by abandoning the religion that made them objectionable. In America, however, there was a new motive for rejecting Orthodoxy: it betokened foreignness, and hence the second generation, especially, found ways to reject it. Jewish socialism, already present in Europe, in America led many to the Socialist party and to the formation of socialist labor unions and newspapers. Meanwhile, as Jews became more affluent, they became leaders in social welfare programs. Doing the Law had been transformed into a modern zeal for righteousness and justice in society.

We can see in Jewish socialism and philanthropy the influence of American experience on traditional Jewish life. It is time now to pursue the American saga of Israel with greater attention. It is true that acculturation has been a fact of all Jewish history since the Jews scattered throughout the lands of.Europe, North Africa, and the Middle East. Moreover, Jewish ritual incorporated pagan and Christian elements, transforming them for Jewish purposes. If this was true in the past, it seems even more the case in America. Briefly, the story of the American Israel is a story of increasing separation between Jewishness the culture and Judaism the organized religion. It is likewise the story of the rise of three major forms of Judaism — Reform, Conservatism, and Orthodoxy — and a number of related religious movements.

American Forms of Judaism

The Reform movement was in the forefront of the effort to turn away from the old model of religioethnic unity to the new one of Judaism as a religion. The Pittsburgh Platform had declared that its subscribers were no longer a nation but instead a religious community. Now the Reformers proceeded to implement their religious community with zeal. By 1889 they had organized in the Central Conference of American Rabbis, and by 1894 they published the *Union Prayer Book* as a new order of synagogue service. Under the new rubric, the synagogue came more and more to resemble a Protestant church of the period. The service was almost entirely in English and was conducted mostly by the rabbi, in contrast to the older Jewish pattern of full congregational participation. Prayer shawls disappeared, as did segregated seating for women, while organs and mixed choirs of men and women were initiated. So far did Reform Jews go in some congregations that they adopted a Sunday Sabbath, more in keeping with the practices of their Christian neighbors. At the same time, the annual cycle of Jewish feasts was less faithfully kept, and other traditional rituals were laid aside.

Still, even the Reform movement at some level cherished the ideal of Israel as a people. Amid this new religion of rationalism and progress, there was a loyalty to the age-old custom of circumcision and the ban on intermarriage with non-Jews, indicating the hidden presence among these "liberated" Jews of allegiance to Israel's religioethnic identity. However, it was the Conservative movement that self-consciously came forward to preserve a Jewish sense of peoplehood. In order to understand Conservatism, we must return to the dismay among many Jews at the path Reform was charting. Throughout the middle years of the nineteenth century, there had been moderates who, while they recognized the need to blend American with Jewish elements, nevertheless saw in tradition a source of nourishment and life. Reform leaders were a vocal minority, but they hardly represented all of the Jewish presence in America. The increasing discontent with their leadership came to a head in 1883, when the first graduating class from Hebrew Union College received rabbinical ordination. At the festive dinner to honor the occasion, two rabbis rose from their places and left the room in horror: the caterer had served shrimp, one of the forbidden foods, for the opening course.

The "shrimp incident," as it came to be called, became a dramatic symbol and catalyst for the movement that began to grow rapidly thereafter. When the Pittsburgh Platform was adopted two years later by Reform rabbis, it provided an added spur. Meanwhile, the great wave of Eastern European immigration had begun, and as we have already seen, immigrant needs also supplied fuel for the Conservative movement. Sabato Morais (1823–1897), the rabbi of a Sephardic synagogue in Philadelphia, emerged as the leader of the Conservatives, and his efforts along with those of others led to the establishment of the Jewish Theological Seminary in New York as an institution to train Conservative rabbis. The association that was formed in 1885 in connection with the seminary introduced its constitution by speaking of fidelity to Mosaic Law and ancestral traditions as well as a love for the Hebrew language — all to become, more and more, badges of ethnic identity.

The seminary had fallen on hard times by 1897 when Morais died, but in the early twentieth century it was revived with the explicit intention of serving the Eastern European Jews. Solomon Schechter (1847–1915) was brought from England to serve as its president. A Rumanian by birth and a distinguished scholar, he attracted an illustrious faculty to the seminary. More than that, he articulated far more clearly than earlier leaders the ethnic emphasis that was to become the identifying mark of Conservatism. In his notion of the "catholic Israel," Schechter expressed his faith that by a kind of mystical inner unity Jews would find the middle way between the full demands of the Law and the requirements of modernity. Consensus, he believed, would arise from the *people*, and that consensus would bind them to their heritage.

In 1918 Mordecai Kaplan (1881–1983) of the Jewish Theological Seminary began a synagogue center movement. Throughout the twenties and thereafter, Jewish centers were popular institutions, adding to the traditional synagogue and its services a host of nonreligious activities. For Kaplan and his supporters, the center should be a place where all Jews, whether observant or not, could feel at home as a people. Meanwhile, Kaplan continued to ponder the relationship between religion and Jewish cultural identity until in 1934 he published *Judaism as a Civilization*, in which he argued that Judaism was a religious civilization rather than a religion. He sought the reestablishment of Jewish community life in America by uniting all Jews, whether Conservative, Reform, Orthodox — or "nonreligious." The following year Kaplan founded Reconstructionism, a movement that, as an offshoot of Conservatism, spread his ideas about the importance of traditional ceremonies and rituals not as expressions of supernatural religion but as distinctive signs of Jewishness. Reconstructionism remained small — with fifty-four groups belonging to the Fellowship of Reconstructionist Congregations and Havurot by 1984 — but it voiced important concerns that were shared by Conservative Jews.

Conservatism found support for its attachment to Jewish ethnic identity in Zionism as well. This movement for the reestablishment of a Jewish nation-state began in its modern form in the late nineteenth century with Theodor Herzl (1860–1904) and his World Zionist Congress. The idea of a return to Israel was attractive to American Jews of Conservative and also, to some extent, Orthodox persuasion. On the other hand, Reform Jews at first strongly opposed Zionism because of their insistence that Judaism meant an organized religion and not a national group. It was not until 1935 that they moved to a position of official neutrality. Meanwhile, small Hasidic sects, the descendants of an eighteenth-century Eastern European mystical movement, also expressed their vehement opposition to Zionism. For them, the worldly ideal of establishing a Jewish nation-state violated the religious hope for the Messiah who, according to tradition, would lead the Jews back to the land of Israel.

With the Holocaust of Nazi Germany (1939–1945), however, Reform and Hasidic Jews were both compelled to rethink their positions. As the news of German atrocities and the full horror of what had happened reached America, Jews of all persuasions were profoundly shaken. The very foundations of their belief in a covenant with God seemed to be called into question. Whatever religious answers they groped toward, Jewish people became convinced that they themselves must take an active role in shaping their future. They could no longer trust the nations of the world and the Western heritage of the Enlightenment. Nor could they any longer wait for their God. Thus, when the modern state of Israel finally came into existence in 1948, it received enthusiastic endorsement and support from American Jewry and has mostly continued to do so. By the late twentieth century, to be Jewish more than ever meant to be part of a people. In Israel American Jews saw their spiritual home.

If Reform stressed Judaism the ethical prophetic religion while Conservatism promoted Jewishness the ethnocultural identity, then Orthodoxy represented the Jewish attempt to maintain the unity of the past. Orthodoxy became a self-conscious movement as first Reform and then Conservative Jewry carved out more "progressive" postures for themselves. It was Orthodoxy with its Eastern European faithful that tried to retain the religious observances of the past and hold on to all 613 commands of the Law — or as much of that as it could. In the terms that we have been using, Reform Judaism, by its emphasis on organized religion as a separate function, tried to make of Judaism an extraordinary (if restrained and Americanized) religion. Meanwhile, Conservatism fostered ordinary religion as it encouraged Jewishness among observant and nonobservant alike, and Orthodoxy, in trying to keep both religion and peoplehood intact, fought to continue the Jewish amalgamation of the two. Still, the lines were not nearly so clear. Conservatism often seemed to share the basic assumption of Orthodoxy that peoplehood and religion were one. And Reform, by the late twentieth century — perhaps influenced by a wave of ethnic pride that swept the United States — had rejected many of the extreme formulations of its past. More and more, cantors in Reform synagogues chanted portions of the service in Hebrew, and, especially among the young, a new devotionalism was springing up. Meanwhile, the new Reform prayerbook *Gates of Prayer* contained noticeably more Hebrew than its predecessor.

The formal divisions within the Jewish community are a good example of how the American experience has been internalized. We will look further in Part II at the related phenomenon of denominationalism that became characteristic of a nation in which church and state are separate. For now, though, we need to look at more of the ways in which Jews were like other Americans of European descent and, as time passed, became even more like them.

First, Jews were already like other Americans, and with their heritage of adaptability in many different host cultures, they were able as a group to rise quickly to middle-class status. They shared with Americans of Calvinist inclination a religion that stressed law and deed. Thus, the "Protestant ethic" did not seem foreign to the newcomers, and they were as ready as their once-Calvinist neighbors to exhibit industry, perseverance, thrift, and prudence. The Jewish tradition of study of the Torah led to a commitment to the values of university study and education, so that many Jews rose quickly to professional status. At the same time, their closely knit families and mutual-assistance patterns provided security and encouragement in the new environment.

Second, Jews changed to become more like other Americans. Nurtured by religious liberty, Judaism should in theory have grown stronger. Yet religious liberty in America meant freedom *from* religion as well as freedom *of* religion. In the Old World of Jewish ghetto and *shtetl*, such choice had not been possible. Thus, it was the voluntary nature of religious commitment in the new land that led, ironically, to the mass defections from Judaism since the late nineteenth century. For those who remained within the Jewish religion, the formal divisions, as we have seen, became an expression of American pluralism. Furthermore, the growth of different forms of Judaism pointed to the fact that in America, unlike the small and self-contained Jewish communities of Europe, no single authority spoke for the Jewish people. While in the Old World the rabbi had given uncontested direction to the *local* community over which he presided, in the *continental* United States various efforts at Jewish ecclesiastical unity met with only moderate success.

Indeed, so diverse had Judaism become that, by the late 1970s, Reform rabbinical candidates at Hebrew Union College were being drawn to the new position called "polydoxy," as articulated by Alvin Reines, one of their professors. In his view different religious outlooks and practices were legitimate so long as they helped a person to affirm his or her Jewishness. While some Jews regarded polydoxy in negative terms, others saw it as a meaningful expression of their Jewishness and, at least in some matters, of openness to tradition. So there was no normative version of Judaism in the American context, and as one Jewish scholar, Joseph L. Blau, has said, it is necessary to talk about the Judaism*s* in the United States. All starting points were seen as valid for religious people in the new land: this was the condition of living among the many.

Meanwhile, in the 1980s Jews formed roughly 2 percent of the American population. The synagogues showed a decline in membership from the middle years of the century, but they were still widely influential. And although the Jews had low rates of attendance at religious services in comparison with other groups, they displayed strong identification with a specific form of Judaism, whether or not they were expressly affiliated with a synagogue. (Perhaps almost half of all

American Jews were so affiliated.) For well over one-third of American Jews, that formal identification was Conservative; indeed, roughly half of all Jews who were synagogue members were Conservatives. By contrast, Orthodox identification hovered from near 7 to 10 percent of the Jewish population. And Reform, although it had experienced signs of vitality and growth, held to the middle position, considerably larger than Orthodoxy but, as in earlier years, smaller than Conservatism.

Whatever their formal allegiance in the second part of the twentieth century, Jewish people continued to read the Bible, yet fewer could say that their beliefs in God or revelation in the Bible were firm. Belief in life after death, underplayed in much of Jewish history, had declined, and more Jews than ever admitted that they never or infrequently prayed. Furthermore, as some strived for greater homogeneity, blending more completely than ever with the general American population, others found new spiritual energy in the mystical tradition that had always persisted as an undercurrent in Judaism. Hasidic Judaism, with its emphasis on the divine spark in every person and its cultivation of intense prayerfulness and devotion to the Torah, appealed to many.

Among the Orthodox in general, a right-wing movement toward strict fundamentalism in interpreting the commands of the Torah was thriving in the 1980s. Among Conservative and Reform congregations, on the other hand, women were serving as rabbis, and the trend was toward their greater and greater participation in both ritual and administration. In synagogue life and in wider, less institutional contexts, feminism was proving a significant force in American Jewish culture. In response to the times, Reform Judaism (and the small Reconstructionist movement, too) addressed the issue of attrition through intermarriage by expanding the age-old rule that being born of a Jewish mother was what made a child Jewish. Now the Jewishness of the father also counted, and having a Gentile mother (but a Jewish father) would not sever the relationship of a newborn child to Judaism.

Throughout the decade, the fortunes and actions of the state of Israel continued to preoccupy American Jews. As the issue of Palestinian rights emerged more sharply, from 1987 events took a new turn in the Palestinian uprising, or *intifada*, in Israeli-occupied territories, and the American Jewish community's response toward Israeli policy became less uniformly favorable than previously. Nor was this response insignificant. Although a small minority of the U.S. population, American Jews made up the largest Jewish population in the world. But they had become many in the land of manyness, and in so doing they had become American.

In Overview

To summarize, the story of American Jewry is the story of both a people and a religion. In three waves of immigration, the Jewish people brought to this country a religious identity forged by common history, mutual suffering, and a sense of chosenness. The revealed religion that was fundamental to this religious identity stressed historical tradition more than nature and organized its cultus around belief in a God who acted in relationship to the community of Israel. Bound to its God by a covenant, Israel consecrated time through regular remembrance and through ethical action, both of them the ways in which observant Jews fulfilled the requirements of the Law, or Torah.

In America differences over how the commandments of the Torah should be observed resulted in the growth of three major forms of Judaism. Reform Jews, who tended to separate Judaism as an organized religion from Jewishness as an ethnic identity, were the most liberal. They loosened social boundaries as they encountered the pluralism of America. Orthodox Jews, by contrast, drew the boundaries tightly and tried to preserve as much of European Jewish culture as possible, blending organized religion and peoplehood. Conservative Jews, who occupied the middle position, also blended organized religion and peoplehood but strived to find a path to fulfillment of the Torah that was more practical in light of modern lifestyles. At present Jewishness as the bond of peoplehood has become more important throughout American Judaism. In this development we see a recent expression of the ancient Jewish heritage, which linked extraordinary religion to the ordinary religion of daily living.

Jews lived in the tension between revealed religion and peoplehood, between extraordinary and ordinary religion, and between manyness and oneness. If they had found a promised land in the New World even as they looked to Zion of old, another group of Americans also lived between two Zions. Roman Catholics came over the sea to reap the promises of America. At the same time, they, too, kept one eye elsewhere — on the domes of St. Peter's in Rome.

SUGGESTIONS FOR FURTHER READING: JUDAISM

Blau, Joseph L. *Judaism in America: From Curiosity to Third Faith.* Chicago History of American Religion. Chicago: University of Chicago Press, 1976.

Eisen, Arnold M. *The Chosen People in America: A Study in Jewish Religious Ideology.* The Modern Jewish Experience. Bloomington: Indiana University Press, 1983.

Encyclopedia Judaica. New York: Macmillan, 1972.

Gaster, Theodor H. *Customs and Folkways of Jewish Life.* New York: William Sloane Associates Publishers, 1955.

————. *Festivals of the Jewish Year.* New York: William Sloane Associates Publishers, 1953.

Glazer, Nathan. *American Judaism.* The Chicago History of American Civilization. Chicago: University of Chicago Press, 1957.

Helmreich, William B. *The World of the Yeshiva: An Intimate Portrait of Orthodox Jewry.* New York: Free Press, 1982.

Hertzberg, Arthur, ed. *The Zionist Idea: A Historical Analysis and Reader.* New York: Atheneum, 1984.

Heschel, Abraham J. *The Sabbath: Its Meaning for Modern Man.* New York: Farrar, Straus, and Young, 1951.

Liebman, Seymour B. *New World Jewry, 1493–1825: Requiem for the Forgotten.* New York: Ktav, 1982.

Meyer, Michael A. *Response to Modernity: A History of the Reform Movement in Judaism.* New York: Oxford University Press, 1988.

Neusner, Jacob. *Israel in America: A Too-Comfortable Exile?* Boston: Beacon Press, 1985.

————. *The Way of Torah: An Introduction to Judaism.* Belmont, CA: Dickenson, 1970.

Rosenthal, Gilbert S. *Contemporary Judaism: Patterns of Survival.* 2d ed. New York: Human Sciences Press, 1986.

Roth, Cecil. *A History of the Jews: From Earliest Times through the Six-Day War.* Rev. ed. New York: Schocken Books, 1970.

Trepp, Leo. *Judaism: Development and Life.* 2d ed. Belmont, CA: Dickenson, 1974.

Waxman, Chaim I. *America's Jews in Transition.* Philadelphia: Temple University Press, 1983.

Wertheimer, Jack, ed. *The American Synagogue: A Sanctuary Transformed.* Cambridge: Cambridge University Press, 1987.

Bread and Mortar: The Presence of Roman Catholicism

When the ships of Christopher Columbus brought the first Marranos to the Americas, they sailed under the flag of Catholic Spain. So it was that Roman Catholics were among the first Europeans to set foot in the New World. Supported by the wealth and power of the Spanish throne, Roman Catholic missionaries determined to convert the natives of the newly discovered lands to Christianity, even as they ministered to the soldiers and other colonials who were establishing the territorial claims of New Spain.

Spanish Missions

As early as 1513, Juan Ponce de Leon made his way into the Florida peninsula. Although no priest accompanied him on the voyage, eight years later he was back, this time with priests to establish missions among the Indians. Understandably, the Indians were hostile to the presence of the foreigners and drove them off. Then, in 1526 two Dominican priests traveling with the party of Vasquez de Ayllon were part of an attempted settlement along the Chesapeake Bay. The settlement failed, as did a series of Spanish ventures in Florida in the following years. Still, by 1565 St. Augustine had been founded, and by 1595 missionary work had begun in earnest. Just over a half century later, the Spanish could boast of nearly forty missions with 26,000 Indians who had heard and accepted the Christian message.

Meanwhile, north of the Gulf of Mexico in the American Southwest, Spanish Catholic missionaries had already begun to work. Francisco Vasquez de Coronado had seen New Mexico in 1540, and three friars from his entourage remained. When Spain officially took control of New Mexico in 1598, the Franciscans began a ministry there. These missions flourished until the 1630s when they began a slow decline, ending about half a century later in a rebellion by the Native Americans in the area. By 1694, though, the missionaries were back, for Don Diego de Vargas had reconquered the territory, and by 1750 the Spanish counted twenty-two missions and 17,500 Indian converts. Similarly, in southern Arizona the Jesuit Eusebio Francisco Kino (1645–1711) founded San Xavier del Bac in 1700 and, with his fabled journeys that led to the establishment of other missions, claimed to have baptized 30,000 Indians.

In California the Franciscan Junipero Serra (1713–1784) would equal the efforts of Kino. Beginning with a mission at San Diego in 1769, Serra was able to plant a line of mission establishments on the main road up and down the California coast. Along an immense stretch of territory, at least 600 miles in length, the California mission system at its peak included twenty-one stations where over 21,000 Indians were engaged not only in Catholicism but also in farming, raising livestock, weaving, and related occupations. The California Franciscans reported that they had baptized thousands more, but by 1821 Mexico had declared its independence from Spain; twelve years later the missions were dissolved by the Mexican government, and Indian converts melted away.

Outnumbered by the Indians, the Roman Catholic missionaries from Spain brought their Native American converts a kind of shotgun Christianity, assisted by soldiers in garrisons never far away. But they were also sincerely convinced of a divine command to bring the Christian message to the Indians. Without the chastened perspective of a later age that would introduce a new regard for the religions of Native Americans, they thought that they were snatching the Indians from Satan — and bringing them civilization as well. For these missionaries, Roman Catholicism represented the one true religion, while European customs and manners epitomized civilization.

French Missions

Roman Catholic efforts in New France were not dissimilar, although the French perhaps encountered even more open hostility on the part of Indian peoples than did the Spanish. The French had begun their involvement in the New World with regular visits by shipping vessels to the Newfoundland coast in the sixteenth century. By the next century they had become interested in colonization, and a French Protestant community, the Huguenots, made plans to establish an outpost in Nova Scotia. While these Protestant settlers would have their own ministers to aid them spiritually, the French government decided that Catholic priests should also go along to convert the Indians. Thus, French Franciscan missionaries entered the New World, later to be joined by Jesuit priests in Quebec.

Here, after 1625, the Jesuits strived to master Indian languages, and later they set up mission stations for the Huron Indians. But the Hurons responded only in token numbers, and this fact combined with attacks by the Iroquois on the Hurons led to the failure of the missions. There were Jesuit martyrs in the process, among them the well-remembered Jean de Brébeuf (1593–1649). Yet ironically, for political reasons the Iroquois subsequently found it necessary to conciliate the French, and by 1668 the Jesuits had taken advantage of the opportunity and opened missions in upper New York.

Work among the Iroquois lasted only about two decades until the English swept into the area, but as early as the 1630s the Jesuits had also been preaching in the Illinois country to various Ottawa peoples. Here, throughout the seventeenth century they had mission stations. St. Ignace, the largest of these, was founded in northern Michigan in 1670, while La Pointe Mission, established in 1665 in northwestern Wisconsin, later acquired fame as the place from which the Jesuit Jacques Marquette (1637–1675) set out to explore the Mississippi River with Louis Joliet. In the interim, French colonies began to encircle the missions, and there was intermarriage with the Indians and a continuing Roman Catholic influence. Meanwhile, after 1680 in what is now the state of Maine, the Jesuits followed the earlier effort by Capuchin priests and worked in missions to the Abenaki Indians.

The voyage down the Mississippi had given the French confidence to enter new territory, and where French trappers and settlers went, the missionaries followed. By the end of the century, priests were working with the Natchez people in the South, and several years later (1703) they formed a parish in what is now Mobile, Alabama. Meanwhile, with a mission near New Orleans, the Jesuits were preaching to the Arkansas, Yazoo, Choctaw, and Alibamon people. New Orleans itself became a settled French colony, and Roman Catholicism grew apace among the Europeans. Further north, a group of transplanted Acadians settled. They were French people from Nova Scotia who had refused to accept British rule there after 1755, and they brought with them to Louisiana their Roman Catholic religion and customs to be handed down to their descendants as part of Creole culture.

English Colonies

By contrast to both the Spanish and French patterns, Roman Catholicism entered the English territories not through missions to Native Americans but through the settlement of English Catholics. When George Calvert, the first Lord Baltimore (1580–1632), acknowledged his Roman Catholicism in England, he resigned as privy councillor to King James I. Still, he did not completely lose favor with the English crown, and later King Charles I decided to grant him a charter to found a colony north of Virginia. Although George Calvert did not live to carry out his plans, his son, Cecil, received the sealed charter in his stead.

Cecil Calvert never came to Maryland himself, but his brother, Leonard Calvert (1606–1647), arrived in 1634 as the first governor of the colony. Religious liberty was guaranteed to all in 1639 by a legal enactment and a decade later by the Act of Toleration. Catholics were a minority in the population, though, and when the Puritans gained governmental power, they repealed the Act of Toleration in 1654 and outlawed Roman Catholicism. Although Lord Baltimore later regained power, by 1688 and the Glorious Revolution in England the Catholic defeat was complete. Ironically, in the colony initially established by a Catholic, Roman Catholics began to pay taxes (1692) in support of the Church of England, and from 1718 until the outbreak of the American Revolution they were refused voting rights.

In New England, after a brief period of toleration in Rhode Island until 1664, Catholics also led a troubled existence. It was only the American Revolution that enabled them to worship freely, and by 1785 there were only perhaps 600 Catholics in New England. Similarly, beginning in 1691, New York applied religious tests to exclude Catholics from public office. Earlier, there had been a Catholic governor, Thomas Dongan (1683), but the era of toleration was short-lived. It was Pennsylvania, however, that provided the best conditions, after Maryland, for Catholic settlement. Germans and some Irish came, the Jesuits worked among them, and by 1770 there were probably 3,000 adult Catholics in Pennsylvania, while Maryland had some 10,000.

Small as the English Catholic presence was in America when compared with the missionary efforts of Spain and France, it was from the English colonies that the constitutional structure emerged within which Roman Catholicism would later flourish. Land that had been claimed by New Spain and New France would become part of the United States in the nineteenth century, and with this territory would come an assortment of Roman Catholic communities. Still more, from overseas hundreds of thousands of Catholic immigrants would pour into the country. But before we pursue the Roman Catholic saga in the United States, we need to understand something of the religion that commanded the loyalty of these Americans.

Roman Catholic Religion

If the religion of Native Americans emphasized a consecration of space and the religion of the Jews emphasized a consecration of time, for Roman Catholics, space and time seemed equally consecrated. From the perspective of space, Catholicism expressed its religious perceptions in its sacramentalism, and from the perspective of time, it articulated its beliefs through its annual liturgical cycle. Meanwhile, the dimensions of space and time were combined in a series of popular devotions that flourished alongside the liturgy.

The Consecration of Space: Sacramentalism

We begin with Roman Catholic sacramentalism. A sacrament in any religion is a sacred sign — a person, a place, an object, or an action that is regarded as holy. More than that, a sacrament is a place where a divine or transcendent world is experienced as breaking into the human one. It is, in other words, a boundary phenomenon; and as the bridge that is affirmed between two worlds, a sacrament is understood to contain, in some mysterious way, the sacred power that it stands for. In a sacrament, therefore, ordinary and extraordinary reality are seen to be present, the one revealing the other even as it disguises it in ordinariness. Coming out of an understanding of the world related to the idea of correspondence, Catholic sacramentalism taught that the material world was so closely analogous to the spiritual one that it could both enclose and disclose the transcendent. Heaven was thought bound to earth by, as it were, a series of links in a chain, and, for example, even an insect was seen in some measure as a reflection of the transcendent world. Matter for Catholics was sacred; the natural world, good and holy.

Catholicism had developed its sacramental sense through the early and middle centuries of Christian history, combining a Jewish legacy with Greek philosophy and the remnants of Greco-Roman popular religion in the Mediterranean lands where Christianity spread. By medieval times, popular Christian belief held to seven sacraments, and these seven became the most concrete expression of a pervasive Catholic sacramentalism. For both medieval people and later Roman Catholics, the seven sacraments were baptism, confirmation, penance, eucharist, holy orders, matrimony, and extreme unction. Five of them formed a series of sacred actions that, ideally, assisted Catholics as they passed — again across a boundary — from one stage in life to the next. The remaining two, penance and eucharist, were meant to aid them, meanwhile, in the regular course of their lives.

Baptism in the name of the Father, the Son, and the Holy Spirit constituted an infant or an adult convert as a member of what Catholics called the communion of saints, the Christian community of all those now on the earth and those who had passed faithfully from this world to the next. Said to obliterate the original sin that these Christians believed was passed down from Adam and Eve, baptism was thought to purify humans and to transform them into children of God. Significantly, baptism featured the symbolic use of water. Just as water washed away the effects of natural pollution, Catholics taught, so the sacrament should cleanse the effects of spiritual stain so that humans could be fit for intimacy with God.

By the same token, confirmation used chrism, or blessed oils, to anoint a Catholic Christian as a sign of his or her spiritual maturation. Just as royal and military leaders had, for centuries, been anointed as they undertook their tasks, so — in Catholic teaching — adults in the communion of saints should be given an effective sign of their status. The bishop who administered the sacrament

gave a physical blow to the candidate in the old and traditional form of the rite —
a further sign that, as an adult in the church, the confirmed (strengthened)
Catholic should be prepared to witness to the faith even to the point of suffering
for it. Similarly, holy orders used chrism to anoint men in a series of steps to the
full Catholic priesthood. Matrimony used the spoken words of a man and a
woman in a pledge of mutual faith and love to make them husband and wife,
sometimes sealing their covenant with an exchange of rings. Extreme unction —
in recent times called the anointing of the sick — once again used blessed oils to
anoint a person in serious illness. The sacrament was meant to give to him or
her the strength to regain physical health or to move successfully through the
time of death.

Before the end, however, Catholics turned to penance and the eucharist
for assistance along the way. Penance demanded the confession of sins and a
sincere act of sorrow spoken by the penitent to a priest. Through the power given
to him in his ordination, Catholics believed, the priest could then forgive the
repentant sinner in the name of the Christian Trinity. Finally, in the eucharist,
Catholics held that Jesus Christ, the Son of God, was made physically and spiritually present to become the food of Christian believers.

Thus, all of the sacraments used material elements and human actions as
vehicles through which sacred power became present for those who believed. But
it was the eucharist that of all the sacraments was the center of Roman Catholic
life and most clearly expressed its sacramental understanding of the world. The
eucharist, which literally means "thanksgiving," was a ritual action to recall both
the biblical Last Supper Jesus had eaten with his disciples and his death on the
cross, in Catholic doctrine as a sacrifice for human sin. More commonly known
as the Mass, the eucharist had existed from early Christian times, but throughout
the Middle Ages it gradually assumed the form in which European Catholics
brought it to the New World. At the heart of the ritual were the elements of
bread and wine that, through a series of sacred words and actions on the part of a
priest, were changed, Catholics believed, into the body and blood of Jesus
Christ. They held that Jesus, present on the altar, was offered to his Father in
atonement, an unbloody sacrifice that yet repeated the sacrifice of Calvary.
Meanwhile, Catholics taught that the priest who offered the Mass was acting not
in his own name but in the name of Jesus. Thus, for Catholics, in the Mass it was
Jesus who was offering himself to his Father. Like the bread and wine, the priest
was a sacramental sign, a vehicle through which the power of Jesus could act.
And as in Jewish ritual, the sacred action was meant to cut through time to make
people present not at a mere commemoration but at the actual event on Calvary.

While the Mass was for Catholics a sacrifice, it was also for them a sacred
meal, a memorial to the last meal Jesus had eaten with his followers and a foretaste of the heavenly banquet. So it was that the bread and wine, now sacramen-
tally the body and blood of Jesus, were consumed at the Mass by the priest, who
offered the bread to other devout communicants. For the action to come full
circle for Catholics, the sacramental bread and wine must be used as they were in

ordinary life. They must nourish human beings and so, Catholics taught, give spiritual grace. Again, the sacrament was seen to cut through time, so that the memorial to the Last Supper and the foretaste of paradise were not simply meant to be signaled but meant to be made real in the lives of participants.

Sacramentalism did not end with the seven sacraments. Rather, it was a pervasive means of conceiving of the church, human life, and even the natural world. In the Catholic scheme of things, the church ideally should be as broad as the human race. In practice, it should include all those born into a territory, a people, a culture. Unlike a sect or denomination, which drew boundary lines between its membership and the world at large, the church sought to include all, both saints and sinners. For Catholicism, the church was the sign of God's presence in the world; it was one, holy, universal (catholic), and apostolic, and from the sacramental perspective the sign of God really *was* God present among humans.

Similarly, the pope of Rome was for Catholics the sign of the church, representing it to God and, at the same time, acting as the conduit through whom God communicated with human beings. Hence, the pope was considered the vicar, or representative, of Jesus Christ, and his solemn and official teachings were popularly regarded as infallible for many centuries. (They were officially so declared by a church council in 1870.) In Catholic understanding, the Roman papacy, with its traditions and trappings, stood equal to the Bible as a source of spiritual authority. Like a new Israel, Rome was seen as the specific human location where God had chosen to communicate with human beings. This was why the church was *Roman* Catholic, and this was why it was also authoritarian.

Finally, at the apex of this structure was Jesus, for Catholics the sign and sacrament of God revealed both in the scripture and in the continuing tradition of the church. In the Catholic view, by taking human flesh Jesus had spoken the clearest word about the goodness of the natural world and the sacredness of matter. If God had, for Catholics, become human in Jesus, then humanness — existence in *this* world — had its worth and value. The church taught that value, and so Roman Catholicism had a thisworldly as well as otherworldly orientation. Indeed, Catholic tradition put spirit and matter together by understanding the church as the Mystical Body of Christ. Likewise, monks and nuns, as members of religious orders that vowed poverty, chastity, and obedience, were thought of theologically as material signs of Jesus in the world and of his kingdom to come. True, monks and nuns were doing as Catholics believed all people would in paradise, neither marrying nor giving in marriage (Matt. 22:30). Yet, Catholics said, they shared basic joys of living: they ate, drank, and worked for and in the church. Hence, in Catholic thought they were witnesses to the messianic age, which although hidden, was already breaking upon the world.

Alongside this major sacramental scheme, Catholicism recognized a more mundane sacramentalism. Any natural object could become a "sacramental," an article in and through which, Catholics believed, humans could encounter the grace of God. Thus, a priest could bless water to make it holy, and he could confer a blessing, too, on a religious painting or statue. People could wear commemorative medals dedicated to Jesus, his mother, Mary, or one of the saints. They could light candles as signs of their prayerful remembrance of a loved one, receive ashes on Ash Wednesday to remind them that they would one day return to the dust, cherish rosary beads as talismans of the Virgin Mary's protection, and acquire and venerate relics of the saints.

The Consecration of Time: The Liturgical Cycle

Just as sacramentalism expressed the Catholic consecration of space, the liturgical cycle expressed its consecration of time. Structured very much like the Jewish annual cycle of feasts and fasts, the Catholic year began with the Advent season, which occurred during the month of December. At this time, believers awaited anew the coming of Jesus Christ. Then on Christmas day Roman Catholics commemorated his historical birth into the world as well as his spiritual birth in human hearts. The season that followed was punctuated with feasts that recalled events recorded in the gospels: the remembrance of the "holy innocents," infants slain by the king, Herod, in his angry search for Jesus; the Epiphany, in which the Magi, or wise men, paid homage at the crib of Jesus in Bethlehem; and the baptism of Jesus by John the Baptist at the Jordan River. Then, as winter drew to a close, Catholics kept a forty-day period of prayer and fasting called Lent. It recalled the forty days that, in gospel accounts, Jesus had spent in the desert before beginning his public ministry, and it culminated in the observances of Holy Week to commemorate the passion, death, and resurrection of Jesus.

Beginning on the Sunday before Easter, known as Palm Sunday, Catholics relived the biblical account of the triumphal entry of Jesus into Jerusalem before his passion and death. They received blessed palms and formed in procession around the church, singing "Hosanna to the son of David" (Matt. 21:9), as had the Jews of old. In the early part of the week, scriptural texts read at each daily Mass told of Jesus's words and deeds during the last days preceding his arrest. Then, on Maundy or Holy Thursday (believed to be originally the same day as the Jewish Passover), Catholics commemorated in a special way the Last Supper and the institution of the eucharist. This was the day on which the oils to be used ritually during the coming year were blessed, and this was also the day on which the priest who said Mass washed the feet of laypeople, a re-creation of the action in which, in the gospel, Jesus had washed the feet of his disciples at the Last Supper (John 13:4–5). For devout Catholics joy and sadness mingled in the liturgy: Jesus was giving the lasting gift of himself in what appeared to be bread and wine; yet Jesus was also about to go to his death for the sins of humankind. As Catholics recalled their Jewish heritage, he was the paschal Lamb to be sacrificed so that his people could pass over from slavery in sin to freedom in grace.

Good Friday was the only day of the year on which Roman Catholics, properly speaking, could not be present at Mass. There was a service that resembled the eucharistic action of the Mass, but unlike any other day the priest did not consecrate bread and wine. Instead, there was a communion service using the reserved sacrament, kept on a side altar after the Holy Thursday Mass. Since Good Friday was the day on which the death of Jesus was memorialized, Catholics felt that it was fitting that they should be without the sacramental action. A sense of sorrow and loss pervaded the scriptural texts of the liturgy, everything serving to underline the significance of what was being commemorated.

But the most sacred day of the church year for Catholics was Easter, and the liturgy used every means available to make the point. A long vigil service the previous evening ended with a Mass at midnight to honor the resurrection of Jesus. The vigil had been filled with the symbolism of new birth and new life: the lighting of a new fire from flint; the blessing of a huge new Easter candle, representing Jesus, which would stand in the sanctuary during the Easter season; the blessing of baptismal water for the succeeding year; and the solemn repetition by the congregation of baptismal vows. In the Mass that followed, the scriptural texts were sprinkled with alleluias: they expressed Catholic joy in the belief that Christ has risen and was still with his people.

Then, forty days after Easter, Catholics celebrated the feast of the ascension of Jesus into heaven, where, they believed, he sat at his Father's right hand, reigning with him in his kingdom. Ten days later, just as the Jews recalled the giving of the Torah (*Shavuot*, Pentecost), Catholics kept the feast of Pentecost. For them, however, it was a commemoration of the coming of the Holy Spirit upon the apostles. In the biblical account, tongues of fire descended on the apostles as they were waiting in an upper room, the fire transforming them with courage and zeal to spread the message of the gospel, the tongues enabling others to understand them, although they could not speak the language of the apostles.

The remainder of the liturgical year was a long series of Sundays after Pentecost, spread through the summer and autumn months, during which successive aspects of the life and teachings of Jesus were considered. Interspersed throughout this period, as through other parts of the year, were major feasts commemorating Jesus, Mary, or the saints. Almost no day in the Roman Catholic year was without its special liturgy, with scriptural texts read at the Mass to bring its lesson home. If a so-called ferial (or, literally, "free") day did occur, the priest used scriptural texts from the Mass of the preceding Sunday, always performing the eucharistic action to consecrate bread and wine.

As in the Jewish calendar, the feasts of the Catholic year were historicized rituals, remembering the traditional events that formed the story of Christian beginnings or the men and women who were its heroes. Still, as in the Jewish liturgy, underneath the symbolism of history lay the symbolism of nature and the material world. Roman Catholics awaited the birth of Christ, for them the light of the world, as the year lay "dying" on the last days before winter solstice. In the Christmas feast, Jesus was presented as if born during the week of solstice, like the first ray of the sun that, ancient religions taught, had conquered the winter darkness at that time. Lent brought a season of fasting during the last days of winter, while Easter came on the Sunday following the first full moon after the vernal (spring) equinox. It was the Catholic feast of new life, held when new life was rising in nature. Appropriately, Catholic customs in many lands included use of Easter eggs, natural symbols of fertility and birth.

Paraliturgical Devotions

In addition to the official liturgy, Catholics could participate in a multitude of paraliturgical devotions (literally, devotions alongside the liturgy) that combined sacramental space and consecrated time. Each Catholic country had its own favorite among them; and in America, therefore, popular devotionalism flourished with imported practices from many lands. These devotions were special, personal ways for Catholics to worship Jesus, venerate Mary, or honor the saints.

Among special devotions to Jesus, the cultus of the Sacred Heart was perhaps the most widespread among American Catholics. Originating in France with the recorded experiences of the nun Margaret Mary Alacoque, who in 1675 claimed a number of times to have seen Jesus, the devotion stressed the love and suffering of Christ. Its iconography included the portrayal of the bleeding and pierced heart of Jesus surrounded by a crown of thorns, often fashioned as a badge that a person could pin to inner or outer clothing. By the middle of the nineteenth century, an official feast honored the Sacred Heart, and meanwhile devout Catholics tried to attend Mass and receive communion on the first Friday of nine successive months. They believed that a promise had been made by Jesus to Margaret Mary Alacoque: if they kept the nine first Fridays, they would not die in a state of serious personal sin, and their salvation would be assured.

Other devotions to Jesus included special worship of the reserved sacrament at a time called Forty Hours, to commemorate the time that, according to tradition, Jesus spent in the tomb before his resurrection. In a period of that length, the communion bread, a small circular wafer, was exposed to public view in a special sacred vessel. There was also Benediction of the Blessed Sacrament, when, in a brief ceremony, the priest raised the sacrament in the same vessel to bless the assembled congregation, making the sign of the cross over them with it. Additionally, there were fourteen Stations of the Cross, usually representations in raised relief along the walls of the church. "Making the Stations" meant moving from station to station, following Jesus, as it were, in meditation along the road to Calvary. Still other Catholics had devotion to the Infant of Prague (Czechoslovakia), a doll-like statue dressed in bejeweled satin with a crown on its head, a representation of the kingship of Jesus even in the child.

Devotion to Mary was even more widespread than paraliturgical devotion to Jesus. In the rosary, Catholics used a chain of beads on which, while repeating prayers to God as Father and to Mary, they recalled traditional beliefs about the mysteries of her life as an inspiration for their own. In use since late medieval times, the rosary was also honored in a feast on October 7. Other Catholics expressed their devotion to Mary by wearing the scapular, two small pieces of brown wool cloth worn over the shoulders as a symbolic undergarment. No one,

Catholics believed, could die unrepentant or unprepared while he or she was wearing the scapular. Beyond these devotions, Catholics venerated Mary under various titles, many of them deriving from the place names of locations in which she was said to have appeared in visions. Marian shrines were erected to honor these apparitions, and these were often the sites of popular pilgrimages. Some of the titles of Mary made their way into the liturgical calendar, and there were, for example, feasts honoring Our Lady of Lourdes (a nineteenth-century French apparition), Our Lady of Good Counsel (a picture acclaimed as miraculous in an Italian church), and Our Lady of Guadalupe (especially popular in the Southwest, the apparition of Mary to a poor Indian near Mexico City).

Meanwhile, those held to be saints were not neglected, and various cultuses honored them, each having its special following among Catholics. Thus, St. Jude was considered the patron of hopeless cases, and St. Rita was called the saint of the impossible. St. Blaise was thought to help in the case of sore throats, and a special blessing for the throat could be had on his feast day. St. Agnes was regarded as patroness of sexual purity, and in the nineteenth century St. Thomas Aquinas became patron of Catholic schools. Each nationality among Catholics had its favored saints, and, indeed, each locality in their countries of origin had its special cultuses. One of the results of the American experience was that St. Stanislas (the Pole) and St. Rocco (the Italian) both received their due among American Roman Catholics.

Other paraliturgical activities were organized by means of special local church groups. Often men could belong to the Holy Name Society, committed to the avoidance of blasphemy and profanity. Women could join the Sodality of the Blessed Virgin Mary, dedicated to promoting chastity in and out of marriage as well as to encouraging the catalog of other virtues Mary was said to embody. One organization was dedicated to the teaching of Christian doctrine, while other groups sewed altar vestments for the liturgy or expressed their devotion to a particular saint through a formal organization.

Hence, to be a Roman Catholic was to be surrounded with sacrament and liturgy from cradle to grave. No day was without its reminders of belief in an invisible world, and each day brought ordinary and extraordinary together. The natural world was not a barrier to the supernatural for Roman Catholics; rather, properly regarded, they held that it led them into the supernatural.

Ethics and Morality

It is not surprising, therefore, that Catholic attitudes toward ethics and morality included the same regard for the natural world that sacramentalism and the liturgical cycle contained. Formulated most clearly by Thomas Aquinas in the thirteenth century, the Roman Catholic ethic grew out of a belief in natural law. This was the law thought to be implicit in the growth and development of any creature — plant, animal, or human. Moral action for Catholics meant action in accordance with this law of nature; immoral action meant unnatural action.

Thus, Catholics pointed to the fact that human beings throughout the world abhorred the killing of one of their own kind. It was, they said, a natural law written in human hearts that murder was wrong. Similarly, they explained, right-thinking people respected the property of others, and stealing also violated the law of nature. It was in matters of sexuality, though, that the implications of natural-law teaching led Catholics down a path different from that to be taken by many of their Protestant neighbors. The sexual act, Catholic thinkers argued, was naturally open to the reproduction of the human species; whatever interfered with that openness violated the divine and natural purpose of sexuality. From this perspective, artificial birth control was considered wrong and sinful. In the later twentieth century, when abortion became an issue, it was still more reprehensible from the point of view of natural-law teaching. Abortion, as traditional Catholics saw it, was murder.

Natural law, however, had been clarified and strengthened for Catholics by revealed law. Like their Jewish and Protestant neighbors, Catholics looked to the Ten Commandments that the biblical Moses had received on Sinai as the source for norms of behavior. They looked as well, with Protestants, to the law taught by Jesus in the Christian gospels. But more clearly than Protestants, they elaborated a scale of offenses against the law. After original sin had been forgiven in the sacrament of baptism, Catholics taught, humans were still capable of committing actual sins of greater or lesser magnitude. There was for them, first, mortal sin, a serious offense that, if unforgiven, they said could condemn a person to damnation for all eternity. And second, there was venial sin, which, though considered less serious, was thought still to weaken a person's resistance to more serious forms of evil and to dull his or her spiritual keenness. Catholics believed that both kinds of sin could be forgiven, if a person were truly sorry, through the sacrament of penance.

Even so, in Catholic thinking sin left its remains after the reception of the sacrament. Once having fallen, Catholics argued, it was always easy to fall again. Beyond that, they taught that the remains of sin meant that after death a person had to undergo a period of suffering and purification before he or she was fit to enter heaven. In the expectation of lessening that time in purgatory, a Catholic might obtain an indulgence through pious acts or prayers specifically recommended by the church for that purpose. There was no tension for a Catholic here: the pope, as the sign of Christ, who was the sign of God, set an indulgence on an act or prayer. Heaven was thought to obey, because, Catholics believed, the pope held authority as the presence of God in the world. Catholics felt assured that the Holy Spirit was with the church and that the believer who trusted would not be led astray. In the sixteenth century, the issue of indulgences was the catalyst for the Protestant Reformation, but in the Catholic scheme of things they played an uncontroversial, if small, part.

For all this legalism in an exacting, personal account of sin and grace, Roman Catholicism, like Judaism, was the religion of a community who collectively considered themselves the people of God. Hence, the ethic of Roman

Catholicism was also and ultimately a social ethic. It dealt with the waging of war and the keeping of peace, with the problem of poverty and the distribution of goods, with the relationship between the church and its claims, on the one hand, and the state and its demands, on the other. In medieval times, Catholicism had existed as Christendom, a public and cultural reality that included both church and state. In the modern era, it still sought to adjudicate the proper roles of church and state, more sensitive perhaps than many to the implications of church–state separation in America. In short, salvation, for Catholics, came to a community, and individuals had to find their place in this communal scheme of things. Nineteenth-century and later popes were particularly strong in pointing to what this meant in terms of capital and labor in an industrialized society, but the message of community and social concern was part of the traditional heritage of Roman Catholicism.

The American Saga of Catholicism

Keeping in mind this traditional heritage, we turn now to the American saga of Catholicism. We need to explore the direction of the changes that the American experience brought, changes that, as we will see, came from both inside and outside the church. Briefly, these changes were brought about by the ethnicity of the American Catholic church and by the pluralism of its setting. Ethnicity refers to the *internal* condition of being many national churches in one church; pluralism, to the *external* condition of being one church among many denominations. Together, the two conditions were aspects of one issue, that of how Roman Catholics should respond to their new American situation. And together, the two conditions generated a tension that in microcosm reflected the larger tension between oneness and manyness characteristic of American society.

Ethnicity

Ethnicity became an important coefficient in the American Catholic experience as the nation expanded into new territory and waves of immigrants poured in. Each ethnic group had evolved its own mix of ordinary and extraordinary religion when in its traditional setting it combined local custom and ethos with general Roman Catholic teaching. There would be organizational problems as worshipers from different European nations tried to share communion plate and pew. Still more, there would be conflict about whose way of being Catholic was right. Both Roman Catholics and their American observers generally wanted to see a single church that could be easily understood and explained. This meant that one or another ethnic group within the church was likely to impart its flavor to the whole. As we will see, this is what happened in Irish ascendancy over American Roman Catholicism.

The Manyness of Religions in America

We have already noticed that the earliest Catholics in the lands that later became the United States were Spanish, French, Native American, and English. Moreover, in colonial times Pennsylvania's Catholics had been mostly German, whereas New England had been the home of a small number of Irish Catholics. From the beginning, there was friction among these nationalities in the church. Different cultures and customs frequently led to different points of view and different practical stands on a series of issues, so that ethnic differences became part of larger misunderstandings. Thus, in Louisiana, French and Spanish Catholics had been hostile toward each other until the Louisiana Purchase of 1803 stirred them to join ranks against their common Anglo-American enemy. By the early nineteenth century, too, newly appointed French bishops were experiencing conflict with the Irish. Still earlier, in the late eighteenth century, Germans had expressed their hostility toward an Anglo-Catholic leadership by the formation of a separate Holy Trinity Church in Philadelphia (1787).

But the most serious ethnic struggles occurred in the second half of the nineteenth century when Irish immigrants became the backbone of American Catholicism and other groups fought to maintain their identity as nationalities within the church. The Irish, mostly poor cotters caught in the potato famine of Ireland, arrived in the 1840s and thereafter in huge numbers; they were bereft of resources and were forced to settle in eastern urban slums. Although their knowledge of the English language helped the Irish to adjust, their lack of literacy and working skills combined with their poverty to hamper them. Because their clergy had helped them in Ireland during the potato famine and also because their clergy had enough education to become cultural brokers in the new and alien setting, the American Irish remained loyal to their religious leaders. It was true that, just as in Ireland, many were attached to the church by little more than baptism. Still, the many who were practicing Catholics marked their religious observance with a distinctive style. Their Catholicism tended toward legalism and literal observance of church law, at the same time emphasizing personal morality and individualistic piety. Often antiintellectual, the Irish encouraged their sons and daughters to serve the church as priests and nuns.

Thus, it was Irish Catholics who, by the sheer power of their numbers — almost 1 million by 1850 — and by their willingness to enter ecclesiastical service, came to dominate the hierarchy of the American church. Moreover, when the Catholic leadership called for the development of a separate parochial school system, it was Irish nuns who for the most part staffed it, enabling them to pass on to generations of Roman Catholic schoolchildren their interpretation of Catholicism. Irish brick and mortar built the church — hence the "mortar" of the "bread and mortar" in this chapter's title. In the middle of the twentieth century, it was still the Irish who were giving American Catholicism its public face. Indeed, the Irish were to Catholicism what mainstream Protestants would be to other religious peoples in America — the dominant one among the many.

Of considerable significance among the Catholic many with whom the Irish dealt were the Germans. Present, as we have seen, from colonial times, they

St. Patrick's Cathedral, New York City. Constructed beginning in 1858, Gothic-style St. Patrick's Cathedral was a proud announcement of Roman Catholic — and Irish — presence in America. The sign on the center-rear building, for the papal visit of 1979, reads "Hardhats welcome the pope."

increased their numbers through immigration after the War of 1812 and steadily expanded until 1855. Indeed, by 1850 there were over 500,000 Germans in the United States. Generally more affluent and better educated than the Irish and other Catholic groups, they often left their eastern ports of entry and headed for the Midwest. Here their settlements spread out in the cities and farmland that described a triangle between Cincinnati, St. Louis, and Milwaukee. The Germans were deeply attached to their language and traditions, wanting them to be used in their churches and schools. Hence, they demanded parishes organized on the basis of nationality rather than territory. With their love of their native music, relaxed observance of the Sabbath, and opposition to the temperance movement, they were often at odds, especially, with the attitudes of the Irish.

From 1855 German Catholics established the Central Verein, a strong organization that continued into the twentieth century. Then in 1871 Peter Paul Cahensly (1838–1923), a businessman in Nassau (Germany), organized the St. Raphaelsverein as a society to aid German immigrants to the New World. In 1891 the society presented a petition to the pope, claiming that immigrants were being lost to Catholicism in huge numbers because they lacked priests and institutions of their own nationality to minister to them. The American church should be multilingual and multinational if it was to succeed, they said. "Cahenslyism," as it came to be called, exaggerated the defections from the American church and brought support from Germans in Europe to the struggle in America against the Irish. Although the movement finally failed in its most ambitious goals, it was a strong indicator of the continuing conflict within American Catholicism.

In the last third of the nineteenth century, however, the immigrant tensions that had begun in an earlier age were complicated by the arrival of new groups. The "new immigration" from 1880 until the First World War brought a steady flow of Southern and Eastern European Catholics. Well over 3 million Italians arrived by 1920 and, among a variety of Eastern European national groups, nearly as many Poles. Yet for various reasons neither ethnic group seriously altered the public face of American Roman Catholicism.

The Italians came mostly from southern Italy and Sicily, poor and illiterate for the most part, and, like the Irish before them, settling in eastern seacoast cities. For the Italians, perhaps more than for most other immigrant groups, religion and culture were interfused, always returning to their source and center in the extended family. This preference for familial over ecclesiastical identification had only been magnified by the recent history of church–state relations in Italy. The pope had been the temporal ruler of the northern Italian Papal States until 1870, and so Italian Catholics had come to extend to the official church the same kind of distrust they felt toward political government. As they immigrated to America, these Italian Catholics were unwilling to give the church either their children, as priests and nuns, or their money, to supply the brick and mortar for new shrines and schools. With their own spirit of relaxed adherence to official rules and regulations, they did not accept the legalism of the Irish.

By contrast, the Poles were intensely devoted to the institutional church. Coming from peasant backgrounds, many who immigrated to America eventually became farmers, but numbers of them settled in cities like Chicago, Milwaukee, Detroit, and Cleveland. For centuries, the Polish people had joined their nationalism to their religion, and so in America, like the Germans, they sought to maintain a distinct national ethos, preserving their language in churches and schools. To some extent, the pattern of conflict was repeated: there were struggles between clergy and laity in different parishes over financial matters, and by the early twentieth century, there was a movement for equal representation with other national groups in the American hierarchy. Indeed, tensions with a non-Polish hierarchy resulted in the formation in Scranton, Pennsylvania, of the separate Polish National Catholic Church in 1904.

Still, most Polish Catholics chose to remain within the Roman Catholic church. And since history was by this time on the side of continued Irish hegemony, the real aim of Polish Catholics was survival more than dominance. The results of their efforts could be measured by the fact that as late as 1950 there were still 800 Polish parishes in the United States. Beyond this, the Polish brought into the American church a series of new devotions, such as that to the Black Madonna (the Virgin) of Czestochowa, and they gave to the church their sons and daughters in Polish Catholic religious communities.

More recently in the twentieth century, Roman Catholic immigration expanded still again. According to U.S. Bureau of the Census figures reported in 1985, there were 16.9 million people of Spanish origin in the nation. This figure represented a decided increase since 1960, when people with Spanish surnames numbered only 3.5 million. Moreover, official figures did not include the many (estimated variously from 3 million to 10 million) who had entered the country without immigration papers. Changes in the U.S. immigration law in 1965 made entry from Central and South America easier, and political and economic conditions in the various countries of origin often also prompted a decision to leave.

Thus, through the arrival of large numbers of Spanish-speaking people, Spanish Catholicism, the earliest European Christianity in America, reappeared in new form. Overwhelmingly, however, this great influx, despite their Catholic heritage, were also the least church oriented of any immigrant group. A swelling Mexican presence had begun in the early twentieth century, spilling over the borders into Texas, California, and the Southwest. Later, by midcentury, Puerto Ricans were entering New York City in heavy concentrations, while the Cuban revolution of 1959 brought Cubans in large numbers to the Miami area, and a record number of Haitians arrived in the country, too. Hispanic Catholics tended to be anticlerical, and, in the United States as in their homelands, many turned from their nominal Catholicism to an intense and active pentecostalism. Still, their liturgies were distinctive, and in their absorption of Catholicism, like the Italians, they displayed strong overlapping between ordinary and extraordinary religion. In their closely knit subcultures, community was not theoretical but lived; organized religion became culture, as the extraordinary elements in

Catholicism merged into ordinariness. So for many years the composition of "public Catholicism" went largely unaltered, not affected one way or another by Hispanics who felt no need to get involved in the official church.

On the other hand, by the late twentieth century the composition of public Catholicism *did* begin to alter because of the Hispanic presence. Hispanics were now some 25 percent of the United States Catholic population, and, whereas in 1972 there had been but one Hispanic bishop in the nation, in 1985 there were eighteen. There was also a national secretariat for Hispanic affairs in Washington, D.C., and six regional offices were scattered throughout the country. Even earlier, by the late sixties in Los Angeles, the militant Catolicos por la Raza (Catholics for the People) had protested the opulence of the church and its seeming indifference toward the political and social struggles of Hispanic peoples. Other Hispanic groups of priests and nuns organized around themes of social justice and empowerment for Hispanic Catholics. Then, in 1971, the first *encuentro*, or national pastoral congress, took place in Washington, D.C. Later *encuentros* were held in 1977 and 1985, addressing the needs and concerns of Hispanic Catholics. Large numbers of laypeople attended, many of them delegates from a grass-roots movement that had by now sprung up. Hispanic bishops, by 1983, characterized the changes as the unfolding of a "new era."

Meanwhile, new Catholic immigrants from Vietnam and elsewhere in Asia added to the changing population of the church. Significantly, too, the small number of African-Americans who were Catholics had shown a sizable increase. In 1985, some 1.2 million, or 5 percent, of the American black community counted themselves as Catholics. Twenty-five years earlier the number had stood at 3 percent. By 1985, also, there were ten African-American Catholic bishops, and the number of priests who were African-American had risen to 350. More indicative than numbers, though, was a new climate. The "black power" movement of the late sixties had been transmuted, so that by 1984 the African-American bishops could write a pastoral letter pointing to the richness of black culture and proclaiming the need to share their experience with others. In this mood, the bishops asked increased leadership authority for black Roman Catholics and called for an end to the racism that had long existed in the Catholic church. Even so, blacks as a people were decisively Protestant, and we will look more closely at African-American religion in Chapter 6.

The black celebration of ethnicity, however, did not go unnoticed by the ethnic groups that had immigrated in years past. Indeed, African-American ethnic consciousness no doubt suggested to some other Roman Catholics their cultural mood in the seventies and eighties, in what the Slovak-American Catholic Michael Novak has called the "rise of the unmeltable ethnic." These ethnic Catholics were drawn to a nostalgic recollection of their past. Being part of the silent majority of the American middle class had proved for them, as it had for other groups, in some ways unrewarding. At the same time, the ethnic organization among blacks (as well as among Indians and Hispanics) urged them toward greater visibility. The many, we might say, interacted with forms of manyness other than their own, so that there was a sustained regard for ethnicity in the American Catholic church. Although the Irish continued to predominate, the age of the monolith simply had not come.

Pluralism and Americanization in Historical Perspective

It is the place here to consider the second major factor that affected the course of Roman Catholicism in the United States — its pluralistic setting. This *external* condition meant that, both for outsiders and insiders, no matter what its theoretical claims to universality, the Catholic church in America was a minority. For outsiders, the Catholic presence was a sometime threatening quantity, and Protestant fears generated a series of nativist and protectionist movements. For insiders, emulation of the American and Protestant mainstream led to a series of attempts by some to "de-Romanize" the church, while others more conservatively sought a retreat into separateness. For these people, the preservation of their ethnic heritages became a way of avoiding the mainstream. Hence, as we have noticed, pluralism and ethnicity were related issues.

We will examine the question of nativism in more detail in the last chapter. Here, however, it is important to note that nativism was a continuing fact of Catholic life throughout much of the nineteenth century and into the twentieth. By 1830 an anti-Catholic weekly called *The Protestant* had been established to counter Roman corruption, and the crusade against Catholicism had begun.

In 1834, in an often-cited incident, a mob set fire to the Ursuline convent in Charlestown, Massachusetts, while in Philadelphia a decade later at least two churches were burned. Meanwhile, associations were formed in order to combat what many Americans saw as the dangers in Catholicism. In 1842 there was the American Protestant Association, and in 1854, the Know-Nothing party. Later, in 1887, the American Protective Association was formed to oppose Catholicism, and then in the 1920s the revived Ku Klux Klan fought against the Catholic church. Fueled by fears inspired by the "otherness" of the assorted "papist" immigrants, these organizations expressed sentiments that were shared by many who did not belong to them. They were monuments to the strains that Protestant America was experiencing as it worked to come to terms with massive immigration.

For some Catholic insiders, nativist harassment was met by a strong desire for retreat and segregation. Hostile toward Anglo-America, many working-class immigrants of German and Polish origins joined the majority of the Irish and their clergy in a strong conservative stance. Led among the hierarchy by Michael A. Corrigan (1839–1902), the archbishop of New York, and Bernard McQuaid (1823–1909), the bishop of Rochester, in the late nineteenth century they labored to isolate the church from the dominance of a Protestant culture. They were especially fearful of the public schools, where, they thought, a kind of common-denominator Protestantism was being promulgated. It was in this atmosphere of caution and reserve that the Catholic school system was born, with the demand by the Third Plenary Council of Baltimore (1884) that every parish establish its own parochial school.

For other Catholic insiders, however, mainstream American culture had an inviting face. Even at the beginning of the early national period, some lay Catholics, in the absence of a prohibition by Bishop John Carroll (1735–1815), had taken a strong hand in parish affairs. Influenced by congregational Protestants, they were often close to calling and replacing their own pastors, sometimes even becoming schismatic by doing so. Trusteeism, as it was called, took advantage of the fact that the civil law had been written to accommodate both church–state separation and Protestant church polity, conferring corporate ownership of church property on the lay trustees of a congregation. Heightened sometimes by struggles between various national groups within the church, trusteeism was a recurring problem for bishops for some sixty years. Trustees invoked their democratic rights, and the old hierarchical and sacramental model was challenged by the new order. Eventually, property rights were vested in the bishop of each diocese as a corporation sole, but not before there had been much disruption of traditional patterns.

The democratic trustees were succeeded in the latter part of the nineteenth century by democratic bishops, who formed a liberal camp in opposition to the conservatives we have already encountered. Led by James Cardinal Gibbons (1834–1921) of Baltimore and even more aggressively by Archbishop John Ireland (1838–1918) of St. Paul, Minnesota, a number of these bishops sought to open Catholic culture outward toward America. They wanted to end every kind of Catholic isolation and to "Americanize" the church. Catholics, they thought, should wholeheartedly embrace the American style and the American way of doing things.

Thus, Cardinal Gibbons actively intervened in 1887 to prevent Rome from condemning the Knights of Labor, an early labor organization supported by Irish Catholics. With the strong endorsement of Cardinal Gibbons and Archbishop Ireland, Bishop John Lancaster Spalding (1840–1916) of Peoria, Illinois, crusaded for the foundation of a Catholic university where graduate theological study could go on. His success was apparent in 1889 when the Catholic University of America opened its doors in the nation's capital. Meanwhile, Archbishop Ireland remained dubious concerning the value of a separate parochial school system and repeatedly urged the American church to live in its own age and its own setting. For Ireland, the Roman Catholic church in America should become an *American* Catholic church. As he and other liberals saw it, the official separation between church and state in the United States was not just a practical arrangement under which Roman Catholicism had managed to thrive. Rather, it was an ideal situation and one that American Roman Catholics should enthusiastically support.

But the liberals did not continue their efforts toward the Americanization of the church with impunity. Matters came to a head in 1899 when Pope Leo XIII published an encyclical letter, *Testem Benevolentiae*, which condemned a number of opinions collectively labeled "Americanism." A key example of this Americanism for the pope was the willingness to regard natural virtues more highly than supernatural ones. Here, natural virtues meant active and "thisworldly" gifts that were congenial to the Protestant American style. Supernatural virtues meant those that were more "passive" and otherworldly in character, like the traditional humility and obedience that were associated with Catholic saints. A second instance of Americanism was the willingness to adapt to the theories and methods of modern popular culture, seen as bringing a relaxation of the ancient rigor of the church. A third instance was a tendency toward individualism in religion, whereas traditional Catholicism had stressed the role of the church in salvation.

Americanism has often been called the "phantom heresy," because as soon as the encyclical letter was published, American bishops unanimously asserted their freedom from the errors named therein. They were not Americanists, the suspected liberal bishops said, nor did they know any Americanists. Pope Leo XIII had effectively put an end to the Americanization of the Catholic church — at least for the time being.

Meanwhile, on the popular level, the second half of the nineteenth century brought to the fore an institution imported from Europe that at the same time fit closely with American Protestant spirituality. The Catholic mission movement gave to the church its own brand of revivalism, helping to stop defections and to excite the piety of ordinary working-class people. Held in a parish, usually for one to two weeks every four or five years, a mission featured traveling preachers whose sermons were designed to stir up fear of eternal punishment, sorrow for what was acknowledged as sin, and recommitment to Roman Catholicism. Like Protestant revivals, missions used mass evangelistic techniques to reach their audiences, the preachers planting a mission cross, preaching with an empty casket to dramatize a point, or tolling a sinner's bell at evening.

Each mission aimed in the context of Catholic sacramentalism at individual conversion or rededication. For the Catholic who came to listen, the sermon was meant to lead to the confessional, where, in Catholic belief, sins were to be forgiven. It was a fact that after the Catholic Counter-Reformation of the sixteenth century, Catholic piety had entered an evangelical and individualistic era. Still, it seemed a fair assessment that the presence of American Protestantism in a general way supported the pattern of Catholic revivalism. Traveling preachers, the use of self-conscious techniques, an emphasis on conversion and stern morality, the preference for emotion over intellect, a pervading individualism — the mission movement shared all of these with Protestant revivalism.

Pluralism and Americanization: The Later Twentieth Century

In the twentieth century, it remained for Rome itself to unleash the forces that would stimulate a new era of Americanization for the church. The Second Vatican Council (1962–1965) — a meeting in Rome of all the bishops of the church with the pope at their head — did not so much *cause* the changes as catalyze them by discarding older forms and admitting new ones. Already, in the fifties, American Catholics had begun to come of age. They were reaching social and economic equality with their Protestant neighbors, and so they were more and more thinking and acting like members of the mainstream. When Vatican II used the work of the American Jesuit priest John Courtney Murray (1904–1967) in its official Declaration on Religious Freedom, it was offering an endorsement of the American way. Although they were no longer alive to savor the fact, the nineteenth-century liberals, the Americanists who thought that church–state separation was an ideal and not just a necessity, had come into their own. The American Catholic experience with religious pluralism, with the manyness of free and individual choices, had helped to shape the teaching of the world church.

Just as significantly, in the wake of Vatican II American Catholicism registered changes in the area of worship and in the area of morality. The results of a long and scholarly liturgical movement were visible when the council paved the way for Mass texts in the language of each nation instead of the traditional Latin. Many accretions to the Mass that had grown up over the years were cut away, while scriptural sermons and congregational singing were stressed. Although the justification for these changes was that they brought the liturgy closer to the pattern of the early church, in fact the changes underlined the verbal content of the service at the expense of the symbolic. In so doing, the changes did not destroy sacramentalism, but they did modify it. The reformed liturgy came closer to the model of Protestant services, a model that we will regard more closely in the next chapter.

At the same time, sociological study suggested that Sunday Mass attendance — always high because failure to attend was considered a serious sin — had declined in the United States. By the early eighties, it had increased only slightly again, and the paraliturgical devotionalism of the past seemed permanently challenged and eroded by the reforms. Once more, Catholics were coming closer in their religious practices and attitudes to their Protestant neighbors.

Beginning in the later sixties as well, a charismatic movement swept the church. In some measure it was a twentieth-century successor to the old nineteenth-century mission revivalism. Yet it went further. Attracting a well-educated middle class that included many clergy, it preferred experience to theology and actively cultivated ecumenical relationships with American pentecostals. The movement stressed the pentecostal baptism of the Holy Spirit, which was thought to bring gifts of prophecy, exorcism, healing, and speaking in tongues. Charismatic religious rhetoric was often borrowed from pentecostals, and so, too, were characteristic gestures such as the raising of hands at prayer and the laying on of hands for healing.

Charismatics often met in private homes during evening hours to conduct their prayer sessions, but they did begin to organize, establishing a Center for Communication and Service in 1969 and sponsoring a Conference on Charismatic

Renewal in Rome in 1975. Annual conventions, usually held at the University of Notre Dame, became huge affairs that used the university's football stadium and basketball arena to accommodate the crowds gathered for Mass. By 1984 perhaps 500,000 Catholics were involved in the charismatic movement, with approximately half of them attending weekly prayer meetings. Not only did prayer groups flourish (some 5,700 of them), but there were also about 100 covenant communities organized more intensely in a pooling of financial resources and decision making. In recent times growth has been slower, and, of course, not all Catholics attracted to the charismatic movement have remained a part of it. But as some ceased participation, new individuals were drawn to charismatic Catholicism, so that the number who have at one time or another been involved is well into the millions. (One 1984 estimate suggested 8 million to 10 million since 1967.) At the end of the eighties, it was clear that the charismatic movement was in the Roman Catholic church to stay. And while the bishops had sometimes regarded charismatics nervously because of fear of heresy, they had, in 1969, cautiously approved the movement. They felt that they needed the zeal of charismatic Catholics at a time when the American church seemed lax.

If there seemed to be laxity — or a different spirit abroad in the church after Vatican II — it was nowhere more suggested than in the area of morality and ethics. Overall, individualism in morality grew at the expense of priority for community. This was evident in a more permissive sexual ethic, which sociological surveys discovered especially among young Roman Catholics. There was more willingness to condone sexual activity outside of marriage and more support for artificial birth control and even abortion. Again, the data suggested that Catholics resembled their Protestant neighbors more closely in the area of sexual morality than they ever had previously. Implicit in the change was a move from a sense of absolutes based on belief in natural and revealed law for a community and a turning toward the situational and the relative. Catholics were moving to an ethic based on history, and the move led them closer to Protestant America.

Meanwhile, individualism was apparent as more and more priests and nuns sought dispensations from their vows to return to lay life. Other priests and nuns in the democratic and collegial spirit fostered by Vatican II demanded greater responsibility in the government of their institutions, while some priests also demanded the right to marry. Similarly, the laity, with church encouragement voicing concern for the management of their parishes, formed councils to assist their priests. While the parishes did not return to nineteenth-century trusteeism, the American democratic model was not difficult to find.

Nor were democracy and an egalitarian spirit hard to find among Catholic women. With a rising feminist consciousness, many came to question the hierarchical stance of their church, seeing it as patriarchal and oppressive to women. Feminist theologians such as Rosemary Radford Ruether and Elisabeth Schüssler Fiorenza led the new morality of resistance and reform from one direction, as did other, more loosely affiliated laywomen from another. By the late eighties — in organizations as diverse as the Institute in Culture and Creation Spirituality, in Oakland, California, and Grailville, in Loveland, Ohio—a broad Catholic feminism had come to mean joining with others who were not Catholic in a movement called ecofeminism. Here environmental activism joined forces with feminism in concern for the earth as Gaia, a living (female) being undergoing a time of purification because of human environmental abuse. Moreover, feminist Catholic women joined with some others who were not Catholic in spontaneous movements like WomenChurch, with its own feminist and earth-based liturgies. There was a mood of experimentation and moral assertiveness in the air, and in this atmosphere some women continued to press their case to be Catholic priests.

The radical, prophetic mood of earth spirituality and female priesthood was an indicator of a final way in which Catholic morality had grown more Protestant and more American. A prophet in the history of religions was a figure who criticized the existing state of things, striving to purify it of perceived corruption and to restore what the prophet saw as fundamental truth. Such a figure stood outside the religious situation in its contemporary form, impelled by a different vision of what ought to be. With this message of criticism, a prophet diverged sharply in character from a priest, whose role was to uphold the standing order by repeating its rituals. Every religion has had something of the prophet and something of the priest in its history, but in the modern West it was certain forms of Protestantism that most strongly cherished the figure of the prophet and Catholicism, by contrast, that most clearly chose the conserving role of the priest. As we will see in the next chapter and in Chapter 11, American Protestantism with its Puritan roots often preached a prophetic morality. On the other hand, Catholicism in its traditional form usually preferred priestly action.

Catholic feminists were, in this context, prophets. But there were other American Catholic prophets, many of them connected with the peace movement. So, for example, the Berrigan brothers, Daniel (b. 1921) and Philip (b. 1923), Roman Catholic priests, led their followers in protest against the Vietnam War, willing to go to jail for their words and deeds. The Berrigans spoke and marched, raided draft headquarters, poured animal blood on records, and inspired dozens of others to behave in kind. Still more, by 1983 even the mood of the Catholic bishops had turned prophetic. In a pastoral letter, "The Challenge of Peace: God's Promise and Our Response," the bishops raised serious questions about war in a nuclear age and became advocates for peace.

Catholic life values informed the left-leaning words and acts of the Berrigans and the bishops. And it was Catholic life values, too, that figured in the complex of motives prompting a militant group of Roman Catholic prophets of the right. In the seventies and eighties, the prolife movement, which included many Catholics, led an antiabortion campaign that escalated from impassioned speeches and the display of enlarged fetal pictures to marches, protests, and sometimes even physical harassment of the clinics where abortions were performed and of the women who chose to undergo them. The antiabortionists resembled the Prohibitionists of an earlier era in the fierceness of their stand and the aggressiveness with which they worked to change laws to reflect their views. Indeed, it was the 1973 Supreme Court decision in *Roe v. Wade*, which held that women had a constitutional right to abortion in the early stages of a pregnancy, that galvanized many into action. And in the 1989 Supreme Court decision in *Webster v. Reproductive Health Services*, a case involving a Missouri statute to discourage abortions, prolifers claimed a partial victory. Here, however, the point is less the politics of prolifers than what they shared with Catholics of profoundly different views. (In fact, polls show that large numbers of Catholics support abortions, especially in certain situations like rape or a threat to the woman's life.) The point is that both Catholics of the left — like feminists, the Berrigans, and to some extent the bishops — and Catholics of the right — like the prolifers — preached and defended traditional life values in a prophetic stance that was new. But the stance of prophecy had more to do with the context of Protestant America than with anything in recent Roman Catholic history.

The last third of the twentieth century saw a Catholicism that had changed remarkably from its small beginnings in America. By the eighties, one-quarter or more of the population was Roman Catholic, but there had been a decline in devotional practice for many of them. Fewer American Catholics thought that the pope was the vicar of Christ or considered him infallible. The reiteration by Pope Paul VI of the church's traditional stand against artificial birth control (1968) alienated many, and the refusal of the church to give official sanction to remarriage after divorce disaffected still others. Still, the use of annulment by Catholic marriage tribunals (church courts) was, in effect, an endorsement of remarriage, and overall statistics showed a marked increase in the number of annulments granted. However, with or without clerical support, in the late eighties more and more American Catholics were, in the earlier words of the priest and sociologist Andrew Greeley, "going their own way." They were picking and choosing, deciding how and in what respects they would be Catholic. With a new voluntary style, Catholics selected what they wanted from the legacy of their church, and they did not all select the same things. Clearly, the habit of pluralism had taken hold.

In one sense, the bread-and-mortar church was still there: the Irish were still noticeable in pulpit and pew, and the diverse ethnic character of the church was still a prominent feature. A huge network of Catholic schools and colleges had scarcely folded up and disappeared. The radical moralists of left and right had gained Catholicism nationwide notice in the media, while the sacraments, still seven in number, gave solace to millions.

Yet the sacramentalism that had shaped the Catholic understanding of religion and human life had begun to crumble. Paraliturgical devotions seemed to melt away after Vatican II, and numbers of Catholics seemed to melt away from church attendance, too. Thousands of priests and nuns had returned to lay life, and new recruits had fallen off sharply. The sexual revolution and a revised sexual ethic signaled a moral sense profoundly different from that of the past. The refusal to accept the authority of the pope and bishops meant that they were no longer regarded, in the same traditional sense, as sacramental signs of Christ. The old order of things, in which ordinary and extraordinary mingled in sacramental unity, was yielding to a new pattern. Ordinary and extraordinary now were more separated and compartmentalized. Like Reform Jews and like mainstream Protestants, as we will see, Roman Catholics by discarding some of their sacramentalism were making clearer distinctions between the two. It was true that American Roman Catholics had made a complex move away from a medieval angle of vision and toward a modern one and that this move had been shared by many in world Catholicism. But the move was complicated by its context "in America." Roman Catholicism was giving way to *American* Catholicism and, if you will, to Protestant-American Catholicism.

In Overview

From the time of Christopher Columbus, Roman Catholicism had been present in North America. Early Spanish and then French missionaries brought their first taste of Christianity to American Indians, while with the arrival of English Catholic colonists in the seventeenth century, Catholicism entered the English seaboard colonies. The religion that was shared by all of these Catholics found holiness in nature as well as biblical and historical tradition. Through its sacramental vision, Roman Catholicism saw the material world as both the symbol and reality of divine things. This understanding crystallized in the seven sacraments of the Catholic cultus, but it was visible throughout the Catholic system. At the apex of the system, for Catholics, was Jesus Christ, whose presence they acknowledged in an annual liturgical cycle commemorating events in the gospel accounts of his life, death, and resurrection. Meanwhile, in a moral system that had developed over the years, Catholics lived their commitment to nature and traditional sources they considered revelation, adhering to natural law, scripture, and church teaching. Like Native Americans and Jews, in both cultus and code they tended to blend extraordinary with ordinary religion.

With this heritage behind it, the Catholic church in the United States faced changes brought by its internal ethnicity and the external pluralism of American culture. Spanish, French, Native American, and English Catholics were joined, as time passed, by German and Irish Catholics and later by Southern and Eastern Europeans and by Hispanic and some African-American and Asian peoples. These groups often strived to maintain the separate boundaries of their ethnic identity, and there were sometimes collisions among them. In this situation of internal manyness with its attendant tensions, the Irish came to dominate by the mid-nineteenth century and continued to do so into the twentieth century. In turn, the pluralism of American culture led to profound changes that swung the Catholic church more and more away from its "Roman" axis. Extraordinary and ordinary religion grew more separate, as Catholic boundaries opened out toward America. By the late twentieth century, catalyzed through the actions of the Second Vatican Council, the Roman Catholic church in America had become an American Catholic church that looked increasingly like the churches of mainstream Protestants.

Who were the people who had so influenced the religions of Catholic and Jewish immigrants? What kind of religion had drawn the many more and more toward itself with its cultural hegemony? It is time now to look at the mainstream Protestantism of America—a Protestantism that in the late twentieth-century, like Catholicism, regarded itself with anxiety and worried about its spiritual condition.

SUGGESTIONS FOR FURTHER READING: ROMAN CATHOLICISM

Abbott, Walter M., ed. *The Documents of Vatican II.* New York: Association Press, 1966.

Chinnici, Joseph P. *Living Stones: The History and Structure of Catholic Spiritual Life in the United States.* Makers of the Catholic Community: The Bicentennial History of the Catholic Church in America. New York: Macmillan, 1989.

Cross, Robert D. *The Emergence of Liberal Catholicism in America.* Cambridge: Harvard University Press, 1958.

Cunningham, Lawrence S. *The Catholic Experience: Space, Time, Silence, Prayer, Sacraments, Story, Persons, Catholicity, Community, and Expectations.* New York: Crossroad, 1987.

Dolan, Jay P. *The American Catholic Experience: A History from Colonial Times to the Present.* Garden City, NY: Doubleday, 1985.

————. *Catholic Revivalism: The American Experience, 1830–1900.* Notre Dame, IN: University of Notre Dame Press, 1978.

————. *The Immigrant Church.* Baltimore: Johns Hopkins University Press, 1975.

Ellis, John Tracy. *American Catholicism.* The Chicago History of American Civilization. Rev. ed. Chicago: University of Chicago Press, 1969.

Greeley, Andrew M. *The Catholic Myth: The Behavior and Beliefs of American Catholics.* New York: Charles Scribner's, 1990.

Hennesey, James. *American Catholics: A History of the Roman Catholic Community in the United States.* Oxford: Oxford University Press, 1981.

McAvoy, Thomas T. *A History of the Catholic Church in the United States.* Notre Dame, IN: University of Notre Dame Press, 1969.

McKenzie, John. *The Roman Catholic Church.* Garden City, NY: Doubleday, Anchor Books, 1971.

Meconis, Charles A. *With Clumsy Grace: The American Catholic Left, 1961–1975.* New York: Seabury, Continuum Book, 1979.

Orsi, Robert Anthony. *The Madonna of 115th Street: Faith and Community in Italian Harlem, 1880–1950.* New Haven: Yale University Press, 1985.

Taves, Ann. *The Household of Faith: Roman Catholic Devotions in Mid-Nineteenth-Century America.* Notre Dame, IN: University of Notre Dame Press, 1986.

Chapter 4

Word from the Beginning: American Protestant Origins and the Liberal Tradition

Probably every schoolchild in America has heard the tale of how the Pilgrims with their Indian friends celebrated the first Thanksgiving, a harvest festival to thank God that they had survived in the New World for the year. Similarly, almost every child has heard the Virginia narrative of how Captain John Smith was saved from certain death at the hands of the Indians by Pocahontas, the daughter of the chief Powhatan, and of how some years later she became a Christian and married John Rolfe.

In light of later American history, these are curious vignettes. They are both tales of ethnoreligious intimacy between English Protestants and Native Americans. The subsequent story of relations between these peoples was not so sunny. There were wars between them; conversion attempts by the English were dubious and marked by tardiness and few missionaries; "empty land" became the characteristic English justification for moving farther into the wilderness that was the Indians' home.

Yet there is a poetic justice about these early tales. If intimacy is based on common elements between different peoples, the two groups did have something in common. For both, manyness was a social condition in which they lived and a feature of their mental landscape. Native Americans, as we have seen, dwelled in nations that in themselves possessed ethnoreligious unity but were surrounded by other, separate Indian nations. English Protestants had left a land in which religious nonconformity meant that they had cultural ties with many of their compatriots but religious differences. Further, just as the many Indian nations had a basic oneness—a similar mentality, ethos, and structure of religious ritual—so the many Protestant groups in America showed a tendency toward religious oneness. In one sense, Protestants came to be the most diverse religious

people in America, counting themselves as members of a plethora of denominational groups. In another sense, though, they were the most unified group in
America, and their common ideal was so persuasive that it became the religious
vision of all Americans. We will pursue much of this latter theme in Part II, but
for now we need to look at the unity of mainstream Protestantism in itself. We
will examine it first as an inherited religious vision and then as an *American*
religious vision. And in this chapter we will especially notice its growth in the
liberal tradition.

The Religion of the Reformation

Protestantism was born in sixteenth-century Europe with the idea of reformation
at its center. In the preaching of the leading Reformers, Martin Luther (1483–
1546) and John Calvin (1509–1564), prophetic protest was lodged against the
priestly religion of medieval sacramentalism. The Reformers saw the many layers
of symbolic and ritual expression that had grown up around Christianity not as
links in a chain to heaven but as obstacles to true communion with God. They
wanted to call the church back to what they considered its original purity. They
wanted to admonish it until, in penitence, it discarded religious practices that
for the Reformers got in the way, substituting the material for the spiritual, the
human for the divine.

In the terms of this text, the Reformers wanted to do two things. First, they
wanted to bring about a clear division between extraordinary religion (attempts
to reach God) and ordinary religion (aspects of human culture). Second, they
wanted to purge Christianity of elements of the idea of correspondence that had
crept in, returning to a purer version of the idea of causality. In other words, they
wanted to emphasize a gap between the divine order of things and the natural
human world. For the Reformers, without God's help through the grace of Jesus
Christ, humans were powerless when their salvation was in question. They were
sinners who on their own could not do anything to win the grace of God. And for
the Reformers, too, just as God must perform a decisive act to save them, so they
must live out their loyalty to him by decisive action in the world. Paradoxically,
although Protestantism separated the world from God, it also led its followers out
of their churches and onto the public stage of history.

Thus, prophetic protest was the original message of Protestantism. And
the prophet, who was believed to be the inspired messenger of God, was its key
religious figure. The prophet called people to a mission that linked traditional
accounts from the past to the present — and to an intended future. Spoken out of a
strong sense of conviction, of being God's emissary, the words of the prophet made
Protestantism the religion of the "Word." Moreover, since words are formed
seemingly without matter — of breath or wind — they could readily be thought
of as "Spirit." It followed that the idea of the spiritual could become the means
by which Protestantism conducted criticism. Prophetic protest was the basic

spiritual principle on which the other, more concrete principles of the Reformation were built.

First among these principles was that of scripture alone. The Word was not any word at all but a specific Word present in the Bible: for the Reformers, it was Jesus and the law that the religion of Jesus enjoined. In the beginning, the gospel of John had announced, there was the Word (John 1:1). Protestants never forgot the scripture as they rebuked the medieval church for its adherence to tradition and the Roman papacy. In Reformation thinking, sacramentalism led away from the truth of the original Word; it was a corruption of the scriptural message of salvation.

The second principle that the Protestant Reformers preached was justification through faith. As they saw it, this principle was intimately bound up with the idea of scripture alone, for they saw justification by faith as the content of the biblical message, the core meaning taught in scripture. Here, justification was a legal term used to connote salvation, and faith meant the trust that human beings felt for God in Jesus. That is to say, faith was not, as in the medieval Catholic church, a collection of doctrinal truths to be accepted. Instead, in Reformation thought it was a response to a divine and trustworthy person. Such faith put the emotional experience of an individual at the center of religion, an emphasis that Protestantism in America would later develop even further. Taken as a complete statement, justification by faith announced that humans could do nothing on their own to gain salvation. It implied the doctrine of total depravity, or corruption, and the huge abyss that in the causal view of things separated the human from the divine.

A third principle on which the Reformation was built was the priesthood of all believers. Here, too, the Reformation departed from the medieval church. The older church, with its sacramental understanding of the role of the priest, saw him as a ritual leader who represented the community before God. In this scheme of things, the community — as one collective entity — offered a common act of worship. Now, with the priesthood of all, Protestants brought individualism into the communal consciousness of the church. If each person was a priest, then each as an individual was offering worship to God. Worship in a group brought the fellowship of common *worshipers* but not, as in the older Catholic sense, of one common act of worship.

The fellowship of common worshipers led to the fourth principle of the Reformation, which was the church. The Reformers saw the need for a social expression of Christianity, and for them the church was the communion of saints. In their understanding, it was the place where those who had received saving faith were gathered, the place where the Word was rightly preached and the sacraments (baptism and the eucharist) were rightly administered. *Preaching* the Word had a new centrality in this definition of the Reformers, and, significantly, administering the sacraments came second to the sermon. Whereas in medieval Catholicism, a sermon might or might not be preached at a eucharistic service, for the Reformers the most important bread to be broken was the bread of the Word. Further, the idea of the communion of saints, while long a part of Christian teaching, still stopped short of the more cohesive metaphor of the Body of Christ. Protestant fellowship was a gathering of the many.

Hence, the basic principles of the Reformation brought a subtle individualism to Christianity. In the context of sixteenth-century Europe, this nascent individualism reflected trends that had already been present in the private spiritual quests of monks and nuns. It also agreed with other trends that were present in the philosophy being taught in the universities of the time. Most importantly, it spoke to the individualism that was growing with a new middle class. Being neither rich nor poor, the middle class knew the condition of having enough to be able to struggle for more but not having enough to rest content. Thus, their place in the middle of society fostered personal striving and, therefore, individualism. In Protestantism the middle class had a religion that fit its vision of the world and its spiritual needs.

Beyond this, the basic principles of the Reformation brought a new emphasis on the content of preaching and with it a new theological consciousness. For Protestants, individuals needed to hear the Word in order to receive a message of faith and salvation. Once they heard it, they needed to ascertain fully what it meant. So the history of Protestantism in Europe and in early America was a history of theological questioning and refinement. In contrast to Catholicism, which mostly remained attached to the theology of the sixteenth century until Vatican II, Protestantism spawned vigorous theological debate. Once the center of religion was no longer the matter of the sacramental order, it became the spirit of comprehension of the Word.

Finally, the basic principles of the Reformation led to a new call for moral action in the world. As in the Old Testament, the Word of the Reformers did not call humans to be idle but instead to witness to their beliefs by their deeds. Protestantism, as we have already noted, led out of the churches and into the world. This meant that while the Word of the Reformation separated extraordinary from ordinary religion, it also aimed to cut away distraction, so that there could be a reunification. Protestants, as well as others, experienced an overlapping of boundaries between extraordinary and ordinary. If the churches led people back to the world, extraordinary religion marched them into the midst of the ordinary. But the overlapping of boundaries between the two did not come, as in medieval Catholicism, through the natural world, which supplied the raw material for ritual action in the sacraments. The overlapping of boundaries came, instead, through the medium of history, that is, through the men and women who, inspired by the preaching of the Word, went forth into the world.

In the Lutheran Reformation of Germany, which spread to the Scandinavian countries, the Protestant movement proceeded cautiously, holding to the sacramental past even as it preached the reforming Word. Luther, compared with Calvin and other continental Reformers, was both a liturgical and theological conservative. Thus, for Luther and his followers, the eucharist was the Word that had become visible. The Mass continued with some changes for about 200 years, and in Sweden attention to liturgical detail clothed the new intent of the worship service in some of the trappings of medieval Catholicism. There were clear signs of the new order, though. Congregational singing indicated the importance of the laity and their response to the liturgical action. New church architecture often placed the pulpit in such a position that it competed with the altar for dominance in the sanctuary space. The Bible was read in the language of the people instead of in Latin, and gradually the eucharist became an occasional, rather than a weekly, celebration. Still, Luther and early Lutherans believed that Jesus was present in the sacrament, and in their attachment to the person of Jesus, they continued a medieval emphasis on the divine humanity. There was warmth more than austerity in the Lutheran reforms and, with the preaching of trust in the compassion of Jesus, a devotionalism that centered on human feelings of closeness to God.

But the Lutheran Reformation did not go far enough for Calvin and for many others. Calvin arrived at his Protestant views independently of Luther, and his emphasis was, as it developed, somewhat different. With his insistence more on the majesty and otherness of God than on the humanity of Jesus, Calvin devised a plan for worship that matched his vision. A Calvinist church in its austerity proclaimed that its God was removed from what was natural or human. With the table of the Ten Commandments the only ornament on the wall, the asceticism of the building directed people to the contemplation of the law. Everything in the service turned on the Word, and the architecture of bareness was itself a sacramental symbol of the gospel message. As new buildings came into existence, the pulpit was placed in the center of the sanctuary and proclaimed that preaching was the essence of the cultus. In order to worship, in Calvin's view, a clear mind rather than stimulation of the senses was required. Thus, hymns, prayers, scriptural lessons, and the sermon all strived to cultivate the clarity of vision that Calvin sought. Communion, in which the presence of Jesus was acknowledged, was at first prescribed monthly and then four times yearly. Above all, for Calvin the presence of Jesus was revealed in the Bible, which was God's law book. Understanding it, he believed, would lead Christians elected for salvation into the world, where they could witness to Jesus by their lives.

In the Reformed free city of Geneva (now in Switzerland), Calvin was able to see his Word made flesh. By a series of political steps taken with the consent, though sometimes reluctant, of the city fathers, he transformed the government into a theocracy, a state ruled by the church. Hence, far more than Luther, Calvin joined the religious and the political, making it possible to view religion as moral action in the public sphere. The impulse of the Calvinist Reformation collapsed extraordinary religion inward toward the ordinary center of things. Moreover, it encouraged a sense of the chosenness of those whom, according to Calvinist doctrine, God had elected for salvation. The sense of chosenness, with a conviction of righteousness not far behind, was hardly complete, at least in Calvin's time. The elect were thought hidden in church and city, and there were no signs to determine clearly who they were. It was understood to be part of God's mystery that the saints should have their identity veiled, even from themselves. The theocratic constitution of the city of Geneva was designed to create a social climate in which the saints could flourish, but Calvin never thought of Geneva as a city in which *only* the saved resided.

With his religion of law and his doctrine of the predestination of saints and sinners, Calvin had begun a spiritual system that led, increasingly, to what the sociologist of religion Max Weber has called innerworldly asceticism. Calvin had initiated the earliest stage of the "Protestant ethic," a moral system that seemed to thrive on the evidence of its own success. Briefly, as believers became anxious about the question of their salvation, they looked to their behavior to seek assurance. One of the signs of saving faith was, they thought, a righteous and reformed pattern of living. Gradually though, believers began in practice to attach more weight to this pattern than to their faith, to put the cart of good deeds before the horse of grace, so to speak. It was not too much of a shift for them to begin to see external righteousness, good works, as a guarantee of salvation — and a guarantee that could be strengthened by more and more good action. Thus, ironically, an ethic of works and work came to flourish at the center of the religion that had taught justification by faith. In America the Protestant ethic would help to mold a continent to Euro-American ways and imprint its character on the public face of the nation. Moreover, it would assist in the assimilation of religious and ethnic groups, such as the Jews, who shared a commitment to the value of law and the ethic of thrift, industry, and hard work — the Protestant ethic.

Unlike Catholicism, which was a very old religion, Calvinism, born in the sixteenth century, was very young. Its structure would be transported to the New World as the major religious influence on the English colonies there. And because it was young, it would continue to grow in America, changing — like Catholicism — in terms of the needs of the new situation, but also changing because it was characteristic of a young (and successful) religion to grow rapidly.

The Reformation in England

Before Calvinism migrated to America, however, it traveled across the English Channel. Here the Reformation had moved from the king through the ranks of government and thence to ordinary people. The Reformation was an act of state accomplished by King Henry VIII (1509–1547) after the pope refused him a divorce sought on the ground that his wife had not given him a male heir. The result of laws passed by Parliament under Henry was the Church of England, and the form of religion that emerged was Anglicanism. Under Queen Elizabeth I (1533–1603), it became the way of comprehension, in which various tendencies in belief were absorbed, or comprehended, in one church. For Anglicanism, theological diversity was acceptable provided there was uniformity in ritual. The *Book of Common Prayer* established the rubrics for that uniformity, and so long as men and women gathered around the same altar table, in effect, they might hold Lutheran, Calvinist, or even Anglo-Catholic opinions as they chose.

Hence, the Anglican church under Elizabeth and afterward sought to find a middle way between Catholicism and Protestantism. Renouncing the papacy and many medieval devotions, open to various Protestant interpretations and practices, it still retained much of the flavor of an older sacramentalism. In this context, there was a growing body of English opinion that Elizabeth's reforms had not gone far enough. Those who shared this view came to be called Puritans, because they sought to purify the church, and their movement flourished in England for a century, encompassing a number of different strands and tendencies. Among the Puritans were Separatists, who thought that the only route to purity was complete separation from the Church of England, and non-Separatists, who thought that the church could be cleansed from within. Among the non-Separatists, moreover, by the 1640s there were some who thought that each congregation should govern itself in complete independence from every other (the Congregationalists or Independents) and others who thought that individual congregations should be related to larger bodies called presbyteries and synods (the Presbyterians). Finally, left-wing Separatist groups, important among them Baptists and Quakers, also arose.

Despite these differences, there was much that every Puritan group shared. For all of them, purifying the church meant purging it of the Roman holdovers from the past and adhering more strongly to Calvinism. Like the nineteenth-century Reform Jews of Germany and the United States, Puritans sought a greater decorum in worship, and they identified it with the austere and simple liturgies of John Calvin. More than Reform Jews, though, they developed the theological rationale that accompanied their ritual reforms. Moreover, as the movement grew, it came to incorporate elements from the left wing of the continental Reformation, more radical than Calvin had been. Puritans began to think of their churches as "gathered," or free — voluntary associations of individuals who had professed their faith with understanding, subscribed to a church covenant or compact, and demonstrated their intent by the upright moral character of their lives. In contrast, both Calvin and Luther had seen churches as territorial, including all the inhabitants of a place.

As in the Calvinist churches of Europe, however, preaching for the Puritans became the central act of public worship. New "meetinghouses" began to displace older churches, and architecture told its story with bare walls and dominant pulpit. As in continental Calvinism, Puritan worship was meant for the ear and the mind, not for the eye. Gone were the ornamental vessels and vestments, the incense and candlesticks, all the accoutrements of a high-church liturgy, which Anglicanism preferred. Instead, there was the simpler rhythm of psalm, scriptural lesson, and prayer, interrupted by the major event of the sermon. Communion occurred only infrequently, and when it was held, it was understood as a sign of faith and love for one another. Sometimes, in order to stress that communion was a meal and to imitate the simple setting of the gospel Last Supper, Puritans sat around a table. Their leaders broke bread from common loaves and then passed the loaves to the rest of the people who broke off their share as well.

Yet in the services there was a new experiential emphasis that went beyond the churches of continental Calvinism. Worship, the Puritans thought, should be spontaneous, the expression of a personal relationship with their God. Thus, early Congregationalists encouraged extempore preaching, often accompanied by heartfelt groans from members of the congregation. Early Baptists (Puritans opposed to infant baptism) thought hymns were artificial and would not allow them in their churches. In emphasizing adult baptism, they stressed that the ceremony was the surrender of a believer to God, an act of decisive choice on his or her part and not, as in the medieval understanding, a sacramental mystery. While this early spontaneity of Puritan worship would later decline, its experiential quality would have important corollaries, as we will see, when the Puritans immigrated to America.

Beyond this, in the spirit of the Calvinism that the Puritans had appropriated, they stimulated a new consecration of time, an austere dedication that expressed their adherence to the idea of causality and their commitment to moral action in history. From the time of their rise under Elizabeth, the Puritans had preached against the holy days, some 165 of them, that interrupted the daily work schedule for religious festivals. For the Puritans, these observances sanctioned "idleness," which invited onslaughts from the devil. Celebrated by Elizabethans with physical activity, sports, and playgoing, the holy days were thought to distract from true religion rather than to encourage it. In Puritan belief, salvation came to those who expressed loyalty to God in the work ethic. Thrift, sobriety, industry, and prudence — all were to be cultivated instead of the moral looseness that for them the holy-day calendar engendered.

※ In place of this old liturgical calendar — even in place of its central feasts such as Christmas and Easter — the Puritans stressed the Sabbath. Kept on Sunday in honor of the resurrection of Jesus, the Sabbath lasted, in the ancient Jewish fashion, from sunset to sunset. On this day, for the Puritans, all work should cease so that humans could spend their time attending to divine things. Meanwhile, the Puritans thought, people should strenuously avoid the frivolous recreation — the sporting, gaming, and playgoing — that Anglicanism permitted. In the Puritan view, such recreation served only to distract men and women from service to God, and it sometimes led them into more serious forms of dissipation and vice.

Puritan Sabbatarianism gained support even among those in the mainstream of the Church of England. And in America, as we will see, it supplied the model for the Sabbath observance throughout the English colonies. In effect, the Puritans in their Sabbath campaign had separated extraordinary religion from ordinary religion. The festival cycle, which had knit natural and supernatural concerns together in an intertwining sequence, was abrogated, while the abolition of all forms of worldly recreation on the Sabbath stressed the separation between human and divine things. Meanwhile, the time taken from the frequent holy days of the older order was freed for the pursuit of work, a pursuit supporting the new demands that industrialization and the factory system would make on people. If the Word of the Reformation led out into the world, its Puritan translation was accompanied by some unforeseen twists. Henceforth, in noticeable ways, church and daily life would begin to occupy separate compartments.

The Reformation in the English Colonies

In America this separation of church and everyday concerns continued and intensified. But the story of European Protestantism in the English colonies is a story of its Americanization. There were strong ties to the past, and the heritage of the Reformation was never lost for the early Protestant settlers. Still, the experience of the new land shaped the older Protestantism in profound ways. It is to the American transformation of Protestantism that we now turn.

The earliest immigrants to the English colonies on the Atlantic coast of North America were Anglicans and Puritans, both with pronounced Calvinist leanings. Moreover, the Puritan movement gradually assumed organizational structure as Congregationalist, Presbyterian, and Baptist churches, all three denominations of the so-called "old dissent" of England. So there was a considerable pattern of religious unity in Protestant America from the first, and that pattern of unity would continue to characterize mainstream Protestantism. The unity, of course, was a unity in diversity, and denominationalism became the framework for American Protestantism.

Unlike a church, which included all of the people born in a given territory, a denomination was a voluntary organization. Thus, by definition it was not universal but particular. As the denomination evolved in Protestant America, it was a group seen as called, or "denominated," out of the larger religious whole; it was construed as a branch of the church, not its entirety. Still, the reasons for belonging to one denomination rather than another were serious and important. The Word did not cut empty air, and often it separated church bodies into two, or three, or more.

The sources for denominationalism lay in the Puritan movement of England, which we have been examining, but in America denominationalism assumed far wider dimensions. American necessities compelled a move away from the old model of a state church (the Church of England) and toward a free-church model. Religious liberty gradually spread until, with the United States Constitution, it became the law of the land. Every church, no matter what its theological claims, became in America a denomination, a voluntary society of gathered members, separate yet not separated from every other Christian church. Moreover, while denominations were not the same as all-inclusive churches, they were also very different from sects and cult movements, as we will see later. They affirmed the world and even in their more critical moods never withdrew totally from it; they accepted the Christian tradition as transmitted by the Reformation and did not claim a new revelation.

From the first, boundary difficulties were involved in this concept of a denomination. To be separate, yet not separated, from the larger church meant to live with ambiguity. The boundaries between a denomination and a church were easily blurred. Thus, Protestantism with its denominational accommodations was always open to amorphousness, always in danger of merging its manyness into a kind of religion-in-general. On the other hand, because the borders dividing one group from the next were relatively weak, there could be a good deal of mutual cooperation between denominations as they sought to make America a Christian nation.

In overview, then, the early denominations brought to America a common Puritan–Anglican past, and they combined it with a common task of settlement in the new land. In this process, they gradually turned more and more away from the Word as theology and toward the Word as experience and action. As we will see, especially in the next chapter, evangelical piety brought a new emphasis on the emotional dimension of religion, even as it continued the separation between ordinary and extraordinary. Meanwhile, the laity, who acted out their beliefs in the world, imprinted their character on the structure of American Protestantism.

Anglican Virginia

In 1607, just four years after the death of Elizabeth I, the Virgin Queen, the first permanent English settlement in the New World was launched. Begun for commercial reasons by London merchants organized as the Virginia Company, the Virginia colony honored in its name and in its religious establishment the legacy of Elizabeth. Here Anglicanism and the *Book of Common Prayer* prevailed. Like the New England colonies that followed, Virginia was founded, in part, to counter the Roman Catholic presence of Spain and France in the New World. The new colony was intended to establish an outpost of Protestant Christianity in the American wilderness, and it was also meant as a base for converting the Indians. Thus, although the fact is often overlooked, the colony of Virginia had a religious as well as a financial motive for its beginnings. Indeed, the (sealed) instructions that authorized the settlement spoke of serving and fearing God and warned that a "plantation" that was not of God's doing would be "rooted out."

For all the Anglicanism of the colony, however, Puritanism—although unofficial—was part of the religious mood of the settlement at Jamestown and later at Henrico. Some settlers had Calvinist leanings, and, underlining the

Puritan seriousness that was woven into the financial and political motives for settlement, the Sabbath observance in Virginia followed a strict order. In fact, honoring the Sabbath demanded more in Virginia, for a time, than it would in New England. Under Sir Thomas Gates in 1610 and Sir Thomas Dale the following year, the law required attendance at divine service and threatened death for a third offense of nonattendance. The law also compelled people to be present at Sunday afternoon catechism and forbade gaming, intemperance, or other violations of the Sabbath peace. Even weekdays were occasions for religious services, which everyone had to attend twice daily, with an extra sermon on Wednesdays. For almost a decade this regime, although never fully enforced, was official law, and even thereafter the Sabbath in Virginia was largely Puritan in style.

As early as 1612, though, with the introduction of tobacco cultivation by John Rolfe, the seeds of another religious style were encouraged. As the decades passed, more and more black slaves from Africa worked the plantations — slaves who, according to Virginia legislators in 1667, could not win bodily freedom through Christian baptism. For this and other reasons, African-Americans were at first given little incentive to become Christian, and they maintained what remnants they could of the traditions of their ancestors, as we will see in Chapter 6. Moreover, although Anglicans were the religious majority, the population was scattered, and religious devotion was not strong. Hence, public piety cloaked a relatively weak Christianity. Just as the Reformation had been an act of state in old England, Protestant Christianity became an act of state in the colony that honored the Virgin Queen.

Thus, Virginia lawmakers provided in 1619 for government support of Anglican clergy. Then, in 1624, when for a variety of reasons the Virginia Company relinquished control of the colony and it became a royal province, the new royal governor wielded legal authority over many aspects of organized religious life. By 1642, legislators prescribed that aspiring ministers show evidence of ordination by an English bishop and conform in all respects to the Church of England on penalty of removal and expulsion from the colony.

But the parish system of England did not work in the vast expanses of the Virginia territory, in which a parish could be sixty miles long. The Virginia accommodation was a system of vestries, groups of lay trustees elected from the men of a parish to run the local congregation's affairs. The system was reinforced in 1662, when legislators intervened again to regularize the vestries, which at the time had been in existence for almost twenty years. Vestry power over the minister who served the parish was considerable, and the 1662 legislation only enhanced that influence. Ministerial tenure and pay typically depended on the vestrymen, so that a lukewarm congregation tended to perpetuate itself by avoiding ministerial appointments that would challenge its people. Ministers themselves tended to be few and often lacking in zeal, and vestry control of clerical positions through annual reappointments further weakened ministerial effectiveness.

By the time plans had been made to send a bishop to the Virginia church, the Civil War in England prevented the move; and missionary efforts among Indians and blacks were also not very successful. By 1720 there were but forty-four parishes in the twenty-nine counties of Virginia, only half of them with ministers. Meanwhile, the Virginia population began to change with the immigration of Scotch-Irish, Germans, and New Englanders. Even as early as 1689 the English Act of Toleration had made religious nonconformity more acceptable, and in 1689 Quaker missionaries had already been working in Virginia for some decades. In sum, the failure of Anglicanism to build a strong establishment created a vacuum into which other forms of Protestantism could move. The weakness of the Church of England in Virginia—and in the other southern colonies as well—helped to determine the future of Protestantism.

Puritan New England

Before it surrendered control of its New World holdings to direct governance by the British crown, the Virginia Company unintentionally fostered settlement outside its territorial claim in what was coming to be known as New England. The Pilgrims, a group of Separatist Puritans (no longer part of the Church of England), contacted the Virginia Company from their settlement in exile in Leyden, Holland. The Pilgrims had fled there when their church came under more and more harassment by the English government for its nonconformity. Now, however, they were dissatisfied by the easy and indulgent life that surrounded them in the Netherlands. With the permission of King James I of England as well as that of the Virginia Company, the small group of Separatists set sail for the New World, intent, ostensibly, on establishing themselves within Virginia territory. But the *Mayflower* sailed off course, and the ship landed on the Atlantic coast well north of Virginia. The Pilgrims were prepared for what followed: still on board ship they had contracted with one another in the Mayflower Compact to form a "body politick" and so to govern themselves. Still, their covenant did not prevent a series of legal and financial problems that plagued them until, in 1691, their Plymouth colony became officially part of the royal colony of Massachusetts.

The Pilgrim landing at Plymouth Rock in 1620 was a symbolic moment in American religious history. But other adventurers came from England before and after the Pilgrim landing, and in the decade from 1620 to 1630 a series of small settlements appeared. However, the significant venture for the religious future of New England and, indeed, the later American nation came with the Puritan settlement of 1630. Founded by non-Separatists—Puritans who were still part of the Church of England—who landed at Salem and then established themselves at Boston, the Massachusetts Bay colony set the pace for the religious life of New England. Like the Pilgrims who preceded them, the non-Separatist Puritans found themselves in a political situation relatively free from direct English

Old Ship Meetinghouse, Hingham. Nineteen miles southeast of Boston, Old Ship Meetinghouse from 1681 reflected the seafaring culture of Hingham with a framed roof that looked like an inverted ship's hull. The spare and simple style likewise reflected Puritan culture.

interference. They were members of the Massachusetts Bay Company, and their company had obtained a direct royal charter for settlement. Cannily, the Puritans brought their charter with them to the New World so that non-Puritan London merchants could exercise little control over their joint-stock enterprise.

In short, the Pilgrims, by landing outside the jurisdiction of Virginia, and the Massachusetts Bay Puritans, by taking their charter to America with them, both managed to carve out virtually independent republics for themselves in the early years. Here they could give substance to their visions of a model religious society that in a number of ways would recall Calvin's Geneva. Here they could work at their "errand into the wilderness," at first, by perfecting their own ordered communities with proper civil and churchly governance and, as time passed, by thinking more and more of their impact on the world. By the second and third generations, a Puritan rhetoric had become standardized in conceptions of Puritan society as a New Israel, a light to the nations, and the like.

Before then, though, there were other colonies in New England, as members of the Massachusetts Bay colony, for one reason or another, struck off on their own. New Hampshire was settled initially by farmers and fishers from England's southern coast, who founded the seaport at Portsmouth in 1630. But Massachusetts and Connecticut families were soon its chief immigrants, and they brought with them the religious convictions of Massachusetts Bay. Connecticut, open to settlement in the 1630s, also, in effect, followed the Massachusetts way, with perhaps a greater conservatism in church organization by the early eighteenth century.

It was Rhode Island, however, that provided a model in some respects different. Rhode Island became a refuge for religious dissidents from the Bay colony who objected to the Puritan establishment in Massachusetts. Roger Williams (1603?–1683) founded the colony in 1636 after he was exiled from Massachusetts for religious views that did not conform to official Puritan doctrine. Here, too, Anne Hutchinson, exiled for challenging Massachusetts church leaders with antinomian ideas of direct guidance by the Holy Spirit, made her way in 1638. And here Quakers and others of independent religious views also found refuge. But the nonconformity of all of these was *Puritan* nonconformity. They sought a purity even greater than that championed by the leaders at Massachusetts Bay, and so, in their commitments, they held a mirror to the Puritan way.

Indeed, the American religious historian Sydney Ahlstrom has told us that Puritanism formed the religious and moral background for as much as 75 percent of the population declaring independence from England in 1776. Hence, Puritan theological understanding and religious practice would be of considerable importance for the American future, something that we will examine further when we look at "public Protestantism" in Chapter 12. Here we need to notice that the growing sense of assurance in all of the New England colonies that they were the New Israel brought with it clear transformations of the Puritanism of old England. In Virginia, the Anglican church might be said to have been transplanted; in New England, the church was formed anew. In a geographical sense,

Virginia was radically different from old England, with large plantations and a sparsely scattered population. In a similar geographical sense, New England was much closer to the English pattern, with its neatly laid-out towns with church and school at the center. But in a religious sense, New England's vision was radical, innovating even on the Puritanism that was already re-forming the English church.

New England's churches were an attempt to bring together gathered communities of totally committed believers within a modified parish structure under a state church. In the traditional sense there was, in fact, little possibility of a parish system without the bishops and organizational structure of Anglicanism. Instead, a congregational system of independent churches flourished under strong clerical leadership. The Cambridge Platform of 1648, the result of a synod meeting that had convened several times since 1646, became an official congregational charter, separating the New England way from Puritan developments across the Atlantic. Meanwhile, the sense of isolation from the corruptions of the Old World and of immersion in the vigor of the New World fostered an increasing belief in New England's chosenness and righteousness. We have already met that belief in the rhetoric of the New Israel and the echoes of a new Geneva in Puritan society. Together these elements led to a form of church–state alliance that, as we will see in Chapter 13, provided the beginnings of a later unofficial civil religion in the United States.

New England Puritanism expressed its sense of chosenness by increased attention to the doctrine of the covenant, which had been part of its English heritage. According to the doctrine, an existing pact, or agreement, between God and his people was modeled on the biblical covenant between God and Israel. As so conceived, the covenant made the Puritans, as members of one community of the elect, God's own people. If they fulfilled their part in the covenant through lives of virtue and righteousness, they believed, their God would be faithful to them. On the other hand, if plague or witchcraft, Indian wars or conservative Anglicans troubled their settlements, these were signs for the Puritans that something was amiss in the Christian commitment of the people.

The idea of the covenant became a practical arrangement in the civil government, which was also established on a covenantal basis, and in the congregational churches, each of which had covenants of association for members. In a further transformation, belonging to the church covenant became more difficult in Massachusetts Bay than it had ever been among the Puritans of England. By about 1636 Puritans began to require a new experiential test for church membership. No longer was it sufficient to confess the Christian faith through intellectual assent. Now an emotional conviction of one's sinfulness and a felt sense of saving faith were required. Thus, no matter how upright the character, no matter how loyal the covenant faith, unless there was a conversion experience, there could be no membership in the church. While the Puritans could never be absolutely certain that all members of the church were people they called "visible saints" — that is, people who were assured of salvation — they had decidedly limited their margin for error. When an individual thought that he or she had felt saving faith, that person went before the elders of the church or, sometimes, the congregation itself. The personal experience was heard and, if acceptable, ratified by community agreement. As for an Oglala Sioux warrior returning from his vision quest, the stamp of the community was necessary to authenticate the private encounter with spiritual forces. In New England the Reformation meant individual seeking, but it also meant community affiliation.

After the first generation, though, the Puritans saw the membership rolls of their churches shrink ominously when their adult children were unable to testify to experiences of conversion as required for church membership. Many of this new generation believed firmly in Puritan Christian teaching and led lives of upright Puritan morality. All that was missing was the emotional encounter with saving faith. Hence, in 1662 a Puritan church synod accepted compromise. The Halfway Covenant, as it came to be called, provided that infant grandchildren of the saints should be baptized and thus made "halfway" members of the church. Children of the saints, though without an experience of saving faith, would likewise be considered halfway church members, provided they met all other requirements. Because voting rights in the colony depended on membership in the church, this action had civic consequences in preserving at least some breadth to the political base of Massachusetts Bay. More importantly for us, some Puritans read the need for the measure as a sign of religious "declension," or decline.

Indeed, when Massachusetts Bay surrendered its quasi-independence in 1691 to become a royal colony, many saw the event as a clear sign of sin. Massachusetts Bay had aimed to link morality and piety with a return to the spirit of biblical times. Now this hope was fading in the complexity of an increasingly ambiguous world. By the third and fourth generations, therefore, many Puritans, instead of looking to a simple restoration of times past, were anticipating times future. These Puritans awaited the *millennium*, the thousand-year reign of Christ as prophesied in the biblical Book of Revelation. In Christian belief an event associated with the second coming of Jesus (the first had been his recorded life in Palestine), the millennium was thought to end history as people knew it and to inaugurate a radically transformed era. In the Puritan context, millennialism—the keen expectation of the impending arrival of the millennium—became a way to hope for the restoration of the past by transposing it into the time to come. Conservatives and radicals at the same time, Puritans both held to their view of the past and looked from past and present to the future. In this double identity they would make a lasting mark on the American religious future. And millennialism would be a significant part of the mark they made.

Pluralist New York and Pennsylvania

South of New England, in what came to be known as the Middle Colonies, it was the Dutch who initially made their mark. As early as 1609 Henry Hudson had explored the river that came to be named after him. Dutch traders established posts there as well as on Long Island Sound and the Connecticut River, and by 1624 there were permanent Dutch residents on Manhattan Island. Not surprisingly, the Dutch Reformed church, with its modified Calvinism, formed the religious backbone of their colony of New Amsterdam. After New Amsterdam became New York in 1664, the Dutch Reformed church continued as the largest religious body, but its congregations struggled, and more and more diversity came to characterize the colony. Initially, the English duke of York, for whom New York was named, was its sole proprietor, and his settlement with the Dutch honored their freedom of conscience and worship. In fact, the first English governors read the settlement to mean support of the Dutch Reformed clergy with public funds.

Nor were the Dutch alone in their enjoyment of religious freedom. The duke of York pursued a policy of toleration for all who professed to be Christian (the Jews were noticeably excluded); and when, in 1693, New York's governor in effect made the Anglican church the official establishment, the change was not significant. At that time, as historian Winthrop Hudson recounts, there were but ninety Anglican families in all of New York, whereas 1,754 Dutch Reformed and 1,355 English dissenter families could be counted.

By the eighteenth century, Protestant pluralism had become the hallmark of New York. The most heterogeneous of the thirteen colonies, the former Dutch possession had become home to groups as various as French Calvinists, German Lutherans, New England Congregationalists, Puritan dissenters of Quaker and Baptist temper, Mennonites, Catholics, and Jews. By that time, New York had had a Roman Catholic governor, and many New Yorkers had come to see religious toleration not simply as practical necessity but also as positive good. These New Yorkers reflected seriously and thoughtfully on the meaning of their colony's pluralism (that is, the existence of many separate but publicly equal religious faiths with none of them having the upper hand). They began to identify what they considered the religious and political benefits of the pluralist arrangement, and they grew in their commitment to the idea of religious equality. Churches found that they could engage in cooperative efforts, and they also found a spur to activism, to voluntary efforts on the part of numbers of believers.

Pennsylvania, the Quaker colony of William Penn (1644–1718), had from the first been ideologically committed to the principle of toleration. Penn aimed to provide a place of sanctuary for European peoples who had experienced religious persecution. And, although Anglicans theoretically received preferred treatment, Penn's colony guaranteed freedom of worship and made a point of its respect for the rights of conscience. Penn extended his respect for diversity even to Native Americans. Aware of the "unkindness and injustice" they had experienced at white hands, he insisted on treating them with equity and negotiated a treaty with them in 1701 on the basis of his reading of this ideal.

Penn's regard for Indian peoples was a sign of one side of the Quaker commitment—that of humanitarian "benevolence" toward all peoples and positive work as service to them. The eighteenth-century reformer and mystic John Woolman (1720–1772), with his crusade against slavery, is a useful early example of this religious direction. But well before members of the Society of Friends (the official name of the Quakers) displayed their concern for human inequity and suffering, they were expressing a radical Puritanism at the center of their worship. The Society of Friends had taken the individualism that was already part of English Puritanism and carried it further still. When in 1681 Penn received his charter to territory in the New World, he had at hand the means to inaugurate his "holy experiment" to relieve oppression *and* to live out the plainness of Quaker worship.

Subject to persecution both in old and New England, the Quakers came to Pennsylvania as a haven where they could follow their conviction that there was something of the divine in every human being. They taught a mysticism of inner light, which for them meant that there was no need for church, creed, or priesthood. In worship they sat quietly together and waited for what they believed to be the promptings of the Spirit before they spoke. Hence, in Quaker religious practice the Reformation's community of saints became a community of contemplation, with a sharing of thoughts gained in prayer as the act of communion. Meanwhile, the bare walls of Quaker meetinghouses were a protest against Anglican ornateness.

Belief in the divine light in all human beings supplied the ground for its logical corollary: conviction of the respect owed Indians, blacks, the suffering, and the downtrodden. So there was, in fact, a theological line from Quaker mysticism to social activism. On the other hand, the sociological realities of life in Pennsylvania began to militate against the radical stance of the Friends. With a religion formed for a prophetic role and with a background that fostered social criticism, the Quakers had become people in power—a religious and political establishment for the colony. At the same time, Quaker successes in commerce were making countinghouse more significant for many than meetinghouse. Although Quakerism was nourished by a stream of immigration from abroad, by the eighteenth century more and more of its Philadelphia elite were turning in the direction of Anglicanism and, eventually, Episcopalianism.

Meanwhile, Pennsylvania's open-door policy of toleration brought an increasing immigration from among the Scotch, Scotch-Irish (Scotch who had earlier immigrated to Ireland), and Germans. The Scotch and Scotch-Irish were Presbyterians, who settled in the Philadelphia area and also moved west and south into the Anglican colonies. The Germans, many of whom were Lutherans, swelled the general colonial population as well, with two-thirds of them settling in Pennsylvania. Pluralism—in fact as well as in theory—ruled the day. By the 1750s the Quakers had given up their place of leadership in the colony, bowing to internal difficulties as well as to discomfort with the role of political leadership as they construed it.

Despite the tensions implicit in the Quaker experiment, Pennsylvania, like New York and Rhode Island—and more than Virginia or especially

Massachusetts Bay — presaged the religious future. In the democracy that would flourish in the new United States, there would be no official religious establishment. And although, until the twentieth century, pluralism would be largely Protestant, pluralism there would be. No one denomination could count on the special blessings of the state. No one denomination could count among its members the majority of the population. Begun as a practical necessity, pluralism would become not merely tolerated but, eventually, preferred. To trace this development is in part to trace the growth of Protestant liberalism from its colonial years into our own time.

Colonial Seeds of Liberalism

The word *liberalism* has its etymological roots in the Latin *liber*, meaning "free." In fact, the words *liberalism* and *liberty* have this common Latin source, an observation that is helpful in recalling what the liberal tradition counts as important. Pluralism, already growing in the colonies, would provide the framework for the new liberal form of Protestant religion. And Protestant liberalism would express in religious terms the political and social accommodations in what became the United States. By the time the liberal tradition fully flowered, it would be emphasizing beliefs like the presence of God in the world (divine immanence), the goodness and even divinity of human nature, the humanity of Jesus, and the millennial fullness of his kingdom about to come on earth. Liberalism would teach optimism about human society and preach a message of social reform that could be achieved through strong and concerted effort. And in certain forms it would privilege experience, putting its premium on a felt individual participation in religion. All of this would add up, in different ways, to religious freedom. Such freedom would mean maximum emphasis on the rights of individual conscience and maximum attention to doctrines and practices that could bring a sense of personal power to human beings alone and in society.

But liberal Protestantism had a long and slow growth in the United States, and — although colonial religion was hardly liberal — the beginnings of liberalism could already be found in colonial developments. Ironically, one important source of the liberal tradition lay in a radical Puritan movement that valued sectarian purity and isolation even more than the leaders of Massachusetts Bay had valued them. That movement was Baptist Christianity.

The Baptists had roots in Holland and in England, but in America it was Roger Williams who promoted Baptist belief and practice in a significant way. In 1639, already exiled from Massachusetts Bay, he established a Baptist church in Providence, convinced at the time that Baptist principles fostered the true body of the church. Williams did not long remain Baptist, but the movement flourished in its New World setting, and Rhode Island grew in reputation as a Baptist center.

What set Baptists apart from other congregational Puritans was their rejection of infant baptism, with its emphasis on the community's role in nurturing Christian belief, and their insistence, instead, that a mature and committed believer was the only appropriate recipient of baptism. In Baptist understanding, therefore, the church was not an umbrella organization that sought to encompass as many as possible. Instead of large numbers — the "comprehension" of all — Baptists sought the purity of the gathered few, those who had freely come to the Christ of the gospels and the way of life they believed he taught. Given this aim, the corollary, for Baptists, was that social arrangements must be created that left individuals free to consent to Christian baptism. Thus, an established church worked against Christian salvation as they understood it, and religious freedom was necessary to insure that only the pure and committed would enter the church.

Rhode Island continued to be an important Baptist stronghold, with leadership, after Williams left the movement, by John Clarke (1609–1676) at Newport. Boston, too, had its Baptist church by 1665, and in the Middle Colonies the Philadelphia Baptist Association (1707) supplied a strong impetus for Baptist growth. Made up of churches in Pennsylvania, New Jersey, and Delaware from its beginning, the association later came to include churches as far away as Maryland, Virginia, New York, and Connecticut. There were links, as well, to Massachusetts and the Carolinas, so that Baptist presence could be found throughout the colonies. By the time of the American Revolution and its aftermath of constitution-making, it was the Baptists who were most vocal, among Christian believers, in demanding an end to religious establishment. The First Amendment owes a good deal, then, to Baptist believers who sought sectarian purity.

When Roger Williams made his way to the New World, he had been a minister and a Separatist Puritan. He was, in theological belief, a staunch Calvinist, and most Baptists continued in America to be strong Calvinists. They emphasized, like Calvin before them, the total "depravity" of human beings, that is, the inability of humans on their own to say or do anything that could merit them salvation. Baptists stressed the unlimited transcendence and sovereignty of a God whom they understood more as distant and authoritative than as near and compassionate. Like other conservative Calvinists, they thought in terms of an atonement, through the death of Jesus, that was limited to those whom God in his inscrutable wisdom had chosen. And Baptists counted grace as a force that could not be resisted and believers as people who, fortified with this grace, were bound to persevere in their faith. The relationship between these beliefs and the political and social matrix of freedom that Baptists demanded seems, in our times, a curious one. Nonetheless, it was real, and there was a religious logic that linked church freedoms to the old Calvinist theology.

Yet the colonial period did see another and significantly modified form of Calvinism — called Arminianism — that, in a different way, contained the seeds of Protestant liberalism. The Baptists already reflected what was to come. Most in the movement were Particular, or Calvinist, Baptists, holding to the doctrine of a limited atonement by Jesus of only the elect, or chosen. But the first English Baptist churches had been General Baptist, affirming a general atonement by Jesus for all human beings. Beliefs in a general atonement had been part of a Dutch pastoral movement that was officially condemned at the Synod of Dort (Holland) in 1618. Named Arminianism after the sixteenth-century Dutch Reformed pastor Jacobus Arminius (1560–1609), who initially gave it direction, this movement emphasized human freedom. It taught that grace could be resisted and that salvation (or condemnation) was not foreordained. Developed by others after the death of Arminius, Arminianism became a religious system that softened the austerity of Calvinism as it was then interpreted — and, as important, stressed human responsibility.

In an echo of the Synod of Dort's condemnation, New England Puritans thought that to call people "Arminians" was to call into question their orthodoxy and to insult their religious integrity. Despite this beginning, however, the history of colonial Puritanism involved, on the whole, a movement from relative Calvinism to relative Arminianism, with Puritanism itself losing its identity in the process. "Creeping" Arminianism eroded the rigor of Calvinist belief and practice, entering New England's churches without great fanfare even though the term itself had become one of condemnation. Indeed, Arminianism grew through a change in the character of the preaching in eighteenth-century churches. More and more, pastors stopped talking about a grim future in hell for the unconverted and talked instead about the requirements of the moral life. Sermons that exhorted to virtue and benevolence replaced sermons that taught predestination. And the shift, of course, meant an unspoken assumption that religious practice, freely embraced, was important, that humans could *do* something that affected their own salvation.

By the end of the colonial period, celebrated preachers like Boston's Charles Chauncy (1705–1787), at the First Church, and Jonathan Mayhew (1720–1766), at the West Church, expounded Arminian teachings with vigor. They were, indeed, "liberal Christians," and their brand of rationalism and moralism was one sign of a liberal Protestantism to come in the new republic.

Rationalism and moralism, however, were no newcomers to the colonial scene. In Anglican Virginia, religious books in seventeenth-century Chesapeake Bay homes showed considerable diversity in reading. But most preferred among writers were a group of English thinkers known to intellectual history as the Cambridge Platonists, among them Henry More (1614–1687), Edward Stillingfleet (1635–1699), and Archbishop John Tillotson 1630–1694). From 1635, these and other Cambridge Platonists were advocates for toleration and breadth in understanding the nature of the church. They sought to settle disputes by referring to a presence of God in the human mind and by using principles established by reason. The successors to the Cambridge Platonists in the English church were called Latitudinarians, people giving wide latitude to matters of dogma, church organization, and rubrics of worship. Their Christian rationalism and interest in matters of morality were not lost on the Virginia tradition that was developing.

Indeed, the eighteenth-century European Enlightenment, especially in its English version, made its mark on readers in Virginia, Massachusetts, and other colonies. With its exaltation of the role of reason, Enlightenment thinking encouraged the earlier rationalism that was already abroad in the colonies, as in England. It might seem at first glance that New England Puritans, with their emphasis on the authority of the Bible, would have little place for human reason beyond attending to the exact meaning and command of scripture. Yet the Puritans, even at their most austere, never rejected what could be learned from reason or nature. God's wisdom, for the Puritans, could be found in the world; they believed that the light of scripture would enable them to use the light of reason and the knowledge gained from nature. In fact, Puritan sermons reflected an educated ministry. Even though Puritans made much of a "plain style," these sermons followed a rigorous logic of reasoned discourse as ministers drew out the meanings they found in scriptural texts.

The budding Puritan rationalism grew and developed in the New England setting, aided by English works that reflected Enlightenment thought and by the emphasis on direct experience that New World surroundings fostered. Here interest in new scientific thought combined with attention to innovations in philosophy. For example, the well-known Puritan minister Cotton Mather (1663–1728) authored some 500 works of varying length and in 1721 fought for inoculation against smallpox. His *Christian Philosopher* was published in the same year, and in it Mather, writing as an amateur scientist and religious poet, placed the book of nature beside the book of biblical revelation as a source of knowledge of things divine.

A contemporary, John Wise (1652–1725), disagreed with Mather on another issue by advocating independence for each Puritan congregation in opposition to Mather's more associational views. But like Mather he supported smallpox inoculation. And in his *Vindication of the Government of New-England Churches* (1717), Wise agreed with Mather on the importance of nature and advanced a theoretical Enlightenment view, equating the "Law of Nature" with the "true sentiments of Natural Reason." Similarly, Jonathan Edwards (1703–1758), although he is most remembered for his leadership in America's First Great Awakening (to be discussed in the next chapter), read widely in science and philosophy. Edwards left a series of important writings in both areas, and he even justified the revival (the Awakening) by a rationalist argument derived from the thought of British philosopher John Locke (1632–1704).

This appeal to reason was an appeal to a *human* endowment, and as the decades passed, more and more attention would be paid to what humans could think and do. Hence, the liberal doctrine of human freedom, of human ability, was subtly being advanced. By the time of the American Revolution, however, for many among the colonial elite the liberalism was no longer subtle.

Liberalism in the American Revolution

During the period of the Revolution, liberal doctrines from abroad were at home among some Protestant Christians in the teachings of "natural religion." Educated upper- and middle-class patriots had learned their natural religion from British thinkers whose books they acquired. These Christians, for example, had read Bishop Joseph Butler (1692–1752), whose *Analogy of Religion, Natural and Revealed, to the Constitution and Course of Nature* (1736) argued forcefully for natural theology by defending the reasonableness of Christianity. They had found inspiration, too, in the works of the Anglican minister Samuel Clarke (1675–1729), who wrote in defense of a rational theology. And they had absorbed the ideas of William Wollaston (1660–1724) in his *Religion of Nature Delineated* (1726), which had been accused of being "deistic."

The deistic label soon became a badge of pride for some, however, in the religious movement called *deism*, which had arisen across the Atlantic and now made its way to America. Although Bishop Butler had written his *Analogy of Religion* to refute the deists and Clarke had also criticized them, deists and deism had entered the Protestant churches through the door of natural religion. And in its pure form deism moved past Protestant Christianity to take a nonchurch form. Etymologically, the term means, literally, "Goddism," since *deus* is the Latin word for "God." Thus, deism and its softer version in natural religion taught a simple creed of belief in a God. But, as important, the deists posited belief in an afterlife of future reward or punishment. The deist creed emphasized a good and moral life, and it looked to nature and its law as source of revelation and guidance. Significantly, deism found organizational expression in the fraternal societies of Freemasonry, an institution and system of belief and practice that we will explore in more detail in Chapter 13. Here the brotherhood supported an ethic of right relationship in one's doings and in dealings with one's fellows.

Deism was carried through the colonies within the Freemasonic lodges. Indeed, as brother Masons, deists played a key role in the political process that brought the new nation into being. The revolutionary organization of the Sons of Liberty and the revolutionary committees of correspondence were tied closely to Freemasonry. Probably fifty-two of the fifty-six signers of the Declaration of Independence were Masons, as were the majority of the members of the Continental Congress. Moreover, nearly every American general in the Revolutionary War was a Mason. Enshrined in the Freemasonic lodges, deism existed cordially beside Protestant Christianity and by so doing moved Protestant Masonic brothers in a liberal direction. For, as we will see in our examination of civil religion later, Masonic symbols were often biblical but could also be understood in terms of deist natural religion, and deist rituals could likewise be so understood.

In sum, deism, although in its most integral version not Christian at all, managed in the New World to make its way into Protestant thought and life. In so doing, it worked to advance the cause of liberal religion. Blending with currents of Arminianism and rationalism, deism furthered the spirit of tolerance that, for practical reasons, flourished amid America's religious pluralism. Religious freedom in America was swiftly becoming the freedom to be liberal.

Early Liberal Heyday: From the Revolution to the Civil War

Although Protestant liberalism did not achieve its classic form in America until well after the Civil War, significant developments were already afoot in the late eighteenth and early nineteenth centuries. These developments occurred in older denominations, and they brought the birth of new ones.

Despite the First Great Awakening, which swept the colonies during the middle years of the eighteenth century, full church membership was probably not large during the latter part of the century. Estimates of membership at the time of the Revolution, for example, have in the past hovered around 10 percent. This observation, of course, has to be balanced against a series of others. For one, church membership was considerably different from church *attendance* at the time of the Revolution; according to new data, perhaps 60 percent of adult whites attended church in 1776. For another, the requirements of full church membership were high in the Congregational churches that now served the heirs of New England's Puritans. They were also forbidding in the Anglican churches, where, until the break with England, no American bishop was available to administer the confirmation that was necessary before taking communion. Moreover, the practice of pewholding meant a financial commitment that restricted membership to people of means.

Still, whether church adherence was as low as many historians have thought, the fact was that late-eighteenth-century contemporaries thought that religion had declined. They blamed this perceived decline on a deism hostile to Christianity, which had reached ordinary people through English soldiers during the French and Indian War (1755–1763) and through French soldiers during the American Revolution (1775–1783). They also felt a disruption in the life of the churches occasioned by the war. With even pastors enlisting and with the countryside turned into a battlefield, church life could hardly have been unaffected. Still more, Anglicanism and an infant Methodist movement had close ties to England and after the war had to undergo reorganization. By 1784 the Methodists had an independent American organization, followed in 1789 by the Protestant Episcopal church, reconstituted out of what had once been Anglicanism.

Finally, late-eighteenth-century observers noted what, in the long run, might occasion the greatest difficulties for church adherence. The United States, from the European point of view, was a new land and a wild land. Institutions and attitudes that were taken for granted in the Old World had to fight to make their way in the new. On the frontier, a church was less necessary than a house, and a Bible was less practical than a hunting rifle or an ax.

American Protestant Origins and the Liberal Tradition

For all of these reasons, Protestant clergy faced the nineteenth century in a mood of anxiety. What concerns us here, though, are the practical consequences of their anxiety in promoting liberal behavior and, if thought follows practice, in ultimately promoting liberal Protestant thought. Thus, among older denominations, the felt need to bring more and more people to the churches generated cooperative efforts. In a key example, by the end of the war the Congregationalists and their denominational cousins, the Presbyterians, had joined forces, regarding themselves almost as a single church and dividing territory as practical need dictated.

In a strict organizational sense, Presbyterians were those who opted for church government through the authority of a presbytery, a ruling body made up of ministers and elders representing a group of local congregations. Congregationalists, instead, insisted on the autonomy of each individual congregation. Although there had been both congregational and presbyterian tendencies among the Puritans, it is fair to say that the congregational way had become the norm in New England. What brought Presbyterianism as a denomination to the New World, however, was largely the immigration of British and, still more, Scotch-Irish Presbyterians. In the tradition of the Scottish Reformer John Knox (1513?–1572), these Calvinist Christians subscribed to the Westminster Confession, a formal statement of faith that had been approved by the British Parliament in 1648.

Presbyterians had been present in the colonies as early as 1611, when a local Presbyterian congregation worshiped in Virginia, and 1630, when other Presbyterians were worshiping in Massachusetts and Connecticut. By 1706 six Presbyterian groups had united in Philadelphia in the first official presbytery in the colonies. But the major impetus to Presbyterian growth came from 1710, when an estimated 3,000 to 6,000 Scotch-Irish immigrated annually until mid-century. These Presbyterian migrants established themselves first in New England and in the Middle Colonies but moved from there throughout the Atlantic colonies. By 1729 the Presbyterian base was large enough to warrant the convening of the first general synod of the church, and it was this group that officially adopted the Westminster Confession.

The needs of the new land, however, began to erode the strict separatism that the Presbyterian stand on the Westminster Confession signaled. Under their Plan of Union in 1801, Presbyterians and Congregationalists cooperated in home missionary efforts on the frontier. Ministers in the two denominations shared each other's pulpits, clergy and laity worked together indiscriminately, and even membership became dual. Under this plan, Presbyterian church adherence swelled from a small 18,000 in 1790 (over a decade before the plan commenced) to more than 220,000 in 1837. Indeed, because congregations could call their own preachers and most turned to Presbyterian ones, the Presbyterians gained the most in numerical terms from the Plan of Union. However, the issue of the plan brought to the fore both conservative and liberal tendencies in the church. Conservatives in the Old School objected more and more to the Congregational affiliation and were concerned over questions of discipline and the allocation of money to missions. Liberals in the New School supported the plan. Thus, New Schoolers were in effect opening themselves to a doctrine of toleration and cooperation that chipped away at the segregation of the pure Calvinist model they had inherited. By 1837, when the Old School party expelled the New Schoolers from the church and two Presbyterian bodies resulted, the extent of the liberal Presbyterian movement was clear.

Similarly, from other quarters liberal practice was softening old denominational separatisms, suggesting by means of cooperative effort belief that human freedom and responsibility had much to do with the kind of Christian society that could be built. In this way of acting, God was implicitly seen as present in the world, helping those who helped themselves. Thus, by the early nineteenth century Protestant voluntary societies, formed without official church ties, were distributing Bibles and tracts and furthering the moral reform of society. For them as for most of the Protestants of this period, the leading problems that American Christianity had to face were "infidelity" and "barbarism." And, above all, the news was that Protestant Christians acting *together*, putting aside their differences, could change things.

If actual practice was generating a liberalism of sorts in older denominations, theological reflection was bringing liberalism to new ones. Liberal Christians in eastern Massachusetts gradually moved toward denominational status, still within the Congregational church but more and more marked by their distinctive views. The seriousness of the growing disagreement within Congregational ranks became apparent in 1805 when Henry Ware, a liberal, was named Hollis professor of divinity at Harvard College. Three years later Andover Seminary was founded by those opposed to what was seen as the liberal takeover of Harvard, which, by 1806, had a liberal as president in Samuel Webber. Signs of cleavage continued to mount. Then in 1819, when liberal leader William Ellery Channing (1780–1842) delivered his sermon "Unitarian Christianity" at a Baltimore ordination, he gave a name and platform to the new movement.

In point of fact, there had been European Unitarians at the time of the Reformation, followers of the Italian Faustus Socinus (1539–1604), who taught the antitrinitarian doctrine that Jesus was a purely human instrument through whom God acted. Later, in eighteenth-century England, the scientist and Presbyterian minister Joseph Priestly (1733–1804) articulated Unitarian ideas, and the Anglican Theophilus Lindsey (1723–1808) broke from the Church of England and in 1774 began a Unitarian congregation. Some New England liberals corresponded with Lindsey, as the publication of his *Memoirs* in 1815 showed.

In the version of Unitarianism that Channing taught and that came to characterize the new American denomination, Jesus was more than an ordinary human. At the same time, although he was Savior, for them he was not God. The Bible was an inspired book, but it was written in ordinary language, they said, and it must be studied and interpreted in the same way as other books were. Most of all, there was a likeness between God and human beings that added up, for Channing and his followers, to a high doctrine of human nature. Humans had a "moral nature" that was the foundation of virtue, and so there could be optimism and enthusiasm about what they might accomplish. Jesus, for these Unitarians, showed the way to the perfection — which was divine — that humans could achieve.

By 1825, 125 churches had come together to form the American Unitarian Association, most of them in Massachusetts close to Boston. Their members were largely of comfortable means and urban in orientation. Well-educated themselves, they thought of their new organization as a publication and missionary society, and in no sense did they think that the views they espoused should constitute a creed. Meanwhile, their churches continued to follow the congregational form and order of service to which the liberals were accustomed.

Unitarians had their country cousins, though, in the Universalists. Universalist views of salvation were expressed in their name, for they held that, through the sacrifice and grace of Jesus, God intended salvation for all. Although there had been universalist preaching in Pennsylvania as early as 1741, in the denominational sense the movement began with the work of John Murray (1741–1815). An English Methodist of Calvinist persuasion, Murray was influenced by another British Methodist, James Relly (1720–1780?), who in his book *Union* (1759) taught the doctrine of universal salvation. Murray arrived in America in 1770 and began preaching on the Atlantic coast, establishing groups of people with universalist convictions. In Gloucester, Massachusetts, he discovered one group already persuaded by Relly's ideas, and Murray stayed to begin the first Universalist church in the United States in the year 1779.

The person who had the most to do with the direction Universalism would take, however, was another convert, Hosea Ballou (1771–1852). With Baptist roots and also with exposure to the thought of Boston liberals who emphasized human goodness and divine benevolence, Ballou published his influential *Treatise on Atonement* in 1805. In it he rejected Calvinist teachings of total depravity and eternal condemnation of the damned. But even more, he rejected the Christian doctrine of the Trinity and the traditional Christian belief in miracles, stressing instead a belief in human goodness and capacity for perfection. Jesus, in Ballou's reading, was not himself God, but he was God's son. And Jesus did not die on the cross as a substitute for humankind in a kind of legal arrangement with God; rather, taught Ballou, he suffered for humans as an expression of his love. Finally, Ballou repudiated the notion of creeds as the bond of Christian community and called in place of them for bonds of faith and goodwill.

In short, the Universalism that Ballou preached had moved close to what would emerge as Unitarian belief. Indeed, the Universalists differed from the Unitarians more in sociological terms (they tended to be rural and poorer) than in theological ones. (The two denominations would join at last in 1961 as the Unitarian Universalist Association.) In the early nineteenth century the Universalist movement prospered, so that by the 1830s there were claims of more than 500 ministers. And throughout the middle decades of the century, Universalist ministers were often leaders in new religious movements, breaking away from even this liberal movement in Protestant Christianity. A 1790 Universalist statement in Philadelphia had condemned war and called for an end to slavery as well as for efforts to educate blacks. And later another and distantly related Ballou—Adin (1803–1890)—with other Universalists from Milford, Massachusetts, would organize the Hopedale Community, an attempt from 1842 to 1856 to give concrete form to theories of common sharing in a Christian community.

The social direction of the Universalist movement was one early sign of what liberalism would come to embody. But there were others, some in surprising places. One key example of the direction that Protestant liberalism could take was the Christian side of the movement known in literary and philosophical circles as New England Transcendentalism. Begun among a group of Boston Unitarians educated at Harvard, many of them ministers, Transcendentalism flourished in a loosely knit club for conversation about literary, philosophical, and religious issues. The acknowledged leader of the movement was Ralph Waldo Emerson (1803–1882), whose small book *Nature* provided its gospel in 1836. Key to this work was a new form of the ancient theory of correspondence, in which Emerson and his friends looked to nature to teach them spiritual truths. They saw in the New England landscape symbolic statements of deeper realities, and by studying nature, they believed, they could uncover the secrets of their inner selves and a corresponding knowledge of the divine.

For the Transcendentalists, intuition—the inner voice—became the key to the discovery of revelation; and nature, as the sacred space that evoked the inner perception of truth, was likewise privileged. Hence, both the inner space of the mind and the outer space of nature suggested for them the presence of a God who was immanent. This was true even though one side of Transcendental thought expressed the belief that the world was only an appearance—an idea derived from ancient Platonic and Neoplatonic philosophy. Of greater significance for us, though, the side of Transcendentalism that pointed to a divine presence in the world also exalted human nature. For Emerson and other Transcendentalists, humans were using only part of the full range of powers they possessed, and there was great optimism regarding their innate goodness and their capacity for reforming their society.

Transcendentalist ministers, either in or out of Unitarianism, began reforming society by their attempted reforms of the church. Orestes Brownson (1803–1876), for example, was influenced by Congregationalists, joined the Presbyterians, became a Universalist minister, spent time as an agnostic, and then returned to Christianity as a Unitarian minister in Walpole, New Hampshire, in 1834. Although he would eventually end his days as a Roman Catholic, in 1836 he established his experimental Society for Christian Union and Progress. He abolished pew ownership to advance his ministry to working-class people, and he preached a doctrine of social reform and progress.

In another example, James Freeman Clarke (1810–1888), a Harvard Divinity School graduate, left a more conventional Unitarian ministry in Louisville, Kentucky, and founded the Boston-based Church of the Disciples in 1841. The new religious society announced its presence with a broad doctrinal statement, flexibility in ritual matters, and, as in Brownson's church, free pews. Similarly, Theodore Parker (1810–1860), another Harvard Divinity School graduate and Unitarian pastor, attempted to reform the church in 1845 in the Twenty-Eighth Congregational Society. Parker had survived strong pressures from other Unitarian ministers to conform to their understanding of gospel and church, and they had expressed their displeasure at his views by ostracizing him. In his new congregation, which eventually became the largest in Boston, with some 7,000 members, Parker abolished the proprietary pew system and a regular collection.

Meanwhile, William Henry Channing (1810–1884), the nephew of William Ellery Channing, ministered to New York City's poor and subsequently, in 1843, worked to form the Christian Union, a religious society organized on watchwords of "Humanity, Wisdom, and Holiness." In 1846, Channing, in Boston, sought to reform the church still more radically by basing a congregation on the thought of the French socialist and communitarian Charles Fourier (1772–1837). Channing's Religious Union of Associationists included members from various denominations who were linked by their adherence to Fourier's principle of Universal Unity. Moreover, Channing was not the only Transcendentalist to seek social reform in Fourierist terms. In West Roxbury, Massachusetts, in 1840, the former Unitarian minister George Ripley (1802–1880) formed the Brook Farm community, a joint-stock company that aimed to express, in a communal-living experiment, Transcendental ideas of freedom and spontaneity. By 1844 Brook Farm became a Fourierist "phalanx," a self-sufficient cooperative community that, in theory at least, would express in its membership all of the different possibilities of human personality and talent.

Ripley's social vision for the Transcendentalists had begun in the concern he felt as a Unitarian minister in a deteriorating Boston neighborhood. He wanted to express the highest possibilities of human nature, to present the ideal in tangible form. Other Transcendentalists also worked to give flesh to their ideals, notably in the antislavery cause. Thus, Theodore Parker made slavery his chief concern and, after the passage of the Fugitive Slave Act of 1850, became an ardent abolitionist. Much earlier, in 1831, Emerson — then a Unitarian minister — had permitted an abolitionist to speak in his church; and he opened his church to the Society for the Abolition of Slavery for its annual meetings. In 1837 Emerson himself spoke at the Second Church in Boston on the issue of slavery.

Other reformist concerns continued to occupy the Transcendentalists, both those who were actively Christian and those with looser religious identities. Emerson, for example, spoke out when the Cherokee were being forced from their ancestral homes in Georgia to make way for whites. He and others supported the peace movement of the era and especially lodged their protest against the Mexican War (1846–1848), tied as it was to the acquisition of territory in which slavery could flourish. Transcendentalists also supported the temperance movement and sided with those who were working for women's rights. In sum, well before the post–Civil War liberal language of establishing the Kingdom of God on earth, the Transcendentalists were, in effect, prompted by similar views of social progress and perfectibility.

Transcendentalism, however, was part of a broader cultural trend. It was one expression of the European and American cultural movement known as Romanticism. The successor to the Enlightenment, this movement flourished after the French Revolution (1789) and became the dominant ideology of the nineteenth century. Like the Enlightenment, the Romantic movement exalted nature, but a nature viewed as organic, free, and spontaneous instead of, as in the Enlightenment, mechanical and ruled by law. More than the Enlightenment, therefore, Romanticism stressed human freedom and its expression through passion or emotion. It found little to fear in strong feeling, for humans, in the Romantic understanding, were basically good. And Romanticism, as already apparent from the Transcendentalists, found significance in the inner life of the individual.

Romantic ideas had found an important theological voice in Germany in the writings of the Reformed minister Friedrich Schleiermacher (1768–1834). His *Christian Faith* (1821–1822) became his masterwork, announcing that religion was the feeling of absolute dependence and that Christianity was the highest but not the only true religion. In America, Schleiermacher's work had helped to shape the Transcendentalists. But it also helped, along with other factors—such as, for example, the reflections of the English Romantic poet Samuel Taylor Coleridge (1772–1834)—to shape a broader movement of Christian Romanticism. Probably the chief exponent of this American movement was the theologian Horace Bushnell (1802–1876). A Yale Divinity School graduate and Congregational minister, Bushnell absorbed home-grown Unitarian ideas along with those of Coleridge, Schleiermacher, and other European thinkers. His "progressive orthodoxy" did not win him much popularity in his own time, but it was later given a full hearing in the seminaries that were training future generations of ministers. Moreover, Bushnell's theology provided a rationale for liberal Protestant practice.

In one sense, it was Bushnell's conservatism, his appreciation for the past, that led him to the liberal theology he formulated. His problem was how to preserve the Protestant Christian heritage in light of new understandings and developments. In this context, he advanced a theory of language that enabled Christians to bring past and progressive present together. This "mediating" theology taught that words were symbolic devices that could only approximate the truth that lay behind and beyond language. In the case of the traditional doctrine of the Trinity, for example, the triform Godhead of Father, Son, and Holy Spirit referred, in Bushnell's explanation, to three different ways in which humans experienced God. But for him the language of the Trinity could not address the question of the inner being of God.

Bushnell thought of language as a social product, and therefore he underlined the importance of the processes by which children were brought, through language, into the cultural community. His *Christian Nurture* (1847) was widely influential in its teaching of the importance of religious education. Here Bushnell countered the revivalist language of the era, with its emphasis on sin and sudden salvation, with a gradualist view of continuing progress from good to better. Behind his thinking lay an organic and developmental view of Christian life: it was something that grew and matured with the years, he believed, through a process nourished by the institutions of family, church, and even nation. In fact, in his later *Nature and the Supernatural* (1858), Bushnell redefined the supernatural (literally, that which is "above the natural") to include everything that was alive. In effect, Bushnell's supernatural could not be separated from nature. His supernatural world participated in the natural one, and his God was immanent in the living world.

Bushnell's ideas pointed the way to what, well after the Civil War, would be called the Social Gospel, and he also laid the groundwork for later liberal Christian acceptance of the biological theory of evolution. In the meantime, the growth of liberal Protestantism was being encouraged from another quarter. Pluralism, present from colonial times, was becoming more plural still, as immigration brought more and more members of European national churches to America. Representatives of groups like the German and Swedish Lutherans and the Dutch and German Reformed had long been present. But now these older national churches were still receiving new members from abroad, and members of new national churches were arriving in America, too. As in Roman Catholicism, extraordinary religion in each national church was blended with ethnic and ordinary religion, so that no one such church was the same as any other. But, unlike Catholic churches, which kept a nominal unity through the institutions of papacy and hierarchy, these national churches in America were, each of them, independent denominations.

Later, slavery and the Civil War would become sources of friction for older, mainstream churches, and so denominations would dissociate into northern and southern factions. Baptists, Methodists, Presbyterians, and (with qualification) Episcopalians divided into separate churches before or during the war. Moreover, although there had been independent black congregations since the late eighteenth century, black denominational growth would receive a major boost after the Civil War, a subject we will examine in more detail in Chapter 6. Considerable acrimony was attached to denominational separations in the Civil War era, and even the new black denominations were not without their growing pains. In an atmosphere of often-passionate adherence to what believers regarded as gospel truth, no one group should be singled out for its "liberalism." Yet the presence of still more of the many would have its results. After passions cooled and new denominations had established their identities, there would be time to look around at the rest of America. Plural presence would shape inner climate as well as external fact, and the liberal endorsement of as much freedom as was consonant with community identity would be strengthened.

From Gilded Age into Twentieth Century

The post–Civil War era was known as the Gilded Age, because beneath the glittering surface of society there was a sense of spiritual malaise. Then America entered the twentieth century, experiencing a continued wave of prosperity until the outbreak of the First World War in 1914 and, in 1929, the Great Depression. From the Gilded Age into the twentieth century Protestant liberalism reached its mature form, making its impact felt in the religious life of many believers. Liberals acted in a broad context in which Protestantism either affirmed American culture, withdrew from it as much as possible, or tried to transform it. And of these three ways in which Protestantism responded to American society, liberalism helped to shape the first and third ways directly and the second indirectly by helping to provoke its rejection of modernity.

With its varied responses to American culture and its liberal impulse, late-nineteenth-century Protestantism was still the religion of the Word. So Protestants formulated new theological statements to guide action in the world. But there was a characteristic American quality to these statements, which distinguished them from an older form of theologizing. If the Word of the gospel, in whatever form, impelled Protestant men and women to moral action, in the postwar version the Word itself took on a pragmatic quality. The gospel Word seemed transparent to the problems and needs of the time, so that wealth and poverty, evolution and science, liberalism and the fear of it became the content of the theological message. In fact, the new Word began not with the gospel but with the situation of the world. Meanwhile, the rank and file among Protestant people were already acting out theologies in the circumstances of their lives. Some Protestants identified so closely with American culture that for them ordinary religion absorbed the extraordinary. Others, in trying to leave the world, discovered again the need for extraordinary religion. And others still, by seeking to change the world, sought a rhythmic alternation between ordinary and extraordinary forms of religion, with the ordinary still in the lead.

In the first place, Protestantism expressed a liberalism come of age by affirming culture through the content of its popular preaching. Perhaps no better example can be found than in the life of Henry Ward Beecher (1813–1887). The clerical hero of the age, Henry Ward was the son of the memorable Lyman Beecher (1775–1863), bellwether for an earlier generation. The elder Beecher had been a famous revivalist and president of Lane Theological Seminary in Cincinnati. A man who had freely moved from the Congregational to the Presbyterian organization in the era of the Plan of Union, he was tried for heresy in 1836 because of the modifications his Calvinism had undergone. The charges against Lyman Beecher were withdrawn, but his uncertain stance between old and new contrasted with the full and warm liberalism of his son. For a forty-year period from 1847 to 1887, Henry Ward Beecher held the pulpit at the Plymouth Church in Brooklyn, New York. Here his sermons drew crowds numbering in the thousands, and the sermons were also widely distributed in pamphlet form.

Henry Ward Beecher had moved far to the left of even the modified Calvinism of his father. His New Theology, as it came to be called, was evangelical liberalism, centering emotionally on an individual relationship with Jesus and leading confidently toward an acceptance of the world. It was the humanity of Jesus that inspired his emotional sermons, and he saw the humanness of Jesus as a sign of natural human possibility. For Beecher, things as they were, were good. The goal of his preaching, with its sentimental warmth, was to lead each hearer to an experiential encounter with the gospel as he saw it. In Beecher's liberalism, church and world became related aspects of one religiocultural whole. The Reformation Protestantism of prophetic protest gave way to a new culture religion, and extraordinary religion was nearly extinguished by ordinariness. Still, there was a biting edge to Beecher's Word, for it led him to speak out on a range of issues from slavery and women's rights to immigration and municipal corruption.

In the Gospel of Wealth, however, the biting edge seemed wholly lost, and so did the self-conscious reflection of Beecher's liberal version of the gospel. For the Gospel of Wealth liberalism became an affirmation of the freedom to prosper, a testimony to prosperity as divine blessing, so that one could live without economic constraint. In short, in the Gospel of Wealth God became immanent in the flow of material good fortune, and human nature became the fitted vehicle for the acquisition of wealth.

A good example of the Gospel of Wealth in popular Protestantism was the preaching of Russell H. Conwell (1843–1925). For the Baptist Conwell and others who agreed, an older Calvinist belief in wealth as God's blessing was transformed into the practical dictum that poverty was sinful and that it was the duty of every Christian to get rich. Conwell's sermon "Acres of Diamonds" was initially delivered in 1861 and repeated some 6,000 times, proclaiming to hearers that there were acres of diamonds in their own backyards, if only they took the trouble to dig them out. Conwell's preaching — and the Gospel of Wealth — was Christian baptism for the burgeoning capitalism of the era. In the age of early millionaires and corporate "robber barons," Conwell and his followers signaled that the church was on the side of the world, especially when it was powerful and rich. Yet there was liberal naiveté in Conwell's Word, even with its Calvinist trappings (the ideas that poverty was a sin and wealth a duty). The confidence, even euphoria, about human nature revealed something more than Calvinism.

The sky was the limit, Conwell was saying, and humans could achieve anything they genuinely chose.

By the last decade of the nineteenth century, the good news of prosperity would be announced again in the kind of Christianity known as New Thought (to be discussed in Chapter 8). In the teachings of Charles (1854–1948) and Myrtle (1845–1931) Fillmore, for instance, God was the divine Supply, and it was up to humans to open themselves to the flow of good. Hence, for the Fillmores and others in the New Thought movement, prosperity was the proper expression of full and free relationship to a divine Source. In their teaching the Gospel of Wealth had achieved a new form—a form that would lead for many out of Christianity and into an independent religious movement.

Popular expressions of Protestant belief in a need to accept the world—as in the cases of Beecher and Conwell—were joined by more intellectual ones. It was here that Protestant liberalism became its most self-conscious and reflective. And it was here that it responded to the challenges of the science and scholarship of the era, including Charles Darwin's articulation of the theory of evolution in his *Origin of Species* (1859). There was continuity between some proponents of the New Theology, like Henry Ward Beecher, and these liberal intellectuals, but New Theology spoke more to the people in the pews, and the intellectuals spoke to an elite.

In its most pronounced form, this liberalism of the intellectuals came to be known as modernism. The Christian task, for modernists, was to realize the gospel in the modern world. Modernists were convinced that any separation between the gospel and the world, between religion and culture, was artificial: in the terms of the text, they sought to collapse ordinary and extraordinary into one continuous reality. In so doing, in some statements they seemed to make modernity the norm by which the Word was measured and to want to restructure the gospel along lines that science and general cultural development provided. For example, modernists wanted to reinterpret traditional biblical accounts, such as the Genesis story of Adam and Eve in the Garden of Eden, in light of modern knowledge. However, although their language sometimes sounded as though the Bible must take second place to the modern world, the thrust behind the modernist reading of culture was a unitive perspective that, as among traditional peoples, blurred the lines between religion and the rest of life.

Even so, the modernist perspective on the Bible was shaped by new scholarship. This scholarship, which emanated mostly from Germany, had been challenging the traditional, literal interpretation of the Bible since the middle of the nineteenth century. Known as the "higher criticism" to distinguish it from the textual ("lower") criticism inherited from the Reformation, the new scholarship emphasized the sources and literary methods that biblical authors employed. Unlike textual criticism, which sought to establish the correct text of manuscripts transcribed before the introduction of the printing press and to reconstruct textual history, higher criticism broadened its concerns. By pointing to possible sources of a biblical author's text, it challenged sacrosanct theories of revelation and inspiration. By suggesting the literary and theological creativity of biblical authors, higher critics likewise inserted biblical books in historical contexts and again cast doubts on direct transmission of a divine Word. In sum, higher criticism raised historical issues and questioned old theories of authorship, dating, and meaning in biblical documents.

Even as the modernists broke with the nineteenth-century norm of literal interpretation of the Bible, they brought to full maturity the nascent liberal challenge to the older Calvinist vision. Whereas the Calvinist religious perspective expressed awe at the transcendence of God—his distance from the human world—the modernists, in their teaching of immanence, saw the presence of God in the world. Whereas Calvinism taught human depravity and the inability of any human act to gain salvation, modernism abolished original sin and taught human goodness. Indeed, modernists shared a basic optimism about creating heaven in the present world through concerted human effort, and so they replaced the traditional heaven of the afterlife with an earthly version.

Moreover, whereas Calvinists had seen Jesus as God's Word clothed in human flesh, modernists saw him as an elder brother, first among the many, who disclosed to humans all that they could know of God. Jesus had the value of God for modernists, but whether he *was* God, as traditional Protestantism had taught, was a question they did not directly address. Finally, whereas the Calvinist Word honed the intellect to doctrinal and spiritual precision, the Word of the modernists urged them to felt experience. In late-nineteenth-century liberal teaching, evangelical pietism, with its emphasis on heartfelt feeling, continued in a new and more sophisticated form. Thus, the intellectual difficulties of new scientific theory and practice were short-circuited by the religion of the heart.

New scientific theory and practice abounded in the "higher criticism" as the most direct challenge to older Protestantism in the Gilded Age and early twentieth century. But the challenge was also symbolized, especially for later generations, by Darwin's publication of evidence from the Galapagos Islands that seemed to confirm the theory of evolution. This theory had actually predated Darwin, but he gave it new impetus with his presentation of evidence and a new reading with his understanding of the "survival of the fittest." Protestant response to Darwin's theory, particularly among people in the pew, was slow in coming. In fact, it was not until the 1920s and the Tennessee trial of John T. Scopes (1925), a biology teacher accused of violating a Tennessee law by teaching the theory of evolution, that the matter evoked great interest and greater passion. Still, earlier Protestant liberals had noticed the existence of evolutionary theory. Although Horace Bushnell had personally rejected the idea of evolution, his own theology was translated by some from a statement about the regeneration of the individual to one about the evolutionary regeneration of society and culture. And Henry Ward Beecher had not been afraid to announce himself a "cordial Christian evolutionist."

In point of fact, many—indeed, most—Protestants who studied Darwin's theory before 1875 saw it as lacking in scientific credibility. They thought of

Christianity as the friend of true science and of Darwinism as a betrayal of scientific truth. But from 1865 to 1875 more and more respected scientists announced their support for evolutionary theory. Hence, after 1875 most articulate Protestant intellectuals began to change their minds. Now they thought that Christian theology needed to be reshaped to make place for the Darwinist theory, and they differed mostly on whether the necessary changes were minimal or more serious. Even further, many of them began to see the idea of evolution as a blueprint for God's way of working throughout the creation.

Liberal acceptance of the world was underlined by acceptance of the theory of evolution, although, as stated before, evolution was at first not the most important issue. Some Protestants, though, refused to accept the world that modernity presented, and they countered liberalism head on in a second response to change. They withdrew from the world as much as they could, and they rejected the worldly forms that, for them, challenged the inherited gospel. Thus, Protestant fundamentalism grew strong in the same climate that fostered a mature liberalism, and the fundamentalist–liberal controversy became the key to Protestantism in the late nineteenth and early twentieth centuries. But fundamentalism, like liberalism, grew out of earlier movements, and we will look further at it in later chapters. The same is the case for other movements that at least partially rejected the world, such as, notably, the holiness-pentecostal movement.

Here, though, we need simply to notice that the presence of liberalism played a significant role in the genesis of movements of withdrawal, particularly the fundamentalist withdrawal. In liberalism, some Protestants saw the face of the enemy not merely out in the modern world but also at home among fellow religionists. For these Protestants, liberalism became, then, a more serious form of betrayal than the defection from the Christian gospel they saw in the world. And so liberalism, indirectly, worked to promote its countermovements.

If one body of liberal Protestants after the Civil War began to affirm culture more strenuously and a second group, reacting both to liberalism and to modernity, partially withdrew from it, there was still a third response. This response was the work of a group of Protestants, many of them liberal, who sought to transform culture through what came to be called the Social Gospel. The new gospel cause had precedents in earlier-nineteenth-century Protestant calls to reform society, such as the ideology of the Transcendentalists and the crusades against alcohol and slavery of many more (a subject we will take up in Part II). Moreover, many of the roots of the Social Gospel lay in evangelical liberalism, although Social Gospelers were less content with social conditions in post–Civil War America than world-affirming liberals had been. Instead, those drawn to the Social Gospel noticed that as business flourished and economic power became concentrated in the hands of a few, large numbers received little pay for their work and led lives of poverty in urban slums. Advocates of the Social Gospel saw the true tasks of Christians as rescuing the poor and renewing the political, economic, and social order. They thought that the Kingdom of God must come on earth; for them, a millennium must be inaugurated through human effort.

Under Washington Gladden (1836–1918), a Congregationalist minister from Columbus, Ohio, the movement began to receive notice in the 1880s. Gladden had first ministered to churches in Massachusetts, where he had become aware of exploitation and poverty that working people faced. Then, in Ohio, his views crystallized in 1884 in the Hocking Valley coal strike, as he saw coal executives who were members of his congregation fight to break the strike and destroy the union movement. In this context, Gladden came to endorse the rights of workers and to stress the adage of "doing unto others as you would have them do unto you." Beyond that, in a mildly collectivist turn, he favored ownership of public utilities by cities and municipalities. Gladden became more and more outspoken in advancing his views, lecturing inveterately and writing some thirty-six books. With this energetic prodding of others regarding social injustice, his influence spread widely in Protestant America, and his impact was considerable.

Later, Walter Rauschenbusch (1861–1918) provided a theological foundation for the Social Gospel in the early twentieth century. Rauschenbusch had labored as a young minister in the Hell's Kitchen district of New York City, and though he returned to his seminary in Rochester as a professor, he never forgot what he had seen. After a decade of seminary life, he published *Christianity and the Social Crisis* (1907), and in 1917 he produced *A Theology for the Social Gospel*, the written version of a series of lectures he had delivered at Yale University. Religion, for Rauschenbusch as for other Protestants before him, led out of the churches and into the world. Now, though, a distinct economic group was targeted to hear the message of the gospel — a gospel that strived to change not only individuals but also the social structures seen as thwarting people. In the Social Gospel, salvation came in the collective reconstitution of society; a personal relationship with Jesus was not enough.

Even more, the Social Gospel could mean taking notice of new social theory, and it could signal a direct attention to new social-scientific thought. Thus, some in the Social Gospel movement were directly inspired by the "Christian socialism" of the English Frederick Denison Maurice and Charles Kingsley as well as by German and Swiss Christian socialist thought. Moreover, a growing American acquaintance with the ideas of Karl Marx and of British socialists in the Fabian Society was making its impact felt, as was a general acquaintance with European political theorists who favored socialism. In one example, William Dwight Porter Bliss (1856–1926), an Episcopalian minister, worked in the Christian Socialist Fellowship and joined the American Socialist party. In another, George D. Herron (1862–1925), a Congregational minister and professor of applied Christianity at Grinnell College in Iowa, became a strong socialist and also, for a short time, a party member.

Among those drawn to the social sciences, political science, economics, and especially sociology could be tapped in the interests of the Social Gospel. Some, for example, supported the development of new "settlement houses," such as, in the most well-known example, that of Jane Addams (1860–1935) in Chicago. Beginning in 1889 at the "social settlement" called Hull House, Addams and her associates worked in slum communities to improve conditions. Others drawn to social science offered more theoretical expressions of their concern. For instance, Richard T. Ely (1854–1943), a Presbyterian turned Episcopalian, studied in Germany and later, as a professor at Johns Hopkins University in Baltimore, melded economics with his reading of Christian ethics. In another example, Albion W. Small (1854–1926), a Baptist who also studied in Germany, founded the first university department of sociology at the University of Chicago (1892). Small participated actively in meetings held by leaders in the Social Gospel movement and, like Ely, brought to his social-scientific work a strongly Protestant moral concern.

In sum, the Social Gospel, with its practical directness, was like more purely intellectual modernism in stressing the ordinary dimensions of religion. But it went beyond modernism in bringing belief in Christian revelation to the task of changing the character of society. In other words, there was insistence on the transcendent, or the extraordinary, in the Social Gospel message, and this was perhaps why some Protestant conservatives could feel comfortable in espousing it. Indeed, the old spirit of prophetic criticism, the Protestant principle, was revived in the movement in a new way. Still, prophetic criticism was directed at the world, not the church, and ordinary religion was strong. The Social Gospel venture sought to order conditions in the here and now as a means of establishing contact with the divine. It strived for the material betterment of human society, so that the Kingdom of God could come through the transformation of the present. Clearly, the God of the Social Gospelers was conceived to be immanent.

Protestant Liberalism in the Later Twentieth Century

The Social Gospel was an enduring legacy for mainstream liberal Protestantism as the twentieth century continued. The popularity of social Christianity waxed and waned with the climate of the times, but the Social Gospel never completely disappeared. Meanwhile, a liberal–fundamentalist split seemed a permanent feature of the Protestant landscape. Sometimes liberals and fundamentalists were organized in separate denominations. But more and more, in the later twentieth century, there were divisions *within* denominations, so that some within the same church might be liberal and others conservative or fundamentalist in orientation.

By the late eighties the most liberal Protestants tended to be Episcopalians, members of the United Church of Christ (heirs to Congregationalism and other traditions), and Presbyterians. (Unitarian-Universalists had effectively moved beyond Protestant Christian boundaries.) Moderate Protestant churches, with memberships that had substantial liberal and conservative factions, included Methodist, Lutheran, and Northern Baptist groups. What is interesting is that for the most part these denominational families numbered among the largest Protestant bodies in the nation for the decade of the eighties. However, that fact needs to be set against another. Baptist churches were the religious preference of perhaps one-fifth of the American population. And among Baptists, nearly half identified with the Southern Baptist Convention, a strongly conservative body.

After the Baptists, Methodist groups constituted the second among Protestant bodies, with some 9 percent of the American population expressing a Methodist preference. Third came the Lutherans, with perhaps 7 percent, followed by Episcopalians, Presbyterians, and members of the United Church of Christ. Taken together, Americans preferring these three most liberal denominations made up roughly 8 to 9 percent of the population.

We have noticed the presence of all of the groups in one form or another since colonial times, and Methodists will concern us especially in the next chapter. Here, though, it should be noted that Lutheran prominence is largely a twentieth-century phenomenon. Lutheran churches had grown quietly, chiefly among German and Scandinavian immigrant groups, in earlier centuries. It was after World War I, however, that Lutheran affiliation jumped, growing rapidly to make Lutheranism the third largest Protestant religious preference in America.

In the midst of their continuing denominational manyness, liberal churches, like mainstream Protestant groups in general, faced a series of common problems. First, the increasingly urban character of American culture caught many Protestants off guard and ill prepared. Protestantism had been a rural religion, and even the Protestantism of more city-oriented liberals had thrived in a simpler, less complex America. Now, however, the future lay with structures of a city life grown significantly more diverse and more complicated. Second, the public separation of American culture from serious and integrated attention to religion also seemed frightening. The growth of radio, television, and film had powerfully affected the social images projected into people's lives. Moreover, people's highly mobile life-styles, the quickening pace of life, and an ascending divorce rate played havoc with older religious values. Despite some prominent exceptions, ordinary religion was flattening the transcendent dimension of life, so that extraordinary religion had a diminished place in the public organization of society.

There was still more to concern later-twentieth-century Protestants. The multiplying pluralism — the manyness — of American culture brought anxiety even to numbers of liberals, leading many Protestants to acknowledge that theirs was a "post-Protestant America." In their view, the path toward the future seemed shrouded and, at times, chaotic. And finally, denominationalism itself often bred difficulty in maintaining boundaries and led to a sense of shapelessness in the Protestant mainstream. Old-line denominations, particularly those with a liberal presence, looked more and more alike, and outside the evangelical and fundamentalist camps, religion-in-general seemed to rule the day.

Given all of these problems, liberal Protestants, along with others, initiated various attempts to resolve them, some of the attempts more and some less successful. Beginning early in the century, for example, some churches tried to speak to urban dwellers by making worship only one facet of their mission. Protestant churches, elaborating on social patterns developed during earlier rural days, held classes and picnics, conducted sporting events, and gave church suppers to reach out to a larger public. Meanwhile, liberal optimism and American cultural materialism were both challenged by the movement called theological realism, or neo-orthodoxy. Originating in Europe, it tried both there and in the United States to bring an end to what it saw as uncritical acceptance of the age of progress. Influenced by the thought of the American Niebuhr brothers, Reinhold (1892–1970) and H. Richard (1894–1962), some Protestants sought again the prophetic Word of their Reformation ancestors. With the Niebuhrs, they believed that there was evil in the present constitution of society, and they were convinced that the mystery of evil could never be completely eradicated by human effort. In tangible ways, these Protestants insisted, the Word must stand in judgment over every political, economic, and social endeavor.

The absence of clear religious symbols and values in most of public life had been accompanied by increasing American pluralism in the private sphere. Both trends probably had something to do with the emergence within Protestantism of the ecumenical movement, which worked for the ultimate reunification of separated churches. Both also probably contributed to the emergence of various movements of cooperative Christianity, which worked not for denominational merger but for union in accomplishing what were perceived as common tasks. Here liberal Protestants took the initiative, and here to a partial degree they succeeded. An international movement of church cooperation and work toward Christian reunion had begun as early as 1910, when a world missionary conference was held in Edinburgh, Scotland. And after other formative meetings, the World Council of Churches came into being in 1948.

But the world movement had actually been predated by an American movement of interfaith cooperation. Without proposing denominational merger as goal, Protestants had experienced the benefits of the American culture of pluralism. And their long tradition of voluntary cooperation left American Protestants advantageously positioned for further organization. There had been a sense among some Social Gospelers that an official church federation could advance the work of social Christianity even more than smaller and less formal cooperative efforts. Then, in 1905, the New York meeting of a group calling itself the Inter-Church Conference on Federation led to plans for the Federal Council of Churches of Christ in America. By 1908, the organization had come into existence, with thirty-three denominations its members. Concern for missions and education was clear, but the Federal Council sought especially to promote Social Gospel projects. Here again, liberalism became less an intellectual movement than a practical comfort with the culture of pluralism, a willingness to work together at mutually conceived tasks. Nor did the liberal flavor of the organization go unnoticed among conservative Protestants. In 1942 the National Association of Evangelicals was established, at least partially because of concern by some that the Federal Council was keeping fundamentalists out of religious broadcasting.

Despite the liberal–conservative rift that continued, Protestant cooperation in America achieved new form with the institution, in 1950, of the National Council of Churches. The old Federal Council of Churches and other coordinating organizations came together to bring the new structure into being. It became the largest cooperative body that Protestants had established, with roughly 33 million members organized in 143,000 congregations. Now, however, Protestants had shed their Reformation exclusivity in collective effort, for a number of Eastern Orthodox bodies held institutional membership in the National Council.

Meanwhile, the mood of cooperation fostered the goal of church union, and the ecumenical movement, in the strict sense, began to have practical results. In the largest effort, the Consultation on Church Union (COCU) was initiated in 1962 to bring together a broad range of denominations. Conversations continued among representatives of denominational bodies, including the Methodist, Presbyterian, and Episcopalian churches, the United Church of Christ, and the Disciples of Christ (to be discussed in the next chapter). Although enthusiasm was at first high, after over a quarter of a century a lack of material success modified the ecumenical vision. COCU (which by then stood for the Church of Christ Uniting instead of the original Consultation on Church Union) retreated in 1988 from its goal of full union to work toward what it termed "covenant communion." Under a more or less federal scheme that paralleled the structure of American government, COCU proposed that member denominations would retain control of their internal affairs. However, it envisioned that there would be cooperative clerical ordinations and baptismal services as well as the mission, education, and welfare cooperation that historically had marked the American Protestant churches.

Still, a number of full denominational mergers did occur. One important union came in 1957, when the Congregational Christian Church joined with the Evangelical and Reformed Church to become the United Church of Christ. Yet another came in 1968, when the United Methodist Church was formed by the joining of the Evangelical United Brethren and the Methodists (who had already, in 1939, brought three separate Methodist bodies together). In the meantime, throughout the century the Lutherans had gradually coalesced, so that the twenty-four separate Lutheran groups of 1900 had, by 1960, mostly joined together in three. Then, in 1988, the American Lutheran Church and the Lutheran Church in America, two of the three largest bodies, completed another historic merger to become the Evangelical Lutheran Church in America. They were joined by the small Seminex group that had already left the Lutheran Church—Missouri Synod (the third of the large Lutheran denominations).

Hence, there were now two major denominations, the more liberal Evangelical Lutheran Church in America and the conservative Lutheran Church—Missouri Synod, organizing Lutheran life in the United States.

Presbyterians, too, worked to achieve denominational merger, succeeding by 1983 in uniting the northern and southern branches of their church, which had divided in the era before the Civil War over the issue of slavery. The new Presbyterian Church (U.S.A.) counted over 3 million adherents, but there were conservative holdouts who continued in separate Presbyterian denominations. A hint of the liberal flavor of the Presbyterian Church (U.S.A.) is conveyed by its 1989 decision regarding its new hymnal. The official volume would contain neither military-inspired hymns, such as "Onward Christian Soldiers" and the "Battle Hymn of the Republic," nor patriarchal ones, such as the Christmas carol "God Rest Ye Merry, Gentlemen" and the classic "God of Our Fathers" (to become "God of the Ages").

Presbyterian avoidance of military and patriarchal imagery was, clearly, a sign of the times. Liberal Protestants dealt with the challenges of the later twentieth century in ways that suggested a fusion of the generally liberal cultural concerns of some other Americans with their own Protestant agenda in the Social Gospel tradition. At the same time, liberal Protestant ways of meeting the larger society suggested a role of leadership in effecting social change. One key instance of liberal Protestantism's involvement was its participation in the fifties and sixties in the civil rights movement. A second, characteristic of the seventies and the eighties, was its openness to feminist concerns.

The civil rights movement was in the most important sense a black revolution, and a distinct African-American religion (to be discussed in Chapter 6) prepared and led its way. Moreover, the events that riveted national attention on continuing twentieth-century oppression of black people pointed to their role as leaders in the struggle. The bus boycott of 1956 in Montgomery, Alabama, began when Rosa Parks, a black woman, decided that she was too tired to relinquish her seat to a white person and to move to the back of a Jim Crow bus. And thereafter, it was Martin Luther King, Jr., a young black cleric, who assumed direction of the boycott. Seven years later, in 1963, he led the historic "March on Washington." And in 1965 King and thousands of other blacks marched in Selma, Alabama.

Nonetheless, white liberal Protestants did have a role to play, part of it official and part less formal. As early as 1952, two years before the U.S. Supreme Court ordered integration in the nation's public schools, the National Council of Churches published an official declaration that segregation by race was opposed to the faith of Christians. The council acted again after the high court's decision, issuing a document that suggested appropriate church action to facilitate the integration ordered by law. And in the midst of the tension generated by civil rights protests, the council established its Committee on Religion and Race to assist its denominational members in their involvement in the struggle. Money to help those victimized by racial hatred was made available, and programs of assistance were initiated. At the same time, the unofficial acts of white liberal Protestants were evident. Members of the clergy marched and allowed themselves to be arrested. They left their congregations to be present in picket lines at distant locations. They took part in sit-ins and in street demonstrations. They joined official leaders in the 1963 "March on Washington."

Liberal Protestant involvement, as already suggested, in some ways repeated the themes of the earlier Social Gospel. But now it advanced that movement to deal with another day. The first Social Gospel had been, essentially, a rescue mission conceived in small-scale social and economic terms and operating in the private sector. The new Social Gospel was politicized, aiming to address the legal and governmental structures that undergirded a perceived social oppression. This Social Gospel saw material rescue as not enough and, in some cases, as a perpetuation of the political and economic base that, it said, guaranteed oppression. In short, this Social Gospel sought more to empower than to rescue.

African-Americans, of course, were already sounding the call to their own empowerment, as the "Black Power" slogan of the later sixties only underlined. And the black gospel of liberation inspired the efforts of a series of others who felt oppressed in American society, not least among them women. The feminist movement generated its own set of leaders; and like the black struggle it sought empowerment of its members through the political, economic, and social structures of the culture. In the seventies and eighties an earlier liberation movement caught up with the churches, and feminism became a major cause among liberal Protestants.

Before feminist liberal Protestants could reform the world, however, they saw a need to put their own house in order. And as the example of the Presbyterian (U.S.A.) hymnal made clear, putting a denominational "house" in order meant, among other things, reforming language. Liberal Protestants, like feminists outside the churches, argued that language and usage pointed, by preference for the masculine, to a social world in which men ruled. More than that, they argued, linguistic choices pointed to the construction of a philosophical — and, in the case of the churches, theological — base to legitimate the rule of men. By repudiating the language they considered sexist in prayer and worship texts, liberal Protestants hoped to promote ideological and social *reconstruction*.

Liberals saw their feminist goals as not merely the best insights of their own democratic society. Rather, they understood them as the core message of the gospel Word, of a Christ in whom there was "neither male nor female" (Gal. 3:28). As they saw the matter, their own (extraordinary) religion compelled them to reform the language of hymnal and prayerbook. Hence, in 1983 the National Council of Churches began publishing its *Inclusive Language Lectionary*, which printed new translations of texts used in worship services that were designed to avoid the language to which they objected. Meanwhile, the denominations were also beginning in different ways, many of them official, to address the problem of textual revision.

But restructured language, for liberals, needed to reflect a restructured church community. Their goal of doing away with male hegemony meant that women as well as men should rule, and so liberals worked to support the ordination of women in the denominations in which, historically, it had been denied them. For some liberal churches, of course, ordination was not an issue. Congregationalists, Northern Baptists, and Disciples of Christ had all ordained women since the late nineteenth century. Moreover, other denominations—Lutherans, Methodists, and Presbyterians—in the 1920s and 1930s created special lay ministerial structures to support a leadership role for women. By the seventies, however, a new feminism was demanding more. In one sign of the times, the Lutheran Church in America ordained its first female minister in 1970. And in the decision that became symbolic of the ministerial question, the Episcopal church approved the ordination of women as priests in 1976. By 1989 Episcopalians had their first woman bishop in Barbara C. Harris, and a traditionalist wing of the church, incensed at her Massachusetts episcopacy and the ordination of women in general, was moving to organize as a special church within the church. At the same time, in a decision just as significant, Joan Salmon Campbell, a black woman, was elected as moderator of the Presbyterian Church (U.S.A.).

A 1989 report from the National Council of Churches showed that in the decade from 1977 to 1986, the number of women in the ministry had almost doubled in the denominations that ordained them. Still, many denominations continued to refuse to ordain women as clergy. Out of 163 denominations that responded in 1977, 76 said that they ordained women; out of 166 denominations reported in the later survey data, a modest 84 supported female ordination. Beyond that, even in the denominations that had a female clergy, women were often relegated to lesser roles, not pastoring churches but working under male pastors or in bureaucratic and educational support services. Feminist liberal Protestants were in the midst of a continuing revolution.

And the feminist case was but one example. By the seventies and eighties liberals were immersed, on a variety of fronts, in the major questions that confronted their culture. Minority rights for Native Americans, for Asian Americans, and for others concerned some. The rights of gays and lesbians, and especially their ordination, occupied others. Environmental pollution, health issues, abortion concerns, the New Age movement, and various new religious movements—these and other questions of the day continued to evoke liberal response. Moreover, liberals insisted that their response was not simply a march to the drumbeat of the times but that they looked to the guidance of the gospel to indicate appropriate action in the world. Even so, in liberal Protestant involvement in social and public concerns, the extraordinary had become ordinary. A felt sense of the sacred was hard to find in the midst of the action in the world the liberals enjoined. In fact, with perhaps a premonition that something was amiss, liberals sometimes tried to counter the prevailing trend toward ordinariness with self-conscious ritual observances in the midst of their social and political activism.

Clearly, the liberal solution to the relationship between Word and world, like the conservative one of withdrawal, was implicit in the Reformation. Even in the sixteenth century, the Word had spoken to believers of an individual communion with God. Even in the sixteenth century, it had emptied monasteries and urged men and women to lives of moral witness in the world. Yet the liberal solution brought to the Reformation heritage a religious sense shaped by *American* history and culture. The liberal solution was Protestant, and it was also very much American.

Even more, the relationship between ordinary and extraordinary religion in the Protestant liberal tradition was complicated by the American social problem of oneness and manyness. If liberal Protestantism faced the danger of dissolving its boundaries, of becoming so amorphous that it merged with American culture-in-general, it also had significantly shaped that culture from its early years. The public face of religion in America was still Protestant, and although there were more strands to the Protestantism than the liberal tradition, liberal Protestantism was a significant part of the story. Changed by the many in a variety of ways, Protestantism yet retained its hegemony, and American culture reflected that fact. Indeed, from another perspective, because it had so fused its identity with America from the years of its foundation, Protestantism maintained itself as a kind of empire, a condition of its — and America's — existence that we will look at again in Part II. In short, throughout the course of its life in the United States, Protestantism — the Word from the beginning — was often close to becoming the word from the Potomac.

In Overview

The Protestantism that began in the Reformation came a long way in the New World of the United States. The sixteenth-century Reformers preached a religion of prophetic protest based on the principles of scripture alone, justification by grace through faith, the priesthood of all believers, and a fellowship of common worshipers. These teachings of the Reformation brought into being a series of churches in which a subtle individualism combined with a new interest in the preaching of the Word and a call for moral action in the world. As Protestant church buildings became simpler and more austere and pulpits more prominent in their sanctuaries, they expressed a cultus and a code that led out of the churches and into public life. Paradoxically, the spirit of Protestantism separated extraordinary from ordinary religion in its emphasis on the gap between God and the material world. But it brought them together in another way in its insistence on a thisworldly ethic.

In England the spirit of Protestantism was reflected in the Church of England and in the many strands of the religious movement called Puritanism. With its Calvinist leanings, Puritanism fostered a spirit of still greater reform and promoted the establishment of English colonies in the New World. New England

and (in the loose sense) Virginia were both settled by Puritans, and so was Quaker Pennsylvania. Gradually, other Protestant peoples, the Scotch-Irish, the Germans, and the Dutch among them, became part of colonial society.

In the context of all that had gone before, the liberal tradition grew slowly in America. The colonists accepted pluralism for practical reasons, but tolerance of manyness gradually came to be seen as advantageous. Moreover, religious freedom—important for dissenters who sought purity of faith—promoted the growth of more and more groups. For many, Calvinism was gradually modified by Arminian ideas, while rationalism, moralism, and—by the time of the Revolution—even deism became discernible themes in Protestant religion.

After the Revolutionary War and a period of concern regarding church membership, Protestant churches rebounded, restructuring in light of the new needs of the times. For many, such as Congregationalists and Presbyterians in their Plan of Union, an early liberalism meant accepting the value of cooperation. For others, a more intellectual agenda governed a move toward liberalism. In urban eastern Massachusetts, late-eighteenth-century liberal Christians became nineteenth-century Unitarians, while their rural relatives turned to Universalism. By the late 1830s a new generation of Unitarians had begun to teach the liberal doctrines of Transcendentalism and, in many cases, to work for reform of church and world. And by midcentury other Protestant Christians were inspired by a Christian Romanticism that had its most articulate American spokesperson in Horace Bushnell.

In the Civil War era, increasing pluralism meant that earlier liberal themes of breadth and tolerance were repeated but emphasized. However, the post–Civil War period and the early twentieth century brought greater challenges to Protestantism from a rapidly changing American society. In general, Protestants either affirmed culture, as in popular evangelical liberalism, the popular Gospel of Wealth, a related New Thought Christianity, and a more intellectual modernism. Or they partially withdrew from the culture and rejected liberal doctrine, as in fundamentalism and the holiness-pentecostal movement. Or, finally, they sought to transform culture, as in Social Gospel activism.

By the late twentieth century, liberalism and conservatism seemed permanent within Protestant life. On their side, liberal Protestants responded to the needs they saw with renewed efforts at interdenominational cooperation and with involvement in the ecumenical movement. Meanwhile, they transformed the older Social Gospel to address issues such as the civil rights of African-Americans and the concerns of women for equality. But the question remained for Protestants whether the success of their version of liberalism had changed it too much into the ordinary religion of present-day American culture.

In the language of the text, boundary questions plagued liberal Protestantism. Conservatives flourished partly because the liberal gospel became less and less clear about what separated Christians from other people of goodwill. More numerous than liberals—and in the late twentieth century more vigorous than they—evangelical Protestants throughout American history responded to the times out of their own reading of the gospel Word. It turned out that, read by a less liberal set of Protestants, the gospel Word said different things, or at least said them in different ways and underlined a different list of priorities. As we will see, in an understanding different from the liberal sense of the term, what the gospel Word said to evangelicals most of all was *mission*.

SUGGESTIONS FOR FURTHER READING: AMERICAN PROTESTANT ORIGINS AND THE LIBERAL TRADITION

Bainton, Roland H. *The Reformation of the Sixteenth Century.* Boston: Beacon Press, 1952.

Bonomi, Patricia U. *Under the Cope of Heaven: Religion, Society, and Politics in Colonial America.* New York: Oxford University Press, 1986.

Bozeman, Theodore Dwight. *To Live Ancient Lives: The Primitivist Dimension in Puritanism.* Chapel Hill: University of North Carolina Press, 1988.

Brown, Robert McAfee. *The Spirit of Protestantism.* New York: Oxford University Press, 1965.

Hudson, Winthrop S. *American Protestantism.* The Chicago History of American Civilization. Chicago: University of Chicago Press, 1961.

Hutchison, William R. *The Modernist Impulse in American Protestantism.* 1976. Reprint. New York: Oxford University Press, 1982.

————. *The Transcendentalist Ministers: Church Reform in the New England Renaissance.* 1959. Reprint. Boston: Beacon Press, 1965.

Marty, Martin E. *Protestantism.* Garden City, NY: Doubleday, Image Books, 1974.

————. *Righteous Empire: The Protestant Experience in America.* New York: Dial Press, 1970.

Morgan, Edmund S. *Visible Saints: The History of a Puritan Idea.* New York: New York University Press, 1963.

Pointer, Richard W. *Protestant Pluralism and the New York Experience: A Study of Eighteenth-Century Religious Diversity.* Religion in North America. Bloomington: Indiana University Press, 1988.

Roberts, Jon H. *Darwinism and the Divine in America: Protestant Intellectuals and Organic Evolution, 1859–1900.* Madison: University of Wisconsin Press, 1988.

White, Ronald C., Jr., and Hopkins, C. Howard. *The Social Gospel: Religion and Reform in Changing America.* Philadelphia: Temple University Press, 1976.

Woolverton, John Frederick. *Colonial Anglicanism in North America.* Detroit: Wayne State University Press, 1984.

Wright, Conrad. *The Beginnings of Unitarianism in America.* 1955. Reprint. Hamden, CT: Archon Books, 1976.

Chapter 5

Restoring an Ancient Future:
The Protestant Churches
and the Mission Mind

Young and beautiful Patty Lumsden had been reared in the Episcopal tradition. She led a privileged life as the daughter of Captain Lumsden, the largest land-owner in a corner of southern Ohio in the early nineteenth century. She seemed aloof, regularly turned down suitors, and wore her fine clothes and jewelry with aplomb. But after having been warned regularly against the lower-class coarse-ness of Methodist circuit riders, she attended a forest meeting to hear one preach. According to the account of what happened, she felt "curiosity" about the event and, below the curiosity, "proud hatred" and "quiet defiance." Yet she found herself, in the course of the preacher's sermon, taking off her earrings and plucking the flowers from her bonnet. With this visible evidence of a radical change of heart, she renounced the world and her former life to embrace the message the Methodist minister brought.

Patty Lumsden's conversion to Methodist Christianity occurred only in fiction, in a climactic scene from an 1874 novel by Edward Eggleston. Titled *The Circuit Rider: A Tale of the Heroic Age*, the novel chronicled the life of the familiar nineteenth-century itinerant minister known to frontier Methodists and others as the circuit rider. The novel's circuit rider was fictional in name but faithful in representing the breed. And in its own time Eggleston's book was an evangelical success. It first appeared in serial form in Henry Ward Beecher's journal *The Christian Union*, and its author, Eggleston, had drawn on Jacob Young's account of his ministerial work in *Autobiography of a Pioneer* (1857). That Eggleston eventually, in 1902, became president of the American Historical Association suggests the historical concern that ran through his work.

Both Young, who rode an Athens, Ohio, circuit in historical fact, and Russell Bigelow, who converted Patty Lumsden in fiction, understood the Christian message as mission. That understanding had flourished in the centuries before the coming of Protestant Christianity. As a monotheistic religion—a faith founded on its belief in one God—Christianity was tied to the vision of one sacred center with universal power, meaning, and significance. In more personal terms, the God of Christians was one who had created *all* peoples, including non-Christians, and to whom all should therefore turn. Hence, intrinsic to the Christian sense of God was an intolerance for the multiplication of sacred centers and forces. The God of the Christian Old Testament was a "jealous" God; he wanted no other Gods in competition with his claims. And in the New Testament of Christianity, Jesus of Nazareth had concretized the divine command in what Christians came to call the Great Commission: "Go ye therefore, and teach all nations, baptizing them in the name of the Father, and of the Son, and of the Holy Ghost" (Matt. 28:19). It followed that those who made their commitment to the creator God through the Word of Jesus should seek to render other Gods obsolete by bringing all people to acknowledge the Christian gospel and to serve the Christian God.

Protestant Christianity, of course, inherited this monotheism and the Great Commission. Moreover, the Reformation supplied a missionary impulse of its own. To make way for its message in lands already considered Christian, the Reformers and their followers had to announce, exhort, convince, and persuade. They must, they thought, alert those already reared in a Christian setting to the deficiencies in their Christianity. It was true that, to some extent, one version of Calvinist teaching dampened this enthusiasm for mission: if God from all eternity had predestined certain individuals to be saved and others to be condemned or damned, mission effort seemed a less all-encompassing requirement. Yet however convincing that view might appear in Europe, in America the realities and demands of a new situation altered the equation. So, after a time, did the evolving sense of selfhood that characterized many American religious leaders.

Furthermore, the specifically Puritan background of much of American public culture carried the message that Americans, like the Hebrews of old, were a "peculiar" people. Americans, according to this way of thinking, were divinely blessed, God's new chosen people. And for the descendants of the Puritans and those who shared their mental world, divine choice brought duties and obligations. Living in a nation they saw as favored by God, they felt that they had been commanded by him to occupy the land and, collectively, to transform its non-Christian inhabitants. In short, as Protestant Christianity adjusted itself to the American experience, the mission mind became a guiding force.

That American experience, as lived by the English and by other Europeans who peopled the Atlantic seaboard, translated an ideology of newness. When, in the fifteenth century, the Europeans "discovered" a "New World," their perception of the land awakened a lasting sense of primitive beginning reclaimed. No matter for them that from the Indian point of view the Europeans invaded an old world, and no matter, later, that from an African point of view they created a totalitarian one of bondage. Anglo-Protestants and other free Western peoples were grasped by the imaginative power of their situation. They felt as if they were walking the Garden of Eden again, and the religion they professed began to reflect their sense of new place and time. In the atmosphere of excitement and expectation, theologies of reformation subtly shifted. Ideas about reforming the church seemed, to many, not to have gone far enough, and these conceptions gave way to newly urgent ideas about the church's *restoration*. *Restoring* the church meant — with focused intensity — doing away with the oldness the centuries had brought, wiping away the effects of time, stress, and corruption to uncover an original and "first-time" vitality.

Gone in this vision was change, and gone were adjustment, accommodation, development, and acculturation. In the New World wilderness, Europeans felt that they could reexperience the time when the church was new and strong. In America, they thought, they could restore the ancient order, uneroded by time or change. Later, biblical imagery would be fed by Enlightenment and then Romantic notions that fictively reconstructed stories of the origins of humanity and the innocence and nobility of "savage" (that is, "primitive" or "new") peoples. History would continue to be dubious in the New World garden. And the attraction of religions that promised to restore the way things were in the original time continued to be strong. The mission mind was enlisted to create a religious agenda in which mission became an imperative to restore the church, to reverse the consequences of time.

But if the mission became one of restoring the once-new purity of times past, concern for newness also pulled toward the future. The paradise of the past, in the Garden of Eden and in its New Testament equivalent, the earliest church, was likewise a paradise of the future. It was the New Jerusalem envisioned and prophesied in the last book of the Christian New Testament, the Book of Revelation, or Apocalypse. According to the predictions of the book as read by Anglo-Protestants and their coreligionists, the second coming of Jesus was linked to a new age, radically different from the current dispensation. As we saw in the last chapter, Protestants believed that the coming of the new age would bring the dawn of the millennium, a 1,000-year period during which Satan, or the devil, would be chained up, and peace and prosperity would prevail.

As centuries passed, people engaged in theological reflection in America seemingly never wearied of speculating on the exact sequence of events that would surround the coming of the millennium. And in time, the mood of intense expectation that accompanied such theologizing was separated from an explicitly Christian scenario. But this is to get ahead of the story. Important now is the observation, already suggested in the preceding chapter, that from the time of the Puritans, millennialism beckoned new Americans toward the time to come even as restorationism drew them toward a past that had been perfect.

Pushed and pulled between past and future, Americans found it easy to live in a mental world colored by narratives and ideologies that reinvented former times and reconstituted dreams of what lay ahead. Church life reflected the polarities of American imagination, and the mission mind spun out its projects as Protestant experience pointed in both directions and found in them little disparity.

Mission on the Home Front

The mission mind was all-encompassing in Protestant America. In fact, it was so inclusive that mission began at home. Even for people who had grown up in a Protestant culture, even for those exposed from childhood to family influences that promoted the religion of Jesus, there was room for the work of the mission mind. All the more so for those children of the Europeans who had left the supports of Christian culture behind them to stake a claim in the new lands to the west or to lose themselves on the urban frontiers of burgeoning industrial cities. The deficiencies that the mission mind discovered in the Christianity of all of these people provided important reasons for revivalism to grow and flourish. As a practiced technique — and art — for evangelizing large groups, revivalism functioned as a tool of the mission mind.

To "evangelize" meant, literally, to "gospel" the masses, to bring the New Testament Word to people thought to be in need of it. Derived from the Greek *euangelion*, an evangel was "good news" and "gospel." And the people who brought the gospel became, by the nineteenth century, proponents of evangelical culture. As heirs to the Puritans with their sectarian concern for purity of scriptural word and equal purity of personal commitment, evangelicals insisted on both. They continued to exalt the Bible and to promote a culture that was based on it. And they continued to underline the importance of personal experience by teaching the doctrine of the "new birth." Being "born again" (as the twentieth-century phrase recaptures the earlier message) meant, as in the time of the Puritans, having an experience of conversion. Once felt and ratified in the presence of other Christian people, conversion led inevitably, for the evangelical, to the task of mission. The good news needed to be shared, and so the process of converting others could go on and on.

In sum, Bible, new birth, and mission became the identifying marks of evangelical culture. The mission mind was, in fact, the hallmark of the mainstream Protestant evangelicalism that became, as we will see in Part II, the "one" religion of the nation. And revivalism, already on the scene by the mid-eighteenth century, became a regular and recurrent feature in American life.

Christianizing Relative, Friend, and Neighbor

The mentality that would elicit the revivals was already present in Puritan times. With their doctrine of chosenness and a covenantal relationship with God, the

Puritans, as we have seen, stressed the significance of inner, emotional states. Personal experience of conversion came to be required in religious New England, and when it was not universally and easily present, adjustments were made in church and community polity, as the Halfway Covenant indicated. But the failure, more and more, to produce full members of the church meant that the Puritans felt they faced a generation of unbelievers in their midst. Not only people from another town or social group but even friends and neighbors, even close relatives and children, became targets for mission enterprise. Preaching became not simply an explanation of the gospel to the convinced and an exhortation to renewal in Christian life. More importantly, it became an avenue of outreach to the unconverted, an opportunity to stir the souls of those near and dear whom, as the Puritans understood the issue, God might choose to save.

Given this way of thinking, it was perhaps only a matter of time before New England was swept by religious awakenings, or revivals. But so were the other Atlantic colonies, beginning in some cases even earlier than New England. Americans were influenced, perhaps, by economic factors and frontier conditions as well as by a pervasive Calvinist sense of sin and the separation anxieties that distance from England created. And so the First Great Awakening spread from place to place.

Historian of American revivalism William McLoughlin assigns the years from 1730 to 1760 to the awakening, but its exact time span as a cultural event is difficult to pinpoint. Indeed, as early as 1726 Theodore J. Frelinghuysen (1691–1748?), a Dutch Reformed pastor in New Jersey, stirred his several congregations by his preaching. Soon the neighboring Presbyterians led by Gilbert Tennent (1703–1764) experienced similar religious excitement. Then, at Northampton, Massachusetts, in 1734, the preaching of Jonathan Edwards sparked a like response; the people groaned, sobbed, and sometimes fell before what they considered the power of God. By 1740 the English Methodist evangelist George Whitefield (1714–1770) was traveling through the colonies and fanning the sparks of revival into fire.

Whitefield and Edwards proved to be this awakening's "stars," memorable preachers who stood out among the others for the quality of their work as well as for the theoretical advances that framed it. Under their words and preaching prowess, numbers of colonists experienced the emotional and physical manifestations that were regarded as clear signs of God's presence. Thousands claimed conversion, and revival leaders thought their mission a success.

Whitefield brought a communications revolution with him, for in his attempts—with Methodism's founder, John Wesley (1703–1791)—to reach the factory workers of England he had turned to open-air preaching. Crowds would gather and swell, held by the magnetic oratory of the speaker. Freed from the constraints of a formal sanctuary, they could more spontaneously express their personal feelings and beliefs about sin and divine mercy. Moreover, the fact that the minister who preached was an itinerant, a traveler who moved from place to place, seemed to excite the crowds, too. There was for them a freshness about preaching that fell from the lips of a stranger, and the newness brought religious excitement in its train.

The vividness of Whitefield's rhetoric as he worked the crowds was cause enough for fame. But it was Edwards who most clearly provided the theological grounding for the new preaching. Bringing together a basic Calvinism and a philosophical immersion in the thought of John Locke, Edwards believed that understanding came to human beings when their senses were directly affected. The logic of this theory, called "sensationalism," was that the more strongly a person's senses were affected, the more clearly he or she would attain knowledge. Furthermore, Edwards added to the five traditional senses (sight, sound, touch, taste, smell) what he called the "sense of the heart." In the sermons that he preached in his Northampton church and elsewhere, he painted striking pictures of, for example, a sinner hanging like a spider by a thread over the abyss of hell. In this way, he thought, God could use him (Edwards) as a tool to excite in the hearts of the people who heard him an awareness of their true spiritual condition. Then, he reasoned, if God had so chosen, the sinner would be converted.

Others agreed. Throughout the colonies, from all reports, strong emotional response to revival preaching was apparent. Probably 30,000 to 40,000 out of a population of about 1 million fell under the words of a preacher and, for believers, the hand of God. Those who had fallen claimed that afterwards they had been raised to new lives of grace. The new birth, in these latter Puritan days, was becoming a mass experience, and it was also becoming, even more than previously, a community experience.

That trend continued when, several decades after a national political community was forged in the American Revolution, another awakening swept the land. Dated by McLoughlin from 1800 to 1830, the Second Great Awakening carried the eighteenth-century memory of revival into new times. In so doing, it became an occasion for modification and change, for further development of revival technique and — to ground it — revival theory.

In the East, Yale College became the site in 1802 for what seemed to those present a remarkable outpouring of the Holy Spirit under the preaching of Timothy Dwight (1752–1817), the grandson of Edwards. As president of Yale, Dwight conducted services in the college chapel that resulted in the conversion of over a third of the students. Lyman Beecher, whom we met in the last chapter — and who was later at the center of the second awakening — was one of Dwight's students. So was Nathaniel W. Taylor (1786–1858), who became the leading theologian of the early-nineteenth-century revival. Furthermore, ministers from Yale and other schools to which the revival spread carried the flame to their congregations in town or countryside.

In the West, the Great Revival — as it came to be called — provoked excitement among thousands. Often coming from fifty miles or farther, people assembled in huge camp meetings, setting up tents where they could remain for several days. Many times preachers who represented different denominations — Methodist, Baptist, and Presbyterian being the most frequent — spoke at the same meeting. At evening meetings the campground became a sacred space with a raised platform for the preacher in the front, a sinner's "pen" where those overcome with a sense of their sinfulness could pray, and behind them space for the rest of the crowd. Here renowned men like James McGready (1758–1817), Peter Cartwright (1785–1872), and Barton W. Stone (1772–1844) held forth. At these meetings and elsewhere in the new revivals, sin was no longer a secret gnawing at an individual's heart. Rather, it was publicly acknowledged by presence in the pen and by other physical signs. Like Roman Catholics with their sacrament of penance, Protestants had found a way to turn private property into public property. In this frontier setting they no longer had to bear alone what they felt to be the burden of sin.

Reports of meetings such as one at Cane Ridge, Kentucky, in 1801 told of people shrieking, crying, and falling into trance. Some of them could not control their motor functions, and they jerked, danced, or even "barked." Sin, for these believers, meant estrangement from God, and now that estrangement could even become alienation from their own bodies. They themselves understood what was happening to them as manipulation and control by the forces of the Holy Spirit or the forces of the devil. But if all the revivals fed on a human sense of estrangement, here the reasons for estrangement were multiplied. Away from eastern cities and from the comforts of more settled territory, people felt themselves to be on the edge of civilization. On the frontier they were surrounded by Indians and "wilderness" country and isolated by distance from those they had left behind. So it was not surprising that they felt a sense of separation, too, from the Christian God.

It was this sense of separation that the mission mind was designed to overcome. Evangelism became the way to try to create community, a community between God and the sinner and a community of saved sinners with one another. Such a community, preachers hoped, might become a way to control what some of them saw as a dangerous tendency toward religious diversity on the frontier. Mission work, they believed, would help keep doctrine "pure," correcting and maintaining it in prescribed form against the "extravagances" that the "wild" country of the frontier seemed to invite.

And here, too, an important geographical element was added to the millennial thinking that lay beneath the revival work of missionary preachers. Controlling the West, bringing what these Protestant Christians regarded as "civilization" to it, was for them part of the command that came with their sense of being the new chosen people of God. As we will see in Chapter 13, when we examine civil religion, by the middle of the nineteenth century Americans were talking about their "manifest destiny" to spread across the continent. The work of the mission mind in the Great Revival of the West signaled, even earlier, the way in which themes of mission, radically new beginning, and expansionism could come together in powerful religious form. Within the frontier mission mind, ordinary and extraordinary religion were joined, and—in Christian terms—natural and supernatural goals were united.

The West, however, was no distant cousin to the East. Theologically speaking, the western and eastern versions of the Second Great Awakening were teaching the same message. The stern Calvinism of Edwards's day was giving way to — as we saw in the last chapter — Arminian views. The old doctrine of predestination was all but forgotten, and optimistic understandings of the role that people could play in their own redemption came to the fore. The message was that Jesus had died for all, not merely for the chosen few. And the corollary was that if humans truly desired salvation, the grace of God would find a way to do its work. In this context, the mission mind could become still more enterprising and could labor even more actively to convert.

The process was epitomized best during this period in the revival theory and practice of Charles Grandison Finney (1792–1875). Beginning in the mid-1820s, this charismatic leader electrified his congregations in upstate New York, the area known as the Burnt Over district because of the revival fires that swept it clean. Finney later widened his field to preach in eastern cities like Philadelphia and New York, and he eventually moved west to become president and professor of theology at Oberlin College in Ohio. More than any other individual, Finney set the pace for revivalism in the later nineteenth century and in the twentieth century as well. He thought carefully and self-consciously about the role of the preacher in bringing on a revival, and he concluded that revivals were not miracles but the natural products of deliberate means.

Thus, Finney introduced a series of "new measures" that were widely imitated by other revival preachers. His speaking style was far more direct than that of previous generations of revivalists: he used the second-person-singular "you," stared boldly, and pointed his index finger at individuals in the crowd. He spoke spontaneously, without prepared notes, and he was often theatrical in delivering the gospel, using body language to effect. Finney instituted inquiry meetings and prolonged services late into the night. At these "protracted meetings" he set up an "anxious bench" in the front where, as in the sinners' pens of the camp meetings, people could receive special attention to evoke the conversion response. Sometimes when he preached and prayed out loud, Finney called individuals by name if he thought their sinful condition grave; and he also encouraged spontaneous public prayer from members of the congregation, both male and female. In fact, reports of women praying out loud in public at Finney meetings, as well as other Finney innovations, shocked the eastern establishment. But his new measures were destined to become standard techniques for professional revivalists thereafter.

At the same time, in his revivals and later at Oberlin, Finney helped to alter an eroding Calvinism still further. He taught a doctrine of perfectionism in which, by trusting and dedicating themselves through the Holy Spirit, Christians would be empowered to work for social reform. Indeed, Finney's ideas became linked to antislavery sentiment during the era, and Oberlin became known for its stand on abolition and for its openness toward other kinds of reform.

It would not be the last time that links were forged, during the nineteenth century, between revivalism and social change. The mission mind was moving from its concern for the welfare of souls to concern for the welfare of bodies. And as the mission mind did so, American evangelicals were moving more and more toward a sense that the beginning of the millennium was in their hands. Jesus would come indeed, for them, but only at the end of a 1,000-year period of blessing that would be inaugurated by the mission effort of the church.

Meanwhile, as revivalism moved to the cities and became more carefully staged and controlled, unrestrained expression of feelings and undirected body movements became largely the style of the past. This kind of emotional and physical abandon would continue within Protestantism in the holiness and pentecostal movements, while revivalism itself came to favor sentimentality. Responding to an altar call by moving to the front of the congregation or signing one's name to a "decision card" became more normal expressions of inner feeling. The change did not come all at once, but in the "businessmen's revival" of 1857–1858 the new kind of revival was evident. Here business people in the cities held noon prayer meetings, in which prayer, testimony, and hymn singing took the place of a sermon. In the meetings religious passion had been socialized in such a way that it was expressed within narrower bounds and an urban class-based propriety ruled.

In some sense, this milder form of revivalism became a challenge to the mission mind. For, as the years passed, Calvinism was disappearing, and so was reference to hell. In the new kind of revivalism, the joys of heaven were stressed in revival hymns that were also tinged with domestic themes of heaven as "home." But how could fervor be maintained without the forbidding specter of hell? How could beliefs about the anguish of the sinner and the joy of the convert be orchestrated if a Calvinist sense of opposites was undercut? The answer came in a dramaturgy of the preacher that was incorporated into the revival format after the Civil War. And the man who became the greatest technician of the new form was Dwight L. Moody (1837–1899).

In Moody, urban revivalism had its most successful innovator, and the late nineteenth century, its most important revivalist. Unlike earlier leaders of the revivals, Moody was a layperson, not an ordained minister. In the 1870s and thereafter he promoted his revivals with shrewd business judgment and dramatic skill. An advance team would precede his arrival in a city, publicizing the revival and generating interest and excitement. At the revival event itself, the famed gospel singer Ira D. Sankey (1840–1908) accompanied him, and the two worked closely to insure the outcome of their meetings. Although carefully staged, Moody's sermons were masterly testimonies to the simple style, filled with Bible stories, anecdotes of home and family, and continuing themes of salvation. Nonintellectual, sentimental, and nostalgic, Moody urged his hearers to a conversion as easy as accepting Christ and filling out a decision card. He wanted his converts to join a church, but which one did not concern him so long as the denomination was evangelical. Salvation for him was joyful, not tortuous, and the Christian life was a surrender to a loving Jesus, not an initiation into theological abstraction.

It was a persuasive, if conservative, message. Bankrolled by wealthy business figures, Moody's revivalism created a world of down-home religious comfort that helped to keep urban dwellers content and attached them more firmly to the middle-class values they already held. For the converts, the content of both hymns and sermons suggested their yearning for a sanctuary where they could feel secure in the midst of urban confusion. The mission mind eased both the spiritual sense of estrangement that came with the notion of sin and the social sense of estrangement that came with urban life. In the large and faceless crowd of strangers at a revival, hymns and sermons brought decision for Christ, feelings of moral purification, and — in the revival moment — an immediate community based on shared emotion.

Twentieth-century revivalism generally followed the path that Moody charted. Early in the century the master revivalist was William A. (Billy) Sunday (1862–1935), a former baseball player who captivated audiences with gestures and antics mimicking the sport, along with slang and colloquial speech. Sunday brought the revival's dramaturgy to new heights as, from 1912 to 1918, his popularity came to a peak. In place after place he preached sermons weaving together themes of fundamentalism and Prohibition (of alcohol) with hostility toward modernists and, in the shadow of the First World War, toward the Germanic enemies of America. God, home, and motherhood became a new trinity, while Sunday enthusiastically affirmed the virtue of patriotism by waving the American flag from his pulpit. Once more, his revivals brought to legions of somewhat bewildered middle-class Americans a haven where they need not feel threatened by the alien world around them.

With the preaching of William F. (Billy) Graham (b. 1918) in the second half of the century, revival dramaturgy adapted to a new time and technology. Revivals became more restrained and media-oriented, but revivalism remained, in many ways, the same. From 1947 and on into the final decades of the century, Graham used radio, film, and television to bring people to their "hour of decision." He became the friend of presidents, his evangelical conservatism in the earlier decades interwoven with a political conservatism as thoroughgoing. But, loyal to President Richard M. Nixon (b. 1913), he was deeply embarrassed when Nixon's guilt in the Watergate scandal of the early seventies became clear, and thereafter he grew more circumspect. By the eighties he was speaking out against nuclear war and, until the war in the Persian Gulf, advocating a peace stand. Graham had begun by preaching that the end of the world was coming soon, entwining mission with millennialism in a familiar American theme. Then in his political middle years his message shifted, as he supported a government establishment based on the belief in the continuance of a strong and thisworldly America. But Graham's antinuclear advocacy mostly returned him to a transformed version of the initial millennialism. For Graham, the world would end soon—unless Americans claimed responsibility and, if they took up weapons of war, did so only for the most just of causes and only without recourse to nuclear means.

To single out Graham and a few earlier revival leaders, though, must not lead us to ignore the pervasiveness of the mission mind in its revival form. Evangelical women, like the popular nineteenth-century lay revivalist and holiness teacher Phoebe Palmer (1807–1874), made their impact, too, differing in style but similar in aims, methods, and effects to evangelical men. And there were thousands upon thousands of revival preachers in the history of evangelical Protestantism in the United States. Revivals seemed to follow one another cyclically, with the religious history of America almost a history of the revivals' waxing and waning. Revivals heightened millennial fervor, and they also encouraged the efforts of those who sought to restore the church. But for restorationists and others, revivals were only instruments, useful for a time but preparations for a more lasting state of affairs. Religious ferment for them required more permanent form if religion was to maintain its role as a significant factor in American culture. In the end, they felt, the mission mind needed a less elusive form of expression: it needed the solidity that organizations give.

Institutionalizing the Mission Mind

The mission mind entered its era of evangelical growth and ascendancy in the nineteenth century, and it is to the eve of that century that we turn to take up our story. By 1790 the new United States had entered a time of rapid development. The population in that year was some 4 million, with one out of every twenty people living west of the Appalachian Mountains. By the time of the Civil War (1861–1865), there were over 30 million people in the country, and about half of them had left the eastern seaboard for new settlements to the west. Church membership, meanwhile, increased ten times from 1800 to 1850, and whereas in 1800 probably only one out of every fifteen persons was a Protestant church member, by 1850 one out of seven belonged to a Protestant church.

A series of voluntary societies sprang up during the period, fueled by a missionary sense of need to bring people to the churches. In this context, the American Home Missionary Society, founded in 1826 as a cooperative venture of Congregational, Presbyterian, and Reformed Christians, was a sign of the times. Flanked by the American Bible Society, the American Sunday School Union, the American Tract Society, and other groups (see the discussion in Chapter 12), the mission society tangibly expressed the commitment of the mission mind. The society sought to organize churches, to support settled ministers in them, and to encourage congregations to bear more and more of the expense of maintaining their minister. Thus, the American Home Missionary Society and the other voluntary agencies that expressed the mission mind pointed, finally, toward the denominations. But as the numbers multiplied in Protestant church pews, all denominations did not benefit equally from the increase. Overwhelmingly the era was a time of Methodist expansion.

Methodists, in fact, numbered well over 1 million by 1850. They formed far and away the largest American Protestant congregation, with the Baptists trailing them by some 500,000. When we consider that the Methodist church had been organized only in 1784, this is an impressive record of growth. And when we look more closely, we can see that the Methodists achieved their success for at least two reasons. First, their religious message fit the mood of Americans in the nineteenth century, entwining concern for mission with perfectionism, millennial optimism, and restorationist themes. Second, Methodist organization was well adapted to new conditions on the frontier and also to more settled areas in the East.

As we saw in the last chapter, there had been an erosion of Calvinist belief among numbers of Protestants even in colonial times. In New England, for example, the character of preaching gradually changed so that ideas of divine sovereignty and human predestination gave way before emphases on morality and, by the end of the eighteenth century, the universal availability of salvation. As people continually experienced success in building up a new country, they found it hard to believe that they could not also succeed at winning their own salvation. So the new style of preaching suited their situation, and new churches like the Universalists and Unitarians appealed to the same dynamic. Like these congregations but with far more numerical success, Methodists—with their teachings of free will, human perfectibility, and universal salvation—were telling Americans what they wanted to hear.

Methodist spirituality and worship were also attractive. John Wesley, Methodism's founder, had been a loyal member of the Church of England and for years saw his movement as part of that church. The hymns that he used in his services were sacramental in their understanding of a eucharistic presence, and he urged Methodists to take communion frequently. But in America these high-church tendencies disappeared, and greater stress was placed on the Bible and on preaching.

Wesley himself had told his American followers that they were at liberty "simply to follow the Scriptures and the Primitive Church." And Americans apparently heeded. It was as though their Wesleyan preachers, cast in what they saw as a "primitive" landscape, rediscovered the earliest Christian church. The formal and elaborate ritual of communion became infrequent and, perhaps in its place, more intimate and communal love feasts became the rule. Whereas the banquet of the Lord's Supper in which the bread of communion was broken and shared was surely scriptural, the spontaneity of the love feast seemed, to Methodists, to capture more clearly the gospel spirit. Moreover, it was a *Protestant* gospel spirit, for the love feast was a banquet of the Word, in which testimonies and witnessings were mingled to create what Methodists called a "melting time." By sharing personal experiences of what they regarded as the power of God and the compassion of Jesus, Methodists thus encouraged one another.

The Circuit Preacher. This lithograph by A. U. Waud appeared in *Harper's
Weekly* in 1867. By that time, the circuit rider had become a national symbol of
religion on the frontier, as Edward Eggleston's novel *The Circuit Rider* (1873)
also suggests.

Methodist zeal for scripture and for modeling the apostolic church found
full expression in new forms of organization. Indeed, the very name "Methodist"
suggests the importance of organization in the evolving Methodist societies.
Methodists were people who were taught to live by a rule, or method, and
Wesley's efforts to structure his movement were part of his legacy to the American church. By 1784, when the Methodist Episcopal Church in America became
an independent entity, it acknowledged two superintendents, or — as they later
were called in an echo of early church polity — "bishops." Thomas Coke (1747–
1814), appointed by Wesley himself, was the first of these, but he was soon joined

by Francis Asbury (1745–1816), whose designation by Wesley was ratified through his election by American Methodist ministers.

Under these and later bishops, the American church was divided into districts. Each district had its presiding elder and, in turn, was carved into circuits, huge areas over which traveling preachers, such as the one who in fiction converted Patty Lumsden, would ride. Preachers aimed to visit Methodists regularly in their far-flung territory. In the interim, in each circuit there were local units called classes, and it was these that the circuit riders visited as they could. But classes conducted worship largely on their own. They met weekly to encourage and to strengthen one another, prayed, studied scripture, and offered testimony. When they could find one, they turned to the services of a lay exhorter, who would preach the gospel and hearten them in their efforts. In short, in the institution of the class, a structure was at hand that could enable Methodists to improvise on a biblical base. The class could perpetuate the mood of new beginning, of self-starting piety and intense personal commitment, that for Methodists evoked the church of apostolic times.

That same impulse toward improvisation on a biblical base was present for Methodists ministers in the structure of the conference. To be a "fully connected" minister meant not merely ordination but also membership in a general conference. Here early Methodism conducted its ecclesiastical business, but here it also experienced times of revival and emotional fervor. In fact, it was only when the camp meetings became the acknowledged sites for revival that conferences turned primarily to legal business. And general conferences were joined by district and annual ones, so that the structure of conference became, for preachers, as all-encompassing as classes for the laity. Methodists, in sum, had successfully institutionalized the mission mind, and their nineteenth-century expansion was one result.

The nineteenth century, therefore, has been called the Methodist era because it was the time when Methodism became the predominant form of American Protestantism. But Methodism also gave its name to the period because it was a generic name for the religious style that swept Protestantism. The older, Puritan form of evangelicalism was yielding to a new, more popular version. Even with their experiential concerns, Puritans had been theological sophisticates who delighted in the well-thought and well-turned sermon. One sign of their predilection was the fact that seven years after their landing, the Massachusetts Bay Puritans founded Harvard College (1836) for the education of a learned ministry. Moreover, Puritans continued to be exercised over theological questions throughout the eighteenth century, and new schools such as Yale (1701) and Andover (1808) were founded because of theological differences. Something of the spirit of John Calvin and his carefully trained legal mind continued in the fundamental appeal to the intellect that characterized a Puritan sermon.

In the nineteenth century, however, it was the mission mind that took precedence over the legal mind of Calvin and the intellectual discourse of the Puritans. Although the Methodists, Baptists, and other major denominations were zealous in founding schools, Protestant Christians also moved more and more away from an intellectual gospel, often preferring the emotional and the experiential. The mission mind permitted theological inattention and a general nonintellectualism, while it fostered sentimental piety and religious individualism. For it was in strongly felt emotion that the mission mind found the springs for action. Hence, the great symbol for the era became the frontier camp meeting.

It was not surprising that the revivals benefited the Methodists most of all, because the revival model fit the teaching of Methodism. Wesley had believed that true religion did not consist in mere intellectual assent to Christianity but, rather, in a felt experience of holiness. Methodist leaders and followers in America agreed. Conversely, revivalism spread a "Methodist" style of religion among other Protestant groups. Hence, we need to look at other groups, too, in order to trace the pattern of evangelical growth. We need to examine the forms in which the mission mind became allied more and more with themes of millennialism and restoration.

Such alliances produced a number of new religious groups in Protestant America. Largest among them was the group that organized in 1832 as the Disciples of Christ, even though its founders — calling themselves "Christians" — did not originally intend to start a new denomination. These leaders, in fact, drew on previous religious ideas and organizations promoting a return to New Testament Christianity. Eighteenth- and nineteenth-century Britain had already spawned groups of restorationist sentiment, and immigration to America brought religious leaders who carried restorationism with them. As early as the post-Revolutionary era, some were preaching the need to follow strict New Testament practice and to abolish the creeds and confessions that divided Protestants into sects and denominations. These ideas were congenial to a new and democratic society that, by cutting its ties with Europe, seemed to be cutting its ties with history in order to begin civilization afresh in the New World "wilderness." Moreover, restoration ideas seemed to point to a way to inaugurate the millennium, for the early church stood symbolically for purity, for the perfection that existed before the corruptions of time had tarnished it. In this conception, last days and first days were the same: the circle would be complete if Americans could restore the wholeness of the beginning. For then, according to belief, the end could surely come.

Already in the 1790s in the Methodist church, rejection of the role of the bishop had led to the departure of a group of Virginia and North Carolina ministers who, by 1794, were calling themselves the Christian Church and proclaiming the Bible their only creed. By the turn of the century, among New England Baptists, a "Christian" movement spread, with the foundation of independent Christian churches and the publication, from 1808, of the earliest religious newspaper in America, the *Herald of Gospel Liberty*. The New England and Virginia–North Carolina Christians were loosely joined in 1820 in the Christian Connection, and when this church formed a general conference in 1831, it contained a significant western faction, members of the Stone movement to be described below. By that time on the western frontier, some churches of Baptist provenance held to restorationist ideas, and many eventually came into the Disciples of Christ with hardly any theological or organizational changes. And in the German Reformed Church, a restorationist movement begun in 1825 by John Winebrenner (1797–1860) led to the establishment of the Church (or Churches) of God.

The largest impetus to an organized restorationism came, however, from the two movements that finally amalgamated to produce the Disciples. Barton W. Stone (1772–1844), who led the first of these movements, was a child of the revival. A Marylander and, by 1796, a Kentucky Presbyterian, he had moved freely in Methodist company during a period of time spent in Georgia. In the camp meetings of the Great Revival, he experienced the fervor of Methodist and Baptist preaching, alongside the Presbyterian. Then in the wake of the Cane Ridge revival of 1801, Stone was questioning the Presbyterian Westminster Confession, with its message of predestination and limited atonement. He became part of a group of revival ministers formally suspended by the Synod of Kentucky in 1803. The group banded together in what they called the Springfield Presbytery, but before ten months had passed they produced "The Last Will and Testament of the Springfield Presbytery." In this document, a landmark of restoration thinking, they officially dissolved their organization to take the Bible as "the only sure guide to heaven." They called themselves "Christians," and they read the Bible as endorsing an Arminian theology and an independent congregational style of church government. The message was evidently attractive, for "Christian" strength gained quickly in Kentucky even as the movement spread to nearly all of the Presbyterian churches in the southeastern part of Ohio. Indeed, by 1830 some 10,000 "Christians" could be counted.

Alexander Campbell (1788–1866), who led the second movement that joined in the Disciples of Christ, had grown up in northern Ireland but in 1809 joined his father, Thomas Campbell (1763–1854), in America. The elder Campbell had come two years earlier and settled in Washington, Pennsylvania, where he accepted a position as pastor in a Seceder Presbyterian church there. But Thomas Campbell's open communion service prompted charges of heresy, and after formal suspension from a church synod he and others began to meet in a body they called a "Christian Association." Campbell announced what became a dictum and byword for the later restoration movement: where the scriptures spoke, he and other Christians should speak; where the scriptures were silent, they should be silent, too. Once again, biblical beginnings were being underlined, and the new order was understood as a restoration of the old.

Alexander Campbell, at twenty-one, had already been drawn to restorationist ideas, and he eagerly embraced his father's views as he became aware of them. By 1812, when the independent Brush Run Church was established, he became its minister and then the leading force in the movement. He taught baptism by immersion as New Testament practice, and by 1815 his church was accepted into the Redstone Baptist Association. In time, Campbell began publishing a magazine to spread his views, but his *Christian Baptist* (1823) gave place in 1830 to *The Millennial Harbinger* when his association with the Baptists came to a formal end. The title of the journal was significant, for it pronounced the link between the recovery of "primitive" Christianity and the coming of the millennium. Meanwhile, those who followed the new movement probably numbered 12,000 by 1830. Like Campbell, they were estranged from Baptist roots by growing theological differences, and like him they would find common cause with the followers of Stone.

Unlike Stone, Campbell was a rationalist, and he had already acquired a reputation for religious debate with opponents. Yet he and his movement shared in numerous ways with the heirs of the revival among the Stonites. Campbell first met Stone during a visit to Kentucky in 1824, and the two leaders noticed their similarities. The name "Disciples of Christ" originated from Campbell, as did the rationalistic tenor of the denomination that emerged in 1832 after leaders of the two groups joined. The Disciples' belief that baptism came before the remission of a person's sins also prevailed in the new church. But the emphasis on restoring the New Testament church, the rejection of creeds as nonscriptural and as obstacles to union, the endorsement of congregational organization — all of these brought Campbellites and Stonites together. From 1830 to 1860 Disciple farmer-preachers spread their message, fanning out from Ohio, Virginia, and Kentucky toward the west. They met Methodist and Baptist competition head on, employing their rationalist inheritance to do so. Some of them, in fact, founded colleges and academies, and by 1849 the Disciples were also beginning the American Christian Missionary Society. At the time of the Civil War, so persuasive had the Disciples become that they numbered 200,000 members.

If there were Baptist and Presbyterian roots for the "Christian" movements that became the Disciples of Christ, Baptists and Presbyterians were hardly eclipsed by the young denomination. Baptist farmer-preachers, though not so mobile as Methodist circuit riders, had spread the revivals in the South and West, bringing to their message a blend of attachment to the older Calvinistic theology and disdain for seminary education. Not so itinerant as the Methodists, Baptists were also not so organized, and their unity came largely on an informal basis. Baptist organization meant independence for each local congregation, but groups of congregations came together in regional associations. Similarly, missionary work brought Baptists together as they formed societies to advance publishing, educational, reform, and philanthropic goals.

Baptist churches often established missionary societies independent of their regional associations, thus laying the groundwork for a denominational mission bureaucracy. In 1832 the American Baptist Home Mission Society came into being to help in the creation of churches and schools and to evangelize Indian peoples and other unchurched individuals. The work of the society eventually extended from the Midwest to the Southwest, to the Rocky Mountain area, and even to the Pacific Coast. Moreover, as the efforts of its home mission society already suggest, Baptists, like Methodists and other Protestant Christians, founded schools to advance their views. The roster of Baptist colleges and seminaries with at least partial ties to the pre–Civil War period is long and distinguished, including such present-day universities as Brown, Baylor, Colgate, and the University of Chicago.

Yet cooperative efforts did not preclude divisions among the Baptists. And the restorationist impulse was at the root of at least one such split. The language of the Landmark Baptist movement (as it came to be called), aimed against non-Baptist groups, evoked the "primitivism" of the early Christian church. As preached by James R. Graves (1820–1893) and his followers James M. Pendleton (1813–1891) and Amos C. Dayton (1811–1865), Landmarkism sought to follow the scriptural dictum to "remove not the ancient landmark, which thy fathers have set" (Prov. 22:28). For these Baptists, the "landmark" meant historic Baptist rejection of other churches and their ministers because they were not considered true representatives of New Testament Christianity. But the new situation that provoked concern for old "landmarks" was complex. It included the growing religious pluralism of the times, the revival-driven evangelical cooperation of Baptists, on the frontier and elsewhere, with other groups, and the formation — dominated by eastern interests — of interdenominational benevolent and missionary societies.

Building on themes that had stirred the Separate Baptists of New England and then the South, Graves first used his position in Nashville, Tennessee, as editor of the *Baptist* to attack non-Baptist churches, their practice of infant baptism, and what he termed their "alien immersions." In 1851 he organized a huge meeting at Cotton Grove, Tennessee, that promulgated a series of stringent resolutions. The five Cotton Grove Resolutions sought to maintain the purity of Baptist churches by increasing their self-segregation from other religious groups. In effect, the resolutions turned self-conscious separation into a doctrinal test of primitivism and, so, religious orthodoxy.

Landmarkism stressed its conviction that the New Testament provided a clear blueprint for church organization and that true churches had always existed in a line without interruption from the first-century church to the present. Unlike invented and humanly contrived churches, Landmarkists taught, true churches were structurally identical to the original church of Christ. Nor were true churches universal entities spread over the globe. Rather, said the Landmarkists, they were particular manifestations of the church of Christ in a given place and time. On these premises, the Landmark movement grew and flourished throughout the South, becoming during the second half of the nineteenth century the most powerful voice in the Southern Baptist Convention (organized in 1845 in the context of tensions that led to the Civil War). Landmarkism was especially strong in the old Southwest, and even in the later twentieth century its influence could still be felt among Southern Baptists, especially in rural places in the middle South and the lower Mississippi Valley.

Trying to restore the old landmarks had put Baptists in touch, in a technical sense, with antimission sentiment, a feature from the 1820s and 1830s of the

Calvinist wing of their denomination. The antimission movement based itself theologically on a strict predestinarian teaching that precluded missionary work because God had already determined who would be saved and who, condemned. But antimission talk and theology provided symbolic expression for fears of loss of local control. Mission opponents worried that new overarching societies, often dominated by easterners, would erode their ability to stand autonomously, to give particular and individual witness to Christianity as communities of neighbors. At a certain point, even Alexander Campbell of the Disciples had been a leader in the antimission movement until he moved on to a position endorsing voluntary mission societies. Thus, restoration "primitivism," especially in the Baptist case, became entangled with the language of antimissionism.

But this fact should not obscure another: antimission rhetoric often cloaked the abiding concerns of the mission mind. As the nineteenth century progressed, even the most adamant Calvinist faced a religious culture that had softened under the Arminian message. Revivals, after all, were Arminian means, and a revival climate, such as existed on the southern and western frontier, promoted the mission mentality. In these terms, what opposition to missions really meant was conviction that missions should be local efforts directed to one's friends and neighbors. In other words, missions should not be universal or organized in large and impersonal mission societies but instead should be designed to bring the near and dear into the true — and local — church. Baptists throughout the South identified with either the primitivist or, opposed to it, the missionary movement within their tradition. But in fact, each side of the divide was united in adherence to mission thinking. Only the form of mission thinking was different.

Moreover, if the primitivist movement within the Baptist fold was particularly aggressive in promoting restorationist thought, it was only exaggerating what other Baptists also believed. Baptist churches, they thought, were New Testament churches, founded by Christ and removed from the corruptions that had entered Christianity during the fourth century or at other points in Christian history. Equally important, for Baptists as for other evangelical Christians, first times were also end times. What happened in New Testament times, they anticipated, would unfold again, and — in a heightened atmosphere of millennial expectation — restoring the true church would inaugurate the new age.

Presbyterians, for example, did not disagree about this general pattern, only about its particulars. Thus, they claimed that their denomination had restored the ancient pattern of church government. For them, the combination of individual autonomy and the larger authority of presbyteries (district bodies with legal authority) and synods (assemblies made up of members of several presbyteries) faithfully followed the New Testament charter. And Presbyterians believed, too, that they maintained true doctrine, reiterating what the Bible taught for their times. In the years after the Civil War and into the twentieth century, however, it is in other new nineteenth-century groups that we can see, especially strongly, the work of the mission mind.

Much of what happened during the post–Civil War era involved the resurgence of premillennial thinking, the belief that Jesus would come *before* the millennium to inaugurate it. While we will look again at premillennial thinking in Chapters 11 and 12, here it is important to note that, as in any form of millennialism, in premillennialism the future was more important than the first times to be restored. All the same, time past and time future were coupled in the religious consciousness of the age. Thus, by 1875 premillennialists were attracting new adherents and preaching their message especially in the form called dispensationalism. Promoted in America by visiting Briton John Nelson Darby (1800–1882), the major leader among the new English group (1831) called the Plymouth Brethren, dispensationalism viewed all of time in terms of distinct ages, or dispensations. During each of the dispensations, according to Darby and his followers, God changed his ways of dealing with human beings. Now, in the nineteenth century, people were living in the penultimate age, the era before the final coming of Jesus that would begin the dispensation of the millennium. But for dispensationalists there was a note of urgency about the times. The millennium, they believed, was imminent. And even though Darbyites also believed that the final events were divinely arranged, they found new work for the mission mind.

In the dispensationalist view, none of the biblical prophecies regarding the end had been fulfilled, but they soon would be. For dispensationalists, the world was growing steadily more evil, the Antichrist would soon control it, and after this period of tribulation, Jesus would return, conquer the Antichrist, and establish his kingdom for 1,000 years. Meanwhile, the members of the true church would, according to scripture, finally meet Jesus in the air (I Thess. 4:15–17), a "rapture" that, dispensationalists said, would occur before the Antichrist came to rule the world. The times were thought short, and Darby and his followers felt impelled to preach so that members of the church could be gathered in and could discover their places in the New Israel. Still, the message that made everything depend on the dispensations that God had divinely ordained became yet another occasion for the work of the mission mind.

Moreover, perhaps more significant than the exact sequence of predicted events in dispensationalist thought was the emphasis of premillennialists on the literal nature of their beliefs. In a general American culture that stressed materiality and tangibility, popular religious thinking clung to inherited beliefs in the miraculous and joined them to new times and concerns. Religion that mattered, more and more, was religion that brought the symbolic squarely into historical time. A series of paradoxes was afoot. People who were antihistory—who preached first times and last times as, essentially, the only meaningful "moments" in time—were insisting on the historicity of what would happen. People who repudiated the sacraments of Catholicism—in which the material sign was thought to become the literal divine presence it symbolized—were introducing by the back door a sacramental consciousness of their own. And people who rejected the magical world of non-Christian "superstition" among Indians, blacks, and pagans were reinstating a magical mentality in which natural laws, as currently understood, would be overruled.

Through it all, the mission mind continued in its work of spreading the news that evangelical Christians wished to share. Dispensationalism was a strong factor in the growth of fundamentalism and, as well, in the growth of the holiness-pentecostal movement. Although there will be more about fundamentalism in Chapter 11, we need to look here at its relationship to the millennial restorationism of the mission mind. In fact, from a more or less strictly defined theological perspective, such as that offered by intellectual historian Ernest Sandeen, fundamentalism had its early roots in the confluence of two cultural streams, one of them premillennial dispensationalism.

Dispensationalist views were spread by a series of summer Bible conferences held at Niagara, Ontario, beginning in 1868. Here a group of conservative evangelicals hammered out their millennial response to the challenges of science and modernity and to the perceived threat of liberalism within Protestant ranks. Their meetings flourished, especially from 1883 to 1897. Those who attended joined to their premillennialism a commitment to rationalistic study and interpretation of the Bible. They took their ideas from the so-called Princeton Theology, the form of biblical interpretation taught by Charles Hodge (1797–1878) and others at Princeton Theological Seminary for the major part of the nineteenth century. In this Princeton understanding, shaped by the new prestige of science during the era, the Bible was seen as a scientific book of facts. Its "scientific" concreteness, therefore, promoted both literalism and regard for its inerrancy. Hence, the literalism that we have already seen as a dispensationalist legacy was fostered, from another side, by Princeton rationalism.

There is much more that can be said about the roots of fundamentalism, however, and we can only scratch the surface here. Understood in a social framework, such as that provided by church historian George Marsden, fundamentalism was and is a Protestant evangelical religious movement that came to national prominence in the 1920s. And it was characterized, most notably, by its militance and antimodernism. With sources in revivalism and the nineteenth-century holiness movement (to be examined below) as well as in the theological traditions identified by Sandeen, the mark of fundamentalism was, especially, its social style. In fact, as the child of American revivalism, fundamentalism acted out its flight from modernity in its own sense of the mission to restore.

That mission to restore was evident in fundamentalism's very name, used self-consciously by Curtis Lee Laws (1868–1946) in a 1920 editorial in the *Baptist Watchman-Examiner*. Laws rejected designations like "Landmarker" or "premillennialist" for those who, he said, still clung to "the great fundamentals." Moreover, his choice was likely enhanced by the continuing success of the twelve small volumes called *The Fundamentals*, published between 1910 and 1915 with the leadership and financial support of the California oil magnate Lyman Stewart (1840–1923) and his brother Milton (1838–1923). Since the late nineteenth century, conservative Protestant evangelicals had been expressing their need to restore the "fundamentals" of their faith, to promote in doctrinal terms the quest for purity expressed in other plans to return to New Testament Christianity. In 1878, for example, the meeting of the Niagara Bible Conference produced a "Niagara Creed" enumerating fourteen such fundamentals of the faith. In 1910 the Northern Presbyterian Church, in the meeting of its General Assembly, listed five. And the booklets that were *The Fundamentals*, although they cited many, were in time popularly understood to affirm a somewhat similar set of five.

This short list thus varied from statement to statement but usually included the inerrancy of the scriptures, the divinity of Jesus, his birth from a virgin, his death on the cross in substitution for the sins of all human beings, and his bodily resurrection and imminent second coming. In this form and in all of the forms in which the fundamentals were announced, they brought to conservative evangelical Protestantism a new insistence on supernaturalism and on absolute surety. This emphasis was especially clear in the concern that conservative evangelicals expressed for scriptural inerrancy. The new doctrine, different from an earlier common evangelical belief that the Bible was inspired and therefore unlike every other book, froze the biblical text so that *all* of its words were seen as guaranteed by the authority of God. Not only was the Bible verbally inspired, fundamentalists said, in its original "autographs," or manuscripts, the Bible avoided error in every historical allusion or statistic, in every quotation or expression of cosmological opinion.

Moreover, the doctrine of inerrancy was linked to a sharp emphasis on the interpretation of biblical prophecy regarding end-time events. Thus, belief in inerrancy became the wall of a fortress, as it were, built to defend the past (as conservatives understood it) from the onslaughts of the present. In this context, the premillennialism of the fundamentalists rejected the assumption of continual human betterment, the message of the age of progress in which, before World War I, the nation had flourished. Instead, in familiar dispensationalist terms the fundamentalists taught that the world was swiftly worsening and that only the power of Jesus in his second coming could save the elect. With its hardheaded dogmatism that argued closely from the biblical text, fundamentalism understood the Bible in terms that for them broke difficulties that science and the modern world — and other Protestants who were liberals — presented. The Word of God was triumphant for fundamentalists. Their mission to restore the Bible to its place of former glory was also a mission to announce the end.

Fundamentalist militance in the 1920s brought its own end, too, in the sense of public attention and respect. Both the climax and the close of the early period of fundamentalist success came in 1925 with the much-reported Scopes trial. John T. Scopes had been accused of violating a Tennessee law that forbade the teaching of — to quote the statute — "the theory that denies the story of the divine creation of man as taught in the Bible." Although liberal Christians would object that the theory of evolution did no such thing, the trial became a forum for expounding fundamentalist and opposing liberal views of the Bible in the context of contemporary science. Scopes had certainly violated the law, and on narrow legal grounds the issue was clear. But the American Civil Liberties Union provided his defense, with Clarence Darrow (1857–1938) squaring off against fundamentalist champion William Jennings Bryan (1860 — 1925). Common report had it that the fundamentalists won the battle but lost the war. At any rate, the years following the Scopes trial were times of regrouping and quieter growth for fundamentalists. It was as if, in cultural terms, they were spent by their mission to banish the symbols of the modern age. Fundamentalists were, for the time being, wearied by their self-appointed task.

However, fundamentalists were joined by still others in the late nineteenth and early twentieth centuries. From yet another quarter the mission mind found its home among Protestant Christians who also desired to restore an ancient future. Holiness and pentecostal people, like those in the fundamentalist movement, at least partially rejected the world and disdained the meaningfulness of historical time.

In terms of its sources, the holiness-pentecostal movement had major roots in the Methodist doctrine of Christian perfection taught by John Wesley and in the Calvinist Keswick theology of sanctification (named for an English town in which annual religious conferences were held beginning in 1875). For the founder of Methodism, there were two distinct operations of grace to be experienced: justification, which came at the time of conversion, and sanctification, which was the spiritual event that brought perfection with freedom from sin. According to the teaching, the second work of grace, or sanctification, would eradicate a deep-seated sinfulness in human beings, something that Wesley himself seems to have understood in progressive terms. In its American version, however, sanctification came to be viewed as a distinct state, one brought by a clearly defined second-blessing experience of the Holy Spirit. The quest for such perfection, or "holiness" — both the experience and the state — had attracted many to Methodism earlier in the nineteenth century.

At the same time, the revivals of Charles G. Finney, as we have already seen, also spread a form of perfectionism. Instead of a state of sinlessness, however, Finney taught a state of empowerment in work for Christian social causes. This Finneyite — and Reformed — version of Christian perfection through the Holy Spirit helped to create a climate in which the theology emanating from Keswick was readily accepted. In fact, though, Keswick views had been inspired by the teaching of three Americans, William E. Boardman (1810–1886), Robert Pearsall Smith (1827–1899), and his wife, Hannah Whitall (1832–1911). Boardman's book *The Higher Christian Life* (1859) both named and helped to spread the so-called "higher-life" movement, which found its home in Baptist, Congregationalist, and Presbyterian churches. For higher-life advocates and the Keswick movement, conversion was just the beginning of the Christian life. Beyond it, sanctification occurred gradually throughout the course of a person's life, and, in a distinct work of grace, the Holy Spirit empowered an individual for Christian service and mission.

Still another impulse for the growth of holiness and pentecostalism came from the premillennial dispensationalism that we have already met in the teachings of John Nelson Darby. Following his conviction that the present dispensation would give way to a new era of the Holy Spirit, Keswick-oriented Christians saw in the rise, initially, of holiness the first stirrings of events that they associated with the second coming of Jesus. Added to these, in the case of pentecostalism, was a new theology that emphasized faith healing. Expressed and spread by "faith homes" that sprang up in the 1880s and 1890s in the Northeast and Midwest, the new theology was not content with historic Christian practices of praying for the sick and anointing them. Rather, it taught, Christ through his atonement had made physical as well as spiritual healing possible.

If Keswick looked to sanctification and also often the second coming and faith homes hoped for restoration of New Testament healing, both aimed at a perfectionism that they thought the Christian world had lost. They understood their mission as to restore the ancient order of things and so to insure the spiritual dimensions of the future. In the last third of the century, as many Methodist churches grew more formal and restrained in worship, a holiness revival was aiming toward that future. After a holiness camp meeting at Vineland, New Jersey, in 1867, the National Camp Meeting Association for the Promotion of Holiness came into existence. Other holiness organizations followed, and for a while holiness remained within the Methodist church, just as earlier, Methodism had remained within Anglicanism. But the Keswick wing of the movement had no connection to Methodism, and as time passed other problems were created by the formal worship protocols that came with the increasingly middle-class status of Methodism. Finally, unavoidable tensions came to a head. By 1893 and thereafter, various holiness associations either seceded or were expelled from the Methodist church, and holiness began an independent history.

The last seven years of the century brought, too, the rapid spread of premillennial dispensationalism and the new healing theology. According to pentecostal historian Grant Wacker, a large minority among Wesleyans and a majority among Reformed believers within the holiness movement expressed their allegiance to both. In this setting, the more traditional of the holiness people formed congregations such as the Church of the Nazarene and the Church of God (later Church of God, Anderson, Indiana). Meanwhile, a more radical element attracted new followers and became known as pentecostalists, spurred on in their efforts by a rediscovered form of New Testament religious experience.

As early as 1895 a Baptist lay preacher, Benjamin Hardin Irwin (b. 1854), claimed he had experienced a baptism of the Holy Spirit and of fire. Irwin had already been preaching in Nebraska that the second blessing of sanctification might not be a full baptism of the Spirit. Instead, there might be a need for further experience to complete the Spirit's work. Now his own claims of an encounter with the Spirit's fire confirmed the theory for him and others. Although a number of holiness leaders thought that Irwin's message was heresy, Fire Baptized groups sprang up in southern states, in Kansas, Oklahoma, and Iowa, and even in Canada. By 1898 Irwin instituted his Fire Baptized Holiness Association of America in Anderson, South Carolina.

The lines of connection between Irwin's teaching and the emerging pentecostals were real. These pentecostals took their cue from the New Testament writings of Paul and from the account of the descent of the Holy Spirit as tongues of fire at Pentecost (Acts 2:1–20). They sought to receive the baptism of the Spirit with speaking in tongues (a form of ecstatic speech) and the additional scriptural gifts of prayer, prophecy, and healing. Buttressed by these spiritual events, they felt, they would be ready for the imminent return of Jesus.

In the late nineteenth century, there had already been reports of tongues speaking at some holiness meetings. And, as in the case of fire baptism, the new pentecostals may have built on these. But the definitive moment for the pentecostal revival came in Topeka, Kansas, at the turn of the century, after Charles F. Parham (1873–1937) founded Bethel Bible College. Parham had been a Congregationalist, a Methodist, and a member of Irwin's own Fire-Baptized Holiness Association. He knew faith healers, claimed that he had been healed himself, and also could, according to reports, heal others. Parham had already decided that the baptism of the Holy Spirit had as its sign the ability to speak in tongues. Indeed, he thought of the "tongues" as foreign languages, miraculously given to believers so that they could spread biblical teaching in foreign parts. Then, in an atmosphere of what was evidently intense community, students sought the Spirit under Parham's direction until, he claimed, beginning with the century on 1 January 1901, "fire fell." Agnes Ozman, one of the Bethel students, reported a full experience of speaking in tongues.

When Parham opened a Bible school in Houston in 1905, the man who played the largest role in the initial spread of pentecostalism came in contact with him and his teaching. William J. Seymour (d. 1923) was an African-American preacher linked to a radical group of Wesleyans called the Evening Light Saints. As a member of the group, he affirmed total sanctification, miraculous healing through faith, and the restoration of the New Testament gifts of the Holy Spirit as joined to the imminent second coming of Jesus. Now Parham carried to Los Angeles the belief in the baptism of the Spirit with speaking in tongues.

There, the fabled Azusa Street revival held strong from 1906 until 1909, the longest continual revival in American history. In a rented hall that had once been an African Methodist Episcopal church and later a stable and warehouse, Seymour made space for his people, who prayed for the restoration of the gifts of the biblical Pentecost. At first only about a dozen came, but the San Francisco earthquake shocked Californians and encouraged religious interest. Then, although news of the meetings had initially been spread by word of mouth, the *Los Angeles Daily Times* began to cover them as curiosities, and the publicity brought out the crowds. Interracial and multiethnic, the followers of the revival were the first sign of the international scope the movement was to assume. Ethiopians and Chinese, Indians and Mexicans, members of various European nationalities, Jews, and, of course, African-Americans prayed and were mutually convinced of the presence of the Spirit among them. They believed they were living in the power of the first, New Testament, times, and they expected that the second coming of Jesus would be soon.

In this atmosphere of miracle and restoration, the millennial faith of the early pentecostal movement was launched, interracial at its inception. It grew in denominations like the Church of God in Christ (founded in 1897 and turned pentecostal in 1907); the Church of God in Cleveland, Tennessee (founded perhaps as early as 1902 and formally pentecostal by 1910); the Pentecostal Holiness Church (formed by the merger of holiness sects and Presbyterian bodies until it reached its enduring form in 1915); and the Assemblies of God (an amalgam of various groups that constituted themselves the General Council of the Assemblies of God in 1914). Pentecostalism flourished, too, in the International Church of the Foursquare Gospel (formally incorporated in 1927 in Los Angeles under the leadership of the charismatic Aimee Semple McPherson [1890–1944]); in the United Pentecostal Church (officially formed as late as 1945 by so-called "oneness pentecostals" as a non-Trinitarian — "Jesus only" — movement); and in numerous other groups.

Throughout pentecostal history the mission mind thrived within the movement, so that it became a worldwide phenomenon, with more members outside the United States than inside. Determining actual numbers is difficult, but estimates have ranged from several million to as high as 29 million in the United States alone in recent times, and from 50 million to as many as 250 million in the world. According to one 1988 report, there were 176 million members of pentecostal churches throughout the world, with the largest numbers coming from the Third World. And there were more than 22.5 million pentecostal believers in North America.

By turning inward for an experience of holiness and for the ecstasy of the Spirit, the holiness-pentecostal movement paralleled fundamentalism in its rejection of Protestant liberalism. And there were further connections between the two. The holiness-pentecostal movement took the scripture as literally as the fundamentalists did. Moreover, both movements sharply divided the extraordinary from the ordinary world in the doctrine (stressed by fundamentalists) or the experience (emphasized by holiness-pentecostal people) of transcendence. For both movements as they became institutionalized, the Word continued to speak out against the world. Yet, different from traditional Protestantism, the message led mostly, until the late twentieth century, not to the public space where history was made but to private quests for God. Both movements sought to restore scriptural purity to the Christian church, and both saw in restoring the beginning the promise of the end, of the imminent return of Jesus. Preferring to live in extraordinary space and extraordinary time, members of both movements found the need for mission a compelling part of their witness. But there was a distinctively modern and American note about these expressions of Protestantism, and, as we will see in later chapters, some of these views were shared by others who did not count themselves heirs to the Protestant tradition.

Christianizing Nearby Strangers

The mission mind found it imperative to convert relatives, friends, and neighbors. But what of the stranger close to home? Should mission reach out to touch those who were culturally alien but geographically near? Initially, the matter was not clear to evangelical Protestants. Was it appropriate for missionaries to work to convert the strange people they encountered in the New World, whom they named the Indians? Later, with the mass arrival of slaves from Africa, the issue of whether to convert or not became clouded in new ways. Should missionaries turn their resources toward converting African-Americans to Christianity?

For Native Americans, the missionaries of Spain, France, and Britain all served as early emissaries of the mission mind. Indeed, converting the Indians became one expression of the imperialism of various European nation-states. In Chapter 3 we glanced at the efforts of early Roman Catholic missionaries from Spain and France among Indian peoples, and in Chapter 1 we gained some sense of the interaction between Protestant missionaries and the Eastern Cherokee.

But these efforts at conversion took place in the context of extended argument about Indians. In one expression, as early as 1550 in Valladolid, Spain, Juan Ginés de Sepúlveda and the Dominican Bartolomé de Las Casas sparred verbally over whether the native peoples of North America were by nature slaves or whether they were human beings who were fit subjects for Christianization. By this time, the Spanish had already decided that Aztec religion, which featured human sacrifice, was demonic. So it was no surprise when Sepúlveda, championing the ancient Greek philosopher Aristotle with his theory of natural slavery, won the debate. Among French Catholics and English Protestants (our concern here), the issue was as clear. Both peoples understood the Indians as savages and therefore as wild and lawless. Indeed, sometimes both understood Indians as even without the capacity for religion. Thus, Massachusetts Bay Puritans viewed local Algonkian peoples as Satan's "minions" and thought their shamanistic rituals embodiments of evil.

These original opinions did not vanish even if, as time passed, they were expressed with more subtlety. The cultural inferiority of Indian peoples was assumed by English Protestant missionaries (as by the missionaries of other European nations). At best, missionaries believed they would "raise" and "elevate" Native Americans with the twin lights of Western civilization and the Christian message. Or, in another version, they would reclaim the Indians as lost American descendants of the ancient tribes of Israel. Or, more cynically, they would stem the tide of barbarity to make the New World safe for white denizens of Western culture. Yet, shaped as they were by assumptions of white and Western superiority, the missionaries were also responding to another impulse. Converting Indians—despite its dubiousness for many whites—was a structural requirement of the mission mind.

English Protestants made it clear that evangelizing the Indians was one of their intentions in colonizing North America. However, the English were slower and less enthusiastic than the Spanish and French in making good on their plans. Even so, there were some early examples of mission. At Martha's Vineyard and Nantucket, the Mayhews, beginning with Thomas, Jr. (ca. 1620–1657), worked among the Algonkian-speaking Indians for well over a century. Thomas Mayhew learned the local Indian dialect, and the work that he began among individual Indians in 1644 led to a regular mission three years later. With perhaps 282 Indians responding to the evangelical message, he went on to found a school in 1652. In seventeenth-century New England, too, John Eliot (1604–1690) learned the Massachuset language and began to preach in it, also translating the Bible and other works for Indian converts. Eliot settled fourteen villages of "praying Indians" where the Massachuset underwent a profound cultural transformation, learning to live permanently in towns, to sustain themselves almost completely by agriculture, and to read and master Christian catechism.

The eighteenth century brought the First Great Awakening and a new impetus to missionary work. In Lebanon, Connecticut, Eleazar Wheelock (1711–1779) established a boarding school for Indians (unpopular with them because of his attempts to transform them culturally, which they found overbearing). Farther south, although Quaker evangelism among the Delaware Indians in Pennsylvania had not been active or enthusiastic, the Presbyterian David Brainerd (1718–1747) spread Christian teaching among them there as well as in New Jersey and New York. After Brainerd's premature death, his brother John (1720–1781) carried on the New Jersey work among the Delaware for almost thirty years. Meanwhile, the Moravian David Zeisberger (1721–1808) studied the Iroquois language and later lived and worked among the Delaware of Pennsylvania, New York, and Ohio for sixty-four years. His literary productions for his Native American converts were numerous, including German-Onondaga and German-Delaware dictionaries, an English-Delaware speller, various Onondaga and Delaware grammatical works, a hymnbook and a collection of sermons, and translations of Moravian worship services.

As these instances suggest, Protestant missions in British North America were tied to a deep sense of the importance of the Word. For these missionaries Indian languages needed to be mastered, and Indian peoples needed to be taught to read so that the Bible could come to them. Introducing Native Americans to Christianity meant introducing them to Christian first times. For the mission mind, restoration must occur even for those who were initially outside the Christian fold. Beyond that, Christianizing the Indians was a task in keeping with the postmillennial mood that dominated much of eighteenth- and nineteenth-century Protestant culture. For those who were postmillennialists, as we will see further in Chapter 12, the concerted efforts of Protestant Christians were needed to bring on the millennium and, at the end of it, the return of Jesus. Hence, working to bring Indians to Christ would, they believed, help prepare the world for end-time events. The mission mind understood its work as part of this universal plan.

Nor did the mission mind rest solely on the work of individuals. Although earlier missionaries had been commissioned by the British Society for the Propagation of the Gospel in Foreign Parts, by 1787 Americans had formed the interdenominational Society for Propagating the Gospel among the Indians. And by 1817 the American Board of Commissioners for Foreign Missions was supporting Cyrus Kingsbury (1786–1870) in work among the Cherokee. We have already noted that, beginning in 1832, the American Baptist Home Mission Society made mission work among American Indians one of its aims. Later in the century, in 1881, the National Indian Association came into existence. Various denominations produced their mission heroes, such as Baptist Isaac McCoy (1784–1846) and Methodist Jason Lee (1803–1845). Meanwhile, the Civilization Fund, established by the U.S. Congress in 1819 for Indian education projects, distributed federal funds through mission schools.

The issue of Indian Removal — the policy to move Indians west of the Mississippi to make way for white settlement in the Southeast — brought controversy to missionaries, who stood on both sides of the question. And entanglement with government and political questions did not cease with the Trail of Tears when, in the 1830s, members of the Five Civilized Tribes (Cherokee, Creek, Choctaw, Chickasaw, and Seminole) were forced to march to the Oklahoma Territory. Even after the Civil War, for example, churches were invited to put forward the names of individuals who could serve as Indian agents. At that time various denominations were active in supervising some seventy-three Indian agencies until, in the 1880s, belated questions were raised about church–state intimacy.

The twentieth century saw Protestant denominations still at work among native North Americans. Much of their effort, as in the past, was traditional, although there was less emphasis on outright evangelism and more on being available and assisting in need. Still further, there was increasing awareness that cultural imperialism was one continuing legacy of mission work. Cultural contact moved two ways, missionaries more and more emphasized. Indian peoples, they said, had a good deal to contribute to the renewal of Christianity. Yet under these terms some efforts were not fully enthusiastic. Evangelical and pentecostal groups, especially, took up the slack, as older denominations seemed less committed to the mission cause. In this context, by 1979 a survey reported some 120,000 Protestants among Native American peoples, distributed in more than forty denominations and other groups as well. Here the mission mind was working, even as its results were questioned.

If biblical restoration figured in the thinking of missionaries as they met Native Americans and if postmillennial anticipation fueled their efforts, the same was true for Protestant missionaries to African-Americans. It was also true that, as for the Indians, there was hesitation before concerted mission work went forward. In this case, though, it was slaveholders who provided the first line of resistance. If slaves were converted to Christianity, they asked, would baptism make them equal to their masters and thus enslaved unlawfully? They asked other questions, too. Was it right for children of God to continue to hold other children of God as slaves? Conversely, were blacks less than human, as many thought, and thus without souls that could be saved? Would introducing them to Christianity turn them into worse slaves because they would hear the New Testament message of equality ("There is neither bond nor free . . . for ye are all one in Christ Jesus" [Gal. 3:28])? Or again, would the process of catechizing take too much time away from work in the master's service?

In partial answer to these questions colonial legislatures, beginning in 1664 in Maryland, began to serve notice that conversion to Christianity would not alter a slave's material condition. By 1706 five other legislatures had joined Maryland in denying any material and legal effects resulting from the Christian baptism of slaves. Meanwhile, missionaries began to urge the Christianization of slaves, alternately pointing to the religious duty of masters and the advantages of Christianity in producing better, more well-behaved servants. Circumstances thus exerted pressure on missionaries to promote their work as a means of controlling a subject population. By 1727, when Edmund Gibson (1669–1748), Anglican bishop of London, wrote a formal letter to urge the conversion of American slaves, he thought it important to point out "the great value of those servants who are truly religious."

Missionary intentions, though, had been present earlier. Already in 1641 the first baptism of a slave was recorded in New England. On the other side of the Atlantic, the English Puritan Richard Baxter (1615–1691) included in his *Christian Directory* (1673) an exhortation to slave masters to make the salvation of the slaves the chief reason for their purchase and employment. But even though the *Directory* was known in the colonies, New England's Puritans were evidently slow in taking its message to heart. American Puritan leaders such as Cotton Mather rebuked New Englanders for their lack of concern for slaves' souls. And before the end of the seventeenth century, Mather had found enough support to organize weekly meetings for a Society of Negroes. Meanwhile, the same John Eliot who preached to the Indians also announced his willingness to preach to blacks if their masters would agree.

More formally, the Church of England's Society for the Propagation of the Gospel in Foreign Parts, founded in 1701, understood its mission to include American slaves. In the South, however, members of the Anglican clergy — especially in Maryland and Virginia — had more than slaveholder resistance to contend with in their mission attempts. By 1724 they were telling the bishop of London, in response to his queries, that they were hindered by the vast size of the parishes to which they ministered. They also complained of their own small numbers and a lack of support from the law, and they pointed to the cultural divide between themselves and the slaves. Indeed, in the end it was African-Americans themselves who held the key to their religious future. Despite the blatant racism of their masters and the subtler racism of the missionaries, it was they who ultimately decided whether and on what terms they were to be Christian, a story we will take up more extensively in the next chapter.

Results in Protestant missionary efforts among the slaves, however, were entwined with the rise of evangelical religion. Baptists and Methodists, and to some extent Presbyterians, brought a revival version of Christianity to African-Americans. Indeed, the First Great Awakening helped catalyze a new Protestant awareness, a new missionary order, and resulting overtures toward the slaves. For a time in the 1780s, white Protestants in the North and the upper South created almost a popular Christian trend in freeing their slaves. Perhaps their gesture aided the conversion enterprise. At any rate, by 1793 perhaps one-fourth of all Baptists were black, and by 1797 nearly one-fourth of all Methodists were black as well. Nineteenth-century proselytism proceeded under the banner of awakening as poorer, less educated white preachers communicated their New Testament enthusiasm to black listeners. There were numbers of new converts among the slaves, and it was even true that some black preachers arose to preach to racially mixed and, on occasion, to all-white audiences. Still, by 1820 most African-Americans had not been deeply influenced by the Christian message.

In this situation it was the growing division between North and South that provided the context for renewed missionary work. As the Methodist and Baptist churches divided into their northern and southern branches in the mid-1840s, concern for converting the slaves grew apace. The new southern denominations underlined the beneficial effects that Christianization would have on slaves' behavior and amenability to control. Meanwhile, missions spread westward aided by the growing conviction of slave masters that the missionaries were right. With evangelism a self-conscious form of cultural control, the Methodist Mission to the Slaves viewed itself as an alternative to antislavery efforts. Methodist missionary and bishop William Capers (1790–1855) published a catechism and sermon book to assist in the oral instruction of slaves, and circuit riders traveled the South with the tool of the catechism.

At the same time, Baptist groups could persuade African-Americans to come into their churches with their dramatic ritual of baptism by total immersion and with their egalitarian spirit. Indeed, there were more blacks than whites in many Southern Baptist congregations before the war, and the Baptists attracted nearly as many converts as the Methodists did. Presbyterians, too, expended efforts toward slave conversion. In keeping with their heritage of a "learned" ministry and a more intellectual approach to faith, Presbyterian clergy and laity together fostered Sabbath schools to carry forward their conversion effort. And significantly, Presbyterian minister Charles Colcock Jones, Sr. (1804–1863) published a catechism for "colored persons" that appeared in two editions (1837, 1843).

By the eve of the Civil War, the missionaries could look to a slave population in which large numbers were at least nominally Christian, although the great majority of the slaves did not belong to the churches. Moreover, even before the war brought emancipation for blacks, missionary work was proceeding among freed African-Americans. Already in 1846 the American Missionary Association, with Congregationalist roots, joined abolition sentiment with evangelical outreach. From its beginnings in Albany, New York, the association supplied missionaries at home, and by the end of the Civil War it had placed well over 500 missionaries in the South. Meanwhile, it founded as many as twenty schools, among them Fisk University in Nashville and Hampton Institute in Virginia, both in 1866.

The 1860s saw the American Missionary Association joined in its southern efforts by other denominational agencies. Thus, in 1864 the Northern Presbyterians established a church committee for freed African-Americans, and two years later the Methodists followed suit with their stronger Freedman's Aid Society. Perhaps most tellingly, it was the mission mind that influenced the national congress to create the Freedmen's Bureau in 1865. With General Oliver O. Howard (1830–1909) — a lay Presbyterian and, by 1869, founder and president of Howard University — its commissioner, the bureau used the educational services of northern churches and their missionary agencies. It is true that the bureau left a mixed legacy, and its failures have been noted by others. What is significant here, though, is that — as in the case of Native Americans — mission zeal and political need forged an alliance that temporarily overrode the wall of separation between church and state.

The mission mind had made its compromises in order to work among African-Americans. Entanglement with the national government in the Freedmen's Bureau was only one instance. More pervasively, in its southern version the mission mind had been willing to preach a consciously one-sided version of the Christian message that stressed obedience to masters, humility before owners, and the like. Still, the missionaries must have said enough about ancient Israel and the bondage of the Jews, on the one hand, and about the return of Jesus and the coming of the millennium, on the other, to inspire the slaves and those newly free. As we will see in the next chapter, it was restorationist (in this case, Old Testament restoration) and millennial themes that most appealed to African-Americans. And when, both before and after the Civil War, they formed their independent churches, restoring first times and preparing for end times proved significant themes. In the twentieth century, evangelical Christianity became the preferred religion of the majority of African-Americans. The mission mind had once again replicated itself among a new group of people.

Nor did the mission mind find among Indians and blacks the only strangers close to home. Notably from the 1840s with the Irish, masses of immigrants began to arrive in the United States. Evangelical Protestants found new people to convert — and to acculturate to America — among European Catholics and Jews and, by century's end, among more religiously diverse East Asians. As we will see in the concluding chapter, Protestant efforts for the immigrants, like those for Native Americans and African-Americans, were ambiguous. Still, from urban settlement houses to the American Society for Meliorating the

Condition of the Jews, at least one facet of their endeavor was unmistakable. Evangelicals continued to exhibit the presence of the mission mind, announcing among nearby strangers the Protestant need to restore the gospel in the shadow of the millennium. Evangelicals continued to look to first times and to anticipate last times even as they skipped over history.

Mission to the World

Home missions expressed an evangelical need to preach the gospel to the unconverted nearby, but they also provided a cultural staging ground for world mission projects. Preaching to relative, friend, and neighbor required organizational support. Thus, the revivals of the early nineteenth century spawned a series of interdenominational societies that, as we have seen, helped to institutionalize the mission mind and to aid in its work. Staffed by volunteers, groups like the American Education Society, the American Bible Society, the American Sunday School Union, and the American Tract Society widened the influence of evangelical Protestantism beyond the boundaries that the denominations by themselves could reach. Yet even before the appearance of these groups, the demands of Christian empire felt by some evangelical Protestants began to prompt them to turn their attention to the world beyond America. In fact, for many Protestants the issue of whether mission on the home front should come before or after mission to the world was a hotly debated issue.

For them and for others, a new evangelical first time became available in the "haystack prayer meeting" of 1806. In that year, according to traditional report, a chance thunderstorm surprised a group of students at Williams College in Massachusetts during their regular meeting for prayer. The students moved under a haystack for shelter and, whether or not affected by the storm, pledged their lives to missionary work abroad. Two years later, under the leadership of Samuel J. Mills (1783–1818), they formed a society to advance their goals and took as their motto "We can do it if we will." In only another two years, now as graduating students at Andover Theological Seminary, members of the group asked the Congregational General Association of Massachusetts for a formal organization to support their work and that of other missionaries.

So, in 1810, began the American Board of Commissioners for Foreign Missions (ABCFM). The board's Congregational base was quickly broadened to include Presbyterian and Reformed membership, and by 1812 the group was sending its first missionaries to India. Mills was numbered among the mission party, and so were Adoniram Judson (1788–1850), Ann Hasseltine Judson (1789–1826) — the first American woman to work abroad as a foreign missionary — and Luther Rice (1783–1836). Then, on board ship, the Judsons and Rice experienced a theological change of heart that also changed denominational involvement in foreign-mission work. The three became certain that adult baptism by immersion was required Christian practice, and they were subsequently baptized in Calcutta (even though Ann Judson left her Congregationalism with some hesitation). News of their conversion spread widely, and American Baptists, as a result, were pushed toward organized work for foreign missions. By 1814 they had formed their own mission board, and it became a strong force within the denomination until Baptists divided over slavery.

The Judsons went on to Burma and engaged in a ministry, filled with hardship and, for Adoniram Judson, even an imprisonment that made him an evangelical hero. Whatever his difficulties, though, he worked to learn the language and to translate the scriptures, with Ann Judson also doing translation work and personal writing on missions. After she died, Adoniram Judson married again in 1834. His second wife, Sarah Hall Boardman (1803–1845), worked in major ways at translation and in other literary endeavors that her husband had initiated, supplying poetry of her own to religious publications. And when, after Boardman's death, Judson again remarried in 1846, his third wife, Emily Chubbuck (1817–1854) — already a popular author under the pen name Fanny Forester — published a biography of Sarah Boardman Judson and other mission literature as well. Clearly, for Adoniram Judson, his three wives, and others of the time, being a missionary meant emphasizing a biblical foundation.

In this mood of evangelical commitment, Burma as well as India and Ceylon (present-day Sri Lanka) became the main theaters of missionary action during the first half of the nineteenth century, with work, too, in Southeast Asia, West Africa, Turkey, Hawaii, and even in a few nations in Latin America. And denominational organizations began to proliferate to support the work. Among the Methodists a missionary society was established in 1819, while the Episcopalians followed suit two years later. Presbyterian Old Schoolers, in turn, left the ABCFM in 1837 to begin their own organization. Even so, there was more interdenominational effort in this period than in the later years of the century.

The millennial doctrine implicit in the call to mission had already been presaged in the eighteenth-century theology of Jonathan Edwards, who linked Christian cooperation in the work of redemption with the coming of the millennium. By the second half of the nineteenth century, the political doctrine of the "manifest destiny" of America to rule the continent had buttressed his message. As many understood the doctrine (to be explored more fully in Chapter 13), America, through the enlightened government of its democracy, would provide the place for the millennium to begin. And as soon as continental expansion was completed, they believed, America would begin the millennial time. Thus, Edwardsean Calvinism was mostly replaced by the emphasis on human agency that came with the revivals and with the political mood. And it was not surprising that, after the revival of 1857–1858, new organizations for mission work appeared, a number of them begun by women.

In the 1850s and in the shadow of manifest destiny, too, the central terms of a debate between two opposing conceptions of mission emerged clearly. Echoing ideas that had surfaced in missionary work among Indian peoples earlier, the debate would continue in the mission projects into the twentieth century. The prevailing position had been that missionaries needed to westernize, or "civilize," non-Christian populations before they could receive Christian teaching. Now, however, Rufus Anderson (1796–1880), foreign secretary of the ABCFM from 1826 to 1866, challenged that view. He opposed the use of English in mission schools, not to mention the commitment to education itself. Anderson thought it misguided to send specialists in agriculture or medicine or various technologies into the field. Missionaries were there, he believed, to proclaim the biblical message. Therefore, they would better spend their time preaching and translating the scripture — and letting indigenous peoples control their own churches.

As he argued his case, Anderson looked to the Christianity of the first century as model. The gospel alone, he said, would perform the work of civilizing. And conversely, those foreigners who acquired the strongest grasp of English would often be furthest from conversion. Anderson, in short, was taking a primitivist stand in a foreign-mission context. First times, for him, provided answers to be applied. That is, restoration of an apostolic foreign-mission strategy was seen to bring the gospel success that he and others desired. In this reading, the millennialism of manifest destiny was cast aside for a millennialism that counted on the gospel itself to inaugurate a new day.

Then, in the 1860s, the Civil War brought a decline in foreign-mission interest and support. Moreover, after the war the antebellum pattern continued. It was home-mission work that occupied Protestants now, as freed slaves, immigrants, the poor, and alcoholics alternately attracted the attention of the mission mind. But after 1880 interest in foreign missions began a decided upswing, and the mission mind seemed permanently launched on projects to encircle the globe.

The millennialism of manifest destiny had not disappeared and, in fact, was now played out in a still more emphatic way. Indicative of the mood of many evangelical Protestants was the book *Our Country* (1885). The work of Josiah Strong (1847–1916), a Congregational minister with substantial Social Gospel credentials and clear expansionist views, *Our Country* articulated a doctrine of Protestant responsibility based on theories of "scientific" racism fashionable at the time. In Strong's reading, the Anglo-Saxon race was inherently superior and so had certain gospel duties and requirements. Anglo-Saxons, argued Strong, possessed both the purest form of government (democracy) and the purest form of religion (Christianity). Therefore, he said, they should spread their culture even as they spread their religion, overcoming the less enlightened ways and beliefs of others in the interest of civilization and of gospel truth.

For foreign missions, the message that could be gleaned from Strong's analysis was that the millennium would be brought on by human effort and that Jesus would return only *after* Americans had established the gospel in human society. There will be more to say about this postmillennial vision in Chapter 12, but its role in Anglo-Saxon triumphalist theories like Strong's should be noted here. For Strong and many of his contemporaries linked the restoration of gospel purity with self-promoting theories about American cultural superiority. Rufus Anderson's foreign-mission primitivism was being supplanted by another kind of mission restoration. In the shadow of Strong and those who agreed, the "civilizers" were often winning the day. And indeed, until at least the 1920s, an elite Protestant establishment, the "upper crust" of Protestant leadership, led the way in missions, with efforts that were clearly postmillennial.

From the other side of the millennial divide, however, premillennialists — strong and growing with the birth of early fundamentalism — looked to their dispensationalist theory of history to spur foreign-mission work. If the return of Jesus was imminent, premillennialists believed, they should do all they could, in the short time that remained, to preach to those who had never heard Christian teaching. Some, convinced by Reformed and Keswick ideas of sanctification by the Spirit as an endowment for service, joined postmillennial "civilizers" in their acceptance of social aid as a function of foreign missions. Others, with more individualist views of sanctification and the Christian life in general, moved toward so-called interdenominational "faith missions." Best exemplified by the China Inland Mission (now the Overseas Missionary Fellowship) — an English mission to China begun in 1865 and, after 1888, including Americans — the faith mission employed laymen and single women as missionaries. Without a denominational sponsoring body or the financial support of an interdenominational one, a faith mission relied on prayer rather than formal fund-raising activity. Faith missions, moreover, encouraged missionaries to blend with native cultures, adopting their dress and language though maintaining strict evangelical preaching on biblical themes.

Two years before the China Inland Mission sent its first North American missionaries to China, still another lay movement, the Student Volunteer Movement for Foreign Missions (SVM), was being initiated. The urban revivalist Dwight Moody, who had helped to inspire the Keswick movement, also created the situation that gave rise to the SVM. At a summer conference Moody sponsored at his Mount Hermon School in Northfield, Massachusetts, some 100 students pledged themselves as future foreign missionaries. Within another year their numbers had increased at least tenfold, and by 1888 the Student Volunteer Movement was formally organized. Led by John R. Mott (1865–1955) and Robert E. Speer (1867–1947), it aimed at "the evangelization of the world in this generation." The lay-controlled SVM became the dominant mission organization until 1920, sponsoring huge "Quadrennial" conventions that acted as catalysts for mission recruitment and producing materials for mission study endeavors. Even in decline, it continued as a separate organization until 1959. Throughout the SVM's history, it was said, it attracted some 20,000 students to careers in Christian missions.

Mott's leadership in the SVM moved in ecumenical directions, and, in fact, he chaired the 1910 world missionary conference at Edinburgh (noted in the last chapter). But the division that came between liberal ecumenists and conservative evangelicals after World War I generally did not trouble the SVM earlier. As new mission stations opened, members of the movement understood evangelical success as evidence of the nearness of the millennium. They generally recognized the evils that went with uncontrolled imperialism; but they thought, optimistically, that these could be replaced by a cultural and spiritual expansionism that was benevolent. Meanwhile, with East Asia supplanting South Asia as the most prominent field for mission labor, Japan, Korea, and, particularly, China became familiar mission terrain. Especially after 1900 and the inauguration of the Open Door policy between the United States and China, considerable impetus was given to the Chinese mission work. And beyond the political situation, the country was so vast that manifold opportunities for interdenominational cooperation and activities could be shared.

Nor was the SVM isolated in its lay approach to foreign missions. The Laymen's Missionary Movement (LMM), which the SVM indirectly helped to spark, was a case in point. Proposed originally by a member of the SVM, the Laymen's Missionary Movement was formed in New York City in 1906. Significantly, it developed out of meetings that took place at the Fifth Avenue Presbyterian Church to remember the student haystack prayer meeting that led to the establishment of the ABCFM. Yet if the LMM harked back a century as it formulated its agenda, its cultivation of the business community in support of mission efforts was decidedly new. It stressed advertising and public relations, so that capitalism became party to Christian enterprise. Bringing a gospel foundation to foreign lands was good business, it maintained. Bringing the gospel was worth capital investment.

The twentieth century also brought new denominational partners in the mission enterprise. Growing numbers of pentecostals sent missionaries abroad, as did other, more and more self-conscious, conservative evangelicals. The Southern Baptist Convention became the largest national supplier of foreign missionaries. At the same time, the proportion of missionaries abroad (those outside of North America and Europe) shifted toward greater American dominance. Whereas in 1900 just over one-quarter of world missionaries were American, by 1925 Americans represented nearly half of all foreign missionaries in the field. Yet for all the numerical increase, the theological conviction that had spurred the mission mind in the nineteenth century was, for many, eroding.

Symptomatic of new times and new questions was the report of the Laymen's Foreign Missions Inquiry in 1932. The work of William E. Hocking (1873–1966), a Harvard philosopher and a liberal, the report was based on a field survey of missions in South and East Asia in 1931. The survey, in fact, had been urged and supported by millionaire industrialist John D. Rockefeller (1839–1937), and its report, *Rethinking Missions: A Laymen's Inquiry after One Hundred Years*, radically criticized Protestant work in missions. The Hocking report moved past the civilizing–Christianizing debate to suggest, more controversially, that conversion should not be the goal of foreign missionaries at all. Instead, missionaries should look for those aspects of their own faith that were echoed in the religions of others. Such similarities, argued the report, should be used as means for inter-faith cooperation and collaboration.

The Hocking report did not sit well with most Protestants. Still, more and more sentiment was expressed among mainstream denominations to turn mission stations over to the control of indigenous peoples. For conservative evangelicals, of course, conversion was the clear and abiding goal of mission effort, and there was often resistance to such indigenous control. In the long term, however, conservative clarity about intentions, along with liberal ambivalence, began to be reflected in the changing configuration of the Protestant foreign-mission establishment.

In the mid-thirties, in the wake of the Hocking report, conservative support for the foreign missions was small despite the commitment that had been made. Conservatives, for example, fielded just over one-quarter of all missionaries in China, only 10 percent of those in Japan, and 16 percent of those in India. But by 1980 conservative evangelicals had taken over the mission establishment, contributing some 32,000 of a total of 35,000 missionaries in the field. Inasmuch as in 1935 the entire number of American missionaries engaged in foreign labors had totaled only 11,000, the magnitude of the new evangelical commitment was all the greater. Still further, new missionaries had increasingly gone to new places. In the 1980s the largest mission field had become Latin America, with over 11,000 North American missionaries there alone. Beyond that, in a historic change that was also ironic, Europe had become an important mission field, and nearly 4,000 North Americans were seeing service there.

Still, the shifts in allegiance and locale were somewhat softened by changing evangelical cultural assumptions. A large contingent of missionaries—nearly 14,000 evangelicals—had moved to a position of support for greater indigenous control and more social assistance. Hence, the latter part of the century brought what American religious historian William R. Hutchison has called a "three-way division" in missionary thought and operation. A small body of ecumenically minded liberals was far outflanked by members of two other groups, who, in turn, expressed the evangelical mission mind in quite different ways. On the one hand were those evangelicals, usually affiliated with large agencies, who were open to indigenous control of mission churches and to some social-service work. On the other hand was the larger body of conservative missionaries who opposed any but traditional missionary patterns.

Those more or less "centrist" missionaries who were affiliated with large agencies reflected organizational changes that had long been occurring, the first as early as 1917. In that year the faith-mission movement decided that there were advantages to central organization and formed the Interdenominational Foreign Mission Association (IFMA). Then, in the forties, came rising evangelical strength and public visibility and, along with both, new organization. In 1945 the largest existing group of evangelicals, those who banded together in 1942 in the National Association of Evangelicals, created as their mission extension the Evangelical Foreign Missions Association (EFMA). This new evangelical missionary organization found in the IFMA a cooperative partner, and the two agencies began to work jointly in numerous ways. By 1960, in fact, they were responsible for sending most American foreign missionaries abroad.

Cooperation between the IFMA and the EFMA was more than practical. In 1966, for example, in the leading instance of theoretical accord, the two groups came together for their Congress on the Church's Worldwide Mission, at Wheaton College in Illinois. Their articulation of principles, the Wheaton Declaration, was a ringing endorsement of evangelical goals for mission. By two decades later, however, within the new unaffiliated missionary agencies even the IFMA and EFMA were suspect. For the 60 percent of Protestant mission workers who were part of the unaffiliated movement, the mission mind should not be compromised by anything that hinted of liberal adaptation.

Indeed, the presence of liberals and the threat of their policies had played a significant role in shaping and catalyzing major aspects of the mission mind. From this perspective, liberals were "complementary" antagonists, necessary enemies to conservative evangelicals in the total cultural system that was mainstream Protestantism. Without liberals, by the late twentieth century the historic commitment of the mission mind would most likely have grown considerably weaker. Liberals reminded conservative evangelicals of who they were and what, as conservatives, they stood for. And what conservatives stood for, by the late twentieth century, was a resurgence of the mission mind. In and through the workings of that mind, conservative Protestants sought to transform ordinary life into the extraordinary. With mission as the call to stand out from the rest of America and be different, conservatives sought to stop time. They disdained ordinary history in favor of a privileged role at the dawn time, the (for them) extraordinary moment of New Testament beginnings. It was this genesis, as they saw it, that they wanted to make visible on the earth again.

With their ritual the proclamation of a sacred book, conservatives scorned liturgical churches in favor of an active call to witness. If they claimed privileged contact with the biblical Word, they also claimed privileged contact with the Bible's proclamation in the sixteenth-century Reformation and with the Bible's embodiment in an earlier American culture. Conservative Protestants argued that they were the true heirs of Puritan forebears, Revolutionary War patriots, and nineteenth-century evangelicals. They saw themselves as working to restore the ancient Word that, they believed, the liberals had all but destroyed. As conservative evangelicals, they felt it was they who would return to the purity and vigor of "first-time" Christianity. And they felt it was they who would create small islands of perfection in a world declining as it awaited the millennium.

In Overview

The churches of mainstream Protestantism had begun in America with a commitment to evangelical themes and ends. To "evangelize" meant to spread the

New Testament Word, and the drive to spread knowledge of the Bible was for them the fruit of a deep personal experience of "new birth." Conversion, in short, bred a need to keep converting.

With this commitment providing the basic structure of religious experience, mainstream Protestants built an evangelical culture that by the mid-eighteenth century found primary subjects for conversion close to home. Christianizing relative, friend, and neighbor became the goal of a series of revivals that were recurring features of the American religious landscape. Beginning with the preaching of George Whitefield and Jonathan Edwards in the First Great Awakening, revivals brought community and intense religious individualism, sincere conversion and thoroughgoing hostility. Whitefield's itinerancy and open-air preaching proved important innovations for later revival technique. Others in the nineteenth century continued to perfect the technique, with Charles Grandison Finney openly pointing to the human role in revivals and employing "protracted meetings" and the "anxious bench." After the Civil War, Dwight L. Moody promoted revivals in the cities and adapted big-business practices to insure success. Meanwhile, revivals were transformed from the intensely emotional and physical experiences of frontier camp meetings earlier in the century to the restrained gatherings of Moody's urban tabernacles, with their altar calls at the end of services.

Twentieth-century revivalism brought, in some cases—like that of Billy Sunday—histrionic preachers and, in others, an evangelical religion-as-usual. But the revivals' cycles had long been buttressed by other, more stable structures for accomplishing the work of the mission mind. These structures were the denominations and the vast network of supporting institutions they built: schools and colleges, publishing houses and periodicals, and voluntary societies for accomplishing evangelical goals.

Among the denominations, the Methodists built so strong a religious organization that it gave its name to an era. Methodist circuit riders and conferences, class meetings and love feasts became the staples of an evangelical culture on the frontier and elsewhere during the first half of the nineteenth century. Methodist perfectionism put its premium on human agency in winning others to Christianity, and it also meant a commitment to restore the New Testament gospel. A series of new denominations, however, took up the restoration theme more explicitly and self-consciously, most prominent among them the Disciples of Christ. These New Testament "Christians" looked as much to the millennium, when they believed Jesus would return, as to the biblical past. Indeed, they sought to restore the past to prepare the way to the future.

Other older denominations shared the restorationist impulse, among them the Baptists. In their Landmark movement, restorationists became a major force in the Southern Baptist Convention during the second half of the nineteenth century. And after the Civil War, inherited restorationist themes were bolstered by the movement of premillennial dispensationalism, which gained more and more adherents. Dispensationalists looked to the imminent arrival of Jesus and then the final dispensation, or age, of the millennium. But they looked equally to biblical beginnings, with their doctrine of the inerrancy of scripture. Moreover, dispensationalism became a leading formative factor in the growth of fundamentalism and of the holiness-pentecostal movement as well.

Fundamentalism itself formed gradually from sources that included, in addition to dispensationalism, a rationalist theology from Princeton Theological Seminary and revival-born ideas and attitudes, including holiness views. By the 1920s fundamentalism had come into its own as a militantly antimodernist movement of Protestant evangelicals. By this time, too, a separate holiness movement had long crystallized from Methodist and Reformed elements, and a series of pentecostal churches had formed, adding to holiness doctrine an experiential emphasis on tongues speaking, faith healing, and other prophetic gifts.

The mission mind, though, did not rest content with rituals and institutions designed to save those near and dear. Instead, it aimed to convert "strangers" in America, beginning with Native Americans and then turning to African-Americans and, by the mid-nineteenth century, to immigrants. After initial hesitation about the goal, numbers of missions to convert Indian peoples and blacks were launched with varying degrees of success. Native Americans were slow to convert, and Puritan — and later — missionary efforts were, in general, less than enthusiastic. Among African-Americans, initial resistance gave way, but by the eve of the Civil War the great majority of blacks were also not church members. Still, for the numbers of African-Americans who belonged, Methodist and Baptist churches were the preferred denominations.

Conversion of the stranger at home led, seemingly inevitably, to attempts to convert the stranger abroad. Fed by the cultural expansionism that was a strong feature of American life in the nineteenth century, Protestant missionaries began to evangelize other nations. They worried, as they did so, about whether they needed to westernize and, as they understood the matter, "civilize" before they could introduce a scriptural foundation. American foreign-mission history stands as a record of that debate. Moreover, as the twentieth century brought firm lines of separation between liberals and conservatives, evangelical mission work passed largely from liberal hands and became the overwhelming property of the conservative wing.

Still, for all that, mainstream Protestants had not been the only evangelical Christians with a dominant role in American religious history. Some Protestants had been happy neither with the ordinary character of mainstream liberal Protestantism nor with its extraordinary manifestations in the evangelical mission mind. Nor, finally, had they been happy with the character of American culture. A nation within the Protestant nation, these people also spilled over its borders, remembering their separate past and wondering if they would also have a separate future. These Americans had African rather than European roots, and, like the Indians before them and the Jews, their religion and nationhood were closely blended. African-Americans, like others among the many, had their own religious center.

SUGGESTIONS FOR FURTHER READING: THE PROTESTANT CHURCHES AND THE MISSION MIND

Anderson, Robert M. *Vision of the Disinherited: The Making of American Pentecostalism.* New York: Oxford University Press, 1979.

Bowden, Henry Warner. *American Indians and Christian Missions: Studies in Cultural Conflict.* Chicago History of American Religion. Chicago: University of Chicago Press, 1981.

Butler, Jon. *Awash in a Sea of Faith: Christianizing the American People.* Cambridge: Harvard University Press, 1990.

Carpenter, Joel A., and Shenk, Wilbert R., eds. *Earthen Vessels: American Evangelicals and Foreign Missions, 1880–1980.* Grand Rapids, MI: William B. Eerdmans, 1990.

Harrell, David Edwin, Jr. *All Things Are Possible: The Healing and Charismatic Revivals in Modern America.* Bloomington: Indiana University Press, 1975.

Hatch, Nathan O. *The Democratization of American Christianity.* New Haven: Yale University Press, 1989.

_____, **and Noll, Mark A., eds.** *The Bible in America: Essays in Cultural History.* New York: Oxford University Press, 1982.

Hughes, Richard T., ed. *The American Quest for the Primitive Church.* Urbana: University of Illinois Press, 1988.

_____, **and Allen, C. Leonard.** *Illusions of Innocence: Protestant Primitivism in America, 1630–1875.* Chicago: University of Chicago Press, 1988.

Hutchison, William R. *Errand to the World: American Protestant Thought and Foreign Missions.* Chicago: University of Chicago Press, 1987.

Jones, Charles Edwin. *Perfectionist Persuasion: The Holiness Movement and American Methodism, 1867–1936.* ATLA Monograph Series, No. 5. Metuchen, NJ: Scarecrow Press, 1974.

Marsden, George M. *Fundamentalism and American Culture: The Shaping of Twentieth-Century Evangelicalism, 1870–1925.* New York: Oxford University Press, 1980.

Mathews, Donald G. *Religion in the Old South.* Chicago History of American Religion. Chicago: University of Chicago Press, 1977.

McLoughlin, William G., Jr. *Modern Revivalism: Charles Grandison Finney to Billy Graham.* New York: Ronald Press, 1959.

_____. *Revivals, Awakenings, and Reform.* Chicago History of American Religion. Chicago: University of Chicago Press, 1978.

Richey, Russell E. *Early American Methodism: A Reconsideration.* Religion in North America. Bloomington: Indiana University Press, 1991.

Sandeen, Ernest R. *The Roots of Fundamentalism: British and American Millenarianism, 1800–1930.* Chicago: University of Chicago Press, 1970.

Weber, Timothy P. *Living in the Shadow of the Second Coming: American Premillennialism, 1875–1925.* New York: Oxford University Press, 1979.

Wood, Forrest G. *The Arrogance of Faith: Christianity and Race in America from the Colonial Era to the Twentieth Century.* New York: Alfred A. Knopf, 1990.

Black Center:
African-American Religion
and Nationhood

Toward the end of August 1619, a Dutch ship slipped into harbor at Jamestown, Virginia. On board were at least twenty "Negars," who were sold as indentured servants to the Virginia colony. So began the African presence in the land that became the United States — an ironic beginning in which, in the land of volunteers, the interrupted lives of nonvolunteers were redirected into channels of oppression. Over the next several decades, there was a continual slow trickle of human cargo into Virginia to labor on the tobacco plantations. By 1649 there were about 300 slaves out of a population of 15,000. After 1660 statutes began to acknowledge slavery and set forth conditions of enslavement, and by the end of the seventeenth century, other Africans were pouring into Virginia and the neighboring Maryland colony.

To the north, as early as 1638 Captain William Peirce brought blacks as slaves from the Providence Island colony to Massachusetts Bay. Shippers and traders across the Atlantic, the Puritans freely engaged in the slave trade and reaped their profits. Thus, the colonies almost without thought started down the road to the bondage of Africans, a road that would bring 427,000 or more blacks to their land. Although this was a small fraction of the nearly 10 million blacks who came to various parts of the New World, by 1865 through natural increase there were about 4 million African-Americans in the United States alone. The importation of African slaves was outlawed in 1808 and, while there was some smuggling, declined thereafter. Still, at the beginning of the nineteenth century there were about 1 million blacks in the country, representing some 20 percent of the population. In short, one person in five was black, and African-Americans had become a significant group. Whether Euro-Americans liked it or not, blacks would have much to do with the future shape of the American experience as religion and as culture.

By and large, these Africans who came as slaves to America had originated from peoples in West Africa and the Congo–Angola region. They included Mandinke, Yoruba, Ibo, Bakongo, Ewe, Fon, and other nations, some of them followers of Islam and many of them practitioners of traditional African religions. In order to understand the religious world the slaves would fashion for themselves in America, we need to look at these traditional West African religions.

West African Religions

In West Africa, in a situation that was roughly analogous to that of Native American cultures, traditional religions were diverse, with each people possessing its sacred accounts of origins, its Gods, and its ritual and magical practices. Yet underneath the diversity, as in the case of Native Americans, there was a common fund of meaning and value. Hence, although it will be necessary to simplify a great deal, it is possible briefly to sketch the "religion" beneath the religions.

Generally, the sacred world of West Africans was one of continuity between different aspects of life. It was based in a strong sense of community, in which individuals understood themselves as part of a people, and no person could live in isolation, either materially or spiritually. Without a sense of original or actual sin in the Judeo-Christian sense, the West Africans considered wrongdoing an offense against one or another among the people, and upon this ground of relationship, their cultures flourished. Similarly, if West Africans were bound to one another by ties of kinship and nationhood in the present, they were tied as closely to the past. The ancestors were never forgotten, and time could not dissolve the relationship with them. Like a continuous thread, memory linked the living to their dead, and ritual reinforced the memory. Burial ceremonies were elaborate affairs with a full list of prescribed customs, from the preparation of the body to continued periods of mourning at set intervals after death. West Africans believed that the ancestors still lived in the land beyond and that they took an interest in their descendants on earth. They might grant fertility and health, or they might punish neglectful kin. As guardians of law and custom, West Africans believed, they mediated between the Gods and ordinary people, sometimes becoming Gods themselves as ancestors of entire clan or kinship groups.

The transformation of some of the ancestors into Gods suggested that, for West Africans, continuity extended to the divine world. There was no sharp break between heaven and earth in the West African scheme of things, but, rather, sacred and profane shaded off into each other. All of life was seen to possess its spiritual power, which could be tapped and used for good or for ill. At the same time, religion sought to sanctify life, renewing it through contact with the Gods. So the Gods were distinguished for West Africans by their extraordinary power. Among them, there was the high God who had created all things, an ultimate fact of life upon which all else depended. In West African thinking, however, once this high God had started up the world, generally he did not interfere with the ordinary conduct of events. Unlike the Judeo-Christian God, the high God from West Africa was usually regarded as nonintervening, and West Africans did not often pay homage in a regular way, instead calling on God from time to time but not making him the object of a cultus. God for West Africans was just *there*, a simple and unavoidable fact of life. He did not change history, and no West African would have expected him to prevent slavery.

But there were other Gods for West Africans besides the high God, and it was these whom they regularly aimed to contact through their rituals. Intermediary Gods might once have been ancestors, as we have already seen, or they might have arisen independently. Associated in West African thought with natural forces or beings like thunder, rain, or animals, these Gods were held to direct the world in its course and to bring good and evil to human beings. Meanwhile, various animal Trickster figures also blurred the West African boundary between the sacred and the profane. Beings who could upset and disturb the governing order, the African Tricksters functioned much like their American Indian counterparts. As hares, spiders, or other small and insignificant creatures, the Tricksters were thought to work chaos, to confound the proud and wise, and to introduce the possibility of a new order into the ordinary flow of events.

Both Gods and Tricksters were remembered in sacred stories. The traditional accounts of the various holy beings in the West African universe explained the origins and interrelationships between Gods and the world. Sometimes, too, these accounts mingled with recollections of the past history of a particular people. Past and present — more than future — were the important moments, and memory was supported by rituals performed to contact the Gods. There could be animal sacrifice, in which gifts of life were intended to honor the Gods, or divination, in which various techniques were believed to discern their will and intentions. Or there could be music and dance in which communion with the Gods might be sought. With the rhythm of drums to set the pace, persons who wanted to contact the Gods danced out their desires until, by what was experienced as a divine reversal, West Africans believed that a God would "mount" the dancer and begin to dance him or her. Possession by a God in West Africa meant the full integration of self with the divine. God was felt to transform the private consciousness of a devoted follower so that the boundary between this world and another seemed to dissolve.

At the same time, West Africans also had their ways to work to acquire power for the ordinary world. Magic of various kinds thrived and was used to attempt to heal illness or to work harm on an enemy, to bring fertility to nature and to women, or to assure the success of a venture in love or war. The cosmos of

West Africans was one in which the extraordinary world shone through the ordinary and a sacred quality colored everyday events. In other words, religious expression became part of the ordinary business of living. Thus, followers of one or another God would often wear special colors and eat designated foods that were identified with the God. They usually turned in worship to a God who had been honored by their parents, and they saw the intermediary Gods not simply as otherworldly beings but as practical intruders who could lend assistance in ordinary concerns.

New Land, New Religion

With the sudden reversal of their fortunes, many West Africans found themselves uprooted from their land and systematically deprived of their kin, their culture, and their Gods. The slave trade was a business, and it depended for its success on transforming human beings into marketable commodities. During the period of middle passage between African ports and New World destinations, blacks were deliberately isolated from those who came from their community or spoke their language. Without the support of kin, friends, speech, or religion, an African would be unlikely to plot a revolt. He or she would be forced to become docile, depending for survival on what little the captors provided. Many Africans died in the holds of ships, and those who managed to survive became slaves under a law code that deprived them of basic human rights. Unlike slavery in West Africa, where captives from enemy societies were treated as dependents who could inherit property and contract marriage, the blacks who came to the English colonies in America kept none of these prerogatives.

Yet legal fiction could never hide the fact that the slaves were people and not inert objects. More than that, they were *a* people who, although they had often been warring enemies in Africa, had also been very much alike. They shared a basic view of life and the relationship of the Gods to the human condition. They spoke for the most part dialects — although not easily translatable into one another — of perhaps two major languages. So there was much that blacks could mutually affirm as they began to take up the remnants of their lives in the New World. Their fundamental ways of looking at religion and at life had been and would remain similar. Their common experience of servitude would give them another and different set of bonds to share.

African-American religion was born among these Africans and their children in succeeding generations. It was built on pieces of a common African past, reconstructed to provide strength and solace in the new situation. It was built, too, on the experiences that the slaves endured in America, mixing their sense of involuntary presence into their religion. And finally, it was built with materials that came to the slaves from the religion of their masters. African-American religion was constructed in part from the Judeo-Christian tradition. Together, these three sources — the West African background, the condition of slavery in the present, the language of European Christianity — provided the elements for a religion to fit the conditions of a distinct people in a new land.

From West Africa, blacks kept many customs and practices that had become habitual. But more than externals, West Africans kept their internal way of ordering life and of looking at the world. Thus, most fundamentally, they continued to see life in terms of a blend of ordinary and extraordinary worlds, bringing together the sacred and the profane and giving meaning to ordinary tasks. The old African Tricksters continued to be present in a new set of tales the slaves told about figures like Brer Rabbit. Small and insignificant, like the hare of Africa, he outsmarted the great and powerful, showing that his cunning was a match for any animal's strength. It was true that Brer Rabbit and his animal friends gave blacks a way to express their hostilities and to celebrate the triumph of the weak (like slaves) over the strong (like masters). But it was also true that the new animal tales contained the same religious philosophy as the West African tales — that chaos was the source of creativity and that by upsetting the standing order with his antics, Brer Rabbit was restoring the situation, making the world vigorous again.

Similarly, the African Tricksters were present in the religious art of conjure, which flourished among the slaves. Here, under the guidance of a root doctor, who resembled in many ways a West African priest-healer, spells were cast and healing practice went on. Conjure aimed to bring extraordinary power to the ordinary details of life. Its magic was believed to kill or cure, work love or create havoc. Using herbs and other natural substances (and sometimes manufactured goods, especially if belonging to the intended subject), root work, as it was called, often made use of a conjure bag. Considered a source of power, like the medicine bundle of a Native American, the conjure bag was intended for some one person, and it was thought to produce its effect when that person knowingly or unknowingly touched it. In their attachment to conjure, African-Americans were expressing their belief that no part of life was without meaning and no situation merely an accident. Like the New England Puritans, they saw life as in the hands of sacred forces. For them, nothing just "happened"; everything had its spiritual cause and cure. Disease, for example, was thought to be the work of an indwelling evil spirit or of the spell cast by an enemy's malice. And, attributed to extraordinary causes, illness was said to be healed by extraordinary means. Physicians, for African-Americans, had to be religious specialists.

Conjure was often also called hoodoo, and by this name it revealed its connections with the religion of voodoo, which grew especially among blacks in New Orleans. By 1850 voodoo was at its height in this city, and its influence was spreading in Louisiana and parts of the South. Based on *vodun*, a Dahomean (West African) religion that flourished in new form in Saint-Domingue (Haiti) and other parts of the French West Indies, voodoo had been present in French Louisiana since its early days, when blacks had come from the Indies. But after the Haitian Revolution of 1804, numbers of new blacks from the West Indies entered New Orleans, many of them with French masters fleeing from the victorious

Negro regime. The influx of these black people succeeded in making New Orleans the capital of voodoo in the United States.

As a system of worship, voodoo made use of drums and dance, song and possession. With priests and, more often, priestesses presiding over its ceremonies, it provided a ritual context in which the West African ideal of personal transformation under the felt power of the God could be realized. Accounts of the voodoo cultus, as they were reported in the public newspapers of the day, were often exotic. They described rituals in which, through the presence of a snake representing the God, the priestess aimed to make contact with sacred power. Then, in trance, she began to deliver messages, and ordinary people in turn became transported. In the cultural mix reflected in the ceremonies were elements derived from Roman Catholic worship, as had also been the case in the West Indies. Thus, as an example, altars, candles, and prayers to the Virgin Mary were often part of the voodoo ceremony. But as in the West Indian setting, Catholic elements were used to express West African or African-American religious meanings.

Root work, or hoodoo, designated the magical and healing practices associated with voodoo. In places where voodoo never reached in its complete form and in times after voodoo had declined, root work continued, becoming part of the ordinary religion of southern, and even northern, blacks. Yet with or without such externals, African ways of seeing the world and interacting with it persisted. When African-Americans turned to Christianity, they brought to it, often without taking notice, the centuries of their prior heritage. We will look for traces of that heritage as we take up the question of black Christianity. And as we do so, we will notice the ways in which the experience of slavery became part of African-American religion, too.

Black Christianity

Most of the slaves who became Christian embraced Protestantism, and this account will chiefly concern them. Yet in Louisiana, where the voodoo cult was centered, and in Maryland some blacks became Roman Catholics. Significantly, Louisiana had been settled by French Catholics, and Maryland by English ones. Moreover, although the formality of Roman Catholic ritual did not offer the opportunities for seeking ecstasy that had been part of West African religion, the sacramental character of Catholicism, with its use of material elements in ritual settings, was attractive. So, too, were the many saints, who functioned, in Catholic belief, as intermediaries with God the Father in somewhat the same way as the many Gods of West Africa had with the high Creator God. Hence, Catholicism enjoyed a modest presence among both slaves and free blacks. That presence continued after the Civil War and into the twentieth century, as we saw in Chapter 3. Still, African-Americans who were Catholic, we remember, were but a small fraction of the total black population.

By contrast, the majority of those who were African-American turned in a different direction. They accepted American Protestantism and changed it to express their own past history and present turmoil. And in the process of doing so, African-Americans grew in a sense of inner autonomy and developed a conviction of separate peoplehood. Their conviction carried them through slavery and continued to support them through the new troubles that emancipation brought. Their sense of inner autonomy enabled them to accept life though it was still lived in slavery. Like their West African kin left behind, African-American Protestants looked to a religion of affirmation in the present, even when the present involved suffering.

The early history of black contact with Christianity in the English colonies was not promising, as we noted in the last chapter. But racism and fear on the part of slaveholders and various practical difficulties on the part of missionaries tell about white problems, not about African-American response. In the end, the most important factor in the Christianization of the slaves was their own decision. And initially African-Americans were hardly excited about embracing Christianity. Instead, they quite clearly expressed indifference to the Anglican missionaries' literary model of religion. They disdained the emphasis on catechetical schools, the reading of the Bible and the *Book of Common Prayer*, and the mastery of Christian doctrine.

As Anglican missionaries gave way before an army of Methodist and Baptist preachers unburdened by the literary model of conversion, however, blacks made it evident that they found this new form of Christianity more attractive. By 1760 the conversion of blacks to the new religion had become noticeable, and throughout the antebellum years of the nineteenth century, we know, the spread of Christianity among the slaves increased. However, as Christianization proceeded apace, it became evident that there were two different forms of Christianity in the world of the slaves.

First was the official Christianity promoted under the auspices of wary masters for slave consumption, a Christianity that stressed humility, obedience, and "good" behavior. Through special plantation missions designed for the purpose, slaves were brought into the church. Yet at their height these missions were never large-scale endeavors, and they hardly reached all the slaves, at least half of whom worked on farms with fewer than twenty laborers. Thus, as late as 1840 the majority of rural slaves had not become members of the church. But in addition to the Christianity that was under white control, there was a second form, more attractive to blacks, which they directed for themselves. It is to this black Christianity that we now turn.

The Invisible Institution

Thriving in the midst of the white-dominated Christianity of the masters, black Christianity has often been called the "invisible institution" — a church or churches without membership rolls and ordained pastors, without official meeting places and approved ceremonies. It had begun under the eyes of the masters when they sometimes permitted their slaves to hold separate services in a local church or chapel. But after about 1830 to 1835, slave revolts in South Carolina, led by Denmark Vesey (1822), and in Virginia, led by Nat Turner (1831), frightened the owner class. Both revolts had been spawned by prophetic and apocalyptic ideas by which the slaves believed they were instruments of divine justice, bringing radical change through catastrophe. So laws were passed to prohibit religious services by slaves without white supervision. The invisible institution became the religion of a double blackness, carried on in the shadows and under cover of the night, always in danger of interruption and punishment so severe that it might mean the death of a slave. Yet the invisible institution made the slaves, more intensely, a community: it brought blacks together as a people, a nation within the nation. Like so many others who were pouring into America from abroad during these years, blacks came to understand themselves as one among the many.

Centering on the life of prayer and worship, the invisible institution created sacred space and time in which members of the slave community could express their religious ideas and sentiments. On some plantations, blacks could go to the praise house, a special chapel constructed for their needs, where regular services, prayer sessions, witnessings, and the like could be held. But most of the time and especially after 1831, blacks held meetings in the woods at evening, secret sessions in the cabin of one of the slaves, or even spontaneous hymn sings. Wherever they made their places for prayer, or "hush harbors," black people could speak their religion into precarious reality. Here prayer was raised only in whispers, and song only in the quietest tones. Lookouts were stationed to give warning of strangers, and often a huge pot or kettle was overturned on the ground because the slaves believed it helped to contain the sound. If someone began to shout in religious excitement, he or she could be sure that the others would quickly silence the dangerous sound.

Just as blacks found sacred space in the hush harbors, they found sacred time in the rhythm of the gathered worship of the community, in the rituals that marked significant moments during the course of each individual's lifetime, and in the distinctive happenings called conversions, which also came to individuals. For the community, sacred time was created through the words of the preacher and the melodies of the spirituals that knit those present together.

In the sermon of the preacher, blacks evolved a sacred art that even today touches the lives of many in the rural South and other parts of the country where it has spread. The sermon was said to be "spiritual" to distinguish it from the more learned style of preaching, in which the words were delivered from a prepared manuscript. Since black preachers were largely uneducated, their calling was thought to be "in the Spirit." So by the early nineteenth century they were turning necessity into virtue, glorying in the freedom that the situation lent them.

In their understanding, the preacher should be possessed by the Spirit, and hence a spiritual sermon, if it was properly inspired, should break into a chanted and, finally, a sung sermon. The preacher might begin by quoting a text from scripture, but as the text fanned out quickly into a context, the preacher began to chant at a swifter and swifter pace, using repetition and association to construct the lines. His chant became an unrhymed poem, with a rough and breathy sound at the end of each line to mark the rhythm. Meanwhile, the congregation became active, interrupting the preacher with shouts and humming in a rhythmic communal accord. Finally, together preacher and people broke into song.

A successful sermon was one in which the prose of everyday life had been left behind in this communal affirmation of the presence of a Spirit who was a giver of poetry and song. And in the rhythmic pulse that told of conviction of his coming, there were echoes of the rhythmic drums of West Africa and the songs of other ages.

Alongside the rhythm of the chanted sermon, there was the rhythm of the spirituals. With words and thematic content based on the Bible, the spirituals were melodies that had developed over the years, probably through a blending of West African and Protestant musical forms. They were above all *communal* songs, in which intense experiences of sacred presence and unity with one another were created. Their fullest expression came in the meetings of prayer or praise at which the preacher chanted and individuals witnessed to the power of Jesus they felt in their lives. At the same time, the spirituals could be sung anywhere, bringing to the everyday world the presence of a sacred world that helped render slavery bearable.

When performed at intentional prayer meetings, spirituals were songs in motion. They were accompanied by hand clapping and head tossing, by cries and moans, and by a form of sacred dancing called the ring shout. In this ritual, largely brought by the slaves from West Africa, a leader lined out the verses of the song while a group of others, called shouters, moved around in a circle. Singers who stood outside the circle made by the shouters gave out the chorus, at the same time tapping their feet and clapping their hands in support of the circle of shouters. With a shuffling step, this inner circle moved quickly to the beat set by the singers and shouted the sounds that gave the ring shout its name. Sometimes, the shout went on all night until the dawn brought release.

Always, the spirituals showed spontaneity and flexibility, so that they could express the moods of various members of the group and draw them into the setting of community. Often someone particularly depressed by a master's cruelty or the loss of a loved one could be heartened by these songs, in which words could be invented to suit the situation by adding new verses to existing choruses. Often, too, the same words and choruses could carry double meanings, so that even as the slaves sang of spiritual freedom in the other world, they also expressed their yearning for physical freedom from bondage. "Didn't my Lord deliver Daniel, and why not every man?" asked one spiritual. "Go down Moses . . . Tell old Pharaoh/To let my people go," sang another — so clear in its allusions to the slave situation that it was reportedly censored. Sometimes the spirituals could even provide a code language by means of which plots were solidified to escape on the "underground railroad" to the North or to Canada. "I am bound for the land of Canaan" might be a signal announcing a slave's intentions to break away to a new life outside the South.

Chanted sermons and spirituals based black people in a community of prayer from which they drew support. That same community was also sensitive to the cycle of each member's lifetime and tried to give recognition and assistance at those times thought specially significant. Thus, especially for a slave who was Baptist, the ritual of baptism was a memorable event when, wearing a white robe, the new church member went down to a stream or pond to be fully immersed in the water. Preacher and people were at hand, the preacher to do the immersing and the people to offer support with their spirituals and their shouts. Likewise, if two persons should marry, the community was there to provide a public witness and to set the seal of its approval on the contract. In a world in which marriage was a doubtful proposition, often broken by the sale of one of the partners, the solemnizing of marriage in the context of the community was important. It affirmed the integrity of partners who, despite the situation, were freely choosing each other. The ceremony was usually simple enough: most often, the couple jumped over a broomstick either together or in sequence. Sometimes, too, a preacher would preside, and the ceremony would be more formal. In either case, an act of public witness had been accomplished. African-Americans had created their own ritual to express commitment, and the couple could begin their life together with a conviction of the blessing of God and their people.

Then at death, if permission had been granted, there was a solemn ceremony. Often held at night so that work during the day would not be interrupted, the funeral procession surrounded by the darkness suggested again the black center out of which African-Americans lived. People might carry pine knots as torches as they moved together to the burial site, singing spirituals along the way. At the grave, the preacher offered some prayers, and a post marked the location. Then as they left, in a custom brought from Africa, people deposited old belongings and broken earthen pots at the burial place, suggestive of the spirit that had broken with its earthly way of living. Usually there was a sermon sometime later, separated from the funeral by an interval ranging from days to months. Here the dead person—and sometimes a number of people who had died in a given period—would be memorialized. Thus, as in Africa, death did not mean forgetfulness but the cultivation of remembrance. Through the ceremony the ancestors lived on in the minds and hearts—and words—of members of the community.

Behind these events by which the community honored its members lay the prior experience of individual conversion, which brought each person into Christianity. In this process, African-Americans thought of God as a "time-God," who would act according to his own divine rhythms. Hence, waiting on

God was built into their religious culture. Conversion, when it came, was seen as initiated by the divine hand—never as the result of human effort or worthiness. Many of the accounts of conversion from among the slaves stressed the action of an arbitrary God who resembled a kind of Great Owner, acting according to caprice rather than logic.

Often of a highly visionary quality, these accounts would begin with a person's experience of "getting awfully heavy." Here conviction of sin was the burden that the convert bore, and that conviction was reinforced by visions in which a little man conducted a tour of hell, where sin was seen to be punished. The experience seemed as oppressive in the extraordinary sphere as slavery was in the ordinary. Crying for mercy and feeling hopelessness in the situation, the soon-convert claimed rescue by the mercy of God. A vision of the Almighty on his throne or of the heavenly regions filled with angelic choruses might accompany this experience. Often, colors of white and gold predominated in these visionary landscapes, along with the green of a country that seemed a plantation paradise. Jesus might be white with golden hair; his outstretched hand might be at once white and gleaming. His message, though, transcended the visual language in which it was cast: it was a message of relief and salvation. The convert felt surrounded by the grace of God and able to overcome all obstacles. Mercy and salvation seemed assured, and shouting with joy, the new convert rushed to tell the rest about the experience.

Thus, the involuntary condition of slavery had been at the same time affirmed and overcome. In the visionary experience, God had been manifestly the Master; he controlled the slave-convert by his will and acted in his own time; he was white or dressed in white; and he presided over a heaven that resembled a giant plantation. Yet, precisely by imaging God in these terms, a slave-convert had at hand the means to relativize the human condition of bondage. The earthly fiction of slavery was decisively modified in the face of the belief in divine ownership. Now God had a prior claim that destroyed the absoluteness of any plantation owner's bill of sale.

Conversion was the focus of religion in the invisible institution. Like other aspects of African-American Christianity, it employed Protestant language to express what was an authentically black understanding, weaving together the West African past and the present condition of slavery. In other words, Protestant themes were *interpreted* through the twin lenses of Africa and of slavery.

In their ideas and experiences of God as one who transformed a person, even physically, without changing the social or historical situation, blacks expressed their ties to Africa. Their freedom, as in Africa, seemed a kind of magical flight, a gift of visionary transcendence, which radically altered the meaning of events. In their experience as they waited on a willful God, African-Americans internalized their outer condition of slavery. They wove together Protestant and plantation themes by their choice of metaphors of Israel and the exodus from Egypt. Just as the biblical nation of the Hebrews had been slaves in ancient

Appliqué quilt, Athens, Georgia. Constructed by former slave Harriet Powers, this quilt (1895–1898) was pieced together from dyed and printed swatches of cotton, with gilt embroidery added. Thematically, biblical stories were joined to astronomy and local lore.

Egypt, so the slaves saw themselves leading lives of bondage in the American Egypt. But just as, in the Bible, Israel had been led to freedom by the power of God and the staff of Moses, so, too, they believed they would one day be free by the power of Jesus and, at the time of the Civil War, the hand of Abraham Lincoln. In a world in which ordinary and extraordinary were one continuous reality, this did not seem incongruous. Rather, every experience and every situation could serve to express the black center of African-American religion.

The Black Church in Freedom

The center began to be visible when the invisible institution became an official black church. Actually, this had started to happen among free blacks in the North by the end of the eighteenth century, although it would be nearly a century later before in both the North and South the church would be autonomous. While not all African-American religion was contained in the black church, from the first, church organization provided a vehicle for religious and even political expression among African-Americans. If blacks were a nation, then their church was a *polis*, an independent city in which they governed themselves and planned their interactions with other peoples. It was no surprise, therefore, that in the twentieth century, the leadership for the black civil rights movement came largely from the church.

As early as 1787 Richard Allen (1760–1831) and Absalom Jones (1746–1818) had founded the Free African Society in Philadelphia, after they were pulled from their knees while praying when they occupied places in a gallery that was closed to blacks in a Philadelphia Methodist church. The insistence on segregated seating showed the limits of Methodist toleration, and the Free African Society provided a community of support for blacks of different religious persuasions until in 1793 Jones organized the Church of St. Thomas (Episcopal), and Allen and the majority formed the Bethel Church (Methodist). By 1816 the movement that Allen had begun took on a more formal character when a number of churches came together as the African Methodist Episcopal Church. Meanwhile, in New York Peter Williams, Sr. (1760?–1834?), left a white Methodist church at the head of a group of blacks and founded, in 1801, the Zion Church. By 1821 it, too, was organizing as a national church, and in 1848 its official name became the African Methodist Episcopal Zion Church.

In the South, before the decade of the 1830s brought heightened fears of black autonomy, Baptist congregations had been particularly open to black independence and control. Because of the nature of Baptist church government, separate black churches had enjoyed a measure of freedom, and black committees within white churches had presided over the spiritual lives of church members who were black. Even after the enforcement of restrictions, some black churches managed to survive. Thus, in 1845 the Baptist Sunbury Association of Georgia was composed of seven black churches that among them had four ordained preachers who were black. Earlier, in 1821, the black Gillfield Baptist Church in Petersburg, Virginia, could boast of a membership of 441 people, making it the largest church in the Portsmouth Association. There were separate black Baptist churches throughout the South and as far as Kentucky and Louisiana in the West. Sometimes they succeeded in wielding considerable authority despite the efforts of white associations to limit or even disband them.

It was after the Civil War, however, that the black church in both the North and the South came into its own. Both the African Methodist Episcopal Church and the African Methodist Episcopal Zion Church sent missionaries to the South, where they worked with great success among the newly freed blacks. At the same time, a series of independent black church organizations incorporated themselves, separating legally from the mainstream Protestant churches. In the space of two decades, the Colored Primitive Baptists (1866), the African Union First Colored Methodist Protestant Church (1866), the Second Cumberland Presbyterian Church (1869), the Reformed Zion Union Apostolic Church (1869), the Christian Methodist Episcopal Church (1870), the National Baptist Convention, U.S.A. (1880), the Reformed Methodist Union Episcopal Church

(1885), and the Independent African Methodist Episcopal Church (1885) all came into existence. Meanwhile, thousands of other blacks continued as congregations organized under the white Baptist and Methodist denominational bodies. Overwhelmingly, whether they established independent churches or remained within white organizations, blacks were Baptists or Methodists. It was through these churches that they had fashioned their own African-American religious expression through the years of the invisible institution, and their loyalty to these churches continued in the decades following emancipation and on through the twentieth century.

There were problems and tensions in this age of the multiplication of African-American churches and church members. Some in the more traditional black churches, like Jewish immigrants and some white Protestants, made an issue of decorum. With middle-class aspirations and values, they were often former house slaves (or their descendants), who had worked close to their masters in a two-class system of plantation slavery. In the new situation they were offended by the spirituals, for example, that were sung by so many. They were upset, too, by a more permissive sexual ethic that prevailed among numbers of free blacks and wanted instead a firm commitment to Victorian morality. Others, who remained in the majority, were mostly former field slaves or their children. On the plantations they had lived without close contacts with whites. Now they felt alienated by the "airs" of the would-be middle class, perhaps recalling the manners of house slaves during the pre–Civil War era. More than that, they sought a church where they could feel at home in a confusing and often hostile world. Like many white Protestants from a similar socioeconomic background, they wanted a religion of the Word—but a Word that could be felt and expressed intensely as well as heard and done.

Yet, despite the difficulties, the black churches succeeded in reaching their members and in providing for them an institutional focus in the uncertain days after emancipation. They became schools in responsibility and community leadership, and their graduates, as already suggested, continued to serve the black community in many capacities. As the nineteenth century drew to a close, at least one-third of all American blacks were church members, with numbers reaching to some 3 million. A century before, only 4 or 5 percent of the black population had been within the church. The record of growth, as these figures indicate, was striking. Furthermore, black churches involved themselves in educational endeavors, supporting universities and seminaries for the training of African-Americans. They helped to organize benevolent societies for mutual aid. In addition to these "sickness and burial" societies, they cooperated in the formation of black fraternal organizations such as the Knights of Liberty and the Grand United Order of True Reformers. In short, they surrounded the members of their congregations with spiritual and material assistance, providing them support as they encountered a world in which they were learning the ambiguities of legal freedom.

Black Religion in the
Twentieth Century

With the twentieth century came changes for the black community that were as consequential as nineteenth-century emancipation. There was, first, a huge migration from southern farms to cities in both the North and the South. Second, there was a growing chorus of nationalistic hopes and aspirations, with blacks searching for ways to make their freedom complete. Thus, whereas 75 percent of African-Americans lived in the rural South before 1900, by the last third of the twentieth century, three-quarters of them were city dwellers, and half of all blacks lived in northern cities. Meanwhile, African-American nationhood was expressed in a series of movements, from the back-to-Africa strategy of Marcus Garvey to an intellectual trend called black theology.

The migration to the North and to industrial cities had considerable implications for black churches. There was a sense of rootlessness and alienation as blacks contended with strange and hostile urban forces. Sociological divisions became more pronounced, and upper, middle, and lower classes more clearly defined. Along with these sharper divisions, preferences in church organization and style of worship only increased in distinctiveness. Like Jews and like Catholics, African-Americans who were upwardly mobile felt the pull of mainstream Protestantism. To be American meant, in some sense, to become more and more like the one center of gravity that Protestantism provided, and so some joined white denominations. At the same time, independent African Baptist and Methodist churches flourished, offering to the black middle classes a sense of religiocultural identity even as they conformed to the protocols of mainline Protestant churches. Furthermore, the new holiness and pentecostal movements attracted some, and a series of smaller movements in northern cities drew others. It was these new religious bodies that seemed to reach out most clearly to those overwhelmed by overt discrimination and the impersonality of city life. Overall, though, Baptists and Methodists predominated. Nearly two-thirds of African-American church members counted themselves Baptists, and almost a quarter identified with Methodism.

The Holiness-Pentecostal Movement

The rise of the holiness churches came toward the close of the nineteenth century, as we recall from the last chapter. African-Americans were prominent in their formation and growth, and we noted their crucial role in the beginnings of pentecostalism after the turn of the century with the Azusa Street revival. Among blacks, it was poor people in the cities who mainly formed holiness and pentecostal churches. Here, in small communal settings, they could express a religious sense that was close to the religion of slave times. With their stress on the felt presence of the Spirit, the holiness-pentecostal churches appealed to an

African-American longing for transcendence through ecstasy. They cultivated the style of preaching that was familiar. They brought along the spirituals in a new development called gospel music, combining themes from the spirituals with blues and jazz and likewise incorporating drums and tambourines. Further, they encouraged the work of healing as a religious exercise — something familiar to blacks from the long tradition of root work and conjure. At the same time, these churches taught perfection — holiness — and so demanded from their followers a disciplined and sanctified life. In this way, they provided a structure to guide people as they tried to order their lives in the midst of unfamiliar urban settings.

Finally, there was something distinctly new about black holiness-pentecostalism. Many of the holiness-pentecostal churches thought of Jesus as a black man, and as they did so, they articulated a regard for blackness in itself. It was from its beginnings in these churches that blackness as a religious and ethnic symbol began the process of transforming African-American religion. That process would have important consequences, as we will see.

Organizationally, the spiritual independence of these churches was expressed in a proliferation of denominations seemingly everywhere. Often their names were a striking reminder of the intensity of religion they fostered. Thus, South Carolina had its Fire-Baptized Holiness Church of God of the Americas (1922), Arkansas its Church of the Living God, the Pillar and Ground of Truth (1925), and Cincinnati its Latter House of the Lord for All People and the Church on the Mountain, Apostolic Faith (1936). The largest of the churches was the Church of God in Christ, originating as a holiness church in a cotton-gin house in Lexington, Mississippi, and later incorporated in Memphis, Tennessee (1897). Reorganized as a pentecostal church (see the last chapter), it spread not only in the United States but also throughout the world, with over 3.7 million members by 1982. Its founder, Charles H. Mason (1866–1961), had moved from holiness to pentecostalism and in the process become a legend in his time, with many white pentecostalists seeking ordination at his hands. Today, among American pentecostal denominations, Mason's church ranks second only to members of the Assemblies of God in its global following.

The Coming of New Cult Movements

If pluralism and independence were hallmarks of the holiness-pentecostal churches, they were even more characteristic of new urban cult movements, thousands of which mushroomed in storefronts and local residences. Many of them were influenced by forms of voodoo and spiritualism (discussed in Chapter 8), but there were also strong connections between these movements and the churches. Pentecostalism had seen in the experience of speaking in tongues a charism, or gift of the Holy Spirit. A person with such a gift was said to be *charismatic* — filled with the Spirit. An individual who thought himself or herself so inspired often left an original church and, with an inner sense of great authority, began a separate religious movement. Likewise, the new charismatic leader often proclaimed a revelation that, adding to the leader's authority, was a major departure from the Christian tradition.

Thus, with a charismatic leader and a new revelation, the religious body that grew up, though relatively small, was clearly distinguished from the religion of the past. Moreover, it encouraged in its adherents an experiential contact with the message of the leader, so that a continuing desire for ecstasy was fulfilled within the movement. Different from a denomination, a cult movement did not see itself as part of a larger church. Different, too, from a sect (as we will see in the next chapter), a cult movement initiated more radical departures from the Christian tradition. But like a sect, a cult movement did enforce the boundaries that marked its members off from the rest of society. By so doing, it strengthened their sense of identity and peoplehood, providing an antidote for the facelessness of city life. It offered strong religious community and a supportive cultural system through which members could find a fusion of extraordinary and ordinary religion seemingly for every need.

A good example of a charismatic leader and his successful cult movement is Father Divine (1877?–1965) and his Peace Mission Movement. The origins of M. J. Divine are mysterious and obscure. Whatever his early years were like, Father Divine must have been a traveling preacher for some time when, according to reports, he appeared in Americus, Georgia, in 1912 and Valdosta, Georgia, in 1914. Here he taught a blend of mysticism and practicality in which, if a person were truly identified with the Spirit of God, health and plenty would result. Most probably, he drew this idea partially from the perfectionism of holiness religion and partially from the mind-cure teachings that, as we will see in Chapter 8, were part of New Thought. Yet Father Divine made the idea his own, and it became the basis of a lifetime of religious leadership.

Before the end of the decade Divine had left Georgia and appeared in New York. He had become convinced of the presence of God within each person and at the same time continued to reflect on the connections between spiritual wholeness and a life with sufficient food and shelter and a modicum of human dignity. Grounded in this mystical yet pragmatic spirituality, he started a religious community and moved to an eight-room house in Sayville, Long Island, in 1919. So began a long era during which Father Divine presided over a community of devoted followers whose lives, they claimed, were transformed by their relationship with him. His hospitality and generosity became legendary, as members of the Peace Mission sat around a laden banquet table. In its implicit theology, if the Father who was also Messiah were present, there ought to be a messianic banquet; and Father Divine did not deny the conclusion of many who followed him that he was God. Yet his implied claim flowed naturally from holiness religion, in which, in the enthusiasm of worship, a person could feel seized and taken over by God and, so, one with God. It could follow, for believers, that such a person be considered God in his or her own person. Further, according to some, Father Divine claimed that he would not die and also held that if a follower were genuinely devout, he or she, too, would neither grow sick nor die. If the report was true, it is not hard to see why. Sickness and death were thought signs of spiritual malfunction, and it followed that the Spirit-filled person, as a man or woman of power, ordinarily should not experience them.

Preaching the doctrine of peace on earth, offering food and shelter at a nominal price, and helping blacks to find employment, often by encouraging the creation of cooperative businesses, Father Divine opened his doors to white followers as well. He would have no discrimination within the walls of his mansions, and while there was strict segregation by sex, integration by race was as strict. When in 1946 he married Edna Rose Ritchings, a white Canadian woman, he became an example of black–white unity for his followers. Indeed, after his death in 1965, Mother Divine continued the movement from its headquarters in Philadelphia, where it had been relocated in 1941.

Meanwhile, in keeping with both holiness and New Thought emphases, drugs, tobacco, and alcohol were banned, and a disciplined life-style was enjoined among members. There were two kinds of followers: an inner group, who surrendered all their possessions to the movement, and an outer circle, who followed less radically. Still, for both groups the Father Divine Peace Mission Movement was an all-encompassing religion. As African-American religion had always done, it saw the ordinary and extraordinary as an indivisible whole. Thus, as an African-American religion, it found in the satisfaction of material needs the outflow of union with God.

The link between ordinary and extraordinary religion seemed omnipresent in the new cult movements. Another case, for instance, was the United House of Prayer for All People, founded by Bishop Charles Emmanuel Grace (1882–1960). "Sweet Daddy Grace," as he was called by his followers, was the beginning and end of their religion. As the names Emmanuel (God with us) and Grace (the gift of God) suggested, they saw him as God present in their midst. Worship was a time when members celebrated their joy in his presence. Song and dance were accompanied by the rhythmic beat of drums and tambourines, with the dancers moving erotically, exclaiming "Daddy! You feel so good!" Many claimed that they had been cured, sometimes by a copy of *Grace Magazine* placed over the chest and sometimes by using Daddy Grace soap. Beyond these, Daddy Grace sold a wealth of other commodities from toothpaste and cookies to emblems and badges, and members were continually urged to contribute money to his cause. While outsiders might find this activity offensive, from the point of view of the believer, giving was intrinsic to the context of worship. Like an African Trickster, Daddy Grace took from his people and profited from his taking. Yet by giving abundantly, his people felt that they experienced even more abundance. For them money was a small price to pay for physical and spiritual transformation, and ordinary reality was inescapably tied to the extraordinary. Using Daddy Grace products underlined the connection they had made.

The Religion of Blackness

Both Father Divine (at least in part) and Daddy Grace had been shaped by the holiness movement, and their movements were distinctive transformations of holiness themes such as ecstasy, healing, revitalization through feeling the presence of God, and sanctification (moral perfection) in everyday life. Another side of holiness-pentecostal religion had been its growing regard for blackness as it reflected on the meaning of the black Jesus. It was in this vein that a different religious movement took root among African-Americans in the twentieth century. Whereas their ancestors in the South had witnessed to visions in which they saw the whiteness of God, blacks now began to look to a God who preferred blackness. Because they were identified with blacks, Father Divine, Daddy Grace (although a mulatto), and other charismatic leaders were implicitly signaling this change. Some, however, grew more explicit, and in a new expression of the interplay between the ordinary and extraordinary, they began to speak of a free black nation.

Even during the time of slavery, when it was common for God to be seen in vision as white, there had been a consciousness of peoplehood among blacks. It had sometimes taken a dramatic turn, as in the slave rebellions of the early nineteenth century and, after 1846, in the formation of the Knights of Tabor, a secret society organized among the slaves to liberate themselves through the use of force. After emancipation and the turn of the century, these stirrings of black consciousness took more concrete form against a background of American racism. There was, in a key example, Marcus M. Garvey (1887–1940), an immigrant from Jamaica who in 1914 established the Universal Negro Improvement Association. In the early twenties, Garvey's star rose, as he preached a gospel of the African heritage based on the affirmation of a black God. To underline the religious character of his message, he was instrumental in the foundation of the African Orthodox Church in New York City in 1921. Anglican in background, the church fostered racial pride and fought against any semblance of white domination in black religion. At the same time, Garvey continued urging blacks to create an independent state for themselves in Africa. Like the Jews in the Zionist movement, the black Israel must mount a campaign for return to the homeland. Although Garvey's dream was interrupted by his deportation in 1927 after accusations of financial fraud, his legacy of a religion of blackness lived on.

Similarly, various groups of Black Jews or Black Hebrews self-consciously promoted the African-American people as the true Israel, accepting the Jewish Talmud as their holy book and observing the Jewish dietary laws. Others, in a similar move that rejected Christianity, turned to Islam as a vehicle for the expression of black ethnoreligious identity. Here, the Moorish Science Temple of America was an early instance. Founded by Timothy Drew (1866–1929) in the year before Garvey's Universal Negro Improvement Association, it thrived in the same atmosphere that fueled the Garvey movement. And the Moorish Science

Temple continued after the death of its prophet. Drew had been influenced by Islam and produced his own version of the Qur'an, the sacred book of Muslims, for his followers. Interspersed with Islamic, Christian, and Garveyite messages, Drew's *Holy Koran* taught the Asiatic origins of American blacks and demanded that they call themselves Moorish (Muslims from ancient Mauretania in Northern Africa) Americans. Noble Drew Ali, as he was renamed, exhorted that before a people could have a God, they must have a nationality.

After the prophet's sudden death in 1929, one of the factions of his movement in Detroit came under the spell of the mysterious Wallace D. Fard (Farrad Mohammad or Wali Farrad). He had appeared in the city in 1930 as a peddler. Thought to be of Arab extraction, he won the confidence of his listeners and gradually began to teach what he claimed was the true religion for black people. When there were too many to meet in a house, Fard and his followers rented a hall. They named it the Temple of Islam, and the movement known as the Black Muslims had begun. Fard continued preaching, urging the black nation to awake to the deceits of "blue-eyed devils." He taught many to read, and he told them that Allah, the true God, was using whites as instruments through whom blacks might learn their own past history and prepare themselves for their future destiny.

Within three years, Fard had established an impressive organization with a temple, a University of Islam (an elementary and secondary school), a Muslim Girls Training Class, and the Fruit of Islam, a military company for the defense of the faithful. Among those who rose to positions of responsibility within the movement was a man from Georgia named Elijah Poole (1897–1975). Renamed Elijah Muhammad by Fard, he became his Minister of Islam, and when Fard disappeared mysteriously in 1934, it was Elijah Muhammad who emerged from the various factions as the leader of a reconstituted Nation of Islam. Fard, he preached to his followers, had been God in their midst, and Fard's birthday in February came to be known among them as Savior's Day.

The voice of Allah was thought to speak now through Elijah Muhammad. In his primer *The Supreme Wisdom* and in continuing issues of the tabloid *Mr. Muhammad Speaks*, he told them what was held as the will of God. After a term in jail during the Second World War because of his refusal to fight, Muhammad returned in 1946 to a movement that grew by leaps and bounds. Like the holiness churches before him, he taught a life of self-discipline and family solidarity. The militancy of his organization was reflected in the Nation of Islam's sacred story of origins, which, as Yakub's history, taught of black superiority and a demonic plot that, over centuries, had produced a bleached-out white race. So, too, the Nation spoke of the formation of a separate national territory for American blacks and warned its members not to vote, hold public office, or serve in the armed forces. As the boundaries were drawn tightly around the community, black pride seemed to be everywhere and, with it, black hope.

Even during the lifetime of Elijah Muhammad, however, there was variant interpretation of the Nation of Islam and the religion of blackness. Malcolm X (born Malcolm Little, 1925–1965), one of Elijah Muhammad's most trusted lieutenants, gradually came to see the message of Islam as universal human solidarity. After a pilgrimage to Mecca, he could no longer endorse the radical separatism of the Black Muslims, and he broke with the movement in 1964 to form the Muslim Mosque, Incorporated, and then the Organization of Afro-American Unity. In this second organization, especially, he had begun to explore the meaning of black nationhood without attaching it overtly to the ideology of Islam. So at the same time, Malcolm X was moving blacks closer to an orthodox and universal Islam and urging them toward a clearer sense of their own identity. The two, as he saw it, were related: people who knew who they were could extend the hand of friendship to those who were different.

Malcolm X was shot to death in 1965 by members of the parent Black Muslim movement, but a decade later, some of his ideas returned. After the death of Elijah Muhammad in 1975, his son, Wallace D. Muhammad (b. 1933), assumed control of the organization. Ironically, the son of the founder carried the movement even further in the direction Malcolm X had taken. It was the dawn of a new day, as a self-assured Wallace D. Muhammad, educated in Egypt and an Arabic speaker, broke with black separatism and moved the Nation toward orthodox Islam. Gone was the origin account of black priority and the inferior moral and physical status of whites. Gone, too, were prohibitions against voting, holding political office, and joining the armed forces. Malcolm X was honored in death with the title of Shabazz (the ancient tribe of Abraham), and a temple in Harlem was named after him. Whites were welcome to join the organization, as a new symbolism of the Qur'an (Koran) as the universal open book was promulgated. The familiar *Mr. Muhammad Speaks* changed its name to the *Bilalian News*, after Bilal, said to be the African convert to Islam who later became the first minister to the original prophet, Muhammad. Meanwhile, a new name — the World Community of al-Islam in the West — announced the rebirth of the movement. Then, in 1980, the movement changed its name again to become the American Muslim Mission. And thereafter it shed even this sign of separateness to proclaim its identity as part of traditional Sunni Islam.

Like Malcolm X, the younger Muhammad re-created his religious inheritance to blend the universal religion of Islam with concern for blackness. Like Malcolm X, too, he expressed his belief that, in America, to be a nation meant to establish ties with other peoples. In other words, Muhammad had loosened the boundaries of the organization. He had made a fundamental decision that he and his people should join America. American and fully Islamic, too, Warith (as he had changed his name) Muhammad acted as official distributor of Arab-donated missionary funds to Muslim organizations in the United States. More honorific for ritual reasons, world Islamic leaders designated him to certify American Muslims for participation in the Islamic annual pilgrimage to Mecca. And Muslim prayer leaders came to be received in associations of black ministers.

There was also negative evidence of the movement's Islamic orthodoxy. In the context of its radical departures from the earlier Nation of Islam, with perhaps

100,000 of the Nation's former members following Warith Muhammad, a countermovement appeared. Led by Minister Louis Farrakhan — toward the end of Elijah Muhammad's career the powerful leader of the Harlem Temple No. 7 — this movement to return to the old Nation of Islam attracted an estimated 20,000 blacks, and splinter movements began to appear, too. Still, by 1989 estimates suggested that roughly 1 million out of 6 million orthodox Muslims in the nation were African-American and that converts to Islam were overwhelmingly black. Rapprochement — to America and to orthodox Islam — was clearly the majority report from the once-separatist movement.

It was significant that, at the other end of the continuum of black religion in the twentieth century, the same fundamental decision to join America had been made. In the civil rights movement of the sixties, it was the more traditional black churches that provided leadership and marshaled their laity to a statement of the religion of blackness. In Martin Luther King, Jr. (1929–1968), the civil rights movement had at once its clearest symbol and its most effective organizer. He came before the public eye for a brief space of twelve or thirteen years before his assassination. His father was a prominent preacher, and King was the product of the black church with its history in slavery and freedom. When he began to employ the tactic of nonviolent resistance, his first model was inevitably that of ancestors who had endured their lot on southern plantations. During King's years at Boston University, theological reading helped to develop his views. Then, beginning with the Montgomery, Alabama, bus boycott of 1955, history provided the stage. As minister of a local Baptist church, King found himself the leader of the boycott movement.

It was the start of a time of public witness, as King moved from place to place in the South and later in the North, feeling impelled by convictions bound to Christian teaching. In Birmingham, Alabama, and Albany, Georgia, in Selma, Alabama, and Washington, D.C., blacks were marching with King at their head. Meanwhile, the U.S. Congress, with a series of new laws, seemed to tread in their steps. There were Civil Rights acts in 1957, 1960, and 1964, and in 1965 came the Voting Rights Act.

Fired by his dream that one day the children of former slaves and former slaveholders would sit together at the same table, King evoked the figure of Moses leading the Jews out of Egypt. His religion of blackness recalled the earlier religion of African-Americans as they sang their spirituals, and it had been nourished in the rural churches that, in honoring a black Jesus, had encouraged self-esteem. On a different front, as King marched, another group of blacks was beginning to articulate for the intellectual community the meaning of the religion of blackness.

There had been precedent for their efforts in the writings of W. E. Burghardt DuBois (1868–1963), a Harvard-educated professor of sociology at Atlanta University at the turn of the century. DuBois had written long reflections on the meaning of the black Jesus and the nature of black spirituality. In the sixties and seventies, a new generation of preachers and scholars took up these themes.

There was, for example, Albert B. Cleage, Jr. (b. 1911), who, in a series of sermons published in 1968 as *The Black Messiah*, declared that Jesus was black and that his true resurrection was the awakening of the black nation. There was Joseph R. Washington, Jr. (b. 1930), who, in *The Politics of God* (1969), saw blacks as the true remnant of the nation of Israel, the suffering servant bearing the sins of all people. And there was James H. Cone (b. 1938), who in a series of works self-consciously set the agenda for the construction of a black theology.

For Cone and for others attracted by his thinking, liberation was the key to theological inquiry into the black experience. The Christian gospels, Cone argued, had revealed Jesus as a religious leader on the side of the oppressed, announcing their impending freedom. Since black people historically had been the most oppressed among the nations, Jesus must be on their side, working against the forces that beat them down. To be a Christian, in this reading, all people must become spiritually black; that is, they must identify with oppressed people and their cause. In *Black Theology and Black Power* (1969) and *A Black Theology of Liberation* (1970), Cone developed these and similar themes.

Much of the material for this theological articulation of the religion of blackness had been reinterpreted from the European Christian tradition, and much of it had little impact on black laypeople. Yet in many ways Cone's work sprang from the same roots as they sprang. In its quest for black empowerment and in its mingling of religion and peoplehood, there were echoes of the African and African-American past. Power was seen to come from heaven to earth and to dissolve the separate worlds of sacred and profane, reconstituting them as one whole.

In the late twentieth century, with perhaps 20 million Protestant church members among their numbers, African-Americans could count over half of their population as belonging to a church. Moreover, African-American church membership was higher proportionately than that of any other religious family. Well over half of black Protestants were attending worship services regularly, and one-quarter were attending occasionally. Among the worshipers, by far the largest black denomination was the National Baptist Convention, U.S.A., with 7.1 million members. Other major African-American denominations included the Church of God in Christ (noted earlier), the National Baptist Convention of America, the African Methodist Episcopal Church, the African Methodist Episcopal Zion Church, the Progressive National Baptist Church, and the Christian Methodist Episcopal Church.

Yet despite the evident use that African-Americans had made of Christianity in creating a religion of blackness and, thus, in struggling for freedom, that freedom was still not complete. In fact, racism flared in the eighties, and on college campuses scattered throughout the nation incidents of racial hatred harked back to a past many thought gone forever. Nor, generally, did blacks' economic situation improve in an American society in which the poor were getting poorer and the rich richer. Nonetheless, by the late twentieth century African-Americans had developed a clear sense of their identity as one people among the many in the United States. Indeed, with little opportunity for cultivating their past, they had markedly demonstrated what it meant to seek for roots. Like American Indians, Jews, and Catholics, they had been pulled toward the one center, the mainstream Protestant axis of American religion. Yet more than Jews and Catholics, blacks had explored the paths of resistance; and like American Indians, they had sought ways to make their separate past a present source of strength.

African-Americans had their churches of middle-class Protestant propriety. They also had the acids of city life, with its drugs and crime, which ate away at the fabric of the black family. Living between these opposites, blacks had learned to bring together old and new to order their world. The African past was over; the African-American present was unfolding.

In Overview

The African-American experience began in the seventeenth-century slavery that brought various West African peoples involuntarily to the New World. While these peoples were diverse, their religious heritage included common elements: a strong sense of community and communal responsibility, an equally strong tie with ancestors, a sense of the nearness of various intermediary Gods, a belief in the ultimate power of a noninterfering high God, and a ritual life that expressed both extraordinary and ordinary religion.

In America, blacks preserved a number of their religious customs and practices. More importantly in the long run, they continued to look at the world according to religious categories that Africa had given them. They mixed ordinary and extraordinary religion in tales of Tricksters like Brer Rabbit and in conjure. As they encountered Christianity, a few blacks became Roman Catholics, but—after a slow start—the largest number became Protestants. In the "invisible institution," these black Protestants created a religion of their own. They found sacred space in public praise houses or in secret hush harbors, and they created sacred time with sermons, spirituals, ring shouts, and various other rituals. As converts who proclaimed they had been "struck dead" by the power of God, blacks both affirmed and overcame the involuntary condition of slavery to express a sense of spiritual freedom.

Meanwhile, in the early nineteenth century, free blacks organized in the African Methodist Episcopal Church and in what became known as the African Methodist Episcopal Zion Church. Under Baptist polity, some enslaved blacks in the South also controlled their churches to a degree. After the Civil War, a series of independent black churches came into existence, and by the twentieth century a religion of blackness was growing among African-American people. A nation within the nation, blacks had already turned to a black Jesus in the northern cities where they belonged to various holiness and pentecostal churches. In numerous smaller movements, they honored blackness in their devotion to black charismatic leaders and to ideologies of chosenness such as those provided by the Black Jews and the Black Muslims. In the civil rights movement of the sixties and the creation of a black theology, the late twentieth century contributed newer versions of the religion of blackness. Even as blacks joined America, the boundaries between themselves and white America were still carefully drawn. African-Americans continued to mingle ordinary and extraordinary religion in the black center.

Yet in America there were other centers and other hopes. As the slaves had been describing their visions of paradise and their children had looked for ways to begin to build a more modest version on earth, other Americans had staked a claim to their piece of a heavenly landscape. Nineteenth-century new religions grew out of the visions of their founders. To imagine in America seemed to mean to create and to construct.

SUGGESTIONS FOR FURTHER READING: AFRICAN-AMERICAN RELIGION

Brown, Karen McCarthy. *Mama Lola: A Vodou Priestess in Brooklyn.* Berkeley: University of California Press, 1991.

Fauset, Arthur H. *Black Gods of the Metropolis.* Philadelphia: University of Pennsylvania Press, 1971.

Frazier, E. Franklin. *The Negro Church in America.* New York: Schocken Books, 1964.

Genovese, Eugene D. *Roll, Jordan, Roll: The World the Slaves Made.* New York: Pantheon Books, 1974.

Hughes, Langston, and Bontemps, Arna, eds. *Book of Negro Folklore.* New York: Dodd, Mead, 1958.

Johnson, Clifton H., ed. *God Struck Me Dead.* Philadelphia: Pilgrim Press, 1969.

Levine, Lawrence W. *Black Culture and Black Consciousness: Afro-American Folk Thought from Slavery to Freedom.* New York: Oxford University Press, 1977.

Lincoln, C. Eric, and Mamiya, Lawrence H. *The Black Church in the African American Experience.* Durham, NC: Duke University Press, 1990.

Long, Charles H. *Significations: Signs, Symbols, and Images in the Interpretation of Religion.* Philadelphia: Fortress Press, 1986.

Malcolm X. *The Autobiography of Malcolm X (As Told to Alex Haley).* New York: Ballantine Books, 1973.

Murphy, Joseph M. *Santería: An African Religion in America.* Boston: Beacon Press, 1988.

Raboteau, Albert J. *Slave Religion: The "Invisible Institution" in the Antebellum South.* New York: Oxford University Press, 1978.

Ray, Benjamin C. *African Religions: Symbol, Ritual, and Community.* Englewood Cliffs, NJ: Prentice-Hall, 1976.

Sernett, Milton C., ed. *Afro-American Religious History: A Documentary Witness.* Durham, NC: Duke University Press, 1985.

Thompson, Robert Farris. *Flash of the Spirit: African and Afro-American Art and Philosophy.* New York: Random House, 1983.

Washington, Joseph R., Jr. *Black Sects and Cults.* Garden City, NY: Doubleday, Anchor Press, 1973.

Weisbrot, Robert. *Father Divine.* Boston: Beacon Press, 1983.

Wilmore, Gayraud S. *Black Religion and Black Radicalism: An Interpretation of the Religious History of Afro-American People.* 2d ed. Maryknoll, NY: Orbis Books, 1983.

NEWMADE IN AMERICA

Two centuries after the original cast came together in early American religious history, they had experienced extensive change. New forms of old religions abounded, and they continued to do so. Yet members of the cast could still be identified by their religious markings, and ties to tradition were real. By the 1800s, however, the ideology of newness was fast offering radical competition to the past. New lands — new places to live and build — were by this time a fact of life for millions, even for many Native Americans, who were being displaced from their ancestral lands by European immigrants. New people — the mix of strangers from many places and traditions — were continuously confronting those who had taken up lives in the new places.

Given all of this change, the religious response was not surprising. For some, the traditions of the past, even as remade for an American context, were no longer adequate. Instead, some began to reach toward religions that were *newmade* in America, religions that in incisive ways cut their ties to tradition and self-consciously struck out in different directions. Religions like Mormonism, Christian Science, spiritualism, theosophy, and New Thought were all examples. So, too, were markedly changed versions of premillennialism like Seventh-day Adventism and of Christian perfectionism like the Shaker and Oneida communities. In these experiments with newness, people were taking parts that no one had foreseen. The original cast were making room for indigenous religious developments.

Visions of Paradise Planted: Nineteenth-Century New Religions

On a spring day in 1820, a teenager named Joseph Smith from a poor family in upstate New York knelt to pray in the woods. He had been confused by the claims and counterclaims of mission-minded sectarians in his area, and not knowing to whom to listen, he had decided to try to listen to his God. Smith was not doing anything exceptional in a district given over to religious excitement and ferment, but what he said happened was extraordinary. According to Smith's account, he watched as a pillar of light came gradually down upon him, and then he saw two "Personages" who filled him with awe. As they stood in the air above him, one pointed to the other, calling the second his beloved son and telling Smith to hear him. When Smith then asked the two persons which of the sects was right and which he should join, he was told that they were all wrong and that he should join none of them.

Sectarianism and Nineteenth-Century New Religions

It was the inaugural vision of a prophet, and the results of Joseph Smith's announced experience live on in a people who count him the founder of their religion—the Mormons. As the account hints, Smith and his followers would think of themselves not as a small sect but instead as a church that was all-inclusive. Still, like members of so many new religions in the nineteenth-century United States, the Mormons were considered by others to be sectarians, that is, members of a sect. This term grows out of sociological scholarship about religion, and it is in the work of Max Weber (1864–1920) and Ernst Troeltsch (1866–

1923) that we find the classic descriptions of sectarianism. For Troeltsch, sects were voluntary societies of people bound to one another by mutual religious experiences of new birth. They lived in small groups separated from the rest of the world, and they emphasized a life of committed love and of law rather than one of free grace. Above all, they lived in expectation of a coming kingdom of God that would end the present world.

A sect was therefore exclusive and conversional. People were not born into one, but they moved into it as the result of some decisive religious experience. This strong religious impulse often urged sectarians to intense missionary effort, but at the same time their gathered groups were the refuge for the few from every society who could give themselves totally to their religious ideal. Thus, sectarians valued intense commitment and a radical life-style over universal availability. Theirs was a chosen society of saints instead of the huge, extended church that included saints and sinners within its membership.

Christianity, which had once itself been a tiny sect within Judaism, spawned continual sectarian movements, especially when it came to be recognized and established. While it would be interesting to trace the growth of these sects over the years from the beginning of Christianity, perhaps the most useful model for American sectarianism is the Radical Reformation of sixteenth-century Europe. This left wing of the European religious revolution departed in major ways from the mainstream of the Protestant Reformation led by Martin Luther, John Calvin, and others. In fact, the radical ideal was so different from that of the main Protestant Reformers that they persecuted sectarians as wholeheartedly as Catholics did. Like Catholics, the Protestant Reformers believed they were attacking those who by their teachings would murder not the bodies but, worse, the souls of human beings.

Although these Radicals were distributed among many sectarian movements throughout Europe, it is possible to identify characteristics that were present in all or most of them. Different from mainstream Protestants and Catholics alike, the Radicals understood the church as a free society of people gathered out of the world. They believed that not all of those who lived in a geographical territory should be part of the church but instead that only those who chose willingly should join. Once, they thought, the Christian church had lived up to that idea; but long ago, in the fourth and early fifth centuries, it had fallen. What the church needed, therefore, was not reformation, as mainstream Protestants thought, but the *restoration* of primitive Christianity.

In this context, the Radicals challenged mainstream Protestants on another front. Luther and Calvin had both preached that salvation was contained in the Word of God. The Word was identified with the gospel, and the gospel with Jesus, so that, although Luther and Calvin had different emphases in their understanding of the matter, salvation, or justification, came for them ultimately through assent to the Word of God. That is, it came through faith in the message that had been preached. By contrast, the Radicals saw the gospel as law, and for them the process of sanctification took the place of the Reformers' justification.

Right living was the essence of true religion, and the church meant to them an association in which people would support one another in their quest for total personal morality. Salvation came, then, by works, by zeal for the kingdom. Jesus became a model of how to live and die more than a sacrificial victim who had gained heaven for all or for some by his atonement. For the Radicals, sacraments (called ordinances) were signs and memorials, teaching events that provided powerful reminders of the truths of Christian history. And since all were called to be saints, the Radicals thought, all were called to be priests both in theory and in practice.

In societies formed on these principles, the things of this world — politics, economics, war — were seen as inconsequential and, indeed, distracting and dangerous in terms of the life of sanctity. More than that, the Radicals believed that they saw signs of a speedy approach of the second coming. In this atmosphere of expectation of the return of Jesus, they disdained any involvement with the state, sometimes treating it with indifference as a relic of the past and sometimes acting with hostility and open provocation toward it. Pacifism, the prohibition of oaths, and the avoidance of magistracies or other government service were all examples of Radical avoidance of the world.

In America, as we have seen, many of these themes were already being echoed in the seventeenth century. The Puritans who settled the Atlantic coast, whether formally Separatists from the Church of England or not, possessed in some ways a distinct sectarian consciousness. Restoration and millennialism, as we noticed, were emphasized. Conversion became the threshold to social and civil participation, and missionary intentions were intrinsic to Puritan self-understanding. Commitment was a requirement for a full Puritan life. Moreover, a series of groups — like the Baptists of Rhode Island, for example — left the main body of the Puritans to seek a greater and more radical purity. On the other hand, the Puritans as a whole had absorbed enough of Calvinist thought to hold to predestinarian views and to be wary of law as a saving force. Enjoined to virtue yet warned against virtue's ability to save, they still found the Christian state necessary. Making war, taking oaths, and serving as magistrates were matters of fact that were also, as the Puritans saw them, matters of Christian duty.

By the nineteenth century, many of the Puritans' descendants were emphasizing Radical themes of restoration and millennialism even more than their forebears. We have traced this development through the evangelical culture of the mission mind. Still, like the Puritans before them, the representatives of evangelical culture stopped short of the full-blown commitment of the Radicals. Theirs were radical themes, to be sure, but played out in a softer, more inclusive style. And theirs, too, were the magisterial themes of the mainstream Reformation, which found an ally in the Christian state and hoped for the Christian transformation of society. It was true that some groups at some periods in the evangelical culture sounded a separatist call. But the separation was, in the main, counterbalanced by other tendencies, so that it never became the entire story. The most accurate description of the Protestant evangelicals will acknowledge that they were hybrids.

But did any separatists in America go further? Did any group descend in an unbroken line from the European Radicals of the sixteenth century? Or, more, did any new groups take up the Radicals' substance and style even though not historically descended from them? In answer to the question of unbroken descent, we can point to religious peoples such as the Amish of Pennsylvania, Ohio, and other areas and the Hutterites of the upper Midwest. These small groups continued to flourish in the New World, and they added to the manyness of American religions. But beyond these, we can look to new sectarian movements that could not trace their lineage directly to the Radicals but that nonetheless strongly resembled them. Such movements could be found in America as early as colonial times, but it was in the nineteenth century that they caught the public eye significantly and that they grew more than at any time before.

Since every historical movement has its particularities, there were, of course, important differences between sixteenth-century Radical views and nineteenth-century American ideas. To cite but one example, the American Mormons placed the fall of the church not in the fourth and fifth centuries but in the time of the earliest apostles. And unlike the Radicals, they emphasized the absolute necessity of a special priesthood and the observation of ordinances (sacraments). Moreover, they sought the restoration of the ten tribes of Israel as much as that of the primitive church.

Nevertheless, if we remember that there were differences, it is interesting to look at the early Mormons and other radically new religious groups that arose in nineteenth-century America as classic instances of sectarianism. Such an approach highlights their departures from the normative Protestantism of the era, both in its liberal and evangelical versions. In other words, from a religious point of view it is not fair to characterize these new groups as "also-rans" among the Protestants. They were not simply smaller or less popular than Baptists and Methodists or even fundamentalists and pentecostals. They pursued a more totalizing vision, one that departed more completely from mainstream American culture. They experimented with forms of ritual and common behavior distinct from what others regarded as standard. We might say that, while mainstream Protestants emphasized the Word and exalted the Bible that contained it, radical American sectarians put their premium instead on the deed—on the major changes in life-style that their religious convictions demanded. From this point of view, in the beginning there was less the Word than the Act.

Thus, like American Indians and like Jews and sometimes Catholics, these movements often succeeded in bringing ordinary and extraordinary religion together. The everyday for them became the center of religious reality, yet their religion meant at the same time the chance to pass beyond the boundaries of the ordinary. As a matter of fact, instead of making the extraordinary ordinary, as in their ways American Indians, Jews, and Catholics tended to do because their practices were given by tradition, the sectarians reversed the process. With the zeal of their newness, they made the ordinary — each detail of daily living — an event touching the extraordinary, a way into another world.

This is where the time and place in which the American sectarians arose is especially important. The nineteenth century was a time of marked political and cultural change. The Great Seal of the United States — visible still on the back of a one-dollar bill — proclaimed in the Latin phrase *novus ordo seclorum* that here was a new order of things. For Americans whose ancestors had been Europeans or who were immigrants themselves, there was tremendous excitement about the possibilities that the new (to them) land created. It was frontier territory — a boundary place once again. It invited them to the boundaries of their own imaginations and abilities, urging them to the purity of life and commitment that could match the stretches of "virgin" land.

For them, it did not matter that the land was not really "virgin" or "new" in any absolute sense but had been peopled by Indian nations for thousands of years. Indeed, those drawn to the nineteenth-century new religions were attracted by the same themes that, as we saw, drew other Americans like the Protestant evangelicals. To eyes inherited from Europe, the land looked fresh and original — like the Garden of Eden before the fall of Adam and Eve. People wanted to match the newness of the land and the newness of the democratic political experiment with a return to old beginnings or a plunge forward into completely new beginnings of their own. Either they would restore Christian origins or, turning the time of beginnings inside out, they would create brand-new societies in the millennium. Their visions would lead to the planting of paradise on American soil.

As we have already begun to notice and will see again in Part II, this millennial fervor was quintessentially American. Although the sectarian movements never involved huge numbers of people relative to the Protestant mainstream, sectarians were acting and living out themes that were central to the culture. At the same time, sectarians in general often could not maintain the purity of their experience for more than a generation or two. So the trajectory of a sect led to religious transformations in which denominational status won the day. Like their Protestant and Catholic neighbors, many sectarians with the passage of time belonged to churches into which they were born, and they often became almost indistinguishable from their nonsectarian associates. (After all, how could someone born in a faith be a "volunteer"?) In America, of course, that is part of the story of how manyness became oneness. For the present, however, we need to look at the early history of some representative sectarian movements in order to understand their religious impulse and their contributions to pluralism.

Here it might be helpful to imagine a broad continuum along which various nineteenth-century new religions were located. At one end were those whose communities, while they maintained their exclusivity and separation from the world, still allowed, relatively speaking, for a modicum of individual initiative and activity among their membership. At the other were those who carried the sectarian principle seemingly as far as it would go, demanding a totalitarian commitment in communal living. Thus, at one end of the continuum we find groups such as Mormons, Seventh-day Adventists, and Christian Scientists, all of whom in their full vigor made considerable demands of their members but stopped short of total community. At the other end we can point to groups such as the Shakers and Oneida Perfectionists, whose members lived together in intensive nineteenth-century communes.

The Mormons

We return to the prophet Joseph Smith (1805–1844), whom we left claiming his first experience of a vision. The group he founded, the Mormons, passed from a time of near-total community living to a time of more individual, but still strongly bonded, membership. Thus, the Mormons are interesting in terms of our continuum because they demonstrate the possibilities of different locations along it. At the same time, to view the Mormons solely for their place on the continuum would be to look at them more sociologically than religiously. We need to find ways to get to what was central to Mormon religion.

These ways are provided in Joseph Smith's account of the revelation he claimed through the heavenly messenger, Moroni. The combination of Smith's anxiety about religious questions and his sometime occupation for clients as a treasure hunter—with a "seerstone" he had discovered—came together in what he reported regarding Moroni and subsequent events. Although the exact sequence of treasure hunting and vision is difficult to pinpoint, Moroni, said Smith, directed him to a place where golden plates were buried, forming a written testimony to the spiritual history of early America. Smith also said that, buried in the same place, he found by direction two stones in silver bows and attached to a breastplate, the Urim and Thummim. After a delay of five years, attested Smith, Moroni allowed him to take the golden plates and the stones. The plates contained what came to be known as the Book of Mormon, and he began to use the stones (seerstones of a higher order) to translate it. Furthermore, he said, Moroni supplemented what was written on the plates with other prophetic words and teachings—most significantly here concerning the future destiny of American Indians and of America itself, the site of a New Jerusalem to come.

Standing beside the Bible as sacred scripture, the Book of Mormon told a sacred history of the tribe of Joseph, descendants of whom came to the American continent in ancient times before the birth of Jesus. According to the Book of Mormon, Lehi and his family left Jerusalem in 600 B.C. and were led by God to North America. But two of Lehi's sons, Laman and Lemuel, were followed by a group of people whose ways had become wicked. Hence, they were cursed by God with dark skin, and from these people, mingled apparently with others, the

American Indians later descended. These Lamanites, as they were called, turned on the white Nephites, the other branch of Lehi's family, and in A.D. 384 succeeded in destroying most of them. But Mormon, one of the Nephites who remained, buried in the Hill Cumorah of upper New York state the plates that contained the Book of Mormon. In addition, he gave a few of the plates to his son, Moroni, who, according to the book, was the last surviving Nephite.

The Book of Mormon, therefore, established the Hebraic origins of American Indians and supplied America with a biblical past. Its revelation was cast as history, and the nature of its account shaped the nature of the movement that grew up around it and Smith. If God acted in history, both in the Bible and in the Book of Mormon, a certain value was placed on the things of time. They were thought important enough to merit God's concern, and so time and history were understood to possess significance in their own right. Action became the essence of religion, and Mormonism early expressed this religious idea in a number of ways.

First, for Mormons revelation was decidedly not a thing of the past. It lived on in the present because, they believed, God continued to speak to the prophet Joseph Smith and his successors even after the Book of Mormon had been translated. Besides these extraordinary revelations, which usually occurred at times of grave crisis, revelation for Mormons came in ordinary ways through the history of the community and its struggles. Time after time, it was troubled by internal dissension and attacked by outsiders. Almost, it seemed, the early Mormons were acting out the account of the wanderings of Lehi and his sons of the House of Joseph, for their history was one of movement from place to place. Although the Mormons did not perceive this connection, they did see themselves as repeating the years of wandering of the first Israel recorded in the Old Testament. Indeed, they looked toward the future time of "gathering," when Zion would be established in the New World.

In 1830, however, they moved to Kirtland, Ohio, and then, in 1837, to Independence and to Far West, Missouri. When the hostility of their neighbors drove them from Missouri, they migrated to Illinois, where they founded Nauvoo; but in 1844, hostility again brought an armed confrontation, and it led to the murder of Smith while he was jailed in Carthage, Illinois. This action by an angry mob did not end the Mormon years of wandering. Under Brigham Young (1801–1877), the main body of the Mormons set out on a journey that brought them at last to the Great Salt Lake in what is now Utah. Here they founded their Zion in the mountains, the state of Deseret.

To understand the Mormons is to understand this history in which they acted out their identity. They were people of pilgrimage, who were still seeking final goodness in Zion. Hence, doing the Word was ever central. At the same time, in their conception of the nature of the church they self-consciously separated themselves from their Protestant neighbors. As we noted earlier, Smith and his followers saw their movement not simply as a restoration of the primitive church, as the Radicals had hoped, but also as a restoration of the ten tribes of

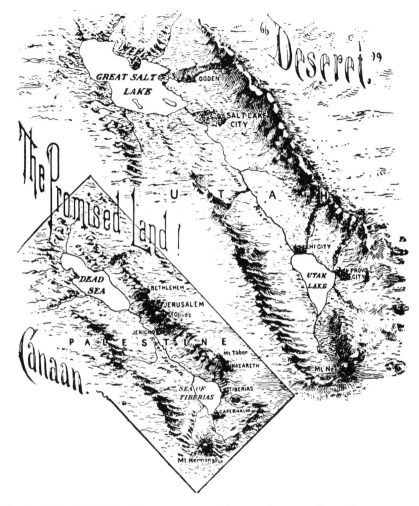

Salt Lake Valley, Utah. This Mormon-inspired drawing (source unknown) was published in William E. Smythe's *Conquest of Arid America* in 1900. Mormon (Old Testament) restorationism is strikingly imaged in the juxtaposition of biblical Canaan and Latter-day Deseret.

Israel. Like the Radicals of the sixteenth century, the Mormons thought that reformation was not enough; but unlike most of them, the Mormons believed that Zion was to be gathered in the flesh.

Even so, with this emphasis on the restoration of the gathered community and on religious action and righteous living, the Mormons did parallel the sixteenth-century Radicals. And to these common features might be added Mormon beliefs concerning the abolition of infant baptism and the coming of the millennium. However, if they resembled the Radicals of another era, the Mormons were also *American* in their religious vision and its enactment. In some ways, their history summed up the tensions between manyness and oneness that have made America a land both of many religions and of one religion. Like all sectarians, they were exclusivistic and yet mission-minded. Like all sectarians, they demanded total commitment in a radical life-style that at some points in Mormon history involved the surrender of excess possessions to the church and the practice of polygamy for religious reasons. Yet paradoxically, their exclusivity often led them to the center of the political process. In order to preserve their separateness, they had to obtain the worldly power that would enable them to form their own societies, independent of the general government around them. Thus, while in Illinois, Smith announced that he was a candidate for the presidency of the United States, and Brigham Young, at the head of Deseret, worked for years for the admission of the Utah Territory to statehood and for a time was its official governor.

Moreover, the content of Mormon revelation was, by implication, more "American" than the religions of most Americans who were part of the mainstream. We have already seen this to be the case in Mormon interest in the history and destiny of American Indians and in their millennial belief in America as the promised land where the New Jerusalem would be located. Beyond this, in their teachings about the nature of God and the nature of human beings, Mormons probed the values of American culture and exalted it to a transcendent status by giving it a theological basis. For they preached—and continue to preach—a doctrine in which the material world was sacred and ultimate. Their God was not an infinite and omnipotent creator of the universe and humanity. Rather, in a universe that had always existed, God was a finite being. As the Mormons saw God, he did not have the world totally under his control. He was a God of space and time, whose existence did not interfere with human freedom and could not prevent evil. He was both Father and Mother, and humans worshiped him by sealing themselves to one another in marriage. Thus, Mormons hoped to rise one day in the spiritual realm to the celestial kingdom where they, too, should be "as Gods."

For Mormons, in the nineteenth century and now, humans were not dependent on God for their existence. They accomplished their tasks through their own efforts, through merit and good work, and through achievement that brought its appropriate reward. Mormons said that their souls had preexisted in a spirit realm before entering their present bodies. But in Mormon teaching there was no pronounced dualism between spirit and matter. Things spiritual were seen as a refined essence of the material world—all spirit as matter—so that God, as well as humanity, testified to the sacredness of matter. Moreover, since it was held that Mormons themselves could become "as Gods," they moved toward a polytheism in which divinity, as a principle, would be embodied in many Gods. Likewise, the Gods that the Mormons aspired to become were said to possess material bodies. Because of this teaching, the human body already held a privileged status. Mormon prohibitions of the use of alcohol, tobacco, and caffeine and their sparing use of meat were indications of their regard for the body.

In an America that in the nineteenth century pursued material success and subscribed to the cult of worldly progress, Mormons taught their neighbors how important matter could be considered. While in the Protestant mainstream old Calvinist beliefs in human depravity and predestination melted away in liberal teachings about human goodness and divine compassion, Mormons went beyond this middle position to a theological stand that, though many dismissed it, was consistent. If, as Mormons said, matter was good and progress was good, they thought this to be the case because revelation had shown the nature of ultimate reality to be both material and progressive. And yet, in a twist that augured the biblical literalism of twentieth-century American fundamentalism, Mormons bound their liberalism to a literal understanding of the teachings of Smith and their later prophets. However, this, too, was consistent with their stand on the sacredness of matter. For them even the revelatory Word should be respected in its material integrity, not made over into abstract, nonmaterial symbols.

The Mormon cultus, or "temple work" as it was called, dramatized these beliefs in ritual activity. After a revelation in 1841, Smith told his people to build a temple in Nauvoo where the Church of Jesus Christ of Latter-day Saints (Mormonism's official title) could present to God the records of their dead. From this time, the Saints dated their practice of baptizing the living for the dead. That is, past- and present-day Mormons expressly immersed themselves in the baptismal waters in the name, usually, of individual relatives who had died without conversion. They hoped, thus, to bring all the worthy dead to salvation. For this reason Mormon genealogical societies sprang up to assist the Saints in uncovering the names of relatives for whom they would perform the temple work.

Meanwhile, in their marriage ceremonies Mormons were encouraged to seal themselves to one another for both time and eternity. Marriage, they held, would continue in the life to come, and full salvation could not be reached for either man or woman without marriage. Indeed, temple work included sealing ceremonies for those who had died before the time of Mormon revelation. In both cases, that of baptism and that of marriage, Mormons continued once again to express their confidence in the sacredness and efficacy of matter. For them, the dead must be subject to material rites, and the sexual as well as spiritual bond of marriage would endure in the world beyond. The millennium would not bring an end to the world and human history but would exalt and perfect both so that Zion in America, though radically different from the present era, would be *in* time and not beyond it.

Finally, the Mormons in their new faith were as American as their Puritan ancestors in New England had been. At Kirtland, at Independence and Far West, at Nauvoo, and finally in Salt Lake City, they tried to build a theocracy, that is, a religiopolitical state in which otherworldly and everyday concerns were governed by one set of authorities. Blending the temporal and the spiritual in this way agreed with Mormon teaching about the importance of matter, and the early theocracies made near-total demands on the Saints. The law of consecration and stewardship at first required each Mormon, on entering the faith, to surrender all goods to the bishop, who would, in turn, give back for use what each Mormon family would need. Later, when this plan did not work for various reasons, Mormons were still required to tithe. And in Utah, although they had had no experience with dry farming, Mormons ventured to construct under their leaders an extensive irrigation system that demanded the community's full commitment to make it work.

Although theocracy officially gave way to statehood for Utah in 1896, the fusion of church and state informally lingered on. Meanwhile, the church continued to be a showcase of organizational efficiency, divided into stakes and wards, with stake presidents and bishops, councils, elders, and priests, and at the head of this empire in the West, a president who inherited the prophetic mantle of Smith. With their combination of otherworldly belief and thisworldly acumen, the Latter-day Saints, like the "visible saints" of the Puritan era, combined spirituality with Yankee shrewdness and wit. The twentieth century brought them wealth and respectability, and in many ways they moved away from the sectarian ideal to become a broad and inclusive church with members in other parts of the world. Yet they retained so much of their past that the sociologist of religion Joachim Wach hesitated to call them a church and labeled them instead an "independent group."

Whether as church or as independent group, though, Mormons are today growing vigorously as a body, and they represent some 2 percent of the general population. Commitment levels are high, and Latter-day Saints have made a strong impact on U.S. culture, especially in Rocky Mountain states like Utah and Idaho. Clearly, the nineteenth-century new religion that was Mormonism has become, in the late twentieth century, an established social entity.

The Seventh-day Adventists

The issue of declining sectarianism is also significant for a second nineteenth-century new religion that continues into our own times. The Seventh-day Adventists have themselves publicly raised the question of whether they are still a sect or, in fact, have become a denomination. Asking this question already indicates an awareness of change within the ranks, but at the same time it points to the connection with their past that Adventists experience. Thus, to understand the sectarian characteristics of even present-day Adventism, we must look to that past, for the various ways in which Adventists have maintained their boundaries against other American religions grew out of their history.

The term *Seventh-day Adventist* came into official existence in 1860, when a general conference of Adventist Christians — bound together by religious, social, and economic ties — decided to adopt it as a designation. Even before 1840, however, there was a growing body of millennialists who awaited the second coming, or advent, of Jesus with the expectation that it was very near. We have already seen that millennialism thrived in various forms within nineteenth-century Protestant Christianity. We know, too, that millennialists flourished on both sides of the Atlantic and that the Plymouth Brethren leader John Nelson Darby was preaching premillennial dispensationalism in North America between 1859 and 1874.

However, premillennial excitement spread in the United States in a movement that preceded Darby's coming by at least two decades. In 1840, in fact, Americans were already rallying around the preaching of a New England Baptist named William Miller (1782–1849) and were becoming known as Millerites. A respected citizen and rather average preacher in his style and mannerisms, Miller drew large crowds as he moved from place to place spreading his conviction that the second coming of Jesus would occur "about the year 1843." Miller had arrived at this conclusion after study of the prophetic books of the Bible and, in particular, of Daniel 8:14: "Unto two thousand and three hundred days; then shall the sanctuary be cleansed." Interpreters generally agreed that a biblical day equaled a year of ordinary time, and for Miller and others the time of the cleansing of the sanctuary was the time, also, of the second coming. Beyond this, Miller taught that the 2,300 years had begun in 457 B.C. when the rebuilding of the city of Jerusalem had been inaugurated. Thus, Millerites thought the end of the present world would come between 21 March 1843 and 21 March 1844, a specific time set by Miller after others had urged him to more and more precision.

Later, when the return of Christ did not occur in March 1844, Samuel S. Snow (1806–1870), a member of the Millerite movement, convinced Miller himself and others that because of differences in the old Jewish calendar the return could be calculated to come on 22 October 1844. While there is no evidence that the faithful donned "ascension robes" to be ready for the day, their expectation was strong and so, too, was their Great Disappointment, as the experience of 22 October was later called. Many, in fact, left the movement. Others accepted the interpretation of Hiram Edson (1806–1882), who declared that, although Christ had failed to appear on earth, in heaven he had entered the holiest part of the Jewish sanctuary as the preliminary to his earthly advent. Still others simply gave up time setting but retained their earlier belief that the end was very near.

It was from among the faithful remnants of the Millerites that the Seventh-day Adventists arose. Prior to the Great Disappointment, a number of Adventists had followed the practice of keeping the ancient Jewish Sabbath (Saturday) instead of Sunday as their weekly day of worship and rest. Influenced by the example of Seventh Day Baptists, some Adventists in Washington, New Hampshire, had become convinced that the Bible should be taken literally and that they should honor the seventh rather than the first day of the week as the Sabbath Day. Among those who later accepted the Sabbath teaching were a former sea captain named Joseph Bates (1792–1872) and a fragile and sickly woman, Ellen G. White (1827–1915), along with her husband, James White (1821–1881). These three provided new leadership for the former Millerites, who were still Adventists and now had become Sabbatarians. In their thinking, Adventism and seventh-day Sabbath keeping were linked by strong ties, for the restoration of the genuine Sabbath prepared Adventists for the second coming. Conversely, they believed that worship on Sunday formed an idolatrous image to the beast that represented the powers of evil in the Book of Revelation (Rev. 13). Such worship, they said, substituted a papal institution for a biblical command in the Ten Commandments.

Because of the unusual character of her religious experience, Ellen White quickly came to prominence in the new movement. According to her report, in December 1844, when only seventeen years of age, she had had a vision in which she saw the Adventists traveling along a path toward the New Jerusalem, all the while lighted on their journey by the message of 22 October. For Adventists, White's account was divine confirmation of their rightness, and when Ellen White claimed further visions, she became for them a charismatic mediator through whom God continued to reveal himself to his people. As the years passed, her reports of visions as well as inspired dreams enabled White to offer pronouncements on a wide variety of concerns, ranging from child nurture and education to missions and church organization. Especially, she addressed issues of dietary reform and health. In keeping with the thought of a number of nineteenth-century health reformers such as Sylvester Graham (from whom the name "Graham crackers" descends), Larkin B. Coles, and James C. Jackson, White saw God calling the Adventist people away from not only alcohol and tobacco but also tea, coffee, and meat, with special prohibitions against pork. She also urged dress reform for women, condemning tightly fitted garments and trailing skirts in the interests of health; and she preached general rules of hygiene to maintain the vigor of the body.

Through the years, as Seventh-day Adventists adhered to their Sabbatarian and dietary practices and continued in their millennial beliefs, they settled close to one another. Thus, a marked localism accompanied their movement. Towns like Battle Creek, Michigan, and Loma Linda, California, became Adventist enclaves, while an empire of Adventist medical and educational organizations sprang up in the United States and throughout the world.

Because of this history, the sectarian character of Seventh-day Adventism was strong. Adventism maintained a separate and exclusive identity through its beliefs in the nearness of the millennium and the prophetic nature of Ellen G. White and through its Sabbatarian and dietary practices. At the same time, its localism illustrated in physical space the boundaries that framed the inner Adventist religious world. On the other hand, like so many other sectarians, Adventists were counterbalanced in their exclusivism by a missionary urge so strong that the story of twentieth-century Seventh-day Adventism is the story of the spread of Adventist world missions. Like other sectarians, too, Adventists have been suspicious of government. The earliest Adventists avoided any relationship to government when they preached their message of an imminent return of Jesus, while later from the early 1850s they began to identify the government of the United States with the beast in the Book of Revelation. Even in the 1880s and later, Adventists remained at the edge of the political process, entering it only if they thought that by doing so they might be able, paradoxically, to delay the coming of the end of this world, the better to preach that it would come soon. Their logic sprang from their millennialism: if the end were soon to come, it was foolish to become involved with worldly government and dispute.

Similarly, Adventists gave wide berth to the waging of war. There was the biblical injunction not to kill as well as the practical difficulty of keeping the Sabbath in an army in which Sunday was the officially recognized day of worship. So Adventists entered military service with noncombatant status, serving generally as medics. Seeking the restoration of the primitive church rather than a reformation of the present one, thinking more of sanctification than of justification, Adventists, like Mormons, resembled the Radicals of the sixteenth century. They preached the gospel, as one Adventist scholar has put it, but they did not cease to preach the law. Like the Mormons, too, though not so markedly, Adventists questioned God's control over the part of the universe that involved humanity; they held that humans with their free will could change the course of events and so the plans of God.

Adventists, indeed, have been paradoxical in more than their desire to delay the end in order to preach the end. Today they look to an advent when the world as we know it will cease to be. Yet with their Sabbatarianism, they just as strongly affirm the material world. Unlike the Sunday observance that expresses faith in the *resurrection* of Jesus, a symbol of spiritual triumph *over* the material world, the Saturday Sabbath points to belief in God's work in creation from which, on the seventh day, he rested. Thus, it honors the natural and material, and it looks to the beginning of things as much as to the end. Implicitly in Adventist theology, the first advent of the divine was in the creation. Hence, the present, for Adventists, becomes a moment stretched between past and future, between destiny done and destiny to come. Standing then within this tension, the present, the time when history is made, was theologically important for Adventists. The implications were that Adventism must take seriously the things of time and that the natural, material world was a significant source of value. So Ellen White, like the prophet Joseph Smith, was the mouthpiece for what Adventists could see as a *progressive* divine revelation, one that took into account the transformations that time and history brought. So, too, the pronouncements that came through White were seriously concerned with matters such as health reform; in her visionary claims, ordinary matters achieved extraordinary status through the divine interference. The world that God had created was seen as sacred. And so, like the Mormons, Adventists took the literal word at face value. Just as the Sabbath meant for them Saturday, creation meant the direct and immediate work of God and not new nineteenth-century teachings such as the theory of evolution and the theory that the earth was older than the Bible had taught.

However, if the Adventists in their sectarianism were paradoxical, they were mirroring an *American* paradox. Curiously, although they worked to maintain their position of distinctiveness among the many, like the Mormons before them, they reflected the oneness of an American religion that was part of American culture. We have seen that Adventists were materialists and millennialists at once and that with their far-flung educational and medical empire they still intensely await the second advent. But the mainstream of American culture was also materialist and millennialist. American cultural materialism is something with which we are all familiar. More than that, we know that Americans in general had been millennialists in the nineteenth century, believing that with the dawn of the Industrial Revolution and the rising power of the young republic, a new age in the history of the world was being inaugurated. In the American republic, they thought, the lion would lie down with the lamb, and peace, plenty, and prosperity would continue to reign. Americans believed they were living in the last, best age of the world, and they thought they were the most fortunate among the human species — ideas we will explore further in Part II.

Thus, other Americans, in the general structure of their beliefs and attitudes, were much like Seventh-day Adventists, while Seventh-day Adventists were much like other Americans. There is an almost humorous commentary on just how much this was the case in the reference of one Adventist apologist of the twentieth century to the "scientifically proven visions" of White. (He meant that the advice attributed to God through the visions had been corroborated by scientific evidence.) Moreover, science was superseded as an indication of Adventist Americanism by Adventist missionary expansionism. After a remarkable foreign-mission effort, world membership in the church stood in 1985 at almost 4.6 million. By contrast, fewer than 650,000 were from the United States. Such evident missionary energy called into question the efforts of mainstream Protestant evangelicals. Matched against Adventism, mainstream Protestant mission work seemed less "American" as an exhibition of missionary enthusiasm than the endeavors of Adventist sectarians.

However, it is perhaps in Adventist ritual that the resemblance to the Protestant and American mainstream is most striking for the casual observer. Adventist services, with the exception of quarterly communion and foot-washing rituals, are largely indistinguishable from general Protestant worship. For the most part, ministers are teachers more than preachers and rational more than emotional, but this is the case in many mainstream Protestant services. It is not so difficult, from the vantage point of a typical Adventist Sabbath observance, to understand the Seventh-day dilemma with which we began: Do affluent and highly educated American Adventists belong to a sect, or are they members of a mainstream Protestant denomination? The Seventh-day dilemma is another form of the American dilemma that we notice again and again. Are Americans many, or are they one?

The Christian Scientists

For still another view of the dilemma, we turn to a third example, that of Christian Science. Mary Baker Eddy (1821–1910), who founded Christian Science, grew up in New England. She was for years a member of the Congregational church, which had descended from Puritan ancestors, and she looked to the past with reverence. Thus, Eddy began her religious quest as part of the American mainstream, as an embodiment of the kind of religion we will examine in Part II as the one religion of America. In the twentieth century, her followers in Christian Science, like Mormons and Seventh-day Adventists, would in many ways be indistinguishable from their mainline Protestant neighbors. Yet in other ways, Christian Science stood as an example of the manyness of American religions.

Sectarians are people who maintain strong boundaries between themselves and the rest of the world. For them, crossing the boundary of the community should occur only infrequently through ordinary exchanges with outsiders. It should come most in the extraordinary encounters that for them define a relationship with God. If this is so, then Eddy's claims of extraordinary religious experience in 1866, like the earlier claims of Joseph Smith and Ellen G. White in its results, inaugurated Christian Science as a distinct sectarian movement.

For years Eddy had moved from place to place, living in boardinghouses in poverty and pain occasioned by the death of a first husband and the unfaithfulness of a second. In this situation she had also suffered from physical complaints, and a chronic spinal affliction had often confined her to her bed for days and weeks on end. Then in 1862 she sought out Phineas P. Quimby, a celebrated mental healer, who began to help and also to teach her. But in 1866, when Quimby died, Eddy felt more bereft than ever. About a month after this traumatic event, she fell on ice and suffered what seemed a concussion and a possible dislocated spine. "On the third day," however, while reading the gospel story of Jesus healing a palsied man (Matt. 9:2), she claimed a profoundly moving experience in which she glimpsed spiritual truth and was instantly healed. She dated the beginning of Christian Science from that moment.

During the longs years before this event, Eddy had grown estranged from the ordinary rhythms of middle-class existence. Yet now her separateness assumed a new and religious form, and in this form it began to attract others. The decade from 1866 to 1875 brought Eddy more years of wandering from one New England mill town to another. But inwardly, these years were a time of quiet thinking and writing. They culminated in 1875 in the publication of the first edition of *Science and Health*, the book that for later Christian Scientists ranked beside the Bible and explained it. Four years later, the Church of Christ, Scientist, was formally chartered, and the story after that, for Eddy and Christian Science, was one of growing wealth, influence, and prestige, a turnabout from the fortunes of those early years.

Still, there was trouble. During this time, the founder and her movement experienced a series of defections, when former students struck out on their own as independent healers, part of the more general mind-cure movement of the period. Perhaps alienated by Eddy's claims to spiritual authority, perhaps inspired by it to experience of their own, these former Scientists in some ways served to enhance the sectarian tendencies of those who remained with Eddy. The original group, now harassed by the accusations and even lawsuits of their former associates, turned within. So the bonds that separated Christian Scientists from the world grew stronger, and their identity grew more distinct.

At the core of this separate existence was the teaching of Mary Baker Eddy and its culminating expression in Christian Science practice. Teaching and practice together, for Eddy and her followers, were the product of a continuing divine revelation. At certain privileged moments in human history, Eddy believed, individuals rediscovered this revelation, and when they did so, they experienced a breakthrough of light and power in their lives. It was in such a moment, for her and the others, that Christian Science had been discovered, and it was in such moments that Christian Scientists would find the power to heal the sick.

At the basis of these healings and the center of this discovery, Eddy said, was Jesus Christ, the only person within human history who fully demonstrated what it meant to be the Son of God. She urged that the revelation of Jesus was a practical ideal for others to imitate, since all people should strive, like Jesus, to realize completely their relationship to God. This meant, she taught, bringing to light the perfection of their actual and God-given natures, instead of accepting the limitations of their apparent natures. For Eddy, Christian Science was the way to break out of a world of illusions. It told people that there were no limits to their authentic spiritual nature as made by God. And it encouraged them to act on the basis of that knowledge through distinctive healing practices.

Based on this view of Christian revelation, Eddy's teaching extended to include a metaphysical reading of the nature of God, human beings, and their world. In her vision God was more than a person, at least in the ordinary and anthropomorphic sense in which "person" had been understood. Besides being a person, Eddy held, God was the divine Principle or Life expressed in the universe. So, for Eddy, God was Soul, Truth, and Love in the world. If gender designations were to be used for the divine Person and Principle, then God was seen as a Father–Mother God, with love (motherhood) as the divine Principle that created spiritual beings and the universe as a reflection of the infinite Mind. It followed for Eddy that, as Mind, God was present in all reality, and — most significant for Christian Science practice — there was no such thing as matter as self-existing reality. God and nature were held to be one, bound by spiritual and not material laws. There was, taught Eddy, only one true Science, the law of this divine Mind; matter was seen as a shadow, a pale correspondent to the truth of God.

Eddy held that for the material sense — the limited sense of reality that people share — matter was completely real. But she thought that from the perspective of God's Mind, the real nature of human beings, as reflecting the divine Principle, was immortal. Seemingly bound by the laws of matter, humans were actually entwined only in their own false conceptions of the nature of things. For Eddy, error was at the bottom of sin and sickness, and therefore the twin evils could be dispelled by truth. This truth was the redemption of what Eddy called "mortal man," and it came for her, as in the Christian gospels, through Jesus Christ. In her view, salvation meant *following the example of Jesus*. At-one-ment with Christ brought an end to separation from God and, consequently, redemption from both sickness and sin.

This vision of the nature of things, with its lingering Calvinist concern regarding evil and its metaphysical idealism, took concrete form in work toward healing the sick. Christian Science practitioners were people who devoted themselves professionally to aiding the healing of others. Their methods were visiting the sick, counseling them, and, above all, praying for them. The work of Christian Science practitioners centered on this prayer, which was understood not as a simple plea to God for help but instead as a meditation on the sick person as seen by and related to God. Practitioners began by going apart to gain a sense of what they considered their own personal relationship with God. Then they quietly tried to discern what they felt was the real (spiritual) truth of each person for whom they worked. This meant, for practitioners, seeing through the illusion of illness to the person as he or she was believed to exist in the sight of God. Practitioners held these thoughts in mind until they felt that they had gained an inner sense of what a patient's problem was and broke its perceived falsity in the truth of God. They worked to focus this sense of truth on the person; and finally, the treatment completed, they firmly expected to receive word that the sick person had been healed.

Although the success of the healing process depended on the Christian Science practitioner, demands were also made of patients. They might be asked to study certain passages from the writings of Eddy, to discipline their thoughts, or to try to realize certain truths about their lives. Meanwhile, Christian Scientists avoided alcohol, tobacco, and sometimes caffeine, wishing to eliminate the presence of drugs of any kind. For a committed Scientist, no medicine could yield genuine well-being. Whether prescribed by a physician or used in the form of socially accepted stimulants or depressants, drugs operated in terms of human belief in their power.

To sum up, Christian Science taught a broad understanding of Christian revelation, expounded a metaphysical system to help modern people understand it, and practiced healing as the logical outcome of its beliefs about Christ and the world. Like the sectarians of the Radical Reformation, Jesus for Christian Scientists was the great exemplar of perfect humanness. Salvation came not through faith alone but, rather, through imitating the model that Jesus had provided. Moreover, like the Radical Reformers, Christian Scientists thought that they were *restoring* the teaching of an early church in which, to a far greater degree than in later centuries, healing had been central. While Eddy would also claim that no one before her had discovered the truth of Christian Science and that all of previous Christian history had missed the revelation, her sometime emphasis on restoration was significant. So, too, was the theology of material error, which led Christian Science to adopt a position toward politics and the social order similar to that of the sixteenth-century Radical Reformers. For if the material world was illusory, participation in its business, attention to its problems, and adherence to its political or social systems could at best be only secondary concerns. True, near the end of her life Eddy founded *The Christian Science Monitor* (1908) to offer a healing approach to social issues. But since, in her view, human conflict and suffering resulted from false belief, entanglement in political and social matters was finally dubious. Eddy believed that a Christian Scientist ought, as much as practicable, to minimize worldly involvement.

If Christian Scientists resembled sixteenth-century Radical Reformers, however, even more did they show themselves to be citizens of nineteenth-century America. Like Mormons and Adventists, even though they tried to separate themselves from mainstream American beliefs and values, they ended up affirming what they denied. First, there was their designation of themselves as Christian *Scientists*. In a century that had witnessed startling advances in science, such as Charles Darwin's discovery of evidence to support the theory of evolution (*The Origin of Species*, 1859), science was a word that carried considerable prestige. For Mary Baker Eddy and her followers, it meant the laws by which God governed the universe, but it also connoted the methods, or rules, used for Christian Science "demonstration" and the certainty with which these rules could be applied. In other words, the assertion was that Christian Science healings, like scientific experiments, were repeatable procedures. They could be counted on, so long as one had studied and practiced correctly.

Thus, Eddy placed her new teaching into a framework that had been supplied by science. Her insistence on discovery and demonstration were instances of the framework, as, of course, was the name by which she chose to designate her new religious movement. So, too, were her continual reference to members of the Christian Science organization as "students" and her steadfast conception of her role as that of teacher. In 1881, just two years after the official incorporation of the church, she received a charter for the Massachusetts Metaphysical College, in which she trained future Christian Science practitioners. Moreover, for years before a church organization of any kind came into being, she taught students her principles in rented rooms.

Second, there was the organizational structure that Eddy built — as American as the business organizations that in the late nineteenth century were becoming giant corporations. Although in the beginning Eddy had not wanted a formal institution at all, her later efforts reversed this direction. She grew dissatisfied with the rudimentary structure she had fashioned through the Church of Christ, Scientist (1879), the Massachusetts Metaphysical College (1881), and the National Christian Science Association (1886). In 1889 she gave up the charter of the college, and in 1892 she dissolved the association. At the same time, she reorganized the Boston church, which she controlled, urging Christian Scientists throughout the country to apply for membership in the Mother Church.

Thus began a process of joint membership in which most Christian Scientists belonged to both a local organization and the Mother Church in Boston. Here a self-perpetuating board of directors assumed a power that would live on after the death of Eddy, while in the branch churches pastors were replaced by readers appointed for three-year terms. Worship under the guidance of the readers did not involve the traditional preaching office but, instead, the reading of assigned passages from the Bible and *Science and Health*, its sanctioned interpretation. In practice, revelation had been given to the nineteenth century only in the scriptural understanding that Eddy opened to her followers, while other teaching was forbidden. Under these circumstances, the Christian Science organization became a model of technical efficiency. The application of bureaucratic principles reflected its American context, and in this respect Eddy's church could compete successfully with the structures built by a John D. Rockefeller or an Andrew Carnegie.

Third, the American background of Christian Science was suggested by the very character of Eddy's life and the lives of those who joined her. In many ways, her problems were the problems of others in the time called the Gilded Age. For this was a time when the surface brilliance of America seemed to hide a spiritual malaise beneath. Recovering from the Civil War and at the same time expanding at a great rate industrially, America was enlarging old cities and creating new ones. People flocked to these cities from the countryside, and people flocked there, too, from abroad, as new waves of immigrants came to America. This was an age of genuine pluralism but also an age of Protestant predicament, as the old symbols of a supernatural order no longer rang true for many Americans.

Into this world, Mary Baker Eddy launched a movement and a message that provided some form of resolution for key anxieties of the era. Herself a product of the social dislocation of the industrial age, Eddy offered followers a bastion of security in the Mother Church. A gifted woman with strong leadership potential at a time when a woman's place was confined to marriage and family, she created through her church a stage on which she and the others who followed her could aspire to act forcefully and effectively. Many of those who joined her were women of midlife and middle-class status (although, to be sure, there were also many—and prominent—men in the church), and what she had to offer them was a purposive life that could be lived *alone*. At a time when community values were breaking down under the impact of urbanization and industrialization, she taught a form of self-reliance through metaphysics and spiritual practice. The cure of illness for these women and men was bound up with their self-initiated action in Christian Science. Meanwhile, the denial of the primacy of the social world that the new religion involved was implicitly a rebuttal to male-oriented America, which had denied a public place to women and their concerns.

In short, Christian Science, like Mormonism and Adventism before it, succeeded in making the ordinary extraordinary. Through the teaching of its founder, Christian Science transmuted the bleak facts of Gilded Age history and sociology. In doing so, Christian Science mined its situation to discover finally what all religions seek as they confront the human situation—a sense of transcendent meaning and purpose. But in the very act of doing so, in the process of turning the ordinary into the extraordinary, Christian Science also made the extraordinary ordinary. Its healings showed believers that the world as it appeared was, after all, malleable. In that conviction Christian Science revealed its American spirit.

Small (with roughly 3,000 churches in the world, most of them in the United States), without an ordained ministry, and without published membership statistics, Christian Science by the late twentieth century appeared to be declining. Yet declining or not, Christian Science was instructive in what it revealed about indigenous and lay-directed American theologizing, and it was equally significant in what it revealed about religious organization and about selectivity in religious practice. In Christian Science a new theological hybrid grew out of a transformed American Calvinism joined to metaphysical idealism. Just as important, in Christian Science, theology met American corporate talent and linked it to a collective quest for healing as a form of religious action. As we will see in later chapters, Christian Science was in some ways a sign of the religious future.

Communalism

The three religious movements that we have so far examined in this chapter, Mormonism, Seventh-day Adventism, and Christian Science, were all examples—case studies, if you will—of sectarianism. Yet while they broke radically with the surrounding world, they still maintained some relative communication with outsiders. This was apparent in the fact that none of the three movements died or disintegrated. Instead, in the twentieth century each of them moved closer to the religious center, taking the route that brought them from a more sectarian to a more denominational status. Their experience followed a pattern that held for many other American sectarians of the period.

Different from the pattern that led from sect to denomination was another in which exclusivity dominated the sectarian venture until in the end it dissolved. This pattern was illustrated in the histories of a variety of communal movements that flourished in the nineteenth century and thereafter all but dis-appeared. Such movements were part of the history of American communalism. Beginning in the eighteenth century and continuing with numerous examples into the present, for some Americans pursuit of the American dream meant creating perfect societies, communities in which all would live together in harmony. Often they saw their planned societies as blueprints for reforms that later would spread throughout America or, in a typical sectarian theme, as inaugurations of the millennium.

We will look briefly at two of these communal sects — the Shakers and the Oneida Perfectionists — to suggest the directions that many of them followed. Each of these communal groups, in the years in which it was successful, was characterized by stronger methods of maintaining its boundaries than those of more "lenient" sectarians. Each was ruled by the magnetic personality of a charismatic leader whose creedal teaching provided a center for the movement. In each society, the sacred story that formed the creed was effectively dramatized through rituals, and in each a code of living translated the Word for ordinary, everyday existence. In objection, we might point to the charismatic leadership of a Joseph Smith, an Ellen White, or a Mary Baker Eddy. Indeed, we might notice the uniqueness of the teaching of each and the ability of their movements to provide cogent rituals and organization for daily living. What then, we might ask, distinguished the communitarians from other sectarians? The answer lies not so much in a difference of structural principles (leader, creed, ritual, everyday ethic) as in the lengths to which communitarians carried these principles. Above all, the difference lay in their adoption of a communal life-style in which they challenged two fundamental principles of social independence — private property and sexual exclusivity in the family.

The Shakers

The founder of the Shakers, Mother Ann Lee (1736–1784), had claimed that she experienced visions from her childhood in Manchester, England. Evidently, she had early become convinced of the sinfulness of human nature, and gradually she had come to identify the root of evil in the act of sexual intercourse. When after her marriage to Abraham Standerin (Stanley) her four children died in infancy, she became even more convinced of this belief. Lee, already a member of an ecstatic group that had broken away from the Quakers under the leadership of Jane and James Wardley, spoke of receiving a vision (1770) in which she saw depicted before her the original sin in Eden. Subsequently, she began to teach the importance of celibacy, and the Shaking Quakers, or Shakers, who followed her visionary directive came to call her Mother Ann, or Ann the Word. When in a later vision she said she had been urged to go to America, a small group of eight believers traveled in 1774 to the land where Lee's reported vision had foretold that the Church of Christ's Second Appearing would be established. The

Shakers settled in New York state and remained there throughout the American Revolution, and although they endured persecution, they continued to preach until the death of Lee in 1784.

It was only thereafter that the United Society of Believers in Christ's Second Appearing became a communitarian body. Living together in "families" of celibates who shared all property in common, the Shakers taught, like Joseph Smith and Mary Baker Eddy, that God was a Father–Mother deity. Since human beings were seen as made in God's image and since they were male or female, for the Shakers it followed that God, too, possessed the equivalent of both genders. Thus God became an ambisexual being. On earth, Shakers began to say, the fullest male manifestation of God had come in Jesus Christ, and the fullest female manifestation, in Ann Lee. Moreover, with the familiar sectarian conviction that they were restoring the New Testament church, the Shakers preached community of property and sexual abstinence. At the same time, they expounded the necessity of a separate government, the Christian duty of pacifism, and, as Eddy would later teach, the power of spirit over physical disease. The millennium was about to begin, they thought, because God had inaugurated his final dispensation, or era, through the second coming of Christ in Ann Lee.

It was in Shaker ritual, however, that the religious teachings of Lee's followers received their strongest expression. Originating in the ecstatic and uncontrollable physical movements of the Shaking Quakers, Shaker dance became the organized enactment of the sacred story of community based on the dual sexuality of God. If, as Shakers thought, God was a dual person, both male and female, and if Jesus Christ and Ann Lee represented, respectively, the power and wisdom of God, then the formal dance of the male and female members of the community revealed that they were members of one body, equally necessary to its existence as a reflection of the divine community. The implication was that they, too, should be power and wisdom for one another as they prayed and worked. Similarly, if the millennium was about to begin or, indeed, had already begun in the coming of Lee, then the Shaker dance dramatized a belief in the millennium already begun. In the dance the barriers between this world and the next were seemingly dissolved, as Shakers experienced the harmonial rhythms that they envisioned would govern the millennial kingdom. When the Shaker dancers continued their stylized movements long into the night — until the movements gradually lost their stylization and the Shakers whirled themselves into ecstasy — they felt that they experienced a union with one another in God and "Mother" Ann and a foretaste of the bliss of paradise.

It is interesting that as the years passed and the mid-nineteenth century brought the Shakers prosperity and success, they maintained contact with their founder by a period of ritual intensity known as "Mother Ann's Work." From 1837, mediums who claimed they could communicate with spirits became important officiants in the rituals. Shakers reported that they had entertained a host of spirit visitors, from American Indians to George Washington. They acted out

From Holy Mother Wisdom To Grove Blanchard. This Shaker spirit drawing, executed in ink on blue-colored paper in May of 1847, announces in part: "Come lovely child, rejoice with me; And beat the drum of victory, For surely I your Mother true, have sent this plate to comfort you."

the visions that their mediums directed, convinced that in the process they were the privileged recipients of heavenly gifts.

Later, in the 1840s, when the period of greatest involvement in spirit activity in the ritual had declined, the Shakers found that some among them, apparently all female, had begun to draw or paint on spiritual and mystical themes. The "spirit drawings" that resulted were gifts, they said, from heaven and often directly from Holy Mother Wisdom, recollections by inspired members of the community of visionary experiences that they had had. At their height, these spirit drawings were executed in bright color and careful symmetry, often emphasizing floral, leaf, and arboreal patterns. Symbols of the Father–Mother God filled them, as did representations of a wealth of material goods (musical instruments, jewelry, exotic foods, and the like) that in their actual lives the Shakers denied themselves.

Spirit drawings declined after 1859. After the Civil War, so did the Shakers, until by the late twentieth century only a few remained in two surviving New England communities. There had been a connection between the vitality of the communities and the vitality of their rituals and religious art, for symbol and rite had acted as ways to remember, ways to re-create the religious way of life that had begun with Lee. In their years of greatest vigor, Shaker societies spread from New York and New England to Kentucky, Ohio, and Indiana, numbering eighteen separate establishments and some 6,000 members. Further, they were renowned not only for the ecstatic disregard of their rituals but also for the quiet and order of their lives. Indeed, the sexual equality dramatized in the ritual dance was reflected, to a great extent, in both the administration and work of the communities. Shaker furniture, with its simplicity, suggested the functional efficiency that regulated community endeavors. Renowned for their practical inventions, for their agricultural seeds and pharmaceutical supplies, Shakers gave every evidence of being as pragmatic as they were mystical. Like Christian Scientists, whose denial of the reality of matter was accompanied by apparent health and prosperity, Shakers blended otherworldliness with thisworldly success.

Perhaps this is not so unusual as it at first appears. Religious groups that thrive seem to be able to balance many concerns, to hold in tension values that are often opposed. They are able, in the total pattern of their lives, to give expression to disparate values that, when held together, yield a resolution felt as completeness. If this is so, then the key to the Shakers' success lay in their ability to combine the celibacy of their daily lives with the ambisexuality of their creed, the order of their everyday world with the disorder of their ritual, and the precision of their business insights with the expansiveness of their mystical flights. Like the other sectarians whose lives we have examined, Shakers knew how to make the ordinary extraordinary, for no detail of life in community was insignificant. The details in some way mirrored what the Shakers had learned from their recollections of the teaching of Ann Lee. The Shakers continued to flourish as long as through ritual and symbol they continued to try to remember — to see in the ordinary events of everyday life extraordinary spiritual gifts.

The Oneida Perfectionists

As with the Shakers, optimism about the millennial age surrounded the efforts of the Oneida Perfectionists, a second case study of sectarian religious community. John Humphrey Noyes (1811–1886), the founder of the Oneida community, had as a young man become convinced that the millennium had already arrived. It had come, he thought, in A.D. 70 when the second coming had occurred, for Jesus had expected the end within a generation of his personal preaching ministry and Jesus, argued Noyes, could not have been wrong.

It followed for Noyes that sinners had centuries ago been separated from the saved and that those who tried to follow Jesus in the nineteenth century need not fear the snares of sin any longer. He thought that such nineteenth-century Christians were saints and perfect beings, since sin had been abolished in the millennial kingdom. Life on earth, said Noyes, should be a foretaste of heavenly bliss. Further, because Christ had indicated there would be no marrying or giving in marriage in heaven, Noyes thought there was something wrong with the ordinary institution of marriage as the nineteenth century understood it. At the heavenly banquet, he said, every food should be available to every guest; on earth, restrictions of the marriage bond seemed to him part of a false, and even sinful, system that should not apply to the perfect.

These thoughts received concrete expression in the communities that Noyes established, first, at Putney, Vermont (1840–1847), and later and more significantly, at Oneida, New York (1848–1879). The Putney community began as a religious association composed of Noyes's own family, but in 1844, joined by others, the Putney group initiated the practice of communism. Two years later, the members of the small community were following their leader's teaching in the twin practices of male continence and complex marriage. Male continence offered a reliable system of birth control through male self-control, for in this practice men completed their sexual activity without ejaculation. Complex marriage, made possible by male continence, meant that every man was "husband" to every woman in the community and every woman was "wife" to every man. Only mutual agreement was needed to engage in sexual relations. At the same time, with an asceticism that belied what looked like sexual license, exclusive relationships between any two members of the community were not tolerated. In Noyes's teaching, sex should become the bond of a community that mirrored the heavenly unity; it should not bring divisiveness that prevented the members of one body in Christ from loving each and all.

When difficulties with outraged neighbors brought trouble to the Putney community, Noyes bought land for the group in northern New York at Oneida. Here began the most successful and best-remembered years of the Perfectionists, who readily engaged in business and manufacture. After 1857 the community profited from the making of steel traps, which they had begun some years earlier, and they also produced a variety of other goods for which they gained a reputation as skilled workers in the crafts. The membership grew until by 1878 it had reached about 300, and meanwhile there were experiments in branch communities that followed the Oneida pattern. Some of the new members freely joined the community, prompted often by Noyes's publications, which forcefully argued the rationale of Oneida Perfectionism. Others, however, were born into the community through unions that were carefully reviewed and approved by Noyes for the production of offspring.

Life in the community, from the many reports of it that have been left, was pleasurable and satisfying, with various kinds of art, literature, and amusements provided. Still, by the time the second generation of Oneida Perfectionists had grown to maturity, internal dissension became a factor in community life. These people had no personal experience of the early struggles that had led to Oneida's foundation. They reacted against the ways of their elders, sometimes by outright agnosticism and sometimes by secret disapproval of what they regarded as the immorality of complex marriage. The misgivings of these Perfectionists, combined with the hostility of outsiders who were shocked by the community's practices, finally led Noyes to flee to Canada and to urge the dissolution of the community. Thus, community life disbanded, Oneida reconstituted itself as a joint-stock company, and ironically the strongest memory the twentieth century has of Oneida is its silverware.

At its height, however, Oneida combined religious theory with a practical efficiency that extended to both ordinary and extraordinary concerns. The ease of life in the community was purchased by a near-monastic discipline embracing all aspects of daily existence. Both complex marriage and communism of property aimed to inculcate detachment, complex marriage by diffusing sexual passion and communism by diffusing intense ambition. Members of the community, moreover, engaged in monastic fashion in the regular and ritualized practice of mutual criticism. Members often requested a criticism from the group, or at times, when they seemed to be causing serious problems, they could be asked to undergo the discipline. Sometimes before all members and sometimes before a selected committee that represented the others, the person to be criticized listened to what was said about his or her actions and the spirit in which they had been performed. The public nature of the proceeding was meant to act as a check, and personal vindictiveness against any one person was discouraged lest it lead to criticism of the critic. At the end of the meeting, criticisms were summarized, advice offered, and encouragement given so that the member would emerge from the experience a more harmonious communitarian. Mutual criticism was found so successful, in fact, that it became a form of treatment for illness. With belief in a connection between mind and body, Oneidans would gather at the bed of a sick member, aiming to hasten recovery by chastening the patient's behavior and attitude. Like Christian Scientists and the many others of the era who had come to believe in the spiritual origins of disease, the Perfectionists seemed convinced that religious means could—and did—cure.

Indeed, Oneidans saw their community as a witness to the end of what Noyes called the "sin-system," a system to which they connected all or most of the evils that troubled Americans of the era. They were convinced that apostasy, unbelief, obedience to mammon, private property, and death were links in a chain that had been destroyed at Oneida. In their place, they thought, the community was building a new chain of redemption, a system established on the restoration of true, original Christianity, of faith and obedience to Christ, of communism, and finally of immortality. In the Oneidan view, Christian love and responsibility would bring freedom, equality, and enduring life to all, for Christian communism had ended the "work-system" and the "marriage-system," replaced by a life that fit the time of the millennium.

Thus, the sectarianism of Oneida, with its carefully drawn boundaries that segregated the community from the world, was meant to provide an exemplary model of what all Christian life should be like. The Perfectionists self-consciously separated themselves in their radical life in community, and yet they saw themselves as the first wave of a future available to all who confessed Christ. Their community intended to reach out to America, and like the other sects we have examined, including the Shakers, the Perfectionists reflected the culture that they tried to avoid in their communities. We have noticed this phenomenon to some extent in the case of the more loosely knit sectarian bodies — the Mormons, Seventh-day Adventists, and Christian Scientists — but it is well to point to the fact that "Americanism" was the heritage of communitarians as well. The material prosperity of Shakers, Perfectionists, and others like them seemed a capsule summary of the American dream. Their millennial expectations — and realizations — complemented the general cultural millennialism of the age, with its faith that a new era was dawning. Moreover, in a land of individualism and pragmatic opportunism, the communities offered a cultural balance and personal sanctuary for those uprooted by industrialization and urbanization. From a historical and sociological point of view, they seemed to be spin-offs of the modernization process that had reached its farthest frontier in America.

In Overview

All of the sectarian movements that we have examined were different, yet all shared certain characteristics. Like sects in general, they were voluntary societies of committed people who guarded the boundaries between themselves and others very closely. Claiming experiences of conversion to a life of love and law, members of the sects could be compared to the Radical Reformers of the sixteenth century in their zeal for the restoration of true Christianity, their stress on right living, their general indifference toward politics, and their millennialism. Not "also-rans" among the Protestants, they embodied a religious vision of their own, imbuing each detail of ordinary life with their sense of its extraordinary religious quality. At the same time, like their Protestant neighbors, sectarians reflected the American experience. Their religious experiments were graphic expressions of the American experiment, emphasizing newness and human possibility with millennial themes. It was no accident that restorationism and millennialism were also important to many evangelical Protestants.

In terms of the degree of their separation from the rest of society, sectarian movements ranged along a continuum. More accommodating movements — like Mormonism, Seventh-day Adventism, and Christian Science — did not demand total community from their members. Their respective histories led them closer and closer to mainstream denominationalism. At the other end of the continuum, movements like those of the Shakers and the Oneida Perfectionists enjoined a style of life in which members participated in total and all-embracing communities. With their concern for the boundaries that separated them from others, all of the sectarian movements were examples of the continuing concern for boundaries in pluralist America. At the same time, whatever their American-ness, sectarians had responded to nineteenth-century situations in religious terms, concerned to mark the boundaries that established their existence in this world, concerned to observe those boundaries, and concerned about how and when to cross them to what they believed lay beyond. Their blend of ordinary and extraordinary religion was not the only one that could have been created, but their blend worked for their time and maintained their continuity as part of the manyness of American religions.

Others, nevertheless, would find the sectarianism of the nineteenth-century new religions too confining or otherwise unpromising. Some would turn, instead, to occult and metaphysical movements that also fed the manyness. It is to these religious traditions that we now turn.

SUGGESTIONS FOR FURTHER READING: NINETEENTH-CENTURY NEW RELIGIONS

Andrews, Edward Deming. *The People Called Shakers.* New York: Dover Publications, 1963.

Arrington, Leonard J., and Bitton, Davis. *The Mormon Experience: A History of the Latter-day Saints.* New York: Alfred A. Knopf, 1979.

Brewer, Priscilla J. *Shaker Communities, Shaker Lives.* Hanover, NH: University Press of New England, 1986.

Bull, Malcolm, and Lockhart, Keith. *Seeking a Sanctuary: Seventh-day Adventism and the American Dream.* San Francisco: Harper & Row, 1989.

Bushman, Richard L. *Joseph Smith and the Beginnings of Mormonism.* Urbana: University of Illinois Press, 1984.

Carden, Maren Lockwood. *Oneida: Utopian Community to Modern Corporation.* Baltimore: Johns Hopkins Press, 1969.

Doan, Ruth Alden. *The Miller Heresy, Millennialism, and American Culture.* Philadelphia: Temple University Press, 1987.

Foster, Lawrence. *Religion and Sexuality: Three American Communal Experiments of the Nineteenth Century.* New York: Oxford University Press, 1981.

Gaustad, Edwin Scott, ed. *The Rise of Adventism.* New York: Harper & Row, 1974.

Gottschalk, Stephen. *The Emergence of Christian Science in American Religious Life.* Berkeley: University of California Press, 1973.

[_____, et al., eds.] *Christian Science: A Sourcebook of Contemporary Materials*. Boston: Christian Science Publishing, 1990.

Holloway, Mark. *Heavens on Earth: Utopian Communities in America, 1680–1880*. Rev. ed. New York: Dover Publications, 1966.

Kephart, William M. *Extraordinary Groups: An Examination of Unconventional Life-Styles*. 3d ed. New York: St. Martin's Press, 1987.

Numbers, Ronald L., and Butler, Jonathan M., eds. *The Disappointed: Millerism and Millenarianism in the Nineteenth Century*. Religion in North America. Bloomington: Indiana University Press, 1987.

Peel, Robert. *Health and Medicine in the Christian Science Tradition: Principle, Practice, and Challenge*. Health/Medicine and the Faith Traditions. New York: Crossroad, 1989.

Shipps, Jan. *Mormonism: The Story of a New Religious Tradition*. Urbana: University of Illinois Press, 1985.

Troeltsch, Ernst. *The Social Teaching of the Christian Churches*. 1911. 2 vols. Translated by Olive Wyon. Reprint. Chicago: University of Chicago Press, 1976.

Weber, Max. *The Sociology of Religion*. 1922. Translated from the 4th ed., rev. (1956) by Ephraim Fischoff. Boston: Beacon Press, 1963.

Chapter 8

Homesteads of the Mind:
Occult and Metaphysical
Movements

The year was 1848, and the place was a ramshackle house in Hydesville, New York. This home to the Fox family—John, a blacksmith; Margaret, his wife; and their two daughters, Maggie, a teenager, and Kate, not yet twelve—became in a series of episodes the site of mysterious knocking sounds. After a week or so of the noise in late March, the two girls or their parents grew anxious, and the girls moved their trundle bed into their parents' bedroom. The new setting made Kate and then Maggie braver; snapping their fingers and clapping their hands, they asked the knocker to make some response. A series of raps came as if in answer, and thus began what seemed a dialogue with an invisible presence. Soon the raps became the talk of the neighborhood, responding to questions and even leading some to claim discovery of the identity of the rapper—a murdered peddler whose remains were said to be buried in the cellar. Such reputed contact with the dead meant that, once again, religious excitement was spreading in the Burnt Over district of upstate New York, already the site of Mormon, Millerite, and Shaker preaching.

For believers, it was the birth of modern spiritualism, and for students of American religions, it was one instance of a growing trend in nineteenth-century America. Occult and metaphysical movements proliferated throughout that era and into the twentieth century. They added to the manyness of religions in America and also expressed a new oneness. Spread by the media and shared by members of the mainstream, the ideas and attitudes of those who joined these movements spilled beyond their boundaries—something we will continue to notice. Here, as we have already seen in so many instances, it is impossible to explore every aspect of the manyness. We can examine only a few major examples to suggest the development of these movements. But before we do, we need to consider the meaning of occultism and metaphysics for American religion.

Occult and Metaphysical Religions

A dictionary will explain that the word *occult* refers to something hidden and mysterious. Yet, what often is not realized is that in the West the occult tradition is another form of *religion*, different from the Judeo-Christian mainstream. Historically, occult religion crystallized in a secret body of knowledge and practice, passed on by a small, select group in every age. During much of Western history, until the Enlightenment of the eighteenth century, however, it was still in touch with major strands of the common European culture. Indeed, the science of the period shared occultism's main beliefs about the nature of the universe and the place of human life within it. And while the Christian church warned against the occult, some of the clergy were familiar with it and agreed with its basic ideas.

After the Enlightenment, though, the new science brought a radical revision in the way educated people viewed the world. As the prestige of science grew and as the church stepped out of the Middle Ages, occultism became, more and more, not only secret knowledge but also rejected knowledge. It had always been an assorted mixture of elements taken from various pagan traditions blended sometimes with material from Judaism and Christianity. Now that mixture was regarded as thoroughly suspect — the remnants of superstition from the early ages of humanity. Thus, by the nineteenth century, to hold occult beliefs meant to run counter to the main trend of culture. If an occultist was aware of the predicament, it meant, therefore, to be self-consciously separated. Alienation from the ordinary religion of culture accompanied occult beliefs and practices.

Here, however, it should be noted that an overview of American religious history reveals at least two forms of occultism. There was, first, a natural and traditional occultism that came to North America with the colonists. It thrived in the seventeenth century and continued strong into the eighteenth, only gradually declining. Even after its general decline, it flourished in rural areas and in small cultural enclaves. Blacks, immigrants from European peasant stock, and Southern Appalachians, as we will later see, all cultivated the occult beliefs and practices that their cultures had passed on to them. Second, there was the occultism of the nineteenth and twentieth centuries, which grew, seemingly spontaneously, from new sources. Popular among middle-class people who were part of the mainstream, it was a self-conscious, educated, and deliberate movement, different from the older and inherited occultism.

Although the lines between the two forms of occult religion were certainly not hard and fast, the two were different from each other in further ways as well. Natural and traditional occultism supported individuals as they tried to cope with everyday tasks. It was at ease with material things and demonstrated a sense of place, of being at home in its world. People planted crops by the signs of the zodiac and doctored themselves using occult anatomical charts, just as their grandparents had. They observed rules about not spilling salt or breaking mirrors, about avoiding black cats and not walking under ladders because, in their world, this was the way things were done, the way that bad luck was prevented, and the way that a person kept in touch with a traditional framework for living. On the other hand, the more self-conscious and deliberate form of occultism sought liberation from a daily round of meaningless existence through a cultivation of higher knowledge and practice. In order to cope with life, it charted the heavens and elaborated on what it considered hidden dimensions of human nature, interested in spiritual more than material things as sources of the present. Homeless in the world, this form of occultism sought, instead, homesteads in the human mind.

Metaphysical religions shared many of the basic ideas of this second and more deliberate form of occultism. In its primary meaning, metaphysics refers to the kind of philosophy that seeks to study the underlying reality of all existence. As the medievalists put it, metaphysics was the science of being as being. In American religious history, however, metaphysics became the theological explanation and religious practice of many groups. Understood literally, metaphysics meant something that went beyond the physical or the material. And, indeed, metaphysical believers in America stressed spiritual theories about life rather than historical traditions — like Judaism and mainstream Christianity — or material elements — like Roman Catholic sacramentalism. Like deliberate occultists, they sought homesteads of the mind. But unlike them, they built their religious systems on more general philosophical language, simpler and more continuous with the ordinary language of culture. And when they turned to religious practice, they were mostly uninterested in ceremonialized ritual forms. Thus, it was easy for metaphysical groups to relate to others among the many in America. Often, their teaching did not seem unusual.

Underlying both the occult and the metaphysical movement was a fundamental religious idea, one with which we are already familiar among American Indians and, to some extent, Roman Catholics. This was the idea of correspondence, in which there were many levels to the universe, all of them replicating one another. In this conception, the microcosm, or small world, of human life reflected the macrocosm, or great world, of the cosmos. There was, for this way of thinking, a sympathy between all things, an underlying harmony among them. Thus, the harmonial religions, as they are sometimes called, strived to bring people into harmony with the macrocosm that surrounded them. Moreover, since harmonialists believed the macrocosm was a larger version of the smaller reality and the world was one thing, it followed for them that action in the microcosm had consequences for the macrocosm. Actions taken by human beings could have some effect on other aspects of the world. If everything was like everything else in harmonial religions, then everything could act on everything else. Through working with elements on a smaller scale, people believed they could take practical action to control larger realities. Thus, magic became a valid activity, grounded in an explicit theory about how the world was put together. It contained no mystery for believers but instead expressed harmony at work. Similarly, in their view, the human mind could act on elements of the world to bring them into harmony with the true structure of things. Mental healing, a leading example, was an ordinary fact of life from this perspective.

It should be clear from this discussion of occult and metaphysical conceptions that believers lived in a mental world with fluid boundaries. A universe in which microcosm and macrocosm shared the same reality and in which any action had truly cosmic repercussions could not be neatly divided into separate compartments. Religion, for the occult and metaphysical movements, as for many other groups that we have viewed, had to do with all of life. But different from other groups, a sense of peoplehood did not locate members within well-defined social boundaries, and a sense of historical tradition could not supply boundaries either. Occult and metaphysical believers floated, seemingly, in universal space. They were cosmic migrants for whom everything was religious and every place was home. So they mingled Western tradition with Eastern imports at times and diffused their message throughout American culture until it became indistinguishable from that culture. Although they had begun from a position of separation, in the end their boundary problems led them to merge with the American mainstream.

Sources of Occultism in the Western Tradition

Before we follow the occult and metaphysical movements through American religious history, however, we need to examine their heritage. For if Jews, Catholics, and Protestants all had roots, so, too, did the occultists of America. Our search for these roots begins in the Hellenistic world during the first three centuries of the Christian era. This was the world shaped by the Mediterranean Sea and the language of ancient Greece (Hellas was another name for Greece). It was a world in which a mixture of Greek, Roman, Christian, Jewish, and other elements fused in various ways to produce a cosmopolitan religiocultural synthesis. When by the end of this period, in the fourth century, Christianity won out and became the official religion of the Roman Empire, elements of that older Hellenistic synthesis provided the ingredients for an occultism that persisted in various systems.

First, as a system, there was Gnosticism, a religious teaching and practice that had grown on the fringes of both the Jewish and Christian traditions. A Gnostic was, literally, one who knew, but the knowledge of the Gnostic was not understood as the rational kind that could be gained from books and logical arguments. Rather, it was considered secret knowledge, accompanied by power to save the person from the present, evil world. In fact, the Gnostic was thought to be someone within whom the saving spark of knowledge had already been planted. According to this belief, once realizing the treasure hiding within the prison house of the body, the Gnostic should begin the process of liberation. By means of the spark of knowledge, the Gnostic could start the long journey leading to reunion with his or her divine counterpart within the Godhead. The goal was mystical merging. Home for the Gnostic was created not here, but in another world.

Second, there was Neoplatonism, a philosophical descendant of the teachings of the Greek philosopher Plato (427?–347 B.C.). Neoplatonism refashioned Platonism to make of it, once again, a Hellenistic religious system. In a variation of the theory of correspondence, Plato had taught that the real world was the world of Ideas, or Forms, on which the physical, material universe was modeled. Thus, the real tree was the abstract idea of a tree that any existing tree reflected. For Plato, too, there was a hierarchy among the Ideas, and the ultimate among them were the Good, the True, and the Beautiful.

Neoplatonism retained Plato's theory of Ideas and the vision of a hierarchy among them. However, it saw the ultimate Idea as the One, followed by Nous, or Mind, which was in turn followed by the World Soul. From the World Soul came individual souls and, even lower in the hierarchy, the manyness of the material world. The religious task, as Neoplatonists understood it, was to reclaim oneself for the One, retracing the path of downward emanation from the One by an upward ascent of the soul. Like the Gnostic, it was clear that the Neoplatonist desired and sought mystical experience — union with the One.

A third occult religious system was provided by astrology. Already in the third millennium (B.C.) in ancient Mesopotamia, Babylonians were observing the heavens with a perception of the world as a whole of interdependent parts. In the Hellenistic era, astrology continued to flourish with the mingling of Babylonians, Egyptians, Greeks, and Romans in the Mediterranean basin, and by the second century A.D., the Roman Claudius Ptolemy wrote what some have called the world's greatest astrological textbook, the *Tetrabiblios*.

While some used astrological materials in an uncombined form and directed their lives by studying horoscopes, many mixed astrology with other religious disciplines. In other words, astrology became a primary ingredient in a religious eclecticism in which various elements blended to yield a new synthesis. Probably the most important example of this process, in terms of its future influence in the West, was a religious philosophy called Hermeticism. This fourth occult system, available at the end of the Hellenistic era, was based on a series of writings attributed to an ancient Egyptian priest called Hermes Trismegistus (the Three-Times-Great Hermes). The writings, which we know today as the *Corpus Hermeticum* and the *Asclepius*, were composed in the second or third century A.D., close to the time of their discovery, and Hermes Trismegistus was, no doubt, a fictional character. Yet for centuries, until critical scholarship proved otherwise, he was revered as a shadowy figure from the early ages of ancient Egyptian civilization, and thus his system possessed great authority within occult circles. Moreover, the Hermetic texts brought together Gnosticism, Platonism, Neoplatonism, astrology, and various other religious philosophies from ancient Greece. They offered a comprehensive synthesis of mystical teaching from pagan sources, establishing a cultus to be followed in the mind, exalting Nous (Mind) as intuition, and giving magical lessons.

Although Christian church fathers such as Lactantius (260?–340?) and Augustine (354–430) preached against the Hermetic texts, other Christians passed on their teachings. So in the Middle Ages some priests practiced magic and astrology. They also engaged in alchemy, a fifth occult system with religious overtones. Alchemy, the ancestor of modern chemistry, was an attempt to change less valuable metals into others regarded more highly, most significant among them, gold. In order to accomplish this, the alchemist, like a monk, was required to lead an ascetic life of self-denial in which great purity of mind and body was demanded. For religious alchemists, the process of creating gold was an external symbol for an internal change the person sought. Here the understood task of the alchemist was to discover the divine spark identified as the Self. The alchemist then sought a reunification with that spark and a merging with the All that was considered divine. Hence, the alchemist pursued the same goal as other occultists. Knowledge was viewed as a secret, saving force that would bring liberation from the present world, realization of the true nature of things, and, finally, mystical union with Self and God.

Meanwhile, at least by the twelfth century, a sixth occult religious system was flourishing. In southern France and Spain, the Kabbalah again blended elements from many different traditions but changed them to give the material a Jewish stamp. In the *Book Bahir* (1180?) and especially the *Zohar* (1280?), Kabbalistic teachings spread. They offered a secret means of interpreting Hebrew scripture through uncovering meanings said to be hidden in the words that were written there. The Torah, for the Kabbalists, was the truth dressed in an earthly garment, and that garment had to be removed to behold spiritual beauty. Behind the God of Hebrew scripture for them lay En-Sof, from whom emanated ten intelligences called Sefiroth. By means of the Sefiroth, Kabbalists believed, En-Sof had created the material world. In a series of correspondences, they explained connections between the Sefiroth and different parts of the human body, different names for God, and different classes of angels.

Like the Hermetic texts, the Kabbalah claimed to be a tradition handed down from the ancient past, in this case from the time of Adam. Like Neoplatonism, it taught the creation of the many (the world) by emanation from the One (here En-Sof). And like Gnosticism, it taught that liberation and the experience of God came through saving knowledge, here concerning the real meaning of the Torah. Eclectic as it was, therefore, the Kabbalah moved into Christian occult circles in the Middle Ages. But as we have noted, occultism was a religious system different from either Judaism or Christianity. Thus, the various occult disciplines found their way into the lives of those who carried on the alternative tradition and transmitted it, in part, to the Renaissance.

The Renaissance, we know, is the name historians give to the movement of cultural rebirth that began in northern Italy in the fourteenth century and spread throughout Europe over the next two centuries. It brought a revival of learning and a new spirit of confidence in human enterprise; and, agreeable to both, it pioneered in a rediscovery of the occult tradition. So the *Corpus Hermeticum*, which had disappeared since antiquity, was brought in its Greek manuscript to Florence, Italy, and translated. Interest in astrology and the Kabbalah flourished, and occult knowledge, officially banned by the medieval church, now gained a new respectability despite that opposition. Learned people translated occult manuscripts and engaged in occult practices. Seemingly overnight, the Renaissance magician became a hero. In England, it was the Elizabethans who became heirs to this Renaissance revival, and so Elizabethan occultism was respected and widely known. With the arrival of the sons and daughters of the Elizabethans in the New World, it came to the English colonies.

Traditional Occultism in the Colonies

Keeping this background in mind, let us look at traditional occultism as it appeared during the early period of American history. Our time span is the seventeenth and eighteenth centuries, from the beginning of settlement to the end of the American Revolution. At the start of this period, both learned and less educated people accepted the occult tradition as it had been handed down. For the learned, it was the basis of the science that they read about in their few and cherished books. For other people, it was the way things were and were done. By the end of the American Revolution, however, there was a clear divergence between the two groups. The scholarly elite had repudiated the old beliefs in favor of a new and more persuasive science. The larger body of people, especially in rural America, continued to adhere to the natural occultism they had received. Still, the times signaled the beginning of a slow decline, even among these populations, in occult belief and practice.

Astrology

There were various practical manifestations of occultism in the colonies. Two of the most prominent were astrology and witchcraft. Astrology came to America from the England of Queen Elizabeth I, who gave her name to the time during which she ruled (1558–1603). Learned Elizabethans had based their astrology on their understanding of the material composition of the universe. They held that it was made up of various combinations of four elements — earth, water, air, and fire — and four qualities — hot, cold, moist, and dry. Here elements and qualities were correlated with each other, so that fire was identified as hot and dry; air, hot and moist; earth, cold and dry; and water, cold and moist. Similarly, human beings were considered to be made up of four basic humors. Choler, or yellow bile, like fire, was thought to be hot and dry; blood, like air, hot and moist; melancholy, or black bile, was understood to imitate earth in being cold and dry, while phlegm was seen as like water in that it was cold and moist. For Elizabethans as for earlier peoples, each of these humors had a definite part to play in the functioning of a healthy body, and when one or the other of them predominated, it stamped its imprint on a person's character.

Within this ordered universe, astrology charted the course of the heavens and related the lives of human beings to the stars. The elements and qualities were thought to be present in the stars, some of which were fire signs and some earth signs, some identified with air and some with water. Similarly, the stars were held to correspond to the humors within human beings, and different stars to govern each of the humors. Moreover, the stars were closely bound up with the calculation of time. In a world in which everything was thought to possess some significance and in which each existing thing was said to correspond with many others in the universe, each moment in time was also considered to have its unique quality. For astrologers, the stars were cosmic clues to the quality of time, and through studying them, astrologers aimed to determine good and bad days for various activities. In other words, astrology taught that there were signs of the times, making it possible to understand the character of a person by the time in which he or she had been born and making it possible, too, to give advice or even foretell the future.

The colonists inherited this world of the Elizabethans. Like them, they continued to make a distinction between two kinds of astrology. First and most common was natural astrology, which concerned the relationship between the stars and other material things such as the rhythms of nature, the weather, and the human body. Second was judicial astrology, which probed the relationship between the stars and human choice and action. This second form of astrology implicitly challenged the Christian doctrine of freedom of the will, because it suggested to many that the stars controlled human destiny. Thus, it had traditionally been most subject to attack and least accepted. The colonists, however, readily used the ideas that they gained from natural astrology. Among the learned, this material was taught in textbooks used at Harvard and Yale, while it appeared in the private libraries of prominent individuals in the late seventeenth and early eighteenth centuries. Among less educated people, it was spread by means of the almanac, which along with the Bible was found in virtually every colonial household.

Probably more widely read than the Bible, the almanac provided its readers with representations of the twelve signs of the zodiac as well as the names and symbols of the seven planets known to antiquity. The zodiac was a zone in the sky created by the path of the planets as they followed the apparent orbit of the sun from sunrise to sunset and again to sunrise. Each sign was assigned 30 degrees of the full 360-degree circle, and in many almanacs these signs were only the most basic in a series of symbols provided by astrological charts and considered useful for farming, weather forecasting, and medicine.

For this last, almanacs usually printed the "anatomy," the picture of a cosmic man surrounded by the signs of the zodiac said to govern parts of his body. Traditionally, Leo ruled his heart and would be shown next to it; Gemini controlled his arms and was appropriately positioned; Pisces was related to his feet and was printed below them on the page. Each day the moon could be found in a different sign of the zodiac. Thus, by locating the moon in relation to the sign, a person could decide whether, according to the system, it was a good or bad day to treat some part of the body medically. For almanac readers, the presence of the moon governed favorable treatment, and by means of the moon the quality of the time was discovered. Hence, astrology formed the basis for an ordinary religion through which people could order their existence and determine their course of action at any given moment. In short, astrology gave them a way to orient their lives.

Witchcraft

Witchcraft was also part of the religious life of the colonists. Like astrology, witchcraft included a learned version, the object of scholarly inquiry, and a nonscholastic type, which attracted more people. The scholarly tradition of witchcraft was carried on most notably in the Pennsylvania German community, especially in the brotherhood established under Johannes Kelpius (1673–1708) in Germantown, now part of Philadelphia. Witchcraft, as the brothers understood it, was the religion of nature that had once dominated Europe and had only gradually yielded before Christianity. The group inaugurated their settlement with the rites of summer solstice according to early German tradition. They built bonfires out of trees and bushes, raised ritual chants, and asked sacred powers they invoked to bless the place where they were making a home. The Woman in the Wilderness, as their community came to be called, offered its inhabitants a blend of pagan, Christian, and Jewish elements. Natural symbols and natural magic were everywhere, for the brothers wore astrological amulets, used incantations in their healing rituals, and studied long hours to learn to control nature by magical means. In their ceremonies, they expressed ideas found in the old heathen religions. Nature, through its fertility, was for the brothers the source of sacred power, and they thought that by orienting themselves toward it and discovering its secrets, they could change reality for the better. So the brothers were actually learned practitioners of magic, using nature to attempt change for what they saw as the greater good.

Among the general population, too, magic was practiced in the colonies. "Cunning folk," as they were called, were witches thought to possess powers sometimes similar to those claimed for Indian shamans. They reportedly could heal the sick, find lost items, locate precious metal with a divining rod, or send a fair wind to a sailing ship. As in the case of the learned magicians among the Germans, these witches drew on special rituals to try to contact the powers of nature. In treasure hunting, for example, after the treasure was believed to be located (with a divining rod), the witch might draw circles around it to protect it, recite words held to have special power to overcome unwilling spirits, and use nails to "pin" the treasure down. None of the gestures was meaningless. Rather, the circles imitated the shapes of nature and centered the object as a source of concern, directing human energy toward it with the intent of safekeeping. The ritual words were forms of speech thought to empower corresponding forces in nature for the protection of the treasure. The nails were symbolic statements meant, like sacraments, to prevent the treasure from being moved.

Other witches were believed to be at work among the colonists, however, and these witches were regarded as evil. Many times they were poor, eccentric, and elderly women, unpopular in their communities because of their begging, their strange ways, or their biting tongues. In any case, these witches were thought to use the old religion of nature to practical advantage under the same principles invoked by German magicians or English cunning folk. The only difference was that they were reputed to invoke their powers to the disadvantage of others. Thus, it was said that they could dry up a cow so that it would not give milk or interrupt the process by which milk became butter. They could allegedly harass their enemies and bring them illness and even, in some cases, death. These feared individuals were joined in popular belief by a fourth and still more disquieting type of witch. This was the Satanic witch, who was thought to have gained power by means of a pact with the devil. Here the influence of Christianity was apparent, and belief in the witch operated as a symbolic counterforce to the power attributed to God. Those considered evil and Satanic witches at times ended up in trouble with the law in the colonies, and the Salem witchcraft episode of 1692 is one example. Actually, however, there had been sixty trials for witchcraft before the Salem episode, and many of the colonies had laws on their books making witchcraft a crime into the eighteenth century.

Events at Salem Village (later Danvers), in the Massachusetts Bay colony, began with Betty Parris, daughter of the town minister, and her cousin Abigail Williams. The two girls, one nine and the other eleven years old, spent many hours with Tituba, a slave from the West Indies, who apparently taught the children something of the magical traditions she had learned. The magic lore attracted other girls in the village, many of them teenagers. Then, when Betty Parris and subsequently Abigail Williams fell into trances — screaming, crying, barking like dogs, and moving on all fours — the diagnosis of witchcraft was pronounced. Neither doctors nor ministers could help, and so events moved to the local courthouse. In a gradual series of escalations, more and more witches were named by the afflicted girls. There was Tituba and then Sarah Good and Sarah Osborne. Before the trials ended, nineteen witches had been hanged, and one, a man, had been pressed to death.

The clearest statement of the strength of colonial witchcraft beliefs was the admission of spectral evidence at the trials. This meant that claims by the girls that they had been attacked or harassed by a phantom in the shape of the accused individual could be used as evidence. So long as the girls attested that they saw the spectral shapes, it did not matter if they were invisible to other people. The accused person could have witnesses that she or he had been miles distant, but the defense was useless because it was believed that the specter of a witch could travel anywhere. Significantly, when spectral evidence was finally banished from the courtroom, the trials came to a speedy end.

The Satanic witchcraft of Salem Village was a negative instance of occult religion in the colonies. For others, the old fertility religion of witchcraft had been more benign, and its ordering of life through nature had been a meaningful way to think and act in an agricultural society. Like astrology, it brought ordinary religion to countless numbers of people and directed their everyday lives in the ways they desired.

The Occult-Metaphysical Revival of the Nineteenth Century

We have seen that as times changed and a new science developed, occult beliefs were rejected among educated colonists. By the time of the Revolution, they were held to be anachronisms, ideas and practices left over from another era. So the tradition, at first rejected because of the triumph of Christianity, was now rejected anew because of the triumph of science and the scientific way of looking at the world. The general population continued to carry on the remnants of the occult tradition it had absorbed, but cultural leaders took a different route. Yet occult and metaphysical religious systems were not gone. Indeed, as we have already seen, a new and deliberate occultism grew rapidly in the nineteenth century, a significant part of it once again among an educated elite. The new occultism was a self-conscious work of construction and reconstruction, and a groundwork for this occultism and its metaphysical counterpart was laid by a group of intellectuals, the American Transcendentalists.

As we saw in Chapter 4, the Transcendentalists found their theological basis in a rediscovery of the theory of correspondence. But while we noted there the results of Transcendental thinking in the context of reform, especially of the church, here we need to stress other aspects of their thought and practice. All of the Transcendentalists began to speak and write in a new way, and with Ralph Waldo Emerson, they began to ponder the meaning of the Oversoul, the World Soul of the Neoplatonists to which individual souls were considered bound. They experimented, too, with new ways of living, sometimes in communities formed to express the One to which they believed all people belonged. Brook Farm and Fruitlands, both Transcendental communes, were two results. Always though, whether or not they chose community life, they followed Emerson (never a member of a commune) in the quest for self-culture. In this nineteenth-century version of the journey toward saving knowledge, each individual was enjoined to turn within and there cultivate the qualities that would lead to harmony with self and universe.

In their own formulation of this teaching, Emerson and the other Transcendentalists, like many with occult and metaphysical interests, were eclectic. They mixed together elements from South and East Asian religious sources, from Neoplatonic philosophy, from European Romantic writers, and from the metaphysical system of the eighteenth-century Swedish mystic Emanuel Swedenborg (1688–1772). From Asia, they took especially the Indian metaphysical belief that the world, God, and human beings all participated in one substance and that beyond the illusion of matter lay the reality of spirit. From Neoplatonism came the complementary teaching about the One and the Many united in the Oversoul, in which every soul had its being.

With the European Romantics, the Transcendentalists participated in the revolt against the intellectual movement of the Enlightenment, which had exalted reason and law. As we already began to consider in Chapter 4, Romanticism was born in a desire to break out of the boundaries imposed by the logical pattern of the mind and the ordering rule of law. Hence, among the Transcendentalists there was a desire to escape from the formality of the Unitarian church and to find religion in the freedom of nature and self. (Since occult and metaphysical themes defied any borders in their universalism, these themes would fit smoothly into Romantic visions of reality.)

Finally, with Emanuel Swedenborg, the Transcendentalists had a model of the way in which many currents of thought could fuse together in a religious system to meet the concerns of the age. The son of a Lutheran bishop and a member of the Swedish nobility, Swedenborg through his education developed a great interest in the natural sciences. In his position as a mining engineer, he traveled widely and wrote extensively on scientific subjects. But his questions concerning life led him to turn to anatomy and to philosophy, while his thinking brought him to conclude that only through intuition could a person know God or the inner nature of reality. Outward experience without such insight, he thought, was incomplete. From 1745, when he claimed revelation from the spiritual world, Swedenborg began to use what he said were visions and communications with angelic beings in a series of spiritual writings. Reviving Neoplatonic and Renaissance occultism, his teachings now rested on the doctrine of the correspondence between natural and spiritual worlds. The natural world, for Swedenborg, had been created in the image of a higher spiritual realm, and both worlds received an influx of the divine. In this explanation, Swedenborg presented an especially detailed description of a succession of spiritual spheres that, he said, surrounded the earth. In Swedenborg's teaching, three were spheres of heaven, and three were spheres of hell. As we will see, later American occultists would build their own systems on a modified version of this idea.

Popular Occult and Metaphysical Movements in a New America

At the time that Transcendentalism flourished, weaving together themes from Asian religion to Swedenborgianism with perceptions drawn from life in America, the United States was undergoing a period of intense change. Emerson, in fact, had capitalized on the change and had traveled widely to many cities and towns where at public meetings he popularized the gospel of Transcendentalism. The world in which he did so was one in which the Industrial Revolution was rapidly spreading across America. A new factory system was centralizing the production of manufactured goods, while a revolution in transportation was making it possible to travel by rail and steamboat many times faster than stage-coaches and sails had allowed. Meanwhile, a nation of migrants was moving westward to people the frontier or cityward to produce large metropolitan centers. The old homesteads, which had housed generations of families, were becoming a thing of the past, supplanted by an emerging urban middle class with some affluence, some education, and some leisure.

People praised the inventions of the age of progress and spoke of the manifest destiny of the United States to reach from one end of the continent to the other. But beneath the optimism and excitement America had become a land of geographical, social, and intellectual dislocation. Migrants and immigrants both had been uprooted from the security of their past. The middle class in the cities, neither very rich nor very poor, was searching for a sense of identity to replace the feeling of being neither here nor there. The ideas that religion had taught through the Judeo-Christian tradition seemed less persuasive in the new situation. At the same time, science, with its growing interest in the theory of evolution, undermined traditional religion from another quarter, and Romanticism encouraged people to step beyond accepted borders. In this world of newness and confusion, the occult and metaphysical movements provided havens for many who felt homeless. They offered sanctuaries where it was hoped that peace and stability could reign, homesteads on a mental landscape to replace the physical ones that, seemingly everywhere, were disappearing.

We will examine some of the most significant of these new movements in the nineteenth century and glance at their continuance into the twentieth. As we do so, our study is touching only a few cases. Beyond them, occult and metaphysical manifestations were widespread, small and not too congenial to organization, part of the newness and manyness that again and again we have seen in the United States.

Spiritualism

The rappings reported by the Foxes in Hydesville, New York, were usually regarded by later spiritualists as the beginning of their movement. But there had

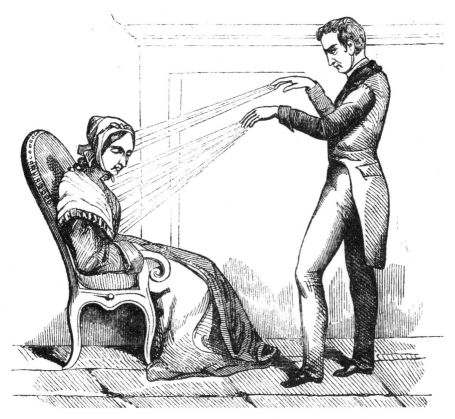

Nineteenth-Century Mesmerism. This anonymous wood engraving from about 1840 depicts a mesmerist directing magnetic "lines of force" toward an entranced female subject who is presumably his patient.

been forerunners of these rappings in America. The Shakers, we recall, in their ecstatic dances and religious exercises had frequently claimed spirit visitors. Meanwhile, in the larger culture, popular Swedenborgianism grew. In one example of the process, John Chapman (1774–1847), better remembered as Johnny Appleseed, became its missionary. As he moved through the Ohio country planting apple seeds and providing saplings to the settlers, he also distributed Swedenborgian literature — introducing to many the tradition that would give spiritualists their metaphysical explanations.

Similarly, mesmerism paved the way for spiritualist groups. Introduced from France in 1836 and often called animal magnetism, mesmerism brought an induced mental — and physical — state, the antecedent of later hypnotism. It was believed to depend on the magnetic transference of a universal fluid from one individual to another. While mesmerism figured in the growth of other occult and metaphysical movements as well, its trance states seemed similar to those in which contact with spirits was reported. Andrew Jackson Davis (1826–1910), whose written work later provided a theoretical grounding for spiritualism, came into contact with mesmerism in his youth. He became convinced that in induced trance states he could see through material objects as a clairvoyant, and later, on his own, he claimed that he made contact with the spirits of Galen, a famous doctor and writer of the ancient world, and Swedenborg. Davis began to acquire a name for himself as a healer and, more importantly here, as a prolific writer. He took Swedenborg's theory of six spheres surrounding the earth and modified it so that each of them became a spiritual plane on the way toward a divine Sun. When all human beings had progressed to the sixth plane beyond the physical, he taught, a new set of spheres would come into existence. The world that Davis saw was one of eternal progress, with spirits on various planes, closer or farther from the earth. Thus, contact, especially with spirits closer to the earth plane, seemed to his followers a realistic possibility.

While Davis, often called the "Seer of Poughkeepsie" (New York), was explaining his views, popular spiritualism was spreading in America. For the many who flocked to séances, spiritualism meant a belief in and practice of communication with the spirits of the dead through the help of human mediums. Those who came were often elderly and often mourning the loss of a loved one. A number of them were prominent individuals, and many, especially among the mediums, were women. To its seekers, spiritualism offered what seemed a reasonable approach to religion in a new time. If religious beliefs were under fire, spiritualism promised empirical evidence, proof that could be seen and heard, that the dead lived on and a world beyond this one existed. Moreover, it often explained the unusual happenings, in which spirits seemed to materialize and strange objects to appear at séances, by an occult form of scientific language. It was eager to open its meetings to objective investigators who might authenticate apparitions and communications. In other words, it sought a blending of science and religion not unlike the blending that had been part of the ancient occult tradition.

Beyond that, spiritualism provided the means for prominent female mediums to assume a leadership role in religion normally reserved, during the period, for men. Their apparent trance states enabled these mediums to speak in public in an age when no respectable woman could easily do so. And these states gave them an authority that, since they were usually inhibited by cultural conventions and often pale and sickly, they could not normally acquire. That a number of female mediums became active in the women's rights movement of the time was testimony to the climate of support for public activity they found in spiritualism. Indeed, spiritualism as a movement embraced the major social causes of the nineteenth century. Andrew Jackson Davis, as an example, wrote, lectured, and campaigned actively for reform during his career and was especially concerned for women's rights and marriage reform. With its individualism expressed through its evolutionary theology of progress and through its personalized form of religious practice, the spiritualist habit of mind led to reform activity that, it was hoped, would increase individual freedom and well-being.

At the same time, spiritualism brought a Romantic approach to religion. As we saw with the lectures and writings of Emerson, other Transcendentalists, and various Protestant liberals, Romanticism was part of the culture. People were often growing impatient with formal religious institutions, and as one alternative they sought inner conviction through personal contact instead. In their felt experiences of communication with spirits, they believed that they were making connection with the further reaches of the natural world, outside the boundaries that organizations had frequently set. They thought, like the Transcendentalists, that the world was one whole and that there were close ties between the spiritual and the material worlds. Spirit, for them, was higher and more perfect matter.

Throughout the time of spiritualist development, however, most spiritualists were more concerned with practice than with theory. Here the medium was central, and she was the necessary agent for communication with another world. Over time, two kinds of mediumship grew up — mental and physical. Mental mediumship involved psychic happenings when the medium achieved a trance state. Her conscious mind seemingly no longer functioned, and, spiritualists believed, a controlling spirit took its place. By the twentieth century, psychic practices in mental mediumship had become formalized. The medium might engage in billet reading by responding to questions submitted on small pieces of paper and directed to a spirit. Or the medium could practice psychometry, in which she aimed to get in touch with vibrations of a physical object and so learn all she could about people (now dead) who had touched it in the past. Again, the medium might prophesy by reading auras, bands of light of different colors believed to emanate from every human being. These auras were thought to record the life history of a person, enabling a spirit to make predictions.

In physical mediumship, the spirits were held to acquire material form at a séance so that they could be seen, heard, and sometimes felt. In the rapping at Hydesville, New York, spiritualists identified one type of physical manifestation. But there were others as spiritualism grew. Sometimes, it was claimed, the spirits tipped over tables, and sometimes they disturbed people at a séance by sending objects through the air. In automatic writing, spirits were said to use the hand of the medium to write their message, and in independent writing, to write, without any material guidance, on paper. On some occasions, spirits reportedly made an object disappear in one place and brought it to another where they rematerialized it. At other times, they were said to use specially constructed trumpets to speak to people at a séance. By the twentieth century, an elaborate system had been worked out with anticipated spirit guides to aid the medium and others present. Among expected spirit visitors at a séance, Indian Chiefs and Spirit Doctors were popular in these roles, Indian Chiefs often as Gate Keepers, who would keep unwanted spirits away, and Spirit Doctors as lecturers or advisers on spiritual subjects. Moreover, mediums sometimes claimed healing gifts through a force thought to flow from their fingers.

While the spiritualists had developed a full ceremonial range for their séances, they were not so successful with larger organization. In the nineteenth century they experienced a ground swell of public interest, especially in the decade after 1848 and during the time after the Civil War. Yet they resisted structure and instead splintered into small groups around different mediums or groups of mediums. After the foundation of the Theosophical Society in 1875, which we will look at next, spiritualists split into some groups who united spiritualist beliefs and practices with Christianity and others who followed theosophy. Finally, in 1893, the National Spiritualist Association of Churches came into existence, featuring a congregational government in which independent churches joined in state organizations. This became the largest and the most conservative of the spiritualist organizations, but it was neither strong nor universal. Today, the number of Americans who are spiritualists can only be guessed; and, in the best estimate, there are probably between 1,000 and 2,000 churches.

The inability of spiritualists to form strong organizations was shared by most of the other occult and metaphysical groups. With their teaching about the unity of matter and spirit, with their blending of religion with an occult form of science, with their reform activism and their stance on women's rights, and with their openness to believers from any background, they were people without boundaries. Moving beyond the most liberal forms of Protestantism, their mental universalism was mirrored in the diffuseness of their organizations. As we have seen before, home was in the mind more than in the structures of society.

Theosophy

If late nineteenth- and twentieth-century spiritualists often tended toward theosophy, this movement itself grew partially out of spiritualism. The two chief founders of the Theosophical Society had met at a farmhouse in Chittenden, Vermont, where in 1874 reports of the materialization of spirits drew spiritualists and others who were curious. Helena P. Blavatsky (1831–1891), world traveler and recent Russian immigrant to the United States, was among them. So was Colonel Henry S. Olcott (1832–1907), corporation lawyer, agricultural expert, and sometime government official, who had already written an account of Chittenden for the New York Sun, in a story copied throughout the world. The two struck up an immediate acquaintance and, drawn by their mutual interest in spiritualism, became fast friends. A year later, with William Q. Judge (1851–1896) and a group of others, they formed the Theosophical Society in New York, an organization to carry on occult research.

It was clear from their statement of intentions that knowledge was the key issue for Theosophists. Indeed, theosophy, in the generic sense, was another name for the occult tradition concerning knowledge of the divine. And while Olcott provided organizational leadership for the group, it was Blavatsky, or

"HPB" as her followers liked to call her, who led the way in the pursuit of occult knowledge. Between 1875 and 1877, she wrote *Isis Unveiled*, a lengthy book that glorified reputed old occult masters and aimed to reveal their secrets for the nineteenth century. Blavatsky wanted to show the presence of a wide-ranging occultism behind the philosophies and religions of the world and especially to show that the Brahmanism of early India and, later, Buddhism were the sources for the other religions. Exhibiting an interest in Asian thought similar to the Transcendentalists', she also taught like them the doctrine of correspondence. Matter, for HPB, was the crystallization of spirit, and magic was possible because of the harmony between earthly and heavenly spheres.

In writing her vast work, Blavatsky claimed that she was aided by Mahatmas, members of a select brotherhood of individuals who, while still human beings, had evolved to degrees of perfection beyond those normally reached by others. The Mahatmas, she said, usually dwelled in the Himalaya Mountains in the isolated country of Tibet, but they possessed magical abilities to materialize at will or to communicate by letters that arrived at their destination as soon as they were sent. Blavatsky had met the Mahatmas earlier in her wanderings, she reported, and they had been directing her life purposively since, not simply for her own sake but in order to help human beings attain greater spiritual growth. Blavatsky claimed that it was for this reason, too, that with even more assistance they helped her to write *The Secret Doctrine* (1888). In this, her major work, she aimed to set forth the root knowledge from which all later religion, philosophy, and science grew. She gave an occult account of the origins of the world and of human life, explaining an Unmoved Mover and Rootless Root of all things as pure impersonal Be-ness. She told, too, of a law of becoming in which each individual reaped what he or she had sowed and was periodically reincarnated to gain in spiritual maturity. Finally, she subscribed to the unity of all souls in the Oversoul, the belief that before her Emerson had affirmed.

Meanwhile, the Theosophical Society slowly assumed its mature form. Its purpose had become threefold. To the quest for occult knowledge, it added its intentions of forming a universal "brotherhood" of all people and of promoting the study of comparative religions. In this change the research group had become a religion, for it now envisioned a way of life. In fact, though, the religion had been implicit from the first, since occult knowledge in itself was never simply sought for rational understanding; it always aimed at salvation through knowledge. Ideally, Theosophists were expected to live according to a disciplined program in which, if they were ordinary members of the society, they were encouraged to perform faithfully the duties of their place in life, to live according to the precept of brotherhood, to meditate and to regulate their diet (vegetarianism was preferred), and to make progress through study and service. In addition to the ordinary class of membership, the society offered a higher degree for an inner circle (the "Esoteric Section"). Here a person was thought to receive the special teaching of the occult masters, or Mahatmas, and at the same time was required to live by the regular discipline already described. At the top of the hierarchy, the masters themselves were believed to form the third degree of membership.

After Helena Blavatsky died, Annie Besant (1847–1933) eventually became the leader of the Theosophical Society. Involved in England in various social-reform movements, she had been drawn to *The Secret Doctrine* and its author. During her era at the head of the society, it grew and prospered so that by 1930 there were 50,000 Theosophists in forty countries, 10,000 of them in the United States. Typically, they were urban, middle-class people, and many among them came from the professions and had achieved prominence. Yet even before the death of Blavatsky and Olcott, the society was beset by factionalism. Thus, in 1895 William Judge led out a huge portion of the American membership to form the independent Theosophical Society in America. Other schisms followed. Once again, the boundary problem was troubling those who strived to live by the occult tradition. Their universalism was also an individualism that made Theosophists willing to pursue their quests wherever they would lead.

At present, the quests surely continue, but it is impossible to provide exact membership statistics for the theosophical groups. Taken together, there are perhaps 40,000 or more Theosophists in the world and, among them, roughly 5,000 in the United States. Thus, from one point of view, interest in theosophical organizations appears to have declined from earlier in the century.

However, small and in decline though they may statistically be, theosophical groups possess an importance for American religious history beyond their numbers. It was the Theosophical Society that provided the first organized conduit for the introduction of Eastern religious thought into the United States. For from the first, Hinduism and Buddhism figured heavily in the society, especially in the knowledge Blavatsky claimed the Mahatmas had taught her. And, in fact, the movement can be read as a spiritual pilgrimage of discovery to the East, a search by "strangers" in America for their religious home abroad.

Moreover, it was the Theosophical Society that offered an institutional model for mixing Eastern and Western materials. The society was an eclectic organization, and its blend of many traditions brought to the fore Western adepts in the occult as well as Eastern ones. Even further, in the climate of the United States, in which popular Transcendentalism, Swedenborgianism, mesmerism, and spiritualism flourished, theosophy absorbed elements from these movements and made the elements its own.

Finally, it was Theosophists who introduced in the late nineteenth century a language of expectation for a "new age." That New Age is with us still, as we will see in Chapter 11, and theosophy has had a good deal to do with the shape and style of its existence. In sum, theosophy culled from traditions East and West an elaborate explanation of nature and humanity, rejecting belief in God in any ordinary sense and supplying instead the complicated details of its occult account of Absolute Reality. That account ended in the society's eclectic form of mysticism. If followers of occult and metaphysical teachings built homesteads of the mind, Theosophists erected large ones.

New Thought

Even before theosophy attracted the attention of some Americans, foundations were already being laid for a third movement within the harmonial religion of the nineteenth and twentieth centuries. New Thought, as it came to be called, took many forms, but different from spiritualism and theosophy, it stressed metaphysical concerns without occult elaboration. In fact, the discussion of Christian Science in the previous chapter dealt with a close relative and with an important historical source for the New Thought tradition. But while Christian Science was a strongly authoritative sect, New Thought followed the pattern of spiritualism and theosophy. It, too, was diffuse and lacked boundaries — so much so that it became in its furthest outreach part of the mainstream of American culture.

The seed for New Thought was contained in the teaching and healing practice of Phineas P. Quimby (1802–1866), the mental healer who had also played a significant role in the life of Mary Baker Eddy. As a young man, Quimby had become interested in mesmerism and had begun to experiment with it when he could find a willing subject. So it was that he met Lucius Burkmar, a person who in mesmeric trance endeavored to diagnose and heal disease. After the two had been working together, Quimby, himself in poor health, sought Burkmar's help and like others was cured. So impressive was his experience that Quimby pondered its meaning until he was satisfied that he had discovered how Burkmar cured disease. He decided that Burkmar's healing depended on a person's inward belief, which, he became convinced, controlled the state of sickness or health. Burkmar inspired belief in his patients, concluded Quimby, and so they were cured of illness. This assessment became the start of a career dedicated to healing the sick, and when in 1859 Quimby opened an office in Portland, Maine, he attracted his most famous patients, among them not only Mary Baker Eddy but also future leaders of New Thought.

Quimby was a practical man who wanted to cure disease. But he was also a theoretically inclined man, and although neither well educated nor a system builder, he pondered the basis of his healing ever more deeply. He came to reject the use of mesmerism, and his writings instead displayed a Swedenborgian influence. No doubt through Swedenborgian friends, Quimby had absorbed the idea of correspondence. He saw human beings as spiritual in nature, and he thought of the soul as in direct relationship with the divine mind. It followed for him that when a person was healed, it was because of the operation of the divine spirit on the human soul. For Quimby, this came about through an awakening by which a patient became aware of his or her inner spiritual nature. Sometimes Quimby identified the means to this awakening with a wisdom or science he called the Christ, and at least once he described his teaching as Christian science.

Far more the systematic thinker for the emerging New Thought movement was Warren Felt Evans (1814–1889). Formerly a Methodist minister, he became in 1863 a member of the Swedenborgian Church of the New Jerusalem, based on the teachings of the Swedish seer. Around the same time, suffering from chronic illness, he sought the help of Quimby, was healed, and—encouraged by Quimby—opened his own healing practice. By 1869 he had produced his first book, *The Mental Cure*, in which he argued that disease was the result of a loss of mental balance that, in turn, affected the body. For Evans, disease was the translation into flesh of a wrong idea in the mind, and the way to get well was to think rightly, restoring harmony between the human spirit and the divine.

The God whom Evans recognized in his numerous works recalled the Neoplatonic Idea of the One. Yet, in incorporating Christianity and reshaping Quimby's teaching, Evans thought of the Christ Principle as an emanation from the One that was present within every person. Union with this Christ Principle, the divine spark within, said Evans, brought wholeness and health. Moreover, he declared that when the basic harmony was disturbed and union with the divine forces was interrupted, another individual—a doctor—could help. If the patient really wanted to get better and trusted the healer, urged Evans, he or she could submit mentally to the doctor. This would bring a flow of thought from the healer to the patient and begin the restoration of harmony.

Above all, Evans seemed convinced of the power of suggestion in healing. His view of the relationship between patient and doctor was built on it. Even further, he could see benefits for the patient in a state of light mesmeric trance in which the sick person could be at once alert and yet submissive to healing influence. Likewise, Evans spoke of the power of conscious affirmation, and it was his thinking that turned New Thought toward the practice. So for later New Thought, the mind cure meant that the sick person must think positively, affirming health in deliberate internal statements and banishing disease as error.

Besides the practice of Quimby and the thought of Evans, the existence of Christian Science and its students contributed to the development of New Thought. Mary Baker Eddy's *Science and Health* from 1875 attracted readers who also read Evans. Those who were uncomfortable within the sharply drawn boundaries of Christian Science under Eddy's authority often found themselves leaving the organization. Indeed, some of the most widely influential early New Thought teachers had been Christian Scientists. Take, for example, the case of Emma Curtis Hopkins (1853–1925). A member of Eddy's 1883 class in Boston and later editor of *The Christian Science Journal* from 1884 to 1885, Hopkins left Eddy's movement to found her own Christian Science seminary in Chicago in 1886. More eclectic and mystical than Eddy, with her speaking and writing she taught a generation of future New Thought leaders from Ernest Holmes, who founded Religious Science, to Charles and Myrtle Fillmore, who initiated Unity, and Malinda E. Cramer and Mona L. Brooks, who began Divine Science.

Beyond the individual contributions of former members of Eddy's Christian Science organization, however, some of Quimby's old students felt that Eddy was not giving credit where credit was due. She owed the discovery of Christian Science far more to Quimby than she had acknowledged, they thought. In this atmosphere, Julius and Annetta Dresser began to practice mental healing in Boston in 1882. Many former Christian Scientists came to them, and the very strength of the Christian Science movement forced them to articulate the meaning of their work more clearly.

By 1882 or 1883, members of the movement were speaking of it as mental science. They had come to believe that thought was the greatest power in the world and that harmony with divine Thought, or Mind, was the way to health and happiness. At the same time, their interest in the ideas of Ralph Waldo Emerson was growing. The writings of Evans showed his acquaintance with Emerson, and in 1887 another writer, Charles M. Barrows, found a forerunner for mental science in the Transcendentalist leader. So began a continuing interest in Emerson until people in the metaphysical movement came to regard him as the father of their movement. For unlike Christian Science, which claimed a basis in divine revelation, proponents of metaphysics sought a foundation in *philosophy* for their ideas.

By the 1890s, mental science was coming to be known as New Thought. First used as a designation in 1889, "this thought," or New Thought, was distinguished from older theology, even though people in the movement for the most part did not see themselves as forming a separate church. Indeed, they had been meeting on Sunday evenings so that those who wished to attend Sunday morning services at traditional churches could do so. Still, by mid-decade, the Church of the Higher Life had been organized in Boston under Helen Van Anderson. Adherents explained that New Thought stood for "exalted living" and had no creed other than love, while among its subsidiary groups was an Emerson Study Club. Even more important to the growth of New Thought was the formation of the Metaphysical Club in Boston in 1895. It became the center for the movement's national and international development, aiming to reach the world with the gospel of New Thought.

By the turn of the century, there was an International Metaphysical League, and among other endeavors it had announced its aim to teach the universal fatherhood and motherhood of God. Meanwhile, New Thought was trying to help people not only to get well but also, by thinking correctly, to become prosperous and successful. Later, from 1915, International New Thought Congresses were held annually, bringing together the many diverse groups who all worked under the banner of New Thought. An organization called the International New Thought Alliance continued to provide leadership through the twentieth century, while the Unity School of Christianity, with its vast publishing enterprise and ministerial training program, became probably the best known of the New Thought institutions. Other New Thought denominations such as Divine Science, based in Denver, and Religious Science, headquartered in Los Angeles, helped to spread belief. Attempts were made to revise traditional religious services so that they might express New Thought ideas, and especially noteworthy, new words were set to older melodies to create appropriate music.

Sometimes, too, poems were set to music, leading to the beginnings of New Thought hymnology.

Yet New Thought's ambivalence about existing in separate churches proved a continuing theme. In its claims to saving knowledge, New Thought was individual more than communal in its emphasis. Like all of the occult and metaphysical movements, it led ultimately to inwardness and to quests for private religious experience. Thus, it made its biggest mark through its publishing, and many of its books became best sellers on the "self-help" market. As an example, Ralph Waldo Trine's *In Tune with the Infinite*, written in 1897, sold well over 2 million copies and continued to be reprinted regularly. Even more, New Thought influenced liberal Protestantism so that many who were part of the mainstream absorbed its ideas and values and began to spread them. Norman Vincent Peale (b. 1898), with his *Power of Positive Thinking* (1952), brought mental healing and the success ethic to millions of people outside the movement, while his other books and magazines continued the trend. Indeed, Peale was only the most successful of a series of writers who brought Americans a similar message. New Thought shared its fundamental assumptions with the occult tradition; but, in the end, its individualism, optimism, and affirmations of health and prosperity dissolved the mystery that surrounded occultism and blended it unobtrusively with mainstream American culture.

Mystical and Psychic Frontiers

If the twentieth century was congenial to New Thought, it also welcomed a variety of other movements of inward exploration. Moreover, it had its theorist to lay the groundwork. William James (1842–1910) brought together the ideas of the occult and metaphysical movements as he had received them through the thought of Emerson and through nineteenth-century American culture. He articulated them in a scholarly context from his chair of philosophy at Harvard University, weaving together, like occultists of old, themes from religion and science. He had been fascinated by the claims of mental healing. Later, his curiosity about altered states of consciousness in religious experience grew, until he experimented with nitrous oxide and even a peyote button. His book *The Varieties of Religious Experience* (1902) stressed the inner, personal nature of religion as different states of mind. James traced these states in great psychological detail throughout the narrative, often giving examples from the private experiences of individuals. Further, from 1885 he played a leading role in the organization and activities of the American Society for Psychical Research.

The philosophy that James came to teach was known as pragmatism, and its central conviction was that truth could be known by its consequences. Put simply, pragmatism taught that what worked in the life of an individual or a society should be considered true. Thus, using James's ideas, individuals might reconcile occult and metaphysical experiences with the world of modern science. In the context of the philosophy of pragmatism, if the occult-metaphysical tradition worked to create a meaningful universe for a person, its truth could not be disputed. For James, the will to believe could erase doubt and uncertainty.

The legacy of William James lived on later in the twentieth century. Meanwhile, others pursued their quests for homes on a mental landscape, leading them toward mysticism and mind-expanding experiments. Noteworthy among them was Aldous Huxley (1894–1963), an English novelist who settled in California. During the fifties, he followed in the tradition of James by experimenting with psychedelic drugs, and in *The Doors of Perception* (1954) he broke ground in describing the experience. Yet Huxley throughout his life was conservative in his use of mescaline and LSD (lysergic acid diethylamide), and his wife afterward reminisced that he had probably used less in a lifetime than many later youthful experimenters would use in a week. Underlying the psychedelic experiments, for Huxley, was his abiding interest in what he called the "perennial philosophy." This term was his way of identifying the major teachings of the occult and metaphysical tradition, which he said lay at the basis of all religion. Nearly a decade before his *Doors of Perception*, he had published an anthology called *The Perennial Philosophy* (1946). Here he identified the perennial philosophy as a metaphysics that saw divine reality within both things and minds. Predicated on that metaphysics, religious practice meant for him seeking identity with the divine spark within and finding there the ground of all being.

Occult-Metaphysical Movements Later in the Twentieth Century

Hence, by the last third of the twentieth century there was a coherent tradition from which to draw in the pursuit of occultism, mysticism, and metaphysical salvation. Moreover, many had been prepared by American culture to turn toward self and universe in their quest for religious certainty. Protestantism, in general, supported the importance of knowledge or belief (the Word) in religion. And liberal Protestantism stressed the presence of God everywhere and, in teaching that human nature was good, underlined American optimism about it. With Protestant liberalism's diffusiveness and lack of strong boundaries, it accustomed people to live comfortably without tight organization. From its place in American culture, the holiness tradition, too, encouraged a perfectionism that, as we saw in the case of Father Divine, could easily be linked to metaphysical views. Meanwhile, the urban and corporate organization of society militated against strong communities. Individuals in their daily lives came to rely more and more on internal resources. So the occult and metaphysical movements blended easily with the cultural mainstream. Because they sought universality and defied institutionalization, they became difficult to count. Because they taught a message so similar to what many were already hearing, they became as difficult to identify. Nearly everyone, it seemed, had an occult or metaphysical belief somewhere among his or her mental furniture.

The religion that the occult and metaphysical movements offered people had its extraordinary aspects, but it was also a way to deal with ordinary life. Astrology gave people a sense of identity and helped them to establish relationships with others with some degree of security. Self-help literature urged them to take steps toward greater health, prosperity, and happiness in their job and life situations. Psychics offered physical healing and spiritual advice on how to deal with whatever problems might arise. Believing they knew the future gave people a way to try to revise it, to take the steps they thought would avoid harm and restore balance in the business of living.

Yet, by the sixties, one side of the occult and metaphysical tradition had begun to attract notice. Like the inner circle of Theosophists who surrounded Helena Blavatsky, many, especially among the young, found a way to unite a desire for saving knowledge and universal harmony with a new sense of boundary definition. The result was a series of short-lived but intense religious movements. These were often collectively described as countercultural, although it is more correct to say that they exaggerated certain tendencies within American culture so that they appeared alien. But probably, the boundaries themselves were alienating. These groups often encouraged members to break ties with families and friends in order to follow the new way of life more totally. They demanded seemingly everything, and converts were willing to surrender to these demands that they felt were ultimately for their benefit.

This description of the new groups evokes the sectarian movements of the nineteenth century with their calls for conversion and their demands for a totally committed way of life. Yet these new movements are referred to in this text as *cult movements*, linking them to some of the African-American movements, like Father Divine's Peace Mission, that we have already explored. As noted in the discussion of Divine and others, the term *cult movement* is reserved for groups that break so radically from the normative religion of the culture that they claim to offer a new revelation to believers. In other words, orthodox Christian or Jewish elements have all but disappeared in the creed of a cult movement. Moreover, added to the claim of new revelation is a sociological structure that depends on a charismatic leader whose presence is vital to the continuance of the movement. That is, the movement, in the form in which it exists, cannot survive the leader's death. And, finally, a cult movement uses its religious ideology and practice to separate its members as totally as possible from others. Neither ideology nor practice follows patterns familiar to the cultural mainstream, and both are used as self-conscious mechanisms of separation.

We might perhaps wish to identify as a cult movement a group like the nineteenth-century Oneida Community, with its practice of complex marriage and its charismatic leadership under John Humphrey Noyes. But what separates Oneida from the movements we are examining now is its Christianity and its relatively more continuous relationship with mainstream culture. In short, Oneida claimed not so much new revelation but new interpretation of old revelation. Noyes and his followers stood squarely within the Christian tradition, if they did reread it in unusual ways. Beyond that, although Oneidans departed from cultural patterns of their time in the practice of complex marriage and other features of their daily routine, they also accepted a good deal that was standard behavioral fare for the nineteenth century. They supported themselves by organizing to advantage in a market economy, producing animal traps and silverware. They delighted in the cultural pursuits of their time, enjoying music, theater, lecture, and discussion. More centrally, their form of worship was continuous with worship in the larger Christian community.

Of course, to call Oneida a sect and a twentieth-century occult-metaphysical group a cult movement is not to place one above the other. (It should go without saying that the term *cult movement*, as used here, is descriptive and *not* negative.) However, more can be said about the occult and metaphysical cult movements that we are looking at. In a feature that distinguishes them from what one might expect in a cult movement concerned with separation, the new occult-metaphysical movements kept their universalism. In their religious explanations they still inhabited cosmic space and time, and they explored essentially mystical terrain. Yet they did so within the boundaries of small and intense religious groups, so that there was a decided contrast between what they believed and how, in sociological terms, they practiced. Still, for those involved, the beliefs did constitute new revelation, and in substantive terms the beliefs — like the practice — ranged far from mainstream religion.

Nor is this the only complication as we look to occult-metaphysical cult movements. Exceedingly numerous and difficult to detail, these movements bore the familiar marks of eclecticism that we have already seen. Indeed, by the late sixties and early seventies they would reconfigure to become part of the New Age movement that continued into the last decade of the century (a movement to be discussed in Chapter 11). Moreover, not all of the cult movements that flourished at this time arose out of the religious family we have been looking at. Some were Eastern in origins and practices. Others took themes such as those concerning the end of the world and made them the basis for their activity. But occult and metaphysical groups grew alongside these others. Probably two of the clearest types were witchcraft covens (groups of witches) and scientific-technological cult movements.

In witchcraft covens, the assumptions of earlier American witchcraft and occultism were more self-consciously present. For believers, the law of correspondence operated to elevate the natural world. It was the macrocosm to which human beings should conform their lives, and witchcraft, or Neopaganism, taught reverence for nature as the power of fertility and life. Through the use of ritual, a coven sought to create harmony for its members and others with the order of the natural world. Ritual, in this understanding, was a magical means to assure the operation of nature, and witches believed that they had discovered the key to the powers of nature, which they could turn to their advantage.

Scientific-technological cult movements linked science with occultism in ways that repeated the blend of religion with science in ancient Western occultism.

For example, UFO cults took their cue from unexplained flying objects in the space age. Members of these groups claimed to have established contact with visitors from outer space and even to have boarded their vehicles. They saw these visitors as higher and more perfect beings who wanted to teach willing human beings a deeper knowledge that would transform their lives. In another well-known instance, Scientology—founded by L. Ron Hubbard (1911–1986)—used an electrical device called an E-meter to help in the spiritual quest. The E-meter, which was said to measure resistance, or tension, within people when they responded to different questions, was meant to help them become "Clear" (like the "clear" button on a calculator). Thus, it was believed, consciousness would be liberated so that it could control matter, energy, space, and time. The goal was total freedom, and the means—as in all the scientific-technological movements—was the pursuit of knowledge as a form of power.

Thus, while witchcraft cults turned people toward the natural world through the magical evocations of ritual, scientific-technological cults taught that the real world lay beyond matter in secret, saving knowledge. For both, as for the occult-metaphysical tradition in general, matter was controlled by the use of elite and secret techniques, part of a heritage of privileged learning. In other words, for both, the mind was the place where sacred pathways began and ended. There, where extraordinary religious experience was seen as possible, strength was sought for the ordinary religion of living. And since the law of correspondence meant for believers that mind equaled world, extraordinary religion could fuse with its ordinary counterpart.

In sum, both twentieth-century occult-metaphysical cult movements and the older American occult and metaphysical movements had developed long and highly elaborate explanations of the nature of humanity and the universe. As important, their ethical systems and ritual demonstrations flowed from the detailed creed of these movements—so much so that the creed became an ethic and a ritual as well. As we have seen, the ethic of these movements was one of universalism, a loosely defined charity toward all. Hence, it often expressed itself in a community life of radical and revolutionary democracy among believers, and it envisioned a world order manifested in similar terms. There had been involvement in reform activities among nineteenth-century spiritualists and other occultists, we know, while the healing practice of New Thought people was intended as action for good in the world. And in the later twentieth century occultism often flourished alongside older visions of a just society of anarchic democracy.

Yet occult and metaphysical movements could also serve to legitimate a conservative social ethic. The Gnostic theories of occult and metaphysical believers supported a division of society into those who were spiritually superior and others who were not. Such spiritual elitism could easily be translated into endorsement of social arrangements as they were. Moreover, this spiritual elitism could combine with a sense of sociopolitical chosenness. As an example, in the 1930s the "I AM" movement encouraged political reformism based on nationalistic themes. Convinced that human life had begun in America, members of the group believed that history would end here, with the nation as a vessel of light to others.

Still, a social ethic was not the most important concern of the occult-metaphysical movements explored here. In the practical workings of social and political organizations, there was, for them, no lasting significance. The world of these occultists was one whose model lay outside human society. The real world, for them, existed in the mind or in the universe. Moreover, ritual, found useful in mysticism and magic, was a way of making the metaphysical world concrete. It, too, led to the mental landscape.

Above all, however, the homesteads of the mind were *American* homesteads. The picking and choosing that eclectic religion brought was congenial in a land where every religion was equal in the eyes of the law and where many peoples and traditions encountered one another. The practicality of occult-metaphysical movements agreed with a general American practicality. Even spectacular journeys into the "other" world, for American occultists, seemed to help them to gain power in this one. In other words, extraordinary religious experience became a way to stimulate energies that would bring useful results. Trying to talk to the dead could help a believing person resolve a present problem. Abiding by theosophical rules could enable a Theosophist to gain confidence in self and universe. Practicing New Thought with commitment could bring a sense of renewed health and good fortune.

Finally, homesteads of the mind were places for people whose only possibility for community had to be created among strangers. In the later twentieth century, with a diminished sense of place and peoplehood, the children of the highway and the divorce court were looking for a refuge. They found it in felt experiences of communion with the All, or divine Mind, through a divine spark within. Seeking union with universal being took the place of existing union with members of a community who had shared a common history. In the end, occult and metaphysical movements appealed because most Americans—with their histories of migration and mobility—were, in a sense, either dislocated persons or descendants of the dislocated.

In Overview

Occult and metaphysical movements have had a long history in the West. Gnosticism, Neoplatonism, astrology, Hermeticism, alchemy, and the Kabbalah numbered among the forms of earlier occultism. As religions, these occult movements and their successors offered secret and, by the nineteenth century, rejected knowledge to Western peoples. During colonial times, a natural and traditional occultism thrived in America in astrology and witchcraft. Even later, traditional occultism continued to flourish among various cultural groups. Then in the nineteenth century new and self-conscious forms of occult-metaphysical movements sprang up. In this context, Transcendentalism provided an eclectic theoretical expression of concerns similar to those of the occult and metaphysical movements. Spiritualism, theosophy, and New Thought gave popular expression to occult and metaphysical religion, while by the turn of the century William James was exploring mystical and psychic frontiers with a psychological frame of reference. In the late twentieth century, a variety of small and intense movements perpetuated the occult-metaphysical legacy, among them witchcraft covens and scientific-technological cult movements. In general, occult-metaphysical movements were popular among middle-class people.

Both the occult and the more generally philosophical metaphysical movements based their theories on the idea of correspondence, held also by American Indians and, to some extent, by Roman Catholics. Like Indians and Catholics, occult-metaphysical devotees mingled ordinary and extraordinary religion. Yet they did more to use the extraordinary to achieve pragmatic and thisworldly results. Even further, without a strong sense of peoplehood, members of these movements tended to be persons without fixed social boundaries. For them, universalism was a condition of living as well as a condition of mind. Occult and metaphysical believers often reflected the upheavals of traditional community in modern urban and industrial society. Frequently, they created mental homesteads to replace the human communities they could not find.

But even as some dislocated Americans found homesteads of the mind, others still felt estranged. For no groups did this observation seem more true than for those who found themselves in the West either as inheritors of a non-Western religion or as converts to one. We turn now to the religions of these cultural strangers in the land. Curiously, as we will see, they were closer to home than they knew.

SUGGESTIONS FOR FURTHER READING: OCCULT AND METAPHYSICAL MOVEMENTS

Bednarowski, Mary Farrell. *New Religions and the Theological Imagination in America.* Religion in North America. Bloomington: Indiana University Press, 1989.

Braden, Charles S. *Spirits in Rebellion: The Rise and Development of New Thought.* Dallas: Southern Methodist University Press, 1963.

Braude, Ann. *Radical Spirits: Spiritualism and Women's Rights in Nineteenth-Century America.* Boston: Beacon Press, 1989.

Brown, Slater. *The Heyday of Spiritualism.* New York: Simon & Schuster, Pocket Books, 1972.

Campbell, Bruce F. *Ancient Wisdom Revived: A History of the Theosophical Movement.* Berkeley: University of California Press, 1980.

Ellwood, Robert S., Jr. *Alternative Altars.* Chicago History of American Religion. Chicago: University of Chicago Press, 1979.

————. *Theosophy: A Modern Expression of the Wisdom of the Ages.* Wheaton, IL: Theosophical Publishing, 1986.

————, **and Partin, Harry B.** *Religious and Spiritual Groups in Modern America.* 2d ed. Englewood Cliffs, NJ: Prentice-Hall, 1988.

Judah, J. Stillson. *The History and Philosophy of the Metaphysical Movements in America.* Philadelphia: Westminster Press, 1967.

Kerr, Howard, and Crow, Charles L., eds. *The Occult in America: New Historical Perspectives.* Urbana: University of Illinois Press, 1983.

Leventhal, Herbert. *In the Shadow of the Enlightenment: Occultism and Renaissance Science in Eighteenth-Century America.* New York: New York University Press, 1976.

MacNeice, Louis. *Astrology.* Garden City, NY: Doubleday, 1964.

Moore, R. Laurence. *In Search of White Crows: Spiritualism, Parapsychology, and American Culture.* New York: Oxford University Press, 1977.

Quinn, D. Michael. *Early Mormonism and the Magic World View.* Salt Lake City: Signature Books, 1987.

Shumaker, Wayne. *The Occult Sciences in the Renaissance: A Study in Intellectual Patterns.* Berkeley: University of California Press, 1972.

PATTERNS OF EXPANSION

AND CONTRACTION

The ancient Chinese classic *Tao Te Ching* is structured on a series of paradoxes surrounding the Tao, held to be the source of all things, and the primordial opposites yin and yang, which in Chinese philosophy issue from it. Although yin and yang are hard to define, in Chinese belief they possess a series of characteristics that alternately antagonize and complement each other. Among these characteristics, yang is considered an expansive, centrifugal force, and yin, a contractive, centripetal power.

Although it may seem odd in discussing religious developments in America after the Civil War to cite a Chinese religious text, the citation is not inappropriate. In the decades following the war, some 300,000 Chinese came to the United States, especially to California. Later the Japanese came to the West Coast, too, over 100,000, for example, from 1901 to 1907. Meanwhile, Americans had mixed feelings, at best, regarding the immigration. On the one hand, the majoritarian culture of the United States, like the yang of the Tao, stretched itself to include peoples who seemed exotic and "other." On the other hand, Americans in a yin modality drew in and retracted their welcome.

This pattern of expansion and contraction also serves as a continuing description for American religion after the Civil War. From the time that is called the Gilded Age, Americans stretched to embrace religious beliefs and behaviors that seemed new, different, and often exotic. Simultaneously, they contracted culturally to keep out the new, to seek purity, and to consolidate. Thus, expansion and contraction formed a cultural system, an expression of the social body's engagement in a collective balancing act. In turning to Eastern religious forms, Americans undertook exercises of religious expansion. Conversely, in forming cultural enclaves where small, distinct regional religions could flourish, Americans demonstrated religious contraction. By the late twentieth century, in their involvement in New Age religion, Americans displayed patterns of religious expansion, and in their enthusiasm for conservative Protestantism they signaled religious contraction.

Chapter 9

East Is West: Eastern Peoples and Eastern Religions

In 1893 the United States celebrated the 400th anniversary of Europeans' arrival in the New World. The Columbian Exposition, named for Christopher Columbus, drew over 27 million people from at least seventy-two countries to its specially erected buildings in Chicago. It was in conjunction with this World's Fair that, during September, representatives of most major religions assembled for the World's Parliament of Religions. In a remarkable spirit of community, they took stock of the religious accomplishments of the century that was ending and planned for an age of unity in the future.

From the perspective of mainline American denominations, the members of the group that met there were decidedly unusual. There was Annie Besant, the rising leader of theosophy, who impressed listeners with her addresses and who, it was rumored, had a devoted Indian swami outside the door of her room to protect her. There was, besides, the persuasive Swami Vivekananda with his dramatic turban and orange and crimson garments, who also addressed the congress. There was the Buddhist Anagarika Dharmapala, later to establish Mahabodhi Societies in America. There was his fellow Buddhist, the Zen Master Soyen Shaku, from whom a Zen lineage in America would derive. And there was George A. Ford, a Presbyterian missionary, who read the paper of a fellow missionary in Syria, closing with a quotation from Baha'u'llah, the founder of a religion called Baha'i.

In the spontaneous community of the parliament, East had come West. It was the inauguration of a new era for American religious history as, more and more, Eastern religions would flourish in the United States. The World's Parliament of Religions signaled the growing American interest in Eastern religions, and at the same time it signaled a period of immigration that brought Asian peoples, as carriers of their indigenous religions, to the country. In both a demographic and religious sense, the pattern was one of expansion.

In the twentieth century, America would be significantly affected by new expressions of pluralism, as the nation observed incoming religions that originated in places scattered through much of the world. If one makes the East Coast of the United States the geographical orientation point, from the Nearer East came Orthodoxy, the Eastern form of Christianity. Nearer geographically as well as spiritually, it was the religion of many Eastern Europeans, Russians, and nationals from the lands of the Mediterranean basin. From the Middle East came Islam, the religion of one-seventh of the world's people and a spiritual relative of Judaism and Christianity. Close behind it came Baha'i, a nineteenth-century new religion that had arisen from the Islam of Persia.

Finally, from the Farther East came the religions of India, China, Japan, Tibet, and Korea. India sent its traditions—collectively called Hinduism by Westerners—in philosophy, action yoga, and, in the later twentieth century, intense devotionalism. China and Japan exported numerous forms of Buddhism, and Japan also contributed a number of movements derived from Shinto. Tibet brought its secret and mystical forms of Buddhism, and even Korea by the late twentieth century had given America a religious movement that blended Eastern and Western themes as the Unification Church of Sun Myung Moon (b. 1920).

Besides their different points of origin, the incoming religions could be distinguished in another way. On the one hand, they were ethnic religions that for centuries had been part of the heritage of the national groups that brought them to America. Thus, they were religions of particular places and peoples, and they blended extraordinary and ordinary religion, mixing the extraordinary into the usual and everyday. Although for Americans these incoming religions seemed on the whole detached from worldly concerns, for most of those who had inherited them they provided ways to live in *this* world more than liberation into another.

On the other hand, the incoming religions were export religions; that is, the religions of converts. Americans from Protestant, Catholic, and Jewish backgrounds began to embrace them, and in so doing they changed the character of these Asian religions. Seekers after the extraordinary, American converts were attracted to Eastern religions because from the (non-Asian) American perspective they were strange and even dramatic. They made it possible for nonnative converts to live an extraordinary religious life, seemingly at the boundary of worlds that they knew. In short, they offered mainstream Americans an avenue to transcendence and a sense of liberation that more traditional Western forms of religion had not provided for them.

These Westerners who pursued extraordinary religion were seekers after "otherness." In accord with the pattern of expansion, they were drawn by the cultural strangeness of Eastern religions from far-off lands. With the exception of Orthodoxy, these religions lay outside the Judeo-Christian tradition. Unlike Native American religions, they did not contain memories of presence in the land predating the later presence of Euro-Americans. Unlike African-American religion, they did not have a background of close interaction with the religions of the white majority. All of this meant that the "otherness" of the East was both historical and geographical, providing an especially powerful symbol for Westerners. So Eastern religions came to stand for and to express to some Americans the "other" reality of a sacred world beyond this one. Paradoxically, the ordinary religion of the immigrants, by its cultural strangeness, became the vehicle for extraordinary religious experience for mainstream Americans.

While Eastern religions were embraced by some Westerners because the religions were considered "other," Easterners themselves felt separate from American life and culture. Eastern Europeans, Middle Easterners, and Chinese- and Japanese-Americans had for decades felt "different" and had experienced harassment and discrimination. To take one example, the Chinese, many of them attracted to the United States as railroad construction workers, were early targets of hostility. So pronounced did West Coast hostility, and even physical violence, against the Chinese become that as early as 1882 Congress passed the Chinese Exclusion Act. The law was only the first in a series of legal measures designed to lessen the Chinese presence, as government policy led to a rapid reduction of the Chinese community, from 107,000 in 1890 to only 75,000 by 1930.

In a second and even starker example, Japanese-Americans also suffered hostility and strictures against them, so that in 1907 the so-called Gentlemen's Agreement between the United States and Japan restricted immigration to nonlaborers. Then in 1913 and 1920 the Anti-Alien Land Laws of California prevented the Japanese from controlling farmlands, making further immigration unappealing. In a Supreme Court decision of 1922, Japanese immigrants were prohibited from becoming naturalized American citizens, and in 1924 the Oriental Exclusion Act cut off the immigration of people who were ineligible for citizenship, effectively halting Japanese immigration. Later events in the twentieth century were not kinder to Japanese-Americans. With the tense years of the Second World War when the United States and Japan were in conflict, Japanese-Americans were forcibly evacuated from their West Coast homes and sent to internment or, as some said, concentration camps.

To sum up, the Chinese, Japanese, and other Easterners felt their foreignness in the United States at the same time numbers of mainstream Americans, alienated from *their* heritage, ironically, were becoming seekers of Eastern wisdom. Both groups were reaching and stretching, moving according to heterogeneous patterns of expansion. Hence, the picture of the East as it came to be present in the West is, from a variety of points of view, a picture of manyness. Many nations, many religions, many ways of embracing these religions, all were part of the horizon of meaning. Once more, the full story cannot be told here, and our approach will be to examine a few cases. Especially in the late twentieth century, when Eastern cult movements spread across America, key examples will suggest the wider religious landscape.

Nearer East: Eastern Orthodoxy

We begin with Orthodoxy, the Christian religious tradition embodied in the various national churches of Eastern European and Eastern Mediterranean lands. Orthodox religious contact with the North American continent had begun as early as 1743, when some Alaskans were baptized by a Russian soldier. By 1792 eight monks had made their way to Kodiak Island, off the coast of Alaska, to build an Eastern Orthodox church there. The native peoples of Alaska welcomed them, and before the end of the century several thousand had become Christian. In the nineteenth century, Orthodox religion continued to grow in Alaska, until by the start of the twentieth century about one-sixth of the population, over 10,000 people, were Russian Orthodox church members. Meanwhile, through a land sale by Russia, Alaska had become a possession of the United States. In 1872 church headquarters was moved from Alaska to San Francisco, where Russians, Greeks, and Serbians from Eastern Europe turned to Russian Orthodoxy. And by the close of the century, the Russian Orthodox had come officially to New York, as Russian immigrants to the United States increased rapidly. Within a decade, from 1906 to 1916, Orthodox church membership increased fivefold, from 20,000 to 100,000 people.

With the twentieth century, Russian Orthodox presence in America was exceeded by the Greek Orthodox church, the result of large-scale immigration beginning at the end of the nineteenth century. Indeed, there were Greek churches in New York and Chicago before 1900, even though the Russian Orthodox leadership had pursued a "pan-Orthodox" policy, welcoming Greeks and other Orthodox peoples and appointing them to positions of clerical authority. The Greeks, however — like other nationals — wanted to worship in their own language and to follow familiar and customary religious patterns. Now, with a huge Greek immigration, that became possible. Membership swelled throughout the century, until in the seventies it had reached a figure close to 2 million. At the same time, the Russian church was over 1 million in number, and another million or so Orthodox peoples were represented in various separate national churches — Albanian, Bulgarian, Rumanian, Serbian, Syrian, and Ukrainian. With this large numerical presence, many came to view Eastern Orthodoxy as a major faith in the United States, ranking behind the traditional three: Protestantism, Roman Catholicism, and Judaism.

Eastern Orthodox Religion

What was the religion that these peoples brought with them to America, and how was it different from Western forms of Christianity? The answer to these

Russian Orthodox Cathedral, Sitka, Alaska. Until 1872, Sitka was the cathedral city for the huge Russian Orthodox diocese that included all of the United States and Canada. This photograph of the cruciform-shaped wooden cathedral dates from about 1900.

questions must take us to the beginnings of Orthodox separation from the Roman (Western) church. Here we learn that, as one student of Orthodoxy has explained, not only the religious answers were different from those of the West but even the questions. While the Roman church asked how Christianity could exist as one body, the Eastern church wondered how it could express community. While the Roman church concerned itself with questions of legal justice through a proper distribution of rights and duties to one another and to God, Easterners sought more intensely for ways to nourish contemplation and an inner life.

Later, with the birth of Protestantism, Eastern Orthodoxy seemed to Westerners even more radically "other" in its religious quest. If Protestantism tended to be a thisworldly religion, Eastern Orthodoxy—for centuries lived out under Muslim rule—looked otherworldly. If Protestantism heard the Word and felt

East is West: Eastern Peoples and Eastern Religions

urged by it to action in the world, Orthodoxy thought of the Word as a precious object surrounded by ritual and found in it a model for prayer. And finally, if Protestantism tended to separate ordinary from extraordinary religion with its sense of a gap between God and sinful human beings, Orthodoxy sought to bring God and humanity together. It created in its liturgical ritual a center for community that could be expressed at many levels, both spiritual and material.

For Orthodoxy, the local community was the church. Organized in self-governing, or autocephalous (literally, "self-headed"), churches, the Orthodox gave first rank of honor to four ancient churches called the patriarchates: Constantinople, Alexandria, Antioch, and Jerusalem. After these four, they recognized eleven other autocephalous churches, among them the Russian and the Greek, which both figured so prominently in America. Below these in later Orthodox history came churches called autonomous, which were self-governing in most ways but not fully independent. And finally came the provinces of Western Europe, North and South America, and Australia.

What held all of these local communities together was their agreed adherence to "right," or "correct," religion. The word *orthodoxy* means just this, and Orthodox churches understood right religion to have two sides. First, it was considered right belief, a union of Christian people in faith and doctrine through acceptance of a common tradition. Inherited through scripture, through the writings of the fathers and other authorities, and through word-of-mouth teaching, tradition established for the Orthodox a living continuity between the generations. It was thought to lead back to the time of Jesus, and it accepted the authority of the seven ecumenical ("worldwide") church councils, the last in A.D. 787, as fundamental to the teaching of the church.

Second, right religion was held to be right worship or communion in the sacraments. Acknowledging the same seven sacraments as the Roman church, the Orthodox understood their own identity in terms of their common worship of God through the sacraments and, especially, through the Divine Liturgy in which the eucharist was celebrated. Like the Mass of Roman Catholicism, the Divine Liturgy recalled the Last Supper of Jesus and his death on the cross of Calvary. In structure it was similar to the Roman Mass, and, in fact, preserved versions of that ritual older than those that had evolved in the West. For the Orthodox, however, more than for the Roman church, the worshiping community was the key to unity. Outward organization was secondary, and true unity in Orthodoxy came from collective presence around the altar table. Those who shared the same worship, or divine "praise," were seen as part of the same religion; for Orthodoxy there could be no clearer test.

The common Christian tradition of the earliest followers of Jesus had developed into Eastern and Western branches over centuries. In the East the cultural temper of the people and the events of their history led to the development of a religious sensitivity different from that of the West. During the eighth and ninth centuries, a controversy over the place of images in the churches helped to crystallize Orthodox thought and practice. This controversy arose between two parties. One group, called the Iconoclasts, were literally image smashers. They were suspicious of any religious art that tried to depict the saints, Mary, Jesus, or the Godhead. For them religious art was a form of idolatry, and they demanded that icons, or religious images, be destroyed. The other group, called the Icon-odules, venerated icons and wanted to preserve them. At issue in the struggle was the question of what Orthodoxy thought of the material world and, ultimately, of the human nature of Jesus. If all matter were evil and led inevitably to idolatry, then it followed for a believer that Jesus could not have taken upon himself the corruption of a human nature. On the other hand, if matter could be a way into the spiritual world, then for the Orthodox Christian the doctrine of the Incarnation, the taking of human flesh by the son of God, was possible.

In the end, the controversy was decided in favor of those who venerated images. Orthodoxy came to be a religion of icons. Behind its iconic preference lay the same sacramental belief that ran through Roman Catholicism. But the Orthodox developed this belief even further, and, especially, they developed it to express qualities of vision and sight. An icon was something that had to be seen, and so it encouraged the gaze of the contemplative person. For the Orthodox, the icon was the place where one could encounter divine things; it was a fixed meeting point where the sacred world could enter this one.

Moreover, icons came to provide a point of reference for understanding the rest of Christianity. The Bible was seen as an icon of Jesus Christ and so the jewel at the heart of the liturgy. Human beings were seen as icons of God, and there was less emphasis on sin in Eastern Orthodoxy than in Roman Catholicism or in Protestantism. Instead, people were encouraged to look within and to seek the image of God in the human through meditation and interior prayer. Similarly, the church was viewed as the icon of the Trinity in which Father, Son, and Holy Spirit were one. Just as the Orthodox affirmed a community of different members in the Godhead, so they believed that there should be a community of different local churches in the larger Orthodox communion. Finally, the most important icon for Orthodoxy was Jesus Christ. He was seen as the image of God's glory and light, as the being in whom the divine had entered the human world to transform it. So the Orthodox portrayed Jesus as a divine king and victor over the forces of evil. Even in representations of the cross, they emphasized their belief in the Godhead of Jesus shining through the human icon, and their images of the crucified Jesus showed him crowned with gold and precious stones.

The Iconoclast controversy was one cultural event that shaped the later history of Orthodoxy. The mystical teaching of the East was a second. From the beginning, the Orthodox had leaned toward contemplation more than activism. Through the centuries, the church fathers of the East contributed to a growing body of mystical literature that became known as hesychastic. Mysticism here means belief in the possibility of an experience of total union between the divine and the human and religious experiences predicated on that belief. Hesychasm became the particularly Orthodox way of understanding mysticism. Coming from the Greek word for quiet, the term *hesychasm* referred to a form of mysticism stressing the need for inner quiet and tranquillity to await what was seen as the transforming light of God. Its goal was a vision of this sought-for light, and its methods were various techniques of physical and mental control. Physically, breathing, posture, and the use of one's eyes were all directed according to specific exercises. Mentally and sometimes verbally, the use of a short prayer, repeated again and again, was held to produce a state of inner quiet. Later in this chapter, when we encounter Hindu and Buddhist meditation practices, we will see similarities. The most "Western" part of the East, Orthodoxy was still Eastern, and its involvement in mystical prayer and mystical technique was a clear sign.

Emphasis on mystical light linked hesychasm to the iconic thought and practice of Orthodox worship. Mysticism, like the veneration of icons, encouraged a form of seeing. The third element that shaped the history of Orthodoxy, however, became a matter of *not* seeing. For while the West, by the sixth century, had come to see and venerate the pope of Rome as the sole head of the church on earth, the East looked at matters differently. There was opposition to a growing Western insistence on the primacy (the firstness) of the pope. Especially troubling was a phrase that had been inserted through papal authority into the traditional creed accepted by the Eastern and Western churches. Whereas in its original form, the creed declared that the Holy Spirit proceeded (came forth) from the Father, the addition to the creed proclaimed that the Spirit proceeded from the Father *and from the Son* (in Latin, *filioque*).

Since the ecumenical councils had earlier forbidden changes in the creed, there was a choice here between the authority of the pope and that of the councils, between the one monarch and the community and its representatives. The Orthodox chose the councils and the community, regarding the papal claims as a departure from the original form of Christianity. In the year 1054 the split between East and West was dramatized when a messenger from the pope left a decree of excommunication for the patriarch (bishop) of Constantinople on the high altar of his cathedral. Thus, 1054 is the traditional date given for the formal break between Eastern and Western churches. The Orthodox, however, point to the year 1204 as the point of no return. It was in this year that the European Christian soldiers who had joined the Fourth Crusade stormed the city of Constantinople (modern Istanbul, Turkey), sacking and pillaging it. This was seen as the final stroke of hostility between the two churches and the event in which, for the East, the damage had become irreparable.

Orthodoxy in America

In every land in which it spread, Orthodoxy blended with the culture of indigenous peoples, survived, and grew. It seemed able to unite extraordinary and ordinary religious concerns, to be an otherworldly and mystical religion that, at the same time, expressed the common life of the people. Indeed, the church was the place where the faithful met their relatives and friends. Often, they came and left in the middle of services, talked to one another during the Divine Liturgy, or stepped outside the church for a longer conversational break. Their priests visited and blessed houses; their religious feasts became community holidays.

In America, Orthodoxy continued to be a religion of mystical contemplation and ethnic solidarity at once. The solidarity, however, was among people from the immigrant generation. In the late twentieth century, Orthodoxy was still "other" from the vantage point of the mainstream. More than Judaism, which though not too much larger had made a major impact on American culture, Orthodoxy remained a religion apart. But overall, there was a decline in Orthodox practice in the United States, as second- and third-generation children of the immigrants grew away from their heritage. For a number of them, Americanization — and the pattern of expansion — meant a weakening of ties with the ancestral faith.

Yet Orthodoxy was sensitive to the needs of its adherents in the New World and offered its own patterns of expansion to accommodate. Like Jews and like Catholics, many of the Orthodox reformed their liturgies to bring them closer to the Protestant and American center. English came into use in services, often alternating with various national languages spoken in the different churches. The calendar of feasts and holy days, which had followed ancient Eastern practice, was altered to bring it into conformity with the Western Christian calendar. In many churches, seats were introduced so that people would not have to stand during the Divine Liturgy as they had in Orthodoxy's lands of origin. Often, instruments and mixed choirs were also used, again bringing the churches closer to other Christian churches in the United States.

Especially, Orthodoxy was affected by the manyness of America. With a multiplicity of national churches entering the country, jurisdictional claims became confused and frequently erupted into disputes. About a dozen or so Orthodox groups had overlapping claims, and disagreements sometimes became long and bitter. By the seventies, there were at least three separate branches of Russian Orthodoxy in the United States (the legacy of the Russian Revolution), three groups of Ukrainian Orthodox church members, and two groups of Syrian Orthodox adherents. Throughout the century, small splinter churches were formed by those who sought to make their religion more universal and more American. Beyond these churches, other Eastern Christians remained outside the Orthodox umbrella but, organized in different national churches and practicing distinctive rites, were linked in communion with the Roman pontiff and were known as Uniates. Finally, still other Eastern Christians — those who had separated from the main body of Christendom even before the Orthodox-Roman break — could also be found in America, the most noteworthy examples being members of the Armenian Apostolic Church and the Coptic Church.

Although, as we noticed, the Greek Orthodox church was numerically preponderant, intellectual and social leadership within Orthodoxy came from the largest of the three branches of Russian Orthodoxy. This was the so-called Orthodox Church in America, with its roughly 1 million adherents and its seminary in New York state. Historical and sociological reasons for the Russian ascendancy were not hard to find. There were, for example, the earlier Russian Orthodox arrival in America and the Russian tradition of clerical initiative, and there were also the class backgrounds of the immigrants (much of the early Greek immigration consisted of unmarried males who were unskilled laborers). Still, today Greek Orthodoxy carries on its theological tradition and maintains its own seminary outside of Boston. And both the Greek Orthodox Archdiocese of North and South America and the (Russian) Orthodox Church in America are constituent members of the National Council of Churches. Both, moreover, participate in the Standing Conference of Canonical Orthodox Bishops in the Americas, an organization formed in 1960 to foster cooperation in the face of Orthodoxy's many divisions.

For all the divisions among the Orthodox and their Eastern religious relatives, Orthodoxy had clearly prospered in the New World. Its manyness could not seem unusual in a setting of pluralism. Its preference for contemplation, as we will see, was a growing choice among other Americans who thought that life in the United States was too cluttered and too fast. In the late twentieth century, an expansive Orthodoxy was in America to stay.

Middle East: Islam

Close to Eastern Orthodox lands of origin and in some cases overlapping them were the homelands of Islamic, or Muslim, peoples. Islam was — and is — a Middle Eastern religion both geographically and spiritually. Located between the Orient and the West, it has shared many of the basic insights of Jews and Christians, but it has also been very different. So in America it became a religion of "otherness," and, with the exception of their recognition of blacks who were Muslims, for many years most Americans hardly knew that Islam existed in the United States. Yet the relationship of Islam to the New World is a long one.

Arab geographers told that their ancestors had sailed the Atlantic from Spain and Portugal, landing in South America as long ago as the tenth century and on the coast of Brazil by 1150. To the north, as early as 1539 Marcos de Niza, a Franciscan friar sent to explore Arizona, had a Moor — "Istfan the Arab" — as his guide. Meanwhile, a sixteenth-century Egyptian, called by Americans "Nosereddine" (Nasr-al-Din), lived in the Catskill Mountain area of present-day New York state. As we have already seen, many West Africans imported to the New World as slaves were Muslims. Moreover, we know that there were Muslims in South Carolina in 1790 because of a reference to them by the state House of Representatives. Then in the 1840s, Arizona was visited again by a Muslim when Hajj'Ali accompanied Arabian camels to the desert in conjunction with a government project. And during the Civil War, descendants of the North African Ben Ali fought on the Confederate side.

As in the case of so many other immigrant groups, however, the general arrival of Muslims in the United States began toward the end of the nineteenth century. Their numbers were initially small, and among them the largest group were Arabs who came from Syria and what is now Lebanon. Although mostly from an agricultural background, these Arab Muslims quickly adjusted to city life. They concentrated their settlements in industrial centers such as New York, Chicago, and Detroit, where they peddled dry goods, operated small businesses, or engaged in unskilled labor. Generally, they were economically successful. Although many had come in their youth with the intention of returning to their lands of origin, most remained in America to the end of their lives.

In addition to the Arabs, other Muslims immigrated to the United States. Among the Europeans, over 3,000 Muslims from Poland, of Tartar origin, settled in New York. And after World War II, when significant numbers of Muslim immigrants began to arrive, they included Albanians and Yugoslavs.

Among South Asians, initial immigration had come earlier. A large number of Indian Muslims immigrated to California agricultural sites in 1906, most of them associated with the mission-minded Ahmadiyya Movement in Islam, a reinterpretation of the Islamic tradition begun in India in 1889 by Mirza Ghulam Ahmad (1835–1908). But the major impetus for South Asian Muslim immigration came with the Immigration Act of 1965, in which Congress abolished the previous system of immigration quotas, which had been based on each national group's representation in the U.S. population in 1890. Under the new system, an annual limit of 170,000 immigrants (since raised to 270,000) was substituted, and by 1978 a limit of 20,000 people per country was instituted. The results shifted immigration patterns in dramatic ways. No longer were European immigrants favored over South and East Asians or other national groups. The law clearly favored diversity, and it added a new demographic motif to the pattern of expansion. Important here, demography was spelled out in religious terms as more and more Indian and Pakistani Muslims immigrated.

By the eighties, Muslim immigrants in America came from more than sixty countries. Arabs, Middle Easterners, Europeans, and South Asians had been joined by Central and South Americans and even Indians from Fiji. Arabs and Iranians constituted the largest immigrant communities, followed, after 1965, by impressive numbers of Pakistanis and Asian Indians. Like Eastern Orthodoxy, American Islam was showing itself to be an ethnic religion, reflecting the national origins of its immigrant constituencies.

However, from the beginning of its history, Islam had thought of itself as a universal religion with a message for all people. It was no surprise, therefore, that there were converts in America. Already in 1888 Mohammed Alexander Russel Webb had become the first mainstream American to embrace Islam. He was a former journalist who had become a diplomat, and after his contact in the Philippines with Indian Muslims, he assumed their faith. Other converts from Protestant, Catholic, Jewish, and Mormon backgrounds came to Islam, mostly through marriage. Meanwhile, African-Americans were attracted by the Islamic message of universal community and equality among all races. They heard with great interest the Muslim tradition that a daughter of Muhammad, the founder of Islam, had married a black man. By the late 1970s, as we noted in Chapter 6, the former Nation of Islam was adopting the doctrines and practices of mainstream Islam and winning the approval of devout Arab Muslims. Other African-Americans were drawn to the Indian Ahmadiyya Movement, with its message of universal peace and unity, and to various Muslim organizations.

Overall estimates of the number of Muslims present in the United States rose from a consensus figure of 2 million or 3 million in 1981 to the approximately 6 million claimed by Muslims themselves and reported in the 1990 *Yearbook of American and Canadian Churches*. Muslims could be found in almost every American town of any size, with significant numbers of them engaged in all of the professions. They were present noticeably in eastern and midwestern industrial and commercial centers and in West Coast cities such as San Francisco and Los Angeles. With a continuing flow of immigrants, a high birthrate, and consistent attractiveness to converts, American Islam grew faster than statisticians could document. Indeed, if current estimates of numbers of followers of the Muslim tradition are correct, Islam in America may be second only to Christianity in size. Under these circumstances, the Islamic rhythm of expansion has been striking, as immigrants, their children, and indigenous American converts have joined in the season of dramatic growth.

The Religious Meaning of Islam

The religion that all of these Muslims acknowledge arose in the seventh century in the Arabian desert. According to traditional accounts, its founder, Muhammad (A.D. 570?–632), lost his father when he was young and grew up in a humble home. But he was a member of a powerful clan, and after he entered the service of a wealthy widow, Khadijah of Mecca, as a merchant, he married her and prospered. At about the age of forty, however, Muhammad reported a series of visions and voice revelations. He said that Allah had informed him, through the angel Gabriel, that he had been chosen as the Messenger of God. The message was said to be at first overwhelming and even terrifying to Muhammad, but it is told that gradually he became convinced of its authenticity, and he began to speak as he said Allah had instructed him.

The message of Allah, as taught by Muhammad, was one of radical monotheism: there was no God but Allah, and Muhammad was his Prophet. Unlike the God-man Jesus acknowledged by Christians, Muhammad was considered only human. The worst sin possible for Muslims was to raise any person to the level of Allah. Yet Islam was the spiritual relative of Judaism and Christianity. Like them, it was a religion of history, concerned with public events and urging human beings to right action in the world. Like them, it gave to humanity a law by which to live and a sacred book, the Qur'an, in which the law was held to be written. Like them, finally, it told of a relationship between God (Allah) and the community that served him. Muhammad brought to Arabia and its people a type of community in which religion and nationhood were joined under the banner of belief in submission to Allah. Before the time of Muhammad, clan kinship had provided the basis for Arabian social organization. Now a new force united the people. In the community of those who followed Allah, called the *umma*, faith overcame the claims of kinship. Muhammad's new community was theoretically open to the entire world.

If Muhammad's teaching echoed Jewish and Christian understandings, Muhammad and his people believed that in Islam the past had been transformed. Muhammad was thought to be the last in a line of prophets that included Abraham, Moses, and Jesus. His message was considered a purification of Judaism and Christianity, fulfilling their best ideals. Thus, while Islam, like Christianity, emphasized the universality of its message, preaching a doctrine of election by grace and final judgment and resurrection, like Judaism it saw religion and politics as one reality. In every land to which it spread, it brought a government by those held to be the elect of Allah, under the requirements of Islamic law. It brought ordinary and extraordinary religion together, just as ancient Israel had done.

This merging of the ordinary and the extraordinary was reflected in the Five Pillars of Islam, basic to the practice of any Muslim. First, a Muslim was required to affirm the central confession of the faith: that there is no God but Allah, and that Muhammad is his Prophet. Second, he or she was bound to perform ritual prayers. Five times a day, at dawn, at noon, in midafternoon, after sunset, and before sleeping, each observant Muslim faced the holy city of Mecca and, using prescribed gestures and vocal forms, prayed. Third, it was a Muslim's duty to give alms by means of a kind of tax and by means of other voluntary offerings. Fourth, during the Islamic month of Ramadan, a Muslim was required to fast from all food and drink from sunup to sunset, taking meals only after dark and before dawn. Fifth, at least once in a lifetime, if health and other circumstances allowed, a Muslim was enjoined to make a pilgrimage to Mecca (in present-day Saudi Arabia). There, the pilgrim should perform the traditional spiritual exercises involving a ceremonial visit to the Kaaba, the holiest shrine of Islam, where the sacred black stone said to have been brought to earth by the angel Gabriel was kept.

The Five Pillars, with their prescriptions for daily prayer, almsgiving, dietary regulation, and even travel, provided Muslims with a way to direct their lives with reference to both everyday and eternal claims. This fusion of the ordinary and the extraordinary was underlined in the Islamic observance of the *sunna*, or customs, which supplemented the teachings of the Qur'an. Handed on from generation to generation and acquiring written form, the *sunna* bound Muslims to the practices believed to have guided the everyday behavior of the first generation in their religion. In other words, the *sunna* were a way to attempt to reach the Islam of the beginning, a way to try to destroy the work of time and gain access to the power in the lives of the early followers of the Prophet.

The later history of Islam saw division into different religious communities. Among these, the Sunni Muslims formed the largest. They aimed to follow the *sunna* of the original Muslim community and honored the early history of Islam with its conquests by religionational leaders called caliphs. The Sunnis were countered in their claims to Islamic orthodoxy by the Shiites, who quarreled with the Sunni version of early Muslim history. The Shiites were followers of the family of Ali, the son-in-law and cousin of the Prophet, who reigned as caliph from 656 until 661, when he was murdered. They considered Ali first in a line of sacred figures called imams, who, for them, came to replace the caliphs of Sunni Islam. Law and authority, they thought, were voiced in every age in the person of the imam. Although long ago the official line of imams had disappeared from public view, for the Shiites the law of the Islamic community continued to be less important than the living lawgiver, the leader considered holy in each era. Moreover, the Shiites awaited the reappearance of an imam from the house of Ali at the end of time. This Mahdi, as he was called, would, they believed, inaugurate the final victory of justice and deliver the dead to resurrection. Intensely emotional in their religion, the Shiites became the dominant Muslims of Persia — modern-day Iran — and an important element in the population of Iraq, Lebanon, and other Islamic states.

Finally, more radical in their religion than either Sunnis or Shiites were the Sufis. These were the mystics of Islam, who wandered from place to place, engaging sometimes in austere practices of self-denial and at other times in the songs and dances that would gain them spiritual renown. They formed themselves into religious communities, or orders, in which a group of disciples followed the mystical teachings of a spiritual master called a *sheikh*. Of these Muslim groups, it was the Sufis who most influenced the cult movements of the late twentieth century in the United States.

Transformations of Islam in America

As the twentieth century found more and more Muslims in the United States, they became another minority among the many — even if, by the eighties, they were to be a large one. Vital and important among them were the African-American converts discussed in Chapter 6. Here, however, we will glance briefly at the lives of the immigrants and their children.

At the beginning of the general period of Muslim immigration to the United States, the fear of losing Islam was an important factor delaying the influx. For the immigrants, to be Muslim in their countries of origin was a matter of birth and culture, but in the United States it could become a question of religious preference. Adults could lose contact with their past, and children could grow up without a strong Islamic foundation, Muslims thought. Thus, significantly, Middle Eastern Christians came to America first, and it was only with some anxiety about their religion that Muslims later began to immigrate.

Like so many other newcomers, they tended to live together in communities that were modeled on their relationships in their countries of origin. Often, in a city neighborhood members of almost an entire Syrian village would live within blocks of one another, renting apartments in huge buildings acquired by one wealthy villager among them.

In these Arab communities in larger cities, tensions sometimes grew between Sunni and Shiite Muslims, with Sunnis building mosques (Islamic places of worship) and Shiites preferring "national clubs." Frequently, however, the strangeness of America and the threat to their heritage led Muslims to ignore the differences of the past in their common affirmation of Islam. Moreover, since Islam had been a religion of community and of law, the mosque and its religious service had never been central. In the old countries, it had been customary for some to meet there for public prayer led by an imam (here simply a prayer leader) at noon on Fridays. So in America mosques were built only slowly, the first at Highland Park (Detroit), Michigan, in 1919. Even in the early seventies, there were only about twenty mosques in the country, with perhaps six official imams for all of them. But by the end of the eighties, that pattern had clearly changed. Mosques could be found in at least 300 American cities. Lists of Islamic associations multiplied, and a student Islamic presence was strong.

Moreover, in the ways in which the mosques functioned, the Americanization of Islam could be seen. No longer simply houses of prayer, they became Islamic centers, multiple-purpose buildings that were much like Jewish synagogues in the twentieth century. Even more, the mosques developed a "Sunday" tendency. Following the lead of their Christian neighbors, Muslims began Sunday schools for their children in order to hand on their religious heritage. Often, Sunday schools were followed by services at noon, which replaced the traditional Friday observances. With the American Islamic emphasis on the education of children, women gained a role of increased prominence. Although Islam had been a male-oriented religion in Muslim countries of origin, the needs of religious education in America were met largely by women. Their positions as teachers in Muslim Sunday schools led to their greater participation in the public life of Islam and a new dependence by Muslim people on women.

Meanwhile, Islamic organization began to acquire a national dimension. Symbolic of what was to come was the Islamic Center in Washington, D.C., the cornerstone of its mosque being laid in 1949. The center, the result of cooperation between Islamic governments abroad and Muslims in the United States, was a statement of new unity among American Muslims. Then, by 1952, the Federation of Islamic Associations, under the leadership of second-generation American Muslims of mostly Lebanese ancestry, provided an organizational umbrella for increasing cooperation among Muslims. Still more important was the formation, in 1963, of the Muslim Students Association. The new organization aimed not only to preserve a sense of Muslim identity and religious activity among students but also to work toward the establishment of pan-Islamic religious community in the nation. By 1981 the Muslim Students Association had given its formal blessing to the creation of the Islamic Society of North America, an organization to foster unity among Muslims from different ethnic groups and to carry forward a mission to non-Muslims. Even earlier, the Muslim World League, with its headquarters in Mecca, supported the formation in 1977 of the Islamic Conference in America. Providing advice about Islamic law and its application, assisting mosques in obtaining imams, and monitoring the media to present Islam in a favorable light, the conference again pointed to greater unification within American Islam.

For most of the twentieth century, however, there was a decline in religious practice among traditional American Muslims. Especially in the third generation, for many Arab-Americans nationalism and politics seemed to take the place that religion once had occupied. As in the case of the Eastern Orthodox, the "otherness" of the Islamic religious heritage led many of the descendants of the original immigrants to discard it. Praying five times daily was not easy in a modern, industrial society. Fasting during the month of Ramadan was an act of religious asceticism totally unsupported by the larger culture. Avoidance of pork products and employment of required ritual slaughter practices for animals intended as food were difficult. Even American banking practices, based on interest received or paid, threatened traditional Muslim beliefs that forbade the taking of interest. The foreignness of Islam was painful to many of the young, who had been educated in American public schools and now looked at their religious history from the vantage point of the American mainstream. The result was a sense of estrangement from the Muslim past, and today perhaps 80 to 90 percent of second- and third-generation Muslims are "unmosqued."

At the same time, Muslims did not run headlong to embrace American culture. The ordinary religion of Islam continued in Muslim communities. As in their lands of origin, family and an extended network of kin formed the basis of community. Women spent much of their leisure time in informal visiting, mostly with relatives, a pattern very similar to that in the mountain tradition of Southern Appalachia, as we will see in the next chapter. Men often gathered in coffee houses (Islam forbade alcoholic beverages) and clubs catering to different ethnic groups. The public male dominance of traditional Islam was apparent in Muslim neighborhoods, in which the main street of business was frequented almost entirely by men. Although many Muslims had stopped praying five times daily, in other ways Islam kept on directing them in their ordinary lives and attitudes toward one another.

Moreover, with the influx of immigrants after 1965, and especially with the increase of the 1980s, critical mass was achieved in the Islamic community. With the solidarity brought by numbers came renewed devotion and dedication to the faith, as the multiplication of new mosques suggests. In short, immigrants found in Islam a way to maintain connection with their past and with members of their community in America. As they expanded the presence of Islam in the United States, their accommodation to America more and more included a reaching back to the Muslim heritage and a reinsertion of it in their new context. Patterns of expansion, for Muslims, could include the religious practice of Islam.

Islam and New Religions: The Example of Baha'i

As a world religion, Islam possessed a dynamism that led to new religious movements throughout its history, and in its spread, it came into contact with many native cultures. Out of the mixture of the Muslim heritage with these other traditions, new religious movements arose. There are many examples of such movements, among them a religion that originated in nineteenth-century Persia (present-day Iran), spread from there into numerous countries, and achieved a notable following in America—the religion of Baha'i.

We recall that the words of Baha'u'llah, the founder of Baha'i, were used to conclude an address at the World's Parliament of Religions in 1893. The history of Baha'i, however, began with a Shiite Muslim, Siyyid Ali Muhammad (1819–1850), later called the Bab, or the "Gate." Like other Shiites he grew up in expectation that someday from the house of Muhammad's cousin and son-in-law Ali a hidden imam, the Mahdi, would return to guide Islam rightly. At the same time, his native Persia was still influenced by Zoroastrianism. This earlier Persian religion taught that, after a universal war between good and evil, a prophet would come to bring in a new age of final justice. Hence, the Shiite teaching about the Mahdi drew on roots in native Persian tradition and like Islam was influenced by Jewish and Christian messianic teachings. Thus, when Siyyid Ali Muhammad, himself a member of the house of Ali, announced in 1844 that he was the Bab, he founded a religion called Babism incorporating ancient expectations of a new prophet to manifest God.

The Bab was martyred in 1850. Among his followers was a young man born as Husayn Ali (1817–1892), later to be known as Baha'u'llah (the Glory of God). Imprisoned after the death of the Bab, Husayn Ali came to see himself as the manifestation of God for the present age, the greatest in a long line of prophets. Thereafter, as Baha'u'llah, he spent the rest of his life, mostly in prison or in exile from Persia, proclaiming his religious vision. (Baha'is have continued to be subject to persecution, as events in the 1980s in Iran testified.) Baha'u'llah taught that just as Islam had been the purification and fulfillment of Judaism and Christianity, Baha'i was the completion of Islam and of all previous religions. It was also, he said, an authentic new religion that in time would establish a new world order. According to Baha'u'llah, each religion had been the expression suited to its era, for revelation in human history was progressive. Now, he announced, the world stood at the threshold of an era of universal unity and peace, an era in which its one religion, fitted to the maturity of the age, would follow the principles of Baha'i. In conjunction with this belief resembling the Christian expectation of the millennium, Baha'u'llah taught the equality of all human beings. For him, men and women, though different, had equal importance and equal work to do. Similarly, all races were seen as equal in the plan of God, and Baha'i encouraged interracial marriage to help promote racial harmony. Even further, it called for a reverence for all living things.

If Baha'u'llah had a vision for the Baha'i community, he also made the vision concrete. Through a ritual and moral program, he gave Baha'is a sense of distinctiveness, so that, paradoxically, this universalist religion maintained a strong sense of boundary and identity. In a special solar calendar the year was divided into nineteen months of nineteen days each, with days added at the end of the year to keep it in time with the sun. Beginning each month, there was a feast day, while nine holy days throughout the year honored specific events in the history and revelation of Baha'i. Likewise, during the nineteenth month of the year, from 2 to 20 March, Baha'is fasted, accepting the ancient Islamic Pillar of the fast and transforming it to their own purposes. In another transformation of Islamic practice, Baha'is retained the custom of prescribed daily prayers. However, they did not pray five times in a day, and they did not use the Qur'an, which had been superseded in their view by the writings of the Bab and especially of Baha'u'llah. Meanwhile, at "firesides" Baha'is came together to discuss the principles of their religion with non-Baha'is.

The United States early proved important in Baha'i development. Beginning no later than 1894, when Ibrahim Khayru'llah began to offer classes in Chicago, the religion was systematically taught. Chicago possessed an ideal location at the center of midwestern America, and it continued to offer a home to a thriving Baha'i movement. In the northern Chicago suburb of Wilmette along Lake Michigan, the Baha'i Mother Temple was built. Large and impressive, it seemed a testimony to the strength of American Baha'i. With its message of a new era of peace and unity, Baha'i drew numbers of Americans, whose nation had been born in hopes for just such a millennium. By the late eighties there were about 110,000 Baha'is in the United States organized in 1,700 local assemblies. As elsewhere in the world, membership was interracial. While participation in partisan politics was forbidden as an offense against unity, efforts on behalf of the United Nations were considered a concrete way to advance this unity. Thus, American Baha'is continued to be active in its service.

With its strong organization, its missionary effort, and its distinctive sense of identity, Baha'i had created a time and space that changed ordinary concerns into extraordinary religion. True to a pattern of expansion, it thrived on the hope of becoming a world faith, and its "otherness" in America, at least from the Baha'i point of view, was only a temporary condition. Baha'i did not intend to merge with American culture but instead to bring Americans to live in accordance with its goal of unifying all human beings.

Farther East: Hinduism

As we turn to movements farther eastward, we look first to India, the land that was as important spiritually to the East as Israel was to the West. India's multifaceted religious system, known to the West as Hinduism, had attracted nineteenth-century Americans when Ralph Waldo Emerson and other Transcendentalists read the *Bhagavad Gita*, the *Laws of Manu*, and other Indian religious classics. Later, Helena Blavatsky and the Theosophical Society explored Hindu teaching as a source of occult and metaphysical thought. Unlike other major religions, however, Hinduism was not nurtured in America through the widespread immigration of South Asians, at least until recently. In fact, until after 1965 Asian Indian immigrants were few, and before that, Hinduism grew in the United States through a series of missionary movements.

We have already seen that, in 1893 at the World's Parliament of Religions, Hinduism caught the eye of the American public in the person of Swami Vivekananda (1863–1902). For Vivekananda, success at the parliament was the beginning of a mission that spread the Indian religious philosophy of Vedanta in the United States. Vedanta Societies sprang up in various places, "churches" to bring the message of the East to Americans who were religious seekers. Then in the 1920s, a new arrival from India, Paramahansa Yogananda (1893–1952), brought to Americans the teachings of yoga. His Self-Realization Fellowship became the first in the series of yogic movements that continued and, in popularized form, were absorbed into American culture. By the sixties and seventies, Hindu devotionalism appealed to some among a new generation of Americans in search of religious meaning. And by the late sixties and seventies, too, more and more Asian Indian immigrants were bringing ethnic Hinduism to America and beginning an important religious shift toward Hinduism as inherited tradition. The culture of religious expansion was visible in both the religious quests of American converts and the religious traditionalism of Asian Indians who used their Hinduism as an adaptive mechanism in their new situation.

Religious Themes in Hinduism

The word *Hinduism* is an all-encompassing term for the religious experience and expression of most of the Indian people. It ranges from a philosophic understanding of the nature of the universe and humanity to popular devotion to one or another of the Gods in many small sects and cult movements. Indeed, a sensitive visitor to India might conclude that there were hundreds of different religions in the country, some of them encouraging knowledge and enlightenment, others urging people to faithfulness in performing their allotted tasks, and still others leading them to strong devotion expressed through ritual. In other words, there was a manyness to Hinduism not unlike the manyness that we have found in American religions from Native American traditions to occultism. Yet, as in other examples of manyness, there were common themes to the Hindu religious movements, and it is possible to speak of Hinduism as a single religion. In this context, we look briefly at Hindu thought and practice.

First, Indian speculation about the cosmos formed the backdrop for Hindu religious expression. Over the centuries, many philosophic Hindus had concluded that the world was one reality and the appearance of separation was an illusion. Behind the material world that people encountered every day, these Hindus posited a vast, impersonal force, or power. They named this power Brahman, and they thought of it as the fundamental reality in the universe. For these Hindus, matter, which gave rise to the sense of separation and distinctiveness, was not so real as it seemed. Beneath its masks, they said, the person who became a realized being could trace the presence of Brahman. Moreover, they thought that within each human being lay the Atman, a spark of sacred power that linked individuals to Brahman. According to their teaching, as a realized being a person would come to know experientially that Atman *was* Brahman. So all beings were one being in this view, and mystical union expressed the truest description of the cosmos.

This religious system, called monism, or the philosophy of oneness, was disputed by other Hindus, who taught dualism. In this latter system, the distinctiveness of spirit and matter, of God and individual souls, formed the basis for any further religious thought or practice. Dualism — the philosophy of twoness and manyness — encouraged Hindus in their fascination with the material world. Its many shapes and colors, sounds and smells often seemed to be intoxicating. Thus, the religious art of India was lavish in its use of color and detail. In like manner, the religious landscape that dualism encouraged was peopled with numbers of Gods and Goddesses, each of them the center of a devoted religious following. Polytheism, or the worship of many Gods, spread through Indian villages and attracted Indian intellectuals as well. It brought a striking sacramentalism to Hindu religious expression, as in it the material world became the vehicle for a journey to what was thought divine.

Indian speculation about the nature of the cosmos was completed by a second background element in all Hinduism. As a people, Hindus were concerned with religious experience and especially religious discipline. Indeed, Hindu thought had often provided maps of the various paths a person might travel in a religious journey through life. Overall, for Hindus, there were three broad routes to God. First, there was the path of devotion. Here, the God-centered culture of India expected that each family would have its statue of a God — Krishna, Vishnu, or another popular deity. Religion then centered on respect and attention paid to the God through the statue. Daily, there would be the practice of *puja*, a kind of hospitality offering in which the God was greeted, bathed, perfumed, clothed, and fed by the head of the household, attended at points by members of the family. Through the faithfulness of a person's devotion to the God, expressed in devotion to the image, it was believed that a Hindu could find the way to salvation. Called *bhakti* — the Indian word for devotion — this religious path stressed the importance of personal feeling expressed in the worship of at least one of India's many Gods and Goddesses. Through love of one, it was thought, a person would do all that was needful, contacting divine power as it was manifested in a single expression.

The second religious path for Hindus was the way of action. Indian society had been established according to a system of classes, or castes. Each person came into the world as a member of one of these castes, and because of this inheritance he or she was heir to a set of prescribed actions and obligations. For example, it was considered the duty of a (male) member of the priestly caste to teach, while it was held to be a warrior's duty to rule and defend society. A merchant's obligation was thought to be to procure food and goods for the other members of society, while a person born into the servant caste was thought to be required to labor at service occupations on behalf of the others. In all of the castes, a woman's normal task was seen as service to her husband and other members of her household. The religious way of action taught that each person must live according to the law for his or her caste, doing what needed to be done without regard to results or satisfaction gained. In other words, it was held that deeds must be performed for their own sake rather than for any fruits they might bring. Performing faithfully the actions required of one's state in life, called *karma*, would, Hindus believed, lead a person to be reborn — reincarnated — in a higher state in a new lifetime. Indeed, *karma* was considered the law of *all* action, leading inevitably to an equal and appropriate effect. As a person sowed, Indians thought, so that individual would reap.

The third religious path for Hindus was the way of knowledge. Here, as in occult and metaphysical movements, knowledge meant more than information, argument, and rational thought. Rather, it was understood as insight into the basic meaning of life, realization of the universal being of Brahman. Called *jnana*, this knowledge came, for Hindus, through cultivation of inner states of mind. Religious teachers, called gurus, gave to others various techniques for physical and mental control that were meant to lead them into higher states of awareness. Often there were exercises for breath and body control, so that there could be interior quiet. Then there would be various methods of meditation, all of them intended to open the way toward a time of spiritual realization of oneness. In other words, the path of knowledge aimed for mystical experience. Its discipline formed a pattern for living that attempted to bring a religious seeker into an altered state of consciousness. Yet, whether that goal was reached or not, the discipline of physical and mental practice directed a person in daily life, providing a religious system that many found satisfying.

Hinduism in America

When Vedanta came to the United States at the end of the nineteenth century, it brought India's most widespread form of monistic religious philosophy to Americans. Swami Vivekananda, India's apostle to the West, had been drawn to the mystic and religious leader Ramakrishna (1836–1886), who combined many aspects of Hindu tradition in his teaching and practice. After the death of Ramakrishna, Vivekananda shaped the movement into an international declaration of

Hinduism, committed to the mystical ideal of Ramakrishna but also to action in the world. Beginning in 1896 with the Vedanta Society he founded in New York, Vivekananda presented Hinduism to Americans in a form that they were likely to understand.

The way of knowledge, or *jnana*, became largely the way of intellectual understanding, as typically, Vedanta Society presented lectures on Vedanta philosophy and offered sessions devoted to the classics of Indian religious literature. *Jnana* gave the society its basic appeal in the United States. Still, the way of action, or *karma*, was important to the movement both in India and in America. In India, Vedanta worked in the Ramakrishna Order to relieve physical poverty. In America, where the swami said there was spiritual poverty, Vedanta worked in the Ramakrishna Mission to teach people its ideas of how to live. The way of devotion, or *bhakti*, while less important, became the "church" devotionalism that accompanied Vedanta in its temple meetings. More than any other export Hindu movement in America, Vedanta conformed to Christian customs, developing a religious service that included hymn and scripture, prayer and sermonic address. *Bhakti* was also present in private shrines that members of the society kept in their homes, offering some form of *puja* on a daily basis.

Vedanta appealed to upper- and middle-class Americans and people from other cultures who had become acquainted with the culture of India and had developed an enthusiasm for Eastern spirituality. Later, it came to appeal to Asian Indian immigrants as well. Teaching that the real nature of people was divine and that it was each person's duty to develop the Godhead within, Vedanta offered ideas that blended with liberal Protestant teachings about the immanence of God and the goodness of human nature. Moreover, with its belief that truth was universal, it agreed with the mood of many Americans seeking a common center beneath the pluralism of sects and denominations. It was significant that Aldous Huxley, the teacher of the "perennial philosophy," was a member of the Vedanta Society and that Vedanta offered the option of monastic vows.

Vedanta continued into the twentieth century as a small (now fewer than 3,500 members) yet stable presence. However, the increasing popularity of Hinduism lay with newer movements that stressed yoga or the way of *jnana*. In a more diffused form, the *karma* teaching also influenced Americans. Through the non-caste-oriented interpretation of Mohandas K. Gandhi (1869–1948), the political and spiritual leader of India during its struggle with Great Britain, the path of *karma* influenced the nonviolent resistance of blacks in the American civil rights movement. Here *karma* became that form of social action demanded by ideas of justice and right and performed regardless of personal consequences. At the same time, Indian *bhakti* movements made little headway, with the exception of the Hare Krishna movement (to be discussed later). Protestant evangelism, Catholic devotionalism, the late-twentieth-century charismatic movement in both Protestant and Catholic circles, even Jewish forms of devotionalism based on Hasidism—all offered chances for emotional fervor in religious expression. So the attractions of *bhakti* were largely being met by Western religious forms. They were also being met — as we will see later in the chapter — by a form of Buddhism called Nichiren Shoshu and — as Part II will discuss — by other nontraditional enthusiasms.

The man who introduced yoga to the United States was Paramahansa Yogananda. Like Vivekananda, he had come to attend a religious meeting. After taking part in the International Congress of Religious Liberals, held by the Unitarians in Boston in 1920, Yogananda remained in America for thirty years. More than Vivekananda, he employed American techniques of gaining publicity to spread his message, beginning a practice that later Hindu gurus on mission to America would also use.

The word *yoga* means union and the discipline thought to bring union. Hence, yoga means teaching and practice that tries to bring about the unification of a person's inner being and an experience by that person of the oneness of all things in Brahman. In the Self-Realization Fellowship that he founded, Yogananda offered Americans a religious philosophy based on yogic teachings. In accordance with this background, a self-realization for Yogananda meant an experiential union with the divine spark within and a mystical encounter with the All-Power in the universe. In a practical sense, the pursuit of self-realization was thought to lead to a life of peace and tranquillity in which health and success came naturally.

The basic principles of classical yoga began with the body. Through a series of physical exercises, called *hatha yoga*, a person tried to release tensions that were held to be obstacles to spiritual peace and happiness. By learning to remain for some time in various prescribed physical postures, called 'asanas, the individual aimed to shift energy from one part of the body to another, believing that this practice would open spiritual centers to receive divine energy and encourage inward quiet. Through control of breathing, called *pranayama*, again quiet was sought, to lead to release into a state of bliss. But this bliss was understood as a state of mind, and the aim of yoga was always mental liberation from the material world. So meditation techniques were central to yoga. In yogic teaching, a person's thoughts must be calmed, and the mind must learn to be aware without thinking anything. Thus, a person might fix inwardly on a sacred sound, called a *mantra*, or focus consciously on a point within the body such as the point between the eyes or below the abdomen. The aim was to reach a state of concentration that was uninterrupted. Then, it was believed, the body with its endless claims would fall away, and a person would realize an eternal oneness.

Beyond this classical yogic teaching, Yogananda promoted a form of yoga called *kriya yoga*. This system, understood as a form of God-realization, placed emphasis on awakening a *kundalini* energy thought to lie at the base of the spine and on directing it upward to the crown. Such a process, Yogananda taught, would bring energy and integration to seven *chakras*, or energy centers, in the body. Through use of the mind in attempted movement of energy and through coordinated forms of breathing and mantra repetition, the yogic practitioner hoped to reach a superconscious state.

Yogananda spread both classical and kriya yoga, with adaptive modifications for an American audience. He told Americans that there was scientific precision to yogic philosophy, he used Western psychological concepts to explain it, and he also introduced Christian ideas in conjunction with his teaching. By the sixties, there were some 200,000 people in the Self-Realization Fellowship, and by the early seventies the movement had forty-four centers in the United States and included both lay members and monastics. Like Vedanta, a Sunday "church" service accommodated the Hindu message to the dominant Christian religious practice of this country, but more than Vedanta, the Self-Realization Fellowship pointed in the direction of the individual religious experience that would become the pattern in the later twentieth century.

From the sixties through the eighties, yoga groups and teachers were a common feature of the American cultural landscape. Church organizations and community centers sponsored short courses in yoga techniques, while television programs enabled people to learn yoga in their homes. Drugstores and newsstands blossomed with paperback books describing various yogic postures and breaths. Yoga became a topic of conversation among groups as diverse as college students, housewives, and working people. In this atmosphere of widely diffused interest in hatha yoga, the appeal of meditation likewise grew. Again, popular books and pamphlets appeared to give instruction, while many yoga teachers explained to their students techniques for meditation and gave them opportunities to practice it. But the seed that Vivekananda and, even more, Yogananda had planted was reaped especially by Transcendental Meditation as led by the Maharishi Mahesh Yogi (b. 1911?).

This popular movement of the times followed the pattern of the Self-Realization Fellowship in a number of ways. The Maharishi, who introduced his teaching to the West in 1959, capitalized on publicity even more than Yogananda had done. Like Yogananda, too, he underlined the scientific aspects of his teaching, providing data claiming Transcendental Meditation (TM) lowered blood pressure, relieved stress, increased intelligence, and even reduced crime in areas in which a significant proportion of the people were meditating. And finally, like the classical aspects of Yogananda's teaching, his was a popularized form of Vedanta religious philosophy, aimed to appeal to ordinary practitioners and not just to an intellectual elite.

Transcendental Meditation was based squarely on the teachings of the Indian spiritual books, the Upanishads, as interpreted by the Vedanta school of Shankara (788–820). But it stressed that it was a simple and natural technique that anyone could practice with striking results. With its background of Hindu openness to many Gods, it felt at home with other religions and attracted many adherents who were also members of other organized religious groups. In fact, in its public presentations frequently it denied that it was a religion at all.

That denial became problematic in 1979, when a U.S. Court of Appeals ruled TM to be a religion and therefore unlawful as part of a public-school curriculum. Yet Transcendental Meditation had continued to teach that it was a form of knowledge—"the science of creative intelligence"—and consequent practice. In fact, in 1974 the World Plan Executive, its general governing organization, founded Maharishi International University at the former site of Parsons College in Fairfield, Iowa. The university has conferred both bachelor's and master's degrees and has become an American hub for the world movement.

Through the International Meditation Society—the overarching TM organization for introducing meditation practice—Transcendental Meditation has taught the practice of two fifteen- or twenty-minute meditation periods daily. Meditators use individual mantras that have been given to them personally in an initiation ceremony that is, in fact, a form of Hindu *puja*. The individual mantra that is conferred at the time of initiation is considered secret.

To date over a million people have taken the basic TM course that introduces meditation practice. But a million people do not continue to meditate, and estimates of how many do so have been as low as the tens of thousands. In recent years, after interest in the basic course dropped in the mid-seventies, a meditation course that aimed to teach the practitioner to levitate was introduced. But the new course created publicity that was often negative, and it did not solve the problem of rekindling strong public interest in TM. Still, those who continued to practice the basic meditation technique said that their lives were made better by the simple procedure they had learned.

If the later twentieth century brought new yogic movements such as Transcendental Meditation to Americans, the times also brought at least one prominent example of *bhakti*. The International Society for Krishna Consciousness (ISKCON) became familiar at many airports where its members, sometimes dressed in colorful pink and yellow robes, offered flowers and solicited donations. Founded in 1965 by A. C. Bhaktivedanta Swami Prabhupada (1896–1977), Krishna Consciousness was based on the teachings of a dualistic sixteenth-century sect established by Chaitanya Mahaprabhu (1486–1533). At the center of the old and new devotional movements was Krishna, a Hindu deity and supreme personal God for his followers. Rejecting the traditional polytheism of popular Hinduism, members of the Chaitanya sect and the Hare Krishna movement were Krishna monotheists. And they hailed Chaitanya Mahaprabhu as an incarnation of Krishna.

Like any intense new religious movement, Krishna Consciousness emphasized the boundaries that separated its members from the rest of the world. It demanded a total surrender to Krishna, a surrender made visible in the monastic style of life led by members. Rising before 4:00 A.M. and eating vegetarian food, they spent their days in work and in prayer, as they danced and repeated again and again the full "Hare Krishna" chant. The vibrations of the chant, they claimed, brought an experience of transcendental consciousness. Celibacy was the preferred life-style, and marriage occurred only under the direction of the spiritual leader, with sexual intercourse exclusively for the production of children. While in recent years members of the society have begun to modify the strictness of some of these practices, community has continued to be a strong requirement.

Since the seventies and the death of its founder, ISKCON has seen a decline, especially in its American convert membership. Although Bhaktivedanta was said to have initiated 5,000 disciples personally, only about 1,000 of them remained after his death. Today, though, there are more than sixty temples belonging to the movement in the United States, and they are generally in cities. Probably 2,500 reside in the temples, and several thousand more come for worship. Increasingly, beginning in the seventies, the devotees who took the place of the former American converts were Asian Indian immigrants. In other words, ISKCON began to move from being an export form of Hinduism to one that incorporated both export and ethnic elements. Indeed, Asian Indians provided what was probably the difference between mild decline and virtual extinction. They brought not only membership but also financial support and a degree of public respectability that had previously mostly eluded the movement.

Other forms of export Hinduism thrived in the congenial climate of late-twentieth-century America. It was a season of religious expansion, and the steady attractiveness of South Asian religious movements persisted, if less spectacularly than in the sixties. Groups like the Divine Light Mission (Guru Maharaj Ji), the Siddhya Yoga movement (Swami Muktananda Paramahansa and later the female Gurumayi Chidvilasananda), Integral Yoga (Swami Satchidananda), the Rajneesh Foundation International (Bhagwan Rajneesh), and the Sri Aurobindo Society (Sri Aurobindo), to name but a few, have persisted despite internal problems and even scandals in some of the movements. But after the new U.S. immigration law of 1965, another story began to unfold — that of South Asian immigrants practicing ethnic forms of Hinduism under new circumstances.

The South Asian participation in ISKCON already suggests one way in which the immigrants made the transition between past and present. But there were other ways, and amalgamation with export Hinduism has not been the preferred pattern. The changed immigration law brought so rapid an increase in the number of Asian Indian immigrants that ethnic Hindus were able to begin to form their own religious institutions. In 1982 alone, as an example, more Asian Indians entered the country than in all of the years before 1960. The 1980 census recorded over 387,000 Asian Indian immigrants, while estimates at mid-decade suggested between 525,000 and 800,000 as permanent residents of the United States. With such a dramatic increase after centuries of virtual absence, the religious results promised to be striking. Add to this the class background of the new immigrants, who overwhelmingly came from professional and educational circles, desired to transmit Indian culture to their children, and decried Ameri-

Dedication of the Rama Temple, Lemont, Illinois. Although the temple was not yet completed, the dedication of its tower was held, significantly, on July 4, 1986. Honoring the hero of the Indian epic *Ramayana* and two other deities, the Rama temple is the main shrine in a larger temple complex at Lemont and is especially favored by South Indians.

can materialism and what they saw as decadent American values. With numbers, financial ability, and cultural and moral concern to spur them, the Asian Indians began to create an American flowering of ethnic Hinduism.

There were, of course, problems in their venture, one of the largest being the heterogeneity in the Asian Indian population itself. With sixteen major languages in India and a series of regional cultures and devotions, no one pattern of Hinduism could speak for all of the immigrants. Yet despite the differences and often because of them, what began to emerge was a temple Hinduism in which the construction of large and impressive shrines became the focus and collective representation for local (in the United States) Hindu communities. By 1986 there were some forty Hindu temples in the nation, and every community of 100 or more families seemed to be planning a temple or building one. Generally, the temples could be distinguished by their architecture, their Gods, their ritual practice, and the like as South Indian, North Indian, ecumenical (meant to have a broad appeal), or sectarian (dedicated to worship as carried on in one Hindu sect). Constructing the temple itself became an act of Asian Indian community, requiring strong financial commitment and work to iron out differences. Thus, whatever their designation, most of the Indian temples expressed some degree of ecumenicity.

Temples, moreover, were cultural centers as much as strictly ritual centers, preserving languages, arts, and practices from the ethnic past. They provided an unusually clear example of how ordinary and extraordinary religion were interwoven in the actual affairs of communities. And, as we have seen in other cases, the temples were adaptive mechanisms, supporting the religious expansionism of these new Americans by enabling them to bring their past into the present. Often prosperous, the temples were sources of pride and identity for Asian Indians. And for mainstream Americans, they signaled a continuing ability to absorb religious diversity in a culture of religious expansion.

Farther East: Buddhism

Krishna Consciousness and some forms of meditation stressed extraordinary aspects of religion, but the general tenor of Hinduism, even in the new temples, supported the framework of daily life as ordinary religion. While this was more true in India, still, in the United States, the discreet Hinduism of the Vedanta Societies and the *karma* ideal of dedication to one's role in life led to involvement in the everyday world. The popularization of yoga in hatha exercise programs and in Transcendental Meditation meant that the "otherness" of Hinduism blended with considerable ease in the pluralism of an expansive American culture. In the case of Buddhism, the pattern was to some extent similar. But Buddhism, perhaps more than Hinduism, emphasized methods for the practice of extraordinary religion in America.

Ethnic Buddhism came to this country with Chinese and, especially, Japanese immigrants of the late nineteenth century. The predominant form of Buddhism was Jodo Shinshu, a branch of Pure Land Buddhism that flourished in the regions from which the immigrants came. In America Jodo Shinshu became the preferred Buddhism of Japanese-Americans, giving them a way of life that fused ordinary with extraordinary religion. However, the late nineteenth century saw wide publicity for export Buddhism in America. This publicity came as a result of the Buddhism that appeared at the World's Parliament of Religions and particularly the Buddhism of the Japanese Zen master Soyen Shaku (1859–1919). There were some Japanese Zen immigrants, of course. But addressed to mainstream Americans, Zen thrived among converts, giving them a way to seek an extraordinary religious experience of enlightenment.

In general, while the first and ethnic form of Buddhism led initially to a "church" religion, the second, mostly convert (export) form led to meditation. A third form, which enjoyed a spurt of growth in the sixties and seventies, was Nichiren Shoshu. This was a missionary type of Japanese Buddhism that was popular in America among both Japanese-Americans and mainstream converts. If we compare these forms of Buddhism with the kinds of Hinduism introduced in America, there are parallels. In both, a predominantly "church" form of the religion, supporting action in the world (one's *karma* in Hinduism), was followed by a religion stressing meditation (for Hindus the way of *jnana*) and, in turn, a mostly devotional and evangelical version (for Hindus the way of *bhakti*). Later we will look more closely at all three.

The Religion of Buddhism

Before we explore the American paths of Buddhism further, we need to examine some basic themes in the religion. Its founder, Siddhartha Gautama (563?–483? B.C.), was considered not a prophet but an example of how to live. Called the Buddha, which means the "enlightened" or "awakened" one, according to tradition he left a prosperous life as a member of the warrior (ruling) caste of India to find an answer to the problem of suffering and death. Tradition has it, too, that he sought help from various spiritual masters without success, all the while practicing great austerities and becoming physically weak. Finally, tradition records, he ended his life of rigorous asceticism and began to meditate for himself, and it was then that one night, sitting under a bo tree, he broke through to enlightenment. From that time, accounts say, he spent his days preaching and teaching others how they, too, might come to this state.

Thus, from the very first, Buddhism stressed religious knowledge. Like occult and metaphysical traditions in America and like some forms of Hinduism, it taught the importance of spiritual "insight," which was understood as enlightenment gained not from reading and studying but through emptying the mind's ordinary contents so that light could enter. The intellectual content of enlightenment in Buddhism was seemingly simple. It was the Four Noble Truths taught by the Buddha. Human suffering had a cause; the cause of suffering was desire; there was a way to end suffering; and the way to end it was to end desire, living in nonattachment to any persons, places, or things. But, for Buddhists, the Four Noble Truths were meant to merge into the one moment of enlightenment when *nirvana* — or unconditioned reality — was experienced. As in Hinduism, the message that the Buddha brought was empirical.

Marking the Buddhist teaching as empirical and practical, the Buddha gave his followers the Noble Eightfold Path. By walking this road, they believed, they might conduct themselves toward enlightenment. Named the Middle Path, it was meant as a way of balance that would avoid extremes of asceticism and self-indulgence as well as all one-sided views and acts. Instead of these, the Eightfold Path called on Buddhists to practice "right" views and intentions, leading to "right" speech, action, livelihood, and effort, and ultimately "right" mindfulness and concentration. Thus, the Eightfold Path traced the pattern of a spiral: it began in the mind at the level of ordinary knowledge, moved from mind to body through forms of speech and action, and then returned to the mind, this time at the level of meditation. It was the pattern of someone who wanted to break through the ordinary dimensions of life into the extraordinary. Hence, it was significant that the Buddha's closest followers from the beginning lived together in a religious order, or community. Buddhist teaching lessened the religious significance of the caste system, urging people to leave their ordinary way of life in pursuit of an extraordinary religious goal.

From the first, this radical community of monks and nuns was joined by lay followers of the Buddha, who continued to occupy their regular stations in life. And gradually Buddhism became a religion that supported the ordinary culture of India. Yet the appeal of the extraordinary world did not leave Buddhism. With expansive zeal, it became the missionary religion of Asia, spreading from India to China and Japan as well as to all of Southeast Asia. Furthermore, as the Buddhist community reflected on the Buddha's message, different understandings of the teaching arose, and different forms of Buddhism resulted.

By the third century B.C., two major schools of Buddhist interpretation had developed. Theravada, which became the Buddhism of Southeast Asia, taught that it carried on the original instruction of the Buddha. Here the emphasis was on the individual, whose goal was to become a solitary spiritual hero, one who would turn within and quench desire completely. In this form of Buddhism, the historical Buddha was revered as an example of what each human being might achieve, and he was revered because of the teaching he had brought. But in the strict teachings of the members of the elite, Buddha was always human, never divine. For them, moreover, Theravada Buddhism was atheistic: there was no God to praise or blame an individual, no God to save or condemn a person. For the Theravadan elite, everything led to an experience of enlightenment, of pure nonattachment in nirvana.

The second major school of Buddhism, Mahayana, became the Buddhism of China and Japan. The larger of the two schools, Mahayana stressed the community. Instead of the solitary monk seeking personal enlightenment, its hero was the *bodhisattva*. He or she was identified as a figure who, on the verge of experiencing nirvana, postponed the time indefinitely out of compassion for human beings and in order to serve them. In this understanding, the accounts of the compassion of Siddartha Gautama, the historical Buddha, were especially remembered, and his compassion was seen as an example to all. Meanwhile, his Buddhahood was considered a quality others, too, could possess. Rather than emphasizing the one historical Buddha, the Mahayana school found Buddhas wherever persons were said to be enlightened.

Gradually, a doctrine of Buddha bodies moved Mahayana toward an elaborate theology of the meaning of Buddhahood. According to the doctrine, there were three expressions of the Buddha. The first was the "body of appearance," or the physical body of the Buddha. The second was the "body of bliss," which was said to appear surrounded by light, the reported reward that the Buddha gained for his spiritual practice and the reported reward, too, of bodhisattvas who saw the Buddha. The third Buddha body, according to the theology, was the "body of essence," the true being of the Buddha as an absolute beyond space and time. In beliefs about the body of essence and to some extent the body of bliss, the Buddha had become in certain ways like a God. Since it was theoretically possible in Mahayana for anybody to become a Buddha, instead of the atheism of Theravada, Mahayana supported a polytheism of many Buddha-Gods.

In time, a third large school of Buddhism joined Theravada and Mahayana. From the third or fourth century A.D., Vajrayana Buddhism grew from Buddhist, Hindu, and other popular religious roots to become the Buddhism, most notably, of Tibet. This form of Buddhism saw the many Buddhas of Mahayana as visualizations of the passions within each human being. In a process of symbolic manipulation, Vajrayana Buddhists aimed to transform these inner forces into visible and audible beings. The point of this procedure was to try to come to terms with each of these forces so that all would merge into a oneness at the center of the self. In other words, Vajrayana sought the mystical goal of union with a divinity within. By dramatizing the inner work in a series of secret initiations and magical techniques, Vajrayana Buddhists were trying to make the spiritual concrete. And by making the spiritual concrete, they hoped to achieve practical control over it.

Each of the three major forms of Buddhism was expressed in many differing sects and schools of interpretation. As new spiritual leaders arose, they stressed aspects of Buddhist teaching that they believed others had missed, and they came to value one or another portion of Buddhist scripture over the rest. Thus, many Buddhist movements focused on a specific Buddhist sutra, or writing, making it central to their devotions and lives. As we examine some of the forms of Buddhism in America, we will look at a few of the Buddhist sects in their teaching and practice.

Buddhism in America

As in the case of Hinduism, there was a long period of preparation in American culture for the arrival of Buddhism. The Transcendentalists had turned to the East as a source of wisdom. More directly, Henry Olcott of the Theosophical

Society had aided the cause of Buddhism both overseas and in the United States, writing a Buddhist catechism that went through forty editions in his lifetime. His spiritual associate, Helena Blavatsky, included Buddhist teaching in her occult works, and her references to Mahatmas identified them as Tibetans familiar with the practices of Vajrayana Buddhism. Both Olcott and Blavatsky formally became Buddhists. Meanwhile, a series of other individuals became Buddhist sympathizers and in some cases converts even before the Theosophical Society appeared.

Buddhism grew even further as its "church," meditation, and evangelical versions came to the United States. Adherents ranged from conventional ethnic followers, who accepted the religion as their birthright, to an elite of purists, both Japanese and mainstream Americans, who sought a Buddhism of the ancient texts. A third group, mostly Americans, became an eclectic following, blending Buddhism with other religious elements.

As early as the 1840s, Chinese immigrants appeared on the West Coast and brought their Buddhism with them. Temples arose in San Francisco's Chinatown district by the middle of the next decade, although in them elements of Taoism and Confucianism (both native Chinese religions) were also incorporated. The most significant early efforts to introduce ethnic Buddhism in America came, however, after the Civil War, and they were the work of the Japanese.

"Church" Buddhism among Japanese immigrants came to Hawaii in 1889 and to California a decade later. The carriers were Jodo Shinshu missionaries of the Nishi Hongwanji movement, one of the 170 or so sects of Buddhism that existed in Japan. A branch of Pure Land Buddhism, Jodo Shinshu, like all Mahayana Buddhism of the Pure Land type, taught faith in a Buddha being called Amida Buddha. According to traditional account, at the time when he became a Buddha, Amida established the Western Kingdom, called the Pure Land, in fulfillment of his previous bodhisattva vows. Now, believers said, it was possible for people, through trust in Amida and devotion to him, to enter the Pure Land after death and there experience enlightenment. Pure Land Buddhism did not consider it necessary to be sinless or to use elaborate meditation techniques. All that one needed to do in Pure Land devotion was to call on Amida with gratitude in the formula "Hail to Amida Buddha." Thus, Pure Land Buddhism put the "other-power" of Amida in place of the "self-power" that Theravada and the other meditation forms of Buddhism taught. Of all the forms of Buddhism, it probably most resembled Christianity with its God of compassion who, through faith in his Son Jesus, brought human beings to an eternal life in paradise.

Because of this resemblance to Christianity, Pure Land seemed most likely of the various Japanese sects of Buddhism to accommodate itself to American culture. Its history in the United States showed how much it did so. From 1899 to 1944 it was largely organized by the Nishi Hongwanji sect as the North American Buddhist Mission, and after that date it became the Buddhist Churches of America. Its membership grew until, in the eighties, about 100,000 people were affiliated in some 100 churches.

From the first, language presented a difficulty for Buddhism in America. Just as Asian Indian missionaries had previously struggled to translate Indian Buddhist ideas into conversational Chinese, so Japanese Buddhist missionaries in America worked to find equivalents in English for Buddhist terms. There were no churches of Buddhism in Japan, and community worship did not take place in a Buddhist shrine except on special occasions. Thus, to use the term *church* when speaking about Buddhism was a concession to American ears. Similarly, Buddhist churches in America began to call their overseer a "bishop," another concession to American Christianity. There were adaptations in worship as well, as Buddhist churches began Sunday services and Sunday schools. Although some worried that these changes might compromise the character of Buddhism, most accepted them as the inevitable result of Americanization. If Japanese-Americans were to retain some meaningful relationship to their religious and cultural past in the American environment, they thought, they must find a practice for themselves and their children that conformed with American customs. Many felt that the Buddhist Churches of America were the necessary compromise. Their ethnic Buddhism enabled Japanese-Americans to unite ordinary and extraordinary religion in a distinctive Japanese-American way of life.

The second form of Buddhism in America, stressing meditation, became represented most notably in Japanese Zen and Tibetan varieties. Zen originated in China as Ch'an Buddhism in the fifth and sixth centuries A.D. From there it was imported in the late twelfth and early thirteenth centuries to Japan where, with Ch'an now become "Zen," it flourished as a combination of Mahayana religious philosophy and Theravada meditation techniques. Thus, the goal of Zen was to bring a person to enlightenment through the practice of meditation. Furthermore, as in China, from the early history of Japanese Zen there were two schools that advocated different methods of meditation and believed that different processes were at work in gaining enlightenment. One school, Rinzai Zen, taught that enlightenment was a sudden event, triggered by unusual circumstances that jolted a person out of ordinary consciousness. Hence, its practice centered on meditation using *koans*, riddles or verbal puzzles meant to baffle the ordinary working mind—as, for example, in the koan-style question "What is the sound of one hand clapping?" The theory was that by pondering a koan, unanswerable by normal reasoning, the mind's hold would be broken and enlightenment would come. The other school, Soto Zen, taught that enlightenment was gradual. Soto Zen practice centered on "just sitting," meditation in which the goal was to quiet the mind and to empty it of all thought.

Soyen Shaku introduced Rinzai Zen at the World's Parliament of Religions. But it was his disciple Daisetz Teitaro Suzuki (1870–1966) who, more than any other person, spread Rinzai Zen in America. From 1897 to 1909, Suzuki worked as an editor for the Open Court Publishing Company in La Salle, Illinois.

After returning to Japan, he wrote prolifically in English about Buddhism, and his many books were widely read in this country. When he came back to the United States in the fifties, he spoke frequently at universities, including one series of lectures at Columbia. Suzuki aided the communication of Zen to non-Oriental Americans by stressing themes that agreed with the contemporary Western philosophy of existentialism. At the same time, he tended to overlook the discipline and ritual attached to the Zen monastic tradition and to disregard its social setting in Japan.

In the late fifties, a group of San Francisco artists and writers that included Allen Ginsberg (b. 1926), Jack Kerouac (1922–1969), and, with qualifications, Alan Watts (1915–1973) and Gary Snyder (b. 1930) combined the interpretations of Suzuki with other elements to form an eclectic "Beat Zen." As a group, they drew on the side of Rinzai teaching that stressed the suddenness of enlightenment and made it into an exaltation of emotional release and freedom. So Beat Zen pursued liberation at the expense of the rigorous and ascetic meditation practices that were part of the Rinzai Zen tradition.

However, both Watts and Snyder went further. Watts, with his many books, was an important popularizer of Zen, using Western scientific and psychological categories in order to present it. In romantic style, he portrayed Zen for his American reader as a new way of life, with expansionist emphasis on its "otherness," its revolution — by Western standards — in inner awareness. Snyder moved beyond the romanticism of Watts to probe the meaning of Zen with greater rigor. With a background in anthropology and literature and an extensive knowledge of Native American religions and ecological concerns, he wrote poetry that expressed themes of interdependence among all living creatures. But he was not content to interpret Zen from the vantage point of this background. He went to Japan to study Zen, learning the language in order to do so and committing himself of a period of monastic training. More than the others, Snyder brought the two sides of Zen — its meditative discipline and its spontaneity — together.

Meanwhile, the more formal and traditional practice of Zen grew with the introduction of Zen centers in California and New York by Sokatsu Shaku Roshi (1869–1954). Soto Zen also took up residence when in 1962 Shunryu Suzuki (1904–1971) established the San Francisco Zen Center, the largest of the American Zen centers. From here and other places, monasteries were organized where individuals might spend either short or extended periods away from society. Finally, in the United States, the Rinzai and Soto lineages were united in a third form of Zen, spread especially by Philip Kapleau's book *The Three Pillars of Zen* (1965). Kapleau (b. 1912) had visited Japan as a reporter in 1946 and less than a decade later studied there under Sogaku Harada, who sought the unification of Zen. In 1966 Kapleau opened the Zen Meditation Center in Rochester, New York, where he applied ideas from his book as a teacher. Different from the emphasis of Suzuki and Watts, Kapleau underlined the importance of the traditional practice of *zazen*, sitting meditation, as well as the relationship between master and student. Even further, at his center he worked to make Zen American, using the English language, adapting rituals, and wearing Western clothes during meditation.

Most American Zen adherents were young, middle-class people, well-educated and white. They were converts from mainstream America, and that fact impressed itself on the character of Zen. It became in America part of the culture of religious expansionism and an extraordinary religion, in which people sought to pursue transcendence. Many of the same things could be said about Tibetan Buddhism in America. Brought to the United States by Buddhist monks fleeing after the Chinese Communist takeover of Tibet, it became noticeable here after 1965. Through Tibetans on university faculties and through the establishment of meditation centers, knowledge of Tibetan Buddhism spread. The esotericism of its teachings and the heavy cloak of symbolism that surrounded them did not deter converts in religiously expansionist America. Moreover, Tibetan Buddhist masters, called *rinpoches*, found a language to express their Buddhist teaching in humanistic psychology. They were able to communicate with mainstream Americans by showing the continuities between Tibetan Vajrayana thought and practice and modern American beliefs. Especially under Tarthang Tulku in Berkeley, California, and Chogyam Trungpa (1939–1987) in Boulder, Colorado, Tibetan Buddhism provided Americans with another type of Buddhism stressing meditation.

Finally, evangelical Buddhism came to America, largely in the form of Nichiren Shoshu. Its membership grew rapidly after its first appearance in America in 1960, and by 1983 it was claimed that there were as many as between 200,000 and 250,000 members in the United States. However, more conservative estimates have suggested that 30,000 or fewer is a likelier figure, and in the eighties, in general, the movement suffered a sharp decline.

Who were the people who turned to this form of Buddhism, and what attracted them? At first, most adherents in the United States came from Japanese ancestry. The few mainstream Americans who joined tended to be men who had married Japanese women, and membership was overwhelmingly middle class, with many of the people involved in small businesses. Yet by 1967, almost all (95 percent) of the new converts were non-Oriental, while in the East and the Midwest, most adherents to Nichiren Shoshu had no connections with Japan. They were younger, less well established, and more diverse than the Japanese-American Buddhists. Beyond that, more than any other Buddhist group, Nichiren Shoshu drew Latins and blacks as well as whites. More than any other Buddhist group, too, it drew working-class as well as college-educated converts.

The religion that these people followed had roots in thirteenth-century Japan. There, according to the traditional account, a monk named Nichiren (1222–1282) was disturbed by the competing claims of the Japanese Buddhist sects and began to preach the centrality of a particular Buddhist holy book, the Lotus Sutra of the Mystical Law. Nichiren is said to have told people that, instead of chanting "Hail to Amida Buddha," they should chant praise to the Lotus Sutra, which explained the fundamental laws of nature. He is said to have told them, too, that Japan had gone astray by turning to Amida and to other forms of Buddhism. By turning to the Lotus Sutra, Nichiren taught, people would find their Buddha-nature within and attain happiness, prosperity, and peace.

Aggressive from the first in its proclamation of this message, the Nichiren movement was reborn in twentieth-century Japan in the Soka Gakkai organization, a lay group convinced that they should use "forceful persuasion" to convert the world. Hence, Nichiren Shoshu came to the United States as a missionary movement — like many other Asian groups but probably more zealous. And it appealed because of its simplicity and its promise of material prosperity and happiness. Although there was a strong philosophical basis for its teaching, it emphasized the devotional practice of the chant *"Nam Myoho Renge Kyo"* ("Hail to the Lotus Sutra"), reverence toward a Gohonzon altarpiece inscribed to recall the Lotus Sutra, and a pilgrimage, if possible, to the headquarters of Nichiren Shoshu in Japan. Each of these provided ways for individuals to act out their cultural reaching in a search for a center — through sound, through sight, through travel. Each of these seemed to promise to release people from a sense of confusion and to give them a surer sense of identity. Indeed, the power behind Nichiren Shoshu had much to do with the power behind all forms of evangelism. Here East met West in their mutual agreement that the proclamation of a sure and simple gospel would enable individuals, by finding a center outside themselves, to find a center within and to experience some form of blessing.

Then by the late eighties, the American immigration law of 1965 and a volatile political climate brought new waves of East Asian immigrants to the United States. With "church," meditation, and evangelical Buddhism flourishing in this country, the new immigrants made ethnic Buddhism a stronger presence, and they changed the way mainstream Americans began to perceive the religion. The large number of East Asians forced the culture of expansion to expand further still, to accommodate traditional religions that were practiced not in the extraordinary context of small and intense export forms but as ordinary ways of life. Estimates were made, for example, of 600,000 Vietnamese, the majority of them Buddhists and many of them in Southern California; of 220,000 Laotians, with temples in Los Angeles, Chicago, and Washington, D.C.; of 160,000 Cambodians, with forty-one temples in the nation; and of over 100,000 Thais, with 40,000 of them in Los Angeles alone. By 1987 the appointment of the first Buddhist chaplain to the U.S. armed forces signaled a Buddhism coming of age. The same year, the establishment of the American Buddhist Congress provided another sign. Formed to explain Buddhism and Buddhists to non-Asian Americans and to articulate a Buddhist community opinion on public policy issues, the congress promised to make Buddhism a visible public presence in a pluralist American society.

East Is West: Syncretism and Community

Increasingly in the late twentieth century, syncretism—the mixture of various elements to form a new religion—became a feature of American life. Syncretism was clearly part of the culture of expansionism. With religious options as available as the foods on a supermarket shelf, it seemed inevitable that people would begin to bring together religious tendencies from various cultures. The result was a proliferation of small religious movements that arose, enjoyed their day, sometimes grew stronger, and sometimes all but vanished. For many, if not most, there was a charismatic leader who combined the magical qualities of a shaman with the saving qualities of a messiah. For many, there was a sense that the activity of the particular religious group was bringing in a new age—something we will look at more closely in Chapter 11. Intense and enthusiastic, these groups stretched to incorporate elements from different religions but also simplified what they took from these religions. Simplicity was present in the mysticism that accompanied such groups when they saw all things as one thing—whether as the manifestation of a universal divine force or as the near-total claims of their own organization. It was present in their gospels of effective, positive action through the use of practical techniques to save themselves and the world. Again and again, simplicity was present in the way these groups reached out to bring East and West together to form one religious universe.

A good example of religious syncretism in the seventies was the Healthy-Happy-Holy Organization (usually known as the 3HO). Founded in the United States in 1969 by the Indian Yogi Bhajan (Harbhajan Singh; b. 1929), it combined under his charismatic leadership forms of Indian yoga, including kundalini and Tantric elements, with the Sikh religion. The Sikh tradition arose in northern India when Nanak (1469–1539) tried to reconcile Muslim and Hindu teachings. Nanak spoke of one God in all religions, a God who could be realized through meditative practices. In America the new religion of the 3HO drew on this multiple background, blending it with millennial expectation of a new age and with American patriotism. Members of the organization led a rigorous communal life, rising at 4:00 A.M., meditating before a picture of Yogi Bhajan, practicing demanding physical forms of yoga, and following a vegetarian diet (with dairy products but not eggs). The requirement of silence underlined the asceticism of community life, while various classes provided knowledge of subjects that harmonized with 3HO ideas. After dinner each evening a session of religious singing using guitars and a folk-rock style closed the day. As it existed at the time of its greatest popularity (the 3HO has gone through many changes), the movement aimed to build a nation, to create a new society in America under God. While conceived in visionary terms rather than in plans for direct political action, the goal of building a nation combined patriotism with a leftist critique of the United States. The 3HO brought together Eastern and Western elements to respond to its era.

The 3HO was but one in an abundant catalog of syncretistic cult movements. But if religious syncretism was present in a series of new and small religious groups, by the late twentieth century it was also becoming a generalized habit of mind for mainstream Americans. Hence, syncretism spilled over the boundaries of distinct religious groups to become a mood and an atmosphere for practicing religion. In this sense, the clearest example at the present time is the New Age movement, which we will explore in Chapter 11. Here, though, the presence of syncretistic religions in America must lead us back to the East and back to the model of religious "otherness" that it gave the West. Both through Eastern peoples practicing their traditional ethnic religions in America and through American converts practicing Eastern export religions or syncretistic religions as "new," the East taught the West to stretch to incorporate what seemed religiously strange. In other words, the East provided the United States with a primary means to pursue the culture of religious expansionism. At the same time, because many in the West were seeking something religiously "other," the East was "at home" in America.

This relationship between East and West highlights the issue of community in America. Among those who inherited Eastern religions, there was natural community and a natural boundary separating each group from other Americans. In the cases of Russian and Greek Orthodox peoples, of Arab Muslims, and of Japanese Buddhists, we saw such communities defining reality for their people and providing for them a seamless fabric of ordinary and extraordinary religion. In the case of converts, there was, instead, a cultivation of instant community with strangers. Converts made self-conscious and deliberate attempts to create a "home" through their association with one another. But like those who joined occult and metaphysical movements, to whom these converts seemed related, their homesteads were ultimately in the mind. A great part of the attraction of Hindu, Buddhist, and syncretistic forms of religion was their overall emphasis on the importance of knowledge and the value of practice in changing a person's mind. Enlightenment, meditation, and inner peace were by definition mental states. They led to a community of the parts of the person in a unified sense of self and, likewise, a uniting with what was conceived as ultimate. Even in American *bhakti*, the focus was on ecstatic states and internal transformations through devotion to God(s). In the process these religions tended to minimize the importance of the human community with its common traditions and history.

For the converts, too, the quest for religion was the quest for the extraordinary. Crossing a metaphysical boundary was important for these converts: it was essential to the experience of conversion. More than that, the quest for a separate extraordinary religion (and the preference for intensity) had long roots in American soil. We have only touched on the common themes that run through American religious history in Part I, but in Part II we will pay more attention to them. Here, though, we need to observe that the bad press given to some of the cult movements has obscured the continuities between converts to Eastern and syncretistic religions and other Americans. The counterculture of the late twentieth century was not counter to culture at all but an expression of one side of American life. Our study of Protestant revivalism and of occult and metaphysical movements has made this apparent.

In this context, the charge that converts to Eastern and syncretistic religions have been "brainwashed" ignores the complexity of culture. To be part of any group is to be told the meaning of the world, to be a member of a particular community with its language and values. No child being born into a society has the choice of accepting or rejecting the language, the values, and the meanings that culture assigns. Hence, if any one group is brainwashed, then we all are. On the other hand, the charge of brainwashing expresses discomfort in the presence of religious expansion. It suggests one form of the religious contraction that we will examine in a different way in the next chapter.

In Overview

The end of the nineteenth century brought the growing visibility of Eastern religions in the United States. As ethnic creations that came with Eastern peoples, these religions united the ordinary and the extraordinary in traditional religious practices. As export religions for mainstream American converts, they gave the extraordinary to Westerners who were seeking "otherness." Both in ethnic and export forms, Eastern religions strengthened the boundaries separating their adherents from mainstream America and at the same time contributed greatly to a culture of religious expansionism.

If we make the Atlantic coast the vantage point, from Nearer East came the religion of Eastern Orthodoxy, a major branch of Christianity that claimed to stand with the major faiths in the United States. Traditionally organized in self-governing local churches, the Orthodox strived for "right" belief and worship, giving expression to their desire for both in their iconic theology and mystical spirituality. From the Middle East came Islam with Arab Muslims and other immigrants as well as converts from, especially, the African-American community. Following the strict monotheism of Muhammad, Muslims inherited a program of religious action in the Five Pillars of their faith. Meanwhile, the new religion of Baha'i, an outgrowth of Persian Islamic culture, made its presence felt in the United States.

From Farther East came Hinduism and Buddhism in both traditional and newer variants. Both religions offered followers spiritual paths through specialized forms of knowledge (yoga, meditation), through "churches" supporting action in the world, and through devotion. Movements linked to Hinduism included the Vedanta Society, the Self-Realization Fellowship, Transcendental Meditation, the International Society for Krishna Consciousness, and many more. Buddhist presence was felt in organizations like the Buddhist Churches of

America, in various forms of Japanese Zen and Tibetan Buddhism, in Nichiren Shoshu, and in other movements as well. Finally, syncretistic religions, such as the Healthy-Happy-Holy Organization, joined charismatic leaders and mystical techniques with a sense of an impending new age, while religious syncretism also existed as a generalized habit of mind. Ministering to ethnic strangers in America, Eastern religions — like the occult and metaphysical movements — also provided American converts with mental homesteads to replace homes and communities often missing in their ordinary lives.

We can learn from the religions of the Nearer, Middle, and Farther East in the late twentieth century. They enable us to see more clearly how many the many really are and how expansive the religious culture is. When we view the religions of America in this light, the mainstream seems to dissolve into thousands of smaller currents. If Easterners, who were foreigners, were more at home in America than they knew, it was because "otherness" was a common feature of life in the United States.

This statement is underlined by the fact that, in America, geography itself marked off areas that were "other." A different landscape meant, for many, a different regional culture and a different regional religion. Indeed, Easterners had many friends in their "otherness," some of them in the mountain hollows of Southern Appalachia, where, as we will see in the next chapter, there was a flourishing regional religion — but also one that illustrated religious contraction.

SUGGESTIONS FOR FURTHER READING: EASTERN PEOPLES AND EASTERN RELIGIONS

Bespuda, Anastasia. *Guide to Orthodox America.* Tuckahoe, NY: St. Vladimir's Seminary Press, 1965.

Ellwood, Robert S., Jr. *The Eagle and the Rising Sun: Americans and the New Religions of Japan.* Philadelphia: Westminster Press, 1974.

———, **and Partin, Harry B.** *Religious and Spiritual Groups in Modern America.* 2d ed. Englewood Cliffs, NJ: Prentice-Hall, 1988.

Ferraby, John. *All Things Made New: A Comprehensive Outline of the Baha'i Faith.* Rev. ed. London: Baha'i Publishing Trust, 1975.

Fields, Rick. *How the Swans Came to the Lake: A Narrative History of Buddhism in America.* Boulder, CO: Shambhala, 1981.

Haddad, Yvonne Yazbeck, and Lummis, Adair T. *Islamic Values in the United States: A Comparative Study.* New York: Oxford University Press, 1987.

Hopkins, Thomas J. *The Hindu Religious Tradition.* The Religious Life of Man Series. Belmont, CA: Wadsworth, 1971.

Kashima, Tetsuden. *Buddhism in America: The Social Organization of an Ethnic Religious Institution.* Westport, CT: Greenwood Press, 1977.

Layman, Emma McCloy. *Buddhism in America.* Chicago: Nelson-Hall, 1976.

Martin, Richard C. *Islam: A Cultural Perspective.* Prentice-Hall Series in World Religions. Englewood Cliffs, NJ: Prentice-Hall, 1982.

Melton, J. Gordon. *Encyclopedic Handbook of Cults in America.* New York: Garland, 1986.

Prebish, Charles S. *American Buddhism.* North Scituate, MA: Duxbury Press, 1979.

Richardson, E. Allen. *Islamic Cultures in North America: Patterns of Belief and Devotion of Muslims from Asian Countries in the United States and Canada.* New York: Pilgrim Press, 1981.

Robinson, Richard H., and Johnson, Willard L. *The Buddhist Religion: A Historical Introduction.* 3d ed. The Religious Life of Man Series. Belmont, CA: Wadsworth, 1982.

Saloutos, Theodore. *The Greeks in the United States.* Cambridge: Harvard University Press, 1964.

Stockman, Robert H. *The Baha'i Faith in America: Origins, 1892–1900.* Wilmette, IL: Baha'i Publishing Trust, 1985.

Tarasar, Constance J., ed. *Orthodox America, 1794–1976.* Syosset, NY: Orthodox Church in America, Department of History and Archives, 1975.

Ware, Timothy. *The Orthodox Church.* Rev. ed. New York: Penguin Books, 1976.

Waugh, Earle H., Abu-Laban, Baha, and Qureshi, Regula B., eds. *The Muslim Community in North America.* Edmonton: University of Alberta Press, 1983.

Williams, Raymond Brady. *Religions of Immigrants from India and Pakistan: New Threads in the American Tapestry.* Cambridge, Eng.: Cambridge University Press, 1988.

Chapter 10

Regional Religion: A Case Study of Religion in Southern Appalachia

Inland from the Atlantic Ocean a mountain range runs in a belt from Newfoundland to Alabama. The southern part of the chain forms a discrete area containing all of the present state of West Virginia, eastern Kentucky and Tennessee, northeastern Alabama, western Maryland, Virginia, North and South Carolina, and northern Georgia. Here geography scorns the fiction of state boundaries, and the region stands in contrast to the lowlands to either side. Southern Appalachia, as it is called, looks toward the east from its sharply rising Blue Ridge chain, its steep escarpment even now a challenge to hardy motorists on twisting mountain roads. Beyond the Blue Ridge is the central district of the Great Valley, extending from north to south with its fertile farmland. Then to the west stands the more horizontal mountain area called the Cumberland Plateau.

In ages past Indian peoples, especially the Cherokee, used these lands as hunting grounds, and the difficulty of entering the region from the east insured that European immigrants for many years regarded the mountains as a natural boundary to their settlements. But by 1750 whites had discovered the Cumberland Gap, a passage carved by nature into the rock near the place where Virginia, Kentucky, and Tennessee now meet. Twenty years later there were white settlers in the land to the south of the Ohio River in Kentucky, and in 1775 the future of western settlement was assured when Daniel Boone (1734–1820) cut the Wilderness Road southwest from the Shenandoah Valley, west across the Appalachians, through the gap, and into Kentucky. The Wilderness Road and, after 1818, the Cumberland Turnpike brought more and more settlers to the New West beyond the mountains. Yet, even as many headed farther west, others chose to remain in the highlands.

The General Study
of Regional Religion

As the years passed and especially after the Civil War, those who remained in the mountains developed a distinctive religion and culture. This religion and culture shared many ingredients from the more general religiocultural synthesis of the nation, but it combined these ingredients in its own way and also added others. We call this synthesis a regional religion, just one among many such regional religions that can be found in various places throughout the United States.

Hence, as this description already hints, a regional religion is shaped by people who live together in a certain geographic area. It is born of natural geography, of past and present human history, and of the interaction of the two. In such regionalism, the common landscape becomes not just an external condition but also an internal influence, transforming the way people view both ultimate and everyday reality. In other words, religion in some measure becomes a function of the spatial location of people and the history of that spatial location *together*. By their physical closeness, humans begin to interact subtly with one another so that they create a particular and regional response to life. Often the geographic closeness is supplemented and supported by similar backgrounds in nationality and in organized religion. Such factors are important agents in strengthening the geographic bond, but regional religion becomes through the blending of all these elements just that — regional.

Moreover, the image of "region" — apart, distinctive, drawn inward — already suggests the role of regional religion in a total cultural system that exhibits both expansion and contraction. Regionalism is, indeed, one response to cultural complexity. In the face of growing pluralism in America, particularly from the late nineteenth century, one response was to "contract." The confusion (for some) of too much manyness, the seeming excesses of the culture of expansion with its new peoples and religions, and the preference by many for the old and the familiar all helped to shape the various regionalisms that developed. In other words, regional religions were not simply responses to contained local situations with their accidental meetings of place, people, and history. Rather, they were also responses to what was happening outside local boundaries or, better, to a fear of boundary-less situations. In short, every religious "inside" had an "outside"; every region, its much larger cultural backdrop. The religious response of regionalism was systemic, and it represented one side in a pattern that included both expansion and contraction.

In this reading, however, the boundaries of "regions" are not necessarily the same as the boundaries of states or cities. Despite the presence of external conditioning factors, regional boundaries follow the natural contours of the land and/or the settlement patterns of people. Besides, insofar as any region is distinct and possesses a separate identity, its ordinary religion, which directs people in everyday life, gives its character to extraordinary religion and changes it in some ways. Finally, "regions" are not simply scarce corners of the United States or any country. They are literally everywhere. And while the number of regions is not infinite, there are far more such regions than at first we may think. To name but a few, we can point to the Hispanic Southwest; to different Native American reservations; to various immigrant sections in large cities (Chinatowns, "Little Italys"); to the North Country of the Dakotas and Minnesota; to Amish country in Pennsylvania, Ohio, and other states; to the Ozarks; to the Deep South; and to the Creole lands of Louisiana. Thus, the sense of cultural "sameness" that we tend to have is to some extent a habit of mind that results from allowing certain sections of the country to set the pace for others — or from focusing on the culture of expansion to the neglect of the culture of contraction.

The Region of Southern Appalachia

As was the case with American Indian cultures, it would be impossible in one chapter to discuss the religions of numerous regions in the United States. Therefore, we focus on just one of the many areas that can be studied, making that area a case study for the concept of regional religion. Our region, Southern Appalachia, is a good one for the purpose. Its separate identity is marked and striking, shaped by its physical boundaries and relative isolation from the rest of the country. Moreover, Americans outside the area early noticed Southern Appalachia as distinctive. When George Tucker's *Valley of the Shenandoah* was published in 1824, it spoke for an emerging awareness of the mountain people as an identifiable group. The sense of separate identity was shared by Southern Appalachians, too, and by 1834 the autobiography of David Crockett (1786–1836) was capitalizing on the frontier mystique of the mountain people. While this sense of difference may lead us to stereotype Southern Appalachians or to dismiss them as a case apart, it may also help us to see clearly what a regional religion is, how it functions, and how it illustrates cultural contraction.

In addition to offering a clear regional identity, Southern Appalachia also offers a chance to study religion with a strong traditional orientation in which both ordinary and extraordinary values are blended. It provides an explicit instance of how regionalism supplies an overarching frame within which religion and culture come together. Even further, Southern Appalachia gives us a chance to study transition in regional religion. Changes and transformations affect any regional religion, not just in the present but continually. In the case of twentieth-century Southern Appalachia, the changes are striking and sometimes dramatic as the culture of contraction for a time takes stronger hold. By standing out so distinctly from their background, the changes help us to follow more closely one pattern of contraction in the culture.

The Manyness of Religions in America

The Origins of the Mountain People

The earliest inhabitants of the highlands were Indian peoples, who gradually yielded their territory before Euro-American settlers. Sometimes they remained on the edges of white settlements for many years. In the culture that came about, traces of their influence could be seen, for example, in folklore and in the healing arts. But for the most part, the regional inhabitants of Southern Appalachia came from European stock.

First, some of their ancestors were English, part of the many who had left to seek their fortunes in the colonies. Second, many of their ancestors were Ulster Scotch, or Scotch-Irish from the north of Ireland. By 1714 the Scotch-Irish were leaving northern Ireland in significant numbers, and their immigration was extensive up to the time of the American Revolution. Even before 1750, there were probably about 100,000 Scotch-Irish in the colonies, settling especially in the Pennsylvania area. Third, others among their ancestors were German, some from the southwestern section of that country but many from the area called the Palatinate around the upper waters of the Rhine River. Mostly farmers, these Germans had been hard pressed by religious wars in the sixteenth and seventeenth centuries. Later their farmlands were laid waste by the invading generals of King Louis XIV of France. So began a migration to England and the English colonies in America, and after 1710 that migration had become rapid and large.

The first pale of settlement for all of these immigrants was the eastern colonies. Some established households in eastern and central Pennsylvania. Others moved southward to the Carolina Piedmont, extending toward the Atlantic coast from the Blue Ridge. A third group made their way to western Pennsylvania and settled in the region around what is now Pittsburgh. As these three areas of population grew denser, Southern Appalachia was still from the point of view of Euro-Americans a wilderness. Sometimes visited by hunters and traders, it was not yet a place that whites could call home.

When the picture gradually began to change after 1770, the valleys of the Southern Appalachian highlands were the first areas to be settled, and poor but ambitious farmers from the Piedmont began the immigration. By 1772 scattered settlements in country that later became part of eastern Tennessee formed the Watauga Association to administer local affairs and to protect against Indian attack. In the beginning many of the immigrants to the mountains were Scotch-Irish, supplemented by others who were English and some who were German. But after 1790, Scotch-Irish and German immigration began to slacken, while English settlers formed a more important element in the population. By 1850 Southern Appalachia had probably 1.6 million people within its boundaries. As we have noted, its culture already possessed a sharp and distinctive regional flavor. From now on, no more migration passed through the region toward the West, for roads had become better elsewhere. Southern Appalachia became physically a place apart.

The religious background of the new mountain settlers could be described as left-wing Protestantism. Like many English settlers in the colonies, the English who came to Southern Appalachia were Nonconformists; that is, they were dissenters from the Church of England, part of the Puritan movement that resulted in Separatist and non-Separatist wings and issued in various Congregational and Presbyterian forms of church government. At the same time, the Scotch-Irish were Presbyterians, followers of the religious revolution that John Knox began in the church of Scotland. The Calvinism of both English and Scotch-Irish settlers was shared by many Germans who were members of the Reformed church. Other Germans were Lutherans and Moravians (Pietists from a Lutheran background), but many followed more radical sects such as the Dunkers and the Mennonites. The Mennonites were a group that arose in the sixteenth century as part of the Radical Reformation, the distinctive religious movement that, as we have already seen, thought that Lutheranism and Calvinism had not gone far enough. Meanwhile, the Dunkers, or Brethren, were a Baptist sect that arose in 1708 out of the Pietist movement in Germany. Practicing baptism by triple immersion and foot washing, the Dunkers were to leave a strong imprint on the emerging religion of the Southern Appalachian mountain people.

The Growth of the Mountain Tradition

Since this religion was regional, we take a closer look at the economic and social life of the Southern Appalachian region. From the beginning, agriculture was key. Mountain people eked out their livings on small and "perpendicular" farms set against steep hillsides. Those who could plant the rich bottomland prospered, but most engaged in subsistence farming on mountain slopes that developed gullies from the rain and suffered from continual erosion and soil depletion. Here corn became the chief crop and the staple of mountain life and diet. It was fed to hogs, which became the major source of animal protein, and it supplied the grain for corn bread and corn whiskey.

Later, forestry and mining became important industries. The region was invaded by a new corporate management class, representatives of "foreign" companies (from other sections of the United States), which harvested wood and extracted coal from the land. Generally, the inhabitants of Southern Appalachia did not profit from these industries. Many signed away mineral rights to their lands without realizing the wealth that they were handing over. Others provided a pool of cheap labor for industries that found their markets elsewhere. Finally, by the middle of the twentieth century, manufacturing became an important industry in the region, once again begun largely by outsiders and employing local people as a ready labor supply to produce goods that usually ended elsewhere.

Thus, from the nineteenth century there was a class system in Southern Appalachian society. Most numerous in the early times were rural dwellers, many of them inhabitants of the hollows formed by nature between the slopes of the mountains. Here, alongside creeks, they built their homesteads and farmed the land. At the entrance to each hollow, where the road into the nearest town passed, there would often be a more prosperous homesteader, perhaps with a small general store and, after the arrival of the automobile, a gasoline pump. At least in the twentieth century, the owner of the general store sometimes owned all or much of the land in the hollow and rented it, with its ramshackle dwellings, to people who were thus tenant farmers.

In addition to these rural mountaineers, a second group of Southern Appalachians formed the commercial and professional classes in the towns. Generally located in the county seats, these townspeople fostered their own variant of Southern Appalachian regionalism and provided centers where rural people could come for goods and services. Finally, as we have already noted, a third group dwelled in Southern Appalachia: the "foreigners," emissaries of industries from outside the region, composed the smallest but wealthiest and most powerful segment of the population. Yet their designation by other Appalachians as foreign suggests that they did not contribute very significantly to the religiocultural ethos of the majority in the area. Our study will take its cue from the population. We will stress the regional religion of rural Appalachians and, when it seems important, look at the variant culture developed by the townspeople.

Among the mountain people, social organization was marked, paradoxically, by both intimacy and isolation. Kinship was the bond of unity, and often most of the residents of any mountain hollow were related to one another. The mountains provided a huge, outdoor mansion, where members of the extended family could be close to and yet far from their relatives. At certain times they would come together—as members of the same church or to help at barn raisings, corn huskings, or quilting bees. At other times they visited one another, and their visits were the cornerstone of social activity in the area.

Yet kinship communities allowed for a huge degree of independence and isolation. Individualism thrived in the mountain fastnesses, and so was born the mixture of pride, stubbornness, and sensitivity to criticism for which mountain people became known. Their rugged life-style offered few opportunities for "getting ahead" in the sense of the American middle class. Education had to fit around the more pressing demands of a rural household and, when it was available, was usually conducted in one-room church-schoolhouses, which were often ill equipped. A steady diet of salt pork, soup beans, and corn bread—much of it fried in heavy grease—often led to poor health. Dyspepsia (indigestion), which foreign travelers in the United States had reported as the national disease in the nineteenth century, continued into the twentieth as the regional complaint of

One-Room Schoolhouse and Church, Floyd County, Kentucky, 1966. Country schoolhouses such as this one often doubled as places for Sunday church services and vacation Bible schools. Outhouse (left rear) and well (right) were typical. The church (facing page), even with its simple wooden construction, is more elaborate than many rural churches.

Southern Appalachia. A system of outhouses and dug wells presented a constant danger of infection.

Mountain Character and Mountain Religion

Within this environment, mountain people regarded themselves and others in distinctive ways. They developed characteristic attitudes toward nature and, beyond it, the supernatural world of their religious heritage. Mountain character was formed of the intersection of traits by means of which Southern Appalachians approached and organized their lives. Although not every dweller in the hills possessed every trait, so many of them came together in the people of the region that it seems fair to call the distinct sets of traits and attitudes the "mountain character." Early a part of the Southern Appalachian heritage, these traits and attitudes continued to thrive into the twentieth century and still are strong today.

Marked by traditional habits of mind, mountain character formed the basis for ordinary religion in the hills. Like many other Americans, mountain people were sometimes mystics and dreamers. Unlike many others, the quality of their landscape led them to foster these traits. Thus, ordinary religion among Southern Appalachians grew out of their temperament and their landscape, the one supporting the other.

For many, perhaps most, who lived in the mountains, nature was a sanctuary, and spiritual power could be found there. People grew up with a sense that they belonged to the mountains, even more to their particular mountain hollow with its creek bed and its walls rising like boundaries between sacred and profane worlds. If they were forced to leave, for example, by economic necessity, they did so with great difficulty. In their new homes, usually in northern cities, they often had trouble coping with the alien character of city life, and at every opportunity, they returned home to visit the hills and their kin. Indeed, by the middle of the twentieth century, many would commute to jobs in Michigan or Ohio, returning on weekends to the mountains. Hence, the relationship of mountain people to their landscape was close. In an expression of the culture of contraction, the hills had become necessary in a spiritual and emotional sense to their survival.

Nature became the center that directed or oriented the lives of mountaineers. Like Native Americans and like followers of various Eastern religions, they bowed to its power, believing that they could have only what nature might grant them. Life, for mountain people, must conform to the patterns nature set. So mountain time was slow and rhythmic, running with the pulse of nature. It was the time of the present, in which people dwelled within the moment, not looking to the future and turning to the past only to support the way the present was lived. For mountaineers, it was the time of *being* more than the time of *doing*. In the twentieth century, it was not unusual to find mountain people at midday sitting in the shade of their front porches, rocking and looking at the landscape, seemingly forgetful of their problems.

Similarly, for mountain people space was natural. It was the space of the particular, not of the abstract. It was the specific place where concrete events occurred and concrete persons or objects were prized. Removed from the throwaway culture of the American mainstream, the traditional mountain person held onto things, as though to gain a new tool was to lose an old friend. As did Native American culture, mountain life fostered regard for material places and objects, giving them a sacramental quality.

Yet unlike Indian peoples, mountaineers viewed nature in the shadow of a supernatural world. If mountain people thought they belonged to the hills, they also thought they belonged to a God beyond nature. Their basic Calvinism taught them that they were subject to him, even as they felt subject to the power of nature. In the mountain view of things, there was some space for free will, but overwhelmingly God controlled the basic lot of people. In this view, destiny had been plotted by the divine will from eternity, and just as a person should live in harmony with nature, so he or she should also conform to the designs of God. Through acceptance and resignation to God's will, mountaineers implicitly believed, a person would become the ally of the power and order that ruled the universe. In this way of thinking, the only freedom was freedom to affirm the basic constitution of the world. Thus, prayer, for mountain people, was not a plea for earthly benefits. Rather, it was an attempt to move into a condition in which a person was thought to yield freely to God. Mountain belief held that God's way was the right way. By living in conformity with it as defined, salvation was held to be assured, and peace in this life was believed to be obtained.

As a counterpoint to this theme of acceptance, however, the mountain relationship with the supernatural world was one of passion and drama. In the mountains, the way to God led through crisis and trouble. Mountain people believed they were here on earth to make a decision — for this world or for the next one, for sin and personal ease or for their immortal souls and God. So the center of the mountain form of extraordinary religion was the crisis moment of conversion when, for believers, an intimate and enduring attachment to the person of Jesus Christ was begun. Here there was little interest in day-by-day development of religious knowledge through a program of education. Instead, for this way of thinking, the power of God entered a person's life all at once, generating an excitement that made the extraordinary stand out sharply against the background of everyday existence. The "thisworldliness" of nature was juxtaposed by mountain people to an otherworldliness based on the conviction that their real life was lived elsewhere.

Mountain character established a way to relate to nature and to what was held to be supernatural, but it also charted human relationships. Once again, a sense of belonging and being "at home" with people was primary. So mountaineers turned to others as blood kin or personal friends. Independent though they proclaimed themselves, emotionally they depended on one another. Indeed, just as mountaineers felt subject to nature and to God, they were also subject to one another. There was little group leadership and community organization, seemingly because to stand out of the crowd in a position of leadership would threaten the basic structure of dependence within each person. No one could lead, because to lead meant to break away and set the pace for others. Similarly, a rupture in the bond of relationship could bring sudden violence, and in earlier times the region was known for its blood feuds and personal vigilante style of justice. Thus, the stolid face of a mountain person was often masking passion.

In the mountains, a stranger was someone from the next county, and a foreigner was a person from outside the region. Every exchange, whether business or pleasure, depended on the quality of relationship between persons. In traditional mountain culture, it was more important to establish the right relationship between persons than to attend to things. Moreover, that right relationship involved a history of other relationships. It was important to know the family of a new friend, and it was important to have had dealings with one or another of the kin. It was necessary to know where a person lived and to be able to say something about the neighbors. The world made sense only if it was familiarized and humanized: to be a stranger in the mountains was to be invisible.

Among the relatives and neighbors who inhabited this close-knit world, there was a definite sense of place and role. People were divided by sex and by age. Men and women lived in socially separate worlds in which deep feelings were not often shared with each other. Traditional churches, in fact, were a graphic reminder of the structure of society in Southern Appalachia. It was customary for men to sit on one side and women on the other. And except for unusual circumstances, such as a conviction of inspiration by the Holy Ghost, women customarily remained silent, allowing men to run affairs and make decisions in the congregation.

Likewise, in running a family farm, men and women had separate cultural assignments. If women were silent in church, in the home they ruled and ordered things. Meanwhile, men conducted the practical affairs of the farm, responsible for animals and crops except in times of special need, when the women might be recruited to help. In young manhood, husbands spoke with the voice of authority, especially as they managed the family's dealings with the world. Yet old age turned the tables, and if a woman lived to be a grandmother, she became powerful. In a world in which childbearing frequently made women old at twenty, those who reached their sixties were venerated. Their healing abilities with herbs or with more occult medicine were often sought by their neighbors, and they freely gave advice to younger people who asked it.

Underlying the network of interpersonal relationships that formed society in the mountains was a basic suspicion of human nature that mountain people shared. They considered human beings powerless and, still more, evil without God. Human life, they believed, was flawed; only the grace of God could heal and redeem it. If a person could trust only relatives and close neighbors, then to be saved meant to become part of the family of God, living in a defined relationship with him. Yet for mountaineers, although the lifeline of grace changed nature, there could be weakness and backsliding still. So, in a culture of paradox, mountaineers belonged to the hills, to God, and to kin, all the while considering each of these relationships precarious. In mountain life, there was always the possibility of violent change.

Organized Religion in the Mountains

The paradoxical structure of mountain character provided the base from which more specific religious beliefs and action sprang. Mountain character, forged in the community regional, expressed its perspective in a distinct religious system that was Protestant Christianity. We look now at the history of Protestantism in Southern Appalachia, and we see it as expressive of the religious culture of contraction.

As the first settlers, many of them Scotch-Irish, trickled into the mountains, they brought with them a Presbyterian era in mountain religion. As in the rest of the country in the era of the American Revolution, probably fewer than 10 percent of the people were formally church members; in the mountains most of those were Presbyterian Calvinists. The Germans did have their own churches, but they formed a minority, and, as we have noted, organized religion itself was a minority phenomenon. To some extent, this would continue to be true as the years passed. Church membership in Southern Appalachia grew, but in the nineteenth century it grew more slowly than in the rest of the country. By the twentieth century, as we will see, Southern Appalachians would have the least official church structure of perhaps any people in the United States.

At the beginning of the nineteenth century, Southern Appalachia, like the East Coast and the New West, entered a period of religious fervor. The frontier version of the Second Great Awakening—the Great Revival—while it began farther to the west in the bluegrass region of Kentucky, came across the mountain passes. Claiming inspiration by the Spirit, preachers rose up to exhort people to seek salvation. At long sessions called "protracted meetings," held outdoors in hastily constructed camp sites, people were alternately threatened by "spiritual" preachers with the fires of hell and consoled by hymn-singing congregations with promises of the joys of heaven. Stretched in the tension between the two, they found themselves turning, with a sense of crisis, to the figure of Jesus. From now on, the episodic conversion experience became the mainstay of Southern Appalachian religion. "Getting religion" became the test of faith, a test that could be passed only by a depth of feeling that broke the monotony of everyday life as the believer sought to cross into an extraordinary world.

Thus, in an expression of a pattern that we noticed in Chapter 5, the older Presbyterian ideal of an educated ministry was supplanted by the presence of the new, "spiritual" preacher. In the mountains, the measure of a preacher's authenticity was his ability to preach without learning or preparation — and with what believers considered the power of the Spirit. His text was the Bible, which he quoted repeatedly from his own memory. Many a preacher, like many of the other descendants of the first generation, had little ability to read. And in another of the mountain paradoxes, the Bible that mountaineers cherished was often known only at second hand. Still, the Bible was of first importance. Mountain people referred to it frequently and disputed vigorously over the meaning of the text.

In this context, the Great Revival brought a sectarian spirit. Many new and Nonconformist churches arose, combining their traditional heritage with the environment of the mountains and the character of the mountaineers. First among them, Baptists took the position of importance formerly occupied by Presbyterians. After the Revolution there was an exodus of Baptists to the west as more and more English people entered the mountains. We have seen that Baptists had a long history in the colonies, beginning with Roger Williams and his foundation of Rhode Island. And, as we recall, General Baptists taught that salvation was open to all. As time passed, however, General Baptist churches, now known as Regular Baptist groups, were again teaching the Calvinist belief in the predestination of the elect and the damned. Meanwhile, Separate Baptists from New England took up the older Baptist belief that salvation was possible for all and, preaching this gospel, moved to North Carolina and Virginia. When they met with scorn and persecution, many fled to the highlands.

Thus, both General and Separate Baptists were preaching in Southern Appalachia. Later, when some members of both churches joined together, there was a further blurring of boundaries. Like Presbyterians, Baptists seemed to teach the Calvinist doctrine of predestination, but they brought to the teaching a vaguely defined sense of freedom of the will that suited the mountain spirit. Moreover, as we know, without a tradition of an educated ministry Baptist farmer-preachers spoke as they said the Holy Ghost had inspired them, spreading their religion in a way that the Presbyterians were unable or unwilling to imitate. With their sense of religious liberty and their simple gospel, they spoke to the inclinations of their mountain neighbors.

Besides the modified Calvinism of Baptist preaching and the availability of lay preachers, what drew people to the Baptists was the biblical ordinances they practiced. Following the Anabaptists of the Radical Reformation, they brought two important rituals to the people of Southern Appalachia. The first was baptism, usually in a running stream and by the process of triple immersion, once for each of the persons of the Trinity. The second was foot washing, in which the actions that the biblical Jesus had performed at the Last Supper (John 13:3–14) were imitated by the people of a congregation.

With the coming of the German Dunkers, both of these practices were found in the mountains in the first decade of settlement. But later, under the gospel of the new Baptist farmer-preachers, these practices spread throughout the region. While Southern Appalachians feared and opposed Roman Catholicism, they had unconsciously absorbed a sacramental sense not unlike that of Catholicism. Their lives in the mountains led them to a regard for nature and the material world. Now they began to find the essence of religion in the practice of those material actions that they believed would provide access to God. Protestant in their attachment to a religion of the biblical Word and individual experience, they accepted a new sacramentalism. Sometimes, too, they turned to other ordinances such as the celebration of the Lord's Supper, performed usually with crackers and wine or grape juice. Yet, perhaps because it smacked too clearly of Roman Catholicism, the communion service was not nearly so important a religious ritual among the mountain people as baptism or foot washing.

Baptist success indicated the direction in which the mountain tradition was developing. The new spirit spread even within Presbyterian ranks, bringing a sectarian movement that resulted in the formation of the Cumberland Presbytery in 1810. Later the Cumberland Presbytery split completely from the parent Presbyterian church as an independent movement. Its leaders were persuaded by English and German traditions of lay preaching in the Baptist churches. Likewise, Cumberland Presbyterians embraced a modified Calvinism and held to an emotional style of preaching. In other words, while still maintaining an institutional affiliation with Presbyterianism, the Cumberland church became an expression of the religion of the mountains.

Larger than the Cumberland Presbyterian movement was the Methodist presence in Southern Appalachia. Methodist bishop Francis Asbury was an untiring missionary to the western frontier. He and other Methodist circuit riders came to the mountains, and with the Great Revival their gospel spread. Even more than the Baptists and the Cumberland Presbyterians, the Methodists, as we have already seen, preached that salvation was available to all. Thus, their preaching of a basic equality in spiritual condition appealed to the mountaineers' love of individual autonomy. Moreover, the Methodists exalted the uneducated preacher in the person of their circuit rider. Like Baptist and Presbyterian preachers, the circuit rider was thought to speak as the Holy Ghost bid, stirring the emotions of the people who listened. Indeed, it was not unusual, as we saw in Chapter 5, for Baptist, Presbyterian, and Methodist preachers to cooperate in a camp meeting, each of them taking over one corner of a field.

Finally, as we have already seen, the "Christian" churches emerged from the context of the Great Revival on the frontier. Coming out of the Presbyterian and Baptist traditions, they preached a more radical doctrine of free grace and called people to unite in the restoration of an authentic New Testament church. As in the early church, they argued, each religious society should be autonomous, conducting its own affairs as the Bible and the Holy Ghost inspired. Thus, with their emphasis on the authority of the Bible, their democratic preference for the local congregation, and their involvement in the problem of predestination versus freedom of the will, the Christians (Disciples of Christ) again conformed in general outline to the religion of the mountains.

By means of the Great Revival, the Southern Appalachian churches increased their membership, which grew throughout the nineteenth century with Baptists and Methodists taking the lead and far surpassing the Presbyterians. By the first decade of the twentieth century, there were over 600,000 Baptists in the region and nearly 475,000 Methodists. Presbyterians numbered fewer than 95,000, while the Disciples of Christ counted almost 70,000 adherents. About 90 percent of all church members were Protestant, but in keeping with mountain habit, the number of church members out of the total population was roughly one-third.

Meanwhile, the nineteenth-century history of Protestantism in Southern Appalachia was a continued saga of sectarianism. Among the Baptists after 1820, the antimission movement attacked the interest in missions that, as we saw in Chapter 5, characterized mainline Baptists along with other Protestant denominations. For Appalachian Antimission Baptists, missionary societies strengthened central control within a denomination, violating the free spirit of the New Testament — and the mountains. God, they thought, had his own independent means to save those whom he had chosen, and human efforts to preach missions were useless. They considered the education of preachers wrong for the same reasons, and so, too, the formation of Sunday schools.

Antimission Baptists became a formidable movement, almost a third as large as the Missionary Baptists and mostly concentrated in the mountains of Southern Appalachia. More than 68,000 strong by the late 1840s, they belonged to various associations, each with a confession of faith printed with the minutes of the annual meeting of the association. Among themselves, the associations exchanged programs, and fellowship was established among those whose principles were in agreement. They called themselves by various names, Primitive Baptist being the most popular, although familiar, too, were Old School, Regular, Antimission, and even Hard Shell Baptists. Still others, with an explicit doctrine of the seeds of good and evil, one of them planted in each human being from the beginning, formed the Two-Seed-in-the-Spirit Predestinarian Baptists. Although this movement began in the late eighteenth century, it flourished in the mountains in the middle of the nineteenth century. At the same time, many of the United Baptists came to share in antimission sentiments.

With the slavery question and the Civil War came an additional source of division for the churches, and agitation over these issues caused many denominations to split. In southern territory, mountain people, with their love of freedom, often found themselves supporting the northern cause. Sometimes, also, the highlands were the scene of bitter clashes between the two armies. But the legacy of the Civil War included more than memories of clashes between North and South. In the new climate of the times, the culture of contraction grew stronger in Southern Appalachia, spurred by a youthful holiness movement. As a protest against formalism in religion, holiness after 1870 gave the mountain people a further way to express the emotionalism of their religion.

Holiness taught that it was important to *feel* God, and it viewed the outward and ecstatic actions that characterized its worship as manifestations of the divine presence. It offered to mountain people a religious system that fitted Southern Appalachian temperament, in which mind, emotions, and body were all involved. With a rhythmic and singsong style of preaching, the holiness preacher, much like the African-American preacher, worked a congregation toward emotional religious expression. The message turned on the scripture and on the purity of life that must be followed in the strict holiness way. Sabbath breaking, alcohol drinking, gambling, cardplaying, and dancing were all prohibited as works of the devil, and sexual temptation was considered the chief of Satan's wiles.

Independent and autonomous like all of mountain religion, holiness flourished. After the turn of the century the pentecostal movement spread along with it, and scores of affiliated or independent pentecostal churches encouraged the experience of speaking in tongues. In the mountains as elsewhere, in small organizations like the Assemblies of God and various Churches of God, pentecostal Christians essentially accepted the holiness way but added to it the elements of tongues speaking and the other New Testament "prophetic" gifts. Furthermore, at about the same time that holiness began to spread, fundamentalism was gathering strength as a religious force. As it moved throughout the country, it found a congenial home in the mountains, where love for the Bible and commitment to its literal meaning had been strong. Thus, fundamentalism as a movement gave official sanction to what mountaineers already believed, at a time when the world beyond the mountains looked more and more threatening.

If the holiness-pentecostal movement and fundamentalism helped to strengthen the post–Civil War culture of contraction in the mountains, they were joined by nondenominational churches. These groups carried the tendencies within mountain religion to their logical conclusion, as one individual or another (usually male) became convinced that God was calling him to preach and exhort. So he would set about establishing a church of his own, often on his property, either in his house or in a separate building he might construct. Like a patron to his neighbors, he invited them to join with him in seeking the Word and will of God. Here all the characteristics of mountain religion came together: the uneducated preacher, the independent church, the primacy of the Bible, and the strong emotionalism of religious worship. The nondenominational church expressed the mountain spirit and advanced its isolationism.

Tradition and Change in the Twentieth Century

At the beginning of the twentieth century, the mountain tradition was strong. In the rural sections of the highlands, it thrived within isolated communities and an inward-turning culture. As the century progressed, the mountain tradition slowly began to decline, but still it endured stubbornly and sometimes showed signs of revival and greater strength. Even today for many the mountain tradition is unforgotten, as its values continue to shape their lives. In the towns of Southern Appalachia, however, change became evident, as more and more Appalachian churches came to resemble those of mainstream religion. We will look first at the "contractive" rural religion of the mountains and then, briefly, at the changes that have brought Southern Appalachians, especially in the towns, closer to the mainstream of American religion and culture.

The Rural Tradition

Recall that the rural tradition was one of both ordinary and extraordinary religion, often fused but also separate to some extent in mountain experience. Ordinary religion was the property of every Southern Appalachian, but especially it was the property of the unchurched. At the beginning of the century, about two-thirds of all mountaineers fell into this category, and as late as the second half of the century over half of the population still did not belong to any religious organization. It was true that, during the interim, church membership grew faster in Southern Appalachia than anywhere else in the nation. Still, the general pattern remained the same as in the past. Here were strongly religious people, seeking after not only ordinary expressions of religion but also a supernatural world. Yet Southern Appalachians did not think that baptism necessarily led into the church. In many a mountain household in eastern Kentucky and elsewhere, people would patiently explain to "foreign" visitors that they cherished the Bible but did not regularly attend a church. On the wall would be a picture of Jesus; on the table, a worn copy of the family Bible.

Ordinary Religion in Rural Appalachia

In this setting in which religion did not always mean the church, the family was the most important religious and social institution, and the church came second. While by the last third of the twentieth century, this picture was sometimes reversed, the strength of family religion was still apparent. Religious beliefs and practices were an ordinary part of living. The Bible was regularly quoted in everyday conversation and in time of trouble. If special help was needed in a crisis, it might be opened at random after a short prayer.

Similarly, particular verses of the Bible were often used by healers. The knowledge of herbs and of medicine had been handed down in many families, sometimes from as far back as the first generation in the mountains, when contact with Cherokee healing was more frequent. Beyond the herbal "root work" of both Indians and mountaineers, however, there was faith healing. The laying on of hands for healing was part of the holiness tradition. Even further, outside the churches, like Indian shamans old "grannies" and men exercised what many claimed was a mysterious ability to blow away the heat of a burn, to stop blood caused by an accident or other unnatural cause, or to cure thrush, a fungus disease that afflicted mountain children.

Often at the center of this kind of healing was the recitation of a particular verse from the Bible in a ritualistic manner. For the treatment of serious bleeding, a healer might recite Ezekiel 16:6, "And when I passed by thee, and saw thee polluted in thine own blood, I said unto thee *when thou wast* in thy blood, 'Live,'" substituting the name of the person for the "thee" of the biblical verse. Among many of the healers, there were special rules for the transmission of their knowledge, and it could be passed down only to certain individuals, perhaps two in a given healer's lifetime. Thus, the healing lore was kept secret, and at the same time it was perpetuated.

Ordinary religion thrived, too, in a series of practices connected with planting. Many sowed their crops by an intricate method based on the signs of the zodiac, justifying their efforts by reference to the biblical account of creation: "And God said, Let there be lights in the firmament of the heaven to divide the day from the night; and let them be for signs and for seasons, and for days, and years" (Gen. 1:14). Yet the appointed days and years of Genesis expressed not so much biblical religion as the harmonial religion of nature. Mountain people often followed ancient horoscopes that correlated the stars with the twelve signs of the zodiac and with corresponding parts of the human body. Based on these sources, planting calendars plotted out each month according to the zodiacal signs. First, each sign appeared at least once in a month, and then it reappeared for a two- or three-day sequence. Some of the signs were considered moist and fruitful, and these were thought best for planting. Seeds sown during "barren" times, it was believed, would result in a poor crop, and all these signs were held to be good for was trimming or destroying (weeds). Moreover, there were special rules for every crop. According to mountaineers, beans should be planted when signs were in the arms (of the human body), and potatoes when signs were in the feet. The new moon was considered a bad day for planting anything, and crops planted under the signs of Taurus and Cancer were reputed to have great ability to withstand drought.

Ordinary religion appeared again in tales of various sorts that mountaineers liked to tell. There were ghost tales and hunting tales, animal stories and snake lore. Sometimes the stories told of an almost Indian sense of kinship with animals, as in the tale of a little girl who daily fed a snake behind a barn with some of her own milk and bread. When a man followed her and discovered what she was doing, he killed the snake—and the girl died, too. Indeed, omens, dreams, and visions seemed to be everywhere in the mountains. These "signs" were for believers avenues to knowledge that supplemented the commonsense view of reality. They added to a sense of meaningfulness by building on beliefs already present.

Mountain people saw signs and heard voices when others experienced nothing. For mountaineers, a person had to curse in order to raise gourds, and he or she had to be bad tempered in order to raise healthy peppers. Many believed that if someone made a feather bed into pillows, that person would have bad luck until the pillows wore out and that if a bird included a hair from someone's head in the nest it was building, that individual's head would ache until the nest crumbled to pieces. There were cradle signs thought to bring good fortune to a newborn baby and to help foresee the future for others. A necklace of corn beads was held to help the baby to have an easy time teething, and a bullet or coin to prevent nosebleed. The creases in the baby's legs, if the same number in both, were considered a guarantee that the next child born would be a girl. The first wood tick found on the baby's body had to be killed with an ax, mountaineers said, if the child was to become a good worker. And if the child was to have a good voice for singing, the tick had to be killed on a bell or banjo.

Similarly, weather signs were used to guide human activity. Forecasters predicted the weather by counting fogs in August, by noting the color of woolly caterpillars, and by observing how close to the ground hornets made their nests. The moon was also thought to control human enterprise. Potatoes planted or pork killed in its light were both believed to come to grief. Soap had to be made at just the right time of the moon, said mountain people, and roofs had to be nailed down at the appropriate interval.

Thus, Southern Appalachians surrounded themselves with a symbolic system based, for the most part, on nature. They used the system to orient themselves in everyday life, seeking to live in harmony by performing each action at the time when they believed nature decreed it should be done. For them, as for Native Americans, adherents to Eastern religions, and Western occultists, there was a correspondence between themselves and nature. A law of resemblance was seen as directing all things. The corollary for mountaineers was that living well meant living in conformance with signs and omens. This religion was not Christian, but it ran deep; and it gave the mountain people a way to guide behavior within the ordinary world.

Extraordinary Religion in Rural Appalachia

Extraordinary religion, however, was not eclipsed by the ordinary religion of the hills. Rather, extraordinary religion flourished, and despite the multiplicity of churches, there was a basic unity in mountain religion. Like any religion, it possessed a creed, or body of beliefs, a code, or moral system for everyday behavior, and a cultus, or ritual expression of its creed and code. Finally, creed, code, and cultus were the property of a community, a group of people who, whatever their differences, identified closely with one another.

The creed of extraordinary religion in the mountains taught that life was a drama involving estrangement from God. Divine predestination and redemption were thought to control a person's destiny, although to some extent human free will entered into the script. Mountain Christians believed that in the Bible a person would find all that was necessary for salvation and that following the Word of the Bible was literally fundamental. At the same time, religion was understood as feeling deeply felt, and the human experience of conversion was prized as the beginning and end of religious life. Thus, while ordinary religion offered mountain people rules for guidance in everyday situations, Christianity in the mountains held out strong feeling as a way to get beyond the ordinary world. Ordinary religion kept people moving through the monotonous round of daily tasks and oriented them within the boundaries of their social world. Extraordinary religion jolted them out of their usual track with sudden emotion and the promise of salvation.

Likewise, the moral code of Christianity provided a new set of rules for everyday behavior. Epitomized by the holiness churches, the code was taught with more or less emphasis by every church of the mountains. It was also put into practice by many who chose not to belong to any church but lived out their religion in a family setting. This code forbade swearing and Sabbath breaking by engaging in labor on the day of rest. It exhorted against drinking, gambling, cardplaying, and dancing. It regarded sexual relationships outside of marriage as sinful.

Yet alongside the code, there was a different, more permissive ethic in the mountains — its legacy from ordinary religion. Purity of life might be the ideal, but in practice there was tolerance for a variety of actions that violated the Christian standard. A relative degree of sexual freedom did exist, and illegitimate offspring were accepted into mountain families without rebuke. "Moonshine," or corn whiskey, provided a ready cash "crop" for a hard-pressed mountain farmer. As we have already noted, an undercurrent of violence ran through mountain society, and ordinary life produced dramas as intense as the experience of conversion. In earlier times, relatives of a victim of murder or violent crime punished the criminal, and no court system prevented this vindication through feuding. By the twentieth century, when feuding days were almost a thing of the past, the automobile provided a new form of sensation seeking. Racing their cars along twisting mountain roads, young men often wrecked a car before they were twenty, bragging that they had "totaled" the automobile. Mountain preaching was silent on these forms of abuse. Rarely did a social ethic enter the usual sermon. Moral injunctions were delivered generally only against private or traditionally identified forms of vice.

But in the mountains, as elsewhere, the center of extraordinary religion lay in cultus, or ritual practice. People understood their religion in terms of what they did, especially when they were at worship. Sacred space was provided, sometimes at meetings in the brush, in cemeteries, or at baptismal streams but especially at the thousands of small churches on country roads or in mountain hollows. The congregations in the churches might number fewer than twenty, with a high proportion of women and girls. Meanwhile, many of the churches were simple, one-room frame or log buildings, and they were usually bare. There was love of simplicity here and fear that ornament of any kind might lead to distraction. Simplicity, however, did not mean formality. A typical congregation wandered into the church gradually, the members exchanging greetings with relatives and friends even though the service might already have started. Often there was kissing all around, regardless of age or sex. On hot summer days, a water dipper was freely passed, and an atmosphere of spontaneity filled the church. In the center of the building, there would be a simple stand as pulpit, while to the front on one side was the amen corner. Leading from here, a group of men lined out the verses of the hymns, while the rest of the men and the women, in the old congregations sitting separately, took up the melody.

Sacred time occurred at intervals throughout the year. Churches held a preaching once a month, and many mountain people divided up their Sundays among various churches so that, nearly every week, they could hear a rousing sermon. But there were other sacred times as well as the Sunday service. The annual baptism ceremony was a special occasion, as was the service of foot washing. In addition, there were protracted meetings (usually annually, when a revival was preached), funeral preachings (often, as among African-Americans, long after death and burial), and decoration services (to lay flowers on the graves of the dead). Like many traditional peoples, mountaineers remembered their ancestors.

Although sectarianism and argument about the meaning of the scripture flourished, in practice sermons were similar in mountain churches. With the Protestant heritage, the Word was central, and preaching accompanied every ritual from a decoration to a foot washing. Held to be called by the Holy Ghost, the preacher was not highly educated and usually boasted of the lack of formal learning. Moreover, the preacher did not command a salary from a traditional mountain congregation, for to do so would have meant working on Sunday—Sabbath breaking. Instead, like the Baptist farmer-preachers, the mountain minister worked at a regular job during the week and preached out of a belief in a calling from God. Sometimes the congregation collected a few coins to help defray expenses, but a person preached because of conviction of a divine gift.

Sermon subjects might be a combination of themes, including Old Testament stories, autobiographical anecdotes by the preacher, and exhortations to personal holiness. Above all, though, the preacher offered a message of sin and salvation, of death and judgment, and of the eternal mercy of God. Sermon style, as we already noticed, resembled African-American preaching. The preacher worked up to a rhythmic chant, pacing back and forth and then rocking forward and backward to do what was called "driving." The listening congregation began to sway forward and backward to the rhythm of the chant, and as they did so, they started to moan, wail, then shriek and shout. There was a call-and-response pattern to the process, a complex ritual exchange. If the preacher could not get into stride or if the people did not respond, the sermon had failed in the eyes of all.

Hymn singing complemented the preacher's efforts. Many of the hymns that Southern Appalachian churchpeople sang were descended from the eighteenth century, some of them composed by such well-known English hymn writers as Isaac Watts (1674–1748) and John Newton (1725–1807). The Anglo-Saxon chant lines of these songs, based on modal scales from British oral tradition, were reminiscent of Roman Catholic Gregorian chant. Their texture was otherworldly, and their words reinforced the music. Often the theme was heaven or divine grace, the fear of damnation or humility before an all-powerful God. Sometimes, too, there were newer gospel hymns that carried the sound of the later country music of the mountains. These were livelier in tempo, and their words were often highly sentimental in a late-nineteenth-century style. Both kinds of hymns were sung in unison, and both were integral to the worship service.

A typical service included hymns and prayers offered spontaneously by the preacher or members of the congregation and, whatever the sequence, was climaxed by the sermon. At the end of the sermon came an altar call, when troubled persons could arise and come forward. With the support of the congregation, they attempted to pray through to what they felt was conversion. Many churches, too, interspersed their services with times when people could "witness"—either to the trouble they had endured, the healing they were seeking, or the manifestations of God's grace that they believed had come into their lives. Then at the end of the service, in a ritual expression of community, the right hand of fellowship was extended.

Among holiness churches, emotional expression was even stronger and the ritual more elaborate. Holiness services were held several times a week, with the length of a typical meeting about two and one-half to three hours. In these settings, self-disclosure by members of the congregation was carried still further than in the other churches. People spoke and witnessed; they prayed together and laid hands on one another for healing; they walked to the altar where, often when the preacher stretched out his hand to touch them, they felt that they were "slain" by the power of the Holy Ghost and fell in a trancelike state at his feet. Some holiness people who were pentecostal experienced speaking in tongues. Others, in holiness fire-handling churches, placed their hands in flame without, they said, being scorched or blistered. Still others, in snake-handling churches, danced with serpents and swallowed strychnine or lye and water, claiming no harm.

The origins of fire handling are unknown, but snake handling began in 1909 in Tennessee. It spread to six states in the mountain area, although it was illegal in all but West Virginia. Following a literal reading of Mark 16:18, "They shall take up serpents; and if they drink any deadly thing, it shall not hurt them," snake handlers acted according to their faith and saw their ritual as a gospel sign. They were a small minority among the mountain congregations, but their ritual expressed how strong their yearning for extraordinary religious experience was: they were willing to endure pain and even death in order to gain a sense of God in their lives.

Like baptism and foot washing, fire and snake handling were considered ordinances, performed because mountaineers believed that the biblical God had so commanded. But like baptism and foot washing, they were also sacraments, actions that signified divine power and by means of the sign were thought to make the power present. Surrounded by nature, mountaineers had in fire and serpents natural elements that led them to supernatural faith. In the ritual setting, they felt empowered, so that they experienced a measure of control over nature and the forces that seemed to dictate the course of their lives.

There was no doubt a connection between the poverty of numerous twentieth-century Southern Appalachians and the experience of these holiness believers. Many of the mountain people had felt control of their lives slip away, the prey of foreign corporations and economic depression. In the churches, these ordinary problems had been transformed to become the raw material of spiritual experience. Moreover, for mountain people, extraordinary religion should be clearly marked. If a person was to make contact with a divine world beyond the borders of this one, that contact should express itself in a manner that was strong and dramatic. So some of the Southern Appalachian people handled fire, and others handled serpents — not unlike other spiritual devotees from different religions in the world. Whatever the path that mountain people chose, the goal was simple: Appalachians wanted what they felt was the presence of God.

Still further, as the discussion already suggests, through their acts of extraordinary religion — as through their practice of ordinary religion — Southern Appalachians situated themselves with reference to the larger cultural system in the United States. After the Civil War and especially in the twentieth century, they became increasingly aware of an external world that impinged on their own. The pluralist, expansionist culture that surrounded them and often wielded economic and political power over them provoked envy and anxiety. In the major form of response we have looked at here, Southern Appalachians reinforced patterns of isolation already present. Typically, mountain people met change with what might be called religious retreat and consolidation. They used tradition to fortify what, even before the Civil War, they had begun to create: a religious world apart. This separate religious world provided relief in the face of new forces they could not control. It also gave to their lives the contemplative cast that is often associated with religious "retreats."

In sum, the contractive power of religion was evident in the late-nineteenth-century and twentieth-century Southern Appalachian experience. The contractive power was expressed through religious ritual that, in both extraordinary and ordinary forms, used signs and symbols to bring a sense of empowerment through separation. Southern Appalachian religion provided the safety that mountain people sought through the presence of a trusted community. This sense of safety made possible the (often ecstatic) practices of extraordinary religion. Further, it "fed" itself, encouraging still more social contact in which patterns of small-group intimacy could be reinforced.

Changing Conditions and Religion in the Towns

We have been viewing the rural Southern Appalachian tradition as a distinct religious system with an identity separate from that of the rest of America, an identity expressed in a religion of contraction. In this context, it is important to notice that some of what has been described as mountain religion was going on outside the highlands, too. We have compared Appalachians at various points to African-Americans and to Western occultists, to Native Americans, Catholics, mainline Protestants, and followers of Eastern religions. What made Southern Appalachian religion regional was not so much the presence of unique elements as the way the elements were combined to form a contractive religious system and the way that the system expressed the experience of life within the mountains and with one another.

But even within the area in which the regional religion of Southern Appalachia flourished, there were other expressions of religion and, as the twentieth century progressed, increasing signs of change. In one such sign, Roman Catholicism maintained a small but growing presence in the mountains from the time that it arrived in the nineteenth century, mostly with the "foreign" element who controlled the economic order. By the second half of the twentieth century, Catholics made up the fourth largest organized religious body in the mountains, ranking after Baptists, Methodists, and Presbyterians. Their presence was still small, especially when compared with the large Baptist population, but in the sixties Catholicism became vocal and visible. Moving away from its position as the church of a managerial elite, it aimed to apply the social teaching of modern popes and to work for what it saw as social justice and the alleviation of poverty.

Meanwhile, as cities multiplied and towns enlarged in the region, more and more urban Protestant churches were similar to those in other parts of the nation. They tended to be conservative — and in that sense still expressed the religion of contraction — but they also tended toward mainstream and middle-class decorum. Their affiliations were with denominations of major importance, so that Southern Baptists, United Methodists, and mainline Presbyterians built substantial edifices, different from the one-room frame structures of the open country. In another sign of change, there tended to be proportionately more church members in the towns than in rural areas, again coming closer to national trends. Social scientists who conducted studies of religious beliefs and attitudes found fundamentalist and otherworldly views declining, general community participation increasing, and the level of education among ministers rising. Churches were becoming more prosperous, and people — while they sometimes expressed the old adherence to a simple way of living — were becoming more interested in gaining material success.

For twenty years, from about 1940 to 1960, the quest for economic prosperity led to a huge out-migration from the area. But in the late sixties and continuing into the seventies, the developing energy crisis brought new employment, as demand for coal to supplement dwindling oil supplies grew. Out-migration became in-migration, and more people began to move into the mountains than to leave. In this setting, the traditional churches still flourished. Although there were signs of confusion in values, the old order provided a framework for the lives of many. Rural religious practices survived, while there were pockets of tradition even in the larger cities.

Even today, a requiem for Southern Appalachian religion would be premature. Exhibiting a pattern of contraction in the presence of fast-paced change, Southern Appalachian religion, despite its diminished existence, may in one sense be the most "American" religion in the nation. Traditionalist Southern Appalachians have held onto a cultural past that reflects an earlier America, and they have wielded that past as a tool to deal with the present. With their stress on the Bible, on preaching the Word, and on experiencing it in a free and democratic congregational setting, mountain people have throughout their history echoed historic mainstream Protestantism.

For all the mountain idealization of the past, however, other characteristics of mountain belief and practice are allied with present-day American religion. The Appalachian preference for crisis leading to a moment of conversion reflects a habit of mind that, as we will see, has remained part of the dominant center of American religion. Appalachian accommodation of paradox likewise continues to be a familiar American cultural trait. And when change came in the twentieth century, even among Appalachian traditionalists, it brought religion in the mountains closer to the religion of the American mainstream. Thus, in the new churches of Appalachian towns and cities were the signs of what we call the one religion of Americans, the religion that we will explore in Part II. And even in the mountain hollows, there were also signs of this one religion.

In Overview

Our study has focused on religion in Southern Appalachia as one example — a case study — of regional religion in the United States. Looking at one instance of how geographical closeness, common histories, and the presence of increasing cultural complexity create a distinctive and contractive response can give us some idea of how the process works in other areas, of how spatial boundaries emphasize religious difference. In the case of Southern Appalachia, Native Americans were supplanted by Euro-American settlers, mostly English, Scotch-Irish, and German. Living together in the mountains, they developed a distinctive "mountain character." Respect for nature was key, but mountaineers always saw beyond nature the controlling power of a supernatural world. Meanwhile, they emphasized ties of kinship and friendship they developed over the years.

With this background, organized and extraordinary religion was mostly Protestant and, in large measure, Calvinist. Fed by the revivals, a sectarian spirit grew among the mountaineers, yet there was much that the different sects held in common even as they disputed. The mountain creed taught predestination as well as the importance of the Bible and of strong feeling in religion. The mountain code stressed personal holiness and yet, influenced by ordinary religion in the mountains, could be permissive regarding human weaknesses. The mountain cultus expressed the centrality of preaching and the significance of ordinances such as baptism and foot washing.

Ordinary religion was pervasive in the hills, where many of the people were unchurched. The bible was quoted and used for divination, healers were thought to possess occult powers, planting took place according to the astrological signs, and natural coincidences were viewed as predictions of human destiny. Especially after the Civil War and through the early and middle years of the twentieth century, this pattern of ordinary and extraordinary crystallized into a religion of contraction, of turning inward in a response that emphasized separation. The horizon of pluralism in a religiously expansionist America signaled changes that many in the mountains hoped to avoid. As changes began to come to Appalachia, however, its religion—already a reflection of historic American Protestantism—became more and more like the contemporary "one religion" of America.

And this was in at least one way typical. For if there was a "one religion" in America, by the late twentieth century it existed not merely in the hypothetical "mainstream" center. Its traces could also be found in less obvious places. It mingled, moreover, with other patterns of expansion and contraction within the culture. At the end of the eighties, the mountain culture of contraction was paralleled by the contractive religion of a strong conservative Protestantism outside the hills. Meanwhile, the religion of expansion flourished and preached a dawning of the New Age.

SUGGESTIONS FOR FURTHER READING: SOUTHERN APPALACHIAN RELIGION

Campbell, John C. *The Southern Highlander and His Homeland.* 1921. Reprint. Lexington: University Press of Kentucky, 1969.

Crabtree, Lou V. *Sweet Hollow.* Baton Rouge: Louisiana State University Press, 1984.

Cunningham, Rodger. *Apples on the Flood: The Southern Mountain Experience.* Knoxville: University of Tennessee Press, 1987.

Dickinson, Eleanor, and Benziger, Barbara. *Revival!* New York: Harper & Row, 1974.

Dorgan, Howard. *The Old Regular Baptists of Central Appalachia: Brothers and Sisters in Hope.* Knoxville: University of Tennessee Press, 1989.

Ford, Thomas R., ed. *The Southern Appalachian Region: A Survey.* Lexington: University of Kentucky Press, 1962.

Gillespie, Paul F., ed. *Foxfire 7.* Garden City, NY: Doubleday, Anchor Books, 1982.

Hooker, Elizabeth R. *Religion in the Highlands.* New York: Home Missions Council, 1933.

Miles, Emma Bell. *The Spirit of the Mountains.* 1905. Reprint. Knoxville: University of Tennessee Press, 1975.

Montell, William Lynwood. *Ghosts along the Cumberland: Deathlore in the Kentucky Foothills.* Knoxville: University of Tennessee Press, 1975.

Photiadis, John D., ed. *Religion in Appalachia: Theological, Social, and Psychological Dimensions and Correlates.* Morgantown: West Virginia University, Center for Extension and Continuing Education, 1978.

Shapiro, Henry D. *Appalachia on Our Mind: The Southern Mountains and Mountaineers in the American Consciousness, 1870–1920.* Chapel Hill: University of North Carolina Press, 1978.

Stephenson, John B. *Shiloh: A Mountain Community.* Lexington: University of Kentucky Press, 1968.

Weller, Jack E. *Yesterday's People: Life in Contemporary Appalachia.* Lexington: University of Kentucky Press, 1965.

Wigginton, Eliot, ed. *The Foxfire Book.* Garden City, NY: Doubleday, Anchor Books, 1972.

———. *Foxfire 2.* Garden City, NY: Doubleday, Anchor Books, 1973.

Chapter 11

Fundamentals of the New Age: An Epilogue on Present-Day Pluralism

Helen Cohn Schucman (1909–1981) grew up in New York City in a family of Jewish ancestry. Her father neither believed nor observed his religion during her childhood, and her mother, the daughter of an English rabbi, at one point explained to the child that she was a Theosophist but was still "searching." Schucman's English governess was a Roman Catholic who prayed the rosary in the child's presence and attended Mass while her charge sat in the hall outside waiting. Like her mother, Schucman herself became a seeker. She wore a Catholic medal, received a Protestant evangelical baptism, and claimed mystical experience during a subway ride. But she fought with her attraction to religion and at the time of her subway experience regarded herself as an atheist. By 1957 she had earned a doctoral degree in psychology, and she subsequently assumed positions as a psychologist at Presbyterian Hospital in New York and as an associate professor of medical psychology at Columbia University's College of Physicians and Surgeons.

In 1965 a stormy relationship with William Thetford, director of Presbyterian Hospital's Psychology Department and Schucman's colleague in medical psychology at Columbia, led to a startling sequence of events. Encouraged by Thetford, who wanted to improve their tense relationship, Schucman began to work with a series of dream images and symbols. According to her own account, she also began to hear an inner voice that grew more and more insistent. "This is a course in miracles," she reported that it kept saying. "Please take notes." Schucman told that she yielded, and from 1965 to 1973 she wrote what became nearly 1,200 pages of material.

When it was published in 1976, A Course in Miracles consisted of a text, a workbook, and a manual for teachers. It announced itself, in its introduction, a "required course," with only the particular time a person took it being "voluntary." It told, too, that it did not aim to teach "the meaning of love" but to remove "blocks to the awareness of love's presence." Dissolving such blocks meant, for the *Course*, forgiveness of self and others, and it meant the foundation for miracles. "Nothing real can be threatened," the text asserted. "Nothing unreal exists." Throughout, the *Course* acknowledged God as Father and Creator, the Holy Spirit, and a "Son of God" identified with the voice that dictated the *Course*. By the late eighties, the work had sold 500,000 copies, and groups of individuals who used it had sprung up across the United States. Called a contemporary form of Christian Science, a restatement of the New Testament, and a Christianized Vedanta, the *Course* eclipsed its genesis in Schucman's life and acquired an independent identity. Although drawn to it, she never came to accept it completely and, in fact, resented the message of much of the material. She died apparently still an atheist.

A *Course in Miracles* is one of the "channeled" documents that claim a place in the New Age movement. Its blend of Christian teaching, especially regarding forgiveness and reconciliation, with themes of the illusoriness of the world and the unreality of appearances expresses a religious mentality flourishing in the late twentieth century. This mentality is ill at ease in establishment settings and uncomfortable with the boundaries of prescribed beliefs. Many who share this habit of mind prefer to describe themselves as "spiritual" rather than "religious." Yet A *Course in Miracles* contains strict limits of its own. Its male-oriented language, its schoolbook format with daily lessons to be practiced, and its insistence on the fixed cosmology it teaches all provide boundaries that in their firmness echo the structured religion of the nation's Protestant past. Indeed, A *Course in Miracles* may be witness to a kind of New Age fundamentalism.

Whether or not that is the case, the *Course* through its evolution and internal message exhibits familiar patterns of expansion and contraction. The work of an atheistic Jew with a theosophical mother and others close to her who were Roman Catholic or Protestant evangelical, it expresses an expansive and universalist creed and ethical code. At the same time, as if reflecting another side of Schucman, who obeyed the voice she disbelieved, the *Course* puts rigorous demands on its students and imposes a near-imperious discipline on their lives. By proclaiming the one truth to be learned and practiced, it functions for them in contractive ways.

Seen in this fashion—as illustrating both expansive and contractive themes—A *Course in Miracles* is symbolic of an American cultural system that finds expression in both. If we think of American culture as the work of the social body that comprises Americans, we understand it not as a series of separate and disparate elements but as a system. In this way of seeing, American culture emerges as a balancing mechanism made up of the forces of expansion and contraction. These forces act antagonistically, but they also produce the complementary powers that make the system work. Expansion and contraction, then, become self-correcting devices for American culture. Each has its strengths, and each its weaknesses. Together they function better than either of them alone, and together they display aspects of religion under conditions of pluralism.

Indeed, by the late twentieth century, religious pluralism—what the text has called manyness—was a marked feature of the American landscape. But it was also, for many, an internalized condition. In other words, for many, pluralism had become an ideology that both described the facts of American life *and* prescribed how to live. For still other Americans, who desired a different, less pluralist country, manyness was a continuing unwelcome fact *and* a philosophic formula that needed to be countered. For both ideological groups and for the countless others who accepted pluralism in less ideological ways, religious manyness would not go away. No religion could be the same under its impact, and all religions needed to reconstitute their claims because of it. Hence, patterns of expansion and contraction grew more pronounced with the pluralism.

As a way of exploring these patterns in the manyness of late-twentieth-century America, we examine in this chapter instances of religious expansion and contraction in contemporary life. As probably the leading example of the culture of religious expansion, we look at the New Age movement. And, similarly, as a leading example of the culture of contraction, we study conservative Protestantism. Then we use these seemingly opposite expressions of religion in America to test the limits of pluralism and to assess the results.

Patterns of Contemporary Expansion: The New Age

The New Age movement has been described as a revival of esoteric and mystical religion, as the expression of a new global culture directed toward human transformation, and as a religious discourse (language) community who speak in similar terms that center on healing. The term *new age* itself, without the capital letters, has been a favorite phrase in American history since at least the time of the Revolution. But use of the term acquired a special self-consciousness, as we saw in Chapter 8, in the theosophical movement of the late nineteenth century, a point to which we will return.

With ties to occult and metaphysical movements as part of its prehistory, the New Age movement began in the late 1960s and early 1970s. One way in which it congealed was through a series of English "light" groups, made up of individuals who came together to "channel" spiritual light to the world and to discuss theosophical writings about the advent of a New Age. Light groups spread from England to this country, and by the early seventies they were part of an international network that expected the imminent arrival of a New Age. Meanwhile, by 1971, the *East–West Journal,* begun that year in Boston under macrobiotic auspices, became a vehicle for the spread of New Age ideas. Changes in the American immigration law likewise facilitated the influx of Eastern teachers and teachings, while at the same time a holistic health movement began to gain momentum, and Native American spirituality became increasingly attractive. In this climate, many Americans — after the decade of the sixties and the Vietnam War era — seemed less spiritually certain of themselves and more open to new and syncretistic teachings.

A movement grew, at first quietly and without mainstream media attention, through a mostly informal network of communication. Bulletin boards in natural food stores, yoga centers, and alternative healing clinics; word-of-mouth messages from chiropractors and massage therapists; local directories of people, goods, and services; multiplying numbers of small, often newsprint periodicals — all helped to announce the New Age. Teachers appeared, and seminars and weekend workshops flourished. Movement leaders began to attract followings, and New Agers increasingly found one another.

Roots of the New Age

Despite its informality and fluidity as a movement, the New Age has long and complex roots in American culture and in religious traditions from abroad. We have encountered most of these sources before, but it is important to identify them here and to point to their contributions to the movement.

From one point of view, the New Age is nothing more than the contemporary manifestation of a popular metaphysical religion that has always been present in American life. In our own time, academic and media attention has tended to solidify and reify what is essentially part of the flux of noninstitutionalized religious culture. New studies are showing that colonial Americans engaged in a full spectrum of religious beliefs and practices, only a small number of which could be fitted within the orthodox boundaries of Christianity. As we saw in Chapter 8, belief in astrology and witchcraft was strong, and popular magico-religious practices abounded. What was true in earlier times continued through the nineteenth and twentieth centuries. Under these circumstances, organized religion in the denominations was but the tip — the one-seventh exposed — of a religious iceberg. Much of American religious history has existed below the surface of historiographical scrutiny.

Moreover, the popular metaphysical religion below the surface responded elastically to new currents that came from abroad or that arose indigenously. Thus, we can trace its history by looking at movements that made their impact in broad and general terms. During the antebellum nineteenth century — a good time to begin — we know that two movements from abroad that swept the nation were mesmerism and Swedenborgianism. And a native movement that excited a huge popular following was spiritualism. We see the three of them come together in Andrew Jackson Davis, the spiritualist seer and theologian whom we met earlier.

Davis, we recall, claimed that he had spoken with the ancient Greek physician Galen and with the Swedish mystic Emanuel Swedenborg. And what Davis described surrounding the meetings were unusual conditions. According to his autobiographical account, he fell easily into a mesmeric trance when in the presence of an "operator." On one occasion, he said, the effects of the trance persisted even after he thought he had emerged from it. He returned to his boardinghouse, got into bed, and fell asleep. It was then, Davis said, that a voice commanded him to get dressed and follow. After a series of dreamlike sequences, in Davis's account, he ran across the frozen Hudson River and ended in a cemetery surrounded by forested land. There he believed that he encountered the spirits of Galen and Swedenborg and was presented with a "magic staff" by Galen.

The conviction of initiatory vision and journey launched Davis's career as clairvoyant and physician, reformer and harmonial philosopher, and major theologian of American spiritualism. Thereafter, in a trance state he delivered a series of 157 lectures on a New York City stage, and they were subsequently published (1847) as *The Principles of Nature, Her Divine Revelations, and a Voice to Mankind*. The huge volume was evidently widely read, for it went through thirty-four editions in the same number of years.

What brought mesmerism, Swedenborgianism , and spiritualism together for Davis and so many others? At least a partial answer is that each in its own way eroded the boundary between natural and supernatural, or matter and spirit, so basic to the Protestant Christianity of the era. And each, as well, erased the distance between ordinary and extraordinary religion, so that the Protestant attempt to keep the two spheres separate was seriously undercut.

Mesmerism, we know, explained the entrancing effect of one individual on another by the existence of a universal fluid that could be transferred from person to person. The fluid was understood as an invisible tide present throughout the universe, and its smooth and unimpeded flow was thought to be necessary for health and wholeness. In a more theological statement, Swedenborgianism taught of a divine influx into the natural world and also posited a God who was understood as the Divine Human. In detailed descriptions of trance journeys to what he claimed to be heaven, Swedenborg gave vivid accounts of angelic mansions, landscapes, garments, and foods that made paradise into a decidedly earthly place. Still more, for Swedenborg, marriage, or "conjugial love," continued in heaven. Meanwhile, those who reflected on spiritualist phenomena mostly believed that spirits could communicate with human beings because spirits and humans were constitutionally similar. What we call spirit, said these spiritualists, was actually a refined form of matter.

Thus, each movement—mesmerism, Swedenborgianism, and spiritualism—conflated what many had previously kept separate. Each movement implicitly argued against boundaries and for expansion. Each movement tended toward metaphysical monism, and each created a cosmology in which ordinary and extraordinary could not easily be distinguished.

By the end of the nineteenth century, mesmerism, Swedenborgianism, and spiritualism had all had their day as popular movements. But a new force continued the challenge to metaphysical boundaries. This new force came not from the occult-metaphysical world but from the latest speculations of science. In 1900, the German physicist Max Planck was countering the orthodox scientific theory that light existed as a wave with evidence that it behaved like a particle. Planck described energy "packets" in which, he said, light was emitted and absorbed. He called the packets *quanta*, and in his work quantum mechanics, the "new physics" of the twentieth century, had its early beginnings. Then, in 1905, Albert Einstein proposed that the energy of light was made up of distinct, speeding, colliding particles. Other elaborations in quantum theory followed. In a curious way, mainstream science seemed now to be repeating the cosmology of the metaphysicians. At the subatomic level, many scientists were saying, matter was not the solid entity that appeared to commonplace observation. Since light acted both like a wave and like a particle, the line between matter and energy was fluid, the boundary not so fixed as it seemed.

New Agers would carry these scientific theories out of the subatomic world and into their own cosmologies, finding in quantum theory, as they understood it, evidence to support their views. But New Age syncretism also found older American material to incorporate, this time in elite, self-conscious formulations of occult-metaphysical belief. The earliest of these older American religious sources was New England Transcendentalism. A second source was the New Thought movement (and, to a certain extent, Christian Science), and a third source came from the legacy of the Theosophical Society.

The Transcendental theory of correspondence, we remember, taught that what was "above" and what was "below" were made of the same elements, replications of each other. Thus, Transcendentalism challenged boundaries and questioned distinctions between sacred and profane. For the Transcendentalists, nature and this world could be broad avenues into the spiritual realm. More than that, the Transcendentalists formed the first movement of American intellectuals that took Eastern religious literature seriously. Emerson and the others found in Asian classics confirmation for the philosophic idealism they had drawn from Platonism and Neoplatonism. The illusory quality of the world was part of their doctrine, even if the Transcendentalists also celebrated nature. Finally, the Transcendentalists were role models for an eclectic and syncretistic future. Dissatisfied with Christianity, even in its liberal Unitarian form, they picked and chose from what was available to them to build their own religious response to life.

When the New Thought movement coalesced toward the end of the nineteenth century, we know that it created in Emerson an ancestor-founder and thus helped to popularize Transcendentalism. New Thought, however, carried Emersonian correspondence in pragmatic directions. If for New Thought mind and world were corresponding aspects of reality, mind (or truth or thought) was "put into practice" in self-conscious ways. In New Thought, believers used the mind in attempts to direct matter. Short, repeated New Thought statements, called affirmations (of what one desired) and negations (of what one denied), provided specifically crafted tools to address individual problems. In effect, New

Thought aimed to conscript "thought" to alter matter, convinced that matter—
in a familiar formula—was not so solid as it seemed. Beyond that, New Thought
believers were unashamed in their desire for the good life on earth. Health and
prosperity were twin issues that concerned them. In keeping with the teaching of
correspondence, they dissolved boundaries once again, finding the sacred in the
world.

Christian Science likewise provided a mental world congenial to what
would become the New Age. Although in its classical form it stressed its interpretation of the Christian gospel and its separation from New Thought, many
Scientists did not make the distinctions that their official theology did. Moreover, as a carrier of the metaphysics of the illusoriness of the world and matter,
Christian Science prepared the way for other versions of its basic philosophy.

Unlike Christian Science and like Transcendentalism, New Thought was
receptive to religious currents emanating from Eastern sources. However, it was
the Theosophical Society that, as we have seen, made a major turn toward Asia.
Moreover, Theosophists united metaphysics with what they regarded as the latest reports of science. They championed belief in a lost continent of Lemuria,
the existence of which was supported by nineteenth-century biologists, and they
rewrote Darwinian evolution into a theory of the evolution of seven "root" races,
the fifth of which included the Aryans. Beyond that, through the reported contact of Helena Blavatsky and others with Mahatmas, or "masters," expectation
grew among Theosophists that one among the masters would come to earth as a
savior figure for humanity. Blavatsky, in fact, borrowed from the Buddhist doctrine of Maitreya Buddha, the Buddha of the final age, to teach that the Lord
Maitreya would come as world teacher to launch a new stage in the human
evolutionary cycle. The presence of the master, then, would inaugurate the New
Age. Indeed, so insistent did Theosophists become concerning the master who
would bring the New Age that they claimed his existence in a young Indian boy,
Jiddu Krishnamurti (1895–1986). Until 1929, when Krishnamurti denied that
he was the world teacher and struck out on his own, Theosophists promoted
their belief through Annie Besant's Order of the Star of the East.

As important as the content of theosophical teaching, however, were the
organizational lineages begun by Theosophists or former Theosophists. The theosophical movement, although weakly institutionalized like other components
of the occult-metaphysical world, still managed to generate perhaps several hundred small organizations that continued its ideas. Chief among them in helping
to shape the late-twentieth-century New Age were the "I AM" movement of
Guy Ballard (1878–1939) and the Arcane School of Alice Bailey (1880–1949).
Ballard claimed that an Ascended Master named Saint-Germain had contacted
him at Mount Shasta to announce, as the master's designated messenger, the
Seventh Golden Age (the "I AM" Age of Eternal Perfection on Earth). Bailey, a
California Theosophist, in turn claimed that Ascended Master Djwhal Khul
(D.K., or "The Tibetan") was sending material to humankind through her. In

Initiation Human and Solar (1922), Bailey—or D.K., from whom she said the material had come—told of a Great White Brotherhood who guided the human race and of the coming of a world teacher who would appear near the end of the century.

Ballard and Bailey had both begun to "channel" in the contemporary sense (although the term itself emerged later, as we will see). They wrote the words that they said the masters had expressly delivered to them as messengers to others. They did not, like an Andrew Jackson Davis, claim simply to speak what came to them when they entered an entranced state. They did, however, parallel the claims of nineteenth-century spiritualist mediums who engaged in automatic writing and appeared on public stages as trance speakers—in both cases, as the mediums believed, used by spirits.

In this context, groups of Ballard's and Bailey's followers received their works as a kind of scripture. But they also placed the new scripture alongside the writings of other major Theosophists, including, especially, Blavatsky and Besant. Moreover, they felt free to innovate, and leaders in the groups announced contact with other masters. Then, by the middle of the fifties, some in the tradition began to perceive the masters differently. In the wake of a series of sightings of unidentified flying objects (UFOs) that had begun in 1947, they now regarded the masters as space commanders. In the technological world of spaceships and their paraphernalia, the space commanders were understood to "transmit" their messages through a "channel," that is, through the claimed human contactee. Thus was born the contemporary language of the "channel."

In perhaps the leading theosophical example of the phenomenon, from 1954 Englishman George King—a yoga adept long familiar with the theosophical tradition—began, according to his own report, to have a series of unusual experiences. He believed that he had been designated by the Venusian Master Aetherius as the "Primary Terrestrial Mental Channel." By 1956, King founded the Aetherius Society in London, and in 1959 he moved to Los Angeles, where his movement grew. Other flying saucer contactee groups, most of them without the explicit theosophical lineage of King and some others, also claimed channeling experiences and transmitted what they said were the messages of beings whom they identified as space commanders.

Hence, technology contributed to New Age syncretism through images drawn from space-age constructs, just as physical science had contributed with models from quantum mechanics. In this climate of enthusiasm for science and its products, social science, too, provided material for the emerging movement. New Agers were attentive to the psychology of Carl G. Jung (1875–1961) with its dream symbolism that aimed to map stages on the way to the discovery of the Self. They were also attracted to humanistic psychology and its themes of self-actualization and self-fulfillment (a subject to be explored more fully in Chapter 14). As early as 1962, at Esalen Institute in Big Sur, California, the human-potential movement became the focus for a generation of seekers. Blending material taken from comparative religion with mystical and meditation theory, small groups worked with psychotherapeutic language and techniques toward goals of emotional growth and consciousness expansion. Esalen became the prototype for other centers that functioned to offer education understood as "growth-oriented," "spiritual," or the like. Smaller, less formal groups also propagated the message, and a wide self-help literature of psychological-spiritual titles arose. Meanwhile, still others turned to the new field of transpersonal psychology, which aimed to study religious states of mind and to incorporate traditional spiritual disciplines as part of research methodology.

Transpersonal psychology was only a short step away from interest in parapsychological phenomena, the paranormal powers that many claimed the human mind possessed. And parapsychology would prove another element that found favor in the New Age movement. As we saw earlier, from 1885 American philosopher and psychologist William James was active in the establishment of the American Society for Psychical Research. The Jamesian tradition was reflected, in 1951, in the organization of the Parapsychology Foundation. Begun as a funding source for parapsychology, it supported experiments, conferences, and publications on parapsychological themes in the decades that followed. By 1957 the foundation was joined by the Parapsychology Society, established by J. B. (Joseph Banks) Rhine for those who, like himself, were engaged in parapsychological research. When, in 1969, the American Association for the Advancement of Science admitted the Parapsychology Society to membership, the move was viewed by some as a sign of new respectability for parapsychology.

Psychological and parapsychological sciences were joined, too, by an alternative form of medical science. In theories of holistic medicine, which grew increasingly popular in the late twentieth century, healing the mind was linked to healing bodily ills. Heirs to a nineteenth-century natural healing movement that we glimpsed in the person of Phineas Quimby and that we will see again in Chapter 14, holistic healers provided yet another source for New Age spirituality. With their concepts that disease is self-created and that individuals have it in their power to heal themselves, the new alternative healers offered habits of thought and action that resonated with the emerging New Age consensus. Likewise, they modeled New Age preferences in their natural pharmacopoeia (herbs, special foods, homeopathic remedies), in their techniques of touch and massage (bodywork) in which physical contact was seen as a healing force, and in their mind–body therapies in general.

Still another—and parascientific—source for the New Age synthesis came from astrology, which functioned for many as symbolic science. As we have already seen, those who followed astrology believed that the qualities shaping human character and destiny were written large on the sky "map" formed by the stars. Even further, in astrological thinking the stars symbolized not only the life paths of individuals but also the quality of time in general. In many cases an astrological "dispensationalism" prevailed, and astrologers claimed to read the coming of different eras in the stars. From this point of view, the Age of

Aquarius, an early name for the New Age, became a symbol for the consciousness that New Agers believed would replace old and outworn beliefs. Understood as the time when the sun would enter the constellation of Aquarius on the day of the spring equinox (the sun is now regarded by astrologers to be in the constellation of Pisces on that day), the Aquarian Age was promoted as an expected new age of the spirit. Although according to strict astrological charting the Age of Aquarius would arrive some 300 years after the last decades of the twentieth century, the concept—like astrological belief in general—became an important ingredient in the New Age.

Even as astrology flourished, another major ingredient in the new synthesis came from the growing presence of Asian peoples and their religions after the changed U.S. immigration law of 1965. Not only did Eastern religions become more visible and accessible, but a large number of new spiritual teachers from Asia arrived on American shores. Often they were willing to modify received tradition in syncretistic ways, as we saw in Chapter 9 in the case of Yogi Bhajan. On their side, those who heard the new teachers accepted their message as one part of a larger religious complex that was still malleable. Beliefs about *karma* and reincarnation, for example, already popularized through the Theosophical Society and its offshoots, received new legitimacy from Eastern sources. Indeed, so persuasive did these ideas become that late-twentieth-century polls suggested that perhaps one-fifth of Americans held reincarnational beliefs. Thus, as Buddhists, Hindus, Sikhs, Sufis, and other Easterners began teaching Americans, they became a strong force in recasting the American occult-metaphysical tradition. Older structures gave way, and new ones were solidified. The American occult-metaphysical tradition found itself changed in the light of the East.

The same process occurred, from another quarter, through American Indian teachers who communicated parts of their spiritual traditions and through the fascination of many non-Indian Americans with native ways. Traditionalists among Indian peoples objected, and even nonnatives warned of mainstream American cultural imperialism. Still, native teachers like Sun Bear (Chippewa) and Rolling Thunder (Cherokee and adopted Shoshone) taught beliefs and practices from their traditions to non-Indian Americans. As a leading case in point, the Bear Tribe Medicine Society, which Sun Bear founded in 1966, flourished with mostly nonnative membership. With an apprenticeship program in Spokane, Washington, and a national and international following, Sun Bear and the Bear Tribe regularly sponsored Medicine Wheel gatherings, weekend camp conferences where he and other native teachers spoke of their religious beliefs and practices to non-Indians. Rolling Thunder, for his part, addressed nonnative audiences and sought as a shamanic healer to help them, even as stories that attributed impressive powers to him grew.

New Agers, to the chagrin of some, appropriated Native American rituals like the sweat-lodge ceremony in various pan-Indian versions. They borrowed American Indian rattles and drums, wore and used feathers, beads, and gemstones,

Sun Bear at California Medicine Wheel Gathering, 1982. Sun Bear, founder of the Bear Tribe Medicine Society, promotes Medicine Wheel gatherings nationally and internationally. The weekend meetings, held usually in outdoor settings, combine Native American ceremonies with workshops or study classes.

engaged in variants of native pipe ceremonies, made pilgrimages to Indian sacred sites, and worked to practice shamanism. Sweat-lodge ceremonies, in fact, became prototypical New Age rituals, and shamanism became a pervasive technique and model for efforts in imaging, mental "journeying," and healing.

American Buddhist and nature poet Gary Snyder, who, we recall, moved from among the San Francisco "beats" to independent stature, was — in his involvement with American Indian themes — perhaps a New Age predecessor. If so, his equal interest in nature and ecology pointed toward another significant source of New Age spirituality. The theme of the earth as a living being and concern for the environment as a common heritage fed into the New Age synthesis, carried by Native American and Eastern traditions and the ecological movement. Thus, as environmental concerns entered the New Age, they were linked to theories of earth changes and purifications appropriated from American Indians and to harmonial ideas derived from Easterners. Together, as we will see, this aggregation of ideas and concerns helped give to the New Age movement a social ethic.

 ## The Religion of the New Age

As all of the ingredients came together to form the emerging New Age synthesis, self-consciousness among participants increased. This self-consciousness was reflected in the designation "New Age," which came to stand for the general collection of beliefs and behaviors within the movement. In fact, though, not every person who identified with the name "New Age" shared every belief or engaged in every behavior that characterized the movement as a whole. Rather, individuals appropriated different elements from the available pool, so that New Agers expressed diversity and fluidity in their membership. In this context, a distinction that has been applied to nineteenth-century spiritualism is helpful in categorizing the religion of the New Age. Historian Robert W. Delp identified a "speculative" and philosophical form of spiritualism, which he contrasted to a more popular "phenomenal" type. For Delp, speculative spiritualism was the spiritualism of Andrew Jackson Davis and other harmonialists; phenomenal spiritualism was represented by the Fox sisters and those who followed the séances, seeking intimate contact with the dead.

If we use this distinction between the speculative and the phenomenal as a way to understand the New Age, we can notice differences between two general groups of movement participants. On the one hand were those thinkers with environmental, transformational, and holistic-health agendas, and, on the other, those "actors" who immersed themselves in New Age practices such as channeling and work with crystals. Of course, speculative New Agers did not simply speculate; related forms of action followed on their theoretical claims. Conversely, phenomenally inclined New Agers did not merely engage in religious practice; they brought an implicit theology to their action. Still, noticing tendencies toward the speculative or phenomenal sides of the movement can help us to see it more clearly.

Similarly, distinctions between ordinary and extraordinary religion are useful when applied to the different tendencies within the New Age. Speculative New Agers made ordinary religion foremost; they sought a reconstitution of society so that it would become what they regarded as integrative and supportive. And they wanted society to enhance the qualities they considered best in human life. On their side, phenomenal New Agers underlined extraordinary religion even as they joined it to the ordinary world; they were spiritual seekers who wanted direct evidence of and contact with the extraordinary. Although the extraordinary world of the phenomenal New Age was usually not supernatural in the traditional sense, it was clearly understood as a transcendent world of entities and encounters not available to ordinary consciousness. In short, the speculative New Age leveled transcendence and elevated ordinariness; the phenomenal New Age brought transcendence into everyday life and, as much as possible, transformed the ordinary.

Seen from this perspective, the speculative New Age ended with an ethical religion, one that stressed a way of life shaped by theoretical reflection. The phenomenal New Age, on the other hand, expressed itself in a strongly ritualized religion, one that emphasized cultic behavior. Still, we recall, a fully functioning religion requires creed, code, cultus, and community. As we meet different manifestations of the New Age, we need to look for the presence of all of these elements. In other words, even an ethical (code-oriented) religion, if it is fully a religion, possesses a shared creed and shared ritual actions in a community. And even a highly ritualized religion, if it, too, is fully a religion, predicates its cultus on a common belief system and encourages certain forms of everyday behavior.

It is not possible, in this brief study, to outline the many ways in which New Age religion displayed — and continues to display — its speculative and phenomenal aspects. Nor is it possible to trace the nuances of the relationships between ordinary and extraordinary that existed — and exist — within the New Age. We can, though, in a general way examine major elements of New Age creed, code, and cultus. And we can also in a general way offer some provisional statements about New Age community.

New Age teaching about the nature of the world and human life has been a modern-day version of the theory of correspondence, a version in which New Age people find in their idea of the universe an ultimate referent. The universe is for them the source of life's many manifestations, and it also possesses an intelligence that they believe guides and guards them on life's pathways. But the relation of the universe to individual human beings is not the same for New Age religion as the traditional relationship between God and his creatures is for Judaism, Christianity, and Islam. Rather, the New Age universe contains all of life and is also manifested within it. As understood by followers of the New Age, the universe exhibits a design and order reflected on a small scale in individual existing things, and it embraces all of these things as part of an integrated whole. Thus, New Agers not only believe that the microcosm of human society reflects the macrocosm of the universe; they especially emphasize their conviction that the notion of separateness, of discrete existence, is finally illusory. In New Age belief, human beings are all expressions of one another and of the universe. With a mystical translation of the language of quantum physics, New Age theology posits a cosmology and anthropology in which matter and energy are different manifestations of one encompassing reality.

Thus, for New Agers, matter and energy are interchangeable, and transformation from one to the other is conceptually simple. More than that, vibrating energy is viewed as a "higher" manifestation of the universe than is matter. Provided the energy is ordered, cohesive, and integrated, New Agers believe, the greater the energy quotient, the greater the good for human life. And once again uniting a popular appropriation of the language of quantum physics to age-old mystical imagery and symbolism, vibrating energy for the New Age is characteristically viewed as light. The early "light centers" that pioneered in the spread of the movement repeated in their name the symbol at the core of New Age belief.

If this description of New Age theology seems to give too much to the metaphysical side of the movement, it can be balanced by reference to New Age doctrine regarding the earth and nature. If the "universe" provides one conceptual foundation for New Age thinking, the "planet" provides another. In its teaching concerning the planet, the New Age reintroduces the theory of correspondence, with insistence on the natural character of the macrocosm. Moreover, for New Agers the earthly macrocosm is emphatically one. For many, the earth is Gaia, the Earth Goddess or Earth Mother. And for all, the earth is a living being, capable of being violated by the rapacious instincts of humans but capable, also, of being regenerated by human efforts at planetary healing.

Theoretical ideas about universal and earthly correspondence, buttressed by conceptual views of the transformational nature of matter-energy, lead further. As in other versions of the doctrine of correspondence, if everything *is* everything else in New Age belief, then everything can also act on everything else. Hence, the New Age universe and planet are conceived as places of magic and miracle. And hence, too, transformation in the New Age is often assumed to be sudden, dramatic, and strongly perceptible.

Perhaps more important, it is in the New Age idea of transformation that we find a conceptual side to the movement linking it especially to traditional forms of American Christianity. For transformation among New Agers is especially understood as a work of healing. In other words, New Agers construe the human situation as in some ways deficient, and the perfection that is possible, for them, is not yet present. There is, indeed, a millennial ring to New Age theology, as its name itself suggests, and adherents think of present-day humans as existing in states that are metaphysical equivalents of sickness or sin. Sometimes, in New Age understanding, that sickness or sin finds material, physical expression. At other times, its expression is largely mental or "spiritual." In both cases, the description of the human situation — in need of healing — echoes, in another key, inherited notions of original sin.

Thus, New Age creed tends to graft to the idea of perfection now, as taught by the theory of correspondence, ideas of *imperfection* and millennial completion suggesting the influence of Christianity. In this logic, what needs to be healed in the future cannot be an exact reflection of the ordered pattern of the universe. What is sick has somehow gone awry and needs to be made right. In this context, the New Age description of reality transforming itself swiftly becomes a New Age prescription for everyday living and for ritual work.

As the discussion already suggests, New Age people take the measure of their code from their creed. In an ethic congenial to Western occult-metaphysical teaching as well as to Asian and American Indian religious traditions, New Agers seek to live according to a perceived law of harmony. If, for them, the microcosm structurally reflects the macrocosm, if human society contains and manifests the energy of the universe, if the individual body is like the body of the earth, then right action for New Age people is harmonious action. Stated differently, the code for New Age living enjoins conformance to the laws of nature and therefore the "natural."

However, in accord with a Christian legacy that speaks of imperfection and future millennial perfection and an American cultural legacy that champions the doctrine of progress, New Agers link harmony to the cultivation of self and to personal transformation. Thus, the ethic of harmony, as read by the New Age, is also an ethic of change. Much as the spiritualist theology of Andrew Jackson Davis viewed the progress of spirits as unending, New Age people view change as continual. The ethic of transformation suggests a goal that is never reached, a perfection that is never quite achieved. The New Age ethic asks believers for a kind of pilgrim's progress; it offers a guide for a journey that is conceived also as a healing. Meanwhile, the ethic emphasizes individual responsibility for one's life and choices. Indeed, one of the preferred New Age ways of reflecting on human action in the world is to see it as a series of lessons to be learned. In this conception, the pilgrim is understood more as a student, and the world has become a New Age schoolhouse.

The general ethic of harmony, change, healing, and learning has been specified by New Age people in numerous ways. It is here that the New Age teacher, favored text, and community lineage become especially significant. Indeed, one might imagine the specific action pathways available for applying the general ethic as options in a vast spiritual emporium of choices. Moreover, New Agers, with their strong predilections for synthesis, often follow multiple disciplines at the same time. For example, a person who seeks to practice the code of forgiveness specified in the *Course in Miracles* may also regularly receive Trager bodywork (a form of massage that aims to facilitate meditative and even mystical states). That person may likewise follow the recommendations of an astrologer and simultaneously practice vegetarianism as part of a spiritual discipline. Moreover, the person may incorporate other suggestions of a particular New Age teacher into daily life.

Beyond the code for the individual, however, there exists the social ethic of the New Age. From the early days of their movement, New Agers have — in keeping with the theory of correspondence — linked the well-being of their lives to the well-being of the world. It is in the New Age language of the "planet" and planetary transformation that this linkage becomes especially clear. Thus, the New Age social ethic has been an environmental ethic, with New Agers concerned about allegations of human abuse of nature and willing to work to undo the damage they believe society has done to the planet. This ethic is connected to New Age theories of earth changes and purifications (appropriated, as we have seen, from American Indian teachers and other sources). The ethic relates environmental healing to reforming action that ranges from ritual means (to be discussed below) to political organization, as in the American version of the political parties called the Greens. New Agers have defended animal rights, have fought food irradiation, and have demonstrated against nuclear power plants. They have lobbied against pesticides and airplane spraying of crops, have promoted organic farming, and have joined in grass-roots businesses to supply what are seen as "environmentally friendly" paper products. They have helped to promote Earth Days and have supported environmental organizations ranging from the established Sierra Club to the newer and more controversial Greenpeace and EarthSave.

Moreover, the New Age social ethic has prompted action intended to increase the well-being of human society, too, particularly through feminism and concern for world peace. Here New Age action has focused mostly on individual and spiritual means and has not, generally, moved toward organization. For example, the New Age has spoken for cooperation over competition, for the "feminine" aspect of male character, and for equal rights for women at home or in public and professional settings. New Age voices have been heard on the boards of mutual funds that avoid investment in military weapons systems, and a New Age sense of mission can be read in automobile bumper stickers recommending that viewers "visualize world peace."

New Age code, however, is closely linked to its cultus, and it is difficult to speak of one without considering the other. That close link exists in any religious system, of course, but in the fluid and informally structured world of the New Age, the connection is especially noticeable. Without the presence of organized "churches," in which ritual religious action conventionally takes place, New Agers blur the line between code and cultus by performing everyday actions in deliberate and self-consciously symbolic ways. Or, conversely, they stage ritual events as ways to affect public and political opinion. As an example of this last activity, the large-scale event known as the Harmonic Convergence — on 16–17 August 1987 — highlighted not only a series of planetary convergences said to be happening in the sky but also patterns of environmental harm New Agers believe humans have brought to the earth. Conceived as a ritual celebration of heavenly events, the widely publicized gatherings and ceremonies also amounted to a New Age exhortation for planetary reform. Similarly, an organized series of annual visualizations for world peace, held simultaneously on 31 January at the same hour throughout the world, have provided collective ritual focus that is also attempted public persuasion.

What is more, the closeness of cultus to code underscores the seriousness with which many of the "phenomenal" rituals of the New Age are practiced. Using crystals and consulting channelers, while seeming to be faddish, have been, for many, purposeful actions. As has been the case, too, for fundamentalism, widespread publicity through the news media has significantly altered the ways in which outsiders view the cultic expressions of the New Age. New Age ritual work is often dramatic and flamboyant. But the preference for drama and flamboyance does not in itself preclude a strong connection between belief, everyday action (code), and ritual behavior.

What can be said, in general, is that New Age cultus provides a series of ritual vehicles for expressing New Age creed and code. As in the case of code, the vehicles are numerous, and their expressions of New Age creed are manifold. All that we can do here is to glance at a few of the general directions in which cultic life in the New Age flows.

One way to approach the issue is to return to the symbol of the quantum and to the matter–energy equation so prevalent in New Age language. When we do so, we notice that some New Age rituals stress the material world and a felt need to bring it into harmony. Here, for example, ritual work seeks to "harmonize" the energies of the body so that they are felt to resonate with larger natural forces and laws. On the other hand, additional New Age rituals seek to facilitate mental journeying into nonmaterial worlds. In these rituals the goal is to stimulate forces of mind and imagination so that they assume control over matter. In both cases, as we will see, the rituals are both symbolic and practical. In other words, they seek to alter the human condition; they aim to heal, even as they act out symbolically the creed and code of the New Age.

As an instance of the first, harmonial, type of ritual work, take, for example, the Japanese method of palm healing known as Reiki, which has been popular among New Age Americans. Gaining attention in the late seventies and the eighties, Reiki posited the existence of "universal life-force energy" and its use through special "attunements" received from a Reiki master. These attunements were thought to enable the individual to receive and transmit life-force energy in a clearer, purer, and more powerful state. Receiving the attunements involved a series of initiatory rituals, as the individual passed through different "degrees" of Reiki attunement. Just as important, when the initiated Reiki practitioner began the actual practice of palm healing, that work also possessed ritual elements. Performed in systematic fashion with specified hand positions and, for the higher degrees, other secret instructions, the practice might take an hour or more. During this time, the client and/or the practitioner might report sensations of heat and cold or body tingling. Reiki would heal, they believed, because Reiki energy could transform bodily organs and functions. In that respect, the ritual acquired practicality and, for believers, provided material proof of the metaphysical system on which it was based.

As an example of the second type of ritual work that has featured the controlled use of imagination, perhaps the leading instance has been New Age shamanism. Shamans, we know, take mental journeys to attempt both to acquire power and to use it. As we have seen, in traditional societies such as those of American Indian peoples, shamanic work was social in its intent and goal, with curing illness a significant focus. Although far less steeped in symbolic lore and, mostly, far less disciplined, New Age shamans have sought similar goals. They have sometimes been encouraged by specific organizations, such as anthropologist Michael Harner's Foundation for Shamanic Studies or adopted Huichol Indian Brant Secunda's Dance of the Deer Foundation. And they sometimes have learned shamanic techniques less formally, through audiotapes or shared experience.

Whatever their introduction to shamanic ritual, practitioners aimed, typically, to "visit" several worlds. In their scenarios, there was usually an underworld where power animals, guardian spirits, and dangers were thought to dwell; a middle world understood as the earth visited in a trance state; and an upper world in which, shamans said, spiritual teachers might be found. Mentally journeying through these various regions with the cultic use of drum, rattle, and/or hallucinogenic plants, the shamanic practitioner sought to live through a story that symbolically expressed the concerns with which he or she began. This story might, for practitioners, illuminate a problem situation in everyday life, offer directions for a healing, aim to effect the healing, or give advice for spiritual growth. Mind, in short, became the ritual focus, and it did so in ways that were not only symbolic but also practical.

Reiki palm healing and shamanic journeying have been forms of New Age ritual, as have been numerous other practices. These two are cited only as illustrations of pervasive cultic activity among New Agers. In fact, seemingly non-ritualistic activity has often acquired quasi-ritual status. The wearing of crystals and other forms of New Age jewelry is one example, with crystals and gemstones thought to possess certain powers to aid individuals, to protect them, or to develop aspects of their character. Similarly, the use of flower and mineral essences provides another example, with these substances also thought to alter mental states in subtle ways that can assist healing or otherwise help to change a person's life situation.

Finally, New Age ritual work might be accomplished alone, but it was often also done in community. Moreover, even when ritual practice was the work of one individual, it was based on beliefs and lifeways that were shared. The cultus of the New Age, therefore, points toward the New Age community.

What can be said about the body of people who, in late-twentieth-century America, follow the New Age? Little is known in the strict demographic or sociological sense, but there are clues that suggest the general nature of the New

Age community. Different scholars have spoken of New Agers as young and urban, as middle-class and upwardly mobile, as better educated than average, and as not particularly alienated from society. High-priced and fashionable weekend workshops and conferences point to the appropriateness of these characterizations. Still, there is a strong working-class component within the New Age movement, although its presence is quieter and less noticeable. And impressionistic evidence indicates that more women are New Agers than men.

In terms of the religious traditions from which New Agers come, evidence suggests representative participation by mainstream American Protestants, Catholics, and Jews, all three. Geographically, New Agers appear to be well represented on both coasts, with California and the Northeast as bellwether regions. New Agers are also strong in parts of the Midwest and probably weakest in the South.

Even more difficult to determine than the sociological characteristics of those who form the New Age community are their numbers. First, in a movement so fluid and individualistic, the criteria for "membership" are disputable. Second, even when criteria are arbitrarily established, information based on the selected criteria is hard to find. At the broadest, we might decide that everyone who held, for example, reincarnational beliefs should be considered in some sense New Age. Since, as we have already cited, surveys suggest that perhaps 20 percent of Americans do accept reincarnation, this would point to a rather large constituency for the New Age. At the narrowest, we could limit membership to those who subscribe to key periodicals, list themselves in New Age directories, or participate in New Age events, such as the Whole Life Expo (an annual New Age gathering and emporium). As another strategy, we might guess that many who are unaffiliated with an organized religious tradition are sympathetic to the New Age. (The unaffiliated represented roughly 7 percent of the population in the mid-eighties, and among baby boomers and those younger significantly more.) And we might add to this number a further percentage to account for those church or synagogue members who also consider themselves New Age. Or, finally, we might accept the results of a *New York Times* survey in 1991, which claimed 28,000 for the New Age.

None of these tactics seems wholly satisfactory however, and the best estimate probably lies somewhere between the extremes. Perhaps, as J. Gordon Melton estimates, New Agers number in the hundreds of thousands among the 250 million and more Americans. But given the readiness with which specific New Age beliefs merge with general American beliefs and values, there may be many more who participate in at least the speculative side of New Age religion.

Sociological descriptions and estimates of size can tell us many things about the components of New Age community, but they tell us little about the community once it has formed and is functioning. Still, there are clues if we look impressionistically at the movement itself. The individualistic nature of participants and the weakness of New Age institutionalization tell us that community is fluid more than fixed, temporary more than permanently established.

Indeed, the homesteads of the mind that characterized the occult-metaphysical tradition throughout American history characterize the New Age synthesis, too. The goal of world community, of a metaphysical oneness with all humankind, is especially attractive for those whose existing community is fragile. Without the historic supports of traditional community, New Agers typically create structures of relationship as they can, ready to move on when circumstance or desire prompts change. Nor is this necessarily a liability in their eyes. With a mentality geared toward personal and social transformation, New Agers view the changing nature of community as metaphysical truth as well as sociological fact.

New Agers discover one another especially by their language. Those who speak of the "universe," of "energy" and "vibration," of "*chakras*" and "etheric entities" acknowledge that they live in similar worlds and begin to share their participation. Beyond that, their language community finds itself in voiced concerns for health and holistic healing, for "saving" the planet, and for "honoring" the feminine aspect of the earth. New Agers often read the same books and subscribe to the same magazines. Their interests have spawned a series of businesses that cater to them and provide places for them to meet one another. New Age networking has been loose but generally effective in bringing people together. And the New Age has so far constructed a community that, for all its imprecision, is felt by those involved to be working. What the community works toward might be seen as a sense of empowerment in a world that, for many, has grown too impersonal, too corporate and bureaucratic, and too resistant to personal leverage. In the small groups that coalesce and dissolve, New Agers have created ad hoc means to meet their felt needs and to give themselves hope for a future that is noticeably better.

In short, New Age community has been as expansive as the New Age itself. It provides a summary statement of the patterns of expansion that form one side of contemporary American culture. Indeed, in a society in which boundaries have historically been everywhere, the New Age promotes a dissolution of boundaries. Its members testify to a pluralism become omnipresent, become, in fact, the very substance of religion. Meanwhile, their ways of seeing ordinary life in light of the extraordinary and, conversely, of bringing the extraordinary into ordinary experience illustrate New Age expansiveness in familiar terms. On many counts, participants in the New Age share a vision of expansion and aim to live according to its pattern.

Patterns of Contemporary Contraction: Fundamentalists and Evangelicals

To examine contemporary fundamentalism and evangelicalism is to resume a study that we began in Chapter 5. Here, though, we look at the reconfiguration of conservative Protestantism that began in the 1930s and 1940s. The mood of the times, for many conservatives, was set by impulses toward contraction.

Sectarianism, always a strong tendency, grew stronger, and dissension — not only with more centrist Protestants but also among one another — was rife. In this context, militant fundamentalists left existing groups within the denominations and established their own fellowships and organizations. In 1932, for example, members of the Baptist Bible Union, part of the Northern Baptist Convention, left the main organization to begin the General Association of Regular Baptist Churches. By 1947 members of the Fundamentalist Fellowship within the convention followed, establishing the Conservative Baptist Association. Presbyterian actions were similar. In 1936 fundamentalists among them created the Orthodox Presbyterian Church, itself subject to division in 1937 when J. Oliver Buswell, Jr. (1895–1977), Carl McIntire (b. 1906), and other premillennialists formed the Bible Presbyterian Church.

Division, however, did not mean conservative decline. While the mainstream of Protestantism was undergoing a time of religious depression in the thirties, fundamentalists were quietly growing, building organizational strength. In 1941, led by McIntire, the more separatist among them formed the American Council of Christian Churches. A year later, moderate fundamentalists established their own organization, the National Association of Evangelicals (cited in Chapter 4 and again in Chapter 5 for its missionary arm). The organizational division reflected a new self-consciousness within conservative circles. The more flexible doctrinal positions of the twenties had hardened by the forties. Likewise, militance was now measured by willingness to depart from mainstream denominations to form independent churches and fellowships. Against this background, the heirs of the earlier fundamentalist movement found their ranks divided between the most militant, who kept the name *fundamentalists*, and those who were relatively moderate, now known as *evangelicals*.

Still further division was to come after World War II. Beginning as early as 1943 with the formation of Youth for Christ, a generation of young and theologically sophisticated conservatives was recruited and trained. By 1948 Harold John Ockenga (1905–1985), founding president of the National Association of Evangelicals and then-president of the new conservative Fuller Theological Seminary, was speaking of the "new evangelicalism." Conceived by Ockenga as "progressive fundamentalism with a social message," this new evangelicalism found other advocates among theologians such as Carl F. H. Henry (b. 1913) and Edward J. Carnell (1919–1967). The movement found, too, a major print vehicle through its periodical *Christianity Today*. And in the mood of the times, new evangelicals championed the work of Billy Graham and formed other parachurch institutions such as Campus Crusade for Christ International (1951).

Moving away from strict dispensational theology and promoting the idea of the kingdom of God as progressively present in the world, the new evangelicals were a major force within conservative ranks until the late sixties. By then, conservative pluralism was again a strong factor, and the evangelical movement itself increasingly spoke with divergent voices. Throughout the period of new evangelical dominance, though, the militants among conservative Protestants—now, as we have seen, called the fundamentalists—expressed displeasure. They denounced Billy Graham and avoided institutions that fostered the new evangelical message. Nonetheless, the end of the sixties was also the end of the old world of fundamentalism. New forces were rising and new times coming that prompted even militant fundamentalists to change.

Fundamentalist and Evangelical: The Search for Conservative Identity

Even as the New Age was emerging in the early seventies, its expansiveness was being countered by new forces of cultural contraction within the conservative Protestant spectrum. And both inside and outside the conservative Protestant world, fundamentalism became an uneasy label. Exactly who should be counted as fundamentalist was not simple to determine. Some wore the designation as a badge of pride, separating themselves pointedly from other conservative Protestants who, they felt, had succumbed to modernity and its erosion of doctrine. Others avoided the name as derogatory even as they shared the views of those who freely called themselves fundamentalists. Still others, while holding to the inerrancy of scripture, were conscious of their departure from dispensational premillennialism and other doctrines and considered the name *fundamentalist* an inaccurate label for their ideas.

In turn, historians and social scientists who viewed the movement from outside had decisions to make about how to define it. Should they regard fundamentalism historically and etymologically—as composed exclusively of those who stood in the lineage of *The Fundamentals*, the volumes published between 1910 and 1915 (see Chapter 5)? Should they consider only premillennial dispensationalists from the turn-of-the-century tradition as fundamentalists? Should they understand fundamentalism as any Protestant form of militant antimodernism, thus including, in a leading example, holiness-pentecostal people under their definitional umbrella? Or should they consider moderates in the National Association of Evangelicals, because of their historical roots, as contemporary fundamentalists?

This battle for the name *fundamentalist* both inside and outside the movement points to the arbitrariness of the term and the difficulty of arriving at a precise taxonomy. At the same time, popular usage in the present provides clues to resolving the dilemma. If we allow the general public to decide the case by what they think and say, we arrive at an understanding of fundamentalism based on the similarities perceived by many among different groups. These similarities are often so striking that outsiders rarely see differences along the conservative Protestant continuum. On the other hand, because these differences do exist, the term *evangelical* seems a useful addition. This term takes seriously the self-designation of moderates since 1942, and its avoids some of the confusion over historical lineages. Thus, for greater clarity, it seems appropriate here to speak of a fundamentalist-evangelical movement.

From this perspective, a number of major groupings command attention on today's conservative Protestant landscape. Groups can be divided theologically, historically, socially, and politically, and overlapping memberships — based on these criteria — are surely visible. Theologically, for example, we can notice strict dispensational premillennialists, militant in their separatism and antimodernism based on their conviction of the sinfulness of the world. On the other side, we see moderates who are members of mainstream denominations, holding to the inerrancy of scripture but willing to grant some latitude in its interpretation and finding the presence of sin in the world but also the presence of grace. Historically, we can isolate those who stand in the tradition of the fundamentalist-modernist controversy from others who come from the holiness-pentecostal wing of conservative Protestantism. Socially, we can point to the differences between a quiet, unflamboyant conservatism existing in thousands of Bible-oriented congregations and a noisier electronic church that has brought widespread notice to conservatives. And politically, we can identify the forces of the New Christian Right and contrast them with radical evangelicals whose views are left of center, as in the frequently cited Sojourner Community.

Dispensational premillennialism, far from disappearing in the late twentieth century, has flourished in the United States since the seventies. With the publication of Hal Lindsey's *Late Great Planet Earth* (1970), the mood of mixed fear and anticipation surrounding expected millennial events grew more tangible. A general belief in the second coming of Jesus was specified more insistently in a scenario of end-time happenings. These included expectation of the rapture of the saints into the air, of a time of tribulation when the Antichrist would rule the world, and of a battle at Armageddon when the army of Christ would defeat Satan and inaugurate the millennium. None of these ideas was new. They had been part of earlier debates among fundamentalist Christians and had emerged, more and more, as hallmarks of the strict and militant side of the movement. Hence, what the seventies and eighties brought was greater popularity for beliefs already available.

But dispensational premillennialism is more than a passive system of beliefs. For contemporary conservatives it represents an active system of reading the Bible and conferring meaning on world events. Not the same as simply reading the Bible literally, dispensational premillennialism provides a future-oriented way to read the Bible prophetically. The Book of Daniel in the Christian Old Testament and the Book of Revelation in the New Testament become preferred texts. Moreover, believers read the notes to the Scofield Reference Bible or the Ryrie Study Bible, with their premillennial glosses on scriptural passages, and they follow weekly newspapers such as *The Sword of the Lord* for premillennialist and prophetic commentary. In this context, to watch the television news each evening becomes an exercise in seeing prophecy unfold. The Bible is not only a history of the past for premillennialists; it is also a chart of the future.

Late-twentieth-century dispensationalist strength is suggested by sales of the Scofield Reference Bible, which from 1967 to the late 1980s amounted to more than 4.2 million copies, some 85 percent of them leatherbound (an indication, perhaps, of serious intent to use). Dispensational strength is suggested, too, by statistics that show Lindsey's *Late Great Planet Earth* as, among Christian booksellers, the most popular trade paperback of the seventies and in the early eighties still among the top ten sellers.

What is it that attracts so many to dispensationalist premillennial views? Along with literal belief in the Bible and a strong separatist tendency, premillennialism points to a religion of cultural contraction among contemporary Protestant conservatives. It is ironic that those who seek such cultural contraction should, in numerical terms, have grown and expanded. But their contraction is an expression, not of demographic size, but of habit of mind and response to complexity in late-twentieth-century life. Implicit in the response of the dispensational message is the idea that the world is growing worse and that human beings cannot by themselves undo the damage and right the situation. Instead, the series of predicted end-time events tells of strong conviction of a need to be rescued, to be snatched away from an untenable situation by a divine and extraordinary power. And if divine rescue is necessary for premillennialists, then until it comes, the believer is seen as best served by avoiding contact with worldly contamination as much as possible. Flight from the world, at least metaphorically, becomes the desired goal.

With cultural contraction markedly present on the fundamentalist end of the fundamentalist-evangelical spectrum, the contractive impulse has been softer among those conservatives who call themselves evangelical. As early as the sixties, theological liberalism entered "new evangelical" ranks when higher criticism of the Bible became more acceptable. Fuller Theological Seminary, once a strict fundamentalist school, began to ratify and use once-condemned methods of biblical interpretation. By 1972, in fact, Fuller had gone so far that it removed from its public statement of faith any reference to biblical inerrancy. Still, Fuller was making distinctions that, its faculty felt, were preserving the essence of biblical authority. If all of scripture was not inerrant, they believed, some parts of it were. When the Bible taught about faith and morality, according to the Fuller position, it could be counted on. It was only history and cosmology in the scripture that reflected a more limited human perspective.

Fuller's move came with controversy, and it prompted public debate on biblical inerrancy. The results included for one denomination, the Lutheran Church—Missouri Synod, an acrimonious division into two. But the changes in new evangelical theology seemed permanent because they spread to major evangelical theological seminaries and college religion programs. Moreover, along with the departure of strict biblical inerrancy came the departure for many of dispensational premillennialism. Evangelicals instead were attracted by psychological study and by social-scientific approaches to religion. They were seemingly making peace with the world, and the world began noticing them more kindly. *Newsweek* magazine proclaimed 1976, on its front cover, as "the year of the evangelical," and *Time* was not far behind a year later with a cover story. Meanwhile, a series of distinct evangelical theological positions arose in the seventies (and multiplied in the eighties). Conservatives—even conservatives who did not consider themselves fundamentalists—did not necessarily agree with others among their number. Earlier divisions seemed to proliferate, and evangelical pluralism was the order of the day.

As the seventies melted into the eighties, evangelicals continued to accommodate themselves to modern-day America. They no longer spurned dialogue with those who disagreed—Catholics, liberals among Protestants, persons within other religious traditions. Academic recognition came; magazines and periodicals grew more nuanced; national presidents, such as Jimmy Carter and Ronald Reagan, professed to be evangelical. Still, evangelicalism was not the same as more liberal mainstream Protestantism: evangelicals continued to exalt the Bible and to insist on the primacy of its authority. They moved toward the world, but they kept returning to their own center. In that sense, we see the continuing presence—weaker though it became—of religion with a measure of contractive power.

If the theological spectrum within the fundamentalist-evangelical movement was broad, the movement also drew on more sources than in its early-twentieth-century version. Heirs to the Princeton Theology, the Niagara Bible conferences, and *The Fundamentals* should not be exclusively identified with the movement. Instead, a major new component has come from the holiness-pentecostal tradition.

Originally holiness-pentecostalism and fundamentalism recognized each other's differences, and both movements marked boundaries and kept their distance. Holiness-pentecostal emphasis on the work of the Spirit, on sanctification, on prophetic gifts, and on strong emotionalism was countered by fundamentalist emphasis on the power of Jesus, on conversion, on biblical proficiency, and on a qualified rationalism. By the late twentieth century, however, these differences were melting away under the light of public, and, especially, media scrutiny. Joined by a characteristic style of preaching, by an emphasis on direct experience, by a championing of biblical authority, and by attention to personal holiness, the two movements recognized their kinship in what seemed an increasingly alien world. Much of the holiness-pentecostal movement grew away from earlier conditions of poverty and insufficiency and, with late-century fundamentalism, acculturated more and more to general American society. Meanwhile, disagreements among earlier fundamentalists yielded the wide spectrum of evangelical opinion that we have been exploring.

Ironically, the most negative publicity for present-day fundamentalism has come because of scandals involving two pentecostal ministers. James (Jim) Bakker (b. 1940), who founded the PTL Club ("Praise the Lord" and "People That Love") and Heritage Village (theme park) and who acquired a large public following through his television ministry, grew up as a conservative pentecostal. He attended Bible college under Assemblies of God auspices and in 1964 was ordained an Assemblies of God minister. Jimmy Lee Swaggart (b. 1935), likewise widely known as a television evangelist, was reared in the Assemblies of God tradition and in 1964 was also ordained an Assemblies of God minister. Accusations of sexual misconduct have dogged both. Additionally, Bakker was brought to trial on twenty-four counts of fraud and in 1989 was convicted and sentenced to prison for forty-five years (since reduced to eighteen). Swaggart, who publicly accused Bakker of adultery, later confessed to paid voyeurism of his own. In 1988 he faced withdrawal of his ordination by the Assemblies of God but himself withdrew rather than submit to disciplinary measures. Significantly, in the midst of the scandal that engulfed Bakker, the PTL founder turned not to another pentecostal minister but to fundamentalist Baptist minister and television evangelist Jerry Falwell (b. 1933). Although Bakker later condemned Falwell for "stealing" his ministry, initially Bakker asked him to guide the evangelical empire he had constructed until the storm passed.

There is much to be pondered in this twin saga of disrepute. Clearly, media and public alike did not distinguish between fundamentalist and pentecostal in their assignment of blame. And as clearly, at least one of the two pentecostals was ready to trust a fundamentalist instead of a fellow pentecostal. Even more, after the damage of the scandals the survival of the ministries of both pentecostals (Swaggart's with growth overseas and Bakker's in much-diminished form) says something about the power of the evangelical message for their followers. That power was largely conveyed not by conventional contact in a specific place but by the electronic medium of television and, to a lesser degree, by the mechanical medium of print.

Noticing the importance of electronics for present-day evangelism points us toward reflection on differing social styles in the fundamentalist-evangelical movement. For the electronic church of the late twentieth century is a striking illustration of one such style. If New Agers could be distinguished by their speculative or phenomenal leanings, fundamentalists and evangelicals can be recognized for their differing tendencies toward privacy and public display, toward a more devotional and contemplative religion and a more vocal and dramatic style. There are, of course, strong promptings within the mission mind (see Chapter 5) to articulateness and action. But to speak on behalf of the Christian gospel may mean "witnessing" to a neighbor: it need not involve mass communications.

In one sense, the social style of the electronic church began almost with the century. The first religious radio broadcast was identical with the first broadcast of the human voice — at a Christmas service in 1906. By 1921, in Pittsburgh, the Calvary Baptist Church was sending its Sunday evening worship service over the airwaves of the new radio station KDKA. Evangelists quickly understood the power that the radio gave, and in 1925 perhaps 10 percent of American radio stations were operating under religious auspices. The Federal Council of Churches was quickly involved on behalf of liberal denominations, and, on their part, fundamentalists produced their own programs and more than stood their ground.

The advent of television meant a new and greater ability to reach mass audiences in a format that could convince and persuade. Christian church leaders recognized their opportunities. At first, though, the prestige of the Federal Council of Churches and its mainstream and liberal denominations swayed decision makers of the major television networks. Mainstream Protestant clergy, joined by Roman Catholics and Jews, received free air time under the category of public service. Conservative Protestants like Rex Humbard (b. 1919), Oral Roberts (b. 1918), and Billy Graham could be seen on television in the fifties, with Graham in a national ABC broadcast of his Madison Square Garden crusade in 1957. But the networks mostly clung to their unofficial policy of giving free public air time to mainstream, more liberal denominations, thus fulfilling a mandated obligation from the federal government to produce public-service programs. Fundamentalists and other evangelicals, if they wanted time on television, had to operate independently and pay their way.

Pay their way they did, and, in fact, conservatives not only purchased air time but also acquired their own Christian television stations and set up distribution networks for their programs. By the 1970s their yearly expenditures jumped to 600 million dollars, and by decade's end there were thirty religious television stations and four networks. But beyond the ability to raise money from audiences to pay for television programming, other changes were afoot that altered the fundamentalist-evangelical future. Network television, so long opposed to paid religious broadcasting, now welcomed it. The Federal Communications Commission had ruled that it would accept paid religious programming as fulfillment of the networks' public-service obligation. At the same time, local television stations, once dominated by network giants, acquired a measure of independence. They quickly discovered that it was lucrative to sell air time on Sunday morning to religious programmers. Long accustomed to receiving free time, mainstream and liberal religious leaders mostly spurned the new order. They fought back by alleging the relatively small audiences of conservatives, their minority status within Protestantism, and their commercialization of religion.

Meanwhile, new technologies increased communications possibilities for a growing evangelical empire. Cable networks, communications satellites from which transmitted signals could be bounced across huge distances, and ultra high frequency (UHF) stations all transformed television and multiplied evangelical outreach. The work of the computer, too, aided the movement. Audience mailing lists could be quickly and efficiently assembled, direct-mail services could be implemented, and personalized solicitation letters could seek financial support. Thus, even as membership in liberal churches was declining in the seventies and conservative church membership was rising, "televangelism" was becoming a vocal means of spreading the conservative gospel. By 1980, some 90 percent of religious television was a commercial enterprise. And the religious leaders who dominated it came from the fundamentalist-evangelical movement. Religious networks such as the Christian Broadcasting Network of Marion Gordon (Pat) Robertson (b. 1930) with its "700 Club," Bakker's PTL Network (until his 1987 resignation), and the Trinity Broadcasting Network brought religious television into millions of homes.

Yet, for all that, most studies showed that religious broadcasts attracted fewer than 2 percent of potential viewers in the places in which the broadcasts were available. Audiences tended to be older (over fifty), composed of more women than men, and with lower- and moderate-income households predominating. Viewers also tended to have less education overall, and they tended to be proportionately more southern, rural, and white. Thus, the typical viewer matched the profile of many who count themselves part of the fundamentalist-evangelical movement, and televangelism was preaching to the already-converted. What at first glance seems to bear the mark of religious expansion on further scrutiny looks contractive.

Moreover, after the scandals involving Bakker and Swaggart, televangelism began to lose support. Scandal, of course, invited criticism from outside, but criticism also came from within fundamentalist-evangelical circles. Indeed, National Religious Broadcasters (NRB), televangelism's major trade association, swiftly drafted new ethical directives. However, scandal was not the only cause of criticism for the social style of the electronic church. If liberals had from the first protested against the commercialization of religion in televangelism, conservatives themselves raised questions. Research shows that most televangelical viewers do not consider religious programming a substitute for attending worship services. In fact, many in the fundamentalist-evangelical community have thought the television evangelists sources of embarrassment and nuisance. And one study of a fundamentalist church in a northeastern industrial city found its pastor condemning many of television's "Christian entertainers" as poor examples of life separate from the world.

Beyond that, the character of the preaching within the televangelical empire subtly shifted, as some evangelicals noticed. Dispensational premillennialism, with it message of impending doom, is not a major ingredient for television success. Although the contractive emphasis of the televangelical gospel is real, entertainment — even "Christian" entertainment — has eroded the self-conscious conservative boundary with the world. The culture of contraction continues in the assumptions of the programming, in its preference for themes of family and domesticity and of personal (often sexual) holiness. But a new and less strident attitude toward the world is also apparent.

Perhaps the television cult of personality fills a void created by a lack of denominational and liturgical emphasis. And perhaps televangelists have succeeded because of their ability to create a feeling of common identity and collective mission. With the strong pluralism that we have seen within fundamentalist-evangelical ranks, both of these explanations are persuasive. On the other hand, untold numbers in the fundamentalist-evangelical community practice a quieter version of their faith than the preaching of televangelists would imply. Local churches and pastors have been more central for most; and if Christian booksellers and their sales are evidence, reading the Bible, biblical commentaries, and other devotional works occupies the time of millions. If so, a more reflective spirituality exists side by side with the flamboyance of media-oriented religion. And within the more reflective spirituality, as within the electronic church, the culture of contraction flourishes.

Divergences in social style within fundamentalism and evangelicalism, however, are matched by divergences in politics. Here, again with media attention and highly visible style, the New Christian Right demands immediate notice. Indeed, the electronic church already sets the stage for the politics of the New Christian Right, for—whatever else the televangelists preach—most preach a superpatriotism.

Pat Robertson is a case in point. The highly visible founder of the CBN and talk-show host of its 700 Club (named after his 1963 campaign to persuade 700 audience members to promise ten dollars monthly in support of his budget), Robertson by the late seventies was moving toward politics. The evangelist interviewed conservative political leaders and talked on television to financial analysts. Still more, he translated the dispensationalist message into a worldly idiom that warned of doom in Washington and a crumbling U.S. Capitol. Then, disillusioned with President Jimmy Carter, whom he had helped to elect (the evangelical Carter, thought Robertson, was soft on national defense), he cochaired the 1980 "Washington for Jesus" rally with its estimated 200,000 participants. The success of the rally encouraged him, and he became more politically vocal. In September 1986 Robertson announced himself a potential presidential candidate, and less than a year later, with his goal of support from 3 million Americans met, he began an official candidacy. Robertson later withdrew from the presidential race when it became apparent that he could not win the Republican nomination. But his active participation until then signaled the power of the New Christian Right and its link with televangelism.

In fact, Jerry Falwell, who reached a huge national audience through his "Old Time Gospel Hour," was the strongest conservative organizer for a religious politics of the right. Falwell's Moral Majority, founded in 1979, grew out of earlier overtures by Washington-based political organizers, including the direct-mail advertiser and fund-raiser Richard Viguerie. But Falwell was no stranger to conservative political sentiment. As early as 1975, his involvement with rallies surrounding the nation's upcoming bicentennial observance had produced warnings from him that America was scorning its heritage under God. Now his Moral Majority grew rapidly, giving voice to a new conservative religious political coalition. At its height the Moral Majority numbered about 4 million members, and by 1987 its budget had risen to roughly 8.4 million dollars. With a name change to the Liberty Federation in 1986, throughout the decade until its dissolution in

1989 the organization acted as bellwether for the New Christian Right. From 1979 through 1987 Falwell himself acted as its president.

Who belonged to the Moral Majority, and — the larger question — who has been a member of the New Christian Right? Falwell claimed that some 30 percent of the members of his organization were actually Roman Catholics, attracted to the Moral Majority by its antiabortion politics. And scholars have noted that the New Christian Right encompasses not only devout conservative Protestants but also sympathizers outside the fundamentalist-evangelical camp. Besides Catholic involvement, there has been, for example, a solid Mormon following and even some Jewish endorsement. A number within mainstream Protestant churches, even liberal ones, have been fellow travelers. Strongest in an area running from the South through the Midwest, the New Christian Right has drawn its membership heavily from the working classes, from people not far from economic difficulty but now bringing in sufficient income for a sustainable life-style. Its appeal has been largest for conservative Christians who are white, rural, and less educated.

Besides the Moral Majority, a series of other religiopolitical organizations have been part of the New Christian Right. Among them Christian Voice, Religious Roundtable, and Concerned Women for America have no doubt received the most notice. Christian Voice began in 1979 and, at the height of its success, counted perhaps 400,000 members. With a large following in the West and Southwest, the organization brought together representatives of at least thirty-seven denominations, independent Baptist, Bible, and Assemblies of God churches being the largest active constituents. Christian Voice has probably been best known for its Morality Report Card, which has rated members of Congress according to their votes on a series of issues of concern to conservatives.

The smaller Religious Roundtable (later simply Roundtable), brainchild of Southern Baptist Ed McAteer, has worked as a loose coalition to teach religious leaders how to organize politically. Its 1980 Dallas meeting, for example, attracted thousands of clergy and laity to hear New Right leaders, televangelists, and even then-presidential candidate Ronald Reagan. In turn, Concerned Women for America developed a mailing list of 100,000 and, like Moral Majority and Christian Voice, has kept a lobby in Washington.

These organizations, with others and with less-organized sympathizers, have taken aim against what they have called "secular humanism," understanding it as the belief that human beings are ultimate and that this life on its own terms is of utmost importance. For the New Christian Right, a liberal politics supports secular humanism, eroding traditional values such as commitment to a strong family, prescribed gender roles, a devout and powerful nation, and an educational system that inculcates received knowledge and inherited ideas of virtue. In place of these, the New Christian Right has offered what it sees as a return to basics and fundamentals, to an America the way it was in an earlier, sounder age. Such an America, for the movement, lived according to the biblical norms to which present-day society needs to return. Thus, the New Christian

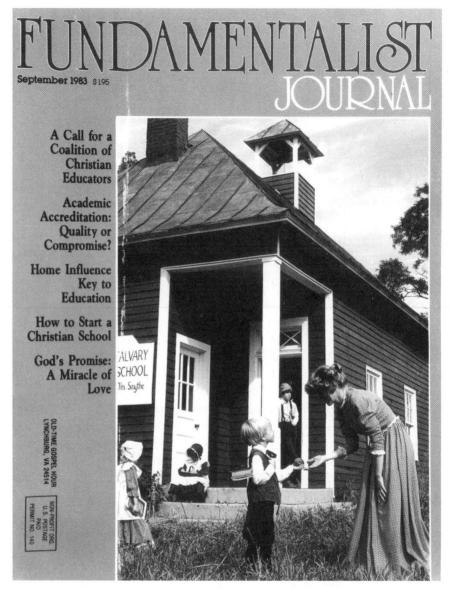

FUNDAMENTALIST

September 1983 $1.95

JOURNAL

A Call for a
Coalition of
Christian
Educators

Academic
Accreditation:
Quality or
Compromise?

Home Influence
Key to
Education

How to Start a
Christian School

God's Promise:
A Miracle of
Love

OLD-TIME GOSPEL HOUR
LYNCHBURG, VA 24514

NON-PROFIT ORG.
U.S. POSTAGE
PAID
PERMIT NO. 140

CALVARY
SCHOOL
Tirs Smythe

Fundamentalist Journal, September 1983. This front cover illustration from the (no-longer-published) *Fundamentalist Journal* evokes the image of an earlier, simpler America when, for editor Jerry Falwell and readers, virtue and education flourished together.

Right has crusaded against abortion and for school prayer, against homosexuality and feminism and for greater government support for religious education, against "atheistic" communism and for a strong national defense.

National organizations have been supported by state and local ones, with conservative pastors using their pulpits to further the ideas and activism of the movement. Employing sophisticated computer technology for direct-mail contacts and fund-raising, organizations in the movement have also been linked to one another. Political action committees (PACs), lobbies, and educational foundations have worked together, so that the PACs—neither tax exempt nor offering tax deductions for contributions—could take advantage of tax-exempt lobbies and tax-exempt and tax-deductible educational foundations. These organizational strategies have been used to effect by the New Christian Right, with the presidential campaigns of Ronald Reagan and those of other political figures as indicators. Media attention and criticism made members of the Right as visible as the televangelists who often campaigned on their behalf, and the movement reached the peak of its influence during the early and mid-eighties. But whether the New Christian Right has actually swayed election outcomes is difficult to determine. Some conservatives claim that as many as 2 million people registered to vote in the Reagan years because of the New Christian Right's efforts. On the other hand, national studies of the electorate suggest that Reagan's success and that of other conservatives were functions of a conservative mood in the nation as a whole rather than the direct result of movement activism.

More to the point here, despite its organizational expansiveness, the New Christian Right exemplifies the religious culture of contraction. With its strong tradition of religious privatism, the fundamentalist-evangelical movement is not finally at ease in a public world. Significantly, Falwell left the Moral Majority in 1987 to pay more attention to his pastoral duties, and two years later he dissolved the organization. And Robertson could not win the Republican nomination to the presidency in 1988 because of insufficient support.

As important, the concerns that have mobilized a segment of the population not usually active in public life—the working class and lower middle class, both religiously separatist in the past—have largely touched areas of personal morality and life-style. Often, too, they have been single-issue concerns. Aside from support for a strong national defense, which fits the dispensational vision of a coming final battle with the forces of the Antichrist and evil, positions regarding abortion, pornography, homosexuality, feminism, school prayer, and the like speak to the ways in which intimate aspects of life impinge on society. In short, the strong organizing ability of the New Christian Right serves to construct a world looking inward more than outward, aiming to promote the vision of an earlier, purer America and make of it social reality.

As we have seen, however, pluralism, which seems everywhere in America, also seems everywhere in the fundamentalist-evangelical movement. Not every conservative Protestant supports the goals of the New Christian Right. In fact, some have been as vocal in their support of a politics of the left, and their radical evangelicalism, as it has been called, has countered the politics of the New Christian Right. A case in point is the Sojourners Community and its *Sojourners* magazine.

Sojourners began as early as 1971 among conservative Baptist seminarians at Trinity Evangelical Divinity School, outside of Chicago. In the context of the Vietnam War era, a small group of students—all white, middle-class, and male—began to think of salvation as the redemption of society as a whole as well as the redemption of individuals. With Jim Wallis as their leader, they started a magazine, the *Post-American*, and a year later they established a community, the People's Christian Coalition. In 1975 they left the impoverished Uptown area of northern Chicago where they were living and moved to the nation's capital. Thereafter they changed the name of their magazine and their community to reflect the self-conscious radicalism of their venture. The church, they thought, was an "alien society" of God's people, a body of "sojourners" present in the world but working for a totally different order.

This language of separation and otherness already suggests the contractive nature of the politics of the left that the Sojourners have practiced. In fact, as an exercise in historical comparison, we can look back to the nineteenth-century revival perfectionism of Charles Grandison Finney with its belief that sanctifica-tion was social and its consequent support for social reform. Believing that they were empowered by the Holy Spirit, perfectionists worked in the nineteenth-century temperance, antislavery, and peace movements to purify society and to rid it of corruption. Thus, their seemingly expansive gestures were ways to con-tract the social body by cleansing it of moral pollution. The line connecting the Sojourners to that nineteenth-century past is tenuous but real. And, historical connections aside, the similarity of the Sojourners' motivation for reform and that of Finneyite perfectionists is striking.

In keeping with the biblical image of sojourners as travelers or pilgrims who stay only for a time, members of the Sojourners Community have under-stood their work as both priestly and prophetic. In priestly vein, they consider their intentional Christian community as a way to support one another on their journey, even as they think of the community as a model of the church of the future. In prophetic style, they believe that people of conscience must partici-pate in the political process. The church's mission, they say, is to challenge the existing order, and they criticize cultural conformity in present-day Chris-tianity. Instead, they identify with the poor, engaging in community organizing, forming tenant unions and food cooperatives, and helping establish day-care centers in the run-down Columbia Heights section of Washington, D.C., in which they live. Beyond that, they move into the more specifically political process through their challenges to government housing policies and, on the foreign front, to U.S. support for governments that they consider repressive. With peace and community reconciliation a stated commitment, the Sojourners are antinuclear publicists and activists. They regularly use *Sojourners* magazine to advance their political views. And Wallis has also edited a series of first-person antinuclear accounts in a book titled *Peacemakers* (1983), which is self-consciously subtitled *Christian Voices from the New Abolitionist Movement*. Meanwhile, they demonstrate, try to gain the ears of members of Congress, and organize against nuclear weapons.

By the late eighties, the community consisted of a core group of some sixty persons, with perhaps several hundred adjuncts, often transient, who aided their work. Members' educational attainments ranged from doctoral degrees to high school educations. The community included not only Baptists but also members of peace churches, mainstream Protestants, Roman Catholics, and those with no church affiliation. Even a Hindu joined the group, one former adjunct has reported.

Despite the diversity, the message Sojourners has proclaimed is the contractive message of conservative Protestantism. Although the mature community has moved to a more reflective and contemplative posture than in earlier years, it is still vocal in condemnation of consumerism, militarism, and greed. Preaching poverty instead of wealth and upholding a strict and traditional sexual ethic, the Sojourners Community is moralistic in its stance. Indeed, in one entire issue of the magazine in 1980, the community made the pro-life agenda its theme. The politics of the left, it turned out, was selective, and Sojourners was seeking to bring America to the biblical foundations the community saw as the source of a viable culture.

The Sojourners Community is instructive for understanding radical evangelical politics. Opposed to the policies of the New Christian Right, radical evangelicals are hardly expansive social joiners. If a "radical" is one who returns to "roots," then these conservative Protestants condemn contemporary society and seek a return to biblical roots. For them, such a return has meant rejecting the arms race. But it has also meant repudiating even a Christian capitalism and rejecting what the Sojourners see as the corrupt sexual morality of a modern-day Babylon. In sum, radical evangelicals have promoted a vision that seeks not a linking of the gospel to modern social philosophies but a return to pure biblical teachings as they understand them. In the language used earlier (in Chapter 5) to describe nineteenth-century evangelicals, theirs is a restoration movement.

The Religion of the Fundamentalist-Evangelical Movement

Nor were radical evangelicals alone in their restorationism. For the restoration of an idealized past has been the desire and goal of all fundamentalists and evangelicals. As we survey the conservative spectrum, its pluralism and seeming fragmentation mask the sources of unity that make conservative Protestants of many stripes part of one movement. These sources of unity come strongly from the religion—the belief and action system—that is at the core of fundamentalist-evangelical identity. To a large extent, we have encountered that religion before, in Chapter 5, when we studied the workings of the mission mind. Now we examine, especially, how the fundamentalist-evangelical movement exemplifies the religion of contraction.

As is the case for New Age religion, speculative and phenomenal themes thread their way through fundamentalist-evangelical religion. In this case, though, the themes are generally more integrated, more interwoven into the collective cloth. For all the pluralism in the conservative Protestant community, fundamentalists and evangelicals agree in their commitment to *both* thought and practice. In other words, there is arguably more fully functioning religion among conservative Protestants than among New Agers.

On the other hand, the joining of ordinary and extraordinary religion is weaker in the fundamentalist-evangelical community. Under the sign of correspondence, New Agers easily mix ordinary with extraordinary, even if speculative and phenomenal New Agers do so somewhat differently. Conservative Protestantism by contrast, pays service to separatism. The Protestant separation of extraordinary from ordinary, the legacy of the Reformation, is underlined in ways that liberal Protestants have long discarded. Yet if fundamentalists and evangelicals call on an extraordinary order that stands in judgment of the ordinary world, they also, through their belief in divine intervention in everyday life, bring the extraordinary close to ordinary concerns. Miracles are never far off in fundamentalist-evangelical circles, and if the extraordinary is sharply distinct from the ordinary, God is also thought to interact in human society for small and even trite concerns. Thus, the extraordinary remains extraordinary, but it also becomes an expected presence in ordinary fundamentalist-evangelical life. The ordinary does not become extraordinary, but it does become the ground for extraordinary action.

Cast against this background, the creed of the fundamentalist-evangelical movement is strongly biblical. With the Christian Bible as the record of a God believed to intervene in human history, the biblical proclamation of extraordinariness becomes the center of fundamentalist-evangelical belief. At both ends of the conservative spectrum — and in the middle — the Bible stands as the ultimate religious authority, inerrant in its religious teaching and honored for its revelatory stature. And those who exalt the Bible accept in some form a set of Christian "fundamentals." The list varies to some degree depending on right or left affiliation, and its doctrinal statements are accepted more literally by some and more symbolically by others. But all agree on the centrality of the life and teaching of Jesus. All acknowledge ideas of human sinfulness, divine grace, and a need for repentance. And all believe in the importance of direct experience for assurance of salvation.

At the fundamentalist end of the theological spectrum, dispensational premillennialism lines out an order of end-time events, with the rapture of the saints, the tribulation, Armageddon, and the final New Jerusalem firm and fixed beliefs. Others in evangelical circles do not subscribe to the ordered list. All, however, hold firm to a sense of divine purpose in human history, to belief in a goal toward which all things and events converge. In this sense, all expect a second and final coming of Christ.

The code of the fundamentalist-evangelical movement is predicated on its creed. If there are sharp boundaries between extraordinary and ordinary — and yet divinely initiated interactions between the two — the fundamentalist-evangelical code requires a sharp separation between the extraordinary life of the Christian and the ordinary proceedings of the world. Seen in individual and personal terms, therefore, the code demands holiness. Behavioral norms draw lines between Christian and world in the action language of a strict and traditional morality, especially regarding sexuality, the use of alcohol, and related issues. Depending on where one stands in the conservative spectrum, these guidelines are more or less austere. But they are always enough to become a mark of difference, to set off the conservative Protestant from the perceived dissoluteness of the world.

Viewed in more social and collective terms, the code becomes a quest for order and a directive to mission. The conservative quest for order translates personal concern for boundaries into community effort for containment. Ordered government, ordered social services, ordered conduct of foreign policy, and the like will, according to the conservative ethic, keep evil at bay and erect the safeguards that protect Christian life. Thus, containment for conservatives means the management of evil, preferably by exorcising it. But containment also implies action to hold together a society congenial to conservative Protestant Christianity. From this perspective, political aims are integral. Both the New Christian Right and the radical evangelicals make programmatic attempts to implement the general conservative impulse toward order.

Similarly, the directive to mission — the continuing expression of the mission mind — is also a boundary concern. We will follow up on this observation in the concluding chapter, but here we can notice that mission acquires a strong boundary-maintaining role in a society as plural as our own. Proclaiming the gospel forcefully, again, can help conservatives keep what they regard as evil outside of their protected community. And it can help to keep the faithful within. Thus, the directive to mission is a conservative ethic that enjoins preaching. Mission achieves dramatic form not only in the exhortations of the electronic church but also in the pulpits of conservative churches and the revival tents of itinerant preachers. And mission takes world form in a vast foreign missionary enterprise, expansive in the sense that it seeks to reach as many as possible but contractive in its goal of rescue and protection from evil. But the directive to mission enjoins, too, personal witnessing by all within daily life. Moreover, the ethic also emphatically proclaims that personal behavior affects society. The example of personal holiness becomes a form of mission for conservatives, as much as does the organized effort of preachers and mission organizations.

Preaching and witnessing point us toward fundamentalist-evangelical cultus. For what conservatives preach and witness to is the cultic life that for them provides divine assurance. The ideal for such a cultic life is direct experience. Thus, for fundamentalists and many others, conversion is primary, while for those with holiness and pentecostal roots, the quest for Spirit blessings and healings may be as significant. For all, the felt sense of the extraordinary — of Jesus or the Spirit — are goals of cultic activity. Hence, cultus takes place in the churches and in regular worship services in which the sermon and prayer that foster devotion are made central. Cultus is expressed, too, through regular biblical reading, study, and devotion and through the practice of private prayer.

But in its preference for direct experience, cultus also acquires spontaneity, a quality of surprise and suddenness that comports with beliefs in surprising and sudden divine interventions in the world. In this way, fundamentalist-evangelical worship replicates the strong sense of boundary that is carried by its creed and code. In fundamentalist-evangelical cultus, the extraordinary is seen to juxtapose itself to ordinary life. Human emotions play out the sense of encounter, becoming in the process cultic confirmations of belief. The most favored worship is strongly experiential, because what is powerfully felt can translate into cultus the striking contrast that is claimed between extraordinary and ordinary.

Still, in the fundamentalist-evangelical movement as elsewhere, ritual is still ritual. Studies of cultus often emphasize its formal and repeated character, and they underline a point that needs notice here. Despite their emphatic regard for experience, fundamentalists and evangelicals, like other religious people, practice cultic activity in patterns of repetition and sameness. Fundamentalist and evangelical conversions are a lot like one another: there are expected rules to be followed. So, too, there are expected rules in even the most spontaneous and emotional churches in contemporary holiness-pentecostalism. Some things are allowed and are considered — however disorderly they may look to outsiders — in good order. Other things are clearly beyond the pale. Similarly, reports of fundamentalist and evangelical prayer experiences, for all their emphasis on the spontaneity of emotion, show unfoldment in expected form. And conservative preachings and witnessings, for all their strongly emotional character, follow logical patterns that can be mapped.

In this context, the quest for order that lies at the base of conservative code is reiterated in ritual. And repeated patterns of separating extraordinary from ordinary, of conversely juxtaposing them, and of marking boundaries suggest the character of conservative community. For creed, code, and cultus are all expressions of a body of people with certain ideas about themselves and the nature of the world around them. These ideas, we have seen, take concrete form in numerous ways. Together we can use the ways to give us clues to the community.

From a sociological and demographic perspective, of course, such clues are unnecessary. We can point to studies that underline the pervasiveness of the fundamentalist-evangelical movement. Sociologists of religion Wade Clark Roof and William McKinney, for example, suggest that some 16 percent of Americans in the seventies and eighties belonged to identifiably conservative Protestant churches. Yet in terms of the numbers who — whatever their church affiliation or lack of one — consider themselves fundamentalists and/or evangelicals, that figure is probably too small. In one study conducted in the early eighties, perhaps 40 percent of Americans said they believed that the Bible was the literal word of God, and in another survey, even more than that number subscribed to a belief in the direct divine creation of human beings.

Conservative Protestantism has tended to be stronger in the South, and it has also flourished best among those who have had less education. On the other hand, some 40 percent of easterners and 25 percent of college graduates hold to at least one conservative religious belief. Nor are present-day conservatives the poorest of the poor. Although their forebears may have numbered among the "disinherited," today's fundamentalist-evangelical movement encompasses working-class people with good job security, lower middle-class people and many who have reached greater affluence. African-Americans share much of fundamentalist-evangelical religion, as do some in other ethnic groups, notably Hispanics and Koreans. But the movement we are looking at is largely white. And its politics (despite its radical evangelical wing) are strongly conservative. Meanwhile, the movement runs the gamut from fundamentalist separatism to evangelical accommodation.

But the gap between separatism and accommodation returns us to the structure and content of fundamentalist-evangelical religion and the clues to community they can provide. Such clues take us beyond questions of who join and who count as members to questions of what kind of community they collectively form. Here we find that the sharp break between extraordinary and ordinary distinguishing fundamentalist-evangelical creed, code, and cultus is reflected, too, in their community. Fundamentalists and evangelicals form a community of the separated, of the extraordinary who believe that they are saved from the sin and chaos of ordinary American society. Committed to maintain a pure community, they also seek to restore a perfect social order. All the same, just as the extraordinary is never fully removed from the ordinary in fundamentalist-evangelical thought and practice — just as for them the extraordinary keeps breaking into the ordinary in unforeseen ways — so the separate community feels it must act in American society. Like the biblical God who interfered in history, fundamentalists and evangelicals are drawn toward the ordinary center of American society. If they aspire to reenact the extraordinary pattern of the revelation they claim, one kind of religious logic requires that they enter the world, make their impact in it, use it, and yet be not of it. Separate from society, they must also exist in its midst.

From this perspective, it is not surprising that fundamentalists and evangelicals have disagreed about the amount and quality of separatism and accommodation to the world that Christian commitment demands. And it is not surprising that their ambivalence has persisted. Creed, code, and cultus suggest that the ambivalence is written into the fundamentalist-evangelical constitution, part of the religious structure of their world. At the same time, creed, code, cultus, and, finally, community tell us that the religious world of fundamentalists and evangelicals is a contractive one. Marking and maintaining boundaries are exercises in sharp definition. Separating extraordinary from ordinary, even if — from the side of the extraordinary — they are rejoined, is an operation performed to insure purity. Doctrinal postures like dispensational premillennialism and organizational ventures like the electronic church and the New Christian Right erect walls to consolidate a community. They seek to maintain a safety zone in the modern world where fundamentalists and evangelicals can find solace and relief. That the contraction is strong, sometimes strident, and other times also irritating to outsiders suggests the degree of expansion that fundamentalists and evangelicals find in present-day America. In sum, the expansive nature of contemporary pluralism is the other side of the coin of fundamentalist-evangelical contraction.

Expansion, Contraction, and the Limits of Pluralism

Pluralism — religious manyness — has multiplied in the contemporary United States without any prospect of ending soon. Truisms about the world becoming a global village are echoed in the polyglot and polynational nature of our own society. With no end to religious manyness in sight, there is also no end to the dynamic of expansion. Thus, religious expansionism, whatever form it takes, will be with us for any future we can predict. And therefore religious contraction will also be present. From one point of view, expansion and contraction need and require each other, and, as we have seen, together they create a system that provides a kind of cultural balance.

Moreover, even a brief comparison of the religions of the New Age and the fundamentalist-evangelical movement suggests similarities. Openly hostile to each other, they are also, in important ways, strikingly alike. For both, a direct experience of personal transformation is at the center of religion, and for both ongoing revelation is primary. God is with us, both groups seem to say; and, whether as the felt presence of Jesus, the words of a channeler, or the claims of a shamanic journey, the extraordinary guides — and transfigures — everyday life for believers. Again, both New Agers and conservative Protestants find in the language of healing powerful metaphors to express their dis-ease in contemporary society. Efforts toward holistic health, faith healing, and prayer for recovery are ongoing concerns in a society that, for many, seems out of joint.

Still more, the positivism of religious therapies is linked to a positivism of language in both movements. New Agers, especially phenomenal New Agers, are as likely as many conservative Protestants to insist on the literalism of their beliefs; fundamentalists and evangelicals are as ready as New Agers to embrace a religious materialism in which miracles are evidence of the presence of the extraordinary. Finally, in both movements, spiritual democracy is regnant orthodoxy. Both groups foster an individual initiative in which each believer is invited to create and authenticate religion on his or her own. Both groups have constructed religions of the nonelite, and both favor do-it-yourself thought and action.

But, we may well ask, what happens when — in the midst of these similarities — levels of manyness increase and types and degrees of pluralism become more intensive and more marked? Cultural-systems theory argues that greater contraction is needed to balance greater expansiveness. More of one requires more of the other.

The results might be imagined as aligned on a kind of cultural seesaw. Extremes of expansion are on one end, and extremes of contraction on the other. If people position themselves on both far ends of the seesaw, achieving balance becomes more difficult than it would be if they took positions closer to the middle. Applying the analogy to the religious and social situation of the United States suggests the difficulties of maintaining balance when forces of expansion and contraction continue to increase incrementally. At the same time, the analogy points to the excitement and challenge of the historical moment. In a game of high skill, all of the players must sharpen their abilities and work to full capacity. In a game of high skill, players may surprise themselves in discovering abilities they did not know they had, in finding their balance in a difficult and sometimes unsteady situation.

Thus, while the numerical limits of pluralism are impossible to predict, in a different sense the limits of pluralism become the boundary markers against which religious cultures test themselves. Among both the people who expand and the others who contract, the limits of pluralism help religious people to define and empower themselves.

In Overview

As religious manyness intensified in late-twentieth-century America, religious cultures of expansion and contraction also flourished. One leading example of the contemporary religious culture of expansion has been the New Age movement, which congealed in the late sixties and early seventies. With roots that include mesmerism, Swedenborgianism, and spiritualism as well as Transcendentalism, New Thought, Christian Science, and theosophy, the New Age has also drawn on quantum physics, on various forms of psychology and parapsychology, and on a growing environmental movement. The New Age reflects, too, forms of Asian and Native American religion, and it turns to alternative forms of healing even as it takes its name, in part, from its astrological beliefs.

These ingredients of New Age religion have been appropriated in different ways by different groups of New Agers. To help sort out the situation, it is useful to adopt a distinction between speculative and phenomenal tendencies within the New Age. For a fully functioning religion, of course, speculative thought and phenomenal action must both be present. At the same time, many New Agers have emphasized the speculative side of religion, while others have turned more to the phenomenal. In the religious creed of the New Age, the theory of correspondence expresses a connection claimed by believers between the universe and themselves. But in this creed, too, matter and energy are seen as interchanging, so that beliefs in transformation and in human perfectibility have been central.

In keeping with these beliefs, the New Age code has stressed harmony, but it has also stressed change. Thus, in the New Age code right action for the individual is viewed as action conforming to the laws of nature, but right action is also seen as action that enhances healing. Similarly, right action for society is thought to be action according to harmonial principles of cooperation instead of warring moralities of competition. But right action also means what New Agers call "healing the planet," in causes ranging from environmentalism to antinuclearism and feminism. Meanwhile, New Age cultus has developed in a seeming kaleidoscope of ritual practices, all of them related to the creed and code. Some of the ritual work has emphasized the more harmonial side of New Age religion, as in the form of Japanese palm healing known as Reiki. Other forms of ritual work have paid more attention to mental factors in efforts toward transformation, as in shamanic journeying. Together creed, code, and cultus have helped to define a New Age community bound both by a common language and by the action that New Agers believe will empower individuals and transform society. With their many sources, diverse membership, and numerous practices, New Agers are a prime example of the religious culture of expansion.

By contrast, the fundamentalist-evangelical movement has clearly expressed the religious culture of contraction in contemporary American society. With the separation, in 1941 and 1942, between strict and moderate fundamentalists, the stage was set for the present fundamentalist-evangelical spectrum. Here strict fundamentalists retained the name *fundamentalist*, moderates were known as *evangelical*, and others, notably from the holiness-pentecostal tradition, also acquired the name *evangelical*. Together these groups, plural as they were, have found common ground. Even so, looking at key theological, historical, social, and political differences yields important sources for understanding them.

Theologically, strict fundamentalists hold to dispensational premillennialism with a sequence of end-time events that includes rapture for the saints, tribulation for the world, Armageddon, and the victorious rule of Christ and the saints. More liberal evangelicals accept higher critical study of the Bible, modify beliefs in biblical literalness and inerrancy, and accommodate themselves to social-scientific approaches to religion and the like. Historically, the late-century fundamentalist-evangelical movement encompasses an older fundamentalist community in the direct lineage of the early-century *Fundamentals*. But it also includes many fellow travelers, most salient among them groups within the holiness-pentecostal tradition (although African-American "Bible-believers" and other ethnic evangelicals, especially with Hispanic or Korean roots, might also be cited).

In matters of social style, most notable have been the exuberance and flamboyance of the electronic church, with televangelists who have succeeded in building huge national followings. But there has been a quieter, more contemplative social style within the fundamentalist-evangelical movement, and its trail can be followed in the sale of millions of Bibles, the proliferation of biblical study groups, and other indicators of personal devotion. Meanwhile, fundamentalists and evangelicals have organized politically in the New Christian Right in support of conservative causes. Here they have worked for a strong national defense and have paid attention to matters that touch domestic life, traditional sexual roles and morality, and the character of public education. Conversely, a small number have understood themselves as radical evangelicals and have worked for what they see as return to a biblical morality of justice and mercy that often translates for them into support for a politics of the left.

What unifies fundamentalists and evangelicals in the midst of these differences is a strong affirmation of the authority of the Bible and the centrality of the life and teaching of Jesus. Thus, the creed of the movement centers on the Bible and belief in a traditional Christian message regarding sin and grace, salvation and divine purpose in human history. The code that follows from the creed has stressed personal holiness for individuals and, in society, a quest for good order as well as missionary action. Related to creed and code, cultus has emphasized preaching and prayer in community worship and has fostered, too, a concern for more intimate experiences understood as conversion and Spirit blessing. Also fostered has been a sustained biblical devotionalism. The fundamentalist-evangelical community that shares the creed, code, and cultus moves between a sense of separation from the world and an impulse toward accommodation.

When we juxtapose the fundamentalist-evangelical community to the New Age movement, structural comparison shows surprising points of similarity. Emphases on direct experience, on ongoing revelation, on the need for healing, on literalness in belief and expectation, and on a democracy of believers characterize both groups. Yet the way each group comes to terms with the extraordinary and ordinary in religion is very much different. New Agers more easily fuse the two with their ruling cosmology of correspondence. Fundamentalists and evangelicals stress the separation between extraordinary and ordinary, but in their belief in the biblical God who acts in history they bring the extraordinary close to the ordinary world. The New Age fusion of extraordinary and ordinary points us toward the expansiveness of New Age religion. On the other hand, the separatist tendency in fundamentalist-evangelical appropriation of both suggests the contractive quality of that religious stance.

As manyness multiplies in contemporary America, the cultural system requires both expansive and contractive religion to achieve balance. But greater plurality means a greater need for both expansion and contraction. And the results are often troubling in their promotion of extremism and hostility between opposing factions. While benefits also come with challenge in the cultural situation, the religions of expansion and contraction have historically been supported by a more centrist religious force that softens oppositions and mediates differences. In other words, for all the manyness within American religious history, there has been a religious common ground, a "one religion," if you will, that smooths disparities and promotes homogeneity.

We have encountered this "one religion" a number of times in our extended examination of the manyness of religions in America. Until now, we have looked at length at that manyness, trying to sharpen our focus on numerous *different* centers of meaning, power, and value that have flourished within the pluralism of the United States. At this point, however, it is the issue of the public oneness that must engage us. In Part II we ask a question fundamental to the study of American religious history: if American religions are so many, how in any way can they be one?

SUGGESTIONS FOR FURTHER READING: THE NEW AGE AND FUNDAMENTALIST-EVANGELICAL MOVEMENTS

Adler, Margot. *Drawing Down the Moon: Witches, Druids, Goddess-Worshippers, and Other Pagans in America Today.* Rev. ed. Boston: Beacon Press, 1986.

Albanese, Catherine L. *Nature Religion in America: From the Algonkian Indians to the New Age.* Chicago History of American Religion. Chicago: University of Chicago Press, 1990.

Ammerman, Nancy Tatom. *Bible Believers: Fundamentalists in the Modern World.* New Brunswick, NJ: Rutgers University Press, 1987.

Balmer, Randall. *Mine Eyes Have Seen the Glory: A Journey into the Evangelical Subculture in America.* New York: Oxford University Press, 1989.

Bednarowski, Mary Farrell. *New Religions and the Theological Imagination in America.* Religion in North America. Bloomington: Indiana University Press, 1989.

Bruce, Steve. *The Rise and Fall of the New Christian Right: Conservative Protestant Politics in America, 1978–1988.* New York: Oxford University Press, 1989.

Ellwood, Robert S., and Partin, Harry B. *Religious and Spiritual Groups in Modern America.* 2d ed. Englewood Cliffs, NJ: Prentice-Hall, 1988.

Ferguson, Marilyn. *The Aquarian Conspiracy: Personal and Social Transformation in the 1980s.* Los Angeles: J. P. Tarcher, 1980.

Flake, Carol. *Redemptorama: Culture, Politics, and the New Evangelicalism.* Garden City, NY: Doubleday, Anchor Press, 1984.

Hadden, Jeffrey K., and Shupe, Anson. *Televangelism: Power and Politics on God's Frontier.* New York: Henry Holt, 1988.

Hill, Samuel S., and Owen, Dennis E. *The New Religious Political Right in America.* Nashville: Abingdon, 1982.

Horsfield, Peter G. *Religious Television: The American Experience.* New York: Longman, 1984.

Hunter, James Davison. *Evangelicalism: The Coming Generation.* Chicago: University of Chicago Press, 1987.

Liebman, Robert C., and Wuthnow, Robert, eds. *The New Christian Right: Mobilization and Legitimation.* New York: Aldine, 1983.

Marsden, George, ed. *Evangelicalism and Modern America.* Grand Rapids, MI: William B. Eerdmans, 1984.

————. *Reforming Fundamentalism: Fuller Seminary and the New Evangelicalism.* Grand Rapids, MI: William B. Eerdmans, 1987.

Melton, J. Gordon, with Clark, Jerome, and Kelly, Aidan A. *New Age Encyclopedia.* Detroit: Gale Research, 1990.

Quebedeaux, Richard. *The Young Evangelicals: Revolution in Orthodoxy.* New York: Harper & Row, 1974.

Reid, Daniel G., et al., eds. *Dictionary of Christianity in America.* Downers Grove, IL: InterVarsity Press, 1990.

Roof, Wade Clark, and McKinney, William. *American Mainline Religion: Its Changing Shape and Future.* New Brunswick, NJ: Rutgers University Press, 1987.

Spangler, David. *Emergence: The Rebirth of the Sacred.* New York: Dell Publishing, 1984.

Toolan, David. *Facing West from California's Shores: A Jesuit's Journey into New Age Consciousness.* New York: Crossroad, 1987.

Wilber, Ken. *No Boundary: Eastern and Western Approaches to Personal Growth.* Boston: Shambhala, 1979.

Washington Giving the Laws to America. In this anonymous engraving, George Washington's Caesar-like appearance, his seated posture giving commandments, and the presence of an angelic messenger combine to suggest the religious character of American law and society.

THE ONENESS OF
RELIGION IN AMERICA

If Americans were so many religiously, how—in any meaningful sense—could they be one? And did they not have to be religiously one in order to produce a viable culture and nation-state? Until now, history has shown that some form of religion provides the most powerful and effective source of unity for a nation. Religion, in fact, supplies the ideologies and prescriptive norms that form a kind of cultural "cement" for a society. Were not Americans, therefore, with their announced agenda of religious freedom and separation of church and state, risking their political experiment almost before it got off the ground? And were they not consequently risking the well-being of the populace and so the social peace of the republic? These were important questions for the new nation in the late eighteenth century. In our own times, with pluralism compounded in ways that eighteenth-century American patriots never dreamed, they are even weightier.

If we begin, though, with the objective evidence of the continuance of the nation and, even more, of the culture that had already achieved rough form in the seventeenth century, the search for reasons becomes compelling. And the search yields at least partial results. We find cultural cohesion for American society in a public Protestantism that affects the religious adaptations of even the most "other" among new Americans. We find the cohesion, too, in a religious nationalism that has been called "civil religion." And we find it yet again in a broad cultural religion that encompasses much of public and private life in our society. Within these three sources of common life, millennialism provides a continuing link. Moreover, through these sources of common life, a national culture succeeds in bringing together many Americans, some of the time.

Chapter 12

Public Protestantism: Historical Dominance and the One Religion of the United States

In 1739 Benjamin Franklin found himself in a crowd of Philadelphians absorbed in the message of George Whitefield, the famous Methodist preacher spreading a religious revival from one end of the colonies to the other. Whitefield was also raising money for an orphanage in Georgia, and Franklin, who had previously disapproved of certain details of the plan, had refused to contribute. Now, though, he was so moved by the speaking gifts of Whitefield in the sermon that, despite his best efforts to stop himself, he emptied his pocket—copper, silver, and gold—into the collector's plate. Franklin was a deist and rationalist, and he stood at the other end of the religious world from the pious Whitefield. Yet, melted by his oratorical powers, Franklin yielded and contributed to the collection. Later, he heard Whitefield speak again out of doors and estimated that the preacher's voice could easily carry to 30,000 people. The quality of the sound must have been as impressive as the strength, for David Garrick, the famous English actor of the period, thought that if Whitefield said the word "Mesopotamia" from the stage, he would move his audience to tears.

Franklin, despite a self-consciously different religious identity, had been persuaded by the golden-tongued Whitefield to join in a mass religious episode. The persuasion was temporary and minimal in Franklin's case: Whitefield got Franklin's money but not his mind and heart. Yet for thousands of others, the persuasion was more lasting. These Americans were responding to a ritual that, as the years passed, continued as a highly visible feature of religion in America. Not only individuals but sometimes entire religious traditions embraced it. Revivalism was a major element among the common themes that made up the one religion of Americans.

Benjamin Franklin's experience with the revival brings to mind the story of the elephant and the blind men in the Introduction. The elephant, we recall, was likened to religion in America — a gigantic creature to be examined piece by piece. Like the blind men of the parable, we have been acquiring knowledge of different parts of the animal. We have been reviewing the separate and distinct religious movements that were and are key examples of the manyness of religions in America. In fact, so separate and distinct have been the various movements we have examined that it seemed as if we were describing different animals and even different species. Not only were there many religious traditions within the geographical boundaries of the United States, but there was manyness *within* traditions. American Indians belonged to separate nations, each with its own religion. Protestants showed as much manyness with their numerous denominations. Catholics demonstrated ethnic identities that created tensions within a supposedly unified church, while occult, metaphysical, and New Age forms of religion seemed almost as numerous as the people who turned to them.

By the same token, even as we immersed ourselves in this religious pluralism, from time to time we could not fail to notice the ways in which different traditions and movements seemed to take on some of the characteristics of the Protestant mainstream. Reform Jews of the late nineteenth century moved their Sabbath services to Sunday morning and imitated the style of Protestant worship. Catholics after Vatican II adopted a leaner and simpler version of the Mass, closer to the demands of the Protestant Reformation. Mormons and Adventists, who affirmed the good life in this world, resembled liberal Protestants in their optimism, while Japanese Buddhists in America spoke of churches, acknowledged bishops, and initiated Sunday services. Meanwhile, blacks who became middle class often gravitated toward congregations that were integrated or that resembled in their style the churches of white mainline Protestantism. In these and other instances, manyness was still thriving, but there were numerous ways in which the boundaries of the separate traditions overlapped the boundaries of Protestantism.

Even further, in the chapters on Protestantism, we noticed in exploring denominationalism, revivalism, and related questions the ways in which Protestants, despite their liberal and conservative differences, often looked alike. As we have already begun to see, that similarity *among* Protestants also became a similarity *with* other Americans. The majority tradition acted in subtle and not-so-subtle ways to wear away the sharp edges of separateness and to bring people toward itself. Hence, in this chapter we examine more directly a theme that we have observed all along — how Protestantism acted as the dominant and public religion of the United States. We notice that the dominant and public religion included the inheritors of the Reformation but also millions of "cultural" Protestants who had through the American experience absorbed aspects of the dominant tradition. Then, in later chapters, we look at related elements of the oneness of religion in America.

Saying that Protestantism acted as the dominant and public religion of the United States means saying that Protestantism became the one religion of the country. Whatever it meant in the personal lives of millions, publicly Protestantism meant acknowledged ways of thinking and acting that were supported by most institutions in society—by the government (though unofficially), the schools, the media, and countless churches and families. If in Part I we saw the many in their manyness by examining different religious communities and their histories, here we face unified social, political, and economic power.

Before we go further, however, some distinctions need to be made. First, religion, we have seen, is both extraordinary—beyond the boundaries of the everyday world—and ordinary—within its limits. In these terms, Protestantism formed the basis for both extraordinary and ordinary religion in the United States. The chief extraordinary religion in America was and is Protestantism, and similarly, the ordinary religion of mainstream American culture possesses characteristics that derive historically from the Protestant experience in the country. Although it is not possible to draw a sharp line between extraordinary and ordinary forms of Protestantism, we can at least see different instances in which one or the other has predominated.

Second, the oneness of religion in America was historically present from the time the English colonies were established. But it also grew with the years, so that various parts acquired new features and became more prominent or—like the Calvinist belief in predestination—gradually faded. Third, the oneness of religion was related to the continuance of a certain community, the early settlers and their offspring, who were of Anglo-Saxon and Northern European stock. But it was also related to the widespread adoption by others of the creed, code, and cultus that the original community handed on. Although many times they were unaware of it, Catholics and Jews, Buddhists and Eastern Orthodox Christians could and did share in public Protestantism. So did countless others from among the many. Hence, as we try to understand the one religion of Americans, we will have to be aware of its complexity.

American Religious History and Public Protestantism

To locate the dominant Protestant community and understand its religion, later shared by others, is to encounter a group of related characteristics. Some were elements of a code of everyday behavior; some were aspects of a cultus, or system of ritual expression; and some were parts of a creed, or set of beliefs. Together these characteristics formed a complete religious system in which the elements interrelated in a coherent whole. One characteristic led logically and psychologically to the next one, and the last characteristic led back to the first. This religious system—called here public Protestantism—did grow and change with the years, but in order to simplify, we will examine only its continuing elements and major moments.

Public Protestantism originated in the Calvinist Christianity of the early Puritan settlers. As we saw in Chapter 4, Puritanism in one form or another was widespread in the colonies. Puritan attitudes and ways characterized public life from Massachusetts Bay to the southern settlements. To put this into statistical terms, out of 154 congregations in the colonies in 1660, nearly 90 percent (138) could be described in the broad sense as Calvinist in inclination. Of these, 75 were Congregational, 41 Anglican, 5 Presbyterian, 4 Baptist, and 13 Dutch Reformed. Eliminating these last leaves over 80 percent who had, generally speaking, not only Calvinist but also Puritan roots. That kind of numerical predominance would continue to be a feature of organized Protestantism in the United States. By the time of the first great revival (the Great Awakening), roughly three-fourths of the colonists still leaned toward Calvinism. By the time of the census of 1790, 83.5 percent of enumerated Americans were counted as English, and they were overwhelmingly Protestant. As late as 1987, 57 percent of all Americans considered themselves Protestant, and again the churches of Calvinist heritage formed the largest block in the listing.

If these large numbers of religious adherents helped to shape public Protestantism, so did the educational earnestness of Puritan Christians. With its opening lines, "In Adam's Fall/We sinned all," *The New England Primer* (1683?) was published in an estimated 7 million copies by 1840. Together the opening lines and the publishing data suggest the enormous religious influence that this single Puritan reader was to have in the early education of other Americans. As we saw in both the Introduction and Chapter 4, New England settlers stressed education from the first. The Massachusetts Bay colonists, we recall, founded Harvard College in 1636, and shortly it was bequeathed 400 books by the young minister John Harvard (1607–1638). By 1639 the first printing press in the colonies was operating from the Harvard College Yard, and the *Primer* as well as the famous *Bay Psalm Book* was printed there.

On the elementary-school level the efforts were strenuous. A legislative act of 1642 made it the responsibility of parents in Massachusetts Bay to educate their children in the "three Rs." Later, towns that had reached the size of fifty families were legally bound to obtain a schoolmaster to teach their children. The Connecticut and New Haven colonies shortly enacted similar laws. Puritans wanted their children to be able to read in order that they might understand the Bible for themselves. Puritan culture meant that people of the Word needed to be literate and that people called by the Word to a vocation in the world also needed to be able to communicate in writing and to use numbers in order to do business. But a Puritan education began and ended in religion, so that the textbooks written for the schools, like *The New England Primer*, spread the message of Calvinist Christianity among the young. As education became more common in the colonies and then in the nineteenth century was mandated by law in state after state, it was not surprising that the early New England textbooks provided

A   In *Adam's* Fall
We Sinned all.

B   Thy Life to Mend
This *Book* Attend.

C   The *Cat* doth play
And after flay.

D   A *Dog* will bite
A Thief at night.

E   An *Eagles* flight
Is out of fight.

F   The Idle *Fool*
Is whipt at School.

The New England Primer. By the late seventeenth century, Massachusetts Bay was printing this text for young students, who would learn the alphabet and the Puritan vision of life at the same time. The primer became an influential model for later American textbooks.

models for the teaching material that came into use. Clearly, New England had established a corner on the material that appeared in educational texts. Into the twentieth century, it was the Puritan vision of American life that predominated in the textbooks used by schoolchildren from coast to coast.

Similarly, the politics of leadership in the colonies helped to create public Protestantism. From the first, many of the people who governed were representatives of a committed elite of Calvinist Christians. In Massachusetts Bay, for example, only men who were church members could vote and hold civil office. In Pennsylvania leadership remained in the hands of the founding Quakers and their descendants into the eighteenth century. The Dutch colony of New Amsterdam (later New York) had Dutch Reformed lay leadership until it fell to the English, while lay members of the Anglican church governed in colonial Virginia. Especially in New England and in Pennsylvania, a self-conscious moral and religious intent pervaded government. Political leaders shaped the civil life of their colonies to reflect their religion. The prestige of their positions lent added public importance to Protestantism.

Besides this prestige through political association, Protestantism enjoyed legal privilege through an official and established Anglicanism in the southern colonies and through a Puritan establishment in New England. Such establishments fell away in the late eighteenth and early nineteenth centuries, but the religious imprint left by early colonial history was not easily erased. As newcomers arrived in the United States, it was natural that they should be taught an esteem for Protestantism along with regard for the institutions of American government and life. Hence, the religious stamp of the colonies lingered on in the public life of the nation, something we will look at further in Chapter 13.

Finally, the usefulness of Calvinist Christianity in helping people to meet the demands of their New World environment also enhanced its stature. Protestantism became dominant, in part, because there was a fit between its thisworldly ethic and the essentials of settling a country. Indeed, Protestantism seemed an ideal religion for those who wanted to "tame" a landscape and lead it from its "wilderness" condition into a replica of the best in Old World civilization. If, as the settlers intended, New England were to resemble a reformed old England and if Virginia were to prove a tribute to the Virgin Queen, Elizabeth I, then hard work, commitment, and frugality must be promoted. At the same time, worship must be kept simple and streamlined, capable of thriving no less in a bare, log chapel than in an elaborate church. Later, as the United States grew and prospered, Calvinist Christianity fitted a culture bent on material progress and industrial efficiency. With its belief in a Word that led into the world and in the religious significance of success, it supported a developing nation. It is only a very recent awareness that has led to major questioning of the goals of the age of progress. Well into the twentieth century, Calvinist Christianity upheld the public aims and intentions of the United States as well as the private ends of millions of its citizens.

The Protestant Code

Earlier in the text, we explored religious systems by looking first at their creeds, or systems of belief, and then moving to consider their ritual and ethical expressions in cultus and code. However, as we investigate the dominant and public Protestantism of America, it will be easier to examine first the everyday attitudes and behavioral styles that form the Protestant code. This code is a large part of the body of connecting religious characteristics that we noted earlier. Present nearly everywhere in Protestant America, the code has expressed itself as clear conditions, institutions, and underlying patterns for behavior within the mainstream. In fact, this code has been the most readily identifiable feature of American Protestant religion and culture — although, as we will see, cultic and creedal expressions are easy to identify as well.

The Conditions: Religious Liberty, Democratic Equality, Separation of Church and State

The code begins with *religious liberty* and *democratic equality*, the social conditions that became a pattern of life, at first unevenly in the colonies and later with more consistency in the young republic. Religious liberty and democratic equality were important ideals for social life even in many colonies with religious establishments. New England Puritans, although they tried to keep Quakers and other dissenters away, had come to the New World in order to enjoy religious liberty for themselves. Meanwhile, in colonies like Pennsylvania and Maryland, pluralism was a fact and religious liberty much of the time a reality. There *were* distinct political inequalities in the English settlements. Full citizenship with voting rights was never the possession of everyone. Religious, racial, sexual, and property qualifications existed, and only a certain class of men were truly "equal." Still, the ideals of liberty and equality were often seen as present in existing conditions by these men of property and "proper" religious preference, and the later history of the United States brought increasing movement toward full realization.

Moreover, the heritage of the Radical Reformation partially influenced many of the colonists. The English Puritans had absorbed a strain of Calvinism that was mingled in their minds with Radical ideas. In New England the congregational form of church government was based on the Radical concept of the gathered or free church, a community of commitment entered without force. The corollary of such a gathered congregational church was religious liberty, for — as proponents reasoned — how could a church be free if people entered it by birth or by provision of a ruler? Thus, religious liberty was a necessity, at least in theory, for the operation of Puritan principles. These principles were tested when Roger Williams was banished from Massachusetts Bay. After his pronounced Separatist convictions led him into trouble with the authorities, he founded the Rhode Island colony, we recall, as a refuge for religious seekers. As leader of the Baptists there, he proved the sincerity of his commitment to religious liberty when he provided a haven for Quakers even though he heartily disapproved of their teachings. And as Baptist churches grew in number and influence in the eighteenth century, their message played an important role in laying the groundwork for religious liberty in the new nation.

When the Constitution was adopted in 1789, religious liberty was legally specified in the *separation of church and state*, or religious disestablishment. Congress could make no law either establishing a religion or prohibiting its "free exercise." Nor could the government require any religious affiliation for officeholding. Legally, this disestablishment referred only to the new federal government, but by 1833 the last state, Massachusetts, had fallen into line and abolished its religious establishment. The reasons for the arrangement were both practical and ideological. With the diversity of religious settlements in the various colonies, it would have proved impossible to unite them except on terms that recognized the religious rights of all. Beyond that, after the adoption of the Declaration of Independence in 1776, Enlightenment teachings about equal and unalienable rights given by nature had become part of the public rhetoric. Even earlier, as we know, British soldiers had brought the Enlightenment to the popular notice during the French and Indian War. So notions concerning natural liberty blended in the climate of the times with other ideas about religious liberty derived from Baptist and free-church sources.

Separation of church and state was a new and, indeed, revolutionary settlement of the religious question. Until the Reformation of the sixteenth century, Europe had understood itself as Christendom—one theoretically unified kingdom of Christ in which spiritual and worldly power were separate aspects of the whole. Even after the Reformation, leading Reformers, such as Martin Luther and John Calvin, and Roman Catholics had agreed that spiritual and worldly government went hand in hand. As we saw earlier, both mainstream Reformers and Roman Catholics persecuted the Radical Reformers, who with their sectarian principle were viewed as dangerous to the church–state unity of Christendom. Official state churches, whether Protestant or Catholic, were the rule in Europe. Holland, the most liberal nation in its tolerance for dissent in the seventeenth and eighteenth centuries, still had a state Reformed church until 1795. England during the same period continued to maintain a religious establishment. Hence, when Americans separated church and state through the new federal Constitution, even though they understood themselves still as Christian and predominantly Protestant, they had created a radically new condition for religion.

The Institutions: Denominationalism and Voluntaryism

This new condition became part of the Protestant code and in turn led to the next characteristics of the dominant and public religion. These were the institutions of *denominationalism* and *voluntaryism*. We have already encountered denominationalism in earlier chapters. The key point here is that conditions of religious liberty, democratic equality, and church–state separation determined the ways in which religious communities could organize most effectively. Since religious associations could not count on state support, they could not hope to include all inhabitants, for the country was being settled by members of many different religious bodies. By the same token, because religious associations did not need to worry about state interference, they were being invited to loosen their boundaries and to mingle freely in society. Thus, one of the factors that in Europe made for the creation of separate and exclusive sects was missing. And thus, under circumstances of official governmental neutrality, an unofficial "establishment" grew up in the United States. The dominant and public religion, recognized and approved by society, was denominational. Denominations thought their specific teachings were important, and they did not consider one religious group exactly the same as any other. Yet they saw themselves as part of the larger spiritual organization of the Christian church, even as they were willing to embrace the idea of separate jurisdictions. Moreover, since religious liberty was a matter of law, nobody could be forced to join a denomination, and no outside assistance could be expected in running its internal affairs or in bringing its Christian witness to others outside the denomination.

The response of denominations to this situation was voluntaryism. Remember that denominations already consisted of groups of volunteers: they were from the beginning *voluntary* societies. Soon, however, voluntaryism became a principle of their activity. Financially, they depended on voluntary support by their members instead of a public tax. Managerially, even during the days of state establishment, Protestantism had fostered lay control of many aspects of each organization, and if anything, the new arrangements only increased this tendency. Then, by the nineteenth century, the denominations looked outward in their voluntaryism. More and more, members of different denominations cooperated, as we have seen, in the formation of voluntary societies beyond their official jurisdictions. Their aims in each case were to spread the fundamentals of the Christian message in America and the world. Despite their doctrinal differences, there were many points on which most of them agreed: the basic importance of the Bible, the use of Sunday schools to spread Christian teaching, the advantages of pamphlet literature about shared Christian ideas, plans for missionary efforts.

So in the space of a few years, national voluntary societies came into existence. Organizations that we have met before, such as the American Board of Commissioners for Foreign Missions (1810), the American Education Society (1815), the American Bible Society (1816), the American Sunday School Union (1824), and the American Tract Society (1825), were all agents of the dominant and public Protestantism of the nation. Run by wealthy and influential lay Protestant citizens, these societies often shared many of the same individuals in leadership roles. Directors of one organization frequently appeared on the board of directors in another. By the 1830s they were controlling what some historians have described as a "benevolent empire."

The Patterns: Activism and the Search to Simplify

Later we will see how voluntaryism spread outward to encompass issues of moral and social reform. Now, however, we need to notice a further interlocking element in the Protestant code. Recall that religious liberty, democratic equality, and separation of church and state were background conditions for religion and that denominationalism and voluntaryism were institutions. With the next item, we encounter a pattern to which everyday behavior conformed. That pattern was *activism*. There were historical roots for the activism that flourished within the Protestant churches, and our study in Chapters 4 and 5 stressed how the Word led into the world. But in America, there were new reasons for religious people to be active. Denominationalism and voluntaryism meant that individuals had to take part in efforts to advance the case for their religion among their fellow citizens. In a young nation that had to build and to plant to insure the future, religious organizations had to do the same. The result was increased religious busyness, a spiritual style that put its premium on public and expressive behavior.

Missionary efforts such as those we explored in Chapter 5 were only part of this story of activism. Despite their cooperation on many counts, the denominations engaged in strenuous competition. To survive without state support meant to dispute the teachings of other churches and to strive to bring more and more people into one's own. Furthermore, the situation demanded the construction of churches, seminaries, and colleges. Especially on the frontier, where institutions arrived after the pioneers, Protestants saw their task as the advancement of Christian civilization. They thought that unless they provided the necessary structures to generate Christian influence, chaos and barbarism would thrive. Of course, the establishment of these institutions was part of the home missionary campaign. Still, people felt that it was not enough simply to speak out for Protestantism. Material efforts had to be made so that buildings could rise. Active people, living an active Christianity, were required.

More than that, this Protestant activism blended indistinguishably with the active style of a growing America. In other words, both the extraordinary religion of Protestantism and the ordinary religion of American culture reflected the activist impulse. Americans, as people, were doers more than thinkers. They loved to speed, and in the nineteenth century they marveled at the invention of rail transportation that typically carried people at seven times the speed of stagecoaches. When steam engines hastened travel on western rivers, Americans delighted in running races with their boats — sometimes to the point of disastrous explosions and accidents. Over a century later, it was much the same. Fast food became a symbol of American culture; the imposition, for a time, of a fifty-five-mile-an-hour speed limit was viewed by many as a national tragedy; and jogging became a national passion. For Americans, to be active was to be oriented rightly; to be fast was to be virtuous.

Religious liberty, democratic equality, and church–state separation were ordinary conditions for the existence of extraordinary religion. Denominationalism and voluntaryism were ordinary institutions, sociologically speaking, that supported the extraordinary commitments of many people. In activism, though, we are faced with a behavioral pattern that had both extraordinary and ordinary aspects. Protestant activism merged with the larger activism of American culture, for Protestantism was indeed *public*. To ask which activism caused the other would be very much like asking a chicken-and-egg question. The relationship between extraordinary and ordinary activism was circular and mutually reinforcing. There were roots in the history of Protestantism. There were other roots that were generated in the American environment. Protestantism strongly influenced American culture, but American culture kept changing Protestantism.

The activist impulse within the churches was related to further aspects of the Protestant code. Among them, *reductionism* affected the way people dealt with religion in general, while *nonintellectualism* affected the way they treated ideas, and *ahistoricism* influenced their attitudes toward the past. Let us look in turn at each of these characteristics of public Protestantism.

Reductionism meant reducing things to their lowest common denominator—to their simplest terms. Such reductionism was related to activism, because activism encouraged a paring away of religion to the bare essentials. If people were to busy themselves in the task of building a Protestant civilization, they did not have much time for elaborations, whether of religion or of anything else. They had to be content with laying out the basic structure. Attention to details would come later, if at all. The ambition of the Protestant goal was underlined by the problems, in many cases, of frontier life, far away from big cities with their intellectual excitement and material goods and services. In America there was, it seemed, limitless space but limited time. So a "bare-bones" approach characterized the spread of Protestantism. As we will see later in the chapter, both creed and cultus came to be very simple—a few clear-cut and easily grasped ideas; an equally simple and effective ritual life. Meanwhile, reductionism itself became part of the behavioral code. People were uncomfortable with ambiguities, and they wanted precise rules for their deeds. For them, either an action was right, or it was wrong. People could live with "yes" or "no," but they could not be comfortable with "it depends."

The results of this pattern of reductionism were evident in both extraordinary and ordinary religion. Within the Protestant churches, crusades such as temperance, to be discussed in more detail later, developed in an all-or-nothing direction. Either people did not drink at all, or, temperance advocates thought, they became disreputable and depraved individuals. Either Christians were "saved" and wholly in the camp of Jesus, or, evangelists believed, they were hell-bound sinners. At the same time, within American culture a related preference for simple rules of behavior was encouraged. The old code of honor between men, for example, required that an insult be righted by a duel. Social shame was a matter of life or death with little in between. Similarly, nineteenth-century Americans frequently reacted to the poor quality of medical care in their society by turning to patent drugs that promised to be miracle cures for every ailment. And, as another instance, writers were fond of describing their period as a time of "ultraisms," their term for radicalisms of many types.

Twentieth-century religion and culture continued to reflect the basic attitude of reductionism. After mid century, we know, conservative Protestant churches grew rapidly while the liberals marked time. Among the reasons was the clear and simple ethic that the conservatives taught. For them, sex outside of marriage was wrong, and Christian witness was right. Gambling and alcohol led to trouble, but love for country and loyalty in war were good. General American culture taught a related message about the clear division between good and evil. Television Westerns had their heroes and villains, the "good guys" and the "bad guys," while when in 1990 Saddam Hussein invaded Kuwait, many considered him an Arab Hitler.

In the area of ideas, reductionism became a more specific nonintellectualism. Active Americans tended to have limited intellectual opportunities and time for thought. Moreover, they were impatient with purely theoretical distinctions that could not be put to practical use. In a widely read nineteenth-century biography, George Washington was praised because he had not studied the impractical "dead" ancient languages of Latin and Greek. In like fashion, the full title of the American Philosophical Society, founded in the eighteenth century, announced that it promoted "useful knowledge." This meant everything from preserving wine to cultivating silkworms, but it did *not* mean abstract theorizing. Later Americans followed in this path. The nineteenth and twentieth centuries saw them develop advanced practical technologies for home, industrial, and wartime use. Yet thoughtful Americans continued to complain that they did not have a national literature or philosophical tradition that rivaled the European contribution. Meanwhile, in the late twentieth century the school systems in many states were in trouble because adequate taxes were not collected to finance them.

If nonintellectualism was a feature of ordinary American culture, it was also a part of the dominant and public Protestantism of the country. Although European Protestantism had flourished in a strongly theological atmosphere and New England Puritanism had encouraged the development of religious thought, the nineteenth century saw an increasing unwillingness among many Protestants to engage in hard theological thinking. With the background of democratic equality and the institution of voluntaryism to stimulate them, lay Protestants felt that theology, as much of it as was necessary, was their province. In their view, they did not require an elite to do their thinking for them.

Beyond that, as the tradition of a learned ministry fell away because of the demands of preaching a simple gospel on the frontier, theology lost its subtlety. Like intellectual activity in general, American theology was expected to be useful. Significantly, the man often called the greatest Protestant theologian that

America produced—Jonathan Edwards—was an eighteenth-century representative of the Puritan and Calvinist traditions who lived well before the age of the largest frontier expansion. In the later twentieth century, the new theologies that Americans expounded were directed toward practical issues—the problems of African-Americans, Hispanics, and women, the goal of economic liberation in Third World countries, the relationship between Christianity and religious nationalism (civil religion).

What nonintellectualism did for the mental "space" of ideas, ahistoricism did for time. Ahistoricism was the refusal to dwell on the past or to feel bound by the events of European history. And like nonintellectualism, it was an example of the reductionist tendency to simplify. Yet in America, this ahistoricism was a complex response, one that was part of Protestantism and also part of mainstream culture. And we have already met it in part in restorationism, a movement that appeared again and again in American religious history.

The Reformation of the sixteenth century urged Christians to forget the centuries of tradition that had intervened between the time of Jesus and its own age. It proclaimed the authority of the Bible alone, and it tried to clear away what it regarded as corruption and superstition. By skipping over the medieval centuries in its quest for meaningful time, the Reformation started Protestantism down a path on which it became easier to disregard history. In Europe, with its history written into the landscape of ancient shrines and churches, tradition still played an important part in Protestant life. In America, though, where no European memorials from the past were located, it was easier to forget. Moreover, the ordinary images and metaphors used to describe America suggested the absence of links with the past. It was called a New World; it had been "discovered" by Europeans; the national government of the United States had been founded on a "revolution." With this background, Americans were far more interested in making history than in reading or honoring it.

Protestant life in the new country both reflected and helped to create the general situation. Churches were forced in one way or another to cut their ties with the past. After the Revolution, Anglicanism, as the established Church of England, was unwelcome in the new United States. So members of that religious community, as we saw, reconstituted themselves as Episcopalians. Likewise, the Methodists, supplied with American bishops, went their own way, separate from the mother country. Neither congregational nor presbyterian forms of church government favored close ties with European religious communities, while in the nineteenth century the religious work on the frontier meant preoccupation with the present. For Protestants as for other Americans, the passage of time in the past seemed dead in comparison with the demands and opportunities of the moment. New denominations sprang up, and the fact that they did not have a past was considered an asset more than a liability. If there was a direction in which Protestants and others looked, it was not the past but the future.

Significantly, many of the new religious movements declared that their roots were in a sacred, biblical time outside the ordinary run of history, and restorationism, as we know, was widespread. Seventh-day Adventism claimed it had sprung up during the time of Enoch before the coming of Jesus. The Churches of Christ said they dated back to the time of Jesus. Christian Science announced it was restoring the healing practices of the early church. In each of these examples and in many others like them, the appeal was to an era that skipped over the centuries of ordinary time. By the twentieth century, as we saw, conservative Protestant churches were illustrating the pattern in their involvement in millennialism, a subject that we will take up again later in the chapter. General American culture repeated the story as well. The original Henry Ford was reputed to have said that history was bunk. The flower children of the sixties wanted to abandon the past as they looked to the dawning of an age of harmony and love. Other young people, who were more conservative, withdrew in large numbers from university history courses as soon as they were no longer required to take them. And the New Age of the last decades of the century—considered as a general movement in culture—self-consciously sought to separate itself from the words and deeds of an establishment past.

The Patterns: Moralism

So far we have seen that certain conditions (religious liberty, democratic equality, the separation of church and state) and institutions (denominationalism and voluntaryism) favored the growth of specific behavioral patterns—the code of Protestant America. Activism, reductionism, nonintellectualism, and ahistoricism were all among these patterns. Probably the most important, though, is the one we will explore now. If any one characteristic gave its overall shape to the Protestant code, that characteristic was *moralism*. The activism of Protestant Americans and their wish to simplify life led to a concern for the rules of action. Morality became the clearest test of Christian commitment and the key element in Christian life.

Moral fervor has long roots in the Judeo-Christian tradition. In our look at the Hebrew prophets, we could not fail to notice their strong ethical impulse. Similarly, when we examined the birth of the mainstream of the Reformation, we saw clearly that belief in the Word of scripture prompted moral action in the world, while we saw, too, the quest for moral purity in the sectarianism of the Radical Reformers. Developments in seventeenth- and eighteenth-century Europe further encouraged a moralistic attitude among Protestants. We have seen that Calvinism came gradually to regard good works and righteousness as central. At the same time, other Protestants began to feel that the descendants of the Reformation had lost their zeal. They were, these critics said, too involved in preserving correct doctrine, and they did not inspire people to an enthusiastic attachment to Christianity. Many of these Pietist critics who sought greater zeal—among them Lutherans, Separatists, and Moravians—later immigrated to America.

In this country, concern for morality combined with Puritan and Enlightenment influences as well as other currents in the culture to produce an ordinary and extraordinary religion of moralism and reform. Even before the arrival of continental Pietists, New England Puritans had fostered their own form of pietism in their demand for an experience of conversion and continuing moral rectitude for full church members. Moreover, Puritan sermons early came to reflect a classic style, so that historians today call them jeremiads. Like the biblical Lamentations of the prophet Jeremiah, jeremiads were sermons of sorrow. They bewailed what were considered the sins of individuals and the community and predicted that these sins would force the hand of God in punishment. These Puritan sermons, often printed and distributed after they were given, set a tone of guilt and need for repentance and action that became characteristic of the public language of America. As we will see in Chapter 13, the same tone was reflected in political speeches and in civil religion. Here it is important to note that the style of the jeremiad led to a felt need for moral purification in society — a feeling that bore fruit in crusades like the temperance and antislavery campaigns of the nineteenth century.

Meanwhile, another strand in Protestantism came to influence the dominant and public religion toward moralism. Gradually, as we saw in Chapter 4, Puritan preaching changed, and especially in and near Boston, ministers of the eighteenth century spread liberal Christianity. Important to this change was their acceptance of Arminian teachings. Recall that Arminianism countered the stern Calvinism of an earlier era with the message that Jesus had died for all people. Conversely, for Arminianism no one's salvation was assured, and each person must strive earnestly to persevere in the Christian life. Morality became the key to authentic Christianity, and the Boston ministers echoed the message by preaching sermons filled with directions concerning how to live.

From another quarter, the moral teachings of Arminianism received encouragement. As we saw in Part I, Enlightenment deism taught a simple creed of belief in God and an afterlife of future reward or punishment. But most important to deistic or "natural" religion was a good and moral life. In effect, what a person believed was not so significant in deism as what that person did or did not do. The real test of religion was moral effort. When the liberal Christians of New England became Unitarians after 1825, their teaching was in many ways close to Enlightenment deism. Until the time of the Civil War, their "moral philosophy" remained the same, providing a background for New Englanders who took action in various moral crusades of the period. Likewise, evangelical Protestants who were stirred by the revivals trod their own moral ground. Like the Puritans of an earlier time, they sought to purify themselves and to remain free from sin. Alcohol, gambling, sexual promiscuity, and even dancing, they thought, could corrupt people and separate them from Jesus. Besides, zeal for the gospel meant for evangelicals a need to labor for moral reform in society.

Hence, by the nineteenth century, Protestant America had a history that urged it toward moralism. One strand, descended from the evangelical side of

Puritanism — and expressing religious contraction, led toward various Protestant movements for immediate purification, either from private vices like alcoholism or from public sins such as slavery. The other strand, brought together from the expansive, liberal side of Puritanism, Enlightenment deism, and, as we will see later, general Protestant perfectionism and millennialism, committed itself to efforts to achieve social justice. This could mean work for antislavery, for women's rights, for peace, or for other reform causes. At the same time, a third strand, derived from general American culture, joined forces with Protestantism in the various reform movements. The reconstruction of society was a goal that stirred many nineteenth-century Americans. Whether as part of an extraordinary commitment to a God beyond this world or as an ordinary venture for common decency, the moral reforms for which Americans labored were the same or nearly so.

To take one example of a campaign largely for moral purity, we glance briefly at the antebellum (pre–Civil War) nineteenth-century temperance movement. Historical evidence concerning early Americans suggests that they drank significant amounts of hard liquor. In fact, estimates of how much alcohol they used range from two and one-half gallons annually for each person in 1792 to seven and one-half gallons in 1823. Benjamin Rush, the eminent physician of the revolutionary and postrevolutionary years, warned in a publication of the dangers of alcohol to body and mind, and members of the American Tract Society, who reprinted the work, agreed. At first, efforts were directed toward moderating the use of alcohol rather than banishing it, although Methodists and Quakers disapproved of liquor entirely. By the early to middle years of the nineteenth century, however, the spread of the right to vote to men without property encouraged social leaders to push to insure a sober electorate. Moreover, the existence of social problems such as poverty and crime also caught the attention of social leaders, who associated these evils with drunkenness.

In this atmosphere, the clergy launched a vigorous campaign for the temperance cause. Congregations repeatedly heard sermons on the evils of drink, and by 1813 the Massachusetts Society for the Suppression of Intemperance came into existence. Then after 1825 the focus of the movement shifted, and total abstinence from alcohol became the cry. Temperance became an absolute proposition, in line with the characteristic American demand for simplicity. The message was that drinking must end *now* as the code of moral purity required. The well-known Lyman Beecher — whom we met in Chapter 4 — began preaching sermons calling for complete renunciation of drink. The American Society for the Promotion of Temperance was born in 1826, immediately waging a successful campaign to get people to sign a teetotaler's pledge not to drink. And after 1833, the American Temperance Society became the national focus of the abstinence crusade.

There was a brief period of decline at the end of the decade, but the movement found new allies in an organization of reformed drunkards and in the work of novelists such as Timothy Shay Arthur, whose *Ten Nights in a Bar Room* (1854)

Family Temperance Pledge. Women organized together and actively promoted the temperance cause, using domestically oriented aids like this one to exert moral pressure. First reason given for signing the pledge is that "moderate drinking tends to drunkenness, while total abstinence directly from it."

became a best-seller. Meanwhile, women staunchly supported the clergy, and in states like Maine (1846), Vermont (1852), and New York (1854), prohibition of alcoholic beverages became the law. Prohibition legislation spread until a total of fourteen states and one territory had laws on their books. Only the tensions over slavery and the shadow of the coming Civil War distracted the reformers and diffused the energies of the temperance workers, so that the heyday of the antebellum movement was over.

Temperance, abstinence, and prohibition, all expressing themes of religious contraction, derived from a desire for purification. Renouncing strong drink, it was believed, would cleanse the body of physical and, more important, moral evil — evil that could weaken an individual's self-control and lead to further sinful and antisocial deeds. By banishing drinking, reformers argued, the body of society would also purge itself — of crime, poverty, and an ignorant and irresponsible citizenry. Both for extraordinary and ordinary reasons, people rallied to the cause of purity, together giving testimony to a dominant and public religion that was both Protestantism and culture.

The cause of purity also motivated a second major crusade of the times — the campaign against slavery. But here the urge to purity was joined more clearly by the yearning of some for greater social justice. From colonial times, there had been opposition to slavery, and in fact one version of the Declaration of Independence had expressed antislavery sentiments. The logic of the doctrine of natural rights, affirming that all were equal, demanded the recognition of the natural freedom of black people. And it was political expediency that led the framers of the Constitution to accept by their silence the working principle of state jurisdiction in matters of slavery. By 1817 the American Colonization Society was seeking to relocate emancipated slaves and free blacks in a territory reserved for them in Africa. But others even at that time thought that the colonization movement was wrong or too timid. Abolition societies already were springing up. Then in 1831 William Lloyd Garrison (1805–1879) began to publish *The Liberator*, a weekly newspaper with militant abolitionist views. His gospel was freedom *now* for black people, and the antislavery movement entered a new phase.

In the New West, converts from the revival preached by Charles Grandison Finney took up the antislavery cause. Among them was Theodore Dwight Weld (1803–1895), who led a group of radical students from Lane Theological Seminary in Cincinnati to Oberlin College in northern Ohio in a dispute over slavery and attitudes toward blacks in general. This linkage between antislavery and revivalism was to yield great success, for Weld had connections with wealthy evangelical Protestants in the East. At the same time, the American Anti-Slavery Society, founded in 1833, took up the cause. In New England, an antislavery society was already active, and liberal ministers gradually began to give public support to abolition. Thus, a coalition of northern evangelicals and liberals joined with other Americans in the crusade against slavery. The mix of Protestantism and politics gave birth eventually to the Republican party and the election in 1860 of Abraham Lincoln (1809–1865), who emancipated the slaves. Ordinary and extraordinary religion mingled freely in the movement, and so did calls for immediate moral purity and for social justice, in an antebellum version of mixed religious contraction and expansiveness. The antislavery movement was a classic case of moral reform in America.

By the end of the century, social justice had become the concern of the liberal Protestant Social Gospel movement, as we saw in Part I. Beyond that, Jewish involvement in socialist causes as well as Jewish and Roman Catholic efforts in the early labor movement signaled that major non-Protestant groups could embrace on their own terms a similar ideal. In Judaism, as we have seen, the ethical heritage of the classical Hebrew prophets supported the new endeavors. In Catholicism, the social teachings of Pope Leo XIII (1810–1903), as well as historic elements in the Catholic tradition, provided theoretical encouragement. Yet, from a practical point of view, the urge to reform society was in the air, for it was a prominent part of the dominant and public religion. So it was not surprising that some Jews and Catholics found the best way to be American was to work for reform.

In the twentieth century, a similar mix of elements could still be seen in various movements for the reform of society. For example, early in the century the enactment of the Eighteenth (Prohibition) Amendment to the Constitution (1919) signaled the opening, a year later, of an era of public abstinence. Moreover, this expression of the dominant Protestant character of America continued long after the death of the amendment in 1933. By the seventies and eighties, as we noted in Chapter 3, the Protestant style had spread to Catholics, who, with the cooperation of Orthodox Jews and conservative Protestants, led a crusade for the "right to life," a national protest against legalized abortion. Here both a felt need for moral purification and perceived demands of extraordinary religion were uppermost.

Earlier, the side of the dominant moralism that demanded social justice for its own sake was more in evidence. President Lyndon B. Johnson (1908–1973) launched the Great Society in the sixties, and civil rights legislation was carried through the Congress. Various programs emerged to fight poverty in urban slums and to upgrade nutritional and educational opportunities for the disadvantaged. Then the war in Vietnam became the focus for a national protest that embraced widely different elements in American society. Ministers and priests joined with flower children and the mothers of soldiers to argue their case against the war. Television news programs and newspapers were filled with accounts of protests, from the ritual burning of draft cards and of the American flag to mass rallies in front of the White House. It was obvious that both people with extraordinary religious commitments and others with more ordinary concerns had joined in these activities. But not to be overlooked in the presence of the call for justice was the fact that the urge to immediate moral purity was also involved in the antiwar movement. Many Americans feared they would bear the guilt of a terrible national sin if they continued to destroy the lives and landscapes of the

Vietnamese. The war, they thought, was "dirty," and people who would remain clean must be free of it.

When, on the heels of the war, the Watergate scandal began to occupy Americans, the same double thread of moralism was in evidence. Many argued that the doctrines of the Enlightenment, written into the Constitution, were being threatened by President Richard M. Nixon, who, they said, was violating the demands of justice and natural right. Others, with Nixon's lawyer John Dean, warned of a cancer growing on the presidency. They saw moral corruption and a consequent need for moral purification. For these Americans, the body of society needed to expel evil and cleanse itself so that it might function once more in health. Again, desires for justice and purity were felt by people with a range of commitments, from the Protestant evangelist Billy Graham to many an agnostic humanist. Hence, moralism knitted together Americans of many persuasions, whether extraordinary or ordinary, and whether Protestant or non-Protestant. The point was that moralism was no longer simply a feature of Protestantism: it had become a general characteristic of American culture.

The Protestant Cultus

Patterns of behavior are related to symbolic statements of the meaning of things, acted out in rituals and thought through in creeds. Our examination of the public Protestant religious system leads us to the ritual actions that were logically and psychologically linked to moralism, activism, and the search for simplicity. These ritual actions can be grouped under the general term *revivalism*, with revivalism understood as a community cultus to stimulate an immediate emotional experience of conversion or religious devotion.

In our exploration of Protestantism in Part I, we saw that the Reformers of the sixteenth century wanted to emphasize a separation between divine and human worlds, thus eliminating much of the Catholic sacramental system that partially closed the gap. As a religious ritual, revivalism was built on this Reformation sense of the distance between God and human beings, and it sought to make the sense of human estrangement from God a strongly felt experience. Likewise, the Reformers had stressed doctrines of the free grace and mercy of God that brought sinners close to him, and revivalism emphasized the belief that grace and mercy came through personal experience. Indeed, early American revivalism increased the Reformation sense of a gap between the divine and the human, thriving on a cosmology in which an all-powerful God, with suddenness and force, overwhelmed a powerless sinner. During the time of conversion or strong devotion, a person was expected to be, literally, out of control, with feelings and often even physical movements considered to be under the power of the Spirit. Paradoxically, the effects of this loss of control were felt as a greater degree of order and control in the later conduct of daily life.

As a ritual, though, revivalism offered a formal and repeated set of practices that might help to bring conversion or strong devotion. Sacred space was marked off, either in a church, a public building, or an open field at a camp meeting. Then during a sacred time created by the service, hymns, prayers, testimonies, and especially revival sermons worked to give to an individual a conviction of the burden of sin and, in earlier forms, of the torments of hell that would result. Alternately, hymns and testimonies evoked feelings of a present joy in conversion and of future bliss in heaven. If being a Christian was seen not as a matter of ideas but as a matter of experience, salvation hung on the sense of emotional liberation and peace that the grace of God was thought to give. Therefore, the older revival practices strived to produce an unbearable tension for believers between sin and possible grace, between the terrors of hell and the anticipated joys of heaven. When the tension had become great enough, the conviction of sin sufficiently painful, in accord with revival theory the believing sinner might, so to speak, be jolted into paradise.

The connections between both the earlier and later, non-Calvinist ritual of the revival and the behavioral patterns of the Protestant code are not hard to find. The activism of the Protestant style was satisfied in active congregations who sang, prayed, gave testimonies, and, more importantly, developed feelings of the burden of sin and the compassion of God. Individuals *worked through* or prayed through to conversion and the attainment of strong feelings toward their God. Especially after the beginning of the nineteenth century, when Calvinism fell away, more and more emphasis was placed on the active role a person played in the entire process.

Further, the Protestant desire for simplification was met by the ritual expression of the revivals. Here religion was distilled to what were believed its essentials: sin and grace, or hell and heaven. There was thought to be no need for an elaborate theology in this way of doing things. Similarly, the practice of the revivals led away from concern for tradition and into a vivid concentration on the present — or a future outside the time of history. Finally, Protestant moralism was served by the revivals. The pattern of overwhelming guilt and the immediate need for moral purification fit the experience encouraged at the revivals, while the authenticity of conversion and devotion was seen as expressed in the reformed character of the lives of Christians. Thus, the private vices that moralism found and sought to cleanse — radically, instantly, and all at once — were the signs for believers of the need for revival, while their eradication was the signal of revival success. Thus, too, the zeal of converts and devoted Christians often led to their involvement in humanitarian reforms, as we saw in the case of the movement against slavery.

Behind the behavioral patterns of Protestantism were the conditions and institutions that had made them possible. Here also there was a fit with revivalism. In a situation of religious liberty, the revivals gave people a democratic God who might come to rich or poor, model citizen or town derelict, with his help. In revival theology there was no elite class to benefit from salvation, except the elite of everybody's people, any one of whom might feel the grace of God. In the legal setting of separation of church and state, the revivals provided, as we saw in Part I, a mission field to be mined by denominations in search of new church members. The voluntaryism of the revival experience helped to fill congregations with volunteers who would work, in and out of official organizations, for the Christianization of America.

Revivalism in American Culture

Thus we gained a first sense of the significance of revivalism in the dominant and public religion of the country through noting in Chapter 5 its presence in Protestant evangelical history. The Protestant mission mind expressed its felt commitment to Christianize relative, friend, and neighbor — and to some extent even stranger — through the revivals. In so doing, the mission mind created a form of cultus that spread beyond its immediate concerns. For if revivalism was part of the history of Protestantism in this country, it was also part of the history of American culture. Like a magnet, Protestantism drew the many toward its center. We noticed in Part I how Roman Catholicism had its parish mission movement that paralleled Protestant revivalism and must have been reinforced by it. Similarly, we observed the twentieth-century upsurge of Jewish interest in Hasidism, a mystical and devotional movement that encouraged pietism. African-Americans for their own reasons also adopted the religion of feeling, and similarly we note that many, if not all, of the nineteenth-century new religions were born in revivalistic fervor. Mormons and Millerites, Shakers and Christian Scientists — all grew out of strong and shared experience. Whether with the charisma of a prophet, the expectation of the millennium, the ecstasy of dance, or the cultus of spiritual healing, these groups encouraged pietism and knit strangers into communities. Although they surely struck out on different paths, there was a oneness to their piety, shaped as it was by the dominant and public religion.

In the late twentieth century, a series of Asian and occult religious movements and then the New Age became for some Americans transformed versions of the old ritual of revival. The message of these religions, of course, is not the Christian gospel, but there has been strong continuity with revival themes. Indeed, one reason why Eastern export *bhakti* groups did not grow larger and more numerous in this country was the presence already within American culture of ways to express devotionalism. Still, in movements like the International Society for Krishna Consciousness and Nichiren Buddhism, individuals became a community not because of shared backgrounds or work but out of the experience of their ritual. In other words, it was *feeling* that made them one and feeling that overcame the estrangement that modern life-styles had created. Likewise, the intertwining of political with religious factors was evident in these movements during the era of the Vietnam War. While Billy Sunday and Billy Graham waved the flag to support American efforts in foreign wars, these men and women evidently cared as deeply but often saw the meaning of America in the context of visions of harmonial world community. Though many Eastern, occult, and political enthusiasts would have been shocked by the relationship, a bond of experiential pietism linked them to the sons and daughters of the Protestant revivals. And in the present the same is the case, as we have seen, for the New Age.

All of these movements represent attempts to reach beyond the boundaries of ordinary life in quest of the extraordinary. While as in every extraordinary religion, elements of the ordinary have been intermingled, these groups have shared the extraordinary religious commitment of Protestantism. But ordinary religion — American culture — took on the revival-bred characteristics of the dominant and public religion as well. During times of conflict like the American Revolution and the Civil War, as we will see in Chapter 13, popular behavior frequently resembled a mass revival. Other collective observances, such as national elections every four years, often evoked the enthusiastic spirit of the revivals.

Outside of war and organized politics, we can see in the second part of this century how general American culture still bears the imprint of the revival. To cite one example of a mass ritual in the revival tradition, there is the Woodstock Rock Festival that gave a generation its name as the Woodstock Nation. During three days in August 1969, 400,000 young people gathered at a farm in New York to hear rock groups perform, to smoke marijuana, to absorb stronger drugs, and to seek an experience of oneness in an atmosphere that has become legendary. Indeed, during the decade of the sixties it seemed that millions were swept into a thisworldly revival. The Broadway musical *Hair* gave Americans the age of Aquarius, a time when, according to its title song, there would be harmony, understanding, sympathy, and trust. In its music and its words, the echo of revival hymns was in the background. For the generation that wanted to make love and not war, feeling and experience were primary values, and immediate community was keenly sought. We will pursue these themes further in Chapter 14, but it should be evident here that they are strongly related to major values engendered by the revivals.

Closer to the present, the New Age Harmonic Convergence of August 1987 — both a religious and a general cultural event — offered another example of a transformed revival cultus. Throngs of New Age sympathizers made their way to special sites, claimed to be places where sacred power was particularly strong and focused. There, rituals to create and express feelings of peace, harmony, and community prevailed, as New Agers greeted expected planetary changes with a demonstration of their own solidarity. Meanwhile, in other, more ordinary places across America, New Agers performed rituals to mark the occasion. They burned pieces of paper listing traits and problems they wanted to release in order to be purified. They buried crystals in the hope of charging and energizing the earth for land and community healing. They met before dawn in public parks and private lands, lit fires that they considered sacred and that they surrounded with mystical symbols, and danced the spiral dance thought to be part of the old religion of the Goddess. At daylight, they exchanged signs of affection in a mood of communal closeness.

More conservatively than the Harmonic Convergence, other aspects of American popular culture expressed their link with the revival. Sentimentality and nostalgia were not only revival features but also common aspects of the everyday world. Messages on greeting cards and Mother's Day celebrations, television movies and popular love ballads proclaimed a world of sentiment that might bind people together into a safe community, leaving problems and pain behind. Here feelings were to be refined, socialized and used as within the revivals, ordering the world and bringing it under control. In short, revivalism provided the pattern for some of the major themes in American popular culture, although the themes were expressed in ways having to do with the present world and not the world beyond. Ritual life in general American culture has absorbed much from the patterns of meaning and behavior stressed in the revivals.

The Protestant Creed

Rituals, in general, are related to creeds, to sacred stories or statements that express basic beliefs. Protestant revivalism is no exception, and the ritual of the revival was connected, again logically and psychologically, to further elements in public Protestantism. These elements formed its religious conception of life. Within that conception, we can isolate three major understandings. First, there was belief in the *importance of the individual*, an idea that assumed significance during the Reformation and became stronger in the American experience of Protestantism. Second, there was conviction regarding a *higher law* that transcended human legislation and institutions. Third, and most prominent, there was affirmation of different forms of *millennialism* and a related perfectionism. We will look at each of these.

Individualism

Revivalism did work to help create community, as we have seen. But as religious experience, we saw, revivalism also focused on individuals. In older forms of revivalism, the individual was understood to be at the mercy of higher forces, as God and Satan wrestled for the soul. In later developments of the ritual, an individual was encouraged to decide by an act of personal will to accept Christ. In both cases, religious belief centered on what each individual experienced in the solitary space of mind and heart. In fact, American Protestant revivalism lived with a tension in which it at once *believed* in individualism and then immediately sought to change it. Revivalism tried to make community out of many undergoing private experiences by establishing a common place and language in which these experiences could become public. Yet through it all, revivalism spoke out of the creed of individualism.

So there is a strong, if problematic, bond between revivalism and American belief in the importance of the individual. Earlier, the Reformation of the sixteenth century had departed from medieval Catholicism by placing the individual at the center of religion. As we saw in Chapter 4, the shift from a sacramental church to one grounded on the Bible meant a new definition of the directness of the relationship between human beings and God. For the rising middle class who embraced Protestantism, the shift was a fortuitous parallel to growing involvement in individual decision and responsibility.

Circumstances in the New World only encouraged the drift toward greater individualism. The presence of vast stretches of land, the clear business opportunities created by the absence of an economic establishment, and the necessity of self-reliance for people uprooted from traditional community ties combined to emphasize individual worth. Patterns of ever-greater mobility developed to increase the trend. The Industrial Revolution shifted huge portions of the population from rural to urban settings. The lure of the frontier attracted others further and further westward. The multiplication of cheaper and more rapid means of transportation promised new opportunities that could be easily reached and also the hope that loved ones could be visited from time to time. By the late twentieth century, the cloverleaf at highway interchanges, the long-distance telephone line, and the fax machine had become major symbols of American life.

The political shape of the nation resembled the socioeconomic pattern of individualism. It was significant that the union formed between the colonies was a federal union—one in which thirteen sovereign states yielded some part of their independence for the benefits of common defense and welfare. Under the loose Articles of Confederation and later the Constitution, the states were like so many separate and individual planets revolving around a federal "sun." Or to use another figure of speech, they were like individual atoms existing within a larger body. In the nineteenth century, the doctrine of states' rights complicated the moral issues raised by slavery. The Civil War spoke not only to the issue of slavery but also to the other issue of how far the rights of individual states could extend. Even so, in the twentieth century the issue of political individualism remained. In national debates concerning the role of the federal government and in questions like the propriety of a national welfare system for the poor or national health insurance for everyone, the question resurfaced.

Meanwhile, the glorification of the common people became part of the political tradition of America. Although in practice democratic equality was a long way from being realized in the eighteenth and early nineteenth centuries, the belief persisted that in America all were equal. Indeed, by the late twentieth century, the power of the belief was being felt as different minority groups— African-Americans, Hispanics, American Indians—and a majority group— women—demanded that the words of the founders be made good. Individuals were considered significant in America, and equality became only the dues paid by society to that fact.

The public school system also played its part in this emphasis on the individual. In texts like the *McGuffey Eclectic Readers* of the nineteenth century, the individualistic virtues that would help a person to succeed were stressed. These schoolbooks promoted such qualities as independence, thrift, industry, and perseverance. Still further, an extensive national literature reflected the significance of each person. Ralph Waldo Emerson's famous essay "Self-Reliance" (1841) became a classic, while by the late nineteenth century Horatio Alger (1832–1899) had written over 100 novels, many of them based on the formula of a rise to success through luck and persistent effort. Alger's boy heroes, a number of them orphaned or at least without a father, were enterprising adventurers who won out over obstacles. They caught the fancy of huge numbers of young Americans, as the sale of some 20 million copies of the Alger stories attests.

It was clear that as part of their ordinary and everyday orientation, Americans valued individuals. But it was organized Protestantism that provided a theological home for individualism, and the Protestant influence on developing American individualism was crucial. Denominationalism and voluntaryism supplied an institutional framework in which individual efforts were the bulwark of church organizations. The activist style relied for its success on the individual involvement of numbers of responsible church members, while the simplifications that Protestantism fostered arose precisely because, in a world in which every individual, however poor or uneducated, counted equally, material and intellectual subtleties had to be reduced to a minimum. Through the various programs for moral reform — many of them directed toward private behavior — it was only as individuals that people could achieve purity, for such morality could never be simply a group affair. Ultimately, a moral act or a moral failure in America rested at the door of a single individual.

It was, finally, the ritual of revivalism that, despite tensions, helped to shape American Protestantism as a religion of individualism. We have already seen the connecting links. Here it is important to note that the content of the preaching in sermon after sermon on the revival circuits had much to do with the spread of an individualistic mentality. The preacher who wished to stimulate his congregation toward conversion or devotional experience was required to deal with individual themes. It was the relationship conceived between the sinner and God that was uppermost in the sermons — not beliefs about the Christian community, the communion of saints, or the general plan of God for the world. Moreover, the substance and style of revival sermons became the substance and style of much ordinary Sunday preaching as well. Week after week, year after year, church congregations heard descriptions of a divine-human relationship in which the individual figured at stage center. It was not surprising that they should conclude that this position was in the very nature of things. The pattern of Protestant revivalism both shaped and reflected the larger pattern of ordinary

American culture. For the dominant and public religion in both its ordinary and extraordinary forms, in the beginning was God — and the individual.

Higher Law

If individualism was basic to the American creed, the sources of public order became a logical next question. In a nation of self-reliant and self-directed individuals, what law or authority could be the final court of appeal? Could equal individuals in the nation be finally submissive to a king, a president, or a written law? Could equal individuals in the churches be forced to obey the dictates of a pope, a bishop, a synod, or elders of a denomination? These questions were complex, and we cannot answer them fully here. Yet a common theme emerged from the questions, and this theme became a tenet of the American creed.

While respect for the written law was a continuing aspect of American life in both church and state, Americans believed that the authority of any written law rested on its agreement with a higher, unwritten law. If written and unwritten law were in conformity, then the written law should be respected and obeyed. But if there was a discrepancy, if the written law violated higher law, then free individuals owed allegiance to the higher order. There was always the possibility that disobedience to human law was the greater virtue.

Sources for this belief were various. The heritage of the Reformation — especially in its Radical form — gave the early colonists a sense of the significance of individual conscience. Puritanism, which adopted the free-church tradition of the Radicals, accepted, at least theoretically, the idea of the rights of conscience. According to the free-church rationale, Puritans could ask, How were churches genuinely free if people were forced to join them? And how could people freely join or refuse to do so unless they listened to the voice of conscience?

The Quakers, with their teaching concerning the "Inner Light," especially stressed a turning within. Their assumption — and the assumption of all Protestants who recognized the idea of conscience — was that if people listened with sincerity, the voice that spoke to them from conscience would be the voice of God. The Baptists, in turn, argued for separate churches in New England and protested the Congregational church establishment. For them conscience became the bar of justice. Moreover, the entire pattern of religious dissent supported this understanding. In order to justify a departure from the established order, an individual needed to find a law beyond private whim. Since the colonists were in the large sense mostly religious dissenters, belief in the rights of conscience was basic to their religious position.

From the heritage of the Enlightenment came another source for American belief in higher law. The idea of a law of nature to which human life must conform had received active support among the Puritans. The rationalism of their intellectual tradition turned easily toward natural law, and this was an important reason for the ready acceptance of Enlightenment beliefs in the colonies. Framed in the political rhetoric of the nation's foundation, higher law became the law under which a God of nature had given unalienable rights to individuals. This law was understood as absolute and fundamental. Patriots believed that it could justify the separation of the colonies from the government of King George III of England, as the Declaration of Independence made clear. According to American patriotic reasoning, political states and their laws must exist as reflections in specific human situations of the higher law of nature. Otherwise, it might become necessary in the course of events to resist them.

Practically speaking, Americans sometimes made use of popular versions of the idea of higher law in order to justify their acquisition of territory from the Indians. For the Puritans, legitimation for conquest was based on the distinction between "civilized" and "savage" peoples. In Puritan assumptions, "savages," by definition, could not be fully human and therefore could not be civilized. Hence, they thought, God required that the wilderness be snatched from their hands and given to people who would turn it into a Christian garden. By the nineteenth century, President Andrew Jackson (1767–1845) could justify the removal of the southeastern Indians to lands farther west by a modified version of the argument. White Americans, ran this legitimation, would as farmers bring a higher state of civilization to Indian lands. Indian peoples retarded progress, the legitimation continued. Removed west of the Mississippi River, perhaps they could be brought to share in civilization.

Although today most condemn the logic of both the Puritans and President Jackson, it is important to see that they were appealing their actions to a law of nature or, more and more in the nineteenth century, a law of progress beyond themselves. By midcentury, as we will explore more fully in Chapter 13, that "law" was given new form as manifest destiny, and in this form it had become a part of the civil religion. In all of these cases, the point of the appeal was that it gave to individuals a transcendent justification for any actions they might take. In a nation in which moralism was a fundamental behavioral pattern, such justification was necessary. It could be and often was self-serving, as in the examples involving the Indians, but it could also support an act of moral courage.

In one memorable instance from the nineteenth century, the American writer and Transcendentalist Henry David Thoreau (1817–1862) spent a night in jail because he had refused to pay his poll tax during the Mexican War. The tax would aid the southern slave power, Thoreau reasoned, and he would have no part of it. This act of civil disobedience had special impact on the twentieth century when Martin Luther King, Jr., learning of it indirectly through Mohandas Gandhi, willingly went to jail many times to advance the African-American struggle for civil rights. In these and other instances of civil disobedience, individuals appealed against the written law to a higher law that, they argued, justified their actions. For many during the era of the Vietnam War, the belief in higher law supported their efforts to resist the draft in various ways and to engage in active protest against the war. Although large numbers of their fellow citizens disapproved of their actions and regarded them as disloyal, these resisters were part of a long tradition of Americans who thought that no human law could be final and that the rights of conscience preceded any government. In our own time, antinuclear protesters violate statutory law, trespass on government or power-plant property, and sometimes destroy it because they believe higher law compels them.

As we have examined it, belief in higher law is an instance of the ways in which ordinary and extraordinary religious values have mingled almost indistinguishably in the American creed. It is difficult to say where the Protestant heritage ended and ordinary American culture began in the affirmation of unwritten law. But because the belief is so clearly tied to the idea of God or transcendence, there is an extraordinary quality about it in every situation. Indeed, the justification of Indian removal is, in this context, especially repugnant because, by appealing to higher law, it brought the idea of God to the service of self-serving human motives. Higher law, if it really was higher, justified the ordinary by reference to the extraordinary. The measure of its power in American life was the measure of the power of Protestantism as the dominant and public religion.

Millennialism

We have noted that higher law was conceived in various ways in the course of American religious history. For some, it meant the voice of the biblical God speaking to conscience. For others, it meant the God of nature at work through his law in governing the world. And for others still, it meant the law itself as an absolute — an almighty nature or an unfailing law of progress. This movement from the biblical God to nature to an abstract law of progress is paralleled in a third belief in the American creed, belief in the coming of the millennium. This belief — and action generated by it — formed what was probably the strongest theme in the one religion of the United States. Significant in public Protestantism, it proved to be more powerful still in civil religion and general cultural religion. In the millennial vision, higher law meant the decree of the God of the future and the unraveling of the inevitable events that would bring about that future. We have already met millennial beliefs in abundance in our survey of religious manyness in America, but now let us review and expand our understanding.

In the strict sense, we recall, millennialism is related to a specific book in the Christian New Testament, the Book of Revelation. According to the book, in a battle of the final age the Word of God will ride forth with his army to fight a beast who embodies evil. After the beast is overcome, the book continues, Satan will be chained up for a thousand years (literally, the millennium), and those who have witnessed to Jesus will rule with him. Then at the close of the thousand-year era will come a war between God and Satan when Satan will be finally defeated (Rev. 19:11–20:10).

In a looser sense, however, millennialism can mean extraordinary religious beliefs, in any tradition, in which there is intense expectation that the end of the present world order is near. Remember that we initially encountered millennialism in the ghost dance religion that spread through the Plains in the nineteenth century. Like the Native American ghost dancers, all millennialists see radical change in the future. They draw strength and religious excitement in the present from their anticipation of the approaching end — or beginning. For common to all millennial beliefs is the faith that with the future a new age will dawn, an age of peace and prosperity and the fulfillment of all hopes.

Finally, millennialism can refer to beliefs outside of any extraordinary religion. The intense expectation of a new era of peace and plenty can take place in terms of ordinary culture. Elation over an age of progress and wonder at the speed of transformation can give rise to popular beliefs that a totally new period in world history is beginning. So millennialism can be a way to make sense of life within the boundaries of the everyday world. Mainstream American culture, especially in the late eighteenth and nineteenth centuries, reflected this kind of millennialism.

As we glance quickly through American religious and cultural history, we find millennial beliefs in abundance. By the third and fourth generations, we recall, the New England Puritans frequently discussed millennial themes, and many of them seemed convinced that the end of the world was coming soon. Thus, Cotton Mather firmly expected the end to come in 1697. When it did not arrive then, he recalculated and predicted 1736 and, later, 1716. By the eighteenth century, we know, some Puritans, like Jonathan Edwards, had begun to believe that the thousand-year period could begin without the physical coming of Christ but instead was a time of intense preparation for it. For Edwards, this understanding was closely tied to the outpouring of God's grace that he believed he had seen in the Great Awakening. The revival had convinced him that a new era was about to dawn in America and that the era would be the beginning of God's millennial kingdom for the entire world.

Since there was general agreement that the prophecies of Revelation were cast in symbolic language, it was possible to interpret them in various ways. By the nineteenth century, we know, two schools of millennial thought arose, which came to be known as premillennialism and postmillennialism. As in dispensationalism, premillennialists believed that Jesus would come *before* the millennium to bring it on by his power. Postmillennialists thought that Jesus would return *after* the millennium had come through the Spirit working in the church. Remember that along with premillennialism went the expectation of a reign of evil through a figure called the Antichrist. Premillennialists believed that many trials and tribulations would occur before Christ came again, and they regarded signs that the world was becoming worse as evidence that the end was near. Conversely, postmillennialists found signs of gradual human betterment to be evidence that the millennium was beginning. At the same time, they thought that by working to spread the gospel and to improve the human condition, they could hasten the coming of the millennium.

We have already met premillennialists not only in the dispensationalists but also in the early Mormons and Millerites and later in the Seventh-day

Adventists. At the same time, liberal Protestants, like the Unitarians, and also moderate evangelicals, like Lyman Beecher, held postmillennialist views. The Methodist teaching of perfection as a second work of grace after conversion was postmillennial in its thrust, and we know that this perfectionism was spread by the revivals until it became a widespread popular belief. By the mid-1830s Charles G. Finney preached the message, while groups as diverse as the Oneida Perfectionists and even the spiritualists held their own versions of the perfectionist creed. These Americans saw a new world open within themselves, with the dream of human perfection either realized or in the process of being realized. Likewise, they were filled with optimism by the signs of progress they believed they saw around them. They read the signs of the times positively, for they were convinced that a new era was dawning and that it would dawn for the whole world in the United States. Yet for both premillennialists and postmillennialists, the Civil War was a time of crisis, and we will return to this theme in the next chapter.

After the Civil War, however, came a resurgence of premillennialism. By 1875 premillennialists were attracting new adherents and preaching their message, especially in the dispensationalist form we have already met. Perhaps more significant than the familiar details of dispensationalist theology was its emphasis on the literal nature of the premillennial beliefs. As we saw in Chapter 5, it was in important part the combination of dispensational and rationalistic beliefs that gave birth to fundamentalism. Hence, wherever fundamentalism thrived, so did premillennialism.

In the later twentieth century, when after a period of decline fundamentalism again became prominent, we know that so, too, did premillennialism. In fact, it attracted considerable attention for fundamentalism in American popular culture, as, we recall, the popularity of Hal Lindsey's book, *The Late Great Planet Earth*, attested. The sense of impending doom, reflected in this book and in the general premillennial message, led many believers to a kind of activism. With so short a time before the end, they wanted to rescue as many people as they could. With premillennialism linked to the mission mind (Chapter 5), for many, revival and foreign-mission activity became a way to hasten the second coming of Jesus. For whatever reasons they worked, premillennialists tried according to their beliefs to save as many as possible before the end.

Premillennial efforts were directed mostly toward the salvation of individuals on otherworldly terms. In general, the premillennialists had little interest in social reform, and the postmillennial logic of the gradual dawning of the millennium as humans created a better society was not theirs. Still, there were people who spread the postmillennial gospel in America after the Civil War. These Americans used new language to express their ideas, and in the Social Gospel movement that we have already encountered they spoke of the millennium as the coming of the kingdom of God. For them, the kingdom was not merely a spiritual reality but a material transformation of human society in which poverty,

ignorance, and disease would be banished. Often with a belief in the basic goodness of America, those who preached and practiced the Social Gospel saw their
task as making America better still. Their work, as they conceived it, was to
build the kingdom of God on earth.

Like fundamentalism, postmillennial commitment to the Social Gospel
went through a period of decline in the early to middle years of the twentieth
century. Still, it never died. In the sixties, liberal Protestantism again threw itself
more completely into postmillennial work. Stimulated by the civil rights movement and the war against poverty, liberal ministers were numbered in the forefront of the various social movements that emerged. For them the message of the
Christian gospel was one of social change. As they read biblical teaching, Jesus
had said that God's kingdom must rise within the human community, not simply
within individual human hearts. So liberals found themselves working to create a
millennium alongside other Americans who were inspired not by the kingdom at
all but by a general humanistic desire to create a more perfect society.

In this last group was millennial belief in the loosest sense of all — the
optimistic expectation that the best of all ages was about to dawn. Indeed, understood in terms of ordinary culture, for many this best of ages had been dawning in
America since the late eighteenth century. Revolutionary and postrevolutionary
rhetoric offered visions of America as the place where the noblest society in
human history would flourish, where there would be peace, abundance, technical progress, and the abolition of life's ills. As the industrial and transportation
revolutions ushered in a series of seeming technological miracles, the enthusiasm
of the age of progress became an ordinary religion of millennialism. Building on
the Puritan understanding of America as a new Israel, ordinary millennialists did
not use the language of Israel any longer, but they still thought of the country as a
promised land. The presence of seemingly endless territory in the early national
period fed the enthusiasm of many, while by mid century the various expansionist adventures of the United States in Texas, in Mexico, and in California were
partially inspired by millennialist ideas.

For other Americans, however, the millennium of ordinary religion came
especially, as suggested above, in the age of convenience and comfort that
seemed to be beginning. With the telegraph of the 1840s and the electric light
of the late 1870s as symbols of an age of technical progress, Americans marveled
at the changes they were witnessing. And by the end of the century, advances in
the knowledge of disease microorganisms were leading to the development of
new ways to prevent sickness.

Meanwhile, the abolition of slavery signaled to many that the goal of
perfection in human society was near at hand. Knowledge of Charles Darwin's
theory of evolution was spreading, and his presentation of evidence in support of
the biological theory (that humans had evolved from other animals) stimulated a
social, or cultural, version. Known as Social Darwinism, it taught that just as
human bodies had evolved, so had human cultures. On the basis of this belief,

numbers of Americans came to see themselves as the most highly evolved people on earth. They became convinced that in their society the age-old vision of the millennium was becoming reality.

The twentieth-century — with its two world wars and painful smaller conflicts — put an end to much of this postmillennial optimism. Tensions long quiet between the races came to new life, and poverty was discovered to be a national problem of greater seriousness than had been thought. By the seventies, there were clear signals that the nation's energy expectations could not be fully met, as long lines at gasoline stations threatened an end to the American romance with the automobile. And by the late eighties, new evidence of environmental fragility seemed everywhere at hand, while violent crime, drug use, and urban blight and decay were major problems. There was strong evidence that Americans were less healthy as a nation than some others and that they were also not close to the best in educational performance tests. Meanwhile, U.S. financial power was declining as other nations prospered.

Yet if the millennium had not exactly dawned, millennialism was still a continuing feature of much American popular life. The social protests of the sixties thrived on millennial anticipation. In the seventies the popularity of science fiction novels and films of the *Star Wars* variety indicated that millennialism was very much alive in the mainstream American imagination — a theme we will explore more fully in Chapter 14. Even further, in the eighties the environmental and New Age movements joined to capture the public language and imagination, so that millions of Americans were observing Earth Day and hoping to help heal the planet. Then, at the end of the decade — when the Berlin Wall crumbled, a rising tide of democratic revolution swept Eastern Europe, and the Soviet Union made cold-war peace with the United States — a resurgence of millennial hope was apparent. The changes and the mood continued in the early nineties.

We have seen millennialism to be part of extraordinary and ordinary religious life in America. Its extraordinary aspect has been both premillennial and postmillennial. Sometimes millennialism has prompted pessimism about the world and urged Christians to rescue as many individuals as they can for Jesus. At other times millennialism has led to a thoroughgoing optimism about human beings and society, inspiring a host of reform efforts to hasten the dawning of the new era. In both cases, millennialism began in Protestantism, but the millennial fervor was shared by other, non-Protestant religious movements. Finally, the postmillennial version of the message was reflected in an ordinary religion of progress with America — as a perfect society — at its center.

In all of these forms, millennialism was closely tied to the behavioral code, the cultus, and the remaining elements of the creed of the dominant and public religion. In both premillennial and postmillennial forms, it was activist — either attempting to save and rescue souls or to bring about the social reform of the nation. In both its forms, also, it expressed the American Protestant urge to simplify. Millennial themes were cast in terms of clear alternatives of good and evil, of war between opposite factions, and of final triumph for good without the intrusion of any evil. Similarly, both forms of millennialism embraced the demands of moralism. Premillennialists sought to purify themselves and other persons by their adherence, according to their beliefs, to the truth of a Christian gospel without liberal corruptions and by leading lives of private virtue. Postmillennialists sought the radical reconstruction of society that their millennium required.

For the two schools of millennial thought, the evangelical model of the relationship between God and the individual provided a ritual foundation. For premillennialists, repentance was necessary for rescue before the tribulation of the end time. For postmillennialists, the fervor of religious awakening was a sign of the nearness of the millennial kingdom. For both, with its pull toward the future, millennialism echoed the message of the revival—that humans were estranged and uprooted from God and from one another. Their millennial society was always *being* made, never made. It was planted in a paradise of future time, in a community not based on a common past and history but on a radical vision of newness. Once again, like the revivals, the millennial creed was built on a community of strangers. Such a community, of course, was consistent with the individualism that was part of the Protestant and American creed, and as we saw earlier, it was connected to the belief in higher law.

The movement from code to cultus to creed has provided a survey of the characteristics that, linked together, form public Protestantism. Interestingly, if we go forward one more step, we will find ourselves back at the beginning—with the social conditions related to the development of the Protestant code. It is easy to take the step. Postmillennialists paid tribute to America as the land of religious liberty and democratic equality, guaranteed by separation of church and state and institutionalized in denominationalism and voluntaryism. In theory, at least, premillennialists could not pay tribute to any worldly government, but in practice they found in the American arrangement the freedom they believed that God intended for them to preach the gospel. So millennialism led back finally to liberty and equality.

In Overview

To sum up, public Protestantism was and is the dominant religion of the United States. Present from colonial times in Calvinistic Christianity, sheer numbers, political and social prestige, economic power, and an early educational monopoly all contributed to the ascendancy of public Protestantism as the "one religion." The many who were not Protestant also contributed to its ascendancy by their acceptance of its influence and by their imitation of its ways. Hence, as both extraordinary and ordinary religion, public Protestantism shaped America.

As a religious system, this public Protestantism offered a code, a cultus, and a creed to Americans, the three elements closely interlinked to form a whole. The code began in conditions of democratic equality and religious liberty, later expressed legally in separation of church and state. These conditions for the existence of religion encouraged the growth of denominationalism and voluntaryism as organizational characteristics of the one religion. Against this backdrop, patterns of activism, a search for simplicity (reductionism, nonintellectualism, ahistoricism), and—most prominently—moralism flourished in the Protestant behavioral code.

Related to the code, the public Protestant cultus of revivalism stressed activism in working through to conversion, simplicity in its religion of bare essentials, and moralism in its emphasis on belief in sin and a need for purification. Historically, the revivals helped to deal with estrangement by creating a place and time in which private feelings could legitimately be expressed in public. In this way people could have a sense of community without confronting their lack of knowledge of one another or their absence of intellectual agreement.

Code and cultus were connected to the creed of public Protestantism in which beliefs about the importance of the individual, higher law, and millennialism were key. While individualism was often more an ideal than a reality and while a higher law could be manipulated to practical advantage, in millennialism public Protestantism shaped and was shaped by a central belief in American culture.

Moralistic in code, revivalistic in cultus, and millennial in creed, the dominant and public religion of America acted as a solvent for the separate centers of the many religions. The dominant and public tradition worked to help break down barriers and to confuse boundaries so that a religious culture of oneness might be formed. As a key element in that oneness, millennialism inevitably led toward the political state on which postmillennialists heaped their expectations and premillennialists, at least theoretically, their suspicions. Civil religion—the religion of nationalism—existed in American religious history as a further way to help weaken boundaries between peoples and bind the many into one. We need to look again at the American flag that Billy Sunday chose to wave.

SUGGESTIONS FOR FURTHER READING: PUBLIC PROTESTANTISM

Brauer, Jerald C. *Images of Religion in America.* Philadelphia: Fortress Press, 1967.

Davidson, James West. *The Logic of Millennial Thought: Eighteenth-Century New England.* New Haven: Yale University Press, 1977.

Handy, Robert T. *A Christian America: Protestant Hopes and Historical Realities.* 2d ed. New York: Oxford University Press, 1984.

Hatch, Nathan O., and Noll, Mark A., eds. *The Bible in America: Essays in Cultural History.* New York: Oxford University Press, 1982.

Hutchison, William R., ed. *Between the Times: The Travail of the Protestant Establishment in America, 1900–1960.* Cambridge Studies in Religion and American Public Life. Cambridge, Eng.: Cambridge University Press, 1989.

McLoughlin, William G. *Revivals, Awakenings, and Reform.* Chicago History of American Religion. Chicago: University of Chicago Press, 1978.

Mead, Sidney E. *The Lively Experiment: The Shaping of Christianity in America.* New York: Harper & Row, 1963.

Niebuhr, H. Richard. *The Kingdom of God in America.* 1937. Reprint. New York: Harper & Row, Harper Torchbooks, 1959.

Richey, Russell E., ed. *Denominationalism.* Nashville: Abingdon Press, 1977.

Roof, Wade Clark, and McKinney, William. *American Mainline Religion: Its Changing Shape and Future.* New Brunswick, NJ: Rutgers University Press, 1987.

Sandeen, Ernest R., ed. *The Bible and Social Reform.* The Bible in American Culture. Philadelphia: Fortress Press, and Chico, CA: Scholars Press, 1982.

Sizer, Sandra S. *Gospel Hymns and Social Religion: The Rhetoric of Nineteenth-Century Revivalism.* American Civilization Series. Philadelphia: Temple University Press, 1978.

Tuveson, Ernest Lee. *Redeemer Nation: The Idea of America's Millennial Role.* Chicago: University of Chicago Press, 1968.

Tyler, Alice Felt. *Freedom's Ferment: Phases of American Social History from the Colonial Period to the Outbreak of the Civil War.* 1944. Reprint. New York: Harper & Row, Harper Torchbooks, 1962.

Weber, Timothy P. *Living in the Shadow of the Second Coming: American Premillennialism, 1875–1925.* New York: Oxford University Press, 1979.

Civil Religion: Millennial Politics and History

Many an American has visited the National Archives Building in Washington, D.C., to see the original copies of the Declaration of Independence and the Constitution. There the documents rest in a special case filled with helium and covered with protective glass to preserve them. Each night they descend into a steel vault where tons of metal prevent any accident or sabotage. Then the next day they rise to be viewed by tourists. Still more Americans have probably attended a ball game and stood in the bleachers with the crowd, singing "The Star-Spangled Banner" to the accompaniment of the local band. And nearly everybody remembers the ceremony that began the class day in primary and secondary school. Teacher and pupils rose and, facing the American flag—each person with hand on heart—recited a pledge of allegiance to the flag and "the Republic for which it stands." Nearly everybody remembers pledging, that is, except for the Jehovah's Witnesses.

Members of this large millennial religious body, which originated as a nineteenth-century new religion, refuse to salute the American flag. Arguing before the Supreme Court in 1940, the Witnesses claimed that the pledge of allegiance was an act of idolatry, homage to an earthly government by people who had made a covenant with God to do his will. In other words, the Witnesses were saying that the pledge of allegiance was a religious act and that, as such, it conflicted with the demands of their own faith. This argument by the Witnesses should prompt us to look again at the ceremonies just described. The solemn preservation and veneration of the Declaration and the Constitution, the singing of the national anthem, and the pledge of allegiance are acts that suggest, by their seriousness and deliberateness, the rituals of organized religion. They are surely attached to ideas about the meaning of America, and they are encouragements to loyal and patriotic behavior. As rituals, they help people to center and orient themselves by reference to the nation.

For well over two decades the religion against which the Jehovah's Witnesses were protesting has been called by many scholars *civil religion*. While there are various definitions of it, civil religion generally refers to a religious system that has existed alongside the churches, with a theology (creed), an ethic (code), and a set of rituals and other identifiable symbols (cultus) related to the political state. As a shorthand definition, we might say that civil religion means religious nationalism. Historically, we know that the term *civil religion* was used by Jean-Jacques Rousseau (1712–1778) in Enlightenment France. And although the term did not come into repeated use in this country until 1967, the phenomenon to which it refers is as old as the beginnings of Western culture.

Thus, ancient Israel understood its government as a theocracy, literally a government by God — through his representatives. In its view of the state, religious and political institutions were united, and one person — a charismatic leader or, later, a king — was responsible for both. Even more, Israel's God was considered the true king, ruling by his law and under a covenant that he had made with the people. Before the idea of a divine covenant with Israel was affirmed, other covenants had been made between warring kings to establish relationships between them. So a covenant was a *political* agreement, and a king, of course, was a political figure, ruling by establishing control over territory. Hence, the empire of the biblical God was the Hebrew state, and as the Hebrew conception of God grew larger, his empire became the universe.

The roots of the majority religion in the United States are, like the roots of all Christianity, bound up with the history of Israel. But a second major source for Western European culture was Greco-Roman. By the time Rome was ruling the Mediterranean world in the first centuries of the Christian era, its empire was linked by a common ideal for living — the Roman Way of Life — and by a ritual centered around the emperor. The head of all the Romans and of the conquered nations, the emperor was thought to possess a spiritual double called his *genius*. Romans considered the genius of the emperor divine, so that throughout the empire people were required to take part in an annual ceremony rendering homage to the genius. In this way, the vast state composed of many ethnic and religious groups maintained a degree of unity. The Roman Way of Life, summed up in ritual homage to the emperor, acted as a social cement to bind the many into one.

With the Jews and, on the Mediterranean coast, some Muslims as clear dissenters, medieval Europe also held to a religiopolitical unity. As we noted in Chapter 12, Christianity united Europeans into Christendom, and religion was a political as well as pious act. Similarly, North America had its native civil religions in the traditional ways of the many Indian nations that populated the land. Here chiefs and holy persons were "civic" authorities in small, independent cultures, and they interpreted the meaning of their nations to other members. Later the European immigrants were not too different. As we saw briefly in Chapter 4, the Puritans readily mixed religion and government. As early as 1749, Benjamin Franklin in Pennsylvania was speaking about the need for "publick religion." A quarter-century afterward, the deliberations of the Continental Congress that gave birth to the United States were filled with attention to religious details.

With this double background, two models for civil faith in Western society had grown up. The first was the Hebrew model in which one nation, bound by ties of blood, history, and language, expressed these bonds in combined religious and political language and actions. The second was the Roman model in which different peoples, with different ethnic heritages, were brought together from the top down, so to speak, through formal ceremonies and ideals. In the United States, civil religion took something from each of these models. For this reason, its nature and its specific history have proved difficult to chart. Briefly, some of the major symbols of American civil religion rose out of Puritan experience, the expression of a people united by ethnic ties and traditions. But the history of civil religion made it increasingly a bond designed to unite *many* peoples from *many* different nations into one state.

The distinction is important. A political state such as the United States means a civil government that contains within its jurisdiction distinct ethnic and religious groups. A nation, in the strict sense, means a group of people bound by language, past history, and real or alleged kinship, like each American Indian culture. A nation-state means a nation that has taken on a formal and political expression so that government is identified with one nation. Modern Japan is a nation-state.

Previous chapters have followed common usage in speaking loosely of the United States as a "nation." But here we need to be careful in our choice of words. Civil religion in this country was an attempt to create a nation and a nation-state, partially on the basis of the English Puritan national heritage, partially on the basis of more universal symbols derived from the Enlightenment, and partially through symbols that grew out of American political history. Yet as the years passed, more and more Americans did not share either the English Puritan national tradition or an ancestry in America during previous eras of its history. At the same time, the Enlightenment, as a cultural event, receded into the past. Thus, civil religion grew less meaningful. At best, civil religion was never more than the expression of many American people some of the time. Still, with its overtones of extraordinary religion, it is an important example of the religion of oneness in this country. It deserves scrutiny if we are to understand religious America.

The Foundations of the Civil Religion

Civil religion grew and changed throughout American history, and its presence was particularly visible in millennial fervor during wartime. Yet its essentials came from the seventeenth and the eighteenth centuries. By the time George

Washington took his oath of office as first president of the United States, the fundamentals of the civil religion were in place. They had arisen out of New England Puritanism, but especially out of the fusion of Puritanism with the engagement of Americans in the Revolutionary War. In this setting, the Puritan past was reinterpreted, linked more strongly to the Enlightenment (it had already been so linked), and joined finally to the historic tradition that Americans were creating by their own deeds in the war—deeds that were widely understood as the beginning of a millennial era. We will look first at Puritanism from the perspective of the civil religion and then at the era of the Revolutionary War. After that, we will be able to examine the civil faith as a religious system and to follow it in later American religious history.

Puritanism and Civil Religion

Centuries after the area we call New England was peopled by the Algonkians, it was colonized by English Puritan nationals, who brought with them a distinct culture and way of life. We encountered these New England Puritans in our study of Protestantism, but we need to look again at their relationship to the civil religion. They came to North America from an England experiencing visible religious dissent and millennial hopes. They grew up on tales of Protestant martyrs who had suffered and died for their convictions during the Catholic reign of Bloody Mary (1553–1558). They had read these tales as evidence of an unending war between God and Satan, and they thought of England as the particular place where that war was being waged.

When they immigrated from England to the colonies along the Atlantic coast of America, the Puritans came to see themselves as the true chosen people from an almost-chosen England. More and more they understood themselves and their projects in terms of a millennial vision inspired by the Protestant martyrs. Their covenant with God was a bond that expressed for them their elect status before him. They considered themselves predestined for paradise, and as "visible saints," they thought they should be busy in doing God's work on earth. The Puritans conceived of this work in two ways. First, they thought they should be an *example* for all the world to see—a society of God's elect in which righteousness had triumphed and sin would reign no more. Second, they believed they had a *mission* to spread the message and the meaning of their gospel to others. Since Puritan society aimed to embody that gospel, the mission for them meant convincing others to live as they (the Puritans) were doing.

Puritan sermons expressed the sense of being an example for others by speaking of New England society as a light to the world and a city upon a hill. The sermons described the mission of Puritanism in the language of destiny and an errand into the wilderness. Being an example and performing a mission, both tasks that were conceived as Puritan obligations under their covenant with God, were also for the Puritans tasks that needed to be done with millennial fervor. By the third and fourth generation in America, as we saw in Chapter 4, the Puritans thought that the days of the world were numbered. In their view, their witness was perhaps the last chance for a sinful world to overcome the deceits of the Antichrist and to seize the truth of the gospel. In short, the Puritans were people who believed they did not have time to lose. For them God's business demanded total dedication in light of their conviction of a millennial future.

What made these themes especially important for American civil religion was that all of them were understood in political terms. Practically speaking, as we have seen, Puritan New England was a theocracy—a church–state aggregation in which government was in the hands of the "saints" (although not in the hands of the clergy). These saints, or fully converted members of the church, ruled the New England colonies in the name of those who were bound together in the civil or political covenant. While not all members of the political covenant were members of the covenant of "grace" (the church covenant), the ideal of the society was that the two should be one. More than that, the Puritans with their Calvinistic heritage formed the political covenant using the church covenant as a model. They came to interpret their government in terms of destined tasks and millennial visions. Government for them was the arm of God reaching into the world through the visible saints to create a society publicly committed to the Word. Although they believed that there might be—and were—sinners in New England, they insisted that the colonies—as public and political communities—should be holy. Indeed, when the Puritans were told they were to be as a city upon a hill, the civil character of religion in Puritan culture was being affirmed, for a city is a *political* unit. In the way the Puritans saw the world, the civil and the religious were fused, and—here at least—ordinary and extraordinary religion were united.

We can see from this description that there was much in Puritan society that resembled Old Testament understandings. The Puritans were aware of the similarities and, as we noted in Chapter 4, envisioned themselves as a New Israel. They linked their millennialism to an older religious model, so that they believed that the experience of the ancient Hebrews had parallels in the story they told about themselves. In other words, if all peoples have a sacred and traditional account about who they are and where they have come from, then the accounts of the ancient Hebrews and the seventeenth-century American Puritans were in some respects alike. When we studied the history of Jewish religion, we noted that the Jews early thought of themselves both as a chosen people and as a suffering people. Among the Puritans, there was the same double message. The Puritans thought of themselves as a chosen people, but they also thought of themselves as a suffering people. We have already glanced at their sense of chosenness, but now let us take a closer look at their conviction of suffering.

We need to remember at the start that suffering arises from subjective experience. We can finally only imagine the depths of other people's suffering, for none of us is able to experience what others feel. Moreover, language in some sense creates suffering. If people say that they are suffering and believe that they are, then they are. These warnings are necessary because it may be difficult for us to recapture the Puritan sense of their own suffering. From the point of view of outsiders, it may not seem nearly so intense, for example, as the suffering of the Jews.

Puritans saw themselves as suffering in two ways. First, they thought of themselves as suffering through outside forces. Like their ancestors during the reign of Bloody Mary, they were persecuted by the Church of England. In their view, the unkindness of the church and its corruption had forced them to make the journey over an ocean. Here they thought of themselves as compelled to live — to use one of their phrases — in a "howling wilderness." They felt surrounded by "savages" (the Indians) in league with the devil. So both their fellow Christians in England and their environment in the New World became for them external sources of discomfort.

Second, the Puritans felt themselves to be suffering from conditions within their own souls. Especially after the first generation in New England, public sermons began to portray the Puritans as guilty sinners. They were not living up to their side of the covenant with God, preachers warned, and therefore all kinds of afflictions were coming to them. Ministers told that God was already forced to punish them through disease and harsh weather, through Indian wars and the failure of many of their children to be converted. We have encountered these sermons of affliction before, for they are the jeremiads that we noted in the last chapter. In fact, these jeremiads were rituals that probably relieved some of the guilt the Puritans experienced. By enumerating what they felt to be their sins and calling loudly for repentance, they were paying back the first penny on the debt they believed they owed to God. If the rest of the debt went unpaid, that was a matter for later concern. The present, at least, had been taken care of.

It is hard to put a finger on the reasons for the Puritan sense of guilt. It is possible that the Puritan break with people in England helped to bring it on. It is also possible that, after the first generation in New England, people looked back on the era of the pioneers with a certain awe. Nothing in the lives of settled farmers and tradespeople could quite match the tales of the heroism of those who had crossed the sea. But there was another reason for Puritan guilt — the sense of millennial chosenness itself. The Puritans had carved a lofty niche for themselves in a divine plan. They understood themselves as the elect nation who in the last ages of the world were giving an example and were possessed of a mission to all nations. As visible saints, they believed that they walked with their God and that they were emissaries of his Word. But the visible saints must have noticed that they and their friends were sometimes walking in unsaintly ways. Like all people, they had feet of clay; like all people, they blundered and made mistakes.

Hence, the gap between the Puritan vision of their role and their experience of themselves must have produced a sense of guilt. The theocratic ideology of the Puritans masked a tension in which being chosen and being sufferers were two aspects of the same story. The connection between these themes is important because, as we will see, much of the Puritan story became the public and official story of later American civil religion. When America became a chosen nation, there would be a good deal of anxiety attached. Americans would simultaneously proclaim their innocence and feel guilty.

The Civil Religion of the American Revolution

By the late eighteenth century, the New England Puritans had thrown in their lot with other colonists in a growing rupture with Britain. In the era of the American Revolution, from the first acts leading up to the war to the final adoption of the Constitution in 1789, a civil religion was born. Much from that civil religion was a new version of the old Puritan story. Other parts of it had been gleaned from the Enlightenment, and still other aspects from the revolutionary experience of Americans. Let us look at each in turn.

The Puritans had been a melodramatic people. Some of the later Protestant search to simplify was already theirs, for their millennialism divided the world into a battlefield between two forces. On one side were God and his saints; on the other, the devil and his agents. In this dualistic world, reality was made up of sharp contrasts — good and evil, heaven and hell, truth and falsehood. Even more, the Puritans thought that there were especially significant divine and human actions, which contrasted sharply with the routine of everyday life. For the Puritan mentality, God acted through "remarkable providences" by which he saved the saints from Indian attack, brought them an exceptionally bountiful harvest, or softened the heart of a sinner for conversion. And humans acted in ways to be remembered when they, too, performed unusual or heroic deeds.

In the eighteenth century, the Puritan way of seeing things by means of dramatic contrasts was intensified by the Great Awakening. Jonathan Edwards, we recall, had worked to make his revival sermons "sensational." For Edwards, the more vivid and striking their language, the more the sinner might realize the terrors of hell and turn earnestly to God to seek salvation. Similarly, the behavior of congregations was also sensational. Accounts of the revivals were filled with references to the moans of anguish, the tears of repentance, the fits of fainting experienced by those who felt they were struck by the power of God. And as the revivals spread throughout the colonies, they brought interaction between people from different parts of the country and a growing sense of community that, some scholars believe, was essential for the occurrence of the American Revolution.

When the Revolution and the events preceding it did come, much of the rhetoric that stirred people, whether from church pulpits, political songs and rallies, or public newspapers, had a Puritan millennial and revivalist ring. As late as the close of the French and Indian War in 1763, Americans had regarded English soldiers with gratitude and had been proud to be part of the British overseas empire. Now, however, they saw the British as Satan's troops in a battle between the forces of good and evil. The Americans were "our Israel," and the

British were the Egyptians at the time of the exodus. Oppressed and persecuted, went the American story, the patriots had been enslaved by the mother country. And so they were engaged in a righteous attempt to gain their freedom. It seems curious to find colonists who owned black slaves using this kind of language. But from the perspective of the Puritan heritage of millennialism, it made considerable sense. The colonists were living out of a powerful story that explained the meaning of reality to them. By their sense of participation in that story, they could exert their fullest efforts to win the war. If they felt guilty for speaking of slavery in the presence of slaves, they probably felt greater guilt for breaking with the land of their ancestors and for in fact having very human motives — like economic considerations — in the midst of their sacred war. But the guilt did not become part of the public rhetoric, and the cries of righteous battle grew louder.

Likewise, descriptions of the war by people involved in events often sounded like descriptions of revivals. Enthusiasm seemed to be everywhere. It gripped the public so that they were carried along by it. Patriots spoke about zeal, the work of Providence, and the need to be awakened. Chaplains left their churches to march off to war, and many in their congregations followed. The American force that tried to conquer Quebec stopped first at George Whitefield's tomb. Meanwhile, newspaper accounts of various battles reported God's "remarkable providences." The British had been overwhelmed, the accounts ran, but the Americans lost hardly a person.

Out of the sensational accounts and the sensational rhetoric, Americans were molding a civil religion in which the only way to see was to see vividly and strikingly. For these Americans, events had to be spectacular to be significant; in some way they had to outstrip every other happening and to outweigh every other event. Making history meant performing these spectacular deeds on the public stage in the presence of witnesses who would record events for future generations. Like the biblical God who acted in history and like the millennial Word of the Book of Revelation who would lead his troops at the final battle, patriotic Americans had to do remarkable deeds in order to make their actions meaningful. Like the Puritans, later Americans were a melodramatic people.

In their melodrama, they had absorbed a large share of the Puritan belief system (its creed) and the Puritan behavioral code (the ethic of the battle with evil). They also perpetuated Puritan rituals (the cultuses) in days of fast and thanksgiving. Ordered by the Continental Congress, these special times were modeled on older Puritan days of public prayer. They were conceived as occasions to call patriotic Americans to repentance for sins that could damage the Revolutionary War effort and to thank God for successes in battle. They were kept throughout the colonies with great seriousness, for Americans who thought themselves engaged in a battle with evil also thought they should be sure that they were righteous. In their view, the God of the covenant and of battles demanded such righteousness of them.

If Puritanism contributed to the civil religion, so did the American Enlightenment. As we say in Chapter 4, with the growing Arminianism of Puritan liberals, morality and human effort had become important. Thus, Puritans were prepared for the moral emphasis of Enlightenment deism — and for its God, who worked by letting human beings work. Further, we know that the Puritans demonstrated an appreciation for what they regarded as God's hand in nature and that by the early eighteenth century that appreciation had begun to assume political form. The Puritans, we saw, grew familiar with the language of reason and nature that had arisen in the European Enlightenment. John Wise thought in 1717 that civil power came from the people, who were by nature free and equal. Others, especially colonial leaders, became acquainted with beliefs about nature's laws and nature's God through Freemasonry.

Organized in lodges in the towns of the colonies, Freemasonry was formally introduced in 1731 when St. John's Lodge was recognized in Philadelphia by the Grand Lodge of London. By 1776 there were over forty lodges, and they offered fellowship to members of other lodges who might be traveling in their area. In fact, the Masonic lodges — as secret societies linked to the occult heritage of the colonies — were like a network of churches of the same denomination: they were one more way in which bonds were formed between the various colonies before the war. The Masons neither approved nor condemned Christianity, but they saw it as one form of religion that had grown strong and would eventually decay. At the same time, the Masonic lodges thought of Christianity as part of a larger whole. That whole included the religion of nature, and it was expressed by the ceremonies of the Masonic brotherhood.

So, as we noticed in Chapter 4, Freemasonry became a way to spread deism. Recall that fifty-two of the fifty-six signers of the Declaration of Independence were Masons and that so were a majority of the members of the Continental Congress. With so many of the leaders on deism's side, it was no wonder that beliefs about the God of nature provided a new source of American unity in the war. Moreover, the concept of the God of nature was familiar also to ordinary people. As we have seen, British soldiers had spread Enlightenment views in America. With the French alliance during the war, a popular grasp of Enlightenment beliefs was only encouraged. At the same time, newspapers, songs, and speeches helped to acquaint Americans with the idea of the God of nature.

In the Freemasonic and Enlightenment view, far from being a God of battles, the supreme power in the universe, we know, was identified with natural law. In other words, the deist God was thought to work through the system he had designed without altering it or interfering. The Masons liked to think of this God as a Grand Architect. In fact, the symbolism of Masonic ceremonies was based on implements from the building trade that were reinterpreted in a spiritual way. And the concept of a God who was a Grand Architect was especially appealing because, like the God of nature, the Grand Architect did not interfere with his creation once he had fashioned it.

Again, God was often regarded as the Great Governor of the universe. In this title, the God of nature had entered political life, since a governor suggested affairs of state. However, for the colonists the ideal governor was one who interfered as little as possible and instead allowed Americans to run things for themselves. So for them the greatest governor was one who governed least. In viewing God as a nonintervening governor, patriotic Americans had a political God who acted like a God of nature, not altering the machinery of state once it had been set in motion. Just as the ancient Hebrews had thought of their God in the political terms of their monarchy and made of him a king, now patriotic Americans were thinking of their God in the terms of their colonial governments and making of him a governor. In both cases, religion and politics had been united. The deist God had become a fit sponsor for civil religion.

Behind all of these ways of speaking of the deist God — the God of nature, the Grand Architect, the Great Governor — there was a sense that God was an absolute power that called into question every human authority. Thus, Americans could appeal their disobedience of British legislation to this God, who had become the higher law that we examined in the last chapter. Identified with natural law, he had *become* natural law and natural right. Not many Americans in 1776 would have accepted this radical way of speaking, but the path was open for a later America to make a different use of the heritage of the Enlightenment if it chose.

Moreover, just as this heritage gave revolutionary Americans a system of beliefs, it also told them how to act and provided necessary rituals. The Enlightenment code of behavior appealed to reason. This ability that all humans possessed within themselves was thought to be an inner law of nature and an inner governor. According to belief, it prompted people to act on its dictates and therefore to become reasonable people. In this understanding, reasonable behavior meant moderate behavior, a golden mean between too much and too little. Above all, it meant moral behavior. For the Enlightenment, reason taught people how to act according to nature, and behaving naturally in the eighteenth century meant behaving morally.

Finally, Enlightenment rituals flourished in the rich ceremonies available in the Freemasonic brotherhood. In the secret cultus of the lodges, Masonry used an architectural symbolism to initiate men (no women were allowed) into Enlightenment religion. The square and compass, tools of building, became emblems of the task of building a perfect human character. Here the square stood for earth, while the compass suggested the sky. The message being taught was clear: out of nature, humans fashioned their character, and by using nature well, they could become perfect human beings. They must be "square" in their dealings with others. They must use the compass to set the boundaries of their aspirations. The square was placed within the compass, and together the two expressed ordinary religion (the square in the center) and extraordinary religion (the compass at the outer limits).

In other ways, the Masonic brothers also dramatized the religion of nature and Enlightenment. The sun was a familiar symbol within the lodges, and during initiation ceremonies, the brothers faced east. Like reason, thought to be the internal light, the sun was regarded as the external light of the world, the center around which all nature revolved. In keeping with this importance given the sun, the two principal feasts of the Masonic calendar were 24 June and 27 December. These were the Christian feasts of Saint John the Baptist and Saint John the Evangelist, so that Christian Masons could observe them fully. But these feasts were also commemorations of summer and winter solstice, the longest and shortest days of the year. They celebrated the sun that had reached its highest point in the heavens and the sun that hung lowest in the winter sky, just before its climb back to summer.

The Enlightenment had provided for Americans a set of universal symbols around which they could build a civil religion. Since the God who was the God of nature and the Grand Architect was also the Great Governor, they could understand the evolution of the United States as a "natural" result that had come through the workings of natural law. They could see the United States also as a great building that had been completed by the Architect; and, indeed, when the new Constitution was adopted in 1789, Americans liked to call it the "new roof." Finally, they could see the civil government as an authentic expression of the Great Governor. They could think of their republic as a place where reason and morality would teach all people to govern themselves, even as they dwelled together in harmony under the law.

On the face of it, there should have been considerable tension between the Enlightenment version of civil religion and the Puritan millennial one. How could a God of battles leading his hosts in an out-and-out-war with evil be reconciled with a morality of the golden mean, the moderate and reasonable way of life? How could rituals built on the Christian call for repentance through the grace of God be harmonized with rituals that celebrated human perfectibility through nature? One answer was that, like all people, Americans did not always live by logic. Even more than most, they were practical and took what they could use from both Puritanism and the Enlightenment as they wished. Moreover, the idea of human perfectibility through nature had its own millennial ring. It looked ahead to the dawning of the age of "progress" and reform, when — as we saw — a postmillennial vision captured much of American culture. Still further, in the nineteenth century Masonry fell into disrepute, and civil religion drew far more on Puritan symbols. As time passed, aided by the public school system and by the Protestant character of the dominant and public religion, Puritanism continued to hold a privileged position within the civil religion.

But in the era of the American Revolution, a third and final factor was involved in civil religion. That factor was the self-creation of Americans out of the history of their struggle with Great Britain. Its presence is easiest to chart through its focused symbolism, so we will begin there. Even before the war broke out, in the midst of protests against the Stamp Act (1765), the practice spread in New England and elsewhere of holding ceremonies around a tree called the Liberty Tree. In Boston this was a huge elm tree in a central location. In other towns and villages, the pattern was similar. Sometimes figures to represent unpopular British or American leaders were hung in effigy from the tree. Sometimes there were liberty processions and speeches under its branches. On at least one occasion, in Rhode Island, a tree received a conscious religious dedication. And whenever they could, British soldiers set upon a town's Liberty Tree to destroy it, as the colonists told the tale, with "diabolical" malice.

In each place where a Liberty Tree stood, it provided a center for community orientation around the values of the Revolution. Sacred stories from many nations had included reference to a tree of the world, or cosmic tree, thought to exist at the center of the earth and to connect it with the sky. In these stories, the tree was a way to climb from earth to heaven. In its American setting, however, the Liberty Tree symbolized the way the colonists were climbing on the limbs of their own aspirations. It stood for their desire to make a mark for themselves and to be remembered longer than any other people on earth. In short, it stood for an ordinary religion of trying to become extraordinary, of human beings trying to become "as Gods."

But the greatest symbol of the godlike quality esteemed by Americans was George Washington (1732–1799). In the revolutionary era, people revered him as a divine man, and in doing so, they expressed their sense of divine abilities present in all. Like later Americans, the colonists were already many. In the figure of Washington, however, they found a person, seemingly larger than life, who could help to make them one. So while he lived, Washington became the center of a cultus. Locks of his hair were treasured, babies were baptized in honor of him, and legends were circulated about his miraculous abilities as a war leader. Actors read speeches in his honor from the stage, and birthday celebrations for him were elaborate even during his lifetime. By 1779 a German-language almanac had already called him the father of his country, while orators everywhere praised him in dramatic terms. When Washington traveled to New York for his first inauguration, his route became the scene for elaborate rituals that expressed American ideas of his greatness. In Philadelphia a new bridge was constructed to float across the river like a triumphal arch, and a little child crowned him. At Trenton several hundred young girls dressed in white serenaded him. At New York accounts spoke of tens of thousands there to greet him.

Interestingly, Washington was compared by his contemporaries to both Jewish and Roman heroes. He was seen as the Moses of his people, freeing them from slavery in Egypt, or he was viewed as Joshua, one of the charismatic war leaders that the bibilical God had chosen to save Israel. Alternately, he was called Cincinnatus, the Roman general who had left his plow to fight for his country and then, when the task was done, had dropped the sword to return to his farm. This double identification with themes both Jewish and Roman expressed the complexity of American civil religion that we noted earlier. Like the civil religion of Israel, it grew out of a dominant national culture (in this case, Protestant). Like the civil religion of Rome, it summed up the pluralism of many different peoples in one state.

By the nineteenth century, the Liberty Tree had all but disappeared as a ritual center for the civil religion, but the cultus of George Washington flourished,

Apotheosis of George Washington, 1802. John James Barralet's stipple engraving reflects popular estimates of Washington's near-divinity in the years immediately following his death. The Washington cultus was one early republican expression of civil religion.

perpetuated especially by the public school system. The same was the case for two other major symbols of the civil religion of the Revolution — the Declaration of Independence and the Constitution. During the revolutionary era, it was the *act* of declaring liberty and not the document that was honored. Similarly, it was the *act* of constitution making, not the original pen, ink, or paper, that was hailed. In fact, John Adams thought that 2 July — the day that Congress declared independence — would be celebrated by future generations, not 4 July — the date that the document was formally approved. And the original document of the Constitution was never publicly exhibited until the twentieth century.

After Congress proclaimed independence, its declaration was solemnly read throughout the colonies. Cannons were fired, cheers raised, toasts made, and liquor consumed. A year later, there were unofficial celebrations with bells and fireworks along with cannons, cheers, and toasts. In 1778 Congress gave official orders to honor the Fourth of July, and a year afterward it told its chaplains to prepare sermons suitable for the event. By the following decade, Americans were giving similar praise to the Constitution. Huge constitutional parades were staged in most of the new state capitals to pay tribute.

The one in Philadelphia, held on the Fourth of July, 1788, after enough states had ratified the Constitution to make it the law of the land, was an elaborate spectacle. According to report, it seemed as if the entire city was either participating or standing in the ranks to watch the eighty-eight divisions that extended for a mile and a half. Exhibits included the "new roof" of the Constitution, erected in a carriage pulled by ten white horses, and the federal ship of state on another float. Meanwhile, tradespeople walked to express their enthusiasm as workers in the new union. There were sacks of federal flour and signs for a federal cabinet shop and a federal printing press. Most significant for us here was the division of the clergy. In it members of different Christian denominations and the Jewish rabbi walked together linking arms — eloquent testimony to the sermon that the parade was preaching. The real ground of unity in the United States was not any of the sects or denominations, said the parade, but the civil religion of the American Revolution that the Constitution summed up.

This attempt to make a new religious statement through the Revolution and to create a religion around it was strikingly expressed in the patriots' search for a design for the Great Seal of the United States. Three committees worked on the problem over six years before, in 1782, a seal was finally adopted. Among the early suggestions were Benjamin Franklin's of Moses dividing the Red Sea in two, Thomas Jefferson's of the children of Israel marching in the wilderness, and John Adams's of Hercules framed by Virtue pointing him up a rugged mountain and Sloth enticing him down paths of pleasure.

The final design rejected both Jewish and classical themes for a symbolic statement that the real religion of the American Revolution was a religion of newness. An eagle with an olive branch and thirteen arrows to represent the states announced, in Latin, *e pluribus unum*; that is, "one from many." On the back of the seal, an uncompleted pyramid was capped by a symbolic eye. Beneath the pyramid was printed *novus ordo seclorum*, "the new order of the ages." There were Masonic overtones to the Great Seal, but the message went beyond Freemasonry and the Enlightenment. Americans were saying that they had brought something new into the world and that they had inaugurated the millennium for which history had waited. The American Revolution itself became a sacred tale of origins, the center and the source for an American civil religion. In the power of their revolution, Americans hoped, they would be able to create one millennial nation from many different peoples.

The Structure of the Civil Religion

By 1790 elements of creed, code, and cultus had come together to form a loose religious system. This system continued into the nineteenth and twentieth centuries, absorbing new elements and discarding old ones but keeping the same basic structure. Let us look briefly at this structure of the civil religion.

The creed of the civil religion rested on fundamental assumptions that the United States was a chosen and millennial nation. Both qualities could be understood either in Christian or in more general terms. Chosenness might come from God, from nature, or from historical events. Millennialism could mean the coming of the kingdom of God or a golden age of peace and prosperity that Americans created for themselves without requiring God. In either case, chosenness was seen as separating Americans from members of other societies in the world. It was thought to burden them with the twin tasks of being an example of democratic equality and fulfilling a mission to bring that democracy to others. Millennialism split the world into simple alternatives of good and evil and at the same time encouraged both optimism and anxiety regarding America's future. Both chosenness and millennialism were attempts to create a nation out of a political state. They were religious concepts that, it was hoped, could forge one people out of many peoples, giving them a history and identity in the American Revolution, interpreted according to Puritan, Enlightenment, and new American themes.

The code of the civil religion was already contained in its creed. Being an example and fulfilling a mission meant that citizens in the chosen nation must engage in public activity. In this morality, loyalty and patriotism as inner qualities were not enough. Rather, as in the majority religion of Protestantism, citizens had to *work* for the collective good. Voting in elections became a symbolic action to sum up the duty of the citizen. But in the ideal formula of the code, civil religion required more. Citizens had to read and be informed so that they might vote intelligently. They had to be willing to enter public life themselves. And if they were male, the ultimate actions that might be required of them were service in their country's armed forces and even death in its defense. Here human sacrifice for religious reasons had not ended but instead was demanded in a new form. Meanwhile, on the domestic side, the code urged Americans to advance economically and technologically so that the millennium would come fully.

However, the code went beyond statements about how individuals should act in the United States. It was a statement about the political community and how it should behave toward the world. Being an example and having a mission were directives for foreign policy, and America would follow them in a series of encounters with other states. Although the United States would not become a world power until the twentieth century, the rhetoric of the American Revolution already predicted as much. From this perspective, world leadership was a self-fulfilling prophecy. Similarly, the wars in which the United States engaged were always fought under the banner of moral crusade. As we will see later, nationalistic missionary labors did not disappear after the Constitution established separation of church and state.

At the same time, the code of the civil religion had its other side. Just as belief in the millennial mission of the Puritans had been linked to themes of guilt and repentance, in the United States the civil religion perpetuated the political jeremiad. In days of fast and thanksgiving and later in oratory and debate bewailing their country's failings, Americans continued to express the tensions of being chosen. Sometimes the guilt led to stronger statements about being chosen and stronger protests of innocence, as America refused to face its problems. This was the case, for example, in many conflicts created in the nineteenth and twentieth centuries by racism and nativism. Sometimes, too, the guilt became a great political upheaval in an attempt at moral purification. This was true in the crisis over slavery that led to the Civil War; and as we noted earlier, this was also the case in the Watergate scandal of the 1970s.

Finally, a cultus for the civil religion was already developed in 1790 and kept on growing in the next two centuries. First, the necessary conditions for ritual had been provided: there were sacred space and sacred time. Sacred space included shrines and significant places like George Washington's home, Mount Vernon, in Virginia, and Independence Hall in Philadelphia. In the planned development of the new capital in the District of Columbia, the city of Washington, with its classical buildings and memorials on a grand scale, furnished an ideal ritual setting. As time went on, historical sites — such as battlefields that had figured prominently in America's wars — offered other sacred places. In the revolutionary era, the Fourth of July and Washington's birthday were already coming to be sacred time. In later years, new commemorations joined them, such as Memorial Day after the Civil War and Armistice Day after the First World War.

Second, there was a catalog of national "saints," individuals to be honored because they embodied the ideals of the civil religion. George Washington was only the first among a community of founders who came to be venerated in the public life of the country — men like Thomas Jefferson, Benjamin Franklin, and John Adams. The nineteenth century brought new heroes and saints, like Andrew Jackson and Abraham Lincoln, while the twentieth century contributed its own figures in men like Franklin Delano Roosevelt and John F. Kennedy.

Third, there were sacred objects as well as sacred figures. The original copies of the Declaration of Independence and the Constitution were the most remembered by the twentieth century, but from the beginning there were other relics of the Revolution. One Liberty Tree destroyed by the British in South Carolina, for example, had its stump preserved by being carved into cane heads.

Last, formal ritual practices were associated with the sacred space and time, commemorating the founders of the republic and venerating the objects that also helped Americans to remember. Fourth of July fireworks and more solemn sermons were early examples. Later, each special time was accompanied by its own ceremonial order of public addresses, processions, or other events. Important in all of these rituals was their use in attempts to unify people so that they would be a political community and a nation. Like all rituals, the rituals of the civil religion were endeavors to change the many into one.

The Meaning of the Civil Religion

Creed, code, and cultus together formed the visible structure of the civil religion. But at a deeper level, its meaning was more than the sum of its parts. At the same time, that meaning was ambiguous. Civil religion pulled in different directions at once, and contradiction was basic to its makeup. Rooted in the Puritan and revolutionary past, it urged Americans toward a millennial future. At first glance, an ordinary religion based on life within the human political community of one country, it had extraordinary aspirations. Because it was firmly based in the Judeo-Christian tradition and, indeed, in Protestantism, it saw America in a transcendent light. Civil religion, therefore, contained a good deal of the power of extraordinary religion.

Beyond that, the civil religion was a self-conscious and deliberate faith conceived by the leaders of the revolutionary era to meet their need for political ideology. Yet there was enthusiasm and spontaneity in the people's response to the new religion. Millennial excitement could not be produced at will: it had to exist first in the people. So the leaders who were trying to make a religion found it already made, the product of a Puritan past and a revolutionary present. All they did was to tap the power that was there and use it for their purposes.

In another contradiction, the civil religion perpetuated the problem that the conviction of chosenness had created for the Puritans. Such conviction led to guilt and anxiety. Belief in a millennium already begun brought fear of corruption and decline. Thus, a combined sense of millennial chosenness and accompanying guilt encouraged people to disguise serious problems that the country faced. To admit that too much was wrong could jeopardize America's belief in its status as a chosen and millennial nation. Acceptable lamentations were often, like Puritan jeremiads, somewhat hypocritical. In the later history of the republic, problems like racism, nativism, and inequities in the economic system tended to be kept hidden, confronted, if at all, only under carefully controlled conditions. These problems violated the basic identity that the civil religion gave to Americans. In that identity, as we have seen, chosen people, living in the millennium, had to be innocent and righteous. Americans could not admit the deepest sources of their guilt without destroying their sense of who they were.

Finally, people who believed that they were chosen and living in the millennium tended, by definition, to be an exclusive community. Yet the civil religion that expressed convictions about millennial chosenness was intended as a way to bind *all* Americans together. How, then, could a religion of exclusivity incorporate the increasingly diverse many? As public consciousness changed and as racial, ethnic, and feminist sensitivities grew in the late twentieth century, how could a religion identified with a white, Anglo-Saxon, and male foundation accommodate those Americans who were self-consciously different? On the face of things, a tradition of exclusivity seemed a narrow basis on which to build for broad social consensus.

Despite these problems within the civil religion, it *was* an attempt to find some basis for public unity in the vulnerable federal republic. In the beginning, the vulnerability had more to do with the newness of the governmental apparatus than the character of the peoples it represented. But by the late twentieth century, government was vulnerable because of the diversity of peoples and interest groups it encompassed. Still, in a political state beset with boundary questions between social groups, civil religion proposed a common and, it argued, natural boundary based on its natural-rights philosophy. Civil religion was an attempt to merge the separate boundaries of the many into a single nation-state.

If there was a central meaning to the civil religion in the midst of these ambiguities, it was in millennialism in politics and history. Whether looking to past or to future, under God or under America, deliberate or spontaneous, hypocritical or sincere, the civil religion revolved around what were considered memorable deeds that Americans had performed to initiate an age unknown before in history. Here, actions had to be striking to be seen; events had to make history to be meaningful. For people who did not like to dwell in the past, Americans were very anxious to achieve a past on a grand scale. The sensationalist philosophy of Jonathan Edwards resounded in later American life, and all paths in the civil religion seemed to lead to millennial politics and history.

Civil Religion in the Nineteenth and Twentieth Centuries

So far we have examined the origins of civil religion in Puritanism and in the era of the American Revolution. We found that the New Israel of the Puritans continued into the revolutionary generation. We also found that the religion of the Enlightenment, as well as a new religion built around the deeds of patriotic Americans, merged with the New Israel. We noticed a distinct creed, code, and cultus in the civil religion that evolved, and despite its ambiguities, we discovered a core of meaning centering on values of millennial politics and history. In our study, we referred at times to the nineteenth and twentieth centuries. Now we give closer scrutiny to civil religion during these two centuries.

The Nineteenth Century

On the whole, nineteenth-century civil religion was rooted in the Puritan and revolutionary heritage. The legacy of the Enlightenment, in the nineteenth century and thereafter, became less clear. Its ethic of the golden mean was cast aside by Americans who were striving for ultimates. At least in the nineteenth century, its Freemasonic rituals came under challenge for their undemocratic secrecy, the clannish political tactics they fostered, and, said many ministers, their godlessness. Yet elements of the creed of the Enlightenment did continue. The proclamations of the Declaration of Independence — that all were equal in the sight of God and that all were endowed with natural rights — were, at least theoretically, sacred beliefs. Still further, Enlightenment ideas continued in new form by blending with a territorial version of millennialism in the age of manifest destiny.

Generally, themes of millennial chosenness, outstanding example as an innocent and righteous nation, and historic deeds and destiny shaped the civil religion. Especially in growing numbers of public schools, the civil religion was expressed in history books and readers that told of the Revolution and its heroes, aiming to inspire young Americans to patriotic behavior. And the civil faith was ritualized in regular annual observances as well as in a series of anniversary commemorations of revolutionary events. Since it is not possible to explore the nineteenth-century history of civil religion fully, we look first at the presence of (extraordinary) biblical millennial themes, especially in the Civil War, and then at a more ordinary millennialism that combined Puritan with Enlightenment ideas. Finally, we glance at how the memory of the Revolution relieved American anxieties and continued to shape the civil religion.

With the War of 1812 (1812–1814), the new conflict with Britain gave impetus to the civil religion. Congress had declared war because of the British impressment of American sailors into maritime service (in the context of a British struggle with France) and because of quarrels with Britain over land in the American West. While a considerable number of Americans opposed the war, once it had begun, many viewed it as a Christian crusade. Public fasts multiplied — some of them observed locally and others throughout the country. Because for political reasons the British had supported Pope Pius VII (1740–1823) against France, in American eyes this identified Britain with the Antichrist. Thus, the war was read as a millennial confrontation. American patriots believed that the last days were at hand, and when the fortunes of the pope sank, this was seen as a sign of fulfillment of the prophecies. For these Americans the War of 1812, like the Revolution, was a holy war.

If the War of 1812 was fought with strong millennial overtones, a half-century later it was the Civil War (1861–1865) that played out these themes as *the* millennial war of the century. The Civil War swept up legions of Americans in what they saw as the final battle between good and evil, as Northerners and white Southerners alike drew on the biblical heritage. In the South, the Confederacy was seen as the authentic New Israel facing the armies of Egypt. White Southerners believed that slavery was in the plan of God, for they considered blacks to be descended from the biblical Ham, the son of Noah who had shamed his father by viewing him naked and drunk (Gen. 9:20–25). According to the Bible, because of Ham's act Noah later cursed him and predicted for him a life of slavery. Hence, said southern whites, the enslavement of blacks was right and just. By contrast, southern whites argued, the northern abolitionists were atheists and unbelievers. War with such people was a defense of the cause of God and religion. For white Southerners, in a millennial vein, this war was the most important struggle through which the country had passed.

In the North, millennial dating convinced Americans that the end was at hand. According to one theory, the Antichrist had come to power in the year A.D. 606. A symbolic reading of the Book of Revelation (Rev. 11:3) indicated that his reign would extend 1,260 years; and therefore, said convinced believers, the Antichrist must fall in the year 1866. Even in the liberal religious circles of Boston, distanced from the literal millennial belief of so much of Protestant America, the vision of Revelation marshaled people to the northern cause. There Julia Ward Howe (1819–1910), who did not believe in miracles or a special revelation in the Bible, wrote "The Battle Hymn of the Republic." She had visited an army camp, and after the experience the poem came to her, filled with images that must have arisen from long-forgotten childhood memories. Published in 1862, the hymn described the coming of Jesus for the biblical final battle. It was written in the dramatic language of the millennium, with echoes of Armageddon interwoven in its evocation of the march of the Union army. The point made by the circumstances of the hymn's composition was clear: beneath the surface of liberal culture in America themes of Armageddon lived on, able to shape the interpretation of events and to give them powerful meaning.

So the war was fought in millennial terms. Then, five days after it ended, Abraham Lincoln was assassinated. He had just begun his second term of office, telling Americans that they should bear malice toward no one and have charity for all. As it happened, the president was shot on Good Friday, and that fact was not lost on others. He had been sacrificed, they said, as Jesus had been on the cross — one victim to redeem all the people. According to their thinking, while the sacrifice of Jesus pointed the way for men and women to enter heaven, the sacrifice of Lincoln brought them together in unity for a better earth. For them, blood had paid the price of liberty. Lincoln's blood, shed for his country, was seen as mingling with the blood of the nameless soldiers who had given their lives for their country. Popular oratory proclaimed these ideas, as a new divine man and event entered the civil religion.

While biblical interpretations — and especially biblical millennialism — dominated during times of greatest crisis for the country, at other moments themes of millennial chosenness became ordinary religion. The clearest example was during the era of "manifest destiny" in mid century (an era that we considered briefly in a Protestant missionary context in Chapter 5). Recall that the Enlightenment God of nature was thought to guarantee natural law and also natural rights. That guarantee had, in effect, allowed Americans to follow the dictates of their own self-interest, breaking the ties with Britain to achieve political and economic independence. The philosophy of natural rights took many turns in the nineteenth century, as it blended with a sense of national chosenness and a belief in the dawning of a new era. The result was the doctrine of manifest destiny that justified the expansionist ventures of Americans in the West.

Natural rights were viewed as rights given by nature to the political community. In the nineteenth-century understanding of these rights, nature grew less philosophical and more geographical. Americans began to think that the physical terrain, in its very contours, *contained* the law. In other words, there were natural boundaries to a country — rivers, oceans, sometimes mountains. According to the doctrine of manifest destiny, the existence of these boundaries was a law written into the landscape — a law that Americans should learn to obey, extending their state from one end of the continent to the other. By doing so, they said, they would be spreading the area of freedom and democracy at the same time that they improved the earth for farming, its predestined and highest use. In this view, true ownership of land came not from written documents but from the higher law of destiny that matched the land with the people most fit to cultivate it. These people, Americans said, were themselves. They argued that clear necessity demanded that they should have new territory, for like a biological organism, the United States ought to stretch to limits intended by nature. And they thought, besides, that the task of Americans was to regenerate conquered peoples by educating them in democracy. Indeed, for these Americans, Providence demanded that the United States absorb surrounding land to fulfill this mission.

The journalist John L. O'Sullivan used the term *manifest destiny* in 1845. In that year, an article in his *Democratic Review* argued regarding the question of Texas that it was America's manifest destiny to expand across the continent. After that, the phrase became a catchword to sum up a spirit and a time, but the ideas it expressed had been present in outline early in the century. Here we cannot trace the growth and changes in the country's commitment to the idea of manifest destiny throughout the century, but it is important to point out the continuance of the past in this new era and, later, into the period of the Spanish-American War of 1898. Mainstream Americans still believed that they were a chosen people, whether they expressed that conception in the language of the Bible, of the Enlightenment, or of nineteenth-century ordinary culture. Likewise, they still believed that they must be an example to the nations and, even more, that they had a mission to perform. Whether they felt Providence, destiny, or the land commanded them, Americans believed that their mission was to establish a millennial age of empire. They were convinced that the natural right and providential plan for Americans was to hold more land.

It is clear from the hindsight of well over a century that Americans had manipulated language and ideals for their own self-interest. But as we noted earlier, this was a problem built into the very structure of the civil religion. Even without the use of the specific biblical language of the millennium, the problem would not disappear. Meanwhile, even as Americans ventured forward aggressively to make their future, they were deeply anxious, and they clung to would-be signs of divine favor tied to their heritage in the Revolution.

For example, when the Marquis de Lafayette (1757–1834) visited the United States as an old man in 1824, Americans staged what amounted to a revival in the civil religion. Lafayette had been the "adopted" son of George Washington. According to accounts at the time, the presence in the flesh of the son intensified the memory of the father, now dead for a quarter of a century. Thus, Lafayette made Washington live again for these Americans through the closeness of past ties with him. And with the presence of Washington came the presence of the Revolution — and the power of the Revolution newly made available. Heaven was surely speaking to them in the visit of Lafayette, Americans thought, for a rainbow hung over his ship both when it arrived and when it departed from port. Moreover, an eagle, the symbolic bird of America, was spotted flying over Washington's tomb as Lafayette walked into it to pay his respects. As Americans shared the news of Lafayette's descent into the tomb, it seemed to them as if they, too, followed him — not to death but to a rebirth in the spirit of the Revolution.

Then, some two years later, the deaths of both John Adams and Thomas Jefferson on the Fourth of July, 1826, awed and impressed Americans. The two had died hours apart on the fiftieth anniversary of the signing of the Declaration of Independence. Once more, Americans believed they had a sign from God as to the significance of their experiment in democracy. Again in the following decade, when the physical remains of Washington were placed in a new marble coffin, his body was declared physically nearly intact. No odor was reported to have offended those present; it was said that the broad temples and chest were still there; and one member of the party, it was told, quickly laid his hand on Washington's head. In these physical remains, Americans had a relic that for them had unusual power. The integrity of Washington's body seemed to them a sign of the integrity of America grounded on its past. Moreover, keeping in touch with the body of Washington was for them a way to keep in touch with the Revolution.

Less dramatically, keeping in touch came not through the deaths of the leaders of the Revolution but through the ceremonial recollection of the events through which they had lived. The fiftieth anniversary of the Declaration (1826), the hundredth anniversary of the birth of Washington (1832), the fiftieth jubilee of the Constitution (1839), the seventy-fifth anniversary of the

Declaration (1851), the centennial of the Revolution (1876), and the centennial of the Constitution (1889) were all such occasions. Americans believed they could draw strength from their past as they faced the tensions that their millennial dreams of progress brought them. The ceremonies of the civil religion worked to reassure them of their cause and motives.

The Twentieth Century

With the twentieth century, civil religion continued to interpret for Americans the meaning of their existence as a political community. With the First and Second World Wars millennial themes were visible. In more peaceful times, the regular ceremonies of the Fourth of July, Memorial Day, the birthdays of Washington and Lincoln, and Thanksgiving recalled the heritage of the past. After the First World War, Armistice Day, later called Veterans Day (1954), joined them. But as time passed and the events of the Revolution became mostly chapters in history books, the power of the civil religion to inspire Americans began to fail. Even more, the second half of the century brought wars in Korea and Vietnam that did not lend themselves easily to familiar millennial interpretations. Moral ambiguity clouded the domestic scene as well, so that civil religion grew to be the faith of fewer Americans, less of the time.

The period preceding the American entry into the First World War (1914–1918) was a time of political isolation from foreign involvements — traditional during much of the country's history before the United States became a world power. Here the ideology of chosenness was expressed through the example Americans understood themselves to give to a "corrupt" world. According to the ideology, in its innocence and righteousness America was a new Eden, a garden of progress and peace. In fact, when Woodrow Wilson (1856–1924) was re-elected to the presidency in 1916, his campaign was built around the slogan "He kept us out of war." The First World War had begun over two years earlier, and Americans had tried to remain neutral. But by 1917 reaction to the loss of American lives through German submarine warfare made that impossible, and the country mobilized for war. Wilson, with a strict Presbyterian upbringing, brought moral earnestness to the effort. Under a committee on public information, the government began a propaganda effort to convince Americans of the righteousness of this new crusade.

Once again, the millennial account of the final battle between the forces of good and evil was recalled. The success of the campaign showed how deeply the millennial pattern was rooted in the American spirit. Motion pictures portrayed the Germans as wicked and barbarian Huns, promoting beliefs that Americans were fighting the agents of Satan. Some states passed laws to forbid teaching the German language in schools and colleges; citizens threw German books out of the libraries; German and Austrian artists and their music were banned from public performances. Speakers appeared at public meetings and at film theaters to deliver brief addresses in support of the war effort. Newspaper editorials and pamphlets repeatedly attacked the Germans as corrupt, and members of the Protestant clergy from their pulpits took up the cry of the New Israel engaged in a holy war against evil.

Billy Sunday — whom we have already met waving the American flag as he preached — declared that he thought that if hell were turned upside down, the phrase "made in Germany" would be seen stamped across the bottom. Meanwhile, Roman Catholic and Jewish leaders supported the Protestant interpretation of the war. Catholics were told that there was a parallel between the sufferings of Israel in the desert on the way to the promised land and the sufferings of America in the massive war effort. Jews in turn were told that they were once again fighting against the forces of oppression, as they had done so many times before in their history. From the side of ordinary American culture, the war whipped patriotism to new religious zeal. By 1918 at least one book — William Norman Guthrie's *The Religion of Old Glory* — was telling Americans of the greatness of their flag, suggesting a ritual for its worship.

According to the phrase that rallied millions of Americans, the war had been fought to "make the world safe for democracy." America had committed itself one more time in a mission to the world, combining extraordinary and ordinary versions of their belief in millennial chosenness to do so. As the "world's policeman," America had entered a new era in international affairs, but it read the new era through the pages of the old story of the civil religion. Then, after another period of isolation, the Second World War (1939–1945) meant a return to the familiar themes, although less intensely than during the Wilson years.

Still, ideas of the dualism of good and evil rode the public airwaves. The totalitarian form of government in the Axis states (Germany, Italy, and Japan) lent itself easily to millennial interpretation. After Americans entered the war in 1941, convinced of the importance of bombing (some would say, despite evidence to the contrary), they used air power in dramatic displays of force. Making history became more destructive than at any time in previous wars, as the night skies were lit by missiles of death. When the United States finally dropped atomic bombs on Hiroshima and Nagasaki, Japan, in 1945, totalitarianism had been countered with a force as total. If the final battle of Armageddon had not come, Americans had done what they could to bring it.

In the midst of these years, Franklin Delano Roosevelt (1882–1945) presided over the country, publicly determined to make America an "arsenal of democracy." Elected to an unprecedented third term in office, he told Congress in January 1941 that America should support the countries that were fighting to defend the Four Freedoms — freedom of speech, freedom of religion, freedom from want, and freedom from fear. In the phrases of his oratory, he was calling all Americans to respond to their mission. For Roosevelt, it was not sufficient to be an example to the nations, as isolationist policy allowed. In so many words, he was urging the Puritans of the New Israel to march again, though they spoke in thisworldly fashion and wore the uniforms of a government theoretically separate from religion.

Less spectacularly, civil religion continued through the annual calendar of public observances in which key moments or individuals from America's past were remembered. Like any ritual of remembrance, these observances were sacramental in nature. They were efforts to make the past present again, attempts to destroy the work of time in order to live in the power of moments remembered as the nation's greatest. Yet by the fifties, a long and gradual period of decline began to affect the observances and the spirit of the civil religion. We cannot follow the whole story here, but as an example let us look at what happened to the annual Memorial Day commemorations.

Memorial Day began in the millennial aftermath of the Civil War, in an America mourning the death of Lincoln and deeply aware of all of the dead. In fact, there were both northern and southern theories of its origins. Northerners recounted that General John A. Logan, commander-in-chief of the Grand Army of the Republic, in 1868 established the observance by his orders. Southerners said the remembrance started in 1866 in Columbus, Mississippi, when women of the town paid homage to the war dead by decorating the graves of both Confederate and Union soldiers. The separate accounts suggest how deep the rupture had been between the two sides. They also suggest the intensity of feeling that marked these early Memorial Day commemorations. As time passed, the presence of veterans who had fought in the war continued to give intensity of feeling to the annual Memorial Day observances, but when the veterans began to die, a bond with the past was broken. Try as they might, later generations could not recapture the spirit that came with the presence of living witnesses to the war.

Then, in the fifties and afterward, time eroded the strength and significance of Memorial Day ceremonies even further. Remember that in both the North and the South, the day had paid tribute to countless soldiers who had given their lives in the cause of their country. By doing so, it had given expression to the sense of unity in the community that remained. By honoring those who died, people renewed their own belief in the need for sacrifice for the good of the entire American community. But the simple formula did not work when applied to the Korean War (1950–1953) and later the Vietnam War (1954–1973), with growing American involvement in the sixties. Many were less sure of the significance of sacrifices in foreign campaigns that were clouded with ambiguity. The community was no longer united in its support of war, and Memorial Day, therefore, could not express traditional themes convincingly.

In the fifties, newspaper editorials complained about the lack of enthusiasm for Memorial Day, while by the sixties, apathy was evident in accounts of poorly attended Memorial Day parades and gaudy souvenirs that cluttered and cheapened the observances. Journalists asked where the spirit of American patriotism had gone, and by the era of the Vietnam War, the answer was that it had become identified with right-wing causes. To be patriotic during the late sixties and early seventies was to make a cultural statement that identified a person with complaints against hippies, draft dodgers, and other long-haired individuals. To be patriotic meant to be a self-declared enemy of the Woodstock generation. Hence, far from being a solemn evocation of national unity, Memorial Day had become a reminder of division. The civil religion in some respects was failing, for the many were not being made into one.

If regular observances of the civil religion like Memorial Day reflected the decline of the tradition, so did the anniversary celebration of America's 200th year. January to December 1976 had been planned as a long remembrance of the events that established the United States. The Fourth of July was to be the high point of the yearlong observance, meant as a tribute to the deeds and values on which America was built. But coming on the heels of the nonvictorious end of the Vietnam War and the resignation of President Richard M. Nixon because of the Watergate scandal, the bicentennial caught many Americans not in the mood for celebration. The American Revolution Bicentennial Administration (ARBA), in charge of official government planning, was plagued with disagreements about how the bicentennial could best be commemorated. When early plans were floated to select one bicentennial city, prime candidates like Boston and Philadelphia thought approvingly of the financial gain for themselves from the influx of tourists. But when, for example in the case of Philadelphia, plans grew more concrete with a specific city neighborhood designated as the focus for the celebration, the city government responded to pressures from neighborhood residents. Local critics argued that the bicentennial would bring strange people, and especially black people, to their doorsteps. People in the Eastwick section of the city did not approve.

Finally, the ARBA settled on a decentralized plan for the bicentennial. No one city would be *the* center of solemnities. Throughout the country, small cities and towns began to erect signs that proclaimed each of them to be an authorized bicentennial city. In fact, the many proclamations mirrored the pluralism of the country at its 200th anniversary. The ARBA had stumbled into a version of America that fittingly summed up national life. In 1976 no one center could speak for all Americans, for there were too many languages to speak and too many stories to be told.

As if to emphasize the existence of different visions of America, the official ARBA had competition in its planning. The People's Bicentennial Commission (PBC), with its newsletter titled *Common Sense*, challenged the ARBA from a leftist perspective. For Americans of the PBC, the story of the American Revolution still had power to inspire, but a new enemy of America replaced King George III. In the late twentieth century, said the PBC, the real enemy of America was the giant corporation, and the power of the Revolution should be harnessed to fight the entrenched business establishment. So on the celebration of the 200th anniversary of the Boston Tea Party in 1973, 25,000 supporters of the PBC rallied for the enactment of their own interpretation of events. On the deck of their ship were oil drums prominently displaying the names of the largest oil companies in the United States. A group of the new Boston protesters threw the drums into the water, using the past to register dissent in the present.

Against this background of conflicting ideas of what America meant, the observances of the civil religion on the occasion of the bicentennial were sometimes lavish but mostly quiet and contained. There were gaudy mementos of every description, as commercial interests hurried to profit from events. But cities awaiting large numbers of tourists did not get nearly so many as they had expected. Police foreseeing fights and accidental deaths in the huge crowds at commemorations found that far less happened than they had anticipated. Generally, Americans observed the Fourth of July soberly more than enthusiastically. There were huge spectacles in big cities, such as a procession of tall ships bearing masts that sailed through New York harbor. But in the atmosphere of the late twentieth century, the civil millennial dream had been interrupted. A new national consensus about the meaning of America had not been formed.

The slow decline did not go unheeded by thoughtful people. In fact, since at least the sixties, a number of scholars had begun to ponder the meaning of America as they examined the role of religion. It was one of these scholars, the sociologist Robert N. Bellah, who by 1967 employed the term *civil religion* to describe the religious system we have been examining throughout the chapter. For some sociologists, like Bellah, and for some historians, like Sidney E. Mead, scholarship about civil religion became an attempt to revitalize the tradition. Bellah's article "Civil Religion in America" spoke of the growing (at that time) conflict in Vietnam as America's third time of trial, a new crisis on the order of the American Revolution and the Civil War. Mead's many essays on the "religion of the Republic"—and later its theology—identified sectarianism as the cause of national disunity and praised the universal religion of the Enlightenment, born in the Revolution. This religion, he thought, offered Americans real hope of unity. In the year before the bicentennial, Bellah published a book-length essay, *The Broken Covenant*. Subtitled *American Civil Religion in Time of Trial*, it began with historical assessment of the power of the traditional American account of origins and, in contrast, found the civil religion of the time empty and broken. Bellah called for a return to what he saw as the true and original meaning of an American covenant, to a millennium brought by God and not by human beings, and to the continuance of the old dreams and visions.

So in their awareness of the lessening hold of the civil religion, descriptive scholars had become theologians and preachers. Their reflection and writing were in fact an attempt to make the civil religion strong again. Although scholars have been less interested in civil religion in recent years and the so-called civil-religion debate is largely over, we can learn much from the decade and more of scholarly exchange. In his article in 1967, Bellah identified the existence of civil religion by studying presidential inaugural addresses to find in them references to God. It is interesting that in the excerpts he included from the 1961 inaugural address of President John F. Kennedy (1917–1963), there were as many references to history or our "forebears" as to God. Later, at the height of the Watergate scandal, President Nixon continually referred to history as the judge of his deeds. He had wanted to make history, and so he had taped presidential conversations in the Oval Office to preserve them. His unwillingness to destroy the tapes — his bond with history — in the end helped bring him down.

In America from the beginning, making history had been closely identified with politics. The public space of government — and the conversations and acts that took place there — gave many Americans a sense of clear direction in the ordinary world. In a key example, in 1823 as an old man Thomas Jefferson wrote to John Adams, including in his letter the wish that the two would meet again in heaven with their colleagues in the Congress. Happiness, for Jefferson, Adams, and many others, meant politics.

Indeed, in the late twentieth century the statement was still true. News accounts revolved around the (often crisis-ridden) doings of the president and Congress, while every four years, the country passed through a season of millennial revival as a presidential election campaign was waged. As Walter Cronkite ended his regular presentations of the evening news on CBS television in the seventies, he told millions of Americans, "That's the way it is." Meant to be a catchphrase to close the broadcast, the statement was philosophical — and religious. The real world, as proclaimed by Cronkite and CBS, was the world of public events and striking deeds. It was the world of political and, sometimes, military action, the account of goals achieved or woefully failed and of public acclaim captured or lost. Americans were still melodramatic people, and they were still sensationalists. That is how they made sense of their world, lived their daily lives, and solemnized their actions in rituals.

Moreover, as the direct memory of Cronkite faded and the century waned, the civil religion still continued to define reality for Americans in extended moments of nationalistic feeling. The Iranian hostage crisis in 1980, the explosion of the space shuttle Challenger in 1986, and the invasions of Grenada in 1983 and of Panama in 1989 all evoked in different ways the patriotic cosmology at the center of the civil religion. When, in 1990, Iraq assumed control of tiny Kuwait and raised fears regarding the international oil supply, American public rhetoric turned more on Iraqi aggression against an "innocent" neighbor than on American defense of and desire for oil. Even with an ambiguous reference by President George H. Bush (b. 1924) to defending "our way of life," the rhetoric stood in the tradition of the "righteous" nation, taking its stand in time and history for the pursuit of transcendent values. The Persian Gulf War that followed (1991) was also fought on these rhetorical terms.

Yet as we have already seen, in such involvement in the historical moment, Americans showed little interest in the chronological account of the unfolding of the past. If they periodically looked to America's time of origins in the Revolution, they looked more to their problems and achievements in the present and to their plans for the future. Civil religion was the triumph of politics and history, but the history involved was, in reality, ahistorical. In an echo of Protestant restorationism, it was the history that Americans performed with an eye to the millennial new day that counted, not the weight of tradition. In effect, as we noticed earlier, the civil religion was caught in a double bind: it needed the past to be meaningful — to give the present a solid foundation. Yet the values it encouraged were values that rejected the past for the future.

As the past became older and the revolutionary events more distant, it was no wonder that many Americans had trouble relating to the founders and their foundation. At the same time, for Americans who were people of color and for immigrants who were newer and more diverse, the ties with the past that did remain in the civil religion proved not especially meaningful. Civil religion could give Americans a creed, a code, and a cultus, but it could not — save in exceptional wartime moments — transform them into one community. Ambiguous in its relationship to tradition, civil religion, with its belief in millennial chosenness, could not awake to the manyness of the present. It was caught between the past and the future. It had no formula for the community that needed to be created in the present from what *all* the people in the United States shared continuously in common.

Still, there was another side to the issue. From the first, civil religion was a religious system that had sprung up in addition to the churches. It had brought ordinary American history into touch with extraordinary religion. Yet unlike being Methodist or Jewish or Presbyterian, being a believer in the national faith did not mean belonging to an organization or breaking ties with a previous church to which a person belonged. Despite the contrary evidence of the Jehovah's Witnesses, a believer in the civil religion might also be a Baptist, a Catholic, or a Mormon. Indeed, a believer in the civil religion might conceivably be an atheist, since a good part of the symbolism of the civil religion could be used without reference to a God. Thus, despite its limitations, to some extent civil religion *was* an answer to the problem of manyness — an overarching religious system under which most of the denominations and sects might find their place. Whatever its problems, civil religion was a "one story" created to form the many into one.

In Overview

We have seen that civil religion is a recent name for religious nationalism as institutionalized in a loose religious system. Its foundations were laid by the New England Puritans and, later, by the patriots of the American Revolution, who linked Puritan millennial themes to Enlightenment religion and the experience and remembrance of their own deeds in the war. By the time of George Washington's first inauguration, the creed, code, and cultus of the civil religion were firmly in place, and through them the ordinary history of the country was linked to extraordinary religion.

The creed proclaimed the United States as a chosen and millennial nation, saddled with the twin charge of providing an example and fulfilling a mission to raise up others to democracy. The code emphasized patriotic behavior by citizens and government, with a view to setting example and accomplishing an American mission. But the code also institutionalized the jeremiad, the public lament about the guilt of America that substituted language for action to correct problems. Interlinked with creed and code, the cultus of the civil faith designated sacred space and time in national shrines and patriotic holy days. It offered national "saints," revered objects, and ritual practices to encourage Americans to keep touch with creed and code. Although there were many ambiguities in the meaning of creed, code, and cultus, the central affirmation was the millennial politics of making history by deeds of greatness.

In the nineteenth century, the War of 1812 and the Civil War carried forward the millennial theme, while the doctrine of manifest destiny applied the theme to the acquisition of land. Then in the twentieth century, the First and Second World Wars heightened millennial fervor, but beginning in the fifties a long period of decline occurred in the civil religion. Celebration of the cultus grew even less enthusiastic at, for example, Memorial Day observances and during the bicentennial. Against this background, a scholarly revitalization movement explored the meaning of the civil faith and tried to revivify and strengthen it. Beleaguered by its problems, civil religion could not create authentic community: it was the religion of, at best, many of the people some of the time. Yet it did offer a framework within which the many could come together as Americans and still pursue their separate religions. And it did provide a focus for national response during public crisis moments from 1980.

However, civil religion was only one piece of the religious territory, so to speak. Although they were many, Americans in their public space had created a dominant culture that, as one, told them who they were, advised them how to act, and provided them with rituals to express these meanings. George Washington was not the only divine man for Americans. Arguing politics and celebrating the Fourth of July were not the only American rituals. Beyond the civil religion there was general American culture. We need further examination of its religious dimensions, for we need to gain a clearer sense of what ordinary religion means in its American setting. As we will see, George Washington shared his power with Elvis Presley, and arguing politics yielded before the public spectacle of the American baseball game.

SUGGESTIONS FOR FURTHER READING:
CIVIL RELIGION

Albanese, Catherine L. *Sons of the Fathers: The Civil Religion of the American Revolution.* Philadelphia: Temple University Press, 1976.

Bellah, Robert N. *The Broken Covenant: American Civil Religion in Time of Trial.* New York: Seabury Press, 1975.

_____, and Hammond, Phillip E. *Varieties of Civil Religion.* San Francisco: Harper & Row, 1980.

Cherry, Conrad, ed. *God's New Israel: Religious Interpretations of American Destiny.* Englewood Cliffs, NJ: Prentice-Hall, 1971.

Gribbin, William. *The Churches Militant: The War of 1812 and American Religion.* New Haven: Yale University Press, 1973.

Herberg, Will. *Protestant—Catholic—Jew.* Rev. ed. Garden City, NY: Doubleday, Anchor Books, 1960.

Hudson, Winthrop S. *Nationalism and Religion in America: Concepts of American Identity and Mission.* New York: Harper & Row, 1970.

Jewett, Robert. *The Captain America Complex: The Dilemma of Zealous Nationalism.* Philadelphia: Westminster Press, 1973.

Mead, Sidney E. *The Nation with the Soul of a Church.* New York: Harper & Row, 1975.

_____. *The Old Religion in the Brave New World: Reflections on the Relation between Christendom and the Republic.* Berkeley: University of California Press, 1977.

Moorhead, James H. *American Apocalypse: Yankee Protestants and the Civil War, 1860–1869.* New Haven: Yale University Press, 1978.

O'Brien, Conor Cruise. *God Land: Reflections on Religion and Nationalism.* Cambridge: Harvard University Press, 1988.

Richey, Russell E., and Jones, Donald G., eds. *American Civil Religion.* New York: Harper & Row, 1974.

Shaw, Peter. *American Patriots and the Rituals of Revolution.* Cambridge: Harvard University Press, 1981.

Strout, Cushing. *The New Heavens and New Earth: Political Religion in America.* New York: Harper & Row, 1974.

Tuveson, Ernest Lee. *Redeemer Nation: The Idea of America's Millennial Role.* Chicago: University of Chicago Press, 1968.

Weinberg, Albert K. *Manifest Destiny: A Study of Nationalist Expansionism in American History.* 1935. Reprint. Chicago: Quadrangle Books, 1963.

Wilson, Charles Reagan. *Baptized in Blood: The Religion of the Lost Cause, 1865–1920.* Athens: University of Georgia Press, 1980.

Wilson, John F. *Public Religion in American Culture.* Philadelphia: Temple University Press, 1979.

Chapter 14

Cultural Religion: Explorations in Millennial Dominance and Innocence

In 1968 the *Whole Earth Catalog* came into existence as a countercultural Sears Roebuck catalog. One of the regulars who contributed to its pages was Gurney Norman. As a strong advocate of composting, Norman in one issue described his composting class for readers. The group began its session with tea, drunk quietly and ceremonially while sitting on cushions. Then the class moved on to a discussion of practical techniques in which questions were aired. Finally, at the end of the meeting each person reverently sprinkled used tea leaves on the compost pile and took away a cup of the half-finished compost and two worms. These items were seed for the compost pile that class members would later begin at home.

It was a small and humble ceremony that Norman and his class followed, but it was nevertheless a definable ritual. Sacred space was created by the cushions on which members of the group sat during the tea ceremony and by the common compost pile at the end. Sacred time was separated from the rest of time by the deliberate acts of drinking tea, sprinkling tea leaves, and taking away the compost. These acts were performed formally and self-consciously with a sense of their symbolic meaning. And clearly, they were related to belief and behavior systems held by class members. Here were people interested in the natural cycle of growth, destruction, and renewal. Here were people about to take up backyard composting on their own.

Gurney Norman and his friends thought themselves different from mainstream Americans, and, especially at that time, in some ways they were. But their ritual in the midst of ordinary life was only one instance of various kinds of ceremonial action that Americans—and all other people—perform regularly. Human beings, whether they hold to organized religions or not, find ways to express in ritual the powers, meanings, and values they see in the world. Everyday life is punctuated with these actions, often even humbler and less deliberate than those in Norman's class. The rituals of ordinary culture are frequently vague and highly diffused. To the untrained eye they may be invisible, but with the background of our continuing study of ordinary religion, we can begin to think about them.

Religion and Ordinary American Culture

In the terms of the text, the composting session of Norman and the others was a series of religious actions. These were ritual gestures related to a creed and a code that in their complete form included all of life. To be sure, the gestures were not a part of any traditional religion, and Norman and his friends would have been the first to protest if we had said that they were. It is clear, for example, that no institution stood behind the composting class, and if the composters thought themselves part of a larger movement, that movement gave out no membership cards, possessed no group statistics, and claimed no constitution. Norman, in the ritual setting, did act as a priestly leader, but his priesthood was temporary and self-appointed. Furthermore, the boundaries of his group were loose and fluid. Members of the class, aside from their composting practices, did not necessarily separate themselves from the rest of society. And while they did share a set of beliefs and actions that united them, they could also be members of other religious groups. Finally, in Norman's ceremonies, no language of the supernatural, no mention of a God, entered the format of the ritual. The message of tea and compost was related to this world without reference to any other.

In our examination of American civil religion, we have already encountered a religious system without formal institutionalization. Custom demanded certain activities, such as Fourth of July ceremonies, but no Church of the Civil Religion distributed membership cards or conducted initiation ceremonies. Except for naturalized citizens, membership came with birth — as general a commitment as being part of American culture. Similarly, while God was acknowledged in much of civil religion, we saw that it was not necessary to affirm God in order to practice it. In the final analysis, the civil faith centered on the political community, with the hope of creating out of the many an American nation-state. Thus, civil religion demonstrated that changing the language — from God to history — did not completely change the religious system. Words are symbols, and as symbols they stand for objects beyond themselves. In the case of civil religion, we saw that even when the words changed, what they symbolized remained. The values of the civil religion were the same or very nearly so, although language might no longer be openly religious. Hence, civil religion is our first example of a diffuse and part-time religion that is still a religion. Without institutionalization and without an absolute need for the language of the supernatural, civil religion exists in recognizable form.

With this background, it should not surprise us that in ordinary culture people often find additional symbolic centers. Besides civil religion, there are other means by which people order their lives and search for meaning within the everyday world. Beyond civil religion, too, there are other ways by which people reach moments of transcendence, using ordinary culture as a way into an "other" world. As we saw in the last chapter, civil religion is only one piece of the religious territory. That means that there is much religious landscape still to explore. In this chapter, we cannot cover all of the terrain, but at least we can take a few steps. We can try to understand tentatively what the religion of culture is about. In the pages that follow, first, we briefly survey major expressions of cultural religion. Second, as a specific case study, we examine in more depth the ways in which the natural world has provided the center for some kinds of cultural religion, as in the composting class. Third, we try to sift through the complexities to arrive at some general conclusions.

Cultural Religion: A Brief Survey

Cultural religion, as we know it today, roughly began to assume its shape in late-nineteenth-century America. In this era, the crisis of the Civil War had passed; industrialization was changing the face of the United States; cities were multiplying in number and in size; and the most massive waves of immigration to date were flooding them. At the same time, such familiar features of American life as organized sports, expanding technologies, and, in literature, Western novels were becoming commonplace. While it would be instructive to study earlier cultural religion in America, here we mostly limit ourselves to this later time and, especially, to the contemporary period. More than looking at the changes in cultural religion through the years, we will identify what cultural religion in the United States looks like in the present. As we will see, there are lines connecting contemporary American cultural religion to the dominant and public religion of Protestantism and to the civil religion. Themes of millennialism — as both a form of dominance and a form of innocence — figure prominently in cultural religion. Linked to the millennialism, quests for religious experience and for a community of feeling appear in many forms of everyday behavior, while voluntaryism is the great given that provides the background. Cultural religion simply carries these themes into a less openly "religious" setting.

The American Ritual Calendar

Probably the most observable aspect of cultural religion at first glance is the American ritual calendar. We have already seen parts of it in the Fourth of July, the birthdays of Washington and Lincoln, Memorial Day, Veterans Day, and Thanksgiving. But there are other special days as well. Encircling the year are a series of holidays (holy days) that bring people together as part of American culture. Thus, the early winter cycle of feasts begins with Halloween, includes Veterans Day and Thanksgiving, and then culminates in Christmas and New Year's celebrations.

At least three of these occasions have historic roots associated with extraordinary religion. Halloween was once All Hallows' Eve, the night before the Catholic feast of All Saints' Day, when — in accord with Catholic belief — all considered hallowed, or holy (the saints in heaven), were remembered. Thanksgiving, we recall, was a harvest festival originating with the Pilgrims, intended to thank God for his blessing on the crops after a successful planting in the New World. Christmas was the commemoration, for Christian believers, of the birth of Jesus Christ. In their twentieth-century American setting, however, these three feasts grew away from their origins. Noticeably, a number of Americans, like some observant Jews and Japanese-American Buddhists, objected to the pervasiveness of the reminders of Christmas in American culture. Many other non-Christians, however, continued to celebrate the feast. For these non-Christians, the holiday trappings of Christmas no longer required Christian interpretation. Nor, for most other Americans and apparently less controversially, did either Halloween or Thanksgiving. Halloween became a beggars' night for neighborhood children; Thanksgiving, a family feast of abundance centering on turkey and trimmings; and Christmas, a winter feast of evergreens, department-store Santas, and conviviality.

On the other hand, without distinct Christian roots, New Year's Eve has been a feast that resembles accounts of pagan festivals. In social gatherings, typically, Americans are expected to behave spontaneously in a night of revelry. Alcohol and food flow freely, and as the clock strikes twelve, people join in a toast to the new year. Below the level of conscious awareness, the social permissiveness and license of the night imitate ancient ways of perceiving — and coming to terms with — time's passage. The old year is running down and being destroyed; a new order is rising. So Americans break their old patterns of behavior by their revelry. They share the creation of a new order later in pro forma New Year's resolutions.

In the first half of the new year, another series of holidays makes symbolic statements about the meaning of life in America. First, there are the remembrances of the civil faith in the January commemoration of Martin Luther King, Jr., and in the February commemoration of the birthdays of Washington and Lincoln, now joined as Presidents' Day; in Memorial Day at the end of May; and in Flag Day on 14 June. Then there is the trinity of Valentine's Day, Mother's Day, and Father's Day, which tell of the importance of feeling and sentiment in the private sphere. In an industrialized society, with its impersonality in work and business, these occasions pay tribute to home, family, and personal affection.

The midsummer feast of Americans is the Fourth of July, when picnic, fireworks, and patriotic displays bring family, friends, and community together. After this the summer weeks pass in some two months of unmarked time — the traditional vacation period. Then, as summer unofficially closes in time for school, comes Labor Day. On this first Monday in September, Americans honor the role of work in the foundation and continuance of their society. And in honoring work and working people, they also show their regard for the Puritan and Calvinist virtues of industry, hard work, and efficiency, through which Americans believe their society became great. Finally, as October returns, Americans commemorate the European "discovery" of the New World in Columbus Day (12 October).

It is worth pausing to reflect on the cumulative meaning of this annual cycle. Eight holidays belong to the calendar of the civil religion, and, of these, four — the Fourth of July, Memorial Day, Veterans Day, and Presidents' Day — are associated with apocalyptic millennial themes that recall catastrophic wars and sacrificial deeds on behalf of country. A fifth, dedicated to the African-American Martin Luther King, Jr., suggests the pluralism that American civil religion seeks to encompass. King's struggles for black civil rights and his assassination evoke, too, the apocalyptic and the millennial. Meanwhile, a sixth holiday of the civil religion, Thanksgiving, is millennial as well, but here a golden age of peace and plenty rather than a final battle is celebrated. A seventh holiday, Flag Day, honors the flag as symbolic of America. Themes of millennialism and sacrifice are implicit, for a flag is a war standard. But Flag Day is a minor occasion, observed legally only in the state of Pennsylvania. Finally, an eighth holiday, Columbus Day, turns, like King Day, on millennial and pluralistic motifs. But here the millennialism resembles that of Thanksgiving — gathering in ideas of hope and promise in the New World. Moreover, remembering Christopher Columbus brings its own set of cultural problems. Its evocation of pluralism is meant to appeal to Southern European ethnic groups, especially to Italian-Americans, to signal the inclusiveness of the civil faith. But other Americans, among them Native Americans, find in the memory of Columbus a symbol of conquest and oppression as well as other social and environmental problems they attribute to Western culture.

At the other end of the spectrum, however, there are at least five holidays in which family or domestic themes are highlighted. Halloween and Christmas belong to children who, on both occasions, receive the gifts and goodwill of neighbors, family, or Santa Claus. Adults, when they participate in these feasts, renew personal bonds with one another through social gatherings or, at Christmas, through family reunions. Similarly, Valentine's Day, Mother's Day, and Father's Day show regard within the context of a close relationship. What all of these occasions have in common is that they seek to honor innocence. There is the natural innocence of children on Halloween and Christmas and the more deliberate innocence of family and friendship on all of the feasts. Coming as they do to interrupt, at least theoretically, the economic cycle of the marketplace, the sanctity ascribed to their domestic themes is underlined.

Labor Day strikes a middle position between public and private, for it is intended to honor each American's contribution to society through productive work. Begun in 1882 by the Knights of Labor, this holiday with its union roots suggests a golden age of equality, when common people create a new America with their work. In the same way as Thanksgiving, it points toward a millennium of peace and plenty. Moreover, like Thanksgiving, it weaves private and domestic themes into the millennial cloth, subtly introducing American innocence again.

Finally, New Year's Eve combines millennialism with innocence in its anticipation of the dawning of a new era when the mistakes and misfortunes of the past will be erased. With its destruction of old forms, New Year's Eve looks toward the world born anew. The symbolism associated with the celebration appropriately summarizes these themes. Old Father Time hobbles along on his cane, his white beard reaching almost to his ankles. Then, at midnight, the diapered infant of the new year appears, fresh and innocent to encounter the future.

We can note, too, that in at least three of the celebrations—Memorial Day, the Fourth of July, and Labor Day—picnics are traditional. These summer feasts provide occasions for many to escape the cares and congestion of urban life and return to a natural setting. Such a return to nature evokes, in its pattern, the innocence of the Garden of Eden and, at the same time, the innocence of the millennial era. The return to nature bypasses history—the world of everyday work—to give an opportunity for rest and renewal.

In sum, the ceremonial cycle of ordinary American culture tells that millennialism—as both dominance and innocence—is as important in general culture as it is in public Protestantism and, as the cycle partially reflects, in civil religion. Furthermore, the cycle shows that millennial dominance and innocence are closely related. Themes of apocalyptic conquest and destruction are not so far as we may think from the innocence of babies and of family reunions. Soldiers of the millennium are conceived as righteous and pure, as persons who do not know evil. The literal meaning of innocence is the same: not knowing evil. Thus, neither the millennial soldier nor the innocent American can be comfortable with the ambiguities of a world that is not black or white but muddled shades of gray.

American Sacred Stories

Traditional sacred stories tell people who they are, where they have come from, what their tasks ought to be, and what their world means. In other words, sacred stories are creeds in narrative form; they tell people the basic beliefs they hold about their human condition. In America such narratives unite the many by providing a common fund of meaning for all to share. In short, these American stories give people a system of beliefs regarding their place as part of one people. The creed is carried by television and film, spread by popular literature and magazines, and embodied in popular heroes and entertainment stars. It surrounds Americans in public places and, through television and the print media, enters the privacy of their homes. More strongly than the gospel of any church, which is heard perhaps once or twice in a week, it shapes Americans from cradle to grave. While its message is complex and many-sided, we can single out a few major themes.

Studies of drama and literature tell us that the thousands of plots enacted on the stage or developed in novels and short stories can be reduced to a very few. The names, personalities, and events on the surface change, but underlying patterns remain the same. We can all name a number of the basic plots: boy and girl meet, boy and girl win each other, a triangle complicates the romance, a trusted friend betrays the family, and other familiar tales. Thus, when television serials and Hollywood films are examined, it should not be surprising to find a limited number of plots repeated time after time. As we watch a dramatized story, we frequently know how things will end. The good side will win; the captive will be rescued; the criminals will be caught and taken to jail. With this near certainty before the story unfolds, the question is, Why bother to watch? Some may argue that the answer is "just for entertainment," but others would say that powerful beliefs about life are being expressed and reinforced in the television and film dramas. We watch and listen because, through the medium of the story, we are being told *what* the world means and *how* it means. With our basic understandings of the nature of things confirmed by the electronic media, we feel better able to go about our lives.

In other words, fictional tales on television and in films work much like the sacred stories fundamental to religious traditions. Like these sacred stories, they establish a world that makes sense and give people a feeling for their place in the scheme of things. These fictional tales come in many artistic styles. Some are Westerns; some are detective or crime stories; some present us with science fiction; and some are old-fashioned soap operas. Yet despite the differences in style, evidence shows that one favorite plot, with variations, dominates in a number of these dramas. This plot organizes a great many stories, and further, it is the skeleton of many of the all-time successes in living room and at box office. Not surprisingly, this preferred plot is related to the millennial Puritan and revolutionary background of American culture and, in fact, is a modified version of it.

The plot might be summarized as trouble in paradise with eventual redemption for the hard-pressed community. Typically, the story turns on a wholesome and innocent society invaded from outside by overwhelming evil. Members of the society are caught off guard and unable to defend themselves because of circumstances. But just in the nick of time, a powerful stranger, also from outside, comes to save them. His past and his background are impressive but unclear; and he seems to want nothing, not even sexual favors, from members of the community. Once he has conquered evil forces through acts of sudden and righteous violence, he leaves members of the redeemed society to continue their peaceful lives as before. Superman, the Lone Ranger, and — with a change of gender — Wonder Woman, all conform to this basic plot outline. So, too, do such science fiction successes as the former television series *Star Trek* and the film *Star Wars*. With some variations, the Rambo films fit the pattern. So also do the older adventures of heroines like Little Orphan Annie and heroes like Dr. Marcus Welby, if subtle forms of manipulation are substituted for righteous violence.

One reason for the popular appeal of these dramas and many like them is that they tap mainstream Americans' fundamental understanding of themselves and their world. To the extent that the many, with their different backgrounds, find themselves caught by the power of the television and film tales, they have joined the mainstream and, in a loose and diffused way, the one religion of Americans. For in the dramas are still visible the themes of millennial dominance and righteous innocence found in the Puritan and revolutionary visions. The saving stranger, though disguised by trappings of role and character, is a transformed version of the messiah of the final battle, the Word riding forth for Armageddon. Hence, the violent destruction of evil in the plot is portrayed as warranted and right. As the stranger fades into the distance, a millennium of peace and justice can reign in the plot's redeemed community.

Popular literature, especially science fiction and Western novels, repeats many of these themes. Gangster and detective stories bring the lonely hero of the Western or science fiction tale into the city, and they also confuse the clear dualism of good and evil as they unfold. We admire the gangster's skill at survival even though we know that he represents evil and in the end must die. We realize that even the detective is guilty in some ways in the corrupt atmosphere of urban life. Still, in their successes and failures, and even more in their traits of character, we see idealized versions of the values that our culture promotes. Here the millennial promise of the New World is realized in self-made people, doers, and go-getters who stand out in their quickness and coolness. The individualism extolled by the American imagination is upheld again in these fictions. We can come away from reading them with belief in the strength of individual action confirmed.

There is not enough space here to treat such criticisms of the prevailing style as anti-Westerns and satiric humor. But generally, these forms of drama and literature succeed precisely because of the strength of the formulas they are criticizing. Thoughtful people applaud the antiliterature because in some ways they are aware of their cultural dependence on the dominant narrative patterns. In the antiliterature, they find a space that gives them a measure of cultural freedom.

Meanwhile, tales of love and romance introduce a more intimate world, so that popular magazines, written especially for men or for women, provide models for personal identity. Generally, millennial themes are even more subdued in this literature, but the perfectionism implicit in the millennial idea lives on as problems of sexual role and relationship are explored. It is worth noticing how much the American *ideal* of individualism provides a background for these books and magazines, even though in actual life they often foster conformity to media models of living.

The Oneness of Religion in America

As an example, magazines for men include *Playboy* and its rivals as well as other periodicals that promote the "masculine" ideal of strength and skill. These magazines tell men how to be men, offering them models of sexual success or masculine achievement. They appeal to men as free and independent individuals able to develop all of their powers and to embody the ideals the magazines present. Although, in the case of *Playboy*, the symbolism it promotes is not nearly so popular as it once was — partly because of feminism and partly because of fears of sexually transmitted diseases — the Playboy and what he represents have acquired an enduring niche in American culture. Similarly, women's magazines such as *Women's Day* or *Good Housekeeping* hold out to women the ideal of the homemaker, even as they encourage women to juggle their home responsibilities when they have jobs and careers. For these magazines, women become Supermoms, capable of excelling at traditional roles even when they must do so only in the time after work and on weekends. Other magazines, like *Cosmopolitan*, cater to women who aim to be free of attachments, successful at career and sex but not encumbered by home and family. Still other periodicals, like *Ms.*, appeal to women with feminist leanings, promoting the message that fulfillment may come with or without men. Each type of magazine gives women a model for imitation. At the same time, each appeals to individualist and perfectionist sentiments with its subtle version of the gospel of achievement — whether as homemaker, home-and-job success, full-time career woman, or feminist.

If television, film, and print provide a web of fundamental beliefs for Americans, so does music, and so do popular singers who embody the themes they sing. Indeed, the entertainment industry provides America with men and women who become ideal types for their fans. All of us have seen or read accounts of film idols mobbed by their admirers and spending hours to sign autographs for them. All of us know about fan mail and fan clubs, fan magazines and the paraphernalia that go with being a star. In fact, entertainment idols are one kind of American hero. Like political leaders, Western roughriders, and self-made men and women who rose from rags to riches, the stars of the entertainment empire demonstrate the qualities that Americans most admire. They are living icons who give people an example in the flesh of the power of the story. We might say that, for those who believe, the heroes are "as Gods." That is why they are called idols. That is why the attention paid to them is similar to the religious worship offered, for instance in India, to avatars, or living persons believed to be incarnations of deities.

This theme might be pursued extensively by studying the many heroes who have inspired Americans at different points in the country's history. But since there is not enough space, let us instead briefly consider the career of one such recent hero, an idol of popular music acclaimed as the "king" of rock and roll. For over twenty years, Elvis Presley (1935–1977) ruled musically, and even after his death, people continued to pay him homage in what became a cult movement of devoted followers. By the late eighties, in fact, some had come to deny his death and believed he continued to live or, as in the gospel account of Jesus, had risen from the dead. What power did Presley have over so many people? What was the source of a popularity that began when he was a teenager, thrived when he was middle-aged and overweight, and continued even after death?

Presley came from humble, working-class origins, and he attracted the attention of the recording industry by a stroke of fortune. But his success, like the success of so many of the symbols of the civil religion, came not from managers but from the people. When RCA Victor released Presley's recording of "Heartbreak Hotel" in 1956, it became an immediate hit and led all competitors for eight weeks. In the same year, Presley gave the public in quick succession "Don't Be Cruel," "Hound Dog," "Blue Suede Shoes," and "Love Me Tender." Moving his hips as he sang, he sent his fans into enthusiastic shouts and shrieks. Teenage girls reportedly came close to hysteria when they saw him, and when Presley finally appeared on national television on the *Ed Sullivan Show*, cameras recorded his movements only from the waist up. The saga of his swift climb to riches and fame thereafter seemed astounding. "Heartbreak Hotel" sold 2 million copies, while a worldwide Presley fan club at one time boasted of 400,000 members. A series of films was produced with Presley in the leading role, and in the first two years of national acclaim, some said, he earned 100 million dollars.

After two years in the army beginning in 1958, Presley returned to private life in the sixties. He continued to be popular, although not nearly in the style of the mid-fifties. Still, with neither personal nor television appearances in the early sixties, he took in 5 million dollars a year simply by making a few recordings and films. Then, in the seventies, a public nostalgic for the innocence of the fifties rediscovered him. Middle-aged men and women, perhaps the same individuals who had been his teenage fans in the past, joined a new generation of young people who revered him. By 1977, he had earned forty-five gold records, each for a song that had sold more than 1 million copies.

When Presley died suddenly in 1977, 25,000 people stood for hours to view his body. They cried as if a family member had passed away, and their cars began to display bumper stickers proclaiming "Elvis lives." T-shirts were sold in front of Graceland, the Presley mansion, printed with the message "Elvis Presley, In Memory, 1935–1977." Jewelry and dinner plates commemorated him; needlepoint could be worked in a pattern to produce his image; an original Presley recording came to cost as much as $500.

Nor did the pattern end with the year of Presley's death. In 1986 Paul Simon's record album and hit song *Graceland* paid evocative tribute to the King, interweaving themes of South African struggle and personal religious pilgrimage. And in 1988 a book and cassette claimed, based on a report from voice analysis of taped conversations, that Presley was still alive. Meanwhile, fans were saying that they had sighted the singer, and a new T-shirt appeared with a list of places where Elvis sightings had reportedly occurred. On the twelfth anniversary of Presley's death (16 August 1989), some 4,000 people kept vigil at the Graceland gravesite, the largest event in a nine-day Elvis International Tribute Week. And almost a year later, in July 1990, a centerspread article in the tabloid *Weekly World News* proclaimed, "Elvis' Tomb Is Empty!" (The basis for the announcement was a psychic's claim.)

From one point of view, much of this strikes the nonbeliever as tasteless commercialism. Yet as in so many other displays of popular religion, people were rendering homage and expressing desire for connection with an avatar or saint. For the millions who championed him, Presley spoke to the inner spirit, assuring them that the values they cared about were real. In short, there were spiritual reasons for Presley's success.

First, he had grown out of the Pentecostal evangelical tradition. During his childhood in Tupelo, Mississippi, he sang with his parents in a trio at church conventions, revivals, and camp meetings. Gospel music was his earliest love, and later some would say that his style was simply an exaggeration of gospel singing. Whether or not that was the case, he took from his evangelical background the strong sentimentality that ran through his music and his personality. People loved Presley because of the "tenderness" of his songs and also because they thrived on stories such as those of how he had given away numerous Cadillacs in compassion for others less fortunate than himself. For many who had never heard a gospel preacher, Presley created the cherished community of feeling that the revivals brought — the millennial moment of common enthusiasm and joy.

Second, Presley's power came from the way he combined black rhythm and blues with white rock and roll. In the lower-class neighborhood in which he was reared, he rubbed shoulders with African-Americans and absorbed something of their musical style. When he came to RCA Victor, he was a white singer with "soul," a youth who looked like many mainstream Americans but who sang with the abandonment and spontaneity of black musicians. At the height of the Eisenhower era of controlled respectability, Presley, overnight dubbed "the Pelvis," sang America's freedom. A teenage rebel, he took the excitement of the revival into a new setting. He made of it sensual and sexual passion, giving people a freedom that was both the liberty of the "natural" and the condition of a paradisal age.

Third, Presley became a legend because, by the seventies and eighties, he was a symbolic reminder to Americans of the innocence of the fifties. In a wave of nostalgia, people looked back to a time when for them old truths were still true, when good and evil were lined out clearly, when the harmless swivel of a singer's hips and the sultry glance of his eye were thought risqué. Presley stood for America's innocence — a shy teenager made good to his own astonishment. And he stood for the golden age of the millennium that Americans recalled in the Eisenhower years, a time they identified with peace and plenty, without environmental crises, financial uncertainty, or public affairs that could not be settled by simple formulas of right and wrong.

Finally, Presley's attraction lingered after his death perhaps because, as the many stories told, he was a victim of his own success. The symbol of spontaneity could not appear freely as he chose. One anecdote recounted how he tried to attend a church service by slipping unobtrusively into a back pew with his body-guards. When people in the congregation began to turn around to stare, he and his friends were forced to leave. The public for which Presley lived became his torture. According to reports, he turned to drugs as stimulants and depressants so that he could sing or sleep as the occasion demanded. When he died with a heart problem, despite official denials, rumors floated that the drugs had in the end destroyed him. (By 1980, Presley's personal physician would be found guilty of malpractice.) The apostle of innocence, Presley had become for devotees an innocent victim, with a heart of gold and a fate to be lamented. Presley's fans had come a long way from the jeremiads of the Puritans, but in identifying with their musical hero, they voiced the collective anxieties that were part of the American heritage. To borrow the words of Richard Nixon about the United States of the time, Presley, like a confused America, seemed a "pitiful giant." Moreover, there were echoes of the Puritan and revolutionary past, for suffering in America was the role of the innocent and the companion of millennialism.

Presley was only one among the heroes and saints, and his songs were only a small number among the ballads and tunes that told people who they were and what their lives meant. Together, heroes and songs, literature and magazines, films and television serials surrounded Americans with popular reminders that reassured and reinforced their system of beliefs. Although the language was dis-guised and not often openly religious, the gospel that popular culture preached through the media was a powerful persuader because it built on what people already believed. More than any organized religious denomination, it was able to capture the public eye and ear. Created by society, it was also creating a society in its image.

American Codes of Living

The ritualization of American life takes place, in part, during an annual calendar of holidays. The beliefs that the rituals express are communicated, too, through the media. However, a religious community expresses itself not just in belief and rite but also in everyday behavior. Hence, we need to examine the codes for living that ordinary culture gives Americans and to discover what patterns of behavior govern their usual interactions with one another. As in the cases of sacred story and ritual, the codes are many, and they are complex. In order to suggest their scope, let us look at a few of the most prominent. As we will see, sports, technology, and popular psychology all provide behavioral codes for many Americans. Later, in our study of nature religion, we will explore the code of living that nature provides.

Organized sports in America are less than a century old. It is true that a few sports became popular in the earlier part of the nineteenth century and that baseball was played as long ago as 1845. But it was in the 1870s and 1880s that organized sports activities became prominent, growing rapidly with the railroads and improved communication. The first professional baseball team came into existence in 1869, a major league followed in 1876, and by the turn of the century, baseball had become a favorite American sport. Meanwhile, football, at first an upper-class activity, became a popular game by 1900. What distinguished baseball and football from other activities such as fishing and solitary running was that they were contests; that is, they were games of competition in which there was a winner and a loser. This characteristic of baseball, football, and other games like them would be important in furthering an American code.

Before we turn to the code, however, let us note the religious overtones that have surrounded public games. Historically, games of sport originated in deliberate religious rituals. Structurally, sports activities still resemble rituals in their form. We have already met one example of religious play in the sacred ball game that was one of the seven rites of the Oglala Sioux. Religious games of various kinds were part of many Native American traditions in this country. They were also part of the European heritage of other Americans. In ancient Greece, funeral games were held in honor of slain heroes, and various Greek city-states held sacred games to offer reverence to one of the Gods. Thus, the Olympic games, held at Olympia, honored Zeus, while the Pythian games at Delphi paid homage to Apollo and the Isthmian games at Corinth celebrated Poseidon.

In an echo of these games, there are many ways in which even the sports of modern America are like deliberate (extraordinary) religious rituals. Both sports events and deliberate religious rituals mark out a separate area for their activities—a "playground" or sacred space. Both also divide the time of their performance from the ordinary passage of minutes and hours. Furthermore, both are examples of dramatic actions in which people take on assigned roles, often wearing special symbolic clothing to distinguish them from nonparticipants. Sports and deliberate religious rituals, through their performances, create "other" worlds of meaning, complete with their own rules and boundaries, dangers and successes. Finally, in sports and deliberate religious rituals, the goal of the activity *is* the activity. While there may be good results from the game or rite, there is a reason implicit in the action for performing it. Play or ritual is satisfying for its own sake, for each is an activity in which people may engage because of the pleasure it gives in itself.

From this perspective sports, with their ordinariness in our society, have provided a ritual-like setting for millions of Americans. By setting up boundaries and defining the space of the game, sports have helped Americans fit a grid to their own experience in order to define it and give it structure. Hence, it is not surprising that public games have given people a code of conduct for everyday living. If the ball field is a miniature rehearsal for the game of life, the message is that life is a struggle between contesting forces in which there is a winning and a losing side. The message, too, is that success depends on teamwork in which members of the winning side conquer the opposing team by pulling together. And in this contest to the end, competition becomes a value in itself and generates a set of accompanying virtues that identify a good team player. Loyalty, fair play, and being a "good sport" in losing are all examples of these virtues. So, too, are self-denial and hard work to achieve victory.

We can notice that the division into two teams who battle each other in the game resembles the dualistic account of the final millennial battle. As in the biblical story of that ultimate war, it is clear in the game that there is a good team (our side) and a bad one (the opposing side). Coaches urge the members of their team to pour all their efforts into winning—as if this were the last game they would play on earth. Each team, in its own understanding, is on the side of right, and so each team must exhibit innocence. Thus, preparatory exercises in self-denial and self-purification by team members—diet, calisthenics, sleep requirements—are expected. Meanwhile, during a game, many players, when they are winning, practice rituals—such as the Catholic sign of the cross, for example—to insure that the winning will continue.

While sports are surely an important feature of most human societies, here we need to look at how they function in an American context. To be understood fully, they cannot be separated from other aspects of this country's life. It is the web of interrelated cultural forms, rather than any one element in isolation, that is persuasive. Hence, the code that the games offer to Americans is one that subtly agrees with themes of millennial dominance and innocence that we have seen before. It is a code that promises to guarantee success in business, industry, or government, for in it individualism bows before the unity of an elect community. Corporate executives may have risen on their merits, but, according to the code, in the executive suite they must be good team players. The same is thought to be true for government officials and Cabinet members, as a series of recent American presidents liked to remark. Finally, within the field with its opposing teams, competition is presented as the ethic of success. Life is seen as a game of winners and losers, and only those who compete are considered worthy. Rigorously prepared for the fight by their previous exercises in self-denial, those who compete to the end are expected to win the day—or, at the very least, to lose with the grace and dignity demanded by the code.

A second code for everyday living comes to Americans from their experience with technology. After the Industrial Revolution of the nineteenth century, Americans saw their agricultural way of life transformed dramatically by mechanization. New forms of transportation—the railroad, the steam engine, and, in the twentieth century, the automobile and the airplane—brought distant parts of the country closer together. With their ability to provide food and manufactured goods for vast numbers of people, these forms of transportation encouraged the growth of cities. The development of the factory system gathered people together under one roof, drawing them away from their farms and leading again to the growth of centers of population. New labor-saving devices cut the amount of time needed to complete many tasks. At the same time, many of these devices lessened the need for human workers and often, therefore, sharply reduced the cost of manufactured goods.

For all intents and purposes, the machine could be seen as bringing the golden age of the millennium to the United States. Many early observers of the Industrial Revolution held this view of what they were witnessing, and accounts of the new machines were often filled with wonder. The Centennial Exhibition held in Philadelphia in 1876 displayed inventions proudly, for they were considered evidence of the plenty brought by the age of progress. But in places where the machine appeared suddenly in a rural setting, a number of Americans saw in it a symbol of the other, apocalyptic millennium. Early viewers of locomotives sometimes used the language of hellfire and demons to describe a train as it plunged through the countryside, its coal-fed fires flaming and its whistle screeching fiercely. For some of America's writers, like Nathaniel Hawthorne and Ralph Waldo Emerson, the roaring engines violated the innocence of an older way of life. Significantly, mechanization had arisen to supply the needs of war. Eli Whitney (1765–1825) created the first system of interchangeable parts in this country in order that firearms could be mass-produced, and after 1798 his factory turned out muskets for the U.S. government.

Thus, whether the new machines were interpreted according to post-millennial or premillennial models, Americans associated them with their futuristic beliefs. And despite the fears of some, for the most part Americans admired their machines and gadgets, while their culture came to reflect the admiration in numerous ways. As early as the eighteenth century, the Enlightenment with its interest in science had fostered the idea that human beings were like machines. By our own era, promoted by a huge advertising industry, technology became a central symbol in American life. People unconsciously adopted the machine as a model for their humanness. They saw their bodies as complex machines; and hence, in many aspects of their lives, they patterned their behavior accordingly. Although technology has not been acknowledged nearly so much as sports as a guide for action, the machine provides many Americans with a code for living.

Stated simply, the technological code demands of Americans that, with the perfection required of a millennial people, they act like their machines. This means, first, that they be as efficient as the technological process. Corporate life is built in part on the image of the machine with well-oiled components, each properly performing its function. Bureaucracies are, implicitly, huge machines in which people are expected to do their jobs efficiently, without attracting undue attention to themselves or creating undue stress by forming time-consuming relationships with their co-workers. Similarly, trade and commerce are streamlined so that people interact with one another in quick, automatic exchanges with no more than the necessary information and action. Unlike the small-town shopkeeper of a century ago, who was a friend and a person who had time to share, the contemporary salesperson is generally groomed to be impersonal. In government the operating model is again that of a vast bureaucratic machine, with each person expected to attend to the assigned job as quickly and impersonally as possible. Meanwhile, the family has shrunk from the extended clan of several generations in one household to the nuclear family of parents and children.

Unlike the extended family with its roots in one place over many years, the nuclear family is mobile. Like the automobile and the train, it can move speedily, ready to pull up stakes and start again somewhere else, if economic interests so demand.

Second, the technological code encourages Americans to be as cool and passionless in public as their machines. The media promote the image of the unflappable individualist — the low-keyed detective or cowboy hero, the rigidly controlled pilot who unleashes weapons of destruction as duty requires, the unexcited business executive who discusses his company's failures with an expressionless face and tone of voice. According to the ethic of the machine, people should always be in control, without strong displays of feeling, either positive or negative. To do otherwise is, for this ethic, to risk impropriety. It is to be marked as not quite acceptable — someone, so to speak, with loose ends trailing. In this model of human behavior, the evangelical search for a community of feeling seems inappropriate. Still, there need not be contradiction. The ethic puts a premium on the man or woman who is cool *in public*. On the other hand, the religion of the heart belongs to the *private* sphere, even as technology provides a public behavioral code that in some respects runs counter to the sentimental leanings of the mainstream. In fact, though, both the ethic of the machine and the ethic of evangelicalism agree in demanding refinement of emotion — the cultivation of "polite" feelings that can be shared with others.

In a third and related aspect, the technological code expects people to be uniform and standard. Like the interchangeable parts produced by the factories, they must be able to replace one another. Here the aim is to be like everybody else so that no one stands out by being different. In this effort, clothing becomes a badge of commonality, and manners provide a way for people to be as indistinguishable as they can. Americans eat the same fast food at chain restaurants, watch the same television shows, and shop at similar regional discount, drug, and grocery stores. Many live in subdivisions in houses that closely resemble their neighbors'. Still more, the code defines no person as absolutely necessary. Because they can replace one another, people — like uniform parts in a machine — are expendable.

The technological code has also altered the way in which Americans think of time. A day on a farm extended from sunup to sunset with the hours measured by natural rhythms — by the location of the sun in the sky, the feeling of weariness in the bones or of hunger. With the introduction of the machine came factory time, measured by the precise movements of the clock. In the nine-to-five day of the contemporary era, each moment is defined like every other moment, qualitatively no different. Like people, time has been divided into interchangeable parts. Many jobs demand exactly the eight hours of the working day, no more and no less.

Finally, the technological code urges people to be consumers. In a paradise of plenty, the products of the machine must be purchased so that the economic wheels of society will turn. Often goods are deliberately planned to wear out quickly in order to be replaced, thus providing jobs and employment for workers. Advertising creates new needs, people keep buying, and the consumer society spends itself to own more and more. Thus, the technological code gives Americans standards of efficiency, coolness, uniformity, mechanical time, and consumption. Ironically, it also gives them a return to another kind of innocence. There is no ambiguity in the world that the machine controls, for it is as precise and measured as interchangeable parts. Seen implicitly by Americans in millennial terms, technology reinforces a view of the world in which it is complex on the surface but ultimately simple.

Much different from the behavioral code derived from the machine is the code that modern psychology provides Americans. Psychology as an organized body of knowledge was born in the nineteenth century at the end of the Romantic revolt against the Enlightenment. While it developed along more rigidly scientific lines in the behavioral school, in forms like humanistic and transpersonal psychology, it was linked to organic and Romantic themes. Like the Enlightenment, we know, the Romantic movement centered on nature. But while the Enlightenment saw nature as an intricate machine moving according to regular and unchanging laws, Romanticists thought of nature as a metaphor for freedom and spontaneity. They linked nature to feeling and emotion, and so, as the discussion of Transcendentalism suggested, one continual theme of the Romantic movement was inwardness.

As we will see when we examine nature religion, by the 1960s a new wave of Romanticism had spread across America. With it came an emphasis on exploring inner frontiers. To turn within became a way to "turn on" to worlds that transcended the humdrum daily routine. Promises of revolutionary new ways to inner knowledge and peace blossomed, and many people sought direction from popular psychology. As they did so, themes of perfection and paradisal innocence thrived. The inner world was acclaimed as good and even divine: nothing ultimately evil, it was believed, could come from confronting its depths. Esalen Institute, along the California coast at Big Sur, and its founder, Michael Murphy (b. 1930), became symbols for a human-potential movement. In 1967 alone, Esalen conducted seminars for 4,000 people, among them 700 psychologists who received instruction in such techniques as sensory awareness and "encounter" therapies. In the initial seven months of the institute's San Francisco branch, 12,000 people came for lectures and seminars. Indeed, as we saw in Chapter 11, the continuing Esalen model became a prototype for major themes in the emerging New Age movement.

The new psychological forms that inspired Esalen enthusiasts were distinguished in several ways from the therapies of the past. First, they did not so much seek to heal the mentally ill as to bring ordinary people with ordinary problems to a greater capacity for happiness and creativity. Second, while the old psychologies had been built on the authoritarian model of the relationship between doctor and patient, in many cases the new therapies stressed community and peer relationships. At other times, they became essentially self-help techniques that closely paralleled the practices, like meditation, of some contemporary religious movements. Third, while the more traditional psychologies had developed a technical language that was scientific, the new forms used a vocabulary that was, sometimes openly and sometimes more subtly, religious. Significantly, the openly religious language was borrowed from Eastern traditions, especially Buddhism, Hinduism, and Taoism (a Chinese religion of nature). Fourth, unlike the therapies of the past, which were seen as lengthy but still temporary processes, the new psychologies aimed to give people instruction in a way of life. Lectures, seminars, and workshops were intensive sessions devoted to the cultivation of techniques that, leaders claimed, could be used for a lifetime.

What were—and are—these therapies? They are too numerous to be detailed fully here, but prominent among them has been the Gestalt psychology of Frederick S. ("Fritz") Perls (1894–1970), in which, aided by members of a working group, a person dramatizes inner conflicts by playing the parts ordinarily taken by different inner voices. Other encounter groups have focused completely on the relationships within the group so that members learn to express positive and negative feelings freely. For some people, the new psychologies harness technology to desires for inner awareness, as in biofeedback machines used to try to distinguish between calm and excited brain-wave patterns and to attempt to control blood pressure, heartbeat, and other automatic processes. Still others, like the followers of Carl G. Jung, have kept dream diaries and seek to understand themselves through the symbolism of their personal stories. And for many, Timothy Leary (b. 1920), a former Harvard professor of psychology, became the leader of a movement for increased self-awareness through drugs and especially LSD.

Along with Fritz Perls, perhaps the most respected theorist of the human-potential movement was Abraham Maslow (1908–1970), a former president of the American Psychological Association. For Maslow, self-actualization was the goal of life and of therapy. This meant for him the fullest use of all the talents and capacities a person had (perfection once again). And it meant spontaneity, initiative, and self-directed action. Closely related to self-actualization for Maslow and his followers was a personal state that he named the "peak experience." Understood as similar to the mystical experiences described in the literature of different religious traditions, a peak experience was thought to dissolve the ordinary sense of separateness so that a person felt at one with the universe and at the same time intensely aware of life all around. "Peakers" were seen as people in touch with themselves and their world. They were reported to be doers and achievers, the ones who realized and actualized themselves. "Nonpeakers" were said to be individuals who were too organized and too tightly controlled.

For Maslow and humanistic psychology in general, control and organization, the key virtues of the technological ethic, were the enemy. Thus, the behavioral code of the movement remained opposed to the code of the machine. Just as the first Romanticism arose as a revolt against the Enlightenment, the new Romanticism has been a revolt against the order of technological society. While the code of the machine draws close boundaries around behavioral expectations, the code of humanistic psychology has encouraged an emotional world in which the boundaries are, theoretically, one's own limits. The movement has stressed what it sees as the free expression of feeling, the formation of communities of openness, and the achievement of health and happiness through mental wholeness. At the same time, it has turned people toward themselves rather than toward the public world, seeing meaning in inner states more than in outer, societal situations.

Some find this ethic alien to American culture, an exotic import, perhaps fed by Eastern religious movements and the like. Yet the code of humanistic psychology is as American as the innocence of the millennium. It is a part of the mainstream and an expression of the one religion of Americans. This is true in two ways. First, from the point of view of numbers, the movement is far more widespread than a simple catalog of those who have participated in a group-process weekend. The millions who read self-improvement magazines and various self-help manuals purchased at the newsstand are being shaped by the psychological code. So are those who attend sessions at their local church on effective parenting, making marriage work, codependency, or subjects of a similar nature. Professional educators have adopted many awareness and encounter techniques as their own, using them regularly in the classroom to facilitate group experience. Radio and television talk shows feature guests who give popular psychological advice, while soap operas daily probe the inner workings of their characters' psyches in the language and style of humanistic psychology. Meanwhile, the New Age movement has made the language of the new therapies fundamental to its own expression.

Second, the new psychologies are an expression of mainstream American culture because the code of inwardness is, as suggested above, a version of the code of millennial innocence. While the ethics of sports and technology draw on the theme of millennial dominance, the ethic of humanistic psychology reverses the coin. It seeks an ideal society of perfect — fully developed, totally good — human beings. It seeks, too, a community of free and spontaneous feeling that signals the planting of paradise among creative, self-actualizing individuals. In our study of civil religion, we saw how innocence was expressed from time to time in American history in political isolationism. Shortly, we will see how it has been expressed historically in American attitudes toward nature. Here it is important to note that turning within has also had long roots in American culture. The Puritans, in fact, kept careful spiritual diaries and autobiographies in order to foster piety and virtue. Although the Puritans did not stress emotional spontaneity, they did pay great attention to their feelings, and they emphasized the importance of inner states. And native Indian peoples, too, were known to cultivate dreams and encourage inner visions.

Throughout American religious history, as we have seen, revivalism taught the importance of right feeling. In the nineteenth century, "self-culture" became a watchword for the Transcendentalists and for the developing occult and metaphysical movements in their own ways as well. A number of Americans turned to an inner world in order to create utopia. The perfectionism that ran through these attempts was a general cultural property of the times, stimulated by factors from Methodist theology to the successes of the age of progress. The innocence that these movements displayed lay both in their belief that they really could achieve perfection and in their certainty that the inner world was a place of virtue.

Hence, the ethic of inwardness in the later twentieth century is based on major interpretive themes that have been part of American culture. The same is true for the religion of nature, a flourishing expression of mainstream America both in the past and at present. In order to increase our understanding of the dynamics of cultural religion, here we use nature religion as a case study. By focusing on how Americans thought, acted, and built community around the symbol of nature, we can gain a better sense of how people use other symbols as well to orient themselves in the ordinary world — and sometimes to go beyond its boundaries in moments of transcendence.

A Case Study in Nature Religion

Studying nature religion is particularly appropriate because theologies have traditionally dealt with three general topics — God, human beings, and the natural world. In looking at the relationship between Americans and nature, we will be following the outlines of major religious systems of the past. Furthermore, because of the overwhelming physical fact of open space in the New World, we will be dealing with an aspect of their environment that deeply impressed Americans. Generally, mainstream Americans saw nature in millennial terms, sometimes by linking it to their plans for dominance and conquest and at other times by seeing it from the perspective of utopian innocence. In a brief survey of nature religion in the past, we will see both of these tendencies at work. Then we will look at the presence of nature religion in the later twentieth century, when rituals like those in Gurney Norman's composting class take place.

Early America

Our study of Native American traditions has already underlined the importance of nature in these religions. What the supernatural God was to the Judeo-Christian tradition, nature was to Indian peoples. While it surrounded them and was the source of their sustenance, they believed nature to be also a friend or many friends to whom they could speak and from whom they could receive answers. Indians thought that their societies should correspond to the natural world as closely as possible and that spiritual wholeness and health came from being in harmony with various animal and plant beings who were other-than-human persons.

Nature in North America struck the Puritans, coming from a European and Judeo-Christian civilization, far differently. Their traditions had often understood nature more abstractly and also in more negative terms. It was mostly a wilderness, and only occasionally, with human cultivation, it became a garden. In this way of seeing things, the wilderness was a place inhabited by wild beasts and nameless terrors. It was understood as a place to which civilization had not penetrated, and it was considered out of control, as expressed by its teeming forests and dense vegetation. For the Romans, the wilderness was inhabited by Gods and demons, often half-human, half-animal in shape. For the people of Central and Northern Europe, the woods were the haunt of trolls, man-eating ogres, and werewolves.

Yet Judaism and Christianity brought another meaning to the wilderness. While in their view God did not reveal himself *in nature* as the sacred powers did in Native American traditions, they did portray him using nature as the background for his visitations. Thus, in the Bible God manifested himself to the Hebrews after they had left Egypt and wandered in the desert of Sinai. Later, God was believed to have come to Christian monks after they fled from the centers of Roman civilization to the Egyptian desert. The wilderness was seen as a barren place, empty of the corruptions of worldly life that had kept people from God. For the monks, the wilderness meant the end of distraction, a silence and openness that could leave them ready for spiritual experience.

At the same time, Judaism and Christianity taught that nature was subservient to human beings. For both religions, just as there was a gap separating human beings from God, there was another separating them from nature. The Bible told people that they were made in the image of God, not in the image of nature (Gen. 1:27). It told them that they should "have dominion over the fish of the sea, and over the fowl of the air, and over the cattle, and over all the earth" (Gen. 1:26). According to a biblical command, they were enjoined to multiply, replenish the earth, and subdue it (Gen. 1:28). This biblical order told Jews and Christians alike that their task was to dominate the wilderness, taming it to the human plan.

Thus, when the Puritans set foot in the New World, their attitudes toward their surroundings were deeply ambivalent. First, they feared the land as wild territory, filled with dangerous beasts and demonic Indians. Because they were an ocean away from European civilization, the wildness they saw in the forests presented a new threat: they feared it might tempt them to forget the control their ancestors had learned and revert to the "savagery" they ascribed to Indians and wild beasts. In spite of the rhetoric of righteousness, the Puritans were suspicious of the depths of their own hearts, afraid that civilization was only a veneer that would melt away in a "savage" environment. Yet even with the fear the Puritans had of the wilderness, they held a second attitude toward it. The Bible told them that their task was to subdue it. Therefore, their errand into the wilderness meant to them carving farms out of the hillsides and plotting towns and settlements. It also meant to them bringing the Indians to Christianity, thus "taming" and "civilizing" them. In these ways, the Puritans hoped to build their millennial city on the hill, the light to the nations that they believed it was their mission to let shine.

And finally, the Puritans looked at their surroundings with qualified approval. If they obeyed the God of the covenant, they thought, they could turn the land into a sanctuary enclosed by the "hedge" of his grace. For Christians, the wilderness had always been the proving ground for God's saints, and now, as the Puritans saw it, away from the corruption of England, they could be tested by God and show the power of his righteousness. At the same time, promotional literature stressed that the New World was "good land," land that could eventually become a paradise.

Hence, while the Puritans saw good wilderness as wilderness transformed into farms and towns, they also saw opportunities that the land gave them. They associated the openness of the country with moral purity and regeneration — with their abiding desire for a return to innocence. With the passage of time, they felt less need for sanctuaries and more desire to expand their presence further into the wilderness. The land at once became a source of vigor and life — a paradise of innocence — and a vast territory to be mastered by the representatives of European civilization. If the Puritans were awaiting Armageddon, they still believed that their efforts could insure that at least some of the wilderness would already be taken from Indian agents of Satan before the end.

Further, the grandeur of the mountains and forests was not lost on sensitive Puritans, and there was a strain of nature mysticism in their response. Thus, as we recall, by the eighteenth century Cotton Mather in the *Christian Philosopher* could see the harmony and order in nature as a second revelation of God. And Jonathan Edwards could ponder his religious experiences in the woods and also create a theology of beauty.

At the time of the Revolution and its aftermath, several strands of Puritan response to the land had become general throughout the colonies. Belief in the freshness and purity of the New World in contrast to the tired corruption of Europe became an important ideological theme in the growing nationalism. A popular play of the period, *The Contrast* by Royall Tyler (1787), celebrated the virtues of rugged and unpolished Colonel Henry Manly and simple Maria Van Rough as opposed to the perfumed decadence of Maria's Europeanized suitor, Dimple. Earlier, during the war, American soldiers had worn hunting shirts on the western frontier, terrifying the British with the shirts' symbolic wildness and at the same time proclaiming the wilderness a source of American strength. Further, Americans wore homespun made from their crops, partly because of the economic blockade of British goods but partly, too, as a ritual expression of their identification with the land. So evocative was the symbol for contemporaries that George Washington took his oath of office to the presidency wearing a suit of homespun.

If nature meant vitality in contrast to the weariness of Europe, it was also a landscape to be tamed. For revolutionary Americans, good land was farmland. Many, like Thomas Jefferson, thought of the future of America as tied to agriculture and simple manufactures. When Hector St. John Crèvecoeur's *Letters from an American Farmer* appeared in 1782, it sang the praises of the "new" person in the new land. For Crèvecoeur and his readers, in the free and open expanses of the countryside, agriculture would yield a bounty, while Europe, on the other hand, was weighted down with its past. By 1803 Jefferson had negotiated the Louisiana Purchase to add a vast tract of land to the territory of the United States. He did so in part for political reasons but also to provide land for the nation of farmers that he envisioned. Hence, in these understandings nature was a place to be dominated and subdued — gently and wisely so that the land would give its fruit.

Beyond this, some Americans did look at their surroundings with feelings of awe and wonder. In his *Notes on the State of Virginia* (1787), Jefferson spoke of the intensity of his feelings on seeing Natural Bridge, and he marveled at the size of mammoth bones that had been discovered. The botanist William Bartram (1739–1823) thrilled at the magnificence of the view from a mountain that he climbed in Georgia, and there were others who expressed similar sentiments.

To sum up, in the revolutionary era the land was considered a millennial symbol of New World purity, a place to be farmed wisely in order to maintain this purity, and a sublime masterpiece to be regarded for its own sake. In all of these ways of looking at the land, Euro-Americans thought of it as "virgin land" or open space. They overlooked the evidence that America had been inhabited for centuries, and they did not recognize in Indian societies the presence of cultures as meaningful as their own. If Native Americans did figure in the way that the environment was seen, they were seen as signs of wildness that lurked in the woods, of danger that lay in the absence of civilizing influences. The nineteenth century would pick up on all of these themes.

Nature in the Nineteenth Century

Romanticism flourished in nineteenth-century America and with it greater interest in the beauties of the natural world. In the 1830s the Transcendentalists, ambivalent about the machinery of the Industrial Revolution, turned to the land. With Ralph Waldo Emerson, their leader, many of them found God more clearly in nature than in the church. In our study at various points we have already followed the general direction of Transcendentalist thought. It is worth reviewing the contents of Emerson's little book *Nature*, however, because Emerson's ideas became the foundation for an increasing religious appreciation of nature among mainstream Americans. Like the Indians, although more abstractly, Emerson thought in terms of a correspondence between human beings, the natural world, and the spiritual. He pondered the meaning of human language, seeing words as "signs," or symbols, of natural facts, of the world around him. Likewise, for Emerson the natural world was a sign — of the world of spirit that went beyond it. In this way of looking at things, humans could understand spiritual truth by looking at nature, where the truth was written in material form.

Nature for Emerson pointed the way to God. To use another term, it was for Emerson the sacrament of God.

With his experience as a practical American, as Emerson looked at nature, he was concerned to explain its uses. First, Emerson wrote, nature was the source of the satisfaction of all physical needs. This was true in agriculture, but it was also true in the developing technologies in which people looked to nature for lessons in how best to construct their machines. Second, the beauty in nature was useful, too, for Emerson because it acted like a tonic for tired minds and bodies and, further, because it gave people moral, artistic, and intellectual inspiration. Third, nature was useful, Emerson declared, because it shaped language and metaphor. Without the world, there would be nothing to name and no way to measure what any inner experience was like. Finally, nature was useful for Emerson because it acted as a discipline. It was simply *there*, so that there was no quarreling with its objectivity and the laws that it followed. More than that, thought Emerson, nature was a moral teacher, instructing people in the laws of right and wrong.

Emerson's statement of the uses of nature was broad, including many uses that others would have considered idealistic and impractical. Yet the fact that Emerson and the other Transcendentalists thought and spoke in terms of nature's uses was important. While, in general, the Transcendentalists saw themselves sitting at nature's feet as humble pupils, other Americans thought that using nature meant, as the biblical book of Genesis had said, in some fashion dominating and controlling it. In their way of seeing things, reverence for nature meant a wise use of natural resources. In the conservation movement near the end of the nineteenth century, wise use would be a strong argument.

Meanwhile, the Transcendentalists expressed their religion of nature, sometimes through solitary walks in the woods and sometimes through the gathering of like spirits in communes. At Brook Farm and at Fruitlands, they attempted social experiments in organic communities where, they believed, harmony and cooperation — as in nature — could replace a competitive way of life. Appropriately, like many other communes in nineteenth-century America, they selected natural settings, away from the distractions of city life. And like these other communes, their societies were expressions of American innocence. At Fruitlands, Bronson Alcott (1799–1888) would not wear wool because to do so exploited sheep. Even further, he would not eat carrots because they did not grow toward the sun. At Brook Farm, members pitched in to perform the hard work of running farm and household. Years later they remembered this period (1841–1847) as the happiest time of their lives. Both of these idealistic experiments in utopian socialism ended relatively quickly (Fruitlands within seven months), but the fact that they existed and survived, even for a time, bore witness to the dreams of Americans. Creating a perfect society and living life in harmony with nature were twin hopes. In their realization, Americans thought, a new era would dawn. It was a nineteenth-century beginning, once again, of the millennium.

Transcendentalism, we know, was linked to a web of occult, metaphysical, and other experimental movements in the nineteenth century, movements that made an impact far beyond the numbers who directly participated in them. Instead of a movie theater, a nineteenth-century American town often had a lyceum, a public building where lectures, concerts, and other entertainments were held. Traveling the lyceum circuit became a way to spread the gospel of nature religion, as various speakers went from town to town to announce their beliefs to others. One area in which they did so was that of health. For these speakers, nature meant more than land and environment. It meant the human body, the laws by which the body was thought to function, and "natural" substances and techniques for healing it. Meanwhile, other Americans expressed related concerns regarding their physical well-being, and nature religion became popular religion through the spread of alternative healing methods. Let us look briefly at what happened.

A favorite on the lyceum circuit at midcentury was the animal magnetizer. This person could perform demonstrations in which a subject, even from the audience, obeyed the magnetist's instructions after being cast into a light sleep and then awakened. But magnetists were often healers, and there were dramatic accounts of their abilities to relieve people of serious illnesses. According to the magnetic theory, as we have seen, a universal energy or fluid flowed through the natural world. The planets and the other stars produced tides or movements in this fluid, so that as it passed through individuals, it produced a state of health. But, according to the theory, if any blockage interfered with the free flow of energy, sickness resulted. However, the magnetic doctor claimed the ability to control the flow of energy by acting on the tides and the blocked situation to redirect magnetic fluid and so restore health.

In his early work, Phineas P. Quimby, whom we met in connection with both Christian Science and New Thought, was one such magnetic doctor. But if mind cure had roots in natural magnetic healing, other late-nineteenth-century healing methods did, too. Techniques of physical manipulation, like osteopathy and chiropractic, were based on theoretical foundations akin to animal magnetism. In chiropractic, for example, health was viewed as the result of the free movement of an energy called "Innate," which traveled down the spinal column. When the chiropractor manipulated a person's spine, the doctor was believed to be freeing the patient from an obstruction so that Innate could continue to give health. Innate was identified with nature, God, or intelligence, both within and outside of a person. Thus, according to chiropractic theory, when healing came, it came from within — and from nature. While in the twentieth century, osteopathy became closely aligned with orthodox medicine, chiropractic continued to function as a separate healing art. Like a ripple in the water, magnetic healing had made many waves, some of them far removed from the occult background of its origins.

But nineteenth-century natural healing went beyond even the loose boundaries of animal magnetism. The old sense of the land as source of vigor and refreshment reappeared in a number of systems of herbal medicine. American Indians, symbols for other Americans of the regenerative power of the wilderness, were seen as natural healers of great ability. As early as 1813 Peter Smith published *The Indian Doctor's Dispensatory* to spread knowledge of the herbal remedies of the Indians. By the 1820s the Thomsonian system of natural herbs was using, among others, Indian herbs, while many mainstream Americans visited "Indian medicine shows" at state fairs throughout the century.

Then in the 1830s homeopathy, a new system from Germany, began to spread in the United States. In its own version of the law of correspondence, it taught that like healed like. In other words, the proper remedy to use for a sickness was one that, in a healthy person, produced the same symptoms as the disease. Combining this rule, called the law of similars, with a second rule, called the law of infinitesimals, homeopathy gave to sick people minute—microscopically small—quantities of specific natural substances in attempting to heal them. With the "infinitesimal" doses that patients ingested, healing was thought to come naturally. Significantly, for part of the century homeopathy rivaled traditional medicine as a healing method. Millions of Americans, alienated by the bleeding, purging, and drugging of medical doctors, had turned to what they saw as nature.

Indeed, the nineteenth century was a century of natural health, as from many quarters people supported the idea that nature had energies to cure people and to keep them strong. After 1840 the water cure, or hydropathy, became popular. The sick submitted to a variety of healing baths, showers, and compresses, hot and cold, in the belief that water could work the cure they sought. Meanwhile, vegetarianism thrived as a way to gain greater health and to preserve the strength a person already had. Nineteenth-century new religions encouraged the general interest in health. As we saw, Ellen G. White, the prophetess of Seventh-day Adventism, advocated a variety of health reforms, including vegetarianism, and her influence was responsible for a continued Adventist interest in health. Likewise, Mormons forbade the use of alcohol, tobacco, and caffeine, and Christian Scientists banished alcohol and tobacco. In these and other cases, people often reasoned that such substances were poisons or drugs that interfered with the natural workings of the body. What interfered with these processes, they said, was wrong. Rather, they thought that people should reverence their bodies as the gifts of God and nature and learn never to abuse them.

Apparent in these healing methods were rituals and a behavioral code built on a creed about the ultimacy of nature. Themes of millennial innocence were expressed in beliefs about the healing powers of American nature and its products. But the other side of millennialism—millennial dominance—also found expression in the symbolism of nature. An example is the fictional career of Davy Crockett during the age of manifest destiny.

The historical *David* Crockett had been three times a U.S. congressman from Tennessee and had died in violent circumstances at the Alamo in the Texan war for independence from Mexico. In 1834 he had published a highly successful autobiography, *A Narrative of the Life of David Crockett*, which traded on the popular image of the rough-and-ready frontiersman in order to make its author a hero. In the same year that the autobiography was published, the first number of an annual almanac about Crockett appeared in Nashville. Building on some of the exploits of Crockett in his autobiography, the almanac embroidered them to such a degree that the exaggerations, already present in the supposedly factual autobiography, became outlandish. This thin volume and several series of others in eastern cities used the device of the almanac, with its calendar information, as a way to entertain the public with anecdote after anecdote about the heroism of a fictional "Davy" Crockett. Filled with lively graphics, the almanacs were in fact nineteenth-century comic books, and the figure of Crockett that they presented told a great deal about the mainstream American feeling for nature. The fact that Crockett almanacs sold extremely well indicated that they had struck a chord in the national spirit.

In many respects, Crockett was the embodiment of an American mentality of innocence. He was portrayed as imbued with the strength of nature, outwitting slick Easterners who did not have the advantage of life in the woods. Yet in his relationship to nature and its forces, Crockett appeared above all as the master of the wilderness. Typically, the anecdotes told of conquests of wild animals, blacks, and Indians, in which he fought with his bare hands instead of a rifle and frequently used his teeth. This fictional Crockett bragged that he had thumbnails at least two inches long, which he dug into eyes or veins without hesitation. He often boasted of killing Indians and, in one gruesome episode, hungry and without a supper, ate two of his red victims. In the descriptions of Crockett in these violent encounters, it was clear that he felt a ruthless ecstasy in the experience of blood. He bragged continually about his identification with wilderness forces: he claimed he was half-horse, half-alligator, and part snapping turtle. Savage like nature, he wanted to out-savage it. As a hunter, he could be seen winning his game by becoming like the thing he hunted. In calmer moments, he contented himself with making pets of the bears and alligators that he conquered. When the spirit of wildness came over him, he preferred to drink blood.

From the point of view of religion, the Crockett depicted in the almanacs experienced moments of mystical oneness with nature through his violence. These times were portrayed as renewing the vigor of the man of the woods — and equally important, as renewing his success in politics. For the fictional Crockett, like the historical one, was a congressman. The almanacs were filled with political and patriotic references — to Congress, to the flag, and to practical expressions of belief in manifest destiny. Crockett continually talked of Mexico, Texas, Oregon, and California. He boasted about the times he had defeated or outwitted the Mexican general Antonio de Santa Anna, spoke of flogging Mexico and annexing Texas, and wanted to extend Uncle Sam's "plantation" throughout the continent. So there was a fusion of civil religion and nature religion in the character of Crockett. And nature religion meant no longer a peaceful millennium of

Crockett and His Bear Sailing Down a Ninety-Foot Waterfall. This graphic
illustrates an anecdote from *Davy Crockett's Almanac, 1847* (New York and
Philadelphia: Turner & Fisher). Crockett's waterfall is in Texas, and he shoots at
Mexicans, emphasizing his dominance both over nature and a political foe.

plenty but instead a cultus of violence in which power came from battling the
wilderness in order to dominate it. Indeed, in one episode, Crockett even proved
himself master of the sun. When it froze, he took bear's grease, worked the sun
loose, and walked away with some of the sunrise in his pocket.

Taming the wilderness and taming nations were similar acts for the fictional Crockett and many historical Americans like him. Millennial dominance,
present in the Revolution in the symbols of hunting shirt and homespun, grew
stronger in the nineteenth century. In Crockett, it expressed itself in an amoral
pornography of violence and racism, but Crockett was a caricature of trends clearly
present in the times. Toward the end of the century, though, a renewed interest

in a nature that was moral was expressed in the conservation movement. The spirit of mastery grew more subtle, as the sense of millennial innocence asserted itself. By this time the Industrial Revolution had changed the face of America. The frontier had all but disappeared, and the cities were growing ever larger. A wave of Romantic nostalgia swept over Americans. They feared that, without the presence of true wilderness, they might lose their youth and purity and become old and corrupt like Europe.

In 1872, preservation of the wilderness was insured legally when President Ulysses S. Grant (1822–1885) put his signature to the bill that created Yellowstone National Park. A little more than a decade later, the state of New York set aside a huge region in the Adirondack Mountains as a forest preserve. Various arguments had moved the legislatures toward their decisions, and it was not until the passage of the Yosemite Act in 1890 that Congress acted with the express intention of preserving the wilderness for its own sake. The apostle of the new movement was John Muir (1838–1914), a Scotch-born naturalist who fell in love with the landscapes of his adopted country, hiking for miles through its forests and climbing its mountains. An admirer of Emerson and of Thoreau, he absorbed the Transcendental teachings into his way of life. He became the first president of the Sierra Club, formed in 1892 to foster exploration of the Pacific coastal mountains and to press for government legislation to preserve the Sierra Nevada Mountains. Muir's books and magazine articles did much to sway the public toward his concern for wilderness preservation. His efforts pointed the way toward the ecological movement of the later twentieth century.

For Muir and his followers, the wilderness was to be preserved as the source of America's innocence and strength. Under Gifford Pinchot (1865–1946), a second—and different—segment of the conservation movement found its leader. A Yale graduate, Pinchot worked as the first professional forester in the country and by 1898 had become head of the Bureau of Forestry in the U.S. Department of Agriculture. For Pinchot, forests should be used wisely by being managed well. This meant that only a certain proportion of the lumber should be harvested each year, while at the same time new trees were planted. In this way, Pinchot and others reasoned, people could enjoy the forests, but they could reap their benefits, too. Here the biblical command to master nature was adapted to forestry in a carefully controlled process. Unlike Crockett with his wild excesses in the almanacs, humans were being asked to act as prudent stewards of nature's gifts. But by the turn of the century, the exaltation of wilderness had become a national movement. Pinchot's work for wise use of resources was overtaken by waves of popular enthusiasm for unspoiled nature.

Nature in the Twentieth Century

The first decades of the twentieth century brought greater intensity to pleas for the preservation of wild land. Especially, the fear of national degeneration surfaced in popular awareness. Many Americans feared that without wild nature to invigorate them, they would become like the rest of the world. They would lose their innocence and strength, like people out of touch with the saving power of sacred story and ritual. Democracy, Americans thought, had grown up in the wilderness; without its presence, they stood in danger of losing their most precious possession. In this mood of anxiety, the Boy Scout movement, originally English, was incorporated in America in 1910 with the intention of giving boys a chance to live close to nature and so to develop the moral and spiritual qualities that the wilderness was thought to foster. As Americans of the time saw it, there was a connection between the forests where the Boy Scouts camped and the Boy Scout Code by which the young people were taught to live.

Meanwhile, "primitivists" began a new campaign for savagery as a source of strength, and hunting, camping, and mountain climbing became popular sports. As early as 1888, Theodore Roosevelt (1858–1919), later president of the United States, organized the Boone and Crockett Club to champion big-game hunting and to build character. In 1914, Edgar Rice Burroughs published *Tarzan of the Apes*, giving expression to the image of the Romantic savage in a figure who became a continuing national fictional hero. And after midcentury, Americans again heard the call of the wild when in 1955 a Davy Crockett revival (with a more sanitized Crockett than the almanac version) reached millions, many young, with its Walt Disney television series and film, *Davy Crockett, King of the Wild Frontier*, and its song success, "The Ballad of Davy Crockett."

Throughout the twentieth century, the religion of nature continued to be an impulse in the national life. Sierra Club, Boy Scouts—joined by Girl Scouts and Campfire Girls—Tarzan, Crockett, and other nature heroes were solidly established on the national scene. Then, beginning in the sixties, the movement gained renewed strength and support under the banner of ecology. Years of concern and efforts to preserve wilderness culminated in 1963 when the National Wilderness Preservation System was created. Congress was convinced that access to wilderness would lead to greater physical and mental health for Americans and that such access would promote their freedom and self-sufficiency. At the same time, ecologists spoke of the delicate balance of nature in any environment and cautioned that humans could upset the balance by their interference. Humans were part of nature, they argued, meant to coexist with other species, not to destroy them. By altering the natural balance of forces, people could bring overpopulation by one species and extinction of another. More important, ecologists declared, human populations could begin to destroy the water they drank, the air they breathed, and the cells of their own bodies, which would sicken and die from the poisons being unleashed into the atmosphere.

Mainstream Americans worried about what they were doing to their environment, and as the Vietnam War became a memory, they turned to the environmental movement as a new cause. As claims rose of more and more cancer-causing chemicals being found in air and food, the movement gained strength. In the seventies, increased fears of the dangers of nuclear power brought still more converts. Nature had become a central symbol by which Americans oriented themselves, expressed in everything from preference for cereals advertised as "natural" to use of earth tones for room decoration and practice of yoga and jogging for health. By the late sixties and early seventies, periodicals sprang up to express and reinforce the ascendancy of nature, among them the *Mother Earth News* beginning in 1970 and the *Whole Earth Catalog* beginning in 1968, with a series of name changes from 1971. Within their pages, the American involvement with nature became an identifiable religious system.

In order to understand more precisely what nature religion involves, let us look at its expression especially in the early years of these publications. There, from the beginning — in an incipient version of New Age religion — we find elements of a creed, a code, and a cultus directed toward the central symbol of nature. There, too, the theme of the innocence of paradise planted offers an exposition of the millennial dream. Expressing their natural creed, from the first both periodicals rejected permanence and saw the world as a process in which they participated. Both preferred to avoid making distinctions and to picture reality as a harmonious merging of elements in one whole. Like the Transcendentalists of the nineteenth century, the periodicals taught correspondence — between self and world, between earth and the rest of the universe. For them, the microcosm reflected the macrocosm, and the two followed the same laws and displayed the same patterns. So it was possible, according to the creed, to see the whole in the part and to find parts repeated in other parts, all together forming the harmony of the world.

Significantly, the *Whole Earth Catalog* declared in its statement of purpose that people were "as gods" and urged them to get good at the role. They were parts of the divine whole, and that whole was symbolized by the image of planet Earth on the cover. The *Mother Earth News*, early more concerned with small-scale organic farming, made it clear that it was committed to the preservation of the ecosystem. And for a time the title page was telling its readers that it was not simply a magazine but a way of life. Thus, the creed of harmony between human beings and the planet was turned into a code for living.

When we examine that code in both publications, it is evident that this is where practical interest has remained. Each has seen living ecologically as normative, and each has provided knowledge and support for doing so in everyday settings. In their view, as part of the greater whole, a person should not seek to dominate the natural world. Rather, he or she should develop a rhythm of relationship with nature. As do Native American traditions, the two publications have taught a reverence for nature in which it must be used caringly and imitated. In the early *Catalog*, for example, books on healing herbs and organic foods were reviewed regularly. There was great interest in shelter in more "natural" circles and squares — domes, zomes, tipis, yurts, and related structures. Within these dwellings, the preferred life-style was communal, and the communities sought country locations where their work would lead them back to nature. At the same time, crafts associated with a preindustrial and rural past were highlighted. Pottery and quilt making, embroidery, weaving, woodcarving, and blacksmithing were cultivated, and, as we have already seen, natural waste disposal through composting was urged. In one issue the *Catalog* advertised its plans for a section on "Death, Old Friend" and asked readers to send photographs and accounts for publication. Like compost, the human body was seen as organic waste that must return to the earth to nourish it.

The *Mother Earth News* has pursued a similar course in showing people how to live naturally. Articles have given explicit directions on planting, canning, or building. The early magazine featured correspondence sections in which readers could express their views and classified sections in which they could advertise their needs to fellow readers. Many wrote seeking others who would farm organically with them or who wanted to form a rural commune. Skills such as dowsing (searching for water through the divinatory use of a branch or twig) have been respected, and natural medicine and homeopathic healing have been favored. Indeed, the kind of natural occultism that we saw in early America and the continued occultism that we found among Southern Appalachian mountaineers were often in keeping with the spirit and advice of the *Mother Earth News*. Such editorial material signaled the presence of a harmonial view of the world and expressed belief in nature religion in daily routine.

If both publications shared a common creed and offered similar advice for a behavioral code, both also supported the cultus of nature religion. The cultus was expressed in a series of rituals, coming from many sources but all reinforcing beliefs and behavior related to the correspondence between human beings and nature. In general, the rituals rose out of Eastern and Western (mostly occult) traditions, out of combinations of either or both, out of humanistic psychology and the environmental movement, and out of the religion that became more and more known as New Age. All were important rites for both publications, because all could express, communicate, and reinforce the central beliefs of nature religion. Thus, all the rituals sought to empower participants for ordinary life according to the tenets of their faith.

In the *Whole Earth Catalog*, advertisements regarding Buddhist or Hindu religious texts were welcome. Yoga and Transcendental Meditation were considered good friends, and the Chinese classic the *I Ching* became almost the Bible of *Catalog* readers. The *Catalog* also expressed enthusiasm concerning the peyote rituals of Carlos Castaneda, described in *The Teachings of Don Juan* (1968). From the West, astrology was favored, palmistry was encouraged, and tarot cards were thought useful. Books in humanistic psychology were regularly advertised, and ecological rituals received considerable attention. Earth flags and the picture of the "whole earth" became fixed points on which people could concentrate for meditation. We have already seen Gurney Norman's rituals for his composting class, and there were other new rituals from various people in the movement as well.

The *Mother Earth News*, especially in its earlier years, likewise welcomed practitioners of Eastern religious rituals in its pages. Correspondents' letters linked them with Zen monasticism, yoga, or Krishna Consciousness. A favorite way for readers to identify themselves was by giving their astrological sign, and when they sought sexual companions, they also indicated which signs were acceptable. Many correspondents exhibited interests that ranged over various ritual expressions of nature religion. They mingled, for example, yoga and meditation with astrology. In humanistic psychology, they spoke of the various groups they were part of, while the *Mother Earth News* printed advertisements on such diverse concerns as Gestalt, bioenergetics, and psychic healing. There were advertisements, too, for earth flags and the like, so that, like the *Whole Earth Catalog*, environmentally related ritual was in evidence.

Hence, the two publications have provided a focus for like-minded and like-hearted people who shared in the religion of nature. They have supported believers in a creed, urged them to live the creed in a daily behavioral code, and shown them how they could find ritual expression for their beliefs and behavior in various cultuses. In all of these expressions of nature religion, they have sought a return in some ways to an older, rural America. Their spirit is the familiar one of millennial innocence that we have seen so many times before. They show us that the occult side of American life has spread to touch the lives of many not closely identified with one specific movement, and with readers' letters, they remind us that creating community in America has been difficult. Meanwhile, the pluralism of their ritual life sums up in its manyness the social history of the country. The Romantic pluralism of nature religion mirrors the pluralism of American society. The merging of cultuses together so freely suggests the tendency of cultural religion to make the many into one.

Finally, the early *Whole Earth Catalogs* and *Mother Earth News* point to the identity of the late-twentieth-century New Age movement as a form of nature religion. These two periodicals, as we have studied them, take us back to the beginning years of the New Age, when it was not yet fully self-conscious. In so doing, they capture the innocence of the emerging movement—its millennial fervor in an embryonic stage. Thus, from the perspective of our study of the two periodicals, we can take a vantage point that corrects the later, more media-driven image of the New Age. The *Whole Earth Catalog* and the *Mother Earth News* tell us that whatever else the New Age has been, it was early an age of the earth.

Much more might be said, of course, about the penetration of nature religion into all segments of our society. Campers, backpackers, and hikers threaten to overrun our wilderness areas, and the advertising industry, in an age of pesticides and additives, has found that a sure way to sell something is to say that it is natural. Nature has meant many things to Americans—a new birth to millennial innocence, a place to be wild (and, as in the millennial age, without a history), an obstacle to master (with the dominance of the millennial history-maker), a resource to be used. In all of these expressions of meaning, nature has given Americans direction, and more often than not, both meaning and direction have been millennial. With this continuing vision, nature has taught mainstream Americans how to live in the ordinary world. By mediating experiences of sublimity and transcendence, it has also provided means of reaching beyond the boundary of the ordinary.

Cultural Religion: Explorations in Millennial Dominance and Innocence

Afterthoughts on Cultural Religion

Our survey has introduced us to cultural religion and provided an overview of the historical and contemporary religious meaning of nature. It is important here that we try to sort out what we have learned. We have been speaking in very broad terms—with a few specific case studies—and we have covered ground rapidly.

First, the complexity of the cultural processes we are studying should not escape us. Although it may seem as if we have traveled far into the religious landscape, there are vast areas that we have not visited and rich materials from the religious history of culture that we have not seen. Second, we should not lose sight of the fact that the religious expressions we have explored are diffused and scattered. The religions that we studied in Part I, organized in specific traditions and movements, were well articulated and easily identifiable. The religion we associate with general American culture, on the other hand, is partial and indistinct. It would not be fair to think of the two forms of religion as the same, but it is fair to see the two as, in some ways, similar. Identifying the religious dimension of culture can help us to understand the power of culture to knit many people together. It can also show us why some stories, persons, and songs are so strongly attracting.

Third, the distinction between ordinary and extraordinary religion needs to be redrawn to take account of cultural religion. In the Introduction and elsewhere, ordinary religion has been described as more or less synonymous with culture, while specific religious organizations have been seen as giving people the fundamentals of extraordinary religion. That distinction is, for the most part, useful. As people who are part of a culture, members of religious organizations easily blend ordinary and extraordinary concerns, or, seeking a sharper definition of their religious identity, they try in various ways to separate the two. On the other hand, the general culture goes its own way, giving people the means to make sense of the world in its everyday reality. Yet, as we have seen in this discussion of cultural religion, sometimes the stories, behavioral codes, and rituals of culture push *beyond* the boundaries of daily routine. Fictional dramas *can* be doorways to a transcendent world. Sports, either alone or with others, can yield moments of ecstasy, while trying to develop human potential can bring peak experiences. Drugs induce chemical mysticism, and the fictional Davy Crockett drank the blood of wildlife to reach a mysticism of violence, however reprehensible. Listening to the voice of Elvis Presley has stretched the limits of the ordinary world for millions of his fans.

Thus, just as people who practice extraordinary religion in one way or another express the ordinary religion of culture, so culture, too, has its moments when it becomes extraordinary. In the late twentieth century, since the role of organized religion has shrunk and since it cannot unify all Americans, it is not surprising to find culture expressing its share of transcendence. Legal declarations of church–state separation and technological revolutions that give prestige to science cannot banish the quest for extraordinary experience from public life.

Fourth, we need to be cautious about determining how effectively cultural religion unites Americans. We can surely say that, like civil religion, it is the (mostly) ordinary religion of many Americans some of the time. In fact, as we see now, civil religion is one expression of the larger presence of cultural religion; and to locate civil religion in this way gives us a clue about how we need to look at the many other aspects of cultural religion we have examined. They are all many smaller circles within the larger circle of culture. Americans who live by the ethic of sports may never become involved in humanistic psychology. Corporate executives who embody the technological ethic may look askance at young couples who build cabins in the wilderness of the Pacific Northwest. Science fiction fans may find country music not to their taste, and readers of feminist journals may scorn readers of *Women's Day*.

On the other hand, there *are* ways in which these smaller circles overlap. Business executives are often avid sports fans, and people in farming communes sometimes practice group-process techniques. Science fiction fans may read feminist journals, and lovers of country music may like to try the recipes in *Women's Day*. Moreover, beyond the overlap we have seen major themes that bind many of these cultural expressions together. Indeed, we have identified the single theme that runs through much of our culture as millennialism. With a long history among us, millennialism has repeatedly appeared in one of two forms. Sometimes it has been the dominating millennialism that takes its cue from visions of a final battle when good will triumph over evil. At other times it has been the innocent millennialism that seeks to make utopias in an uncorrupted landscape. Both kinds of millennialism provide Americans with an ordinary religion that yet contains extraordinary moments. Both direct them in the course of their lives, interpreting the meaning of things, offering occasions for ritual, and providing ways to seek empowerment for daily life. With millennialism as the unifying center, dominance and innocence have been two sides of the same cultural coin. Those who dominate and win try to find ways to prove their innocence. Those who stress innocence discover that the world will not go away and that the same struggles for power beset utopia as trouble any human venture.

Furthermore, dominance and innocence share the dualistic way of looking at life that millennialism brings. Good *or* evil, right *or* wrong, this *or* that provide a framework for thinking and acting. The instincts of the dominant and public center — of public Protestantism — are at home here. Moralism, the search for simplicity, and the activism of doers and achievers are part of the millennial theme. Significantly, though, in many expressions of cultural religion, especially in the nineteenth and twentieth centuries, American individualism is countered by expressions of community. Ideologies of teamwork and cooperation are as frequent as those of solitary success. While American cultural religion pays lip service to the nation's historic individualism, it also preaches a need to live and act together. And in its cultivation of unity among the many, once again cultural religion has learned from the values taught by public Protestantism. Voluntaryism is to be encouraged, it suggests; but in a land of different peoples and different traditions, cultural religion teaches that the only way to be alike is to feel alike. So the community that cultural religion seeks to create is, finally, a community of feeling.

In Overview

As a religious system, cultural religion — although diffuse and loose — provides a mostly ordinary expression of the one American religion. A brief survey of its manifestations, especially in contemporary times, has shown familiar elements of cultus, creed, and code. But whether these three shape or are shaped by a mainstream American community remains problematic.

The cultus of cultural religion is present in the annual ritual calendar that evokes themes of millennial dominance in patriotic holidays and millennial innocence in familial and sentimental feasts. The creed of cultural religion unfolds in thematic popular stories spread, for example, by television, film, literature, and entertainment stars. Commitment to ideas of millennial dominance appears in recurring plot structures of violent redemption for a besieged community, while perfectionism is embodied in men's and women's magazines and the ideal of millennial innocence lives on in the legacy of Elvis Presley. Finally, the code of cultural religion expresses norms of behavior guided by mentalities of millennial dominance and perfectionistic innocence in the ethics of sports, technology, humanistic psychology, and nature. In a case study of nature religion as one form of cultural religion, we explored its presence in early America and then in the nineteenth century. In the later twentieth century, we noted its continuing power and its expression in the *Whole Earth Catalogs* and the *Mother Earth News*.

This study of cultural religion has tried to suggest its complexity in impressionistic ways. Such thinking about cultural religion has hinted at new approaches to conceiving the boundaries between ordinary and extraordinary religion. In the end, in order to assess the impact of cultural religion we need to place it beside the other expressions of the one religion. In the forms of public Protestantism, civil religion, and general cultural religion, the one religion seeks to dissolve the differences in American life in a final unity. The power of the one religion is evident in the facts that most of the time it works in public and part of the time it also works in private. Hence, we are left on one side with many religions, each trying to maintain its separate identity, and on the other, with one religion trying to unite them. But to say this does not tell us much about the relationships between the two. For if culture is complex, so are these relationships. And there are many questions still to answer.

What was it like to be white, Anglo-Saxon, and Protestant in the land of the many? What did it mean to be among the many in the land of white, Anglo-

Saxon Protestants? And finally, what did the presence of other minorities do to the experience of separate groups among the many? These are important boundary questions. They are also important questions about the interactions of ordinary and extraordinary religion. We need to address these questions, at least briefly, and we will do so next in the concluding chapter.

SUGGESTIONS FOR FURTHER READING: CULTURAL RELIGION

Albanese, Catherine L. *Corresponding Motion: Transcendental Religion and the New America.* Philadelphia: Temple University Press, 1977.

————. *Nature Religion in America: From the Algonkian Indians to the New Age.* Chicago History of American Religion. Chicago: University of Chicago Press, 1990.

Carroll, Peter N. *Puritanism and the Wilderness: The Intellectual Significance of the New England Frontier, 1629–1700.* New York: Columbia University Press, 1969.

Cawelti, John G. *The Six-Gun Mystique.* Bowling Green, OH: Bowling Green University Popular Press, 1970.

Fuller, Robert C. *Alternative Medicine and American Religious Life.* New York: Oxford University Press, 1989.

————. *Americans and the Unconscious.* New York: Oxford University Press, 1986.

Goethals, Gregor T. *The TV Ritual: Worship at the Video Altar.* Boston: Beacon Press, 1981.

Huizinga, Johan. *Homo Ludens: A Study of the Play Element in Culture.* 1938. Reprint. Boston: Beacon Press, 1955.

Jewett, Robert, and Lawrence, John Shelton. *The American Monomyth.* 2d ed. Lanham, MD: University Press of America, 1988.

Lewis, R. W. B. *The American Adam: Innocence, Tragedy, and Tradition in the Nineteenth Century.* Chicago: University of Chicago Press, 1955.

Marx, Leo. *The Machine in the Garden: Technology and the Pastoral Ideal in America.* New York: Oxford University Press, 1964.

McLuhan, Marshall. *The Mechanical Bride: Folklore of Industrial Man.* 1951. Reprint. Boston: Beacon Press, 1967.

Nash, Roderick. *Wilderness and the American Mind.* 3d ed. New Haven: Yale University Press, 1982.

Nelson, John Wiley. *Your God is Alive and Well and Appearing in Popular Culture.* Philadelphia: Westminster Press, 1976.

Novak, Michael. *The Joy of Sports: End Zones, Bases, Baskets, Balls, and the Consecration of the American Spirit.* New York: Basic Books, 1976.

Nye, Russel. *The Unembarrassed Muse: The Popular Arts in America.* Two Centuries of American Life Bicentennial Series. New York: Dial Press, 1970.

Reich, Charles A. *The Greening of America.* New York: Random House, 1970.

Williams, Peter W. *Popular Religion in America: Symbolic Change and the Modernization Process in Historical Prespective.* Rev. ed. Urbana: University of Illinois Press, 1989.

Many Centers Meeting

In 1834 a group of Roman Catholic nuns, the Ursulines, were conducting a convent school in Charlestown on the outskirts of Boston. The institution had attracted the daughters of some of Boston's first families as well as those of wealthy families in the vicinity. These pupils were Protestant and, specifically, Unitarian. As liberals, their parents were drawn to the educational advantages that contact with Catholicism might provide. They felt little sympathy for what they regarded as the narrowness of Congregationalism in the public schools. On the other hand, the citizens who lived and worked in the vicinity of the Charlestown convent were poorer people, suspicious of "papist superstition" and resentful of upper-class Unitarians who seemed to prefer the mysteries of Catholicism to the heritage of the Reformation.

Writers of the period had been warning of the dangers of Catholicism. They said that the Catholic church was trying to convert Protestant children, especially females, so that it could gradually gain control. In other words, they believed that a papist plot was afoot and that the plot was a conspiracy. Supported by respected Congregational institutions and ministers, the fears of Catholicism and of education at the Charlestown convent spread. Lyman Beecher, whom we have already met several times, turned his revivalistic preaching to the cause of anti-Catholicism and warned of the connection between the pope and despotism. In this emotionally charged atmosphere, a series of circumstances provided the final impetus. Then in August, a mob of working-class citizens lit a torch and burned the convent and a nearby farmhouse down. They were well organized, and there were hints that some of Boston's prominent citizens might have been involved. From their point of view, they had shown the Catholics of Massachusetts and the world what the true heirs of the Reformation thought of the papist church and its plot. They had also let Protestant liberals know what some other Protestants thought of compromise.

With the dynamics of social class and ideology added to the issue of religious preference, the affair at the Charlestown convent was a symbol of the complexity and ambivalence of Protestant attitudes toward the many. On the one side, there was suspicion, hatred, and fear, as exemplified by the working people who came, many of them, from the brickyards at Charlestown. Fed by class jealousy and outrage at liberal ideology, these feelings were nourished, too, by the extraordinary religious commitment of the Reformation, as interpreted in the Puritan tradition. On the other side, there was a fascination with the many and a pragmatic willingness to use their resources to perceived community advantage. The Unitarians' attraction for things Catholic, an expression of their own sense of their cosmopolitan breadth and upper-class "freedom" from old prejudices, marked these liberal Christians as "worldly wise." It also marked their disapproval of the rigorous legacy of Puritanism that still thrived and of the classes that were its carriers.

From the point of view of our discussion, events at the Ursuline convent were an early expression of Protestant cultural expansion and contraction. For the incident underlined, once again, the boundary question. This time it was the boundary question of the one religion, of the dominant and public mainstream, as it tried to determine its own borders in the presence of outsiders. For some, like the strict Congregationalists, it was important to maintain strong boundaries, preserving integrity in a situation seen as threatening. Here foreign religious ideas seemed a source of disorder that might lead to a rearrangement or reconstruction of the Protestant heritage. For others, like the liberal Unitarians, it was preferable to be open for exchanges. Liberals felt comfortable with greater expansiveness. They were willing to go out farther and to absorb more inside. We might say that their sense of religious identity was more diffused than that of their stricter fellow Protestants.

With these observations as general background, in this chapter we examine in more detail the ways in which the one religion of Protestantism responded to the many religions of other Americans. Then we review what we have already seen to some extent in Part I — the ways in which these many religious traditions responded in America to Protestantism. Finally, we look briefly at the ways in which the many responded to one another. All of these cultural exchanges involved boundaries, and by the late twentieth century, all of them had led to some restructuring in the relationships among various religious centers.

In general, patterns were visible in the history of these relationships. Participants in each religion, or religious center — Protestant or part of the many — moved toward others in exchanges that loosened boundaries. But other participants in each center retreated in fear or out of a desire to maintain the purity of its past identity. Sometimes this form of behavior included conscious concern about those in other religious centers, either in missionary efforts or in warnings against the dangers of outside influences. Sometimes the movements of members of one center toward another or away from it were ambivalent, resulting in a complicated series of interchanges.

At least in the first three centuries in America, the response of the dominant and public tradition was more negative than positive toward the religions of the many. And because the one center *was* dominant — in power — this meant various kinds of discrimination and disability for religions among the many. In contrast, the response of the many religious traditions toward public Protestantism was more evenly divided between those who wanted to maintain a separate identity as a community and those who wanted to "Americanize" by becoming more like mainstream Protestants. Lastly, the response of members of the many religions toward one another was more often negative than positive. Let us look at each of these responses.

Defensive Deities: The One Confronts the Many

Protestantism was the religious giant in the land. Yet Protestants generally displayed anxiety toward the cultural "invaders" who were adopting America as their home. So the main thrust of Protestant response to different religions was a contractive one, separation and retreat into purity. Convinced of Anglo-Saxon chosenness and superiority, Protestants barred gates more than opened them. In a sense, the "others" were for Protestants social "dirt," which polluted the body politic and religious. Thus, in the interests of both ordinary and extraordinary religion, from the mainstream Protestant point of view it was necessary to purge the community of any contamination. Foreign religions and their representatives, in the midst of the New Israel, became matter out of place. To rid the public space of these sources of social disorder, Protestants thought, ritual purification was necessary.

We saw in the Introduction how charged with danger the boundaries of the human body were. In many societies individuals believed that they had to be careful about the food they ate and even about what happened to their hair and nail parings lest they fall into the wrong hands. In similar vein, the Protestant quest for public cleanliness was an attempt from the Protestant point of view to preserve the social body — to keep the wrong substances from entering and corrupting it and to prevent its energies from being drained away by alien forces. Thus, while this impulse toward social purity led Protestants to engage in some ugly border wars, we need to recognize that the impulse itself is a powerful element in all religions. Defending the Gods, historically, has been a constant religious enterprise.

In the instance of American Protestantism, the result was discrimination against different religious and ethnic groups. Generally, both the ordinary and extraordinary religions of these groups appeared threatening to the mainstream. The reaction of Protestants was, as in the example of the Ursulines, a mingling of social, economic, political, and more openly religious elements. From the beginning, American Indians felt the brunt of Protestant fears. As we saw in the discussion of nature religion, beneath the Puritan attitude toward Indians was the fear that, far from the centers of European civilization, Euro-American Christians would forget what the centuries had taught them and revert to the savagery they imagined in the Indians. Symbolic of this "savagery," for Puritans, was the "heathen" worship that Indian cultures practiced and the moral codes associated with them. Puritans thought that Indians were cannibalistic and sexually promiscuous. They feared captivity by the Indians, especially for women. They aimed as much as possible to avoid cultural contact between the two peoples.

Similarly, Protestants feared nonhierarchical encounters with their black slaves. When the slaves were freed, the dominant culture continued to uphold, as much as it could, the tradition of separate societies with as little contact as possible. At the same time, the nineteenth-century influx of immigrants challenged Protestants with new religiocultural contacts that they preferred to keep at a minimum. From the Protestant point of view, foreign peoples on all sides seemed ready to overwhelm them, and so Protestants felt they had to fight to maintain their moral superiority as the chosen nation. Indeed, the various reform movements that Protestants led in the nineteenth century appear in a different light if we remember this general background of contact with "other" cultures. And in the twentieth century, movements in the dominant culture to rid the body politic of various forms of corruption take on new meaning. The Red Scare of the twenties and the McCarthy congressional hearings of the fifties, both directed against Communists, suggested public expressions of an old religious fear. Even the Watergate purge of government in the seventies, with its references to the Germanic dominance of the White House by Nixon's aides, H. R. Haldeman and John Ehrlichman, echoed the theme.

In spite of the contractive attempt to maintain its boundaries against alien cultures, Protestantism showed an ambivalence, as we will see. The long era of unrestricted immigration is a strong statement to that effect; and as we look at Protestant restrictive behavior, we need to remember this second side to the story. First, though, let us examine two cases of Protestant resistance to different religiocultural groups. We look first at Protestant attitudes toward Roman Catholicism and then at Protestant attitudes toward Judaism. In both cases, Protestant fears became general cultural fears of the outsider.

The Roman Catholic "Plot"

Extraordinary religion played a strong role in Protestant fears of Roman Catholicism. Conforming to their Reformation heritage, American Protestants thought of the pope as Antichrist in the millennial drama. In familiar pattern, they believed they stood on the side of the Lamb in the war between good and evil, while the pope and the church he headed were emissaries of Satan. For most colonial and nineteenth-century Protestants, in fact, Catholics were not even Christians. Their leaders were thought to be engaged in a secret and powerful plot to take over the world. Protestants saw Catholics as imperialists of the first order, and they ascribed to priests and nuns an immorality they feared would wreck the moral order of America. Often this meant Protestant fears that, like blacks and Indians, Catholics were engaged in wild sexual promiscuity and also that, like blacks and Indians, they were cunning and deceitful.

When they looked at Catholics, and when they looked at each group among the "others," Protestants, in their desire to defend their boundaries, probably displaced their own forbidden fantasies by attributing them to others. In this reading, the urge to moral purity, heightened by the presence of aliens, prompted them to deny the side of themselves they did not wish to see. The hidden sources of Protestant guilt could be acknowledged when they became the open "sins" of Catholics and Jews, Indians and blacks. In emotional terms, the dynamics of projection worked to produce the Protestant image of Catholics and the rest of the "others." By regarding these "others" as they did, Protestants could look safely at the shadow side of themselves.

By the revolutionary era, a second element helped to shape the Protestant attitude toward Roman Catholics. The Enlightenment view of Catholicism mingled with older Protestant ideas. The thinkers of the Enlightenment had themselves been molded by protest against what they regarded as the medieval superstition of the Catholic church. Its priestcraft had kept people in intellectual darkness, they thought, preventing them from seeing the light of true knowledge. Its papal and authoritarian system, they believed, had deterred them from acknowledging the sovereignty of reason, the inner governor and source of light.

Finally, in the nineteenth century, when waves of immigration began to flood America, social and economic reasons joined the other sources of Protestant fear. Roman Catholic immigrants were mostly Irish and very poor. As Protestant Americans saw it, they strained the social services that government and private agencies could provide, often arriving penniless and blighting the cities with their slums, their diseases, their lack of cleanliness, and their foreign ways. According to Protestants, they brought unwelcome competition for jobs and so reduced the wages that the market would pay to all.

Already in the seventeenth century, although there were few Catholics in the English colonies, there had been clear anti-Catholicism, especially in Maryland and Massachusetts Bay. In Maryland, Protestants felt threatened by the Catholicism of the proprietor of the colony, Lord Baltimore. In Massachusetts Bay, the strong Puritan atmosphere led to a vigorous anti-Catholicism, too. When in 1690 war broke out with France and Spain — the other European landlords on the continent — there was new cause for anti-Catholic sentiment, so that by 1700 Rhode Island was the only colony to grant Catholics complete civil and religious rights. The eighteenth century continued this story of legal disabilities for Catholics, now justified by new wars with Catholic France.

During the Revolution the alliance with France against Britain in 1778 brought an era of relative toleration. Still, despite the spirit of the Declaration of

Independence, state constitutions after the war continued to limit the role that Catholics could play in government. It was in the nineteenth century, however, that old fears of Catholic power revived, as the immigrants began to come. The trusteeship controversy within Roman Catholicism—over the question of lay control of church property—generated unfavorable publicity. New Protestant converts, born of the zeal of the Finney revivals, spread anti-Catholicism in the various voluntary societies they joined. Religious newspapers by 1827 began to warn their readers of the tyrannies of the pope and the dangers of the Catholic church. And by 1832 the New York Protestant Association was founded, aiming to promote the Reformation by public discussions that would bring the (in its view, negative) character of Catholicism to light.

In this climate of opinion, the burning of the Ursuline convent in 1834 was the first act in a continued Protestant war against nunneries. Two years later, after several books were published claiming to reveal the horrors of convent life, Maria Monk's *Awful Disclosures of the Hotel Dieu Nunnery of Montreal* appeared. Monk's book professed to be the work of an escaped nun, and among her "awful disclosures" were alleged secret sexual unions between priests and nuns. The children born of these relationships, according to Monk, were strangled in infancy after being duly baptized. Their bodies, she said, were hidden in a secret passage that linked the convent to the home of the priests.

Actually written in New York at the urging of a group that included several Protestant ministers, the book, needless to say, was noticed. Although the Hotel Dieu was finally searched by trustworthy investigators who found no evidence to support even the floor plan of the convent as described by Monk, many still believed the allegations of her book and subsequent publications. The Reformation had brought Protestants a new religious spirit, and they regarded celibacy as an unnatural state. Moreover, mysteries that took place behind the cloistered walls of a convent, so different from the openness eulogized in a democratic republic, also disturbed Protestant Americans. Together, they believed, celibacy and secrecy could add up to no good. So the rumors flew, and convents were subject to harassment.

At the same time, Protestants believed they had new cause for worry as rumors spread of a papal plot to take control of the Mississippi Valley with the aid of European despots. Lyman Beecher wrote his *Plea for the West* (1835), warning of Catholic plans to use schools as a way to win converts and so win the country. For this reason, he urged, Protestant schools and colleges had to be established in the new territories. In the East, Catholicism became embroiled in other scholastic controversies as church leaders protested against the reading of the King James (Protestant) Version of the Bible in the public schools. Further, Catholics were upset by many of the textbooks that their children were required to use because they thought that the books presented an unfair and untrue picture of Catholicism. In Philadelphia, these and similar issues provoked a confrontation between Protestants and Irish Catholics that led in 1844 to the burning of two Catholic churches in the Kensington suburb of the city. Spurred on the Prot-

SHALL IT COME TO THIS?
ROMISH INTOLERANCE MUST NOT TRIUMPH!

"DANGER IN THE DARK"
IS DESTINED TO BE READ BY EVERY AMERICAN.

THE AIM OF POPE PIUS IX.

"BEWARE! THERE IS DANGER IN THE DARK!"

The Aim of Pope Pius IX, 1855. This titled cartoon from a Protestant nativist flyer advertised the Reverend Isaac Kelso's *Danger in the Dark*, an anti-Catholic novel. With the cartoon's depiction of the pope destroying the U.S. Constitution, note the irony of the caption's allusion to "Romish intolerance."

estant side by the publicity given to the issue by the American Protestant Association, the discontent between the two factions brought a state of civil riot and mob action to Philadelphia.

There had been political insensitivity on the part of the Catholic bishops in these and other instances, but the roots of the problem, as we have seen, ran deep. Protestants continued to form organizations to counter what they perceived as the Catholic threat. Through many of the best-known voluntary societies — the American Tract Society, the American Home Missionary Society, and others — anti-Catholic attitudes were spread. Then in the mid-1840s Protestant nativism assumed political form as the Native American party, which demanded that the naturalization law be changed to require a twenty-one-year wait before an immigrant could become a citizen. A five-year wait had been the law of the land since the presidency of Thomas Jefferson, but the nativists reasoned that it took twenty-one years for a native-born American to receive full rights as a citizen. Foreigners, though adults, should expect a similar waiting period. In fact, nativists thought that the lengthy prohibition would cut down on the number of Catholic immigrants who became citizens, thus lessening their political power to control public policy through the ballot box.

By the early 1850s, the secret Order of the Star Spangled Banner, known in its public activities as the Know-Nothing party, had come into existence as the enemy of Roman Catholicism. With local, county, state, and national councils, the order was tightly and effectively organized for its purposes. Its members, bound by the elaborate ritual of their secret society, "knew nothing" when publicly questioned. But they staged write-in campaigns during the elections and succeeded in bringing their slates of candidates to office in local contests. Later, the Know-Nothing party began to carry states — Massachusetts, Delaware, and Pennsylvania among them. In 1854 it sent a delegation of about seventy-five congressmen to Washington, D.C., all united on anti-Catholic principles. So confident was the party that it hoped to capture the White House in 1856. However, without a majority in the Congress, the party could not translate its programs into law, and, in the end, the movement failed.

Political nativism was swept away by the slavery controversy that erupted shortly later in the Civil War. However, the country experienced another strong resurgence of anti-Catholic sentiment in the 1870s and especially in the 1880s, when the heaviest immigration in American history began. When in 1886 a bomb exploded in the midst of the police officers called to Chicago's Haymarket Square during an anarchist meeting, the incident triggered a renewal of nativism, directed now against Jews as well as Catholics. By 1887 the American Protective Association formed to defend Protestant boundaries by never voting for a Catholic and, if members were able, by never hiring one. Anti-Catholic feeling continued for roughly the next fifty years and lingered in subdued form until the present. Thus, by 1915, the revived Ku Klux Klan had made Catholicism one of its targets. Meanwhile, theories of "scientific" racism alleged that the Teutonic, or Northern European, "race" was superior and that therefore the Protestant peoples — the Germans and the English — were the lifeblood of the nation. On the other hand, for those convinced, it followed that the Mediterranean "race," represented by Southern European Catholic immigrants, would weaken the strength of America.

When in 1928 New York's governor, Alfred ("Al") Smith (1873–1944), ran for the presidency on the Democratic ticket, his Catholicism became a key issue in his defeat. America was not ready to elect a Roman Catholic president until 1960, when, not without questions concerning his religion, John F. Kennedy won the office. The second half of the twentieth century had brought a new era for Catholicism. Now anti-Catholic sentiment was more discreet, and when it surfaced, it presented itself as educated, sophisticated, and "polite." The best example was Protestants and Other Americans United for the Separation of Church and State (POAU), which after 1948 warned of the growing authority of the Catholic church in the United States. The POAU found the possibility of federal aid to parochial schools particularly disturbing, and a good deal of Protestant anxiety was expressed through the public controversy stimulated by the organization.

The Jewish "Conspiracy"

Unlike anti-Catholicism, anti-Semitism did not become a serious factor in American life until the later nineteenth century. There were reasons. First, the Puritan belief in the covenant had fostered a strong identification with the biblical Israel. According to their self-understanding as chosen people and visible saints, Puritans believed they had inherited the mantle of divine election that had formerly protected the Jews. As descendants of the people who Puritans saw as having played an honored role in God's plan, seventeenth-century Jews did not inspire the hatred and alarm that Catholics did. Second, outside the heritage of extraordinary religion, there were social, political, and economic reasons why Jews appeared less threatening. From the beginning, their presence in the colonies was minimal — smaller even than the presence of Roman Catholics. Moreover, no Jewish power, such as the Catholic powers of Spain and France, opposed English presence in North America. Finally, early Jewish immigrants did not drain public welfare programs. They were largely tradespeople able to earn their own livings. When problems did arise, individual Jews turned to the Jewish community for help and support.

Still, there *were* reasons for Protestants to erect barriers against the Jews. As a religious organization, the Christian church was born out of conflict with the Jewish synagogue. The gospels, written during the period of struggle, reflected the attempts of the Christian movement to assert its own identity not only positively but also negatively. In other words, Christians aimed to show how and why in their view the Jews were wrong. So the gospels, and especially the gospel of John, portrayed the Jews as disobeying God and rejecting his prophets. The ultimate rejection had come, according to Christian accounts, when Jews refused to recognize the messiah in their midst and even persecuted and crucified him. By the third century, condemnation of the Jews had escalated, and the Christian scholar Origen (185?–254?) was saying that all the Jews had killed Christ. A tradition had been formed. Throughout the Middle Ages and into the era of the Reformation, the charge that the Jews were Christ-killers stuck, often combining with other factors to lead to episodes of persecution of the Jews.

Meanwhile, because the medieval church prohibited usury (lending money with an interest charge), European Jews became identified with moneylending and banking to accommodate Christian demands. So began a continuing Jewish association with business and financial interests, an association in which prominent members of the Jewish community lent money to their Christian neighbors, prospered materially, and frequently attracted their resentment. From the Christian point of view, there was something suspicious—even wrong—with wealth that was obtained not by productive work but from unproductive money. According to this reasoning, seeds planted in the ground would grow and reproduce their kind. Hands skilled at their work would create the arts and crafts needed by society. But, the argument concluded, money could not be planted and, in its own form, could not be used. Therefore, according to the rationale, it must be an agent of the devil.

These ideas, the common possession of all Christians before the Reformation, continued among both Protestants and Roman Catholics after the sixteenth century. So despite their identification as the New Israel, American Protestants shared extraordinary and ordinary forms of ambivalence toward Jews. Even in colonial times, therefore, prohibitions against atheists and non-Christians slowed Jewish immigration, while the Jews also suffered legal disabilities. Yet in comparison with the restrictions the Jews had endured in Europe, America seemed the promised land, and the Jewish community prospered. It was not until the era of the Civil War that anti-Semitism became noticeable, as Jews in both the North and the South were blamed with profiteering from the war and with treason. In an order later reversed by President Abraham Lincoln, General Ulysses S. Grant commanded all Jews to leave the Tennessee military district. The citizens of one Georgia town agreed to banish them, too; and meanwhile, Congress legislated that only Christians could serve as chaplains to the Union army.

After 1880 the huge immigration of Eastern European Jews, poor and distinctly foreign, brought Jewish people increasingly to public attention. At the same time, the success of older Jewish Americans, sometimes greater than that of Protestant Christians, aroused hostility. Jews found themselves barred from prestigious social clubs and summer resorts. College fraternities began to exclude Jewish students at eastern schools, while, increasingly, Jews faced difficulties in obtaining housing. By the 1890s anti-Semitic feeling crystallized around the suspicion that Jews were responsible for an international conspiracy to base the economy on the single gold standard. The prominence of European Jewish banking families, such as the Rothschilds, fueled these fears, for the Rothschilds and other Jews were thought to have a corner on the world gold market. This was a populist era when many Americans were organizing politically to protect the silver standard. They believed that the "free" coinage of this second metal, while it produced inflation, would ease conditions, especially for farmers and working people.

The People's, or Populist, party began in 1889, backed by southern and western agricultural organizations, and through the regular Democratic party as well as through its own political machinery, it made its presence felt. Beginning with legislation in 1878, the government subsidized silver producers and farmers by requiring the purchase of silver bullion for coinage. Then in 1890 the Sherman Silver Purchase Act raised the amount of silver to be purchased by the treasury to twice the former amount. When a financial panic swept the country in 1893, the steady drain of gold from the treasury to purchase silver became a matter of serious concern. At a special session of Congress, the Silver Purchase Act was repealed.

Farmers and working people felt betrayed, and after President Grover Cleveland (1837–1908) obtained a gold loan from the Rothschilds, anti-Semitism flared. Many thought that America had sold out to an international banking conspiracy headed by the Jews. The Populists, through their own party and within Democratic ranks, expressed the sentiments that these Americans shared. At the Democratic convention in 1896, William Jennings Bryan gave the "Cross of Gold" speech that won him the presidential nomination. "You shall not crucify mankind upon a cross of gold," he declared in a long-remembered statement.

Whether or not he was consciously aware of it, Bryan's rhetoric undercut the Protestant cultural boundaries. He had Jews to enforce the linked charges that the Jews were Christ-killers and that they were banking conspirators with the Populist cry for free silver. And he had done it with innuendo and suggestion, so that Jews had not directly been named, but everybody knew that Jews were meant. Others were more direct. During these years anti-Semitic rhetoric and literature became an open part of American life. Indeed, the pattern continued until after the Second World War, so that the first half of the twentieth century brought the Jews little relief from anti-Semitism.

An often-cited example is the Leo Frank case in Atlanta in 1913. There, new city dwellers from rural areas felt tense and uncomfortable, for cities had long been symbols of evil for Americans. In addition, the physical and emotional problems of adjustment increased tension, and there were periodic eruptions of violence, such as a race riot in Atlanta in 1906. In this atmosphere of conflict and fear, the Southern Baptists, who played a large role in the religious life of the city, thought of immigrants as one of the largest threats to America. The Jew, historically identified with cities rather than farms, stood as a strong symbol of all that these Americans hated and feared.

So when thirteen-year-old Mary Phagan was assaulted and murdered one night at the National Pencil Factory, her employer, Leo M. Frank, was immediately suspected. Although Frank had witnesses to his whereabouts during the fatal day and evening, he was placed on trial for the crime. He admitted having seen the Phagan girl alive on the day before the night of the crime (nobody would admit to having seen her later), and strands of her hair as well as blood-stains were found in a workroom opposite his office. Furthermore, he possessed something of a reputation for making advances toward his female employees. Thus, although many years later his name was cleared, Frank was railroaded through a trial in the midst of public outrage toward him. It was no surprise when the jury found him guilty. Public oratory and newspaper editorials made identifications between the northern Jew, the evils of the city, and the death of the "little factory girl." Stories circulated that Frank's Jewish friends had tried to bribe the jury, while his lawyers received anonymous threats. After fruitless appeals all the way to the U.S. Supreme Court, Frank's sentence to death by hanging was commuted by the governor of Georgia to life imprisonment. But shortly after the decision, in 1915 the prison was stormed, and Frank was kidnapped and lynched.

The same year as Frank's murder, the revived Ku Klux Klan began directing its attacks against Catholics and Jews, as well as blacks, as we have already seen. The new Klan was an identifiably Protestant organization with its own chaplains and hymns that it adapted specially to express its creed and code. By 1923 it had grown to nearly 3 million members, a militant reminder of the threat felt by many Protestants in a mixed society. During this decade, too, Henry Ford in 1920 championed the American publication of the *Protocols of the Elders of Zion*, the fabricated account of a conference of nineteenth-century Jews planning to overthrow Christianity and to gain control of the world. Significantly, in the *Protocols* the gold standard was to be the Jewish weapon in the attempted subversion. Once again, religious and economic prejudices were linked in a work that became a continuing justification for anti-Semitism.

In the cases of Frank, the Klan, and the *Protocols*, hatred of Jews was crude and blatant. But now a "polite" form of anti-Semitism began to spread, as Harvard and other universities questioned their admissions policies and introduced quota systems because they feared that Jews would alter the traditional Anglo-Saxon character of their institutions. A decade later, in the thirties, public sentiment against the Jews only grew stronger, as the Great Depression and the growth of European Fascism stimulated American fears. As we will see, many Catholics as well as Protestants became openly anti-Semitic — that fact a pointed reminder that in speaking of the boundaries of Protestant identity we are speaking about the cultural Protestantism that was the dominant and public religion of the land. In this blend of ordinary and extraordinary religion, Jews had come to stand for many of the ills that troubled the republic. For numbers of Americans, Jewish unbelief challenged Christianity, Jewish wealth wrongly outstripped that of the leaders of the New Israel, and Jewish cosmopolitan identification with the city corrupted the wholesome rural flavor of America. Within the boundaries of the one religion, Jews had come to represent a looming threat at the gates.

Overtures toward the Many

In spite of its defensiveness, the dominant and public religion did initiate exchanges with the "others." The record was far from being all negative, however insecure the mainstream had been. Perhaps the single most important sign was the fact that only with the twentieth century did the era of unlimited immigration end. There were strong economic reasons, of course, for the open immigration policy of the United States. But the millennial belief of Americans that they stood at the dawn of a golden age, that they were an example and possessed a mission to all peoples, was also involved. Thus, immigration continued throughout the nineteenth and into the twentieth century until a series of congressional measures in 1917, in 1921, and then in 1924 reduced it drastically. The laws of 1921 and 1924 introduced a quota system, which clearly favored Northern Europeans in its restrictions. Then, as we have seen, in 1965 the law of 1924 gave way to one that restricted immigration but not on the basis of national origins. In a further legislative testimony to a new mood in America, Congress in 1973 passed the Ethnic Heritage Act, providing funds for programs that would improve public understanding of different cultural groups within the United States.

From the beginning of the mainstream encounter with the many, however, there was a series of exchanges, or moves, each of them a different way of meeting the "others." In general, we may single out three. The first move, sometimes linked to fear of being swept away in foreign religions and cultures, was the traditional attempt to do missionary work among them. Here extraordinary religion led the way, but in various projects to assist the social welfare and cultural integration of African-Americans, American Indians, and immigrants, ordinary religion was involved as well. The second move, in a different mood, was an outward turning toward the "others" with a sense of interest and qualified openness. Again, extraordinary religion was prominent, since Protestant liberalism and, in the twentieth century, the ecumenical movement were carriers for this kind of exchange. Finally, the third move was an expansive preoccupation with the "others" that drew the mainstream into a strong attraction toward those who were different. Played out mostly within ordinary religion — through general culture, this expansiveness found expression in literature and the arts. We will glance briefly at each of these moves toward the many.

As we saw in Chapter 5, Protestant missionary efforts began during the time of English colonization of the New World. They were a basic expression of the mission mind, so that Puritans and their successors worked among Native Americans and African-Americans into our own times. What is relevant about this mission work here, though, is its ambivalence. Racism was always a characteristic of American culture, and the religion of Protestant chosenness bore its share of responsibility. Thus, missionary work was in some ways a veiled expression of Protestant cultural contraction — of a retreat from cultural contact with those who were different. The emotional "logic" seemed to be that by transforming Indian and African-American peoples, so that they more and more resembled mainstream Protestants, their otherness might be neutralized. Difference would be muted, and the threat for members of the mainstream who wanted to remain culturally intact would be lessened. By the same token, "others" who were Jewish or Catholic also felt the impact of Protestant missionary efforts, efforts that sometimes intertwined with the anti-Semitism and anti-Catholicism we have already examined.

In the case of Jewish people, as early as 1667, well before any Jews settled in Boston, Increase Mather (1639–1723) had published a set of sermons directed to Jewish conversion. Because of the small number of Jews in the country, however, it was only in the nineteenth century that missionary efforts became significant. By 1823 the activities of the interdenominational American Society for Meliorating the Condition of the Jews prompted the publication of a Jewish periodical as a rebuttal. Jews did not look kindly on the work of Christian missionaries, as succeeding issues of *The Jew* made clear. Later in the century, a number of denominations — among them Episcopalians and Baptists as well as Old School and United Presbyterians — sponsored official or semiofficial efforts to convert the Jews. In general, the Jews did not welcome them.

Protestants also worked to convert Catholics, and by 1842 the American Tract Society established plans to send missionary agents to them. Two years later, the American Protestant Society was holding monthly prayer sessions for the conversion of Catholics and fielding missionaries as its active agents. The society was subsequently incorporated into the American and Foreign Christian Union, and its labors became more extensive, spreading especially to areas where Protestants could encounter Catholic immigrants. Likewise, the American Home Missionary Society worked to spread Protestantism in the New West, where Catholic influence was likely to be met. The official Catholic response to Protestant mission work directed toward Catholics was, of course, negative, and numbers of lay Catholics also resented and feared Protestant overtures. These Catholics read Protestant missionizing as an expression of anti-Catholicism.

Nonetheless, by the 1890s, when immigration had become the largest in American history, Protestants, we recall, were working in settlement houses among Jewish and Catholic immigrant groups. Here and in other expressions of the Social Gospel movement, they brought economic assistance and American cultural influence to the newcomers. Just as the government throughout the nineteenth century had tried to acculturate and to "civilize" the Indians, and just as the Freedmen's Bureau after the Civil War had tried to do the same for African-Americans, the organizations to assist the immigrants brought the ordinary religion of Americanism to their doorstep.

Yet if missionary outreach was one move toward the "others," a second move was one of attention and interest without missionary aspirations. The liberal, upper-class Unitarians who sent their daughters to the Ursuline convent at Charlestown in 1834 were examples of this second move. Here there was belief that a different cultural tradition could add to the heritage of the mainstream.

There was, as the image of the school expresses, a willingness to be taught. In fact, part of this willingness came from practical considerations, a situation, we remember, that was repeated in the West in these decades. In the new land, there were few opportunities for a solid education. Catholicism, which had long experience through its teaching orders of nuns and priests, sometimes supplied the community's needs.

However, it remained for the twentieth century to bring Protestantism to a more organized openness regarding the many. The changes that resulted in the ecumenical movement were complex, involving developments on the world religious scene and within religious organizations outside of Protestantism. As early as 1928, the National Conference of Christians and Jews had been formed for the mutual educational benefit of both groups. The conference was publicly active in a number of ways, among them the inauguration of Brotherhood Day and, later, National Brotherhood Week. Then, we recall, two years after the establishment of the World Council of Churches, the National Council of Churches came into existence in America in 1950. As an expression of the ecumenical movement, the council aimed to study the faith and life of the churches in relationship to one another. It also wanted to understand the meaning of the unity and universality that Christians had traditionally associated with the church and to find ways to make the unity and universality more than an ideal. Organizationally, it included among its members representatives of various Eastern Orthodox churches, and so dialogue beyond Protestant boundaries had become possible within its ranks.

After 1960 the ecumenical movement began to gain rapid ground in a world religious climate changed by the election of Pope John XXIII (1881–1963) and his plans for Vatican Council II. An example of the new mood was the suggestion by the Jewish scholar Will Herberg for a book exploring interfaith questions to be written by the Protestant theologian Robert McAfee Brown and the Catholic priest and scholar Gustave Weigel. In the resulting work, *An American Dialogue: A Protestant Looks at Catholicism and a Catholic Looks at Protestantism* (1960), Protestantism was viewing Catholicism in a new way—without a desire either to convert or to be converted. Protestant identity remained, yet positive exchanges were being conducted across the boundary of another religious world.

The third Protestant move toward the many was a more romantic cultural expansion toward "otherness"—a move that recalls the general cultural expansion we examined in Part I. Outside the mainstream, this "otherness" flourished, so that when Protestants looked to the many, in some ways they recognized human possibilities that their own culture did not encourage them to express. "Reverse" acculturation was almost inevitable, as the dominant and public religion found that strange religions and cultures were often close to home. Thus, the nineteenth-century Unitarians who sent their children to the Catholic convent school had been at least aware of the trappings of medieval culture that came with Catholicism. Later the Transcendentalists were drawn by this

Catholic heritage. Ralph Waldo Emerson, after he traveled in Europe, had come away with a strong sense of the ritual power in Roman Catholic sacramentalism. Indeed, at least two of the Transcendentalists became prominent Catholic converts, and both Isaac Hecker (1819–1888) and Orestes Brownson (1803–1876) were devoted members of their new church.

Yet the mainstream made its closest contacts with the "others" within ordinary religion, through general culture, and often through literary and artistic means. The Euro-American relationship with Indian Americans was a case in point. Although a long heritage had taught whites to shrink from association with "savage" and "uncivilized" Indian peoples, the same history told them that the Indian was a noble creature of the forests. As a romantic relationship with the wilderness grew in the nineteenth century, the Indian came to stand for the purity and regeneration that uncorrupted nature gave to America.

For example, in the *Leatherstocking Tales* of James Fenimore Cooper (1789–1851), the frontier life of Natty Bumppo, or Leatherstocking, embodied the qualities of the "noble savage." A guide for other whites, often extricating them from dangerous situations, Leatherstocking maintained close ties with Indian peoples. He had learned their ways and could survive in the forest. He could respect their code of honor and sympathize with their plight under the pressures created by the coming of more and more whites. Yet Natty Bumppo often boasted that he was a man "without a cross" (of blood), and he continued to stand on the boundary—never quite an Indian, but never an ordinary white man either.

Even more than Leatherstocking, David Crockett in his autobiography spoke proudly of his Indian skills. He could, he boasted, use his tomahawk to chop a tree, to obtain some honey, or to break ice when the river was frozen. And just as the Indians did, Crockett in the autobiography succeeded in hunting by becoming like the animals he stalked and killed. In the pages of the autobiography Crockett demonstrated many times his readiness for wild and "savage" actions. If Crocket thought American Indians ran naked in the woods, he had his tale of how, in an accident during a trip to float some logs down the Mississippi, he had lost his clothes. If Indians could not read or write, Crockett bragged of his own difficulties with book learning. Crockett was a hero and a great congressman, as the autobiography told it, because of his closeness to wilderness forces. Crockett had become an ideal American, a character to be admired and imitated, because he had become like an Indian.

In our own era, the fascination with Native American cultures, if anything, has grown stronger. Children play "Indian," wearing Plains Indian war bonnets to express their identification with the first Americans. College students avidly read accounts of Indian culture like *Black Elk Speaks*, told from the Indian point of view, while films such as *Little Big Man*, *A Man Called Horse*, and *Dances with Wolves* seek to offer insights into native cultures. At the same time, a flowering of Indian crafts, especially in the Southwest, has brought Navajo jewelry and blankets and Pueblo pottery and baskets into demand. Indian designs appear on towels and bed linens, adding a Native American flavor to interior decorating.

There is not enough space to explore all of the ways in which the mainstream has reached out to the many and taken elements to itself. German Christmas tree customs, Italian spaghetti and pizza, and Chinese food are all instances. Even more, African-American music and entertainment have transformed twentieth-century art forms, and what is most distinctive about American music has been what blacks have brought to it. Gospel, jazz, and blues owe their genesis to African-American music. Elvis Presley, we recall, took part of his success from the "soul" quality he gave to white rock and roll.

Finally, the presence of "otherness" had led to *discontinuity* within the dominant religion. In the mood of cultural expansiveness that we have already seen in Part I, mainstream religion has become partial to meditation and contemplation as well as to activity. It has absorbed elements of the occult, has found its children living in communes, and has listened to the messages of new and foreign religious movements. Even among the middle class, casual clothes and expansive life-styles have symbolized a departure from the etiquettes of the past. The public face of American religion has come to look different in the presence of the "others."

Acculturative Religion: The Many Encounter the One

Throughout Part I, we noticed the ways in which religious people among the many tried to come to terms with the dominant and public religion of the mainstream. Generally, they either turned, in an exercise of contraction, to the resources within their own communities, attempting to preserve their original identity in the new situation. Or they decided, on an expansive note, to turn outward, becoming as American as they could, even as they preserved some of the heritage of the past. Or lastly, they employed missionary efforts — either in traditional churches like Roman Catholicism, or in sectarian groups and new religious movements that maintained strong boundaries against the world and at the same time worked zealously to win converts to their cause. Inasmuch as we have examined these moves in some detail, let us simply review them here.

First, the many used their distinctive rituals and ways of life to preserve their religiocultural identity. In the case of African-Americans, during their years in slavery preservation of remnants of the African past was present. More than that, when they began to use a Christian religious language, they evolved their own African-American form of Christianity that sought not to imitate the mainstream but to express themselves. In the style of their preaching, in spirituals, in marriage and funeral customs, and in the blend of idea and emotion that characterized their worship, blacks spoke and acted their ordinary and extraordinary religion within the circle of African-American identity. In root work and voodoo and later in religious movements that made blackness central, they drew a line between themselves and white society.

For Native Americans, the story was similar, although in their case the boundaries were not so much encouraged by mainstream culture as maintained in spite of it. Christian missions and government agencies alike tried to break down Indian nations' ways and to replace tradition with Christianity and modernity. The results were often destructive to tradition, leaving Indian peoples in a demoralized state. Still, many fought back and preserved their religious and ethnic identity. In the later twentieth century, the return to tradition became a movement that penetrated reservation cultures. The peoples who had separated themselves most effectively from outsiders, usually because of historical accident, found themselves often in a more integral condition than other, more "Americanized" Indians.

In the examples of the Hopi and the Oglala Sioux, we saw how ordinary and extraordinary religion worked together to create an interlinked world of belief, behavior, and ritual drama. In other cases, Christian elements were reinterpreted to maintain the boundaries between Indian and white society. For example, the Rio Grande Pueblos of New Mexico accepted Roman Catholic ritual as a new resource that could be added to their already full ceremonal life. More radically, the Paiutes who created the ghost dance transformed Christian millennialism into an expression of Indian renewal in which it was believed that the remnants of white culture would be swept away and a new earth restored to Native Americans.

Among whites, the non-Protestant religions also used boundary markers to tell themselves and their Protestant neighbors that they were different. The Jewish dietary laws expressed a commitment to the religion of Israel and likewise distinguished Jews in a public way from Gentiles. After 1880 the emergence of Conservatism and the self-consciousness of Orthodoxy underlined the Jewish desire to keep alive past traditions. Similarly, the growth of the parochial school system among Catholics indicated the strength of the Roman refusal to be assimilated to mainstream Protestantism through the cultural persuasion of the public schools. And we have already seen within Judaism and Catholicism strong currents of rejection of Protestant missionizing.

In a related move, within Roman Catholicism different ethnic groups strived to maintain their religious traditions in the face of the dominant Irish power—closer, for them, to the Protestant mainstream. Germans and Poles fought to keep their native languages in religious services. Italians steadfastly continued their devotions to their favorite saints, lavishing attention on traditional statues and lighting candles in the saints' honor. Different ethnic groups blended extraordinary religion with distinctive folk customs in various church feasts. They kept marriage and funeral customs that they had brought from their countries of origin, using their separate practices as badges of identity for themselves and for others.

The Oneness of Religion in America

Meanwhile, the new religious movements that arose in America also adopted badges of identity. Seventh-day Adventists adhered to rigorous dietary laws, and Christian Scientists distinguished themselves with their characteristic ritual of healing. Mormons created a separate society with temple ceremonies forbidden to outsiders and, again, distinctive dietary practices. Shakers lived apart in celibacy, and spiritualists drew a boundary between themselves and other Americans through their practice of communication with the dead in séances. Twentieth-century Anglo-American followers of Krishna wore saffron robes and sandals and chanted publicly in honor of their God.

In these and similar instances—and in the cases of the many Eastern religions whose ethnic representatives settled in the United States—people worked to separate themselves from the mainstream, turning instead to the traditions they had inherited or the new religions they had embraced. Far from wanting to be like the followers of the dominant and public religion, they chose to be different in order, as they saw it, to be themselves.

Yet, second, a countermove among the many brought them closer to the mainstream. In America, to be different most of the time seemed to carry negative consequences. The dominance of the one religion insured that its mentality would affect others, and the sense of chosenness that characterized mainstream Protestantism made its mark on general American culture. Even as the public religion tried to maintain its boundaries against outsiders, it made clear where power and authority lay. So acculturation to Protestant America changed the religions of the many. Instead of excluding American culture, numbers among the many went out to meet it and incorporated it into their world.

For example, the Reform movement that spread through nineteenth-century Judaism brought changes that made it more "American." Protestant "decorum" became a feature of worship, and for a period Sunday services and Protestant-style hymns came into use. Theological liberals reinterpreted the meaning of Israel, so that the ethics of the biblical prophets provided support for the voluntaryism and activism of the American religious style. Jewish scholarship, traditionally focused on the Torah and the Talmud, came both in America and abroad to mean achievement at the university and in Gentile society. Meanwhile, Reform, Conservatism, and Orthodoxy took shape as forms of American Judaism that in many ways paralleled mainstream denominationalism.

Lay Catholics early identified with the host culture as, in the nineteenth century, they struggled with their bishops to control church property through a system of democratic lay trustees. Later, a series of liberal bishops sought to "Americanize" the church until a message from Rome put a stop to the most open attempts. At the same time, Irish clerical leadership showed in its activism, moralism, and search for simple, nonintellectual answers how close to the mainstream it was.

In the twentieth century, a new generation of Catholic scholars, both in this country and abroad, looked at the era of the Reformation more kindly, fostering ecumenical dialogue with Protestants. When Vatican Council II opened world Catholicism to change, American Catholics quickly showed signs of their movement toward Protestant America. The English Mass became an appeal to the biblical Word of God with a corresponding deemphasis on the more elaborate aspects of sacramentalism. Many of the symbolic badges of Catholicism, such as Friday abstinence from meat and old-style paraliturgical devotions in the churches, began to disappear. The Catholic mission movement of the nineteenth century had its successor in the charismatic movement that brought pentecostal tongues and revivalistic fervor to many members of the church. Individuals and groups, such as the radical Berrigan brothers and the conservative prolifers, engaged in prophetic-style "Protestant" moral crusades. Democracy reinforced belief in the rights of private conscience as many priests and nuns left their religious orders and many laypeople made decisions about moral issues like birth control that countered traditional Catholic teaching.

For African-Americans, emancipation brought a social revolution with accompanying religious changes. Class divisions, often disguised during the years in slavery, came into the open, and religious preferences came to reflect the new situation. Holiness and pentecostal churches became havens in the cities for African-Americans, providing religious experience and a perfectionist behavioral code shared by many Protestants in the mainstream. Likewise, Baptist and Methodist churches, affiliated with white denominations, introduced middle-class blacks to the controlled and more formal worship preferred by other Protestants. Black religious leadership in the civil rights era of the 1960s and afterward did draw on its own traditional resources. But it also drew on the mainstream of the Protestant theological tradition, as reflected in the seminary education of church and social leaders like Martin Luther King, Jr. Blacks were gaining political power and socioeconomic success in white society to the extent that they learned to speak the cultural language. Black Protestantism had been a key factor in the process.

Among Native Americans, some followed the strong suggestion of church and government, leaving the reservation and adopting white ways and white society. Others, while they remained at home, became Christian. They substituted beliefs in the universal God of Christianity and his son, Jesus, for inherited religious beliefs and expressed their sentiments in Christian worship instead of traditional ritual. Acceptance of Christianity frequently went along with willingness to be educated in government programs and to live in new housing, even on the reservation. By the later twentieth century, tribal councils, elected according to mainstream democratic rules, governed the reservations. Indian traditionalists often found themselves in conflict with many aspects of reservation life.

Sects followed a typical pattern in which, more and more, they became denominations. By the same token, in their attempts to create separate and exclusive religious societies, they often ended by reflecting the dominant religion and culture they were seeking to escape. For instance, America became a central symbol for the Mormons, who, in their millennialism, shared the expectation of Zion that linked many members of the mainstream. Likewise, Mormon theology affirmed material abundance. It carried Arminian doctrines of free will to their logical conclusion, seeing unlimited possibilities for human beings to become "as Gods." And like mainstream Protestants, Mormons made theology second to the moralism and activism of their lives, preferring to act their religion more than to think it.

The pattern was similar in other new religious movements. They reflected the general cultural millennialism of America, sometimes in specific teachings about the end of the world, as in the cases of the Shakers and the Seventh-day Adventists. They displayed, as well, the pragmatic American quality that made of religion a means to success and abundance in the world. Thus, like the Mormons, the Seventh-day Adventists affirmed the material world they found in American culture. Christian Science and the New Thought movement fulfilled mainstream culture more than they departed from it, while spiritualism and theosophy were also built, in their own terms, on respect for modern science. The mental homesteads provided by occult and metaphysical movements were only prominent examples of the general tendency in postindustrial America to create private havens where personal relationships and interests were primary. The evangelical cultivation of a private relationship with Jesus, the revivalistic quest for right personal feeling, and the conservative tendency to overlook the socioeconomic problems of public life were not too different in style from these occult and metaphysical worlds.

Even further, estrangement was the common bond that linked members of the sects and cult movements with the mainstream. In the twentieth century, the new religious movements that turned to Eastern and Western occult and mystical ideas often tried to leave American society. Yet time and again, they came to imitate it. Their expression of innocence as they embraced nature was one example of the larger innocence of American culture, part of its religion of chosenness. Their use of various techniques, such as meditation, yogic exercises, or rhythmic chanting, reflected the general American search for tools that worked. And New Agers in many ways resembled the fundamentalists and evangelicals they spurned. More deliberately, ethnic peoples who inherited Eastern traditions sought to "Americanize" their religious expression. Japanese Buddhists spoke of their churches and bishops. Muslims attended their mosques on Sunday, instead of the traditional Friday. Eastern Orthodox Christians introduced the English language into the Divine Liturgy and placed Western-style pews in their churches.

In short, the many were ambivalent about their manyness. While they did not wish to throw away their distinctive religious approaches, they often, consciously or not, reflected elements in the dominant and public religion. The process was complex, for it did not mean simply imitating Protestants in order to win approval or despite dislike for them. Rather, it involved internal changes

Many Centers Meeting

within the separate communities so that creeds, codes, and cultuses became expressions of new powers, meanings, and values. Americans were forming a new people. Every American faith, in a sense, became new religion.

Even the revived emphasis on ethnicity in the later twentieth century did not alter this ambivalence. Whether built on nostalgia for the past or on militance regarding group status in the present, the mood of separatism has been only one move in a complex dialectic in which the many try to find a public space. In other words, emphasis on ethnic separateness is at least partially a strategy to insure a viable place in present-day American society. The "others" in the twentieth century belong to *American* religions, and for them the boundaries have been redrawn.

Finally, a third move appeared among some but not all of the many. Like representatives of the mainstream, these individuals labored as missionaries of extraordinary religion, trying to bring members of the one religion into their separate communities. For traditional churches, missionary work was an old and familiar activity, not to be neglected in the new situation. The chief example was Roman Catholicism. With its self-understanding as a universal church and its long history of missionary involvement, Catholicism countered Protestant efforts with its own.

Many Catholic parishes held inquiry classes for members of other denominations. And the Catholic mission movement of the nineteenth century had as its secondary goal the aim of making Protestants better acquainted with the Roman church. Catholic schools, which in the nineteenth century sometimes catered to Protestants, hoped to influence their charges in the direction of the Catholic faith. Meanwhile, bishops who debated Protestant preachers, either in person or through the press, wanted ultimately to convince them of the truth of Catholicism. Likewise, when the Transcendentalist Isaac Hecker became a Roman Catholic convert and priest, he founded the Paulist order (1858), dedicated to missionary work in Protestant America. In the twentieth century, radio and television helped Catholicism to make its message known; and in a well-remembered example, Bishop Fulton J. Sheen (1895–1979) engaged in a media ministry from 1930 to 1957. The millions who watched his *Life Is Worth Living* series after 1951 were learning how Roman Catholics saw the world.

However, it was the small religious groups, the sects and cult movements, that expended the most intensive efforts in missionary work. Paradoxically, the strength of their boundaries, based on a conviction of exclusive possession of religious truth, led them to go out toward others. Like fundamentalist and evangelical Protestants, they felt they must witness to the truth and rescue as many individuals as they could from the confusion of the world. Hence, missionary work, both theoretically and practically, was part of the very substance of these movements. For instance, Shaker preachers followed the revivals to gain converts, and later it became customary for young Mormon men to spend two years in missionary work. In a more subdued twentieth-century example, Christian Scientists have established reading rooms in the business districts of cities and towns across America to attract shoppers. At the other end of the religious spectrum, Jehovah's Witnesses publish *The Watchtower* twice a month in 106 languages, with a circulation of over 18 million copies. At the same time, individual Witnesses, called "publishers," spend hours in weekly door-to-door visitation.

Among the newer movements, members of the International Society for Krishna Consciousness were initially known for selling flowers in airport terminals to finance their ventures and also to find a way to speak to mainstream Americans. Members of Sun Myung Moon's Unification Church went from door to door for similar purposes. Followers of Eckankar, a group that teaches soul travel, or astral projection, continue to distribute literature on college campuses, while members of the International Meditation Society lecture on campuses, in public libraries, and elsewhere in order to introduce people to Transcendental Meditation. In these and other cases like them, aggressive missionary work has been a way to maintain the religious identity of the group and at the same time to argue for the place of the new religion in mainstream society. Members of these groups are saying, in effect, that the gates lead in as well as out.

Colliding Atoms: The Many Face the Many

So far we have looked at the responses of the one religion to the many and, in parallel ways, of individual groups among the many to the one. But the many also had to come to terms with one another, and it is to a consideration of this process that we now turn. Studies from both the social sciences and the humanities are necessary to fill out the picture, but at least we can glance at the major lines of interaction among the "others" to complete our discussion. In what follows, we look briefly at the main directions of these relationships.

In general, members of the various groups frequently responded negatively to one another. Members of small and intense religious groups, who thought themselves in possession of unique and privileged truth, could work to evangelize other religious peoples. Or they could denounce others as wrong and confused or accuse them of deliberate falsification. On the other hand, members of ethnic religious communities had their own reasons to experience friction with others among the many.

Each of the groups shared a common outsider status and a common realization of the dominance of the one religion. And on the level of ordinary religion, many of the groups competed with others for the attention and resources of the mainstream. To a certain extent, because the one religion was public and dominant, it succeeded in convincing all Americans of its importance. Hostility toward one group among the many by another of these "outgroups" allowed the first group to feel closer to the mainstream. By expressing such hostility, a group could also express its identification with the one religion and so take on stature from the relationship. By the same token, hostility by one group toward the others could underline its own sense of distinctiveness. By drawing a sharp line between itself and the many, a group could articulate its separate identity and its difference.

Still, on occasion members of the various groups did respond positively to one another. From the perspective of extraordinary religion, missionary efforts were attempts to communicate with others, while within the boundaries of ordinary religion, various groups could share support and encouragement. While their common status as outsiders could lead them apart, it could also bring them closer together. Many groups found that there was strength in unity. Banding together gave them leverage in their relationship with the mainstream, and so they learned to be friends.

One example of a negative response by a distinct group among the many toward another is Roman Catholic anti-Semitism. Like all Christians, Roman Catholics inherited the images of Jews as Christ-killers and as conspiratorial moneylenders. Indeed, the medieval church emphasized these ideas, and until the aftermath of Vatican Council II the Roman Catholic liturgy for Good Friday spoke of the "perfidious Jews."

In a prime American instance of Catholic anti-Semitism, during the 1930s Father Charles E. Coughlin (1891–1979) influenced millions of Americans through his radio sermons from Royal Oak, Michigan. A commentator on many of the political and economic issues of the time, he was telling his listeners by the latter part of the decade that the greatest dangers facing America were Communism and the wealthy financial interest. Linking the two together, thought Coughlin, were the Jews. They had been key leaders in the Communist movement in Russia, he said, and during the Spanish Civil War, they had spread Communist propaganda, opposing the Catholic General Francisco Franco. For Coughlin, Nazism, like Fascism, was a defense against Communism, and European Jews were persecuted because they were in alliance with Communism and frequently unpatriotic. Likewise, in an old argument, Coughlin complained that most of those who controlled the world's wealth were Jewish and that with their money they dominated the press and shaped public opinion to their purposes. Coughlin added insult to injury by calling on Jews to accept Christ as a way to banish the "Jewish problem." He reprinted the *Protocols of the Elders of Zion* in his weekly newspaper and, in general, continued to spread anti-Semitism until he was ordered to be silent by his religious superiors.

A second example of the tensions that could arise between groups among the many occurred in the relationship between African-Americans and Jews. Often African-Americans followed Jews into older inner-city neighborhoods. Thus, the landlords and storekeepers with whom blacks dealt were often Jewish. When rents and prices were high, money scarce, and buildings overcrowded and run-down, blacks expressed their anger toward the Jews. Blacks believed, too, that, like other whites, Jews discriminated against them in hiring and employment practices. And they resented the fact that Jews lived in wealthy suburban neighborhoods where African-Americans could not obtain housing, even if they had the money to pay for it. From the Jewish perspective, there was also a good deal of antiblack feeling. Stereotyped attitudes toward blacks were common. Like other whites, Jews at times thought of African-Americans as lazy, intemperate, and not too intelligent. And they saw blacks as rowdy and culturally strange. When African-Americans supported quota systems in the university and on the job, Jews, remembering their own experiences with quotas, fought their efforts. So the two communities, both outsiders, found themselves at odds with each other. Like countless groups among the many, estrangement from the mainstream was accompanied by estrangement from each other.

While we could find numerous other instances of suspicion, tension, and even hatred among the many, there *were* positive moves by members of different groups. Some took the risk of establishing communications across the boundary, and some joined forces to achieve mutually desirable goals. For example, let us look at the cases of Catholic-Jewish and Jewish-black relations once again. In both instances, there were ongoing efforts to achieve communication, and alliances were forged.

Vatican Council II set the stage for a new era in Roman Catholic–Jewish discourse. In a formal document, the Declaration on the Relationship of the Church to Non-Christian Religions (1965), the council addressed the ancient charge that the Jews were Christ-killers. It explicitly rejected the notions that all Jews or the Jews of its day were responsible for the death of Christ. Further, it warned that the Jews ought not to be characterized as "cursed by God," and it spoke of a common heritage shared by Catholics and Jews. Some Jews thought that the language of the document did not go far enough, since the specific accusation that the Jews were guilty of deicide (the murder of God) was not condemned and since no contrition was expressed for the church's long history of anti-Semitism. Moreover, some were disappointed because the document did not flatly reject attempts to convert the Jews. Still, the council had taken a major step forward for Catholic-Jewish relations.

In recent times, Jews and Roman Catholics (like other Christians) have engaged in Jewish-Christian dialogue. Sometimes, at the grass-roots level, interested Catholics have been present for the Passover *seder* with Jews in home settings, and Jews have attended Roman Catholic services to learn about them. Lay Catholics have discovered the importance of the Law in Jewish life, and, conversely, Jews have become familiar with Christian theological concepts.

While Jewish-Catholic relations have developed in the context of extraordinary religion, Jewish-black relations have been part of ordinary life. Jews and African-Americans had much in common, for both had experienced years of suffering and persecution at the hands of white Christians. Both thought of themselves as separate nations, and both blended ordinary and extraordinary religion with their nationhood in distinctive religioethnic identities. During the civil rights struggle of the sixties, Jews were prominent among the whites who supported the black effort. They contributed substantial funds, and they marched beside blacks in demonstrations and protests. On the whole, they have expressed more concern than other whites about racism and have been more willing to hire blacks when they were employers. Jews have been active in the foundation of the National Association for the Advancement of Colored People (NAACP), an organization to win black equality through legal contests in the courts. They have also made efforts on behalf of black education. Although blacks have had neither the wealth nor the occasion to return the gestures in kind, they have on occasion formed social and political alliances with Jews for mutual goals. And the dialogue between the two groups has been characterized by frankness and honesty.

For the many in general, alliance has been the key to positive relationships in ordinary life. Just by sharing the status of "otherness," the many in the long run have made it more acceptable to be different. And indeed, if historian R. Laurence Moore is right, the best way to be an "insider" in America has been to be an outsider. Moreover, the example of one group has sometimes provided a model for others. Thus, in the twentieth century the black-power movement of the sixties spurred the expression of a more militant ethnic and religious awareness among American Indians, Hispanic Americans, and even the descendants of various Catholic immigrant groups — the "white ethnics." Here there was imitation more than alliance on the practical level, but on the psychological plane the relationship between the rise of different ethnic movements seemed clear.

In more concrete terms, regional religion often provides an example of alliance among the "others." As we saw in our study of Southern Appalachian religion, many small and unconventional churches in the mountains shared a mentality and way of life different from that of the contemporary Protestant mainstream. These churches often disagreed on doctrinal points and specific ritual practices, but in many ways they resembled one another. More than that, the mountaineers who did not belong to any church were generally linked to church members in more religious ways than they were separated from them. The overwhelming majority of the people of Southern Appalachia agreed on fundamentals of belief and behavior that involved both ordinary and extraordinary religion. Though many in their church allegiances or lack of any, they were one in their dealings with the world outside the mountains. They were united in their spirit of cultural contraction.

Similarly, party politics has offered a vehicle for alliance. The Democrats, historically, have been identified as the party of the poor and the immigrant, the African-American and the Jew. Through a coalition of these groups, the party often successfully challenged a dominant elite, obtaining social programs and policies intended to benefit the many. Banding together politically, in fact, has been a step in becoming like the established culture by learning to be seen and heard, to "make history," so to speak. However, it is also an exercise in learning to form networks among the many. It is a commitment to engage in exchanges across boundaries.

Finally, missionary work went forward among the many. It thrived not only in attempts to convert members of the mainstream but also in efforts to acquaint the many with the truth as seen by one particular group. We have already looked at these efforts in the relationship of the many to the one, and the pattern of their outreach toward one another was similar, if not the same. Pluralism meant that each could witness to all and that each could listen to the message presented by all. Against a backdrop of religious liberty and organizational voluntaryism, missionary activism was often a way to survive and grow. So in ordinary and extraordinary terms, the many learned to speak to one another.

Summing Up the Present

We have moved rapidly to look at relationships between the religions and religion of the United States. In so doing, there has been danger of oversimplification, for movements of exchange between peoples are usually subtle, ambiguous, and complicated. Still, the idea of boundaries — between ordinary and extraordinary and between the one and each of the many — has been helpful. In a culture of pluralism, the question of boundaries is crucial, for it is on the boundaries that most of the issues lie. In our own day, some of the sharp edges have softened for the mainstream and the "old" immigrant religions, but as new, strongly committed religious groups arise, boundaries are once again tightly drawn.

Meanwhile, as the many centers meet, the old moves are still there. The one religion is anxious about its dominance, while the many seek to challenge it in the preservation of their separate identities. Patterns of housing, job, and educational discrimination still exist for African-Americans, American Indians, and other groups. Christian Scientists come off slightly worse than others in some books, while the term *cult* is a signal for condemnation. Southern Appalachian Bible believers who migrate to northern cities are sometimes derided as "hillbillies." At the same time, in their desire to remain apart, Asian Indians erect lavish temples, suggesting by the character of the architecture their wish to separate themselves. Arab Muslims sometimes live in ethnic neighborhoods. Pueblo Indians prefer their adobe villages, laid out with central plazas for the performance of sacred dances.

Although some among the many retreat from the mainstream, others seek greater assimilation. Some Catholic Poles and Jews still change their surnames to blend into the "melting pot," even as other ethnics have proclaimed themselves unmeltable. Seventh-day Adventists discuss whether or not they have become a denomination, while some fundamentalists edge closer to the mainstream. Blacks move to the suburbs, and Catholics, with their own colleges, attend major public universities. Jews, to the disappointment of rabbis, frequently intermarry and drift away from affiliation with a synagogue.

When the many meet the many, they often find reason to be hostile to one another. Native Americans and Hispanic Catholics in Santa Fe, New Mexico, resent and live in mutual suspicion of each other as well as of the often-Protestant Anglo-American inhabitants of the city. African-Americans and

Italian-Americans express mutual rage and fear in the context of crime in a New York City borough. American Arabs and Jews face each other tensely in view of their different stances regarding the Middle East.

To sum up, throughout American religious history Protestant attitudes toward the many have been ambivalent, ranging from a defensive fear and hostility to, on the other hand, conversion attempts, qualified openness, and expansive fascination. The attitudes of the many toward public Protestantism have divided mainly between those who wished to preserve their old ways in the new land and those others who wanted to become more American and — it followed — more Protestant. At the same time, representatives of some groups have tried to win converts from the one (mainstream) religion. Finally, as the many have encountered one another, they have frequently exchanged insecurities by voicing mutual suspicions and accusations. Still, some have found common worlds to share and have made alliances, while others have expressed their social and religious commitments in missionary work directed toward different groups and persons among the many.

What does this all mean, and to what does it all add up? The United States of America is among the most pluralistic religious and social experiments in history. Its people live in a social situation complicated by great diversity. Religions abound, and so do peoples, their beliefs, styles of worship, and moral codes. Community is fragile and temporary, and estrangement is probably the one thing that many have in common. While the vast machinery of government and of the corporate industrial complex continues, the frictions that face Americans are a recurring feature of life. The manyness of groups and movements heightens impulses for everyone to mark boundaries carefully. At the same time, the one religion of millennial chosenness, innocence, and hidden guilt fosters anxiety regarding the boundaries to the cultural mainstream.

Living with so many boundaries has proved a difficult task for Americans. There is a tremendous gap between the millennial goal of community and the realities of estrangement only thinly veiled. Faced with the problems of impersonality that accompany the corporate organization of any modern urban and industrial society, Americans have been beset with the serious *religious* problem of crossing the human boundaries that hinder community. That problem has had a long history: it began with the first collision between Native American ways of seeing and European interpretations of Indian life. And it began with the political realities of a power situation in which, though insecure and fearful, Puritans could dissolve their fright in a growing millennial fervor that expressed both dominance and innocence. The balance of political power has always complicated the picture of religious America.

Still, to live without a public center — a one religion — seems humanly impossible. Shared sources of power, meaning, and value, however loosely expressed, must provide some kind of bonding, or society would lose all cohesion and fall apart. To live without the many who form so significant a part of religious America seems equally impossible. Although sometimes less fully organized and less visible, the many have deeply affected American life—which would not be American without them.

American religious reality is a dialectic between the one and the many. The one religion suits active and energetic people who desire clear and simple directives for their work. Its evangelical warmth seeks to provide solace for Americans uprooted by a society ever on the move. Huge numbers, strong institutionalization, wealth, and political prestige have given it a clear role of leadership in shaping America. So in Part II we paid attention to the one religion in its various forms. At the same time, the many possess ordinary and extraordinary religious capital of their own. Their ways of living within boundaries and learning how to cross them tell us many things about human possibility and realization that the story of the one religion cannot tell. In a word, both America and American religious history would be diminished without the many. Their stories need to be told with a sense of texture and a feel for detail that hints of who they are and what material and spiritual resources they have acquired. This the chapters tried to do in Part I.

The coexistence through several centuries of one religion and many religions is, of course, a fact of American life. But it is also a significant ordinary and extraordinary religious achievement, an achievement that suggests a potential to be tapped and a basic fund of regard and respect to be counted. Still more, the tension between the one and the many is not simply a burdensome condition with which American religious history has been saddled and with which it has dealt in a successful way. Rather, the tension created by point and counterpoint is an asset. The tension has meant a more complex, more ambiguous, and finally more "live" religious situation for all Americans. To say this, however, is not to say all. In the end, we need to return to the problem of forging community in the New World.

Over the years, as pluralism grew stronger, the problem of creating community became more acute. People spoke but often not to one another; they heard sermons and gave speeches but frequently did not communicate. Instead, they bypassed their differences and their mutual fears. Sometimes they did so through pragmatic and functional interactions, cooperating when a set of circumstances could be manipulated politically for joint advantage. They jockeyed their concerns to create a "new" order of things in which the old ways of thinking remained largely unexamined and unchanged. Interfaith and multidenominational efforts were accepted styles of relating among some religious groups, but they were styles in which people mostly did not face their differences.

At other times Americans chose a community of feeling—private emotion that through a complex religious etiquette could legitimately be expressed in public. Shared feeling could make the "others" no longer other and knit the many into one. Significantly, the shared feeling that could evoke community most effectively, again and again, seemed to be the violent feeling that generated attitudes of millennial dominance and, as their underside, righteous innocence. Americans never looked more like a community than when, under the banner of their civil religion, they marched to war. Fired with the rhetoric and passion of millennialism, Americans found community in their historic venture but not in the humbler, more modest need of individuals and groups to speak to one another.

Under the terms of the millennial covenant, in all honesty they could *not* speak. The chosen, like an army in a colonial fortress, could not let down the bridge to the "others." To do so might lessen the monopoly of the dominant center and lead to a situation of *decenteredness*, to a loss of purity and the creation of a new religious center. The many, beleaguered and precarious, could not begin the conversation either. They were too involved in the task of defining and maintaining their boundaries — their side of the territory. So behind the problem of community in America is another one. The ordinary and extraordinary religious problem of America is finally the content of the one religion and the many religions insofar as they share, in certain respects, a pronounced culture of contraction in the present and an overexpansive millennial dream for the future. In short, caught between boundaries and dreams, the one and the many have found it difficult to maintain balance.

Dreams, we know, are not reality. Although they can be the source of creativity and vital energy, they can also weave illusions that leave people ill-prepared to cope with daytime problems. And dreams can also mask fears that constrict the waking lives of dreamers. In the case of millennialism, the irony of the dream is large. Bound to the vision of an expansive new heaven and new earth, millennialism is an *old* dream from an *Old* World. Although it thrived in the context of the discovery of a continent, millennialism is largely a product of the European heritage and the European imagination. Up until this time in our study, we have stressed the Americanness of American religions and religion, but now at the core of the new, we must confront the presence of the old. Millennialism represents what Europeans have thought over centuries more than a fresh response to a new situation. Its continuing versions, evoking either Armageddon or paradise, prevent the realities of New World existence from being adequately seen and met.

In short, millennial time is not *lived-through* time; and it cannot help Americans to know and care for one another. It is true that in the midst of their millennial dream Americans have tossed fitfully at times — as if half awake or just about to awaken. Yet as a product of their waking, a completely American religion has not yet come to be. People in the New World are still learning to do something really new.

SUGGESTIONS FOR FURTHER READING: MANY CENTERS MEETING

Ahlstrom, Sydney E. *A Religious History of the American People.* New Haven: Yale University Press, 1972.

Billington, Ray Allen. *The Protestant Crusade, 1800–1860: A Study of the Origins of American Nativism.* 1938. Reprint. Chicago: Quadrangle Books, 1964.

Dinnerstein, Leonard, ed. *Antisemitism in the United States.* New York: Holt, Rinehart & Winston, 1961.

————, Nichols, Roger L., and Reimers, David M. *Natives and Strangers: Ethnic Groups and the Building of America.* New York: Oxford University Press, 1979.

Douglas, Mary. *Purity and Danger: An Analysis of Concepts of Pollution and Taboo.* London: Routledge & Kegan Paul, 1966.

Gaustad, Edwin Scott. *Historical Atlas of Religion in America.* Rev. ed. New York: Harper & Row, 1976.

————. *A Religious History of America.* Rev. [3d] ed. San Francisco: Harper & Row, 1990.

Handlin, Oscar. *The Uprooted.* New York: Grosset & Dunlap, 1951.

Higham, John. *Strangers in the Land: Patterns of American Nativism, 1860–1925.* 2d ed. New Brunswick, NJ: Rutgers University Press, 1988.

Hudson, Winthrop S. *Religion in America.* 4th ed. New York: Macmillan, 1987.

Lippy, Charles H., and Williams, Peter W., eds. *Encyclopedia of the American Religious Experience: Studies of Traditions and Movements.* 3 vols. New York: Charles Scribner's, 1988.

Marty, Martin E. *Modern American Religion.* Vol. 1, *The Irony of It All, 1893–1919.* Chicago: University of Chicago Press, 1986.

————. *Modern American Religion.* Vol. 2, *The Noise of Conflict, 1919–1941.* Chicago: University of Chicago Press, 1991.

————. *A Nation of Behavers.* Chicago: University of Chicago Press, 1976.

————. *Pilgrims in Their Own Land: 500 Years of Religion in America.* Boston: Little, Brown, 1984.

————. *Religion and Republic: The American Circumstance.* Boston: Beacon Press, 1987.

Melton, J. Gordon. *The Encyclopedia of American Religions.* 3d ed. Detroit: Gale Research, 1989.

Moore, R. Laurence. *Religious Outsiders and the Making of Americans.* New York: Oxford University Press, 1986.

Roof, Wade Clark, and McKinney, William. *American Mainline Religion: Its Changing Shape and Future.* New Brunswick, NJ: Rutgers University Press, 1987.

Williams, Peter W. *America's Religions: Traditions and Cultures.* New York: Macmillan, 1990.

————. *Popular Religion in America: Symbolic Change and the Modernization Process in Historical Perspective.* Rev. ed. Urbana: University of Illinois Press, 1989.

INDEX

Page numbers in bold indicate pages on which terms are defined.

Social ethic, 365

Social Gospel, 137–39, 144, 147, 414, 426–27

Society for the Propagation of the Gospel in Foreign Parts (SPGFP), 179

Sojourners, 382

Soka Gakkai, 318

Soto Zen, 316

Southern Appalachia, 526
agriculture of, 328
Baptists in, 335–36, 346
Bible in, 339–40
Calvinism in, 332
changing conditions of, 346–47
class system in, 329
cultus of, 343–44
Disciples of Christ in, 337
earliest inhabitants of, 327–28
extraordinary religion in, 341–45
fundamentalism of, 338
Great Revival in, 335–37
holiness-pentecostalism in, 338
Methodists of, 346
mountain character in, 330–31
ordinary religion in, 339–41
organized religion in, 334–38
Presbyterians in, 334–35, 336, 346
as region, 324, 326
relationships within, 333–34
religious background of, 328
sectarianism in, 337
social organization of, 329
view of nature in, 332–33

Spalding, John Lancaster, 93

Spanish Catholicism, 91–92

Spanish Civil War, 524

Spanish Missions, 74–75

SPGFP (Society for the Propagation of the Gospel in Foreign Parts), 179

Spirit drawings (Shaker), 243

Spiritualism, 250, 261–66, **354**

Spiritualist mediums, 357

Spirituals, black, 201

Sports, 474–76

Stewart, Lyman, 170

Stone, Barton W., 165, 166

Strong, Josiah, 184

Student Volunteer Movement for Foreign Missions (SVM), 185

Sunday, William A. (Billy), 159, 455

Sunni Muslims, **296**, 297

Suzuki, Daisetz Teitaro, 315

SVM (Student Volunteer Movement for Foreign Missions), 185

Swaggart, Jimmy Lee, 375

Swedenborg, Emanuel, 261, 353

Swedenborgianism, **354**

Syncretism, **43**, 45, 319–21

Tarzan, 492

Taylor, Nathaniel W., 155

Technology, 476–79

Televangelists, 374–75, 391

Television, 375–78, 469

Temperance movement, 411–12

Tennent, Gilbert, 154

Textual criticism, 135

Thanksgiving, 467

Theocracy, 436

Theology for the Social Gospel, A (Rauschenbusch), 138

Theosophy, 266–68, 356

Theravada (Buddhism), 312–13. *See also* Buddhism, schools of

Thetford, William, 350

Thomsonian system, 488

Thoreau, Henry David, 423

3HO (Healthy-Happy-Holy Organization), 319–20

Three Pillars of Zen, The (Kapleau), 316

Tibetan Buddhism, 317

Time
black religion and, 200
Catholic consecration of, 81–82
Jews and, 60–63
new religions and sacred, 408–9
sacred, 463
in Southern Appalachia, 343

TM (Transcendental Meditation), 306–7

Tongues speaking, 174

Torah, 59, 60, 64, 71, 72

Transcendental Meditation (TM), 306–7

Transcendentalism, 147
and correspondence, 260
and Hinduism, 301
and nature, 129, 355, 486
and reform, 129–30
as Romanticism, 131

Transpersonal psychology, 358

Treatise on Atonement (Ballou), 128

Trickster, 28–29, 31–32, 195, 197

Troeltsch, Ernst, 220